The Information Age

Economy, Society and Culture

Volume I

The Rise of the Network Society

The Rise of the Network Society

Second Edition

Manuel Castells

First edition published 1996
Reprinted 1997 (three times), 1998 (three times), 1999 (twice), 2000
Second edition published 2000
Reprinted 2001

Blackwell Publishers Ltd
108 Cowley Road
Oxford OX4 1JF
UK

Blackwell Publishers Inc.
350 Main Street
Malden, Massachusetts 02148
USA

British Library Cataloguing in Publication Data
A CIP catalogue record for this book is available from the British Library.

Library of Congress Cataloging-in-Publication Data
Castells, Manuel.
    The rise of the network society / Manuel Castells. — 2nd ed.
        p. cm. — (Information age ; v. 1)
    Includes bibliographical references and index.
    ISBN 0-631-22140-9 (pb : alk. paper)
    1.   Information technology—Economic aspects. 2. Information technology—Social aspects. 3. Information society. 4. Information networks. 5. Technology and civilization. I. Title.

HC79.I55 C373 2000
3303.48'33—dc21
                                                                                00-037832

Typeset in 10.5 on 12 pt Sabon
By Ace Filmsetting Ltd, Frome, Somerset
Printed in Great Britain by T.J. International Limited, Padstow, Cornwall

This book is printed on acid-free paper

For Emma Kiselyova-Castells,
without whose love, work, and support
this book would not exist

Contents

Figures

Tables

Acknowledgments 2000

The volume you have in your hands is a substantially revised edition of this book, originally published in November 1996. The current version was elaborated and written in the second half of 1999. It aims at integrating important technological, economic, and social developments that took place in the late 1990s, generally confirming the diagnosis and prognosis presented in the first edition. I have not modified the key substantive elements of the overall analysis: mainly because I believe that the core argument still stands as presented, but also because all books are of their time, and must eventually be superseded by the development and rectification of the ideas they contain, as social experience and research add new information and new knowledge. Besides updating some of the information, I have corrected a few mistakes and have tried to clarify and strengthen the argument wherever possible.

In so doing, I have benefited from many comments, criticisms, and contributions from around the world, generally expressed in a constructive and cooperative manner. I cannot do justice to the richness of the debate that this book has engendered, to my great surprise. I just want to express my heartfelt gratitude to readers, reviewers, and critics, who took the time and effort to think about the issues analyzed in these pages. I cannot claim to be aware of all the comments and discussions in a variety of countries and in languages which I do not understand. But, by thanking those institutions and individuals who, by their comments and the debates they organized, have helped me to better understand now the questions I treated in this book, I wish to extend this acknowledgment to all readers, and commentators, wherever and whoever they are.

First of all, I would like to express my gratitude to a number of

reviewers whose thoughts have been influential for my own better un-
derstanding and for the eventual rectification of some elements of my
research. Among them are: Anthony Giddens, Alain Touraine, Anthony
Smith, Peter Hall, Benjamin Barber, Roger-Pol Droit, Chris Freeman,
Krishan Kumar, Stephen Jones, Frank Webster, Sophie Watson, Stephen
Cisler, Felix Stalder, David Lyon, Craig Calhoun, Jeffrey Henderson,
Zygmunt Bauman, Jay Ogilvy, Cliff Barney, Mark Williams, Alberto
Melucci, Anthony Orum, Tim Jordan, Rowan Ireland, Janet Abu-
Lughod, Charles Tilly, Mary Kaldor, Anne Marie Guillemard, Bernard
Benhamou, Jose E. Rodriguez Ibanez, Ramon Ramos, Jose Felix
Tezanos, Sven-Eric Liedman, Markku Willennius, Andres Ortega,
Alberto Catena, and Emilio de Ipola. I wish to thank especially the
three colleagues who organized the first presentations of this book,
thus launching the debate: Michael Burawoy in Berkeley, Bob Catterall
in Oxford, and Ida Susser in New York.

I am also indebted to the numerous academic institutions that invited me, in 1996–2000, to submit the research presented in this book
to collegial critique, and, especially to all the people who came to
my lectures and seminars, and provided their intellectual feedback.
This book has been presented and debated, in chronological order,
at the University of California at Berkeley; Oxford University; City
University of New York, Graduate Center; Consejo Superior de
Investigaciones Cientificas, Barcelona; Universidad de Sevilla; Universidad de Oviedo; Universitat Autonoma de Barcelona; Institute of
Economics, Russian Academy of Sciences, Novosibirsk; The Nether-
lands Design Institute, Amsterdam; Cambridge University; University
College, London; SITRA–Helsinki; Stanford University; Harvard
University; Cité des Sciences et de l'Industrie, Paris; Tate Gallery, Lon-
don; Universidad de Buenos Aires; Universidad de San Simon,
Cochabamba; Universidad de San Andres, La Paz; Centre Européen
des Recoversions et Mutations, Luxembourg; University of California
at Davis; Universidade Federal de Rio de Janeiro; Universidade de São
Paulo; Programa de Naciones Unidas para el Desarrollo, Santiago de
Chile; University of California at San Diego; Higher School of Economics, Moscow; and Duke University. I also want to thank the many
other institutions and organizations that invited me to share my work
with them in these four years, although I was not able to respond to
their kind interest.

A special mention goes to my friend and colleague Martin Carnoy
of Stanford University: our continuing intellectual interaction is most
important for the development and rectification of my thinking. His
contribution to the revision of chapter 4 (on work and employment)
in volume I has been essential. Also, my friends and colleagues in Bar-

celona, Marina Subirats and Jordi Borja, have been, as during most of my life, sources of inspiration and healthy criticism.

I also want to thank my family, the main source of my strength. First, my wife, Emma Kiselyova, for her support, love, intelligence, and patience, in the midst of a most strenuous period for both of us, and for her determination in keeping me focused on substance rather than on image-making. My daughter, Nuria, who managed during these years to support her father from a distance, while producing a doctoral dissertation and a second child. My sister, Irene, who never stopped being my critical consciousness. My step-daughter, Lena, who enriched my life with her warmth and sensitivity. My son-in-law, Jose del Rocio Millan, and my brother-in-law, Jose Bailo, with whom I have spent many hours discussing our work and our lives. And last, but certainly not least, the source of joy in my life, my grandchildren Clara, Gabriel, and Sasha.

I also want to acknowledge my copy-editor, Sue Ashton, whose contribution has been essential in bringing order and clarity to this book, both in the first and second editions. I also want to thank the editorial, production, and promotion staff of my publisher, Blackwell, and particularly Louise Spencely, Lorna Berrett, Sarah Falkus, Jill Landeryou, Karen Gibson, Nicola Boulton, Joanna Pyke, and their co-workers. Their personal effort for this book has gone way beyond the usual standards of professionalism in the publishing world.

As for my doctors, customary characters of my trilogy's acknowledgments, they have continued to do their remarkable job, keeping me afloat during these critical years. I would like to reiterate my gratitude to Dr Peter Carroll and to Dr James Davis, both with the University of California at San Francisco, Medical Center.

Finally, I wish to express my deep and genuine surprise at the interest generated by this very academic book around the world, not only in university circles but in the media, and among people at large. I know this is not so much related to the quality of the book as to the critical importance of the issues I have tried to analyze: we are in a new world, and we need new understanding. To be able to contribute, in all modesty, to the process of construction of such an understanding is my only ambition, and the real motivation to continue the work I have undertaken, as long as my strength will allow.

Berkeley, California
January 2000

The Association of American Geographers: Fig. 6.1 *"Largest absolute growth in information flows, 1982 and 1990,"* Federal Express data, elaborated by R. L. Michelson and J. O. Wheeler, "The flow of information in a global economy: the role of the American urban system in 1990," *Annals of the Association of American Geographers*, 84: 1. Copyright © 1994 The Association of American Geographers, Washington DC.

The Association of American Geographers: Fig. 6.2 *"Exports of information from the United States to major world regions and centers,"* Federal Express data, 1990, elaborated by R. L. Michelson and J. O. Wheeler, "The flow of information in a global economy: the role of the American urban system in 1990," *Annals of the Association of American Geographers*, 84: 1. Copyright © 1994 The Association of American Geographers, Washington DC.

Business Week: Table 2.10 *"Stocks valuation, 1995–1999: the Standard & Poor 500's top growth stocks,"* Bloomberg Financial Markets, compiled by *Business Week*. Copyright © 1999 McGraw Hill, New York.

University of California: Fig. 4.9 *"Percentage of working-age Californians employed in 'traditional' jobs, 1999."* Copyright © 1999 University of California and The Field Institute, San Francisco.

University of California: Fig. 4.10 *"Distribution of working-age Californians by 'traditional jobs' status and length of tenure in the job, 1999."* Copyright © 1999 University of California and The Field Institute, San Francisco.

University of California Library: Fig. 4.11 *"The Japanese labor market in the postwar period,"* Yuko Aoyama, "Locational strategies of Japanese multinational corporations in electronics," University of California PhD dissertation, elaborated from information from Japan's Economic Planning Agency, *Gaikokujin rodosha to shakai no shinro*, 1989, p. 99, fig. 4.1.

CEPII-OFCE: Table 2.3 *"Evolution of the productivity of business sectors (% average annual growth rate),"* database of the MIMOSA model. Copyright © CEPII-OFCE.

CEPII-OFCE: Table 2.4 *"Evolution of productivity in sectors not open to free trade (% average annual growth rate),"* database of the MIMOSA model. Copyright © CEPII-OFCE.

The Chinese University Press: Fig. 6.5 *"Diagrammatic representation of major nodes and links in the urban region of the Pearl River Delta,"* elaborated by E. Woo, "Urban Development," in Y. M. Yeung and D. K. Y. Chu, *Guandong: Survey of a Province Undergoing Rapid Change.* Copyright © 1994 Chinese University Press, Hong Kong.

Table 4.29 excerpted from Lawrence Mishel, Jared Bernstein and John Schmitt, and Economic Policy Institute, *The State of Working America 1998–1999.* Copyright © 1999 Cornell University. Used by permission of the publisher, Cornell University Press.

Defence Research Establishment Ottawa: Fig. 7.3 *"War deaths relative to world population, by decade, 1720–2000,"* G. D. Kaye, D. A. Grant and E. J. Emond, *Major Armed Conflicts: a Compendium of Interstate and Intrastate Conflict, 1720 to 1985,* Report to National Defense, Canada. Copyright © 1985 Operational Research and Analysis Establishment, Ottawa.

Economic Policy Institute: Fig. 4.8 *"Employment in the temporary help industry in the United States, 1982–1997,"* analysis of Bureau of Labor Statistics data by Lawrence Mishel, Jared Bernstein and John Schmitt, *The State of Working America 1998–99.* Copyright © Cornell University Press/Economic Policy Institute, Ithaca and London.

The Economist: Fig. 2.2 *"Estimate of evolution of productivity in the United States, 1972–1999 (output per hour),"* Bureau of Labor Statistics, elaborated by Robert Gordon in "The new economy: work in progress," in *The Economist,* pp. 21–4. Copyright © 1999 The Economist, London (24 July). Reprinted by permission of the publisher.

The Economist: Fig. 2.9 *"Declining dividends payments,"* in "Shares without the other bit" in *The Economist,* p. 135. Copyright © The Economist, London (20 November). Reprinted by permission of the publisher.

The Economist: Fig. 5.1 *"Media sales in 1998 of major media groups,"* company reports; Veronis, Suhler and Associates; Zenith Media; Warburg Dillon Read; elaborated by *The Economist,* 1, p. 62. Copyright © 1999 The Economist, London (11 December). Reprinted by permission of the publisher.

The Economist: Fig. 5.2 *"Strategic alliances between media groups in Europe, 1999,"* Warburg Dillon Read, elaborated by *The Economist,*

1, p. 62. Copyright © 1999 The Economist, London (11 December). Reprinted by permission of the publisher.

Harvard University Press: Fig. 4.3 *"Index of employment growth by region, 1973–1999;"* an earlier version of this figure appeared in *Sustainable Flexibility*, OCDE/GD(97)48; elaborated by Martin Carnoy in the forthcoming *Sustaining the New Economy: Work, Family and Community in the Information Age*, Cambridge, Mass.: Harvard University Press, Copyright © 2000 by the Russell Sage Foundation.

Harvard University Press: Fig. 4.4 *"Part-time workers in employed labor force in OECD countries, 1983–1998;"* an earlier version of this figure appeared in *Sustainable Flexibility*, OCDE/GD(97)48; elaborated by Martin Carnoy in the forthcoming *Sustaining the New Economy: Work, Family and Community in the Information Age*, Cambridge, Mass.: Harvard University Press, Copyright © 2000 by the Russell Sage Foundation.

Harvard University Press: Fig. 4.5 *"Self-employed workers in employed labor force in OECD countries, 1983–1993;"* an earlier version of this figure appeared in *Sustainable Flexibility*, OCDE/GD(97)48; elaborated by Martin Carnoy in the forthcoming *Sustaining the New Economy: Work, Family and Community in the Information Age*, Cambridge, Mass.: Harvard University Press, Copyright © 2000 by the Russell Sage Foundation.

Harvard University Press: Fig. 4.6 *"Temporary workers in employed labor force in OECD countries, 1983–1997;"* an earlier version of this figure appeared in *Sustainable Flexibility*, OCDE/GD(97)48; elaborated by Martin Carnoy in the forthcoming *Sustaining the New Economy: Work, Family and Community in the Information Age*, Cambridge, Mass.: Harvard University Press, Copyright © 2000 by the Russell Sage Foundation.

Harvard University Press: Fig. 4.7 *"Non-standard forms of employment in employed labor force in OECD countries, 1983–1994;"* an earlier version of this figure appeared in *Sustainable Flexibility*, OCDE/GD(97)48; elaborated by Martin Carnoy in the forthcoming *Sustaining the New Economy: Work, Family and Community in the Information Age*, Cambridge, Mass.: Harvard University Press, Copyright © 2000 by the Russell Sage Foundation.

Harvard University Press: Fig. 4.12 *"Annual growth of productivity,* employment, and earnings in OECD countries, 1984–1998;" data from OECD, compiled and elaborated by Martin Carnoy in the forthcoming *Sustaining the New Economy: Work, Family and Community in the Information Age*, Cambridge, Mass.: Harvard University Press, Copyright © 2000 by the Russell Sage Foundation.

Harvard University Press: Fig. 7.1 *"Labor force participation rate (%) for men 55–64 years old in eight countries, 1970–1998,"* A. M. Guillemard, "Travailleurs vieillissants et marché du travail en Europe," *Travail et emploi*, September 1993, and Martin Carnoy in the forthcoming *Sustaining the New Economy: Work, Family and Community in the Information Age*, Cambridge, Mass.: Harvard University Press, Copyright © 2000 by the Russell Sage Foundation.

Harvard University Press: Table 4.23 *"Employment in manufacturing, major countries and regions, 1970–1997 (thousands),"* International Labor Office, *Statistical Yearbook*, 1986, 1988, 1994, 1995, 1996, 1997; OECD, *Labour Force Statistics, 1977–1997* (Paris: OECD, 1998); OECD, *Main Economic Indicators: Historical Statistics, 1962–1991* (Paris: OECD, 1993), compiled and elaborated by Martin Carnoy in the forthcoming *Sustaining the New Economy: Work, Family and Community in the Information Age*, Cambridge, Mass.: Harvard University Press, Copyright © 2000 by the Russell Sage Foundation.

Harvard University Press: Table 4.24 *"Employment shares by industry/occupation and ethnic/gender group of all workers in the United States, 1960–1998 (percent),"* US Department of Commerce, Bureau of the Census, *1 Percent Sample, US Population Census, 1960, 1970,* compiled by Martin Carnoy in the forthcoming *Sustaining the New Economy: Work, Family and Community in the Information Age*, Cambridge, Mass.: Harvard University Press, Copyright © 2000 by the Russell Sage Foundation.

Harvard University Press: Table 4.25 *"Information technology spending per worker (1987–1994), employment growth (1987–1994), and unemployment rate (1995) by country,"* derived from OECD, *Information Technology Outlook, 1995* (Paris: OECD, 1996, fig. 2.1); employment growth from OECD, *Labour Force Statistics, 1974–1994*; unemployment rates from OECD, *Employment Outlook* (July 1996), compiled and elaborated by Martin Carnoy in the forthcoming *Sustaining the New Economy: Work, Family and Community in the Information Age*, Cambridge, Mass.: Harvard University Press, Copyright © 2000 by the Russell Sage Foundation.

Harvard University Press: Table 4.26 *"Main telephone lines per employee (1986 and 1993) and Internet hosts per 1,000 population (January 1996) by country,"* ITU Statistical Yearbook, 1995, pp. 270–5; Sam Paltridge, "How competition helps the Internet," OECD Observer, no. 201 (Aug.–Sep.) 1996, p. 201; OECD, Information Technology Outlook, 1995, fig. 3.5, compiled and elaborated by Martin Carnoy in the forthcoming *Sustaining the New Economy: Work, Family and Community in the Information Age*, Cambridge, Mass.: Harvard University Press, Copyright © 2000 by the Russell Sage Foundation.

Harvard University Press: Table 4.27 *"Men's and women's employment/population ratios, 15–64 years old, 1973–1998 (percent),"* OECD, Employment Outlook (July 1996, table A); OECD, Employment Outlook (June 1999, table B), compiled by Martin Carnoy in the forthcoming *Sustaining the New Economy: Work, Family and Community in the Information Age*, Cambridge, Mass.: Harvard University Press, Copyright © 2000 by the Russell Sage Foundation.

Humboldt-Universität zu Berlin: Table 7.2 *"Potential lifelong working hours, 1950–1985,"* K. Schuldt, "Soziale und ökonomische Gestaltung der Elemente der Lebensarbeitzeit der Werktätigen," unpublished dissertation, p. 43. Copyright © 1990 Humboldt-Universität zu Berlin, Berlin.

Iwanami Shoten Publishers: Table 4.28 *"Percentage of standard workers included in the* chuki koyo *system of Japanese firms,"* Masami Nomura, *Syushin Koyo*. Copyright © 1994 Iwanami Shoten, Tokyo.

International Labour Organization: Fig. 4.2 *"Total fertility rates for nationals and foreigners, selected OECD countries,"* SOPEMI/OECD, elaborated by P. Stalker, *The Work of Strangers: a Survey of International Labour Migration*. Copyright © 1994 International Labour Organization, Geneva.

Kobe College: Fig. 7.2 *"Ratio of hospitalized deaths to total deaths (%) by year, 1947–1987,"* Koichiri Kuroda, "Medicalization of death: changes in site of death in Japan after World War Two," unpublished research paper, 1990, Department of Inter-cultural Studies, Kobe College, Hyogo.

MIT Press: Fig. 6.11 *"Barcelona: Paseo de Gracia,"* Allan Jacobs, *Great Streets*. Copyright © 1993 MIT Press, Cambridge, MA.

MIT Press: Fig. 6.12 *"Irvine, California: business complex,"* Allan Jacobs, *Great Streets.* Copyright © 1993 MIT Press, Cambridge, MA.

Notisum AB: Table 7.3 *"Duration and reduction of working time, 1970–1987, "* L. O. Pettersson, "Arbetstider i tolv Lander," *Statens offentliga utrednigar,* 53. Copyright © 1989 Notisum AB, Frölunda.

OECD. Table 2.2 *"Productivity in the business sector (percentage changes at annual rates),"* in *Economic Outlook,* June. Copyright © 1995 OECD, Paris.

Polity Press: Table 2.6 *"Cross-border transactions in bonds and equities, 1970–1996,"* IMF 1997, *World Economic Outlook. Globalization: Challenges and Opportunities,* Washington, DC, p. 60, compiled by David Held, Anthony McGrew, David Goldblatt, and Jonathan Perraton, *Global Transformations,* p. 224. Copyright © 1999 Polity/ Stanford University Press, Cambridge. Reprinted by permission of the publisher.

Polity Press: Table 2.7 *"Foreign assets and liabilities as a percentage of total assets and liabilities of commercial banks for selected countries, 1960–1997,"* calculated from IMF, *International Financial Statistics Yearbook* (various years), elaborated by David Held, Anthony McGrew, David Goldblatt, and Jonathan Perraton, *Global Transformations,* p. 227. Copyright © 1999 Polity/Stanford University Press, Cambridge. Reprinted by permission of the publisher.

Polity Press: Table 2.8 *"Direction of world exports, 1965–1995 (percentage of world total),"* calculated from IMF, *Direction of Trade Statistics Yearbook* (various years), elaborated by David Held, Anthony McGrew, David Goldblatt, and Jonathan Perraton, *Global Transformations,* p. 172. Copyright © 1999 Polity/Stanford University Press, Cambridge. Reprinted by permission of the publisher.

Polity Press: Table 2.9 *"Parent corporations and foreign affiliates by area and country, latest available year (number),"* UNCTAD, 1997 (*World Investment Report: Transnational Corporations, Market Structure and Competition Policy*), 1998, compiled by David Held, Anthony McGrew, David Goldblatt, and Jonathan Perraton, *Global Transformations,* p. 245. Copyright © 1999 Polity/Stanford University Press, Cambridge. Reprinted by permission of the publisher.

Population Council: Table 4.22 *"Foreign resident population in West-*

ern Europe, 1950–1990," H. Fassmann and R. Münz, "Patterns and trends of international migration in Western Europe," *Population and Development Review*, 18: 3. Copyright © 1992 Population Council, New York.

Routledge: Fig. 2.8 "*Share of growth from high-tech sector in the United States, 1986–1998,*" US Commerce Department, elaborated by Michael J. Mandel in his article "Meeting the challenge of the new economy," in *Blueprint*, Winter, on-line edition. Copyright © 1999 Routledge, London.

Statistics Bureau and Statistics Center: Table 4.17 "*Japan: percentage distribution of employment by occupation, 1955–1990,*" *Statistical Yearbook of Japan*. Copyright © 1991 Statistics Bureau and Statistics Center, Tokyo. Reprinted by permission of the publisher.

Every effort has been made to trace copyright owners. If notified, the publishers will be pleased to rectify any errors or omissions in the above list at the first opportunity.

Acknowledgments 1996

This book has been 12 years in the making while my research and writing tried to catch up with an object of study expanding faster than my working capacity. That I have been able to reach some form of completion, however tentative, is due to the cooperation, help, and support of a number of people and institutions.

My first and deepest expression of gratitude goes to Emma Kiselyova, whose collaboration was essential in obtaining information for several chapters, in helping with the elaboration of the book, in securing access to languages that I do not know, and in commenting, assessing, and advising on the entire manuscript.

I also want to thank the organizers of four exceptional forums where the main ideas of the book were discussed in depth, and duly rectified, in 1994–5, in the final stage of its elaboration: the special session on this book at the 1994 Meeting of the American Anthropological Association, organized by Ida Susser; the Department of Sociology Colloquium at Berkeley, organized by Loic Wacquant; the international seminar on new world trends organized in Brasilia around Fernando Henrique Cardoso, as he was assuming the presidency of Brazil; and the series of seminars on the book at Tokyo's Hitotsubashi University, organized by Shujiro Yazawa.

Several colleagues in several countries read carefully the draft of the book, in full or specific chapters, and spent considerable time commenting on it, leading to substantial and extensive revisions of the text. The mistakes that remain in the book are entirely mine. Many positive contributions are theirs. I want to acknowledge the collegial efforts of Stephen S. Cohen, Martin Carnoy, Alain Touraine, Anthony Giddens, Daniel Bell, Jesus Leal, Shujiro Yazawa, Peter Hall, Chu-joe Hsia, You-tien Hsing, François Bar, Michael Borrus, Harley Shaiken,

Claude Fischer, Nicole Woolsey-Biggart, Bennett Harrison, Anne Marie Guillemard, Richard Nelson, Loic Wacquant, Ida Susser, Fernando Calderon, Roberto Laserna, Alejandro Foxley, John Urry, Guy Benveniste, Katherine Burlen, Vicente Navarro, Dieter Ernst, Padmanabha Gopinath, Franz Lehner, Julia Trilling, Robert Benson, David Lyon and Melvin Kranzberg.

Throughout the past 12 years a number of institutions have constituted the basis for this work. First of all is my intellectual home, the University of California at Berkeley, and more specifically the academic units in which I have worked: the Department of City and Regional Planning, the Department of Sociology, the Center for Western European Studies, the Institute of Urban and Regional Development, and the Berkeley Roundtable on the International Economy. They have all helped me, and my research, with their material and institutional support, and in providing the appropriate environment to think, imagine, dare, investigate, discuss, and write. A key part of this environment, and therefore of my understanding of the world, is the intelligence and openness of graduate students with whom I have been fortunate to interact. Some of them have also been most helpful research assistants, whose contribution to this book must be recognized: You-tien Hsing, Roberto Laserna, Yuko Aoyama, Chris Benner, and Sandra Moog. I also wish to acknowledge the valuable research assistance of Kekuei Hasegawa at Hitotsubashi University.

Other institutions in various countries have also provided support to conduct the research presented in this book. By naming them, I extend my gratitude to their directors and to the many colleagues in these institutions who have taught me about what I have written in this book. These are: Instituto de Sociología de Nuevas Tecnologías, Universidad Autónoma de Madrid; International Institute of Labour Studies, International Labour Office, Geneva; Soviet (later Russian) Sociological Association; Institute of Economics and Industrial Engineering, Siberian Branch of the USSR (later Russian) Academy of Sciences; Universidad Mayor de San Simon, Cochabamba, Bolivia; Instituto de Investigaciónes Sociales, Universidad Nacional Autónoma de Mexico; Center for Urban Studies, University of Hong Kong; Center for Advanced Studies, National University of Singapore; Institute of Technology and International Economy, The State Council, Beijing; National Taiwan University, Taipei; Korean Research Institute for Human Settlement, Seoul; and Faculty of Social Studies, Hitotsubashi University, Tokyo.

I reserve a special mention for John Davey, Blackwell's editorial director, whose intellectual interaction and helpful criticism over more than 20 years have been precious for the development of my writing, helping me out of frequent dead ends by constantly reminding me that books are about communicating ideas, not about printing words.

Last but not least, I want to thank my surgeon, Dr Lawrence Werboff, and my physician, Dr James Davis, both of the University of California at San Francisco's Mount Zion Hospital, whose care and professionalism gave me the time and energy to finish this book, and maybe others.

Berkeley, California
March 1996

Prologue: the Net and the Self

"Do you think me a learned, well-read man?"
"Certainly," replied Zi-gong. "Aren't you?"
"Not at all," said Confucius. "I have simply grasped one thread which
links up the rest."

Sima Qian, "Confucius"[1]

Toward the end of the second millennium of the Christian era several events of historical significance transformed the social landscape of human life. A technological revolution, centered around information technologies, began to reshape, at accelerated pace, the material basis of society. Economies throughout the world have become globally interdependent, introducing a new form of relationship between economy, state, and society, in a system of variable geometry. The collapse of Soviet statism, and the subsequent demise of the international communist movement, has undermined for the time being the historical challenge to capitalism, rescued the political left (and Marxian theory) from the fatal attraction of Marxism–Leninism, brought the Cold War to an end, reduced the risk of nuclear holocaust, and fundamentally altered global geopolitics. Capitalism itself has undergone a process of profound restructuring, characterized by greater flexibility in management; decentralization and networking of firms both internally and in their relationships to other firms; considerable empowering of capital *vis-à-vis* labor, with the concomitant decline in influence of the labor movement; increasing individualization and diversification of

---

1 Recounted in Sima Qian (145–*c*.89BC), "Confucius," in Hu Shi, *The Development of Logical Methods in Ancient China* (Shanghai: Oriental Book Company, 1922), quoted in Qian (1985: 125).

working relationships; massive incorporation of women into the paid labor force, usually under discriminatory conditions; intervention of the state to deregulate markets selectively, and to undo the welfare state, with different intensity and orientations depending upon the nature of political forces and institutions in each society; stepped-up global economic competition, in a context of increasing geographic and cultural differentiation of settings for capital accumulation and management. As a consequence of this general overhauling of the capitalist system, still under way, we have witnessed the global integration of financial markets, the rise of the Asian Pacific as the new dominant, global manufacturing center, the arduous economic unification of Europe, the emergence of a North American regional economy, the diversification, then disintegration, of the former Third World, the gradual transformation of Russia and the ex-Soviet area of influence in market economies, the incorporation of valuable segments of economies throughout the world into an interdependent system working as a unit in real time. Because of these trends, there has also been an accentuation of uneven development, this time not only between North and South, but between the dynamic segments and territories of societies everywhere, and those others that risk becoming irrelevant from the perspective of the system's logic. Indeed, we observe the parallel unleashing of formidable productive forces of the informational revolution, and the consolidation of black holes of human misery in the global economy, be it in Burkina Faso, South Bronx, Kamagasaki, Chiapas, or La Courneuve.

Simultaneously, criminal activities and Mafia-like organizations around the world have also become global and informational, providing the means for stimulation of mental hyperactivity and forbidden desire, along with all forms of illicit trade demanded by our societies, from sophisticated weaponry to human flesh. In addition, a new communication system, increasingly speaking a universal, digital language, is both integrating globally the production and distribution of words, sounds and images of our culture, and customizing them to the tastes of the identities and moods of individuals. Interactive computer networks are growing exponentially, creating new forms and channels of communication, shaping life and being shaped by life at the same time.

Social changes are as dramatic as the technological and economic processes of transformation. For all the difficulty in the process of transformation of women's condition, patriarchalism has come under attack, and has been shaken in a number of societies. Thus, gender relationships have become, in much of the world, a contested domain, rather than a sphere of cultural reproduction. A fundamental redefinition of relationships between women, men and children has followed, and thus, of family, sexuality, and personality. Environmental consciousness has permeated down to the institutions of society, and its values have won political appeal, at the price of being belied and manipulated in the daily practice of corporations and bureaucracies. Political systems are engulfed in a structural crisis of legitimacy, periodically wrecked by scandals, essentially dependent on media coverage and personalized leadership, and increasingly isolated from the citizenry. Social movements tend to be fragmented, localistic, single-issue oriented, and ephemeral, either retrenched in their inner worlds, or flaring up for just an instant around a media symbol. In such a world of uncontrolled, confusing change, people tend to regroup around primary identities: religious, ethnic, territorial, national. Religious fundamentalism – Christian, Islamic, Jewish, Hindu, and even Buddhist (in what seems to be a contradiction in terms) – is probably the most formidable force for personal security and collective mobilization in these troubled times. In a world of global flows of wealth, power, and images, the search for identity, collective or individual, ascribed or constructed, becomes the fundamental source of social meaning. This is not a new trend, since identity, and particularly religious and ethnic identity, has been at the roots of meaning since the dawn of human society. Yet identity is becoming the main, and sometimes the only, source of meaning in an historical period characterized by widespread destructuring of organizations, delegitimation of institutions, fading away of major social movements, and ephemeral cultural expressions. People increasingly organize their meaning not around what they do but on the basis of what they are, or believe they are. Meanwhile, on the other hand, global networks of instrumental exchanges selectively switch on and off individuals, groups, regions, and even countries, according to their relevance in fulfilling the goals processed in the network, in a relentless flow of strategic decisions. There follows a fundamental split between abstract, universal instrumentalism, and historically rooted, particularistic identities. *Our societies are increasingly structured around a bipolar opposition between the Net and the self.*

In this condition of structural schizophrenia between function and meaning, patterns of social communication become increasingly under stress. And when communication breaks down, when it does not exist any longer, even in the form of conflictual communication (as would be the case in social struggles or political opposition), social groups and individuals become alienated from each other, and see the other as a stranger, eventually as a threat. In this process, social fragmentation spreads, as identities become more specific and increasingly difficult to share. The informational society, in its global manifestation, is also the world of *Aum Shinrikyo*, of the American militia, of

Islamic/Christian theocratic ambitions, and of Hutu/Tutsi reciprocal genocide.

Bewildered by the scale and scope of historical change, culture and thinking in our time often embrace a new millenarianism. Prophets of technology preach the new age, extrapolating to social trends and organization the barely understood logic of computers and DNA. Postmodern culture, and theory, indulge in celebrating the end of history, and, to some extent, the end of reason, giving up on our capacity to understand and make sense, even of nonsense. The implicit assumption is the acceptance of full individualization of behavior, and of society's powerlessness over its destiny.

The project informing this book swims against streams of destruction, and takes exception to various forms of intellectual nihilism, social skepticism, and political cynicism. I believe in rationality, and in the possibility of calling upon reason, without worshipping its goddess. I believe in the chances of meaningful social action, and transformative politics, without necessarily drifting toward the deadly rapids of absolute utopias. I believe in the liberating power of identity, without accepting the necessity of either its individualization or its capture by fundamentalism. And I propose the hypothesis that all major trends of change constituting our new, confusing world are related, and that we can make sense of their interrelationship. And, yes, I believe, in spite of a long tradition of sometimes tragic intellectual errors, that observing, analyzing, and theorizing are a way of helping to build a different, better world. Not by providing the answers – that will be specific to each society and found by social actors themselves – but by raising some relevant questions. This book would like to be a modest contribution to a necessarily collective, analytical effort, already underway from many horizons, aimed at understanding our new world on the basis of available evidence and exploratory theory.

To take some first steps in this direction: we must treat technology seriously, using it as the point of departure of this inquiry; we need to locate the process of revolutionary technological change in the social context in which it takes place and by which it is being shaped; and we should keep in mind that the search for identity is as powerful as techno-economic change in charting the new history. So, having said this, we will depart on our intellectual journey, following an itinerary that will take us to numerous domains, and across several cultures and institutional contexts, since the understanding of a global transformation requires a perspective as global as possible, within the obvious limits of this author's experience and knowledge.

Technology, Society, and Historical Change

The information technology revolution, because of its pervasiveness throughout the whole realm of human activity, will be my entry point in analyzing the complexity of the new economy, society, and culture in the making. This methodological choice does not imply that new social forms and processes emerge as a consequence of technological change. Of course, technology does not determine society.[2] Nor does society script the course of technological change, since many factors, including individual inventiveness and entrepreneurialism, intervene in the process of scientific discovery, technological innovation, and social applications, so that the final outcome depends on a complex pattern of interaction.[3] Indeed, the dilemma of technological determinism is probably a false problem,[4] since technology *is* society, and society cannot be understood or represented without its technological tools.[5] Thus, when in the 1970s a new technological paradigm, organized around information technology, came to be constituted, mainly in the United States (see chapter 1), it was a specific segment of American society, in interaction with the global economy and with world geopolitics, that materialized into a new way of producing, communicating, managing, and living. That the constitution of this paradigm took place in the United States, and to some extent in California, and in the 1970s, probably had considerable consequences for the forms and evolution of new information technologies. For instance, in spite of the decisive role of military funding and markets in fostering early stages of the electronics industry during the 1940s–1960s, the technological blossoming that took place in the early 1970s can be somehow related to the culture of freedom, individual innovation, and entrepreneurialism that grew out of the 1960s' culture of American campuses. Not so much in terms of its politics, since Silicon Valley was, and is, a solid bastion of the conservative vote, and most innovators were meta-political, but with regard to social values of breaking away from established patterns of behavior, both in society at large and in the business world. The emphasis on personalized devices, on

2   See the interesting debate on the matter in Smith and Marx (1994).
3   Technology does not determine society: it embodies it. But nor does society determine technological innovation: it uses it. This dialectical interaction between society and technology is present in the works of the best historians, such as Fernand Braudel.
4   Classic historian of technology Melvin Kranzberg has forcefully argued against the false dilemma of technological determinism. See, for instance, Kranzberg's (1992) acceptance speech of the award of honorary membership in NASTS.
5   Bijker et al. (1987).

interactivity, on networking, and the relentless pursuit of new technological breakthroughs, even when it apparently did not make much business sense, was clearly in discontinuity with the somewhat cautious tradition of the corporate world. The information technology revolution half-consciously[6] diffused through the material culture of our societies the libertarian spirit that flourished in the 1960s' movements. Yet, as soon as new information technologies diffused, and were appropriated by different countries, various cultures, diverse organizations, and miscellaneous goals, they exploded in all kinds of applications and uses that fed back into technological innovation, accelerating the speed, broadening the scope of technological change, and diversifying its sources.[7] An illustration will help us to understand the importance of unintended social consequences of technology.[8]

As is known, the Internet originated in a daring scheme imagined in the 1960s by the technological warriors of the US Defense Department Advanced Research Projects Agency (the mythical DARPA) to prevent a Soviet takeover or destruction of American communications in the event of nuclear war. To some extent, it was the electronic equivalent of the Maoist tactics of dispersal of guerrilla forces around a vast territory to counter an enemy's might with versatility and knowledge of terrain. The outcome was a network architecture which, as its inventors wanted, cannot be controlled from any center, and is made up of thousands of autonomous computer networks that have innumerable ways to link up, going around electronic barriers. Ultimately ARPANET, the network set up by the US Defense Department, became the foundation of a global, horizontal communication network

6   There is still to be written a fascinating social history of the values and personal views of some of the key innovators of the 1970s' Silicon Valley revolution in computer technologies. But a few indications seem to point to the fact that they were intentionally trying to undo the centralizing technologies of the corporate world, both out of conviction and as their market niche. As evidence, I recall the famous Apple Computer 1984 advertising spot to launch Macintosh, in explicit opposition to Big Brother IBM of Orwellian mythology. As for the countercultural character of many of these innovators, I shall also refer to the life story of the genius developer of the personal computer, Steve Wozniak: after quitting Apple, bored by its transformation into another multinational corporation, he spent a fortune for a few years subsidizing rock groups that he liked, before creating another company to develop technologies of his taste. At one point, after having created the personal computer, Wozniak realized that he had no formal education in computer sciences, so he enrolled at UC Berkeley. But in order to avoid embarrassing publicity he used another name.
7   For selected evidence concerning the variation of information technology diffusion patterns in different social and institutional contexts, see, among other works: Bertazzoni et al. (1984); Guile (1985); Agence de l'Informatique (1986); Castells et al. (1986); Landau and Rosenberg (1986); Bianchi et al. (1988); Watanuki (1990); Freeman et al. (1991); Wang (1994).
8   For an informed and cautious discussion of relationships between society and technology, see Fischer (1985).

of thousands of computer networks (comprising over 300 million users in 2000, up from less than 20 million in 1996, and growing fast) that has been appropriated for all kinds of purposes, quite removed from the concerns of an extinct Cold War, by individuals and groups around the world. Indeed, it was via the Internet that Subcomandante Marcos, the leader of Chiapas' *Zapatistas*, communicated with the world, and with the media, from the depths of Lacandon forest. And the Internet played an instrumental role in the development of Falun Gong, the Chinese cult that challenged the Chinese Communist party in 1999, and in the organization and diffusion of the protest against the World Trade Organization in Seattle in December 1999.

Yet, if society does not determine technology, it can, mainly through the state, suffocate its development. Or alternatively, again mainly by state intervention, it can embark on an accelerated process of technological modernization able to change the fate of economies, military power, and social well-being in a few years. Indeed, the ability or inability of societies to master technology, and particularly technologies that are strategically decisive in each historical period, largely shapes their destiny, to the point where we could say that while technology *per se* does not determine historical evolution and social change, technology (or the lack of it) embodies the capacity of societies to transform themselves, as well as the uses to which societies, always in a conflictive process, decide to put their technological potential.[9]

Thus, around 1400, when the European Renaissance was planting the intellectual seeds of technological change that would dominate the world three centuries later, China was the most advanced technological civilization in the world, according to Mokyr.[10] Key inventions had developed in China centuries earlier, even a millennium and a half earlier, as in the case of blast furnaces that allowed the casting of iron in China by 200BC. Also, Su Sung introduced the water clock in AD 1086, surpassing the accuracy of measurement of European mechanical clocks of the same date. The iron plow was introduced in the sixth century, and adapted to wet-field rice cultivation two centuries later. In textiles, the spinning wheel appeared at the same time as in the West, by the thirteenth century, but advanced much faster in China because there was an old-established tradition of sophisticated weaving equipment: draw looms to weave silk were used in Han times. The adoption of water power was parallel to Europe: by the eighth century

9   See the analyses presented in Castells (1988b); also Webster (1991).
10   My discussion of China's interrupted technological development relies mainly on an extraordinary chapter by Joel Mokyr (1990: 209–38) and on a most insightful, although controversial, book, Qian (1985).

the Chinese were using hydraulic trip hammers, and in 1280 there was wide diffusion of the vertical water wheel. Ocean travel was easier for the Chinese at an earlier date than for European vessels: they invented the compass around AD 960, and their junks were the most advanced ships in the world by the end of the fourteenth century, enabling long sea trips. In military matters, the Chinese, besides inventing gun powder, developed a chemical industry that was able to provide powerful explosives, and the crossbow and the trebuchet were used by Chinese armies centuries ahead of Europe. In medicine, techniques such as acupuncture were yielding extraordinary results that only recently have been universally acknowledged. And, of course, the first information processing revolution was Chinese: paper and printing were Chinese inventions. Paper was introduced in China 1,000 years earlier than in the West, and printing probably began in the late seventh century. As Jones writes: "China came within a hair's breadth of industrializing in the fourteenth century."[11] That it did not, changed the history of the world. When in 1842 the Opium Wars led to Britain's colonial impositions, China realized, too late, that isolation could not protect the Middle Kingdom from the evil consequences of technological inferiority. It took more than one century thereafter for China to start recovering from such a catastrophic deviation from its historical trajectory.

Explanations for such a stunning historical course are both numerous and controversial. There is no place in this Prologue to enter the complexity of the debate. But, on the basis of research and analysis by historians such as Needham, Qian, Jones, and Mokyr,[12] it is possible to suggest an interpretation that may help to understand, in general terms, the interaction between society, history, and technology. Indeed, most hypotheses concerning cultural differences (even those without implicitly racist undertones) fail to explain, as Mokyr points out, the difference not between China and Europe but between China in 1300 and China in 1800. Why did a culture and a kingdom that had been the technological leader of the world for thousands of years suddenly become technologically stagnant precisely at the moment when Europe embarked on the age of discoveries, and then on the industrial revolution?

Needham has proposed that Chinese culture was more prone than Western values to a harmonious relationship between man and nature, something that could be jeopardized by fast technological innovation. Furthermore, he objects to the Western criteria used to measure technological development. However, this cultural emphasis on a

---

11 Jones (1981: 160), cited by Mokyr (1990: 219).
12 Needham (1954–88, 1969, 1981); Qian (1985); Jones (1988); Mokyr (1990).

holistic approach to development had not impeded technological innovation for millenniums, nor stopped ecological deterioration as a
result of irrigation works in southern China, when the conservation of
nature was subordinated to agricultural production in order to feed a
growing population. In fact, Wen-yuan Qian, in his powerful book,
takes exception to Needham's somewhat excessive enthusiasm for the
feats of Chinese traditional technology, notwithstanding his shared
admiration for Needham's monumental life-long work. Qian calls for
a closer analytical linkage between the development of Chinese science and the characteristics of Chinese civilization dominated by the
dynamics of state. Mokyr also considers the state to be the crucial
factor in explaining Chinese technological retardation in modern times.
The explanation may be proposed in three steps: technological innovation was, for centuries, fundamentally in the hands of the state;
after 1400 the Chinese state, under the Ming and Qing dynasties, lost
interest in technological innovation; and, partly because of their dedication to serve the state, cultural and social elites were focused on arts,
humanities, and self-promotion *vis-à-vis* the imperial bureaucracy.
Thus, what does seem to be crucial is the role of the state, and the
changing orientation of state policy. Why would a state that had been
the greatest hydraulic engineer in history, and had established an agricultural extension system to improve agricultural productivity since
the Han period, suddenly become inhibited from technological innovation, even forbidding geographical exploration, and abandoning the
construction of large ships by 1430? The obvious answer is that it was
not the same state; not only because they were of different dynasties,
but because the bureaucratic class became more deeply entrenched in
the administration due to a longer than usual period of uncontested
domination.

According to Mokyr, it appears that the determining factor for technological conservatism was the rulers' fears of the potentially disruptive impacts of technological change on social stability. Numerous forces
opposed the diffusion of technology in China, as in other societies,
particularly the urban guilds. Bureaucrats content with the status quo
were concerned by the possibility of triggering social conflicts that
could coalesce with other sources of latent opposition in a society that
had been kept under control for several centuries. Even the two en-
lightened Manchu despots of the eighteenth century, K'ang Chi and
Ch'ien Lung, focused their efforts on pacification and order, rather
than on unleashing new development. Conversely, exploration and
contacts with foreigners, beyond controlled trade and the acquisition
of weapons, were deemed at best unnecessary, at worst threatening, because of the uncertainty they would imply. A bureaucratic state

without external incentive and with internal disincentives to engage in technological modernization opted for the most prudent neutrality, as a result stalling the technological trajectory that China had been following for centuries, if not millenniums, precisely under state guidance. A discussion of the factors underlying the dynamics of the Chinese state under the Ming and Qing dynasties is clearly beyond the scope of this book. What matters for our research purposes are two teachings from this fundamental experience of interrupted technological development: on the one hand, the state can be, and has been in history, in China and elsewhere, a leading force for technological innovation; on the other hand, precisely because of this, when the state reverses its interest in technological development, or becomes unable to perform it under new conditions, a statist model of innovation leads to stagnation, because of the sterilization of society's autonomous innovative energy to create and apply technology. That the Chinese state could, centuries later, build anew an advanced technological basis, in nuclear technology, missiles, satellite launching, and electronics,[13] demonstrates again the emptiness of a predominantly cultural interpretation of technological development and backwardness: the same culture may induce very different technological trajectories depending on the pattern of relationships between state and society. However, the exclusive dependence on the state has a price, and the price for China was that of retardation, famine, epidemics, colonial domination, and civil war, until at least the middle of the twentieth century.

A rather similar, contemporary story can be told, and will be told in this book (in volume III), of the inability of Soviet statism to master the information technology revolution, thus stalling its productive capacity and undermining its military might. Yet we should not jump to the ideological conclusion that all state intervention is counterproductive to technological development, indulging in ahistorical reverence for unfettered, individual entrepreneurialism. Japan is of course the counter-example, both to Chinese historical experience and to the inability of the Soviet state to adapt to the American-initiated revolution in information technology.

Historically, Japan went, even deeper than China, through a period of historical isolation under the Tokugawa Shogunate (established in 1603), between 1636 and 1853, precisely during the critical period of the formation of an industrial system in the Western hemisphere. Thus, while at the turn of the seventeenth century Japanese merchants were trading throughout East and South-East Asia, using modern vessels of up to 700 tons, the construction of ships above 50 tons was prohib-

13   Wang (1993).

ited in 1635, and all Japanese ports, except Nagasaki, were closed to foreigners, while trade was restricted to China, Korea, and Holland.[14] Technological isolation was not total during these two centuries, and endogenous innovation did allow Japan to proceed with incremental change at a faster pace than China.[15] Yet, because Japan's technological level was lower than China's, by the mid-nineteenth century the *kurobune* (black ships) of Commodore Perry could impose trade and diplomatic relations on a country substantially lagging behind Western technology. However, as soon as the 1868 *Ishin Meiji* (Meiji Restoration) created the political conditions for a decisive state-led modernization,[16] Japan progressed in advanced technology by leaps and bounds in a very short time span.[17] As just one significant illustration, because of its current strategic importance, let us briefly recall the extraordinary development of electrical engineering and communication applications in Japan in the last quarter of the nineteenth century.[18] Indeed, the first independent department of electrical engineering in the world was established in 1873 in the newly founded Imperial College of Engineering in Tokyo, under the leadership of its dean, Henry Dyer, a Scottish mechanical engineer. Between 1887 and 1892, a leading academic in electrical engineering, British professor William Ayrton, was invited to teach at the college, being instrumental in disseminating knowledge to the new generation of Japanese engineers, so that by the end of the century the Telegraph Bureau was able to replace foreigners in all its technical departments. Technology transfer from the West was sought through a variety of mechanisms. In 1873, the machine shop of the Telegraph Bureau sent a Japanese clockmaker, Tanaka Seisuke, to the International Machines exhibition in Vienna to obtain information on the machines. About ten years later, all the bureau's machines were made in Japan. Based on this technology, Tanaka Daikichi founded in 1882 an electrical factory, Shibaura Works, which, after its acquisition by Mitsui, went on to

14 Chida and Davies (1990).
15 Ito (1993).
16 Several distinguished Japanese scholars, and I tend to concur with them, consider that the best Western account of the Meiji Restoration, and of the social roots of Japanese modernization, is Norman (1940). It has been translated into Japanese and is widely read in Japanese universities. A brilliant historian, educated at Cambridge and Harvard, before joining the Canadian diplomatic corps, Norman was denounced as a communist by Karl Wittfogel to the McCarthy Senate Committee in the 1950s, and was then submitted to constant pressure from Western intelligence agencies. Appointed Canadian ambassador to Egypt, he committed suicide in Cairo in 1957. On the contribution of this truly exceptional scholar to the understanding of the Japanese state, see Dower (1975); for a different perspective, see Beasley (1990).
17 Kamatani (1988); Matsumoto and Sinclair (1994).
18 Uchida (1991).

become Toshiba. Engineers were sent to Europe and to America. And Western Electric was permitted to produce and sell in Japan in 1899, in a joint venture with Japanese industrialists: the name of the company was NEC. On such a technological basis Japan went full speed into the electrical and communications age before 1914: by 1914 total power production had reached 1,555,000 kw/hour, and 3,000 telephone offices were relaying a billion messages a year. It is indeed symbolic that Commodore Perry's gift to the Shogun in 1857 was a set of American telegraphs, until then never seen in Japan: the first telegraph line was laid in 1869, and ten years later Japan was connected to the whole world through a transcontinental information network, via Siberia, operated by the Great Northern Telegraph Co., jointly managed by Western and Japanese engineers and transmitting in both English and Japanese.

The story of how Japan became a major world player in information technology industries in the last quarter of the twentieth century, under the strategic guidance of the state, is now general public knowledge, so it will be assumed in our discussion.[19] What is relevant for the ideas presented here is that it happened at the same time as an industrial and scientific superpower, the Soviet Union, failed this fundamental technological transition. It is obvious, as the preceding reminders show, that Japanese technological development since the 1960s did not happen in an historical vacuum, but was rooted in a decades-old tradition of engineering excellence. Yet what matters for the purpose of this analysis is to emphasize what dramatically different results state intervention (and lack of intervention) had in the cases of China and the Soviet Union, as compared to Japan in both the Meiji period and the post-Second World War period. The characteristics of the Japanese state at the roots of both processes of modernization and development are well known, both for *Ishin Meiji*[20] and for the contemporary developmental state,[21] and their presentation would take us excessively away from the focus of these preliminary reflections. What must be retained for the understanding of the relationship between technology and society is that the role of the state, by either stalling, unleashing, or leading technological innovation, is a decisive factor in the overall process, as it expresses and organizes the social and cultural forces that dominate in a given space and time. To a large extent, technology expresses the ability of a society to propel itself into technological

19 Ito (1994); Japan Informatization Processing Center (1994); for a Western perspective, see Forester (1993).
20 See Norman (1940); Dower (1975); Allen (1981a).
21 Johnson (1995).

mastery through the institutions of society, including the state. The historical process through which this development of productive forces takes place earmarks the characteristics of technology and its interweaving in social relationships.

This is not different in the case of the current technological revolution. It originated and diffused, not by accident, in an historical period of the global restructuring of capitalism, for which it was an essential tool. Thus, the new society emerging from this process of change is both capitalist and informational, while presenting considerable historical variation in different countries, according to their history, culture, institutions, and their specific relationship to global capitalism and information technology.

Informationalism, Industrialism, Capitalism, Statism: Modes of Development and Modes of Production

The information technology revolution was instrumental in allowing the implementation of a fundamental process of restructuring of the capitalist system from the 1980s onwards. In the process, this technological revolution was itself shaped, in its development and manifestations, by the logic and interests of advanced capitalism, without being reducible to the expression of such interests. The alternative system of social organization present in our historical period, statism, also tried to redefine the means of accomplishing its structural goals while preserving the essence of these goals: that is the meaning of restructuring (or *perestroika*, in Russian). Yet Soviet statism failed in its attempt, to the point of collapsing the whole system, to a large extent because of the incapacity of statism to assimilate and use the principles of informationalism embodied in new information technologies, as I shall argue in this book (volume III) on the basis of empirical analysis. Chinese statism seemed to succeed by shifting from statism to state-led capitalism and integration in global economic networks, actually becoming closer to the developmental state model of East Asian capitalism than to the "socialism with Chinese characteristics" of official ideology,[22] as I shall also try to discuss in volume III. None the less, it is highly likely that the process of structural transformation in China will undergo major political conflicts and institutional change in the coming years. The collapse of statism (with rare exceptions, for

22 Nolan and Furen (1990); Hsing (1996).

example, Vietnam, North Korea, Cuba, which are, nevertheless, in the process of linking up with global capitalism) has established a close relationship between the new, global capitalist system, shaped by its relatively successful *perestroika*, and the emergence of informationalism, as the new material, technological basis of economic activity and social organization. Yet both processes (capitalist restructuring, the rise of informationalism) are distinct, and their interaction can only be understood if we separate them analytically. At this point in my introductory presentation of the book's *idées fortes*, it seems necessary to propose some theoretical distinctions and definitions concerning capitalism, statism, industrialism, and informationalism.

It is a well-established tradition in theories of post-industrialism and informationalism, starting with classic works by Alain Touraine[23] and Daniel Bell,[24] to place the distinction between pre-industrialism, industrialism, and informationalism (or post-industrialism) on a different axis from the one opposing capitalism and statism (or collectivism, in Bell's terms). While societies can be characterized along the two axes (so that we have industrial statism, industrial capitalism, and so on), it is essential for the understanding of social dynamics to maintain the analytical distance and empirical interrelation between modes of production (capitalism, statism) and modes of development (industrialism, informationalism). To root these distinctions in a theoretical basis, which will inform the specific analyses presented in this book, it is unavoidable to take the reader, for a few paragraphs, into the somewhat arcane domains of sociological theory.

This book studies the emergence of a new social structure, manifested in various forms, depending on the diversity of cultures and institutions throughout the planet. This new social structure is associated with the emergence of a new mode of development, informationalism, historically shaped by the restructuring of the capitalist mode of production towards the end of the twentieth century.

The theoretical perspective underlying this approach postulates that societies are organized around human processes structured by historically determined relationships of *production, experience,* and *power.* *Production* is the action of humankind on matter (nature) to appropriate it and transform it for its benefit by obtaining a product, consuming (unevenly) part of it, and accumulating surplus for investment, according to a variety of socially determined goals. *Experience* is the action of human subjects on themselves, determined by the interaction

23 Touraine (1969).
24 Bell (1976). First published 1973, but all quotes are from the 1976 edition, which includes a new, substantial "Foreword 1976."

between their biological and cultural identities, and in relationship to their social and natural environment. It is constructed around the endless search for fulfillment of human needs and desires. *Power* is that relationship between human subjects which, on the basis of production and experience, imposes the will of some subjects upon others by the potential or actual use of violence, physical or symbolic. Institutions of society are built to enforce power relationships existing in each historical period, including the controls, limits, and social contracts achieved in the power struggles.

Production is organized in class relationships that define the process by which some human subjects, on the basis of their position in the production process, decide the sharing and uses of the product in relationship to consumption and investment. Experience is structured around gender/sexual relationships, historically organized around the family, and characterized hitherto by the domination of men over women. Family relationships and sexuality structure personality and frame symbolic interaction.

Power is founded upon the state and its institutionalized monopoly of violence, although what Foucault labels the microphysics of power, embodied in institutions and organizations, diffuses throughout the entire society, from workplaces to hospitals, enclosing subjects in a tight framework of formal duties and informal aggressions.

Symbolic communication between humans, and the relationship between humans and nature, on the basis of production (with its complement, consumption), experience, and power, crystallize over history in specific territories, thus generating *cultures and collective identities*.

Production is a socially complex process because each one of its elements is internally differentiated. Thus, humankind as collective producer includes both labor and the organizers of production, and labor is highly differentiated and stratified according to the role of each worker in the production process. Matter includes nature, human-modified nature, human-produced nature, and human nature itself, the labors of history forcing us to move away from the classic distinction between humankind and nature, since millenniums of human action have incorporated the natural environment into society, making us, materially and symbolically, an inseparable part of this environment. The relationship between labor and matter in the process of work involves the use of means of production to act upon matter on the basis of energy, knowledge, and information. Technology is the specific form of this relationship.

The product of the production process is socially used under two forms: consumption and surplus. Social structures interact with production processes by determining the rules for the appropriation, distribution, and uses of the surplus. These rules constitute modes of production, and these modes define social relationships of production, determining the existence of social classes that become constituted as such classes through their historical practice. The structural principle under which surplus is appropriated and controlled characterizes a mode of production. In the twentieth century we lived, essentially, with two predominant modes of production: capitalism and statism. Under capitalism, the separation between producers and their means of production, the commodification of labor, and the private ownership of means of production on the basis of the control of capital (commodified surplus), determined the basic principle of appropriation and distribution of surplus by capitalists, although who is (are) the capitalist class(es) is a matter of social inquiry in each historical context, rather than an abstract category. Under statism, the control of surplus is external to the economic sphere: it lies in the hands of the power-holders in the state – let us call them *apparatchiki* or *lingdao*. Capitalism is oriented toward profit-maximizing, that is, toward increasing the amount of surplus appropriated by capital on the basis of the private control over the means of production and circulation. Statism is (was?) oriented toward power-maximizing, that is, toward increasing the military and ideological capacity of the political apparatus for imposing its goals on a greater number of subjects and at deeper levels of their consciousness.

The social relationships of production, and thus the mode of production, determine the appropriation and uses of surplus. A separate yet fundamental question is the level of such surplus, determined by the productivity of a particular process of production, that is by the ratio of the value of each unit of output to the value of each unit of input. Productivity levels are themselves dependent on the relationship between labor and matter, as a function of the use of the means of production by the application of energy and knowledge. This process is characterized by technical relationships of production, defining modes of development. Thus, modes of development are the technological arrangements through which labor works on matter to generate the product, ultimately determining the level and quality of surplus. Each mode of development is defined by the element that is fundamental in fostering productivity in the production process. Thus, in the agrarian mode of development, the source of increasing surplus results from quantitative increases of labor and natural resources (particularly land) in the production process, as well as from the natural endowment of these resources. In the industrial mode of development, the main source of productivity lies in the introduction of new energy sources, and in the ability to decentralize the use of energy throughout the production and circulation processes. In the new, informational mode of development the source of productivity lies in the technology of knowledge generation, information processing, and symbol communication. To be sure, knowledge and information are critical elements in all modes of development, since the process of production is always based on some level of knowledge and in the processing of information.[25] However, what is specific to the informational mode of development is the action of knowledge upon knowledge itself as the main source of productivity (see chapter 2). Information processing is focused on improving the technology of information processing as a source of productivity, in a virtuous circle of interaction between the knowledge sources of technology and the application of technology to improve knowledge generation and information processing: this is why, rejoining popular fashion, I call this new mode of development informational, constituted by the emergence of a new technological paradigm based on information technology (see chapter 1).

Each mode of development has also a structurally determined performance principle around which technological processes are organized: industrialism is oriented toward economic growth, that is toward maximizing output; informationalism is oriented towards technological development, that is toward the accumulation of knowledge and towards higher levels of complexity in information processing. While higher levels of knowledge may normally result in higher levels of output per unit of input, it is the pursuit of knowledge and information that characterizes the technological production function under informationalism.

Although technology and technical relationships of production are organized in paradigms originating in the dominant spheres of society (for example, the production process, the military–industrial complex) they diffuse throughout the whole set of social relationships and social

---

25 For the sake of clarity in this book, it is necessary to provide a definition of knowledge and information, even if such an intellectually satisfying gesture introduces a dose of the arbitrary in the discourse, as social scientists who have struggled with the issue know well. I have no compelling reason to improve on Daniel Bell's (1976: 175) own definition of *knowledge*: "Knowledge: a set of organized statements of facts or ideas, presenting a reasoned judgment or an experimental result, which is transmitted to others through some communication medium in some systematic form. Thus, I distinguish knowledge from news and entertainment." As for *information*, some established authors in the field, such as Machlup, simply define information as the communication of knowledge (see Machlup 1962: 15). However, this is because Machlup's definition of knowledge seems to be excessively broad, as Bell argues. Thus, I would rejoin the operational definition of information proposed by Porat in his classic work (1977: 2): "Information is data that have been organized and communicated."

structures, so penetrating and modifying power and experience.[26] Thus, modes of development shape the entire realm of social behavior, of course including symbolic communication. Because informationalism is based on the technology of knowledge and information, there is an especially close linkage between culture and productive forces, between spirit and matter, in the informational mode of development. It follows that we should expect the emergence of historically new forms of social interaction, social control, and social change.

Informationalism and capitalist perestroika

Shifting from theoretical categories to historical change, what truly matters for social processes and forms making the living flesh of societies is the actual interaction between modes of production and modes of development, enacted and fought for by social actors, in unpredictable ways, within the constraining framework of past history and current conditions of technological and economic development. Thus, the world, and societies, would have been very different if Gorbachev had succeeded in his own *perestroika*, a target that was politically difficult, but not out of reach. Or if the Asian Pacific had not been able to blend its traditional business networking form of economic organization with the tools provided by information technology. Yet the most decisive historical factor accelerating, channeling and shaping the information technology paradigm, and inducing its associated social forms, was/is the process of capitalist restructuring undertaken since the 1980s, so that the new techno-economic system can be adequately characterized as *informational capitalism*.

The Keynesian model of capitalist growth, which brought unprecedented economic prosperity and social stability to most market economies for almost three decades after the Second World War, hit the wall of its built-in limitations in the early 1970s, and its crisis was manifested in the form of rampant inflation.[27] When the oil price in-

---

26 When technological innovation does not diffuse in society, because of institutional obstacles to such diffusion, what follows is technological retardation because of the absence of necessary social/cultural feedback into the institutions of innovation and into the innovators themselves. This is the fundamental lesson that can be drawn from such important experiences as Qing's China or the Soviet Union. For the Soviet Union, see volume III. For China, see Qian (1985) and Mokyr (1990).

27 I presented some years ago my interpretation of the causes of the 1970s' worldwide economic crisis, as well as a tentative prognosis of avenues for capitalist restructuring. Notwithstanding the excessively rigid theoretical framework I juxtaposed to the empirical analysis, I think that the main points I made in that book (written in 1977–8), including the prediction of Reaganomics under that name, are still useful to understand the qualitative changes that operated in capitalism during the last two decades of the twentieth century (see Castells 1980).

creases of 1974 and 1979 threatened to spiral inflation out of control, governments and firms engaged in a process of restructuring in a pragmatic process of trial and error that continued into the 1990s with a more decisive effort at deregulation, privatization, and the dismantling of the social contract between capital and labor that underlay the stability of the previous growth model. In a nutshell, a series of reforms, both at the level of institutions and in the management of firms, aimed at four main goals: deepening the capitalist logic of profit-seeking in capital–labor relationships; enhancing the productivity of labor and capital; globalizing production, circulation, and markets, seizing the opportunity of the most advantageous conditions for profit-making everywhere; and marshaling the state's support for productivity gains and competitiveness of national economies, often to the detriment of social protection and public interest regulations. Technological innovation and organizational change, focusing on flexibility and adaptability, were absolutely critical in ensuring the speed and efficiency of restructuring. It can be argued that without new information technology global capitalism would have been a much-limited reality, flexible management would have been reduced to labor trimming, and the new round of spending in both capital goods and new consumer products would not have been sufficient to compensate for the reduction in public spending. Thus, informationalism is linked to the expansion and rejuvenation of capitalism, as industrialism was linked to its constitution as a mode of production. To be sure, the process of restructuring had very different manifestations in areas and societies around the world, as I shall briefly survey in chapter 2: it was diverted from its fundamental logic by the military Keynesianism of the Reagan administration, actually creating even greater difficulties for the American economy at the end of the euphoria of artificial stimulation; it was somewhat limited in Western Europe because of society's resistance to the dismantling of the welfare state and to one-sided labor market flexibility, with the result of rising unemployment in the European Union; it was absorbed in Japan without dramatic changes by emphasizing productivity and competitiveness on the basis of technology and cooperation rather than by increasing exploitation, until international pressures forced Japan to offshore production and to broadening the role of an unprotected, secondary labor market; and it plunged into a major recession, in the 1980s, the economies of Africa (except South Africa and Botswana) and Latin America (with the exception of Chile and Colombia), when International Monetary Fund policies cut the money supply and reduced wages and imports in order to homogenize conditions of global capital accumulation around the world. Restructuring proceeded on the basis of the political defeat of organized labor in major capitalist countries, and the acceptance of a common economic discipline by countries of the OECD area. Such discipline, although enforced when necessary by the Bundesbank, the Federal Reserve Board, and the International Monetary Fund, was in fact inscribed in the integration of global financial markets that took place in the early 1980s using new information technologies. Under conditions of global financial integration, autonomous, national monetary policies became literally unfeasible, thus equalizing basic economic parameters of restructuring processes throughout the planet.

While capitalism's restructuring and the diffusion of informationalism were inseparable processes on a global scale, societies did act/react differently to such processes, according to the specificity of their history, culture, and institutions. Thus, to some extent it would be improper to refer to an "informational society," which would imply the homogeneity of social forms everywhere under the new system. This is obviously an untenable proposition, empirically and theoretically. Yet we could speak of an informational society in the same way that sociologists have been referring to the existence of an "industrial society," characterized by common fundamental features in their sociotechnical systems, for instance in Raymond Aron's formulation.[28] But with two important qualifications: on the one hand, informational societies, as they exist currently, are capitalist (unlike industrial societies, some of which were statist); on the other hand, we must stress the cultural and institutional diversity of informational societies. Thus, Japanese uniqueness[29] or Spain's difference[30] is not going to fade away in a process of cultural indifferentiation, marching anew toward universal modernization, this time measured by rates of computer diffusion. Nor is China or Brazil going to be melted in the global pot of informational capitalism by continuing their current high-speed developmental path. But Japan, Spain, China, Brazil, as well as the United States, are and will be more so in the future, informational societies, in the sense that the core processes of knowledge generation, economic productivity, political/military power, and media communication are already deeply transformed by the informational paradigm, and are connected to global networks of wealth, power, and symbols working under such a logic. Thus, all societies are affected by capitalism and informationalism, and many societies (certainly all major societies)

28   Aron (1963).
29   On Japanese uniqueness in a sociological perspective, see Shoji (1990).
30   On the social roots of Spanish differences, and similarities, *vis-à-vis* other countries, see Zaldivar and Castells (1992).

are already informational,[31] although of different kinds, in different settings, and with specific cultural/institutional expressions. A theory of the informational society, as distinct from a global/informational economy, will always have to be attentive to historical/cultural specificity as much as to structural similarities related to a largely shared techno-economic paradigm. As for the actual content of this common social structure that could be considered to be the essence of the new informational society, I'm afraid I am unable to summarize it in one paragraph: indeed, the structure and processes that characterize informational societies are the subject matter covered in this book.

The Self in the Informational Society

New information technologies are integrating the world in global networks of instrumentality. Computer-mediated communication begets

---

31 I should like to draw an analytical distinction between the notions of "information society" and "informational society," with similar implications for information/informational economy. The term "information society" emphasizes the role of information in society. But I argue that information, in its broadest sense, e.g. as communication of knowledge, has been critical in all societies, including medieval Europe which was culturally structured, and to some extent unified, around scholasticism, that is, by and large an intellectual framework (see Southern 1995). In contrast, the term "informational" indicates the attribute of a specific form of social organization in which information generation, processing, and transmission become the fundamental sources of productivity and power because of new technological conditions emerging in this historical period. My terminology tries to establish a parallel with the distinction between industry and industrial. An industrial society (a usual notion in the sociological tradition) is not just a society where there is industry, but a society where the social and technological forms of industrial organization permeate all spheres of activity, starting with the dominant activities, located in the economic system and in military technology, and reaching the objects and habits of everyday life. My use of the terms "informational society" and "informational economy" attempts a more precise characterization of current transformations beyond the common-sense observation that information and knowledge are important to our societies. However, the actual content of "informational society" has to be determined by observation and analysis. This is precisely the object of this book. For instance, one of the key features of informational society is the networking logic of its basic structure, which explains the use of the concept of "network society," as defined and specified in the conclusion of this volume. However, other components of "informational society," such as social movements or the state, exhibit features that go beyond the networking logic, although they are substantially influenced by such logic, as characteristic of the new social structure. Thus, "the network society" does not exhaust all the meaning of the "informational society." Finally, why, after all these precisions, have I kept *The Information Age* as the overall title of the book, without including medieval Europe in my inquiry? Titles are communicating devices. They should be user-friendly, clear enough for the reader to guess what is the real topic of the book, and worded in a fashion that does not depart excessively from the semantic frame of reference. Thus, in a world built around information technologies, information society, informatization, information superhighway, and the like (all terminologies originated in Japan in the mid-1960s – *johoka shakai*, in Japanese – and transmitted to the west in 1978 by Simon Nora and Alain Minc, indulging in exoticism), a title such as *The Information Age* points straightforwardly to the questions to be raised, without prejudging the answers.

a vast array of virtual communities. Yet the distinctive social and political trend of the 1990s was the construction of social action and politics around primary identities, either ascribed, rooted in history and geography, or newly built in an anxious search for meaning and spirituality. The first historical steps of informational societies seem to characterize them by the pre-eminence of identity as their organizing principle. I understand by identity the process by which a social actor recognizes itself and constructs meaning primarily on the basis of a given cultural attribute or set of attributes, to the exclusion of a broader reference to other social structures. Affirmation of identity does not necessarily mean incapacity to relate to other identities (for example, women still relate to men) or to embrace the whole society under such identity (for example, religious fundamentalism aspires to convert everybody). But social relationships are defined *vis-à-vis* the others on the basis of those cultural attributes that specify identity. For instance, Yoshino, in his study on *nihonjiron* (ideas of Japanese uniqueness), pointedly defines cultural nationalism as "the aim to regenerate the national community by creating, preserving or strengthening a people's cultural identity when it is felt to be lacking, or threatened. The cultural nationalist regards the nation as the product of its unique history and culture and as a collective solidarity endowed with unique attributes."[32] Calhoun, although rejecting the historical newness of the phenomenon, has also emphasized the decisive role of identity in defining politics in contemporary American society, particularly in the women's movement, in the gay movement, in the civil rights movement, movements "that sought not only various instrumental goals but the affirmation of excluded identities as publicly good and politically salient."[33] Alain Touraine goes further, arguing that "in a post-industrial society, in which cultural services have replaced material goods at the core of production, *it is the defense of the subject, in its personality and in its culture, against the logic of apparatuses and markets, that replaces the idea of class struggle.*"[34] Then the key issue becomes, as stated by Calderon and Laserna, in a world characterized by simultaneous globalization and fragmentation, "how to combine new technologies and collective memory, universal science and communitarian cultures, passion and reason?"[35] How, indeed! And why do we observe the opposite trend throughout the world, namely, the increasing distance between globalization and identity, between the Net and the self?

32 Yoshino (1992: 1).
33 Calhoun (1994: 4).
34 Touraine (1994: 168; my translation, his italics).
35 Calderon and Laserna (1994: 90; my translation).

Raymond Barglow, in his illuminating essay on this matter, from a socio-psychoanalytical perspective, points to the paradox that while information systems and networking augment human powers of organization and integration, they simultaneously subvert the traditional Western concept of a separate, independent subject: "The historical shift from mechanical to information technologies helps to subvert the notions of sovereignty and self-sufficiency that have provided an ideological anchoring for individual identity since Greek philosophers elaborated the concept more than two millennia ago. In short, technology is helping to dismantle the very vision of the world that in the past it fostered."[36] Then he goes on to present a fascinating comparison between classic dreams reported in Freud's writing and his own patients' dreams in the high-tech environment of 1990s' San Francisco: "Image of a head . . . and behind it is suspended a computer keyboard . . . I'm this programmed head!"[37] This feeling of absolute solitude is new in comparison to classic Freudian representation: "the dreamers . . . express a sense of solitude experienced as existential and inescapable, built into the structure of the world . . . Totally isolated, the self seems irretrievably lost to itself."[38] Thus, the search for new connectedness around shared, reconstructed identity.

However insightful, this hypothesis may be only part of the explanation. On the one hand, it would imply a crisis of the self limited to a Western individualist conception, shaken by uncontrollable connectedness. Yet the search for new identity and new spirituality is on also in the East, in spite of a stronger sense of collective identity and the traditional, cultural subordination of the individual to the family. The resonance of *Aum Shinrikyo* in Japan in 1995, particularly among the young, highly educated generations, could be considered a symptom of the crisis of established patterns of identity, coupled with the desperate need to build a new, collective self, significantly mixing spirituality, advanced technology (chemicals, biology, laser), global business connections, and the culture of millenarianist doom.[39]

On the other hand, elements of an interpretative framework to explain the rising power of identity must also be found at a broader level, in relationship to macro-processes of institutional change, to a large extent connected to the emergence of a new global system. Thus, widespread currents of racism and xenophobia in Western Europe may

36 Barglow (1994: 6).
37 Barglow (1994: 53).
38 Barglow (1994: 185).
39 For the new forms of revolt linked to identity in explicit opposition to globalization, see the exploratory analysis undertaken in Castells et al. (1996).

be related, as Alain Touraine[40] and Michel Wieviorka[41] have suggested, to an identity crisis on becoming an abstraction (European), at the same time that European societies, while seeing their national identity blurred, discovered within themselves the lasting existence of ethnic minorities in European societies (a demographic fact since at least the 1960s). Or again, in Russia and the ex-Soviet Union, the strong development of nationalism in the post-communist period can be related, as I shall argue in volume III, to the cultural emptiness created by 70 years of imposition of an exclusionary ideological identity, coupled with the return to primary, historical identity (Russian, Georgian), as the only source of meaning after the crumbling of the historically fragile *sovetskii narod* (Soviet people).

The emergence of religious fundamentalism seems also to be linked both to a global trend and to an institutional crisis. We know from history that ideas and beliefs of all brands are always in stock waiting to catch fire under the right circumstances.[42] It is significant that fundamentalism, whether Islamic or Christian, has spread, and will spread, throughout the world at the historical moment when global networks of wealth and power connect nodal points and valued individuals throughout the planet, while disconnecting, and excluding, large segments of societies, regions, and even entire countries. Why did Algeria, one of the most modernized Muslim societies, suddenly turn to fundamentalist saviors, who became terrorists (as did their anti-colonialist predecessors) when they were denied their electoral victory in democratic elections? Why did the traditionalist teachings of Pope John Paul II find an indisputable echo among the impoverished masses of the Third World, so that the Vatican could afford to ignore the protests of a minority of feminists in a few advanced countries where the progress of reproductive rights contributes precisely to diminishing the number of souls to be saved? There seems to be a logic of excluding the excluders, of redefining the criteria for value and meaning in a world where there is shrinking room for the computer illiterate, for consumptionless groups, and for under-communicated territories. When the Net switches off the self, the self, individual or collective, constructs its meaning without global, instrumental reference: the process of disconnection becomes reciprocal, following the refusal by the excluded of the one-sided logic of structural domination and social exclusion.

Such is the terrain to be explored, not just declared. The few ideas

40   Touraine (1991).
41   Wieviorka (1993).
42   See, for instance, Colas (1992); Kepel (1993).

advanced here on the paradoxical manifestation of the self in the informational society are only intended to chart the course of my inquiry for the reader's information, not to draw conclusions beforehand.

A Word on Method

This is not a book about books. While relying on evidence of various sorts, and on analyses and accounts from multiple sources, it does not intend to discuss existing theories of post-industrialism or the information society. Several thorough, balanced presentations of these theories are available,[43] as well as various critiques,[44] including my own.[45] Similarly, I shall not contribute, except when necessary for the sake of the argument, to the cottage industry created in the 1980s around postmodern theory,[46] being for my part fully satisfied with the excellent criticism elaborated by David Harvey on the social and ideological foundations of "post-modernity,"[47] as well as with the sociological dissection of postmodern theories performed by Scott Lash.[48] I certainly owe many thoughts to many authors, and particularly to the forebears of informationalism, Alain Touraine and Daniel Bell, as well as to the one Marxist theorist who sensed the new, relevant issues just before his death in 1979, Nicos Poulantzas.[49] And I duly acknowledge borrowed concepts when I use them as tools in my specific analyses. Yet I have tried to construct a discourse as autonomous and nonredundant as possible, integrating materials and observations from various sources, without submitting the reader to the painful revisiting of the bibliographical jungle where I have lived (fortunately, among other activities) for the past 12 years.

In a similar vein, while using a significant amount of statistical sources and empirical studies, I have tried to minimize the processing of data to simplify an already excessively cumbersome book. Therefore, I tend

43   A useful overview of sociological theories on post-industrialism and informationalism is Lyon (1988). For the intellectual and terminological origins of notions of "information society," see Nora and Minc (1978) and Ito (1991a). See also Beniger (1986); Katz (1988); Williams (1988); Salvaggio (1989).
44   For critical perspectives on post-industrialism, see, among others, Woodward (1980); Roszak (1986); Lyon (1988); Shoji (1990); Touraine (1992). For a cultural critique of our society's emphasis on information technology, see Postman (1992).
45   For my own critique of post-industrialism, see Castells (1994, 1996).
46   See Lyon (1994); also Seidman and Wagner (1992).
47   Harvey (1990).
48   Lash (1990).
49   Poulantzas (1978: esp. 160–9).

to use data sources that find broad, accepted consensus among social scientists (for example, OECD, United Nations, World Bank, governments' official statistics, authoritative research monographs, generally reliable academic or business sources), except when such sources seem to be erroneous (such as Soviet GNP statistics or the World Bank's report on adjustment policies in Africa). I am aware of limitations in lending credibility to information that may not always be accurate, yet the reader will realize that numerous precautions have been taken in this text to form conclusions usually on the basis of convergent trends from several sources, according to a methodology of triangulation with a well-established, successful tradition among historians, policemen, and investigative reporters. Furthermore, the data, observations, and references presented in this book do not really aim at demonstrating but at suggesting hypotheses while constraining the ideas within a corpus of observation, admittedly selected with my research questions in mind but certainly not organized around preconceived answers. The methodology followed in this book, whose specific implications will be discussed in each chapter, is at the service of the overarching purpose of its intellectual endeavor: to propose some elements of an exploratory, cross-cultural theory of economy and society in the Information Age, *as it specifically refers to the emergence of a new social structure*. The broad scope of my analysis is required by the pervasiveness of the object of such analysis (informationalism) throughout social domains and cultural expressions. But I certainly do not intend to address the whole range of themes and issues in contemporary societies – since writing encyclopedias is not my trade.

The book is divided into three parts which the publisher has wisely transformed into three volumes. They are analytically interrelated, but they have been organized to make their reading independent. The only exception to this rule concerns the Conclusion, in volume III, which is the overall conclusion of the book, and presents a synthetic interpretation of its findings and ideas.

The division into three volumes, while making the book publishable and readable, raises some problems in communicating my overall theory. Indeed, some critical topics that cut across all the themes treated in this book are presented in the second volume. Such is the case, particularly, of the analysis of women and patriarchalism, and of power relationships and the state. I warn the reader that I do not share a traditional view of society as made up of superimposed levels, with technology and economy in the basement, power on the mezzanine, and culture in the penthouse. Yet, for the sake of clarity, I am forced to a systematic, somewhat linear presentation of topics which, while relating to each other, cannot fully integrate all the elements until they have been discussed in some depth throughout the intellectual journey on which the reader is invited by this book. The first volume, in the reader's hands, deals primarily with the logic of what I call the Net, while the second (*The Power of Identity*) analyzes the formation of the self, and the interaction between the Net and the self in the crisis of two central institutions of society: the patriarchal family and the nation-state. The third volume (*End of Millennium*) attempts an interpretation of historical transformations in the last lapse of the twentieth century, as a result of the dynamics of processes studied in the first two volumes. It is only at the end of the third volume that a general integration between theory and observation, linking up the analyses concerning the various domains, will be proposed, although each volume concludes with an effort at synthesizing the main findings and ideas presented in the volume. While volume III is more directly concerned with specific processes of historical change in various contexts, throughout the whole book I have tried my best to accomplish two goals: to ground analysis in observation, without reducing theorization to commentary; and to diversify culturally my sources of observation *and of ideas*, as much as possible. This approach stems from my conviction that we have entered a truly multicultural, interdependent world, which can only be understood, and changed, from a plural perspective that brings together cultural identity, global networking, and multidimensional politics.

1

The Information Technology Revolution

Which Revolution?

"Gradualism," wrote paleontologist Stephen J. Gould, "the idea that all change must be smooth, slow, and steady, was never read from the rocks. It represented a common cultural bias, in part a response of nineteenth century liberalism to a world in revolution. But it continues to color our supposedly objective reading of life's history . . . The history of life, as I read it, is a series of stable states, punctuated at rare intervals by major events that occur with great rapidity and help to establish the next stable era."[1] My starting-point, and I am not alone in this assumption,[2] is that, at the end of the twentieth century, we lived through one of these rare intervals in history. An interval characterized by the transformation of our "material culture"[3] by the works of a new technological paradigm organized around information technologies.

By technology I understand, in a straight line from Harvey Brooks and Daniel Bell, "the use of scientific knowledge to specify ways of

---

1   Gould (1980: 226).
2   Melvin Kranzberg, one of the leading historians of technology, wrote "The information age has indeed revolutionized the technical elements of industrial society" (1985: 42). As for its societal effects: "While it might be evolutionary, in the sense that all changes and benefits will not appear overnight, it will be revolutionary in its effects upon our society" (1985: 52). Along the same line of argument, see also, for instance, Nora and Minc (1978); Dizard (1982); Perez (1983); Forester (1985); Darbon and Robin (1987); Stourdze (1987); Dosi et al. (1988a); Bishop and Waldholz (1990); Salomon (1992); Petrella (1993); Ministry of Posts and Telecommunications (Japan) (1995); Negroponte (1995).
3   On the definition of technology as "material culture," which I consider to be the appropriate sociological perspective, see the discussion in Fischer (1992: 1–32), especially: "Technology here is similar to the idea of material culture."

doing things in a *reproducible* manner."[4] Among information technologies, I include, like everybody else, the *converging set* of technologies in micro-electronics, computing (machines and software),
telecommunications/broadcasting, and opto-electronics.[5] In addition,
unlike some analysts, I also include in the realm of information technologies genetic engineering and its expanding set of developments
and applications.[6] This is not only because genetic engineering is focused on the decoding, manipulation, and eventual reprogramming of
the information codes of living matter, but also because biology, electronics, and informatics seem to be converging and interacting in their
applications, in their materials, and, more fundamentally, in their conceptual approach, a topic that deserves further mention below in this
chapter.[7] Around this nucleus of information technologies, in the broad
sense as defined, a constellation of major technological breakthroughs
took place in the last two decades of the twentieth century in advanced
materials, in energy sources, in medical applications, in manufacturing techniques (current or potential, such as nano-technology), and in
transportation technology, among others.[8] Furthermore, the current
process of technological transformation expands exponentially because
of its ability to create an interface between technological fields through
common digital language in which information is generated, stored,
retrieved, processed, and transmitted. We live in a world that, in the
expression of Nicholas Negroponte, has become digital.[9]

The prophetic hype and ideological manipulation characterizing most
discourses on the information technology revolution should not mis-
lead us into underestimating its truly fundamental significance. It is,
as this book will try to show, at least as major an historical event as
was the eighteenth-century industrial revolution, inducing a pattern
of discontinuity in the material basis of economy, society, and culture.
The historical record of technological revolutions, as compiled by
Melvin Kranzberg and Carroll Pursell,[10] shows that they are all
characterized by their *pervasiveness*, that is by their penetration of all

---

4 Brooks (1971: 13) from unpublished text, quoted with emphasis added by Bell (1976: 29).
5 Saxby (1990); Mulgan (1991).
6 Hall (1987); Marx (1989).
7 For a stimulating, informed, although deliberately controversial, account of the convergence between the biological revolution and the broader information technology revolution, see Kelly (1995).
8 Forester (1988); Edquist and Jacobsson (1989); Herman (1990); Drexler and Peterson (1991); Lincoln and Essin (1993); Dondero (1995); Lovins and Lovins (1995); Lyon and Gorner (1995).
9 Negroponte (1995).
10 Kranzberg and Pursell (1967).

domains of human activity, not as an exogenous source of impact, but as the fabric in which such activity is woven. In other words, *they are process-oriented*, besides inducing new products. On the other hand, unlike any other revolution, *the core* of the transformation we are experiencing in the current revolution refers to *technologies of information processing and communication*.[11] Information technology is to this revolution what new sources of energy were to the successive industrial revolutions, from the steam engine to electricity, to fossil fuels, and even to nuclear power, since the generation and distribution of energy was the key element underlying the industrial society. However, this statement on the pre-eminent role of information technology is often confused with the characterization of the current revolution as essentially dependent upon new knowledge and information. This is true of the current process of technological change, but so it is of preceding technological revolutions, as is shown by leading historians of technology, such as Melvin Kranzberg and Joel Mokyr.[12] The first industrial revolution, although not science-based, relied on the extensive use of information, applying and developing pre-existing knowledge. And the second industrial revolution, after 1850, was characterized by the decisive role of science in fostering innovation. Indeed, R&D laboratories appeared for the first time in the German chemical industry in the last decades of the nineteenth century.[13]

11   A full understanding of the current technological revolution would require the discussion of the specificity of new information technologies *vis-à-vis* their historical ancestors of equally revolutionary character, such as the discovery of printing in China probably in the late seventh century, and in Europe in the fifteenth century, a classical theme of communications literature. Without being able to address the issue within the limits of this book focused on the sociological dimension of technological change, let me suggest a few topics for the reader's attention. Electronic-based information technologies (including electronic printing) feature incomparable memory storage capacity and speed of combination and transmission of bits. Electronic text allows for substantially greater flexibility of feedbacks, interaction, and reconfiguration of text, as any word-processing writer will acknowledge, thus altering the process of communication itself. On-line communication, combined with flexibility of text, allows for ubiquitous, asynchronous space/time programming. As for the social effects of information technologies, I propose the hypothesis that the depth of their impact is a function of the pervasiveness of information throughout the social structure. Thus, while printing did substantially affect European societies in the modern age, as well as medieval China to a lesser extent, its effects were somewhat limited because of widespread illiteracy in the population and because of the low intensity of information in the productive structure. Thus, the industrial society, by educating citizens and by gradually organizing the economy around knowledge and information, prepared the ground for the empowering of the human mind when new information technologies became available. See, for an historical comment on this earlier information technology revolution, Boureau et al. (1989). For some elements of the debate on technological specificity of electronic communication, including McLuhan's perspective, see chapter 5.
12   M. Kranzberg, "Prerequisites for industrialization," in Kranzberg and Pursell (1967: I, ch. 13); Mokyr (1990).
13   Ashton (1948); Clow and Clow (1952); Landes (1969); Mokyr (1990: 112).

What characterizes the current technological revolution is not the centrality of knowledge and information, but the application of such knowledge and information to knowledge generation and information processing/communication devices, in a cumulative feedback loop between innovation and the uses of innovation.[14] An illustration may clarify this analysis. The uses of new telecommunications technologies in the past two decades have gone through three distinct stages: the automation of tasks, an experimentation of uses, and a reconfiguration of applications.[15] In the first two stages, technological innovation progressed through learning *by using*, in Rosenberg's terminology.[16] In the third stage, the users learned technology *by doing*, and ended up reconfiguring the networks, and finding new applications. The feedback loop between introducing new technology, using it, and developing it into new realms becomes much faster under the new technological paradigm. As a result, diffusion of technology endlessly amplifies the power of technology, as it becomes appropriated and redefined by its users. New information technologies are not simply tools to be applied, but processes to be developed. Users and doers may become the same. Thus users can take control of technology, as in the case of the Internet (see below in this chapter, and in chapter 5). There is therefore a close relationship between the social processes of creating and manipulating symbols (the culture of society) and the capacity to produce and distribute goods and services (the productive forces). For the first time in history, the human mind is a direct productive force, not just a decisive element of the production system.

Thus, computers, communication systems, and genetic decoding and programming are all amplifiers and extensions of the human mind. What we think, and how we think, become expressed in goods, services, material and intellectual output, be it food, shelter, transportation and communications systems, computers, missiles, health, education, or images. The growing integration between minds and machines, including the DNA machine, is canceling what Bruce Mazlish calls the "fourth discontinuity"[17] (the one between humans and machines), fundamentally altering the way we are born, we live, we learn, we work, we produce, we consume, we dream, we fight, or we die. Of course, cultural/institutional contexts and purposeful social action decisively interact with the new technological system, but this system has its own, embedded logic, characterized by the capacity to translate

14 Dizard (1982); Forester (1985); Hall and Preston (1988); Saxby (1990).
15 Bar (1990).
16 Rosenberg (1982); Bar (1992).
17 Mazlish (1993).

all inputs into a common information system, and to process such information at increasing speed, with increasing power, at decreasing cost, in a potentially ubiquitous retrieval and distribution network.

There is an additional feature characterizing the information technology revolution in comparison with its historical predecessors. Mokyr[18] has shown that technological revolutions took place only in a few societies, and diffused in a relatively limited geographic area, often living in isolated space and time *vis-à-vis* other regions of the planet. Thus, while Europeans borrowed some of the discoveries that took place in China, for many centuries China and Japan adopted European technology only on a very limited basis, mainly restricted to military applications. The contact between civilizations at different technological levels often took the form of the destruction of the least developed, or of those who had predominantly applied their knowledge to non-military technology, as in the case of American civilizations annihilated by Spanish conquerors, sometimes through accidental biological warfare.[19] The industrial revolution did extend to most of the globe from its original West European shores during the next two centuries. But its expansion was highly selective, and its pace rather slow by current standards of technological diffusion. Indeed, even in Britain by the mid-nineteenth century, sectors that accounted for the majority of the labor force, and at least half the gross national product, were not affected by new industrial technologies.[20] Furthermore, its planetary reach in the following decades more often than not took the form of colonial domination, be it in India under the British empire; in Latin America under commercial/industrial dependency on Britain and the United States; in the dismembering of Africa under the Berlin Treaty; or in the opening to foreign trade of Japan and China by the guns of Western ships. In contrast, new information technologies have spread throughout the globe with lightning speed in less than two decades, between the mid-1970s and the mid-1990s, displaying a logic that I propose as characteristic of this technological revolution: the immediate application to its own development of technologies it generates, connecting the world through information technology.[21] To be sure, there are large areas of the world, and considerable segments of the population, switched off from the new technological system: this is precisely one of the central arguments of this book. Furthermore, the speed of technological diffusion is selective, both

18   Mokyr (1990: 293, 209ff).
19   See, for instance, Thomas (1993).
20   Mokyr (1990: 83).
21   Pool (1990); Mulgan (1991).

socially and functionally. Differential timing in access to the power of technology for people, countries, and regions is a critical source of inequality in our society. The switched-off areas are culturally and spatially discontinuous: they are in the American inner cities or in the French *banlieues*, as much as in the shanty towns of Africa or in the deprived rural areas of China or India. Yet dominant functions, social groups, and territories across the globe are connected at the dawn of the twenty-first century in a new technological system that, as such, started to take shape only in the 1970s.

How did this fundamental transformation happen in what amounts to an historical instant? Why is it diffusing throughout the globe at such an accelerated, if uneven, pace? Why is it a "revolution?" Since our experience of the new is shaped by our recent past, I think the answers to these basic questions could be helped by a brief reminder of the historical record of the industrial revolution, still present in our institutions, and therefore in our mind-set.

Lessons from the Industrial Revolution

Historians have shown that there were at least two industrial revolutions: the first started in the last third of the eighteenth century, characterized by new technologies such as the steam engine, the spinning jenny, the Cort's process in metallurgy, and, more broadly, by the replacement of hand-tools by machines; the second one, about 100 years later, featured the development of electricity, the internal combustion engine, science-based chemicals, efficient steel casting, and the beginning of communication technologies, with the diffusion of the telegraph and the invention of the telephone. Between the two there are fundamental continuities, as well as some critical differences, the main one being the decisive importance of scientific knowledge in sustaining and guiding technological development after 1850.[22] It is precisely because of their differences that features common to both may offer precious insights in understanding the logic of technological revolutions.

---

22 Singer et al. (1958); Mokyr (1985). However, as Mokyr himself points out, an interface between science and technology was also present in the first industrial revolution in Britain. Thus, Watt's decisive improvement of the steam engine designed by Newcomen took place in interaction with his friend and protector Joseph Black, professor of chemistry at the University of Glasgow, where Watts was appointed in 1757 as "Mathematical Instrument Maker to the University," and where he conducted his own experiments on a model of the Newcomen engine; see Dickinson (1958). Indeed, Ubbelohde (1958: 673) reports that "Watt's development of a condenser for the steam, separated from the cylinder in which the piston moved, was closely linked up with and inspired by the scientific researches of Joseph Black (1728–99) the professor of chemistry at Glasgow University."

First of all, in both cases, we witness what Mokyr describes as a period of "accelerating and unprecedented technological change"[23] by historical standards. A set of macro-inventions prepared the ground for the blossoming of micro-inventions in the realms of agriculture, industry, and communications. Fundamental historical discontinuity, in an irreversible form, was introduced into the material basis of the human species, in a path-dependent process whose inner, sequential logic has been researched by Paul David and theorized by Brian Arthur.[24] They were indeed "revolutions," in the sense that a sudden, unexpected surge of technological applications transformed the processes of production and distribution, created a flurry of new products, and shifted decisively the location of wealth and power in a planet that became suddenly within the reach of those countries and elites able to master the new technological system. The dark side of this technological adventure is that it was inextricably tied to imperialist ambitions and inter-imperialist conflicts.

Yet this is precisely a confirmation of the revolutionary character of new industrial technologies. The historical ascent of the so-called West, in fact limited to Britain and a handful of nations in Western Europe as well as to their North American, and Australian offspring, is fundamentally linked to the technological superiority achieved during the two industrial revolutions.[25] Nothing in the cultural, scientific, political, or military history of the world prior to the industrial revolution would explain such indisputable "Western" (Anglo-Saxon/German, with a French touch) supremacy between the 1750s and the 1940s. China was a far superior culture for most of pre-Renaissance history; the Muslim civilization (taking the liberty of using such a term) dominated much of the Mediterranean and exerted a significant influence in Africa and Asia throughout the modern age; Asia and Africa remained by and large organized around autonomous cultural and political centers; Russia ruled in splendid isolation a vast expanse across East Europe and Asia; and the Spanish empire, the laggard European culture of the industrial revolution, was the major world power for more than two centuries after 1492. Technology, expressing specific social conditions, introduced a new historical path in the second half of the eighteenth century.

This path originated in Britain, although its intellectual roots can be traced back all over Europe and to the Renaissance's spirit of discovery.[26] Indeed, some historians insist that the necessary scientific know-

23 Mokyr (1990: 82).
24 David (1975); David and Bunn (1988); Arthur (1989).
25 Rosenberg and Birdzell (1986).
26 Singer et al. (1957).

ledge underlying the first industrial revolution was available 100 years earlier, ready to be used under mature social conditions; or, as others argue, waiting for the technical ingenuity of self-trained inventors, such as Newcomen, Watt, Crompton or Arkwright, able to translate available knowledge, combined with craft experience, into decisive new industrial technologies.[27] However, the second industrial revolution, more dependent on new scientific knowledge, shifted its center of gravity towards Germany and the United States, where the main developments in chemicals, electricity, and telephony took place.[28] Historians have painstakingly dissected the social conditions of the shifting geography of technical innovation, often focusing on the characteristics of education and science systems, or on the institutionalization of property rights. However, the contextual explanation for the uneven trajectory of technological innovation seems to be excessively broad and open to alternative interpretations. Hall and Preston, in their analysis of the changing geography of technological innovation between 1846 and 2003, show the importance of *local* seedbeds of innovation, of which Berlin, New York, and Boston are crowned as the "high technology industrial centers of the world" between 1880 and 1914, while "London in that period was a pale shadow of Berlin."[29] The reason lies in the territorial basis for the interaction of systems of technological discovery and applications, namely in the synergistic properties of what is known in the literature as "milieux of innovation."[30]

Indeed, technological breakthroughs came in clusters, interacting with each other in a process of increasing returns. Whichever conditions determined such clustering, the key lesson to be retained is that *technological innovation is not an isolated instance.*[31] It reflects a given state of knowledge, a particular institutional and industrial environment, a certain availability of skills to define a technical problem and to solve it, an economic mentality to make such application cost-efficient, and a network of producers and users who can communicate their experiences cumulatively, learning by using and by doing: elites

27   Rostow (1975); see Jewkes et al. (1969) for the argument, and Singer et al. (1958) for the historical evidence.
28   Mokyr (1990).
29   Hall and Preston (1988: 123).
30   The origin of the concept of "milieu of innovation" can be traced back to Aydalot (1985). It was also implicitly present in the work of Anderson (1985) and in the elaboration by Arthur (1985). Around the same time, Peter Hall and I in Berkeley, Roberto Camagni in Milan, and Denis Maillat in Lausanne, together for a brief period with the late Philippe Aydalot, started to develop empirical analyses of milieux of innovation, a theme that, rightly so, has become a cottage research industry in the 1990s.
31   The specific discussion of the historical conditions for the clustering of technological innovations cannot be undertaken within the limits of this chapter. Useful reflections on the matter can be found in Gille (1978) and Mokyr (1990). See also Mokyr (1990: 298).

learn by doing, thereby modifying the applications of technology, while most people learn by using, thus remaining within the constraints of the packaging of technology. The interactivity of systems of technological innovation and their dependence on certain "milieux" of exchange of ideas, problems, and solutions are critical features that can be generalized from the experience of past revolutions to the current one.[32]

The positive effects of new industrial technologies on economic growth, living standards, and the human mastery of a hostile Nature (reflected in the dramatic lengthening of life expectancy, which did not improve steadily before the eighteenth century) over the long run are indisputable in the historical record. However, they did not come early, in spite of the diffusion of the steam engine and new machinery. Mokyr reminds us that "per capita consumption and living standards increased little initially [at the end of the eighteenth century] but production technologies changed dramatically in many industries and sectors, preparing the way for sustained Schumpeterian growth in the second half of the nineteenth century when technological progress spread to previously unaffected industries."[33] This is a critical assessment that forces us to evaluate the actual effects of major technological changes in light of a time lag highly dependent on the specific conditions of each society. The historical record seems to indicate however that, in general terms, the closer the relationship between the sites of innovation, production, and use of new technologies, the faster the transformation of societies, and the greater the positive feedback from social conditions on the general conditions for further innovation. Thus, in Spain, the industrial revolution diffused rapidly in Catalonia, as early as the late eighteenth century, but followed a much slower pace in the rest of Spain, particularly in Madrid and in the south; only the Basque Country and Asturias had joined the process of industrialization by the end of the nineteenth century.[34] The boundaries of industrial innovation were to a large extent coterminous with areas that were prohibited to trade with the Spanish American colonies for about two centuries: while Andalusian and Castilian elites, as well as the crown, could live from their American rents, Catalans had to provide for themselves through their trade and ingenuity, while being submitted to the pressure of a centralist state. Partly as a result of this historical trajectory, Catalonia and the Basque Country were the only fully industrialized regions until the 1950s and the main seedbeds of

32   Rosenberg (1976, 1982); Dosi (1988).
33   Mokyr (1990: 83).
34   Fontana (1988); Nadal and Carreras (1990).

entrepreneurialism and innovation, in sharp contrast with trends in the rest of Spain. Thus, specific social conditions foster technological innovation that itself feeds into the path of economic development and further innovation. Yet the reproduction of such conditions is cultural and institutional, as much as economic and technological. The transformation of social and institutional environments may alter the pace and geography of technological development (for example, Japan after the Meiji Restoration, or Russia for a brief period under Stolypin), although past history does bear considerable inertia.

A last and essential lesson from the industrial revolutions that I consider relevant to this analysis is controversial: although they both brought a whole array of new technologies that actually formed and transformed an industrial system in successive stages, at their core there was fundamental innovation in the generation and distribution of energy. R. J. Forbes, a classic historian of technology, affirms that "the invention of the steam engine is the central fact in the industrial revolution," followed by the introduction of new prime movers and by the mobile prime mover, under which "the power of the steam-engine could be created where needed and to the extent desired."[35] And although Mokyr insists on the multifaceted character of the industrial revolution, he also thinks that "the protestations of some economic historians notwithstanding, the steam engine is still widely regarded as the quintessential invention of the industrial revolution."[36] Electricity was the central force of the second revolution, in spite of other extraordinary developments in chemicals, steel, the internal combustion engine, telegraphy and telephony. This is because only through electrical generation and distribution were all the other fields able to develop their applications and be connected to each other. A case in point is the electric telegraph which, first used experimentally in the 1790s and widely in existence since 1837, could only grow into a communication network, connecting the world on a large scale, when it could rely on the diffusion of electricity. The widespread use of electricity from the 1870s onwards changed transportation, telegraphy, lighting, and, not least, factory work by diffusing power in the form of the electrical engine. Indeed, while factories have been associated with the first industrial revolution, for almost a century they were not concomitant with the use of the steam engine that was widely used in craft shops, while many large factories continued to use improved water-power sources (and thus were known for a long time as mills). It was the electrical engine that both made possible and induced large-scale

35   Forbes (1958: 150).
36   Mokyr (1990: 84).

organization of work in the industrial factory.[37] As R. J. Forbes wrote (in 1958):

> During the last 250 years five great new prime movers have produced what is often called the Machine Age. The eighteenth century brought the steam-engine; the nineteenth century the water-turbine, the internal combustion engine and the steam-turbine; and the twentieth the gas-turbine. Historians have often coined catch-phrases to denote movements or currents in history. Such is "The Industrial Revolution," the title for a development often described as starting in the early eighteenth century and extending through much of the nineteenth. It was a slow movement, but wrought changes so profound in their combination of material progress and social dislocation that collectively they may well be described as revolutionary if we consider these extreme dates.[38]

Thus, by acting on the process at the core of all processes – that is, the necessary power to produce, distribute, and communicate – the two industrial revolutions diffused throughout the entire economic system and permeated the whole social fabric. Cheap, accessible, mobile energy sources extended and augmented the power of the human body, creating the material basis for the historical continuation of a similar movement toward the expansion of the human mind.

The Historical Sequence of the Information Technology Revolution

The brief, yet intense history of the information technology revolution has been told so many times in recent years as to render it unnecessary to provide the reader with another full account.[39] Besides, given the

---

37 Jarvis (1958); Canby (1962); Hall and Preston (1988). One of the first detailed specifications for an electric telegraph is contained in a letter signed C.M. and published in *Scots Magazine* in 1753. One of the first practical experiments with an electrical system was proposed by the Catalan Francisco de Salva in 1795. There are unconfirmed reports that a single-wire telegraph, using Salva's scheme, was actually constructed between Madrid and Aranjuez (26 miles) in 1798. However, it was only in the 1830s (William Cooke in England, Samuel Morse in America) that the electric telegraph was established, and in 1851 the first submarine cable laid out between Dover and Calais (Garratt 1958); see also Sharlin (1967); Mokyr (1990).
38 Forbes (1958: 148).
39 A good history of the origins of the information technology revolution, naturally superseded by developments since the 1980s, is Braun and Macdonald (1982). The most systematic effort at summarizing the developments of the early information technology revolution was conducted by Tom Forester in a series of books (1980, 1985, 1987, 1989, 1993). For good accounts of the origins of genetic engineering, see Elkington (1985) and Russell (1988). For an authoritative history of computing, see Ceruzzi (1998). For the history of the Internet, see Abbate (1999) and Naughton (1999) .

acceleration of its pace, any such account would be instantly obsolete, so that between my writing this and your reading it (let's say 18 months), microchips will have doubled in performance at a given price, according to the generally acknowledged "Moore's law."[40] Nevertheless, I find it analytically useful to recall the main axes of technological transformation in information generation/processing/transmission, and to place them in the sequence that drifted toward the formation of a new socio-technical paradigm.[41] This brief summary will allow me, later on, to skip references to technological features when discussing their specific interaction with economy, culture, and society throughout the intellectual itinerary of this book, except when new elements of information are required.

Micro-engineering macro-changes: electronics and information

Although the scientific and industrial predecessors of electronics-based information technologies can be found decades before the 1940s[42] (not the least being the invention of the telephone by Bell in 1876, of the radio by Marconi in 1898, and of the vacuum tube by De Forest in 1906), it was during the Second World War, and in its aftermath, that major technological breakthroughs in electronics took place: the first programmable computer, and the transistor, source of micro-electronics, the true core of the information technology revolution in the twentieth century.[43] Yet I contend that only in the 1970s did new information technologies diffuse widely, accelerating their synergistic development and converging into a new paradigm. Let us retrace the stages of innovation in the three main technological fields that, although closely interrelated, constituted the history of electronics-based technologies: micro-electronics, computers, and telecommunications.

40   An accepted "law" in the electronics industry, originated by Gordon Moore, chairman of Intel, the legendary Silicon Valley start-up company, today the world's largest and one of the most profitable firms in micro-electronics.
41   The information reported in this chapter is widely available in newspapers and magazines. I extracted much of it from my reading of *Business Week, The Economist, Wired, Scientific American*, the *New York Times, El Pais* and the *San Francisco Chronicle*, which constitute my daily/weekly information staple. It also comes from occasional chats on technology matters with colleagues and friends around Berkeley and Stanford, knowledgeable about electronics and biology and acquainted with industry sources. I do not consider it necessary to provide detailed references to data of such general character, except when a given figure or quote could be hard to find.
42   See Hall and Preston (1988); Mazlish (1993).
43   I think that, as with the industrial revolutions, there will be several information technology revolutions, of which the one constituted in the 1970s is only the first. Probably the second, in the early twenty-first century, will give a more important role to the biological revolution, in close interaction with new computer technologies.

The transistor, invented in 1947 at Bell Laboratories in Murray Hill, New Jersey, by three physicists, Bardeen, Brattain, and Shockley (recipients of the Nobel Prize for this discovery), made possible the processing of electric impulses at a fast pace in a binary mode of interruption and amplification, thus enabling the coding of logic and of communication with and between machines: we call these processing devices semiconductors, and people commonly call them chips (actually now made of millions of transistors). The first step in the transistor's diffusion was taken with the invention by Shockley of the junction transistor in 1951. Yet its fabrication and widespread use required new manufacturing technologies and the use of an appropriate material. The shift to silicon, literally building the new revolution on sand, was first accomplished by Texas Instruments (in Dallas) in 1954 (a move facilitated by the hiring in 1953 of Gordon Teal, another leading scientist from Bell Labs). The invention of the planar process in 1959 by Fairchild Semiconductors (in Silicon Valley) opened up the possibility of the integration of miniaturized components with precision manufacturing.

Yet the decisive step in micro-electronics had taken place in 1957: the integrated circuit (IC) was co-invented by Jack Kilby, a Texas Instrument engineer (who patented it), and Bob Noyce, one of the founders of Fairchild. But it was Noyce who first manufactured ICs by using the planar process. It triggered a technological explosion: in only three years, between 1959 and 1962, prices of semiconductors fell by 85 percent, and in the next ten years production increased by 20 times, 50 percent of which went to military uses.[44] As a point of historical comparison, it took 70 years (1780–1850) for the price of cotton cloth to drop by 85 percent in Britain during the industrial revolution.[45] Then, the movement accelerated during the 1960s: as manufacturing technology improved and better chip design was helped by computers using faster and more powerful micro-electronic devices, the average price of an integrated circuit fell from $50 in 1962 to $1 in 1971.

The giant leap forward in the diffusion of micro-electronics in all machines came in 1971 with the invention by an Intel engineer, Ted Hoff (also in Silicon Valley), of the microprocessor, that is the computer on a chip. Thus, information-processing power could be installed everywhere. The race was on for ever-greater integration capacity of circuits on a single chip, the technology of design and manufacturing constantly exceeding the limits of integration previously thought to be physically impossible without abandoning the use of silicon material.

44 Braun and Macdonald (1982).
45 Mokyr (1990: 111).

In the mid-1990s, technical evaluations still gave 10–20 years of good life for silicon-based circuits, although research in alternative materials was stepped up. The level of integration has progressed by leaps and bounds in the past two decades. While technical details have no place in this book, it is analytically relevant to indicate the speed and extent of technological change.

As is known, the power of chips can be evaluated by a combination of three characteristics: their integration capacity, indicated by the smallest line width in the chip measured in microns (1 micron = 1 millionth of 1 meter); their memory capacity, measured in bits: thousands (k), and millions (megabits); and the speed of the microprocessor measured in megahertz. Thus, the first 1971 processor was laid in lines of about 6.5 microns; in 1980, it reached 4 microns; in 1987, 1 micron; in 1995, Intel's Pentium chip featured a size in the 0.35 micron range; and projections were for reaching 0.25 micron in 1999. Thus, where in 1971 2,300 transistors were packed on a chip the size of a thumbtack, in 1993 there were 35 million transistors. Memory capacity, as indicated by DRAM (dynamic random access memory) capacity, was in 1971, 1,024 bits; in 1980, 64,000; in 1987, 1,024,000; in 1993, 16,384,000; and projected in 1999, 256,000,000. As for the speed, mid-1990s 64–bit microprocessors were 550 times faster than the first Intel chip in 1972; and MPUs are doubling every 18 months. Projections to 2002 forecast an acceleration of micro-electronics technology in integration (0.18 micron chips), in DRAM capacity (1,024 megabits), and microprocessor speed (500+ megahertz as compared to 150 in 1993). Combined with dramatic developments in parallel processing using multiple microprocessors (including, in the future, linking multiple microprocessors on a single chip), it appears that the power of micro-electronics is still being unleashed, thus relentlessly increasing computing capacity. Furthermore, greater miniaturization, further specialization, and the decreasing price of increasingly powerful chips made it possible to place them in every machine in our everyday life, from dishwashers and microwave ovens to automobiles, whose electronics, in the 1990s standard models, were already more valuable than their steel.

Computers were also conceived from the mother of all technologies that was the Second World War, but they were only born in 1946 in Philadelphia, if we except the war-related tools of the 1943 British Colossus applied to deciphering enemy codes, and the German Z-3 reportedly produced in 1941 to help aircraft calculations.[46] Yet most allied effort in electronics was concentrated in research programs at

46   Hall and Preston (1988).

MIT, and the actual experimentation of the calculators' power, under US army sponsorship, took place at the University of Pennsylvania, where Mauchly and Eckert produced in 1946 the first general purpose computer, the ENIAC (electronic numerical integrator and calculator). Historians will recall that the first electronic computer weighed 30 tons, was built on metal modules nine feet tall, had 70,000 resistors and 18,000 vacuum tubes, and occupied the area of a gymnasium. When it was turned on, its electricity consumption was so high that Philadelphia's lighting twinkled.[47]

Yet the first commercial version of this primitive machine, UNIVAC–1, produced in 1951 by the same team, then under the Remington Rand brand name, was extremely successful in processing the 1950 US census. IBM, also supported by military contracts and relying partly on MIT research, overcame its early reservations about the computer age, and entered the race in 1953 with its 701 vacuum tube machine. In 1958, when Sperry Rand introduced a second-generation computer mainframe machine, IBM immediately followed up with its 7090 model. But it was only in 1964 that IBM, with its 360/370 mainframe computer, came to dominate the computer industry, populated by new (Control Data, Digital), and old (Sperry, Honeywell, Burroughs, NCR) business machines companies. Most of these firms were ailing or had vanished by the 1990s: this is how fast Schumpeterian "creative destruction" has proceeded in the electronics industry. In that ancient age, that is 30 years from the time of writing, the industry organized itself in a well-defined hierarchy of mainframes, minicomputers (in fact, rather bulky machines), and terminals, with some specialty informatics left to the esoteric world of supercomputers (a cross-fertilization of weather forecasting and war games), in which the extraordinary ingenuity of Seymour Cray, in spite of his lack of technological vision, reigned for some time.

Micro-electronics changed all this, inducing a "revolution within the revolution." The advent of the microprocessor in 1971, with the capacity to put a computer on a chip, turned the electronics world, and indeed the world itself, upside down. In 1975, Ed Roberts, an engineer who had created a small calculator company, MITS, in Albuquerque, New Mexico, built a computing box with the improbable name of Altair, after a character in the *Star Trek* TV series, that was the object of admiration of the inventor's young daughter. The machine was a primitive object, but it was built as a small-scale computer around a microprocessor. It was the basis for the design of Apple I, then of Apple II, the first commercially successful micro-

---

47   See the description by Forester (1987).

computer, realized in the garage of their parents' home by two young school drop-outs, Steve Wozniak and Steve Jobs, in Menlo Park, Silicon Valley, in a truly extraordinary saga that has by now become the founding legend of the Information Age. Launched in 1976, with three partners and $91,000 capital, Apple Computers had by 1982 reached $583 million in sales, ushering in the age of diffusion of computer power. IBM reacted quickly: in 1981 it introduced its own version of the microcomputer, with a brilliant name: the Personal Computer (PC), which became in fact the generic name for microcomputers. But because it was not based on IBM's proprietary technology, but on technology developed for IBM by other sources, it became vulnerable to cloning, which was soon practiced on a massive scale, particularly in Asia. Yet while this fact eventually doomed IBM's business dominance in PCs, it also spread the use of IBM clones throughout the world, diffusing a common standard, in spite of the superiority of Apple machines. Apple's Macintosh, launched in 1984, was the first step towards user-friendly computing, with the introduction of icon-based, user-interface technology, originally developed by Xerox's Palo Alto Research Center.

A fundamental condition for the diffusion of microcomputers was fulfilled with the development of new software adapted to their operation.[48] PC software also emerged in the mid-1970s out of the enthusiasm generated by Altair: two young Harvard drop-outs, Bill Gates and Paul Allen, adapted BASIC for operating the Altair machine in 1976. Having realized its potential, they went on to found Microsoft (first in Albuquerque, two years later moving to Seattle, home of Bill Gates's parents), today's software giant, which parlayed dominance in operating-system software into dominance in software for the exponentially growing microcomputer market as a whole.

In the last 20 years of the twentieth century, increasing chip power resulted in a dramatic enhancement of microcomputing power. By the early 1990s, single-chip microcomputers had the processing power of IBM only five years earlier. Furthermore, since the mid-1980s, microcomputers cannot be conceived of in isolation: they perform in networks, with increasing mobility, on the basis of portable computers. This extraordinary versatility, and the capacity to add memory and processing capacity by sharing computing power in an electronic network, decisively shifted the computer age in the 1990s from centralized data storage and processing to networked, interactive computer power-sharing. Not only did the whole technological system change, but its social and organizational interactions as well. Thus, the aver-

48 Egan (1995).

age cost of processing information fell from around $75 per million operations in 1960 to less than one-hundredth of a cent in 1990.

This networking capability only became possible, naturally, because of major developments both in telecommunication and computer-networking technologies during the 1970s. But, at the same time, such changes were only made possible by new micro-electronic devices and stepped-up computing capacity, in a striking illustration of the synergistic relationships of the information technology revolution.

Telecommunications have been revolutionized also by the combination of "node" technologies (electronic switches and routers) and new linkages (transmission technologies). The first industrially produced electronic switch, the ESS-1, was introduced by Bell Labs in 1969. By the mid-1970s, progress in integrated circuit technologies had made possible the digital switch, increasing speed, power, and flexibility, while saving space, energy, and labor, *vis-à-vis* analog devices. Although ATT, parent of the discoverer Bell Labs, was initially reluctant about its introduction, because of the need to amortize the investment already made in analog equipment, when in 1977 Canada's Northern Telecom captured a share of the US market through its lead in digital switching, the Bell companies joined the race and triggered a similar movement around the world.

Major advances in opto-electronics (fiber optics and laser transmission) and digital packet transmission technology dramatically broadened the capacity of transmission lines. The integrated broadband networks (IBNs) envisioned in the 1990s could surpass substantially the revolutionary 1970s proposals for an integrated services digital network (ISDN): while the carrying capacity of ISDN on copper wire was estimated at 144,000 bits, the 1990s IBNs on optic fibers, if and when they can be realized, though at a high price, could carry a quadrillion bits. To measure the pace of change, let us recall that in 1956 the first transatlantic cable phone carried 50 compressed voice circuits; in 1995, optical fibers could carry 85,000 such circuits. This opto-electronics-based transmission capacity, together with advanced switching and routing architectures, such as the asynchronous transmission mode (ATM) and transmission control protocol/interconnection protocol (TCP/IP), are the foundation of the Internet.

Different forms of utilization of the radio spectrum (traditional broadcasting, direct satellite broadcasting, microwaves, digital cellular telephony), as well as coaxial cable and fiber optics, offer a diversity and versatility of transmission technologies, which are being adapted to a whole range of uses, and make possible ubiquitous communication between mobile users. Thus, cellular telephony diffused with force all over the world in the 1990s, literally dotting Asia with unsophisticated pagers and Latin America with status-symbol cellular phones. In 2000, technologies were available for a universal-coverage, personal communication device, only waiting for a number of technical, legal, and business issues to be sorted out before reaching the market. Each leap and bound in a specific technological field amplifies the effects of related information technologies. The convergence of all these electronic technologies into the field of interactive communication led to the creation of the Internet, perhaps the most revolutionary technological medium of the Information Age.

The creation of the Internet

The creation and development of the Internet in the last three decades on the twentieth century resulted from a unique blending of military strategy, big science cooperation, technological entrepreneurship, and countercultural innovation.[49] The origins of the Internet lie in the work of one of the most innovative research institutions in the world: the US Defense Department's Advanced Research Projects Agency (ARPA). When in the late 1950s the launching of the first Sputnik alarmed the American high-tech military establishment, ARPA undertook a number of bold initiatives, some of which changed the history of technology and ushered in the Information Age on a grand scale. One of these strategies, developing an idea conceived by Paul Baran at Rand Corporation in 1960–4, was to design a communications system invulnerable to nuclear attack. Based on packet-switching communication technology, the system made the network independent of command and control centers, so that message units would find their own routes along the network, being reassembled in coherent meaning at any point in the network.

When, later on, digital technology allowed the packaging of all kind of messages, including sound, images, and data, a network was formed that was able to communicate its nodes without using control centers. The universality of digital language and the pure networking logic of the communication system created the technological conditions for horizontal, global communication.

The first computer network, named ARPANET after its powerful sponsor, went on-line on September 1, 1969, with the first four nodes of the network being established at the University of California, Los Angeles, Stanford Research Institute, University of California, Santa

---

49   For excellent histories of the Internet, see Abbate (1999) and Naughton (1999). See also Hart et al. (1992). On the contribution of "hacker" culture to the development of the Internet, see Hafner and Markoff (1991); Naughton (1999); Himannen (2001).

Barbara, and University of Utah. It was opened to research centers cooperating with the US Defense Department, but scientists started to use it for their own communication purposes, including a science fiction enthusiasts' messaging network. At one point it became difficult to separate military-oriented research from scientific communication and personal chatting. Thus, scientists of all disciplines were given access to the network, and in 1983 there was a split between ARPANET, dedicated to scientific purposes, and MILNET, directly oriented to military applications. The National Science Foundation also became involved in the 1980s in creating another scientific network, CSNET, and – in cooperation with IBM – still another network for non-science scholars, BITNET. Yet all networks used ARPANET as their backbone communication system. The network of networks that formed during the 1980s was called ARPA-INTERNET, then INTERNET, still supported by the Defense Department and operated by the National Science Foundation. Having become technologically obsolete after more than 20 years of service, ARPANET was closed down on February 28, 1990. Then, NSFNET, operated by the National Science Foundation, took over as the backbone of the Internet. Yet, commercial pressures, the growth of private corporate networks, and of non-profit, cooperative networks, led to the closing of this last, government-operated Internet backbone, in April 1995, ushering in the full privatization of the Internet, as a number of commercial spin-offs of NSF's regional networks joined forces to form cooperative arrangements between private networks. Once privatized, the Internet did not have any actual overseeing authority. A number of *ad hoc* institutions and mechanisms, created throughout the development of the Internet, took some informal responsibility for coordinating technical configurations and brokering agreements in assigning Internet addresses. In January 1992, under the initiative of the National Science Foundation, the Internet Society, a non-profit organization, was given responsibility over pre-existing coordinating organizations, the Internet Activities Board, and the Internet Engineering Task Force. Internationally, the main coordination function remains the multilateral agreements in assigning domain addresses throughout the world, a very contentious matter.[50] Despite the establishment in 1998 of a new, American-based regulatory body (IANA/ICANN), in 1999 there was no indisputable, clear authority over the Internet, either in the US or in the world – a sign of the free-wheeling characteristics of the new medium, both in technological and cultural terms.

For the network to be able to sustain exponential growth in the

---

50   Conseil d'Etat (1998).

volume of communication, transmission technology had to be enhanced. In the 1970s, ARPANET was using 56,000 bits-per-second links. In 1987, the network lines transmitted 1.5 million bits per second. By 1992, the NSFNET, backbone network behind the Internet, operated at transmission speeds of 45 million bits per second, enough capacity to send 5,000 pages per second. In 1995, gigabit transmission technology was in the prototype stage, with capacity equivalent to transmitting the US Library of Congress in one minute.

However, transmission capacity was not enough to establish a worldwide communication web. Computers had to be able to talk to each other. The first step in this direction was the creation of a communication protocol that could be used by all kinds of networks, a seemingly impossible task in the early 1970s. In the summer of 1973, Vinton Cerf and Robert Kahn, computer scientists doing research at ARPA, designed the basic architecture of the Internet, building on work toward a communication protocol conducted by Kahn at his research firm, BBN. They called a meeting at Stanford, attended by researchers from ARPA and various universities and research centers, including PARC/Xerox, where Robert Metcalfe was working on packet-communication technology that would lead to the creation of local area networks (LANs). Technological cooperation also included various groups in Europe, particularly the French researchers associated with the Cyclades program. Working on the basis of this Stanford seminar, Cerf, Metcalfe, and Gerard Lelann (from Cyclades) specified a transmission control protocol that would accommodate the requests of different researchers, and of different existing networks. In 1978, Cerf, Postel (from UCLA), and Cohen (from USC) split the protocol in two parts: host-to-host (TCP) and internetworks protocol (IP). The resulting TCP/IP protocol became the standard for computer communication in the US by 1980. Its flexibility allowed the adoption of a multilayered structure of links between computer networks, which showed its capacity to adapt to various communication systems and to a variety of codes. When, in the 1980s, telecommunication carriers, particularly in Europe, imposed as international standard a different communication protocol (the x.25) the world came very close to being split into non-communicable computer networks. Yet, the capacity of TCP/IP to accommodate diversity ultimately prevailed. With some adaptation (assigning x.25 and TCP/IP to different layers of the communication network, then setting up links between the layers, and making the two protocols complementary) TCP/IP was able to win acceptance as the common standard for computer communication protocols. From then on, computers were able to encode, and decode, for each other data packages traveling at high speed in the Internet network. Another instance of technological convergence was still necessary for computers to communicate: the adaptation of TCP/IP to UNIX, an operating system enabling access from computer to computer. The UNIX system was invented by Bell Laboratories in 1969, but became widely used only after 1983, when Berkeley researchers (again funded by ARPA) adapted to UNIX the TCP/IP protocol. Since the new version of UNIX was financed with public funds, the software was made available just for the cost of distribution. Networking was born on a large scale as local area networks and regional networks connected to each other, and started to spread anywhere where there were telephone lines and computers were equipped with modems, an inexpensive piece of equipment.

Behind the development of the Internet there was the scientific, institutional, and personal networks cutting across the Defense Department, National Science Foundation, major research universities (particularly MIT, UCLA, Stanford, University of Southern California, Harvard, University of California at Santa Barbara, and University of California at Berkeley), and specialized technological think-tanks, such as MIT's Lincoln Laboratory, SRI (formerly Stanford Research Institute), Palo Alto Research Corporation (funded by Xerox), ATT's Bell Laboratories, Rand Corporation, and BBN (Bolt, Beranek & Newman). Key technological players in the 1960s–1970s were, among others, J. C. R. Licklider, Paul Baran, Douglas Engelbart (the inventor of the mouse), Robert Taylor, Ivan Sutherland, Lawrence Roberts, Alex McKenzie, Robert Kahn, Alan Kay, Robert Thomas, Robert Metcalfe, and a brilliant computer science theoretician Leonard Kleinrock, and his cohort of outstanding graduate students at UCLA, who would become some of the key minds behind the design and development of the Internet: Vinton Cerf, Stephen Crocker, Jon Postel, among others. Many of these computer scientists moved back and forth between these various institutions, creating a networked milieu of innovation whose dynamics and goals became largely autonomous from the specific purposes of military strategy or supercomputing link-ups. They were technological crusaders, convinced that they were changing the world, as eventually they did.

Many of the applications of the Internet came from the unexpected inventions of its early users, inducing a practice and a technological trajectory that would become essential features of the Internet. Thus, in the early stages of ARPANET, the rationale for computer link-ups was the possibility of time-sharing through remote computing, so that scattered computer resources could be fully utilized on-line. Yet, most users did not really need that much computer power, or were not ready to redesign their systems in accordance with the communication requirements. But what really caught fire was e-mail communication between the network participants, an application created by Ray Tomlinson at BBN, and this remains the most popular use of computer communication in the world today.

But this is only one side of the story. In parallel with the efforts of the Pentagon and big science to establish a universal computer network with public access, within "acceptable use" norms, a sprawling computer counterculture emerged in the United States, often intellectually associated with the aftershocks of the 1960s' movements in their most libertarian/utopian version. An important element of the system, the modem, was one of the technological breakthroughs emerging from the pioneers of this counterculture, originally labeled "the hackers" before the term took on its malignant connotation. The modem for PCs was invented by two Chicago students, Ward Christensen and Randy Suess, in 1978, when they were trying to find a system to transfer microcomputer programs to each other through the telephone to avoid traveling in the Chicago winter between their distant locations. In 1979 they diffused the XModem protocol which allowed computers to transfer files directly without going through a host system. And they diffused the technology at no cost because their purpose was to spread communication capabilities as much as possible. Computer networks that were excluded from ARPANET (reserved to elite science universities in its early stages) found a way to start communicating with each other on their own. In 1979, three students at Duke University and the University of North Carolina, not included in ARPANET, created a modified version of the UNIX protocol which made it possible to link up computers over the regular telephone line. They used it to start a forum of on-line computer discussion, Usenet, which quickly became one of the first large-scale electronic conversation systems. The inventors of Usenet News also diffused freely their software in a leaflet circulated at the UNIX users conference. In 1983, Tom Jennings designed a system to post bulletin boards on PCs, by adding a modem and special software that allowed other computers to link up with a PC equipped with this interface technology. This was the origin of one of the most original, grassroots networks, Fidonet, which by 1990 was connecting 2,500 computers in the US. Because it was cheap, open, and cooperative, Fidonet was particularly successful in poor countries around the world, such as Russia, especially among countercultural groups,[51] until its technological limitations, and the development of the Internet, brought most of its users into the shared world wide web. Conferencing systems, such as Well in the San

---

51   Rohozinski (1998).

Francisco Bay area, brought together computer users in networks of affinity.

Ironically, this countercultural approach to technology had a similar effect to the military-inspired strategy of horizontal networking: it made available technological means to whoever had the technical knowledge and a computing tool, the PC, which soon began a spectacular progression of increasing power and decreasing price at the same time. The advent of personal computing and the communicability of networks spurred the development of bulletin board systems (BBS), first in the United States, then worldwide. Bulletin board systems did not need sophisticated computer networks, just PCs, modems, and the telephone line. Thus, they became the electronic notice-boards of all kinds of interests and affinities, creating what Howard Rheingold named "virtual communities."[52] In the late 1980s, several million computer users were using computer-mediated communication in cooperative or commercial networks that were not part of the Internet. Often, these networks used protocols that were not compatible, so they shifted to Internet protocols, a move that, in the 1990s, assured their integration into the Internet and thus the expansion of the Internet itself.

Yet by 1990 the Internet was still difficult to use for the uninitiated. There was very limited graphic transmission capability, and it was extremely hard to locate and retrieve information. A new technological leap allowed the diffusion of the Internet into the mainstream of society: the design of a new application, *the world wide web*, organizing the Internet sites' content by information rather than by location, then providing users with an easy search system to locate the desired information. The invention of the world wide web took place in Europe, in 1990, at the Centre Européen pour Recherche Nucleaire (CERN) in Geneva, one of the leading physics research centers in the world. It was invented by a group of researchers at CERN led by Tim Berners-Lee and Robert Cailliau. They built their research not on the ARPANET tradition, but on the contribution of the hackers' culture of the 1970s. In particular, they partly relied on the work of Ted Nelson who, in 1974, in his pamphlet "Computer Lib," called upon people to seize and use computer power for their own benefit. Nelson imagined a new system of organizing information which he called "hypertext," based on horizontal information links. To this pioneering insight, Berners-Lee and co-workers added new technologies adapted from the multimedia world to provide an audiovisual language to their application. The CERN team created a format for

52 Rheingold (1993).

hypertext documents that they named hypertext markup language (HTML), designed in the Internet tradition of flexibility, so that computers could adapt their specific languages within this shared format, adding this formatting on top of the TCP/IP protocol. They also set up a hypertext transfer protocol (HTTP) to guide communication between web browsers and web servers, and they created a standard address format, the uniform resource locator (URL) which combines information on the application protocol and on the computer address holding the requested information. Here again, URL could relate to a variety of transfer protocols, not just HTTP, thus facilitating general interface. CERN distributed world wide web (www) software free over the Internet, and the first web sites were established by major scientific research centers around the world. One of these centers was the National Center for Supercomputer Applications (NCSA) at the University of Illinois, one of the oldest NSF supercomputer centers. Because of the decline of uses for these machines, NCSA's researchers, as in most other supercomputer centers, were looking for new tasks. So were some staff members, including Marc Andreessen, a college student doing part-time work at the center for $6.85 an hour. "In late 1992, Marc, technically capable, and 'bored off his ass,' decided it was fun to take a crack at giving the Web the graphical, media rich face that it lacked."[53] The result was a web browser called Mosaic, designed to run on personal computers. Marc Andreessen and his collaborator Eric Bina posted Mosaic free on the NCSA web in November 1993, and in the spring of 1994 several million copies were in use. Andreessen and his team were then approached by a legendary Silicon Valley entrepreneur, Jim Clark, who was getting bored with the company that he had created with great success, Silicon Graphics. Together they founded another company, Netscape, which produced and commercialized the first reliable Internet browser, Netscape Navigator, released in October 1994.[54] New browsers, or search engines, developed quickly, and the whole world embraced the Internet, literally creating a world wide web.

Network technologies and pervasive computing

In the late 1990s, the communication power of the Internet, together with new developments in telecommunications and computing, induced another major technological shift, from decentralized, stand-alone microcomputers and mainframes to pervasive computing by intercon-

53   Reid (1997: 6).
54   Lewis (2000).

nected information-processing devices, coming in multiple formats. In this new technological system computer power is distributed in a communicated network built around web servers using common Internet protocols, and enabled with access capability to mega-computer servers, usually differentiated between database servers and application servers. Although the new system was still in the process of formation at the time of writing, users were accessing the network from a variety of single-purpose, specialized devices distributed in all spheres of life and activity, at home, at work, at shopping, at entertainment places, in transportation vehicles, and ultimately everywhere. These devices, many of them portable, can communicate among themselves, without needing their own operating system. Thus, computing power, applications, and data are stored in the servers of the network, and computing intelligence is placed in the network itself: web sites communicate with each other, and have at their disposal the necessary software to connect any appliance to a universal computer network. New software programs, such as Java (1995) and Jini (1999) designed by Bill Joy at Sun Microsystems, enabled the network to become the actual information-processing system. The networking logic epitomized by the Internet became applicable to every domain of activity, to every context, and to every location that could be electronically connected. The ascent of mobile telephony, spearheaded by Finland's Nokia, Sweden's Ericsson, and America's Motorola, created the possibility of accessing the Internet from mobile devices. Third-generation mobile phones, unveiled by Nokia and Ericsson in 1997, could transfer data at 384 kilobits per second outdoors and 2 megabits indoors, compared to copper line's ability to carry 64 kilobits per second of data. Furthermore, the extraordinary increase of transmission capacity with broadband communication technology provided the opportunity to use the Internet, or Internet-related communication technologies, to transmit voice, as well as data, through packet switching, thus revolutionizing telecommunications – and the telecommunications industry. According to Vinton Cerf, "Today you go through a circuit switch to get a packet switch. Tomorrow you'll go through a packet switch to get a circuit switch."[55] In another technological vision, Cerf asserted that "during the latter half of the next decade – that is around 2005–2010 – there will be a new (technological) driver: billions of devices attached to the Internet."[56] So, ultimately, the communications network will be packet switched, with data transmission accounting for the overwhelming share of traffic, and voice transmission being but

55   Cerf (1999).
56   Quoted in *The Economist* (1997: 33).

one, specialized service. This volume of communication traffic will require a gigantic expansion of capacity, both trans-oceanic and local. The building of a new, global telecommunications infrastructure based on fibre-optic and digital transmission was well underway at the turn of the century, with transatlantic fiber-optic cable transmission capacity approaching 110 gigabits per second in 2000, in comparison with about 5 gigabits in 1993.

The frontier of information technology at the turn of the millennium appeared to be the application of a chemically based and/or biologically based nanotechnology-approach to chip making. Thus, in July 1999, the journal *Science* published the results of experimental work by computer scientist Phil Kuekes of Hewlett-Packard's laboratory in Palo Alto and chemist James Health of UCLA. They found a way to make electronic switches using chemical processes instead of light, thus shrinking the switches to the size of a molecule. While these ultra-tiny electronic components are still some way away from operational stage (at least for a decade), this and other experimental programs seem to indicate that molecular electronics is a possible avenue to overcoming the physical limits of increasing density in silicon chips, while ushering in an era of computers 100 billion times as fast as a Pentium microprocessor: this would make it possible to pack the computing power of a hundred 1999 computer workstations into a space the size of a grain of salt. Based on these technologies, computer scientists envisage the possibility of computing environments where billions of microscopic information-processing devices will be spread everywhere "like pigment in the wall paint." If so, then computer networks will be, materially speaking, the fabric of our lives.[57]

The 1970s' technological divide

This technological system, in which we are fully immersed at the dawn of the twenty-first century, came together in the 1970s. Because of the significance of specific historical contexts for technological trajectories, and for the particular form of interaction between technology and society, it is important to recall a few dates associated with essential discoveries in information technologies. All of them have something essential in common: while mainly based on previously existing knowledge, and developed in prolongation of key technologies, they represented a qualitative leap forward in the massive diffusion of technology in commercial and civilian applications because of their accessibility and their decreasing cost with increasing quality. Thus, the

57   Hall (1999a); Markoff (1999a, b).

microprocessor, the key device in spreading micro-electronics, was invented in 1971 and began to diffuse by the mid-1970s. The micro-computer was invented in 1975 and the first successful commercial product, Apple II, was introduced in April 1977, around the same time that Microsoft started to produce operating systems for micro-computers. The Xerox Alto, the matrix of many software technologies for 1990s' personal computers, was developed at PARC labs in Palo Alto in 1973. The first industrial electronic switch appeared in 1969, and digital switching was developed in the mid-1970s and commercially diffused in 1977. Optic fiber was first industrially produced by Corning Glass in the early 1970s. Also by the mid-1970s, Sony started to produce VCR machines commercially, on the basis of 1960s' discoveries in America and England that never reached mass production. And last, but not least, it was in 1969 that the US Defense Department's Advanced Research Projects Agency (ARPA) set up a new, revolutionary electronic communication network, which would grow during the 1970s to become the current Internet. It was greatly helped by the invention by Cerf and Kahn in 1973 of TCP/IP, the interconnection network protocol that ushered in "gateway" technology, allowing different types of networks to be connected. I think we can say, without exaggeration, that the information technology revolution, as a revolution, was born in the 1970s, particularly if we include in it the parallel emergence and diffusion of genetic engineering around the same dates and places, a development that deserves, to say the least, a few lines of attention.

Technologies of life

Although biotechnology can be traced all the way back to a 6000 BC Babylonian tablet on brewing, and the revolution in microbiology to the scientific discovery of the basic structure of life, DNA's double helix, by Francis Crick and James Watson at Cambridge University in 1953, it was only in the early 1970s that gene splicing and recombinant DNA, the technological foundation of genetic engineering, made possible the application of cumulative knowledge. Stanford's Stanley Cohen and University of California at San Francisco's Herbert Boyer are generally credited with the discovery of gene-cloning procedures in 1973, although their work was based on research by Stanford's Nobel Prize winner Paul Berg. In 1975 researchers at Harvard isolated the first mammalian gene, out of rabbit hemoglobin; and in 1977 the first human gene was cloned.

What followed was a rush to start up commercial firms, most of them spin-offs from major universities and hospital research centers, clusters of such firms emerging in northern California, New England, Maryland, Virginia, North Carolina, and San Diego. Journalists, investors, and social activists alike were struck by the awesome possibilities opened up by the potential ability to engineer life, including human life. Genentech in south San Francisco, Cetus in Berkeley, and Biogen in Cambridge, Massachusetts were among the first companies, organized around Nobel Prize winners, to use new genetic technologies for medical applications. Agro-business followed soon; and micro-organisms, some of them genetically altered, were given an increasing number of assignments, not least to clean up pollution, often generated by the same companies and agencies that were selling the superbugs. Yet scientific difficulties, technical problems, and major legal obstacles derived from justified ethical and safety concerns slowed down the much-vaunted biotechnological revolution during the 1980s. A considerable amount of venture capital investment was lost and some of the most innovative companies, including Genentech, were absorbed by pharmaceutical giants (Hoffman-La Roche, Merck) who, better than anybody else, understood that they could not replicate the costly arrogance that established computer firms had displayed toward innovative start-ups: to buy small, innovative firms, along with their scientists' services, became a major insurance policy for pharmaceutical and chemical multinationals to both internalize the commercial benefits of the biological revolution and to control its pace. A slowing down of this pace followed, at least in the diffusion of its applications.

However, in the late 1980s and in the 1990s a major science push, and a new generation of daring scientist entrepreneurs, revitalized biotechnology, with a decisive focus on genetic engineering, the truly revolutionary technology in the field. Genetic cloning entered a new stage when, in 1988, Harvard formally patented a genetically engineered mouse, thus taking the copyright of life away from God and Nature. In the next seven years, an additional seven mice were also patented as newly created forms of life, identified as the property of their engineers. In August 1989 researchers from the University of Michigan and Toronto discovered the gene responsible for cystic fibrosis, opening the way for genetic therapy. In February 1997, Wilmut and his collaborators at the Roslin Institute in Edinburgh announced the cloning of a sheep, which they named Dolly, realized from the DNA of an adult sheep. In July 1998 the journal *Nature* published the findings of a potentially even more significant experiment: the research by two biologists at the University of Hawaii, Yanagimachi and Wakayama, who proceeded with a massive cloning of 22 mice, including seven clones of clones, thus proving the possibility of the sequential production of clones, under more difficult conditions than sheep cloning, since mice embryos have a much faster development than sheep. Also in 1998, scientists at Portland State University succeeded in cloning adult monkeys, although without being able to reproduce the conditions of their experiment.

In spite of all the media hype – and the horror stories – human cloning is not on the cards for anyone, and, in strict terms, it is indeed physically impossible, since living beings form their personality and their organism in interaction with their environment. Animal cloning is economically inefficient because, if practiced on a massive scale, it would raise the possibility of the complete destruction of the entire livestock in the event of an infection – since all animals of a given kind would be vulnerable to the same deadly agent. But other possibilities emerge, particularly in medical research: the cloning of human organs, and the large-scale cloning of genetically engineered animals for the purpose of experimentation, and for the replacement of human organs. Furthermore, rather than replacing organs with organ transplants, new biological research, with powerful medical and commercial applications, aims at inducing self-regenerating capabilities in humans. A survey of potential applications in process in the late 1990s revealed the following projects, all of them expected to be operational between 2000 and 2010, all of them related to inducing self-regeneration or growth of organs, tissue, or bones in the human body by biological manipulation: bladder, in project by the company Reprogenesis; urinary conduct by Integra Life Sciences; maxilar bones by Osiris Therapeutics; insulin-producing cells, replacing the pancreas function, by BioHybrid Technologies; cartilage by ReGen Biologics; teeth by a variety of companies; spinal cord nerves by Acorda; cartilage breasts by Reprogenesis; a complete human heart, on the basis of genetically manipulated proteins already tested as being capable of producing blood vessels, by Genentech; and liver regeneration, on the basis of tissue on which liver cells are planted, by Human Organ Sciences.

The most decisive frontier of biological research and application is genetic therapy and genetic prevention on a large scale. Behind this potential development is the effort initiated in 1990 by the US government to sponsor and fund a $3 billion, 15-year collaborative program, coordinated by James Watson, bringing together some of the most advanced microbiology research teams to map the human genome; that is, to identify and locate the 60,000–80,000 genes that compose the alphabet of the human species.[58] The map was expected to be com-

---

58   On the early development of biotechnology and genetic engineering, see, for instance, Hall (1987); Teitelman (1989); Bishop and Waldholz (1990); US Congress, Office of Technology Assessment (1991).

pleted in 2001, ahead of schedule. In April 2000, the University of California teams assembled in a research center at Walnut Creek completed the sequence of three of the 23 human chromosomes. Through this and other efforts, a continuous stream of human genes related to various diseases are being identified. This effort prompted widespread reservations and criticism on ethical, religious, and legal grounds. Yet, while scientists, regulators, and ethicists debated the humanistic implications of genetic engineering, researchers-turned-business-entrepreneurs took the short path, setting up mechanisms for legal and financial control of knowledge of the human genome. The most daring attempt in this sense was the project initiated in 1990 in Rockville, Maryland, by two scientists, J. Craig Venter, then with the National Institute of Health, and William Haseltine, then at Harvard. Using supercomputer power, they sequenced in only five years parts of about 85 percent of all human genes, creating a gigantic genetic database.[59] Later on, they split and created two companies. One of these companies, Venter's Celera Genomics, raced the Human Genome Project to complete the sequencing in 2000. The problem is that they do not know, and will not know for some time, which gene's piece is what or where it is located: their database comprises hundreds of thousands of gene fragments with unknown functions. What was then the interest? On the one hand, focused research on specific genes may (and does in fact) use to its advantage the data contained in such sequences. But, more import-antly and the main reason for the whole project, Craig and Haseltine have been busy patenting all their data, so that, literally, they may one day own the legal rights to a large portion of the knowledge to manipulate the human genome. The threat posed by such a development was serious enough that, while on the one hand they have attracted tens of millions of dollars from investors, on the other hand, a major pharmaceutical company, Merck, gave in 1994 substantial funding to Washington University to proceed with the same blind sequencing and to make the data public, so that there would be no private control of bits and pieces of knowledge which could block development of products based on a future, systematic understanding of the human genome. And the publicly funded Human Genome Project published its results to prevent private ownership of genetic knowledge. The lesson for the sociologist of such business battles is not just another instance of human greed. It signals an accelerating tempo in the spread and deepening of the genetic revolution.

The development of genetic engineering creates the possibility of acting on genes, making humankind able not only to control some

59 See *Business Week* (1995e).

diseases, but to identify biological predispositions and to intervene in such predispositions, potentially altering genetic fate. In the 1990s, scientists were able to identify precise defects in specific human genes as sources of various diseases. This prompted the expansion of the apparently most promising field of medical research, gen-etic therapy.[60] But experimental researchers hit a wall: how to deliver a modified gene with an instruction to correct the defective gene in the body to the proper place, even when they knew where the target was. Investigators generally used viruses, or artificial chromosomes, but the rate of success was extremely low. Thus, medical researchers started to experiment with other tools, such as tiny fat globules designed to carry tumor-suppressor genes directly into cancer tumors, a technology used by firms such as Valentis and Transgene. Some biologists think that this engineering mentality (one target, one messenger, one impact) overlooks the complexity of biological interaction, with living organisms adapting to various environments and changing their predicted behavior.[61]

When and if gene therapy starts yielding results, the ultimate goal of genetic-based medical therapy is prevention; that is, identifying genetic defects in human sperm and eggs, and acting on the human carriers before they develop the programmed illness, thus eliminating the genetic deficiency from them, and from their offspring, while there is still time. This perspective, of course, is full of promise as well as of dangers. Lyon and Gorner conclude their balanced survey of developments in human genetic engineering with a prediction and an admonition:

> We could in a few generations do away with certain mental illnesses, perhaps, or diabetes, or high blood pressure, or almost any affliction we selected. The important thing to keep in mind is that the quality of decision making dictates whether the choices to be made are going to be wise and just . . . The rather inglorious way that the scientific and administrative elite are handling the earliest fruits of gene therapy is ominous . . . We humans have evolved intellectually to the point that, relatively soon, we will be able to understand the composition, function, and dynamics of the genome in much of its intimidating complexity. Emotionally however, we are still apes, with all the behavioral baggage that the issue brings. Perhaps the ultimate form of gene therapy would be for our species to rise above its baser heritage and learn to apply its new knowledge wisely and benignly.[62]

60 *Business Week* (1999a: 94–104).
61 Capra (1999a); Sapolsky (2000).
62 Lyon and Gorner (1995: 567).

All indications point toward the full blossoming of genetic engineering, and its applications, in the early years of the new millennium, thus triggering a fundamental debate about the now blurred frontier between nature and society.

Social context and the dynamics of technological change

Why were discoveries in new information technologies clustered in the 1970s, and mostly in the United States? And what are the consequences of such timed/placed clustering for their future development and for their interaction with societies? It would be tempting to relate directly the formation of this technological paradigm to the characteristics of its social context, particularly if we remember that in the mid-1970s the United States and the capitalist world were shaken by a major economic crisis, epitomized (but not caused) by the oil shock of 1973–4: a crisis that prompted the dramatic restructuring of the capitalist system on a global scale, actually inducing a new model of accumulation in historical discontinuity with post-Second World War capitalism, as I proposed in the Prologue of this book. Was the new technological paradigm a response by the capitalist system to overcome its internal contradictions? Or, alternatively, was it a way to ensure military superiority over the Soviet foe, responding to its technological challenge in the space race and nuclear weaponry? Neither explanation seems to be convincing. While there is an historical coincidence between the clustering of new technologies and the economic crisis of the 1970s, their timing was too close, the "technological fix" would have been too quick, and too mechanical, when we know from the lessons of the industrial revolution and other historical processes of technological change that economic, industrial, and technological paths, while related, are slow-moving and imperfectly fitting in their interaction. As for the military argument, the Sputnik shock of 1957–60 was answered in kind by the massive technological build-up of the 1960s, not the 1970s; and the new major American military technology push was launched in 1983 around the "Star Wars" program, actually using and furthering technologies developed in the preceding, prodigious decade. And while the Internet originated from research sponsored by the Defense Department, it was not in fact used in military applications until much later, at about the same time as it started to diffuse in countercultural networks.

In fact, it seems that the emergence of a new technological system in the 1970s must be traced to the autonomous dynamics of technological discovery and diffusion, including synergistic effects between various key technologies. Thus, the microprocessor made possible the microcomputer; advances in telecommunications, as mentioned above, enabled microcomputers to function in networks, thus increasing their power and flexibility. Applications of these technologies to electronics manufacturing enhanced the potential for new design and fabrication technologies in semiconductor production. New software was stimulated by the fast-growing microcomputer market which, in turn, exploded on the basis of new applications and user-friendly technologies churned out from software writers' minds. Computer networking could expand by using software that made possible a user-oriented world wide web. And so on.

The strong, military-induced technological push of the 1960s prepared American technology for the leap forward. But Ted Hoff's invention of the microprocessor, while trying to fulfill an order for a Japanese hand calculator company in 1971, came out of knowledge and ingenuity accumulated at Intel, in close interaction with the milieu of innovation created since the 1950s in Silicon Valley. In other words, the first information technology revolution clustered in America, and to some extent in California, in the 1970s, building on developments of the two preceding decades, and under the influence of various institutional, economic, and cultural factors. But it did not come out of any pre-established necessity: it was technologically induced rather than socially determined. However, once it came into existence as a system, on the basis of the clustering I have described, its development and applications, and ultimately its content, were decisively shaped by the historical context in which it expanded. Indeed, by the 1980s, capitalism (specifically, major corporations and governments of the club of G-7 countries) did undertake a substantial process of economic and organizational restructuring, in which new information technology played a fundamental role and was decisively shaped by the role it played. For instance, the business-led movement toward deregulation and liberalization in the 1980s was decisive in the reorganization and growth of telecommunications, most notably after the 1984 divestiture of ATT. In turn, the availability of new telecommunication networks and information systems prepared the ground for the global integration of financial markets and the segmented articulation of production and trade throughout the world, as I shall examine in chapter 2.

Thus, to some extent, the availability of new technologies constituted as a system in the 1970s was a fundamental basis for the process of socio-economic restructuring in the 1980s. And the uses of such technologies in the 1980s largely conditioned their uses and trajectories in the 1990s. The rise of the network society, which I shall attempt to analyze in the following chapters of this volume, cannot be understood without the interaction between these two relatively autonomous trends: the development of new information technologies and the old society's attempt to retool itself by using the power of technology to serve the technology of power. However, the historical outcome of such a half-conscious strategy is largely undetermined since the interaction of technology and society depends on stochastic relationships between an excessive number of quasi-independent variables. Without necessarily surrendering to historical relativism, it can be said that the information technology revolution was culturally, historically, and spatially contingent on a very specific set of circumstances whose characteristics earmarked its future evolution.

Models, Actors, and Sites of the Information Technology Revolution

If the first industrial revolution was British, the first information technology revolution was American, with a Californian inclination. In both cases scientists and industrialists from other countries did play an important role, both in the discovery and in the diffusion of new technologies. France and Germany were key sources of talent and applications in the industrial revolution. Scientific discoveries originated in England, France, Germany, and Italy were at the roots of new technologies in electronics and biology. The ingenuity of Japanese companies has been critical in the improvement of manufacturing processes in electronics and in the penetration of information technologies into everyday life around the world through a flurry of innovative products, from VCRs and faxes to video games and pagers.[63] Indeed, in the 1980s, Japanese companies came to dominate semiconductor production in the world market, although by the mid-1990s American companies by and large had retaken the competitive lead. The whole industry evolved toward interpenetration, strategic alliances, and networking between firms of different countries, as I shall analyze in chapter 3. This made differentiation by national origin somewhat less relevant. Yet not only were US innovators, firms, and institutions at the origins of the revolution in the 1970s, but they have continued to play a leading role in its expansion, which is likely to be sustained into the twenty-first century, although we shall undoubtedly witness an increasing presence of Japanese, Chinese, Korean, and Indian firms, as well as important European contributions in biotechnology, advanced chemistry, software, and telecommunications.

63 Forester (1993).

To understand the social roots of the information technology revolution in America, beyond the myths surrounding it, I shall recall briefly the process of formation of its most notorious seedbed of innovation: Silicon Valley. As I have already mentioned, it was in Silicon Valley that the integrated circuit, the microprocessor, the microcomputer, among other key technologies, were developed, and that the heart of electronics innovation has beaten for four decades, sustained by about a quarter of a million information technology workers.[64] In addition, the San Francisco Bay area at large (including other centers of innovation such as Berkeley, Emeryville, Marin County, and San Francisco itself) was also at the origins of genetic engineering and is, at the turn of the century, one of the world's leading centers of advanced software, genetic engineering, Internet design and development, and multimedia computing design.

Silicon Valley (Santa Clara County, 30 miles south of San Francisco, between Stanford and San Jose) was formed as a milieu of innovation by the convergence on one site of new technological knowledge; a large pool of skilled engineers and scientists from major universities in the area; generous funding from an assured market with the Defense Department; the development of an efficient network of venture capital firms; and, in the very early stage, the institutional leadership of Stanford University. Indeed, the unlikely location of the electronics industry in a charming, semi-rural area of northern California can be traced back to the establishment in 1951 of Stanford Industrial Park by Stanford University's visionary Dean of Engineering and Provost, Frederick Terman. He had personally supported two of his graduate students, William Hewlett and David Packard, in creating an electronics company in 1938. The Second World War was a bonanza for Hewlett Packard and other start-up electronics companies. Thus, naturally, they were the first tenants of a new, privileged location where only firms that Stanford judged innovative could benefit from a notional rent. As the Park was soon filled, new electronics firms started to locate down freeway 101 toward San Jose.

The decisive event was the moving to Palo Alto in 1955 of William Shockley, the inventor of the transistor. And this was a fortuitous development, although it reflects on the historical inability of established electronics firms to seize revolutionary micro-electronics technology. Shockley had solicited the support of large companies on the East Coast, such as RCA and Raytheon, to develop his discovery into industrial production. When he was turned down he took a job in Silicon Valley,

---

64   On the history of formation of Silicon Valley, two useful, easy-reading books are Rogers and Larsen (1984) and Malone (1985).

with a subsidiary of Beckman Instruments, mainly because his mother lived in Palo Alto. With the support of Beckman Instruments he decided to create there his own company, Shockley Transistors, in 1956. He recruited eight brilliant young engineers, mainly from Bell Labs, attracted by the possibility of working with Shockley; one of them, although not precisely from Bell Labs, was Bob Noyce. They were soon disappointed. While learning the fundamentals of cutting-edge micro-electronics from Shockley, they were turned off by his authoritarianism and stubbornness which led the firm into dead-ends. In particular, they wanted, against his decision, to work on silicon as the most promising route to the larger integration of transistors. Thus, after only one year they left Shockley (whose firm collapsed) and created (with the help of Fairchild Cameras) Fairchild Semiconductors, where the invention of the planar process and of the integrated circuit took place in the next two years. While Shockley, after repeated business failures, finally took refuge in a Stanford professorship in 1963, the "Fairchild Eight," as soon as they discovered the technological and business potential of their knowledge, left Fairchild one by one to start their own firms. And their new recruits did the same after some time, so that one-half of the 85 largest American semiconductors firms, including today's leading producers such as Intel, Advanced Micro Devices, National Semiconductors, Signetics, and so on, can be traced back to this spin-off from Fairchild.

It was this technology transfer from Shockley to Fairchild, then to a network of spin-off companies, that constituted the initial source of innovation on which Silicon Valley and the micro-electronics revolution were built. Indeed, by the mid-1950s Stanford and Berkeley were not yet leading centers in electronics; MIT was, and this was reflected in the original location of the electronics industry in New England. However, as soon as knowledge was available in Silicon Valley, the dynamism of its industrial structure and the continuous creation of start-up firms anchored Silicon Valley as the world's micro-electronics center by the early 1970s. Anna Saxenian compared the development of electronics complexes in the two areas (Boston's Route 128 and Silicon Valley) and concluded that the decisive role was played by the social and industrial organization of companies in fostering or stymieing innovation.[65] Thus, while large, established companies in the East were too rigid (and too arrogant) to constantly retool themselves toward new technological frontiers, Silicon Valley kept churning out new firms, and practicing cross-fertilization and knowledge diffusion by job-hopping and spin-offs. Late-evening conversations at the

65   Saxenian (1994).

Walker's Wagon Wheel Bar and Grill in Mountain View did more for the diffusion of technological innovation than most seminars in Stanford.

As I have elaborated elsewhere,[66] another key factor in the formation of Silicon Valley was the existence of a network of venture capital firms early on.[67] The significant factor here is that many of the early investors originated from the electronics industry, and thus they were knowledgeable about the technological and business projects on which they were betting. For instance, Gene Kleinert, of one of the most important venture capital firms in the 1960s, Kleinert, Perkins, and partners, was one of the Fairchild Eight engineers. In 1988, it could be estimated that "venture capital accounted for about one-half of the new product and service investment associated with the information and communication industry."[68]

A similar process took place in the development of the microcomputer, which introduced an historical divide in the uses of information technology.[69] By the mid-1970s Silicon Valley had attracted tens of thousands of bright young minds from around the world, coming to the excitement of the new technological Mecca in a quest for the talisman of invention and money. They gathered in loose groups, to exchange ideas and information on the latest developments. One such gathering was the Home Brew Computer Club, whose young visionaries (including Bill Gates, Steve Jobs, and Steve Wozniak) would go on to create in the following years up to 22 companies, including Microsoft, Apple, Comenco, and North Star. It was the club's reading, in *Popular Electronics*, of an article reporting Ed Roberts's Altair machine which inspired Wozniak to design a microcomputer, Apple I, in his Menlo Park garage in the summer of 1976. Steve Jobs saw the potential, and together they founded Apple, with a $91,000 loan from an Intel executive, Mike Markkula, who came in as a partner. At about the same time Bill Gates founded Microsoft to provide the operating system for microcomputers, although he located his company in 1978 in Seattle to take advantage of the social contacts of his family.

A parallel story could be told about the growth of genetic engineering, with leading scientists at Stanford, UC San Francisco and Berkeley bridging into companies, first located in the Bay area. They would also go through the process of frequent spin-off, while keeping close ties with their alma maters.[70] Comparable processes took place in Bos-

---

66   Castells (1989b: ch. 2).
67   Zook (2000c).
68   Kay (1990: 173).
69   Levy (1984); Egan (1995). For an interesting case study of the complex interaction between technological creativity and business strategies, see Hiltzik (1999) on the experience of one of most important centers of innovation in Silicon Valley, Xerox-PARC.
70   Blakely et al. (1988); Hall et al. (1988).

ton/Cambridge around Harvard–MIT, in the research triangle around Duke University and the University of North Carolina, and, more importantly, in Maryland around major hospitals, national health research institutes, and The Johns Hopkins University.

The conclusion to be drawn from these colorful stories is twofold: first, the development of the information technology revolution contributed to the formation of the milieux of innovation where discoveries and applications would interact, and be tested, in a recurrent process of trial and error, of learning by doing; these milieux required (and still do in the early twenty-first century, in spite of on-line networking) the spatial concentration of research centers, higher-education institutions, advanced-technology companies, a network of ancillary suppliers of goods and services, and business networks of venture capital to finance start-ups. Secondly, once a milieu is consolidated, as Silicon Valley was in the 1970s, it tends to generate its own dynamics, and to attract knowledge, investment, and talent from around the world. Indeed, in the 1990s Silicon Valley benefited from a proliferation of Japanese, Taiwanese, Korean, Indian, and European companies, and from the influx of thousands of engineers and computer experts, mainly from India and China, for whom an active presence in the Valley is the most productive linkage to the sources of new technology and valuable business information.[71] Furthermore, because of its positioning in the networks of technological innovation, and because of its built-in business understanding of the rules of the new information economy, the San Francisco Bay area has been able to jump on any new development. In the 1990s, when the Internet was privatized, and became a commercial technology, Silicon Valley was also able to capture the new industry. Leading Internet equipment companies (such as Cisco Systems), computer networking companies (such as Sun Microsystems), software companies (such as Oracle), and Internet portals (such as Yahoo!) started in Silicon Valley.[72] Moreover, most of the Internet start-ups that introduced e-commerce, and revolutionized business (such as Ebay), also clustered in Silicon Valley. The coming of multimedia in the mid-1990s created a network of technological and business linkages between computer-design capabilities from Silicon Valley companies and image-producing studios in Hollywood, immediately labeled the "Siliwood" industry. And in a run-down corner of San Francisco (South of Market), artists, graphic designers, and software writers came together in the so-called "Multimedia Gulch" that threatens to flood our living rooms with images coming from their fevered minds – in the

71　Saxenian (1999).
72　Reid (1997); Bronson (1999); Kaplan (1999); Lewis (2000); Zook (2000c).

process creating the most dynamic multimedia design center in the world.[73]

Can this social, cultural, and spatial pattern of innovation be extrapolated throughout the world? To answer this question, in 1988 my colleague Peter Hall and I began a several years' tour of the world that brought us to visit and analyze some of the main scientific/technological centers of this planet, from California to Japan, New England to Old England, Paris-Sud to Hsinchu–Taiwan, Sophia-Antipolis to Akademgorodok, Szelenograd to Daeduck, Munich to Seoul. Our conclusions[74] confirm the critical role played by milieux of innovation in the development of the information technology revolution: clusters of scientific/technical knowledge, institutions, firms, and skilled labor are the furnaces of innovation in the Information Age. Yet they do not need to reproduce the cultural, spatial, institutional and industrial pattern of Silicon Valley or, for that matter, of other American centers of technological innovation, such as southern California, Boston, Seattle, or Austin.

Our most striking discovery is that the largest, old metropolitan areas of the industrialized world are the main centers of innovation and production in information technology outside the United States. In Europe, Paris-Sud constitutes the largest concentration of high-technology production and research; and London's M4 corridor is still Britain's pre-eminent electronics site, in historical continuity with ordnance factories working for the crown since the nineteenth century. The displacement of Berlin by Munich was obviously related to the German defeat in the Second World War, with Siemens deliberately moving from Berlin to Bavaria in anticipation of American occupation of that area. Tokyo–Yokohama continues to be the technological core of the Japanese information technology industry, in spite of the decentralization of branch plants operated under the Technopolis Program. Moscow–Szelenograd and St Petersburg were and are the centers of Soviet and Russian technological knowledge and production, after the failure of Khrushchev's Siberian dream. Hsinchu is in fact a satellite of Taipei; Daeduck never played a significant role *vis-à-vis* Seoul-Inchon, in spite of being in the home province of dictator Park; and Beijing and Shanghai are, and will be, the core of Chinese technological development. And so are Mexico City in Mexico, São Paulo–Campinas in Brazil, and Buenos Aires in Argentina. In this sense, the technological fading of old American metropolises (New York/New Jersey, in spite of its prominent role up to the 1960s, Chicago, Detroit,

73   Rosen et al. (1999).
74   Castells and Hall (1994).

Philadelphia) is the exception at the international level, linked to American exceptionalism of frontier spirit, and to its endless escapism from the contradictions of built cities and constituted societies. On the other hand, it would be intriguing to explore the relationship between this American exceptionalism and the indisputable American pre-eminence in a technological revolution characterized by the need to break mental molds to spur creativity.

Yet the metropolitan character of most sites of the information technology revolution around the world seems to indicate that the critical ingredient in its development is not the newness of the institutional and cultural setting, but its ability to generate synergy on the basis of knowledge and information, directly related to industrial production and commercial applications. The cultural and business strength of the metropolis (old or new – after all, the San Francisco Bay area is a metropolis of about 6.5 million people) makes it the privileged environment of this new technological revolution, actually demystifying the notion of placelessness of innovation in the Information Age.

Similarly, the entrepreneurial model of the information technology revolution seems to be overshadowed by ideology. Not only are the Japanese, European, and Chinese models of technological innovation quite different from the American experience, but even this leading experience is often misunderstood. The role of the state is generally acknowledged as decisive in Japan, where large corporations were guided and supported by the Ministry of International Trade and Industry (MITI) for a long time, well into the 1980s, through a series of bold technological programs, some of which failed (for example, the Fifth Generation Computer), but most of which helped to transform Japan into a technological superpower in just about 20 years, as Michael Borrus has documented.[75] No start-up innovative firms and little role for universities can be found in the Japanese experience. Strategic planning by MITI and the constant interface between the *keiretsu* and government are key elements in explaining the Japanese prowess that overwhelmed Europe and overtook the US in several segments of information technology industries. A similar story can be told about South Korea and Taiwan, although in the latter case multinationals played a greater role. India and China's strong technological bases are directly related to their military–industrial complex, under state funding and guidance.

But so was also the case for much of the British and French electronics industries, centered on telecommunications and defense, until the 1980s.[76] In the last quarter of the twentieth century, the European

75   Borrus (1988).
76   Hall et al. (1987).

Union proceeded with a series of technological programs to keep up with international competition, systematically supporting "national champions," even at a loss, and without much result. Indeed, the only way for European information technology companies to survive technologically has been to use their considerable resources (a substantial share of which comes from government funds) to make alliances with Japanese and American companies, which are increasingly their main source of know-how in advanced information technology.[77]

Even in the US it is a well-known fact that military contracts and Defense Department technological initiatives played decisive roles in the formative stage of the information technology revolution; that is, between the 1940s and the 1970s. Even the major source of electronics discovery, Bell Laboratories, played the role of a national laboratory: its parent company (ATT) enjoyed a government-enforced monopoly of telecommunications; a significant part of its research funds came from the US government; and ATT was in fact forced by the government from 1956, in return for its monopoly on public telecommunications, to diffuse technological discoveries into the public domain.[78] MIT, Harvard, Stanford, Berkeley, UCLA, Chicago, Johns Hopkins, and national weapons laboratories such as Livermore, Los Alamos, Sandia, and Lincoln, worked with and for Defense Department agencies on programs that led to fundamental breakthroughs, from the 1940s' computers to opto-electronics and artificial intelligence technologies of the 1980s' "Star Wars" programs. DARPA, the extraordinarily innovative Defense Department Research Agency, played in the US a role not too different from that of MITI in Japan's technological development, including the design and initial funding of the Internet.[79] Indeed, in the 1980s, when the ultra-*laissez-faire* Reagan administration felt the pinch of Japanese competition, the Defense Department funded SEMATECH, a consortium of American electronics companies to support costly R&D programs in electronics manufacturing, for reasons of national security. And the federal government also helped the effort by major firms to cooperate in micro-electronics by creating MCC, with both SEMATECH and MCC locating in Austin, Texas.[80] Also, during the decisive 1950s and 1960s, military contracts and the space program were essential markets for the electronics industry, both for the giant defense contractors of southern California and for the start-up innovators of Silicon Valley and New England.[81]

---

77 Castells et al. (1991); Freeman et al. (1991).
78 Bar (1990).
79 Tirman (1984); Broad (1985); Stowsky (1992).
80 Borrus (1988); Gibson and Rogers (1994).
81 Roberts (1991).

They could not have survived without the generous funding and protected markets of a US government anxious to recover technological
superiority over the Soviet Union, a strategy that eventually paid off.
Genetic engineering spun off from major research universities, hospitals, and health research institutes, largely funded and sponsored by
government money.[82] Thus, the state, not the innovative entrepreneur
in his garage, both in America and throughout the world, was the
initiator of the information technology revolution.[83]

However, without these innovative entrepreneurs, such as those at
the origin of Silicon Valley or of Taiwan's PC clones, the information
technology revolution would have had very different characteristics,
and it is unlikely that it would have evolved toward the kind of decentralized, flexible technological devices that are diffusing through all
realms of human activity. Indeed, since the early 1970s, technological
innovation has been essentially market driven:[84] and innovators, while
still often employed by major companies, particularly in Japan and
Europe, continue to establish their own businesses in America and,
increasingly, around the world. This gives rise to an acceleration of
technological innovation and a faster diffusion of such innovation, as
ingenious minds, driven by passion and greed, constantly scan the industry for market niches in products and processes. *It is indeed by this
interface between macro-research programs and large markets developed by the state, on the one hand, and decentralized innovation stimulated by a culture of technological creativity and role models of fast
personal success, on the other hand, that new information technologies came to blossom.* In so doing, they clustered around networks of
firms, organizations, and institutions to form a new socio-technical
paradigm.

The Information Technology Paradigm

As Christopher Freeman writes:

> A techno-economic paradigm is a cluster of interrelated technical, or-
> ganizational, and managerial innovations whose advantages are to be
> found not only in a new range of products and systems, but most of all
> in the dynamics of the relative cost structure of all possible inputs to
> production. *In each new paradigm a particular input or set of inputs
> may be described as the "key factor" in that paradigm characterized by*

82 Kenney (1986).
83 See the analyses gathered in Castells (1988b).
84 Banegas (1993).

falling relative costs and universal availability. The contemporary change
of paradigm may be seen as a shift from a technology based primarily
on cheap inputs of energy to one *predominantly based on cheap inputs
of information derived from advances in microelectronic and telecommunications technology.*[85]

The notion of the technological paradigm, elaborated by Carlota Perez,
Christopher Freeman, and Giovanni Dosi, adapting the classic analysis of scientific revolutions by Kuhn, helps to organize the essence of
current technological transformation as it interacts with economy and
society.[86] Rather than refining the definition to include social processes beyond the economy, I think it would be useful, as a guide to
our forthcoming journey along the paths of social transformation, to
pinpoint those features that constitute the heart of the information
technology paradigm. Taken together, they are the material foundation of the network society.

The first characteristic of the new paradigm is that information is
its raw material: *these are technologies to act on information*, not just
information to act on technology, as was the case in previous technological revolutions.

The second feature refers to the *pervasiveness of effects of new technologies*. Because information is an integral part of all human activity,
all processes of our individual and collective existence are directly
shaped (although certainly not determined) by the new technological
medium.

The third characteristic refers to the *networking logic* of any system
or set of relationships using these new information technologies. The
morphology of the network seems to be well adapted to increasing
complexity of interaction and to unpredictable patterns of development arising from the creative power of such interaction.[87] This topo-
logical configuration, the network, can now be materially implemented,

85   C. Freeman, "Preface to part II," in Dosi et al. (1988a: 10).
86   Kuhn (1962); Perez (1983); Dosi et al. (1988a).
87   Kelly (1995: 25–7) elaborates on the properties of networking logic in a few telling
paragraphs: "The Atom is the past. The symbol of science for the next century is the dy-
namical Net . . . Whereas the Atom represents clean simplicity, the Net channels the messy
power of complexity . . . The only organization capable of nonprejudiced growth, or unguided
learning is a network. All other topologies limit what can happen. A network swarm is all
edges and therefore open ended any way you come at it. Indeed, the network is the least
structured organization that can be said to have any structure at all . . . In fact a plurality of
truly divergent components can only remain coherent in a network. No other arrangement
– chain, pyramid, tree, circle, hub – can contain true diversity working as a whole." Although physicists and mathematicians may take exception to some of these statements, Kelly's
basic message is an interesting one: the convergence between the evolutionary topology of
living matter, the open-ended nature of an increasingly complex society, and the interactive
logic of new information technologies.

in all kinds of processes and organizations, by newly available information technologies. Without them, the networking logic would be too cumbersome to implement. Yet this networking logic is needed to structure the unstructured while preserving flexibility, since the unstructured is the driving force of innovation in human activity. Moreover, when networks diffuse, their growth becomes exponential, as the benefits of being in the network grow exponentially, because of the greater number of connections, and the cost grows in a linear pattern. Besides, the penalty for being outside the network increases with the network's growth because of the declining number of opportunities in reaching other elements outside the network. The creator of local area networks technology, Robert Metcalfe, proposed in 1973 a simple mathematical formula showing how the value of a network increases as the square of the number of nodes in the net. The formula is $V = n^{(n-1)}$ where n is the number of nodes in the network.

Fourthly, related to networking but a clearly distinct feature, the information technology paradigm is based on *flexibility*. Not only processes are reversible, but organizations and institutions can be modified, and even fundamentally altered, by rearranging their components. What is distinctive to the configuration of the new technological paradigm is its ability to reconfigure, a decisive feature in a society characterized by constant change and organizational fluidity. Turning the rules upside down without destroying the organization has become a possibility because the material basis of the organization can be reprogrammed and retooled.[88] However, we must stop short of a value judgment attached to this technological feature. This is because flexibility could be a liberating force, but also a repressive tendency if the rewriters of rules are always the powers that be. As Mulgan wrote: "Networks are created not just to communicate, but also to gain position, to outcommunicate."[89] It is thus essential to keep a distance between assessing the emergence of new social forms and processes, as induced and allowed by new technologies, and extrapolating the potential consequences of such developments for society and people: only specific analyses and empirical observation will be able to determine the outcome of interaction between new technologies and emerging social forms. Yet it is essential as well to identify the logic embedded in the new technological paradigm.

Then, a fifth characteristic of this technological revolution is the growing *convergence of specific technologies into a highly integrated system*, within which old, separate technological trajectories become

88 Tuomi (1999).
89 Mulgan (1991: 21).

literally indistinguishable. Thus, micro-electronics, telecommunications, opto-electronics, and computers are all now integrated into information systems. There still exists, and will exist for some time, some business distinction between chip makers and software writers, for instance. But even such differentiation is blurred by the growing integration of business firms in strategic alliances and cooperative projects, as well as by the inscription of software programs into chip hardware. Furthermore, in terms of technological system, one element cannot be imagined without the other: computers are largely determined by chip power, and both the design and the parallel processing of microprocessors depend on computer architecture. Telecommunications is now but one form of processing information; transmission and linkage technologies are at the same time increasingly diversified and integrated into the same network, operated by computers.[90] As I analyzed above, the development of the Internet is reversing the relationship between circuit switching and packet switching in communication technologies, so that data transmission becomes the predominant, universal form of communication. And data transmission is based on software instructions of coding and decoding.

Technological convergence increasingly extends to growing interdependence between the biological and micro-electronics revolutions, both materially and methodologically. Thus, decisive advances in biological research, such as the identification of human genes or segments of human DNA, can only proceed because of massive computing power.[91] Nanotechnology may allow sending tiny microprocessors into the systems of living organisms, including humans.[92] On the other hand, the use of biological materials in micro-electronics, although still very far from a generalized application, was already at the experimentation stage in the late 1990s. In 1995, Leonard Adleman, a computer scientist at the University of Southern California, used synthetic DNA molecules, and with the help of a chemical reaction made them work according to the DNA combining logic as the material basis for computing.[93] Although research has still a long way to go toward the material integration of biology and electronics, the logic of biology (the ability to self-generate unprogrammed, coherent sequences) is increasingly being introduced into electronic machines.[94] In 1999, Harold

90   Williams (1991).
91   Bishop and Waldholz (1990); *Business Week* (1995e, 1999b).
92   Hall (1999b).
93   Allen (1995).
94   See, for an analysis of trends, Kelly (1995); for an historical perspective on the convergence between mind and machines, see Mazlish (1993); for a theoretical reflection, see Levy (1994).

Abelson and his colleagues at MIT's computer science laboratory were trying to "hack" the *E. coli* bacterium so that it would be able to function as an electronic circuit, with the ability to reproduce itself. They were experimenting with "amorphous computing;" that is, mapping circuitry into biological material. Because biological cells could only compute as long as they were alive, this technology would combine with molecular electronics, by packing millions or billions of these biologically based switches in very tiny spaces, with the potential application of producing "smart materials" of all kinds.[95]

Some experiments of advanced research in human–computer interaction rely on the use of adaptive brain interfaces that recognize mental states from on-line spontaneous electroencephalogram (EEG) signals, based on artificial neural network theory. Thus, in 1999, at the European Union Joint Research Center in Ispra, Italy, computer scientist Jose Millan and his colleagues were able to show experimentally that people wearing a compact EEG helmet could communicate through conscious control of their thoughts.[96] Their approach was based on a mutual learning process whereby the user and the brain interface are coupled and adapt to each other. Therefore, a neural network learns user-specific EEG patterns while subjects learn to think in such a way that they are better understood by the personal interface.

The continuing convergence between different technological fields in the information paradigm results from their shared logic of information generation, a logic which is most apparent in the working of DNA and in natural evolution and which is increasingly replicated in the most advanced information systems, as chips, computers, and software reach new frontiers of speed, storage capacity, and flexible treatment of information from multiple sources. While the reproduction of the human brain, with its billions of circuits and unsurpassable recombining capacity, is strictly science fiction, the boundaries of information power of today's computers are being transgressed month by month.[97]

From the observation of such extraordinary changes in our machines and knowledge of life, and with the help provided by these machines and this knowledge, a deeper technological transformation is taking place: that of categories under which we think all processes. Historian of technology Bruce Mazlish proposes the idea of the necessary

> recognition that human biological evolution, now best understood in cultural terms, forces upon humankind – us – the consciousness that

95   Markoff (1999b).
96   Millan et al. (2000).
97   See the excellent prospective analysis by Gelernter (1991).

tools and machines are inseparable from evolving human nature. It also requires us to realize that the development of machines, culminating in the computer, makes inescapable the awareness that the same theories that are useful in explaining the workings of mechanical contrivances are also useful in understanding the human animal – and vice versa, for the understanding of the human brain sheds light on the nature of artificial intelligence.[98]

From a different perspective, based on the fashionable discourses of the 1980s on "chaos theory," in the 1990s a network of scientists and researchers converged toward a shared epistemological approach, identified by the code word "complexity." Organized around seminars held at the Santa Fe Institute in New Mexico (originally a club of high-level physicists from Los Alamos Laboratory, soon joined by a select network of Nobel Prize winners and their friends), this intellectual circle aims at communicating scientific thought (including social sciences) under a new paradigm. They focus on understanding the emergence of self-organizing structures that create complexity out of simplicity and superior order out of chaos, through several orders of interactivity between the basic elements at the origin of the process.[99] Although this project is often dismissed by mainstream science as a non-verifiable proposition, it is one example of the effort being made in different quarters toward finding a common ground for the intellectual cross-fertilization of science and technology in the Information Age. Yet this approach seems to forbid any integrating, systemic framework. Complexity thinking should be considered as a method for understanding diversity, rather than as a unified meta-theory. Its epistemological value could come from acknowledging the self-organizing character of nature and of society. Not that there are no rules, but that rules are created, and changed, in a relentless process of deliberate actions and unique interactions. Thus, in 1999, a young researcher at the Santa Fe Institute, Duncan Watts, proposed a formal analysis of the networking logic underlying the formation of "small worlds;" that is, the widespread set of connections, in nature and in society, between elements which, even when they do not communicate directly, are in fact related by a short chain of intermediaries. For instance, he shows, mathematically, that if we represent systems of relations by a graph, the key to generating a small-world phenomenon

98   Mazlish (1993: 233).
99   The diffusion of chaos theory to a broad audience was largely due to the bestseller of Gleick (1987); see also Hall (1991). For a clearly written, intriguing history of the "complexity" school, see Waldrop (1992). I have also relied on personal conversations with Santa Fe Institute researchers during my visit to the Institute in November 1998. I am particularly grateful to Brian Arthur for sharing his thoughts.

(which epitomizes a networking logic) is the presence of a small fraction of very long-range, global edges, which contract otherwise distant parts of the graph, while most edges remain local, organized in clusters.[100] This accurately represents the logic of local/global networking of innovation, as documented in this chapter. The important contribution of the complexity theory school of thought is its emphasis on non-linear dynamics as the most fruitful approach to understanding the behavior of living systems, both in society and in nature. Most of the work of the Santa Fe Institute researchers is of a mathematical nature, not an empirically based analysis of natural or social phenomena. But there are researchers in a number of fields of science using non-linear dynamics as their guiding principle, with increasingly important scientific results. Fritjof Capra, a theoretical physicist and ecologist at Berkeley, has integrated many of these results in an outline of a coherent theory of living systems in a series of books, particularly in his remarkable *Web of Life*.[101] He built on the work of Nobel Prize winner Ilya Prigogine. Prigogine's theory of dissipative structures demonstrated the non-linear dynamics of self-organization of chemical cycles, and allowed new understanding of the spontaneous emergence of order as a key characteristic of life. Capra shows how cutting-edge research in areas as diverse as cell development, global ecological systems (as represented by the controversial Gaia theory, and by Lovelock's "Daisyworld" simulation model), neuroscience (as in the work of Gerald Edelman or Oliver Sacks), and studies on the origins of life based on emerging chemical network theory, are all manifestations of a non-linear dynamics perspective.[102] Key new concepts, such as attractors, phase portraits, emergent properties, fractals, offer new perspectives in making sense of observations of behavior in living systems, including social systems – thus paving the way for a theoretical linkage between various fields of science. Not by reducing them to a common set of rules, but by explaining processes and outcomes from the self-generating properties of specific living systems. Brian Arthur, a Stanford economist with the Santa Fe Institute, has applied complexity theory to formal economic theory, proposing concepts such as self-reinforcing mechanisms, path dependency, and emergent properties, and showing their relevance in understanding the features of the new economy.[103]

In sum, the information technology paradigm does not evolve toward its closure as a system, but toward its openness as a multi-edged

100   Watts (1999).
101   Capra (1996).
102   Capra (1999b).
103   Arthur (1998).

network. It is powerful and imposing in its materiality, but adaptive and open-ended in its historical development. Comprehensiveness, complexity, and networking are its decisive qualities. Thus, the social dimension of the information technology revolution seems bound to follow the law on the relationship between technology and society proposed some time ago by Melvin Kranzberg: *"Kranzberg's First Law reads as follows: Technology is neither good nor bad, nor is it neutral."*[104] It is indeed a force, probably more than ever under the current technological paradigm that penetrates the core of life and mind.[105] But its actual deployment in the realm of conscious social action, and the complex matrix of interaction between the technological forces unleashed by our species, and the species itself, are matters of inquiry rather than of fate. I shall now proceed with such an inquiry.

104 Kranzberg (1985: 50).
105 For an informative, casual discussion of recent developments at the crossroads of science and the human mind, see Baumgartner and Payr (1995). For a more forceful, if controversial, interpretation by one of the founders of the genetic revolution, see Crick (1994).

2

The New Economy: Informationalism, Globalization, Networking

A new economy emerged in the last quarter of the twentieth century on a worldwide scale. I call it informational, global, and networked to identify its fundamental distinctive features and to emphasize their intertwining. It is *informational* because the productivity and competitiveness of units or agents in this economy (be it firms, regions, or nations) fundamentally depend upon their capacity to generate, process, and apply efficiently knowledge-based information. It is *global* because the core activities of production, consumption, and circulation, as well as their components (capital, labor, raw materials, management, information, technology, markets) are organized on a global scale, either directly or through a network of linkages between economic agents. It is *networked* because, under the new historical conditions, productivity is generated through and competition is played out in a global network of interaction between business networks. This new economy emerged in the last quarter of the twentieth century because the information technology revolution provided the indispensable, material basis for its creation. It is the historical linkage between the knowledge–information base of the economy, its global reach, its network-based organizational form, and the information technology revolution that has given birth to a new, distinctive economic system, whose structure and dynamics I shall explore in this chapter.

To be sure, information and knowledge have always been critical components of economic growth, and the evolution of technology has

indeed largely determined the productive capacity of society and standards of living, as well as social forms of economic organization.[1] Yet,
as argued in chapter 1, we are witnessing a point of historical discontinuity. The emergence of a new technological paradigm organized
around new, more powerful, and more flexible information technologies makes it possible for information itself to become the product of
the production process. To be more precise: the products of new information technology industries are information-processing devices or
information processing itself.[2] New information technologies, by transforming the processes of information processing, act upon all domains
of human activity, and make it possible to establish endless connections between different domains, as well as between elements and agents
of such activities. A networked, deeply interdependent economy
emerges that becomes increasingly able to apply its progress in technology, knowledge, and management to technology, knowledge, and
management themselves. Such a virtuous circle should lead to greater
productivity and efficiency, given the right conditions of equally dramatic organizational and institutional changes.[3] In this chapter I shall
try to assess the historical specificity of the new economy, outline its
main features, and explore the structure and dynamics of a worldwide
economic system emerging as a transitional form toward the informational mode of development that is likely to characterize the coming
decades.

Productivity, Competitiveness, and the Informational Economy

The productivity enigma

Productivity drives economic progress. It is by increasing the yields of
output per unit of input over time that humankind eventually mast-
ered the forces of nature and, in the process, shaped itself as culture.
No wonder that the debate over the sources of productivity is the cornerstone of classical political economy, from the Physiocrats to Marx,
via Ricardo, and remains at the forefront of that dwindling stream of
economic theory still concerned with the real economy.[4] Indeed, the
specific ways of increasing productivity define the structure and dy-

---

1   Rosenberg and Birdzell (1986); Mokyr (1990).
2   Freeman (1982); Monk (1989).
3   Machlup (1980, 1982, 1984); Dosi et al. (1988b).
4   Nelson and Winter (1982); Boyer (1986); Dosi et al. (1988b); Arthur (1989, 1998);
Krugman (1990); Nelson (1994).

namics of a given economic system. If there is a new, informational economy, we should be able to pinpoint the historically novel sources of productivity that make such an economy a distinctive one. But as soon as we raise this fundamental question we sense the complexity and uncertainty of the answer. Few economic matters are more questioned and more questionable than the sources of productivity and productivity growth.[5]

Academic discussions on productivity in advanced economies ritually start with reference to the pioneering work of Robert Solow in 1956–7 and to the aggregate production function he proposed within a strict neoclassical framework to explain the sources and evolution of productivity growth in the American economy. On the basis of his calculations he contended that gross output per man doubled in the American private non-farm sector between 1909 and 1949, "with 87½% of the increase attributable to technical change and the remaining 12½% to increased use of capital."[6] Parallel work by Kendrick converged toward similar results.[7] However, although Solow interpreted his findings as reflecting the influence of technical change on productivity, statistically speaking what he showed was that increasing output per hour of work was not the result of adding more labor, and only slightly of adding capital, but came from some other source, expressed as a statistical residual in his production function equation. Most econometric research on productivity growth in the two decades after Solow's pathbreaking work concentrated on explaining the "residual," by finding *ad hoc* factors that would account for the variation in the evolution of productivity, such as energy supply, government regulation, education of the labor force, and so on, without succeeding very much in clarifying this enigmatic "residual."[8] Economists, sociologists, and economic historians, supporting Solow's intuition, did not hesitate to interpret the "residual" as being equivalent to technological change. In the most refined elaborations, "science and technology" were understood in the broad sense, namely as knowledge and information, so that the technology of management was considered to be as important as the management of technology.[9] One of the most insightful, systematic research efforts on productivity, that by

---

5   Nelson (1981); for a worldwide perspective on the sources of growth of multifactor productivity, see World Bank (1998).
6   Solow (1957: 32); see also Solow (1956).
7   Kendrick (1961).
8   See, for the USA, Jorgerson and Griliches (1967); Kendrick (1973); Denison (1974, 1979); Mansfield (1982); Baumol et al. (1989). For France, Sautter (1978); Carre et al. (1984); Dubois (1985). For international comparison, see Denison (1967) and Maddison (1984).
9   Bell (1976); Nelson (1981); Freeman (1982); Rosenberg (1982); Stonier (1983).

Richard Nelson,[10] starts from the widespread assumption of the central role of technological change in productivity growth, thus recasting the question about the sources of productivity to shift the emphasis toward the origins of such change. In other words, the economics of technology would be the explanatory framework for the analysis of the sources of growth. However, this analytical intellectual perspective may in fact complicate the matter even further. This is because a stream of research, particularly by economists of the University of Sussex's Science and Policy Research Unit,[11] has demonstrated the fundamental role of institutional environment and historical trajectories in fostering and guiding technological change, thus ultimately inducing productivity growth. Therefore, to argue that productivity creates economic growth, and that productivity is a function of technological change, is tantamount to stating that the characteristics of society are the crucial factors underlying economic growth, by their impact on technological innovation.

This Schumpeterian approach to economic growth[12] raises an even more fundamental question concerning the structure and dynamics of the informational economy. Namely, what is historically new about our economy? What is its specificity *vis-à-vis* other economic systems, and particularly *vis-à-vis* the industrial economy?

Is knowledge-based productivity specific to the informational economy?

Economic historians have shown the fundamental role played by technology in economic growth, via productivity increase, throughout history and especially in the industrial era.[13] The hypothesis of the critical role of technology as a source of productivity in advanced economies seems also able to comprehend much of the past experience of economic growth, cutting across different intellectual traditions in economic theory.

Furthermore, the analysis by Solow, repeatedly used as the starting-point of the argument in favor of the emergence of a post-industrial economy by Bell and others, *is based on data for the 1909–49 period of the American economy, namely the heyday of the American industrial economy.* Indeed, in 1950 the proportion of manufacturing employment in the US was almost at its peak (the highest point was reached

---

10   Nelson (1980, 1981, 1988, 1994); Nelson and Winter (1982).
11   Dosi et al. (1988b).
12   Schumpeter (1939).
13   David (1975); Rosenberg (1976); Arthur (1986); Basalla (1988); Mokyr (1990).

Table 2.1 Productivity rate: growth rates of output per worker (average annual percentage change by period)

Country	1870–1913	1913–29	1929–50	1950–60	1960–9
United States[a]	1.9	1.5	1.7	2.1	2.6
Japan[b]	–	–	–	6.7	9.5
Germany[a]	1.6	–0.2	1.2	6.0	4.6
France[c]	1.4	2.0	0.3	5.4	5.0
Italy[c]	0.8	1.5	1.0	4.5	6.4
United Kingdom	1.0	0.4	1.1	1.9	2.5
Canada	1.7	0.7	2.0	2.1	2.2

[a] Initial year for period 1870–1913 is 1871.
[b] Initial year for 1950–60 is 1953.
[c] Initial year for 1950–60 is 1954.
Source: Historical Statistics of the United States: Colonial Times to 1970, Part 1, Series F10–16

in 1960), so that by the most usual indicator of "industrialism" Solow's calculations were referring to the process of expansion of the industrial economy. What is the analytical meaning of this observation? If the explanation of productivity growth introduced by the aggregate production function school is not substantially different from the results of historical analysis of the relationship between technology and economic growth over longer periods, at least for the industrial economy, does this mean that there is nothing new about the "informational" economy? Are we simply observing the mature stage of the industrial economic system whose steady accumulation of productive capacity frees labor from direct material production for the benefit of information-processing activities, as it was suggested in the pioneering work of Marc Porat?[14]

To answer this question, let us look at the long-term evolution of productivity growth in advanced market economies (see table 2.1 for the so-called G-7 countries and table 2.2 for OECD countries). For the purpose of my analysis, what is relevant is the change of trends between *five* periods: 1870–1950, 1950–73, 1973–9, 1979–93, and 1994–9.

However, as my analysis is dependent on available secondary sources, the data between periods are not really comparable. First, I will analyze the data for selected countries, for different periods, up to 1993. Then I will focus on the US in the period 1994–9 because it was at that time and in that country that the new economy appeared to manifest itself.

14 Porat (1977).

Table 2.2 Productivity in the business sector (percentage changes at annual rates)

	Total factor productivity[a]			Labor productivity[b]			Capital productivity		
	1960ᶜ–73	1973–9	1979–93ᵈ	1960ᶜ–73	1973–9	1979–93ᵈ	1960ᶜ–73	1973–9	1979–93ᵈ
United States	1.6	–0.4	0.4	2.2	0	0.8	0.2	–1.3	–0.5
Japan	5.6	1.3	1.4	8.3	2.9	2.5	–2.6	–3.4	–1.9
Germanyᵉ	2.6	1.8	1.0	4.5	3.1	1.7	–1.4	–1.0	–0.6
France	3.7	1.6	1.2	5.3	2.9	2.2	0.6	–1.0	–0.7
Italy	4.4	2.0	1.0	6.3	2.9	1.8	0.4	0.3	–0.7
United Kingdom	2.6	0.6	1.4	3.9	1.5	2.0	–0.3	–1.5	0.2
Canada	1.9	0.6	–0.3	2.9	1.5	1.0	0.1	–1.1	–2.8
Total of above countriesᶠ	2.9	0.6	0.8	4.3	1.4	1.5	–0.5	–1.5	–0.8
Australia	2.3	1.0	0.5	3.4	2.3	1.2	0.2	–1.5	–0.7
Austria	3.3	1.2	0.7	5.8	3.2	1.7	–2.0	–3.1	–1.5
Belgium	3.8	1.4	1.4	5.2	2.7	2.3	0.6	–1.9	–0.7
Denmark	2.3	0.9	1.3	3.9	2.4	2.3	–1.4	–2.6	–0.8
Finland	4.0	1.9	2.1	5.0	3.2	3.2	1.4	–1.6	–0.8
Greece	3.1	0.9	–0.2	9.1	3.4	0.7	–8.8	–4.2	–2.1
Ireland	3.6	3.0	3.3	4.8	4.1	4.1	–0.9	–1.2	0.2
Netherlands	3.5	1.8	0.8	4.8	2.8	1.3	0.8	0	–0.2
New Zealand	0.7	–2.1	0.4	1.6	–1.4	1.6	–0.7	–3.2	–1.4
Norwayᵍ	2.3	1.4	0	3.8	2.5	1.3	0	–0.3	–1.9
Portugal	5.4	–0.2	1.6	7.4	0.5	2.4	–0.7	–2.5	–0.8
Spain	3.2	0.9	1.6	6.0	3.2	2.9	–3.6	–5.0	–1.5
Sweden	2.0	0	0.8	3.7	1.4	1.7	–2.2	–3.2	–1.4
Switzerland	2.0	–0.4	0.4	3.2	0.8	1.0	–1.4	–3.5	–1.3

Total of above smaller countries[f]	3.0	0.9	1.1	5.0	2.5	2.0	-1.5	-2.8	-1.1
Total of above North American countries[f]	1.6	-0.4	0.4	2.3	0.1	0.9	0.2	-1.3	-0.7
Total of above European countries	3.3	1.4	1.2	5.1	2.6	2.0	-0.7	-1.4	-0.7
Total of above OECD countries[f]	2.9	0.6	0.9	4.4	1.6	1.6	-0.7	-1.7	-0.9

[a] TFP growth is equal to a weighted average of the growth in labor and capital productivity. The sample-period averages for capital and labor shares are used as weights.

[b] Output per employed person.

[c] Or earliest years available, i.e. 1961 for Australia, Greece and Ireland; 1962 for Japan, the United Kingdom and New Zealand; 1964 for Spain; 1965 for France and Sweden; 1966 for Canada and Norway; and 1970 for Belgium and The Netherlands.

[d] Or latest available year, i.e. 1991 for Norway and Switzerland; 1992 for Italy, Australia, Austria, Belgium, Ireland, New Zealand, Portugal and Sweden; and 1994 for the United States, Western Germany and Denmark.

[e] Western Germany.

[f] Aggregates were calculated on the basis of 1992 GDP for the business sector expressed in 1992 purchasing power parities.

[g] Mainland business sector (i.e. excluding shipping as well as crude petroleum and gas extraction).

Source: OECD, *Economic Outlook*, June 1995

Because I use different statistical sources I cannot compare levels of productivity growth rates between the periods before and after 1969, but I can reason on the evolution of growth rates within and between periods for each source.

Overall, there was a moderate rate of growth of productivity for the 1870–1950 period (never surpassing 2 percent for any country or subperiod, except for Canada), a high rate of growth during the 1950–73 period (always over 2 percent, except for the UK) with Japan leading the charge; and a low growth rate in 1973–93 (very low for the US and Canada), always below 2 percent in total factor productivity, except for Italy in the 1970s. Even if we account for the specificity of some countries, what appears clearly is that *we observe a downward trend of productivity growth starting roughly around the same time that the information technology revolution took shape in the early 1970s*. Highest growth rates of productivity took place during the 1950–73 period when industrial technological innovations which came together as a system during the Second World War were woven into a dynamic model of economic growth. But by the early 1970s, the productivity potential of these technologies seemed to be exhausted, and new information technologies did not appear to reverse the productivity slowdown for the next two decades.[15] Indeed, in the United States, the famous "residual", after accounting for about 1.5 points of annual productivity growth during the 1960s, made no contribution at all in 1972–92.[16] In a comparative perspective, calculations by the reliable Centre d'Etudes Prospectives et d'Informations Internationales[17] show a general reduction of total factor productivity growth for the main market economies during the 1970s and 1980s. Even for Japan, the role of capital in productivity growth was more important than that of multifactor productivity for the 1973–90 period. This decline was particularly marked in all countries for service activities, where new information-processing devices could be thought to have increased productivity, if the rela-

15   Maddison (1984); Krugman (1994a).
16   See Council of Economic Advisers (1995).
17   Centre d'Etudes Prospectives et d'Informations Internationales (CEPII) (1992). I have relied on key information in the 1992 report on the world economy prepared by CEPII, on the basis of the MIMOSA model of the world economy elaborated by the researchers of this leading economic research center linked to the French Prime Minister's office. Although the database has been produced by this research center, and thus does not coincide entirely in its periodization and estimates with various international sources (OECD, US government statistics, etc.), it is a reliable model that allows me to compare very different economic trends in the whole world, and for the same periods, without changing the database, thus furthering consistency and comparability. However, I have also felt the necessity of relying on additional sources from standard statistical publications, which I have cited where necessary. For a presentation of the characteristics of this model, see CEPII–OFCE (1990).

tionship between technology and productivity were simple and direct. Evidently, it is not.

Thus, over the long term[18] (reserving for the moment the observation of trends in the late 1990s), there was a steady, moderate productivity growth, with some downturns, in the period of formation of the industrial economy between the late nineteenth century and the Second World War; an acceleration of productivity growth in the mature period of industrialism (1950–73); and a slowing down of productivity growth rates in the 1973–93 period, in spite of a substantial increase in technology inputs and acceleration in the pace of technological change. Thus, on the one hand, we should expand the argument on the central role of technology in economic growth to past historical periods, at least for the Western economies in the industrial era. On the other hand, the pace of productivity growth in 1973–93 does not seem to covariate with the timing of technological change. This could indicate the absence of substantial differences between the "industrial" and the "informational" regimes of economic growth, at least with reference to their differential impact on productivity growth, thus forcing us to reconsider the theoretical relevance of the distinction altogether. However, before surrendering to the enigma of vanishing productivity growth in the midst of one of the fastest and most comprehensive technological revolutions in history, I shall advance a number of hypotheses that could help to unveil the mystery. And I shall relate these hypotheses to a summary observation of productivity trends in the United States in the late 1990s.

First, economic historians argue that a considerable time lag between technological innovation and economic productivity is characteristic of past technological revolutions. For instance, Paul David, analyzing the diffusion of the electrical engine, showed that while it was introduced in the 1880s, its real impact on productivity had to wait until the 1920s.[19] For new technological discoveries to be able to diffuse throughout the whole economy, thus enhancing productivity growth at an observable rate, the culture and institutions of society, business firms, and the factors intervening in the production process need to undergo substantial change. This general statement is particularly appropriate in the case of a technological revolution centered around knowledge and information, embodied in symbol-processing operations that are necessarily linked to the culture of society, and to the education/skills of its people. If we date the emergence of the new technological paradigm to the mid-1970s, and its consolidation to the

18   Kindleberger (1964); Maddison (1984); Freeman (1986); Dosi et al. (1988b).
19   David (1989).

Table 2.3 Evolution of the productivity of business sectors (% average annual growth rate)

Country	1973/60[a]	1979/73	1989/79[b]	1985/79	1989/85[b]
Total factor productivity					
United States	2.2	0.4	0.9	0.6	1.4
Japan	3.2	1.5	1.6	1.5	1.6
W. Germany	3.2	2.2	1.2	0.9	1.7
France	3.3	2.0	2.1	2.1	2.0
UK[c]	2.2	0.5	1.8	1.6	2.2
Productivity of capital					
United States	0.6	−1.1	−0.5	−1.0	0.7
Japan	−6.0	−4.1	−2.6	−2.3	−3.0
W. Germany	−1.5	−1.3	−1.1	−1.8	0.0
France	−1.9	−2.5	−0.9	−1.8	0.4
UK[c]	−0.8	−1.7	0.3	−0.7	1.9
Productivity of labor (output per person/hour)					
United States	2.9	1.1	1.5	1.3	1.8
Japan	6.9	3.7	3.2	3.0	3.4
W. Germany	5.6	4.1	2.4	2.3	2.5
France	5.6	3.9	3.3	3.7	2.7
UK[c]	3.5	1.5	2.5	2.6	2.4

[a] The period starts in 1970 in Japan, 1971 in France, and 1966 in the UK.
[b] The period ends in 1988 in the United States.
[c] For the UK the work factor is measured in number of workers and not in hours worked.
Source: CEPII–OFCE, database of the MIMOSA model

1990s, it appears that society as a whole, business firms, institutions, organizations, and people, hardly had time to process technological change and decide on its uses. As a result, the new techno-economic system did not yet characterize entire national economies in the 1970s and 1980s, and could not be reflected in such a synthetic, aggregate measure as the productivity growth rate for the whole economy until the 1990s.

However, this wise, historical perspective requires social specificity. Namely, why and how *these* new technologies had to wait to deliver their promise in enhancing productivity? What are the conditions for such enhancement? How do they differ depending on the characteristics of technology? How different is the rate of diffusion of technology, and thus its impact on productivity, in various industries? Do such differences make overall productivity dependent on the industrial mix of each country? Accordingly, can the process of economic maturation of new technologies be accelerated or restrained in differ-

Table 2.4 Evolution of productivity in sectors not open to free trade (% average annual growth rate)

Country	1973/60[a]	1979/73	1989/79[b]	1985/79	1989/85[b]
Total factor productivity					
United States	1.9	0.6	−0.1	−0.1	0.0
Japan	0.1	0.3	−0.2	−0.1	−0.4
W. Germany	1.4	0.9	0.7	0.0	1.6
France	2.4	0.6	1.6	1.6	1.7
UK[c]	1.3	−0.3	1.2	0.5	2.3
Productivity of capital					
United States	0.4	−0.6	−1.2	−1.4	−0.7
Japan	−7. 9	−4.5	−5.3	−4.3	−6.7
W. Germany	−2.4	−2.2	−1.6	−2.7	0.1
France	−1.7	−3.2	−0.6	−1.6	0.9
UK[c]	−1.1	−2.6	−0.1	-0.9	1.1
Productivity per person/hour					
United States	2.5	1.1	0.4	0.4	0.3
Japan	4.0	2.6	2.1	1.8	2.6
W. Germany	4.3	3.2	2.4	2.1	2.8
France	4.7	2.7	2.8	3.3	2.1
UK[c]	2.2	0.5	1.5	1.0	2.3

[a] The period starts in 1970 in Japan, 1971 in France, and 1966 in the UK.
[b] The period ends in 1988 in the United States.
[c] For the UK the work factor is measured in number of workers and not in hours worked.
Source: CEDII–OFCE, database of the MIMOSA model

ent countries, or by different policies? In other words, the time lag between technology and productivity cannot be reduced to a black box. It has to be specified. So let us have a closer look at the differential evolution of productivity by countries and industries over the past two decades, restricting our observation to leading market economies, so as not to lose the thread of the argument in excessive empirical detail (see tables 2.3 and 2.4).

A fundamental observation concerns the fact that the slowdown of productivity took place mainly in service industries. And since these industries account for the majority of employment and GNP, its weight is statistically reflected in overall productivity growth rate. This simple remark raises two fundamental problems. The first one refers to the difficulty of measuring productivity in many service industries,[20]

---

20 See the interesting effort at measuring services productivity by McKinsey Global Institute (1992). However, they focused on just five services industries which were relatively easy to measure.

particularly in those that account for the bulk of employment in services: education, health services, government. There are endless paradoxes, and instances of economic nonsense, in many of the indexes used to measure productivity in these services. But even when considering only the business sector, measurement problems are substantial. For instance, in the US in the 1990s the banking industry, according to the Bureau of Labor Statistics, increased its productivity by about 2 percent a year. But this calculation seems an underestimate because growth in real output in banking and other financial services is assumed equal to the increase in hours worked in the industry, and therefore labor productivity is eliminated by assumption.[21] Until we develop a more accurate economic analysis of services, with its corresponding statistical apparatus, measuring productivity in many services is subject to considerable margins of error.

Secondly, under the term "services" are lumped together miscellaneous activities with little in common except being other than agriculture, extractive industries, utilities, construction, and manufacturing. The "services" category is a residual, negative notion, inducing analytical confusion, as I shall argue in some detail below (chapter 4). Thus, when we analyze specific service industries we observe a great disparity in the evolution of their productivity in the past two decades. One of the leading experts in this area, Quinn, observes that "initial analyses [in the mid-1980s] indicate that measured added value in the services sector is at least as high as in manufacturing."[22] Some service industries in the US, such as telecommunications, air transportation, and railroads, displayed substantial increases in productivity, between 4.5 and 6.8 percent per year for the period 1970–83. On a comparative basis, the evolution of labor productivity in services as a whole shows wide disparity between countries, increasing much faster in France and Germany than in the US and the UK, with Japan in between.[23] This indicates that the evolution of productivity in services is to a large extent dependent on the actual structure of services in each country (for example, much lower weight of retail employment in France and Germany vis-à-vis the USA and Japan in the 1970s and 1980s).

By and large, the observation of stagnant productivity in services as a whole is counterintuitive to observers and business managers, who have been witnessing staggering changes in technology and procedures in office work for more than a decade.[24] Indeed, detailed analysis of

21   Council of Economic Advisers (1995: 110).
22   Quinn (1987: 122–7).
23   CEPII (1992: 61).
24   Business Week (1995a: 86–96); Osterman (1999).

accounting methods for economic productivity reveals considerable sources of measurement error. One of the most important distortions in US calculating procedures refers to the difficulty of measuring software and R&D investment, a major item of investment goods in the new economy, yet categorized as "intermediate goods and services," and not showing up in final demand, thus lowering the actual rate of growth of both output and productivity. An even more important source of distortion is the difficulty in measuring prices for many services in an economy that has become so diversified and has submitted to rapid change in the goods and services produced.[25] It has been argued, by Paul Krugman, among others, that difficulties in measuring productivity are not new, so that, overall, all periods being equally prone to error, there is a productivity slowdown. However, there is indeed something new in the accounting error of productivity when it refers to an economy in which "services" account for well over two-thirds of GDP, and information-based services represent over 50 percent of employment, and when it is precisely this fuzzy "service sector" that we have trouble measuring with traditional statistical categories. In sum, it may well be that a significant proportion of the mysterious productivity slowdown results from a growing inadequacy of economic statistics to capture movements of the new informational economy, *precisely because of the broad scope of its transformation under the impact of information technology and related organizational change.*

If that is the case, manufacturing productivity, relatively easier to measure for all its problems, should offer a different picture. And this is indeed what we observe. Using the CEPII database, for the US and Japan multifactor productivity in manufacturing in 1979–89 increased by an annual average of 3 percent and 4.1 percent respectively, dramatically upgrading the performance of 1973–9, *and increasing productivity at a faster pace than during the 1960s.* The UK displayed a similar trend, although at a slightly slower pace than productivity increases in the 1960s. On the other hand, Germany and France continued their slowdown in manufacturing productivity growth, with annual increases of 1.5 percent and 2.4 percent respectively in 1979–89, way below their past performance. The better-than-usually-thought performance of manufacturing productivity growth in the US in the 1980s is also documented by the US Department of Labor, although the periods selected and methods used offer a lower estimate than CEPII's database. According to its calculations, output per hour in the manufacturing sector went from 3.3 percent annual increase in 1963–72 to 2.6 percent in 1972–8, and again 2.6 percent in 1978–87, hardly a

---

25   Council of Economic Advisers (1995: 110).

spectacular drop. Productivity increases in manufacturing are much more significant in the United States and Japan in the sectors that include electronics manufacturing. According to the CEPII database, in these sectors productivity increased by 1 percent per year in 1973–9, but it exploded by 11 percent per year in 1979–87, accounting for the largest share of total increase in manufacturing productivity.[26] While Japan displays similar trends, France and Germany experienced a decline of productivity in the electronics industry, probably as a reflection of the accumulated technological gap in information technologies *vis-à-vis* America and Japan.

So perhaps, after all, productivity was not really vanishing in the 1980s and 1990s but could have been increasing through partly hidden avenues, in expanding circles. Technology, and the management of technology involving organizational change, seem to have diffused from information technology manufacturing, telecommunications, and financial services (the original sites of technological revolution) into manufacturing at large, then into business services, gradually to reach miscellaneous service activities, where there are lower incentives for the diffusion of technology and greater resistance to organizational change. An indication of the relationship between technology, organizational change, and productivity can be provided by the 1997 study by Brynjolfsson of 600 large US firms, focusing on the impact of organizational structures on the relationship between computers and productivity. Overall, Brynjolfsson found that investments in information technology were correlated with higher productivity. But firms sharply differed in their productivity growth depending on their management practices: "Strikingly, the most productive users of IT tend to employ a synergistic combination of a customer-focused business strategy, and a decentralized organizational structure. In contrast, firms that simply graft new technologies onto old structures (or vice versa) are significantly less productive."[27] Thus, organizational change, training of a new labor force, and the process of learning by doing, fostering productive uses of technology, should eventually show up in productivity statistics – on the condition that statistical categories are able to reflect these changes.

At last, in October 1999, the US Commerce Department's Bureau

---

26   CEPII (1992); see tables 2.3 and 2.4 in this chapter, and CEPII (1992: 58–9). Data on manufacturing productivity do not coincide with those of the US Bureau of Labor Statistics (BLS) because of different periodization and calculation procedures. However, trends in both sources coincide in not showing a slowdown in manufacturing productivity growth during the 1980s: according to BLS data there was a stabilization of growth rates; according to CEPII data, there was an increase in growth rates.
27   Brynjolfsson (1997: 19).

Figure 2.1 Productivity growth in the United States, 1995–1999 (index of output per hour of all people in non-farm businesses; 1992 = 100, seasonally adjusted
Source: US Bureau of Labor Statistics as reported by Uchitelle (1999)

of Economic Analysis paid some attention to the matter, and changed some of its accounting categories. Besides changing the basis for calculating inflation, the most important change concerning productivity measurement was to consider for the first time business spending on software as an investment, thus counting it as part of GDP. Following these changes, on November 12, 1999, the US Labor Department released new calculations of labor productivity for the period 1959–99. According to these new statistics, US productivity grew at an annual rate of 2.3 percent in the golden period of 1959–73, then declined to between 1.4 and 1.6 percent in 1973–95. Then, from the third quarter of 1995 to the third quarter of 1999, productivity growth climbed to an annual rate of 2.6 percent, with the third quarter of 1999 posting an annualized rate of 4.2 percent, the biggest jump in two years (see figure 2.1).[28] Commenting on these developments, Alan Greenspan, chairman of the Federal Reserve Board, stated that "although it is still possible to argue that the evident increase in productivity growth is

28   Uchitelle (1999).

ephemeral, I find such arguments hard to believe."[29] Indeed, Greenspan had previously lent strong credibility to the emergence of the new economy by asserting, in his report to the US House of Representatives on February 24, 1998, that:

> Our nation has been experiencing a higher growth rate of productivity – output per hour worked – in recent years. The dramatic improvements in computing power and communication and information technology appear to have been a major force behind this beneficial trend ... The sharp acceleration in capital investment in advanced technologies beginning in 1993 reflected synergies of new ideas, embodied in increasingly inexpensive new equipment, that have elevated expected returns and have broadened investment opportunities. More recent evidence remains consistent with the view that capital spending has contributed to a noticeable pick-up in productivity –and probably by more than can be explained by usual business cycle forces.[30]

In fact, only a substantial productivity increase could explain the economic boom in the US in 1994–9: 3.3 percent of annual GDP growth, with inflation below 2 percent, unemployment under 5 percent, and an increase, albeit moderate, in average real wages.

While business circles, in America and in the world, appeared to embrace the notion of a new economy, along the lines I suggested above, some respected academic economists (including Solow, Krugman, and Gordon) remained skeptical. And yet, even the statistical evidence provided to refute the notion of significant productivity increase, associated with information technology, seems to confirm the new trend in upward productivity growth, on the condition that data are interpreted in a dynamic perspective. Thus, the study most often cited to object to an upturn of productivity growth in the late 1990s is the one posted on the Internet in 1999 by a leading productivity economist, Robert Gordon.[31] As shown in figure 2.2 and table 2.5, Gordon observed un upswing in productivity growth in the 1995–9 period, at about 2.15 percent per year, almost doubling the performance during 1972–95. However, decomposing productivity growth by sectors, he found that the overwhelming proportion of productivity growth was concentrated in computer manufacturing, which increased its productivity in 1995–9 at the stunning rate of 41.7 percent per year. While computer manufacturing represents just 1.2 percent of output in America, the productivity increase was so large that it aug-

---

29   Quoted in Stevenson (1999: C6).
30   Greenspan (1998).
31   Gordon (1999).

Figure 2.2 Estimate of evolution of productivity in the United
States, 1972–1999 (output per hour)
Source: US Bureau of Labor Statistics as elaborated by Gordon (1999)

Table 2.5 Evolution of US productivity by industrial sectors and periods

	% *Increase at annual rate*		
Sector	*1952–72*	*1972–95*	*1995–9*
Non-farm private business	2.63	1.13	2.15
Manufacturing	2.56	2.58	4.58
Durables	2.32	3.05	6.78
Computers	–	17.83	41.70
Non-computers	2.23	1.88	1.82
Non-durables	2.96	2.03	2.05

Source: US Bureau of Labor Statistics as elaborated by Gordon (1999)

mented the overall productivity rate in spite of the sluggish performance of the rest of manufacturing, and of the economy as a whole. In a
static vision of economic growth the conclusion would be that there is
just one dynamic sector in the economy built around information technology, while the rest of the economy continues in its slow growth.
But we know from history,[32] and from case studies of industries and
companies in the 1990s,[33] that the uses of technological innovation
come first in the industries which are at their source, then they spread
to other industries. So, the extraordinary growth of productivity in

32   Rosenberg (1982); Rosenberg and Birdzell (1986); Hall and Preston (1988).
33   Hammer and Camphy (1993); Nonaka (1994); Saussois (1998); Tuomi (1999).

the computer industry could, and should, be interpreted as the shape of things to come, not as an abnormal blip in the flat landscape of economic routine. There is no reason why this productivity potential, once unleashed by its producers, should not diffuse in the economy at large, albeit with uneven timing and uneven spatial spread, provided, of course, that there is organizational and institutional change, and that labor adapts to new production processes. But, in fact, firms and workers will have little choice because competition, both local and global, imposes new rules and new technologies, phasing out those economic agents unable to follow the rules of the new economy.[34] This is why the evolution of productivity is inseparable from the new conditions of competitiveness.

Informationalism and capitalism, productivity and profitability

Yes, in the long term productivity is the source of the wealth of nations. And technology, including organizational and managerial technology, is the major productivity-inducing factor. But, from the perspective of economic agents, productivity is not a goal in itself. Neither is investing in technology for the sake of technological innovation. This is why Richard Nelson, in an insightful paper on the matter, considers that the agenda for formal growth theorizing should be built around the relationships between technical change, firm capabilities, and national institutions.[35] Firms and nations (or political entities of different levels, such as regions or the European Union) are the actual agents of economic growth. They do not seek technology for the sake of technology or productivity enhancement for the betterment of humankind. They behave in a given historical context, within the rules of an economic system (informational capitalism, as I proposed above), which will ultimately reward or penalize their conduct. Thus, *firms will be motivated not by productivity, but by profitability,* and *growth of value of their stocks.* For which productivity and technology may be important means, but certainly not the only ones. And *political institutions*, being shaped by a broader set of values and interests, *will be oriented, in the economic realm, toward maximizing the competitiveness of their constituent economies. Profitability and competitiveness are the actual determinants of technological innovation and productivity growth.* It is in their concrete, historical dynamics that we may find the clues for understanding productivity's vagaries.

34 Shapiro and Varian (1999).
35 Nelson (1994: 41).

The 1970s were at the same time the likely birth date of the information technology revolution and a watershed in the evolution of capitalism, as I argued above. Firms in all countries reacted to an actual or feared decline in profitability by adopting new strategies.[36] Some of them, such as technological innovation and organizational decentralization, while essential in their potential impact, had a relatively long-term horizon. But firms looked for shorter-term results that could show up in their book-keeping and, for American firms, in their quarterly reports. To increase profits, for a given financial environment and with prices set by the market, there are four main ways: to reduce production costs (starting with labor costs); to increase productivity; to broaden the market; and to accelerate capital turnover.

With different emphases, depending on firms and countries, all were used during the last two decades of the twentieth century. In all of them, new information technologies were essential tools. But I propose the hypothesis that one strategy was implemented earlier and with more immediate results: the broadening of markets and the fight for market share. This is because to increase productivity without a prior expansion of demand, or the potential for it, is too risky from the investor's point of view. This is why the American electronics industry desperately needed military markets in its infant years until investments in technological innovation could pay off in a broad range of markets. And this is why Japanese firms, and after them Korean firms, used a protected market and clever targeting of industries and segments of industries at the global level as ways to build up economies of scale in order to reach economies of scope. The real crisis of the 1970s was not the oil prices shock. It was the inability of the public sector to keep expanding its markets, and thus income-generating employment, without either increasing taxes on capital or fueling inflation through additional money supply and public indebtedness.[37] While some short-term answers to the profitability crisis focused on labor trimming and wage attrition, the real challenge for individual firms and for capitalism as a whole was to find new markets able to absorb a growing productive capacity of goods and services.[38] This is at the root of the substantial expansion of trade relative to output, and, later, that of foreign direct investment in the last two decades of

36 Aglietta (1976); Boyer (1986; 1988a); Boyer and Ralle (1986a).
37 The critique by the monetarist school on sources of inflation in the American economy seems to be plausible; see Friedman (1968). However, it omitted the fact that expansionary monetary policies were also responsible for unprecedented, stable economic growth in the 1950s and 1960s. On this point, see my own analysis in Castells (1980).
38 The old underconsumption theory, at the heart of Marxian economics, but also of Keynesian policies, still has relevance when placed in the new context of global capitalism. On this issue, see Castells and Tyson (1988).

the twentieth century. They became the engines of economic growth throughout the world.[39] It is true that world trade grew at a lower rate in these years than during the 1960s (because of a lower rate of economic growth overall), but the critical figure is the relationship between the expansion of trade and GDP growth: in 1970–80, while world's GDP grew at an annual 3.4 percent, exports of merchandise trade grew at 4 percent per year. In 1980–92, the corresponding figures were 3 percent and 4.9 percent. There was a substantial acceleration of world trade, when measured in value, in the second half of the 1980s: an average annual growth of 12.3 percent. And although in 1993 world trade experienced a downturn, in 1993–5 it continued to grow at rates over 4 percent.[40] For nine major manufacturing sectors considered in the CEPII model of the world economy,[41] the proportion of internationally traded manufactured goods in total world production was in 1973 15.3 percent, in 1980 19.7 percent, in 1988 22.2 percent, and in the year 2000 was projected to reach 24.8 percent. As for foreign direct investment, scanning the globe in search of better production conditions and market penetration, see the section below.

To open up new markets, linking in a global network valuable market segments of each country, capital required extreme mobility, and firms needed dramatically enhanced communication capabilities. Deregulation of markets and new information technologies, in close interaction, provided such conditions. The earliest and most direct beneficiaries of this restructuring were the very actors of techno-economic transformation: high-technology firms and financial corporations.[42] The global integration of financial markets since the early 1980s, made possible by new information technologies, had a dramatic impact on the growing disassociation of capital flows from national economies. Thus, Chesnais measured the movement of internationalization of capital by calculating the percentage over GDP of cross-border operations in shares and obligations:[43] in 1980, this percentage was not over 10 percent in any major country; in 1992, it varied between 72.2 percent of GDP (Japan) and 122.2 percent (France), with the US standing at 109.3 percent. As I will show below, this trend accelerated during the 1990s.

By extending its global reach, integrating markets, and maximizing comparative advantages of location, capital, capitalists, and capitalist

39   I refer the reader to the excellent overview of global economic transformations by Chesnais (1994).
40   GATT (1994); World Bank (1995).
41   CEPII (1992: MIMOSA model).
42   Schiller (1999).
43   Chesnais (1994: 209).

firms substantially increased their profitability particularly in the 1990s, restoring for the time being the preconditions for investment on which a capitalist economy depends.[44] This recapitalization of capitalism may explain to some extent the uneven progress of productivity. Throughout the 1980s there was massive technological investment in the communications/information infrastructure that made possible the twin movements of deregulation of markets and globalization of capital. Firms and industries that were directly affected by such dramatic transformation (such as micro-electronics, microcomputers, telecommunications, financial institutions) experienced a surge in productivity as well as in profitability.[45] Around this hard core of new, dynamic, global capitalist firms and ancillary networks, successive layers of firms and industries were either integrated in the new technological system or phased out. Thus, the slow movement of productivity in national economies taken as a whole may hide contradictory trends of explosive productivity growth in leading industries, the decline of obsolete firms, and the persistence of low-productivity service activities. Furthermore, the more this dynamic sector constituted around highly profitable firms becomes globalized across boundaries, the less it is meaningful to calculate productivity of "national economies," or of industries defined within national boundaries. Although the largest proportion of GDP, and of employment, of most countries continues to depend on activities aimed at the domestic economy, rather than at the global market, it is indeed what happens to competition in these global markets, in manufacturing as in finance, telecommunications or entertainment, that determines the share of wealth appropriated by firms and, ultimately, by people in each country.[46] This is why,

44 For the US, a good measure of profitability, for non-financial corporations, is the after-tax profit per unit of output (the higher the ratio, the higher the profit, of course). The ratio stood at 0.024 in 1959; went down to 0.020 in 1970 and 0.017 in 1974; bounced back to 0.040 in 1978, to decline again to 0.027 in 1980. Then, from 1983 (0.048) it kept an upward trend that accelerated substantially during the 1990s: 1991, 0.061; 1992, 0.067; 1993, 0.073; third quarter 1994, 0.080. See Council of Economic Advisers (1995: 291, Table B-14).

45 CEPII (1992). Profitability was high from the 1980s in electronics, telecommunications, and finance as a whole. However, cut-throat competition, and risky financial deals, did cause a number of setbacks and bankruptcies. Indeed, without the US government bailout of a number of savings and loan associations, a major financial crash could have been a very serious possibility.

46 The decisive role played by global competition in the economic prosperity of the nation is widely accepted all over the world, except in the United States, where, in some economists' circles, and in sectors of public opinion, there is still the conviction that because exports only accounted for about 10 percent of GNP in the early 1990s, the country's economic health depends essentially on the domestic market (see Krugman 1994a). Although the size and productivity of the American economy does make it much more autonomous than any other country in the world, the idea of quasi-self-reliance is a dangerous illusion

together with the search for profitability as the driving motivation of the firm, the informational economy is also shaped by the vested interest of political institutions in fostering the competitiveness of those economies they are supposed to represent.

As for *competitiveness*, it is an elusive, indeed controversial, notion that has become a rallying flag for governments and a battleground for real-life economists opposing academic model-makers.[47] One reasonable definition, by Stephen Cohen and colleagues states:

> Competitiveness has different meanings for the firm and for the national economy. A nation's competitiveness is the degree to which it can, under free and fair market conditions, produce goods and services that meet the test of international markets while simultaneously expanding the real incomes of its citizens. Competitiveness at the national level is based on superior productivity performance by the economy and the economy's ability to shift output to high productivity activities which in turn can generate high levels of real wages.[48]

Naturally, since "free and fair market conditions" belong to the unreal world, political agencies acting in the international economy seek to interpret such a principle in a way that maximizes the competitive advantage of firms under their jurisdiction. The emphasis here is on the *relative position of national economies* vis-à-vis *other countries*, as a major legitimizing force for governments.[49] As for firms, competitiveness simply means the ability to win market share. It must be emphasized that this does not necessarily rely on eliminating competitors, since an expanding market can make room for more firms – this, in fact, is a frequent occurrence. However, enhancing competitiveness does usually have a Darwinian undercurrent, so that best business practices are generally rewarded in the marketplace, while laggard firms are phased out in an increasingly competitive world that has, indeed, winners and losers.

So, competitiveness, both for firms and countries, requires strength-

---

that is in fact not shared by either business or government elites. For arguments and data concerning the critical role of global competition for the American economy, as for all economies in the world, see Cohen and Zysman (1987); Castells and Tyson (1989); Reich (1991); Thurow (1992); Carnoy et al. (1993b).

47   The debate over productivity versus competitiveness as keys to renewed economic growth raged in American academic and political circles during the 1990s. Paul Krugman, one of the most brilliant academic economists in America, can be credited with triggering a necessary debate by his vigorous critique of the notion of competitiveness, unfortunately tainted and obscured by manners inappropriate to a scholar. For a sample of the debate, see Krugman (1994b); for a reply, Cohen (1994).

48   Cohen et al. (1985: 1).

49   Tyson and Zysman (1983).

ening market position in an expanding market. Thus, the process of worldwide market expansion feeds back into productivity growth, since firms must improve their performance when faced with stronger competition from around the world, or when they vie to win market shares internationally. A 1993 McKinsey Global Institute Study on manufacturing productivity in the US, Japan, and Germany found a high correlation between an index of globalization, measuring exposure to international competition, and the relative productivity performance of nine industries analyzed in the three countries.[50] Thus, the linkage path between information technology, organizational change, and productivity growth goes, to a large extent, through global competition. This is how firms' search for profitability and nations' mobilization toward competitiveness induced variable arrangements in the new historical equation between technology and productivity. In the process, they created, and shaped, a new, global economy.

The historical specificity of informationalism

A complex picture emerges regarding the process of historical development of the new informational economy. This complexity explains why highly aggregated statistical data cannot reflect directly the extent and pace of economic transformation under the impact of technological change. The informational economy is a distinctive socio-economic system in relationship to the industrial economy, but not because they differ in the sources of their productivity growth. In both cases, knowledge and information processing are critical elements in economic growth, as can be illustrated by the history of the science-based chemical industry[51] or by the managerial revolution that created Fordism.[52] *What is distinctive is the eventual realization of the productivity potential contained in the mature industrial economy because of the shift toward a technological paradigm based on information technologies.* The new technological paradigm changed first the scope and dynamics of the industrial economy, creating a global economy and fostering a new wave of competition between existing economic agents as well as between them and a legion of newcomers. This new competition, played out by firms but conditioned by the state, led to substantial technological changes in processes and products that made some firms, some sectors, and some areas more productive. Yet, at the same time, creative destruction did occur in large segments of the

50   McKinsey Global Institute (1993).
51   Hohenberg (1967).
52   Coriat (1990).

economy, also affecting firms, sectors, regions, and countries disproportionately. The net result in the first stage of the informational revolution was thus a mixed blessing for economic progress. Furthermore,
the generalization of knowledge-based production and management
to the whole realm of economic processes on a global scale requires
fundamental social, cultural, and institutional transformations which,
if the historical record of other technological revolutions is considered, will take some time. This is why the economy is informational,
not just information-based, because the cultural–institutional attributes
of the whole social system must be included in the diffusion and implementation of the new technological paradigm, as the industrial
economy was not merely based on the use of new sources of energy for
manufacturing but on the emergence of an industrial culture, characterized by a new social and technical division of labor.

Thus, while the informational, global economy is distinct from the
industrial economy, it does not oppose its logic. It subsumes it through
technological deepening, embodying knowledge and information in
all processes of material production and distribution on the basis of a
gigantic leap forward in the reach and scope of the circulation sphere.
In other words: the industrial economy had to become informational
and global or collapse. A case in point is the dramatic breakdown of
the hyperindustrial society, the Soviet Union, because of its structural
inability to shift into the informational paradigm and to pursue its
growth in relative isolation from the international economy (see volume III, chapter 1). An additional argument to support this interpretation refers to the process of increasingly divergent development paths
in the Third World, in fact ending the very notion of "a Third World,"[53]
on the basis of the differential ability of countries and economic agents
to link up with informational processes and to compete in the global
economy.[54] Thus, the shift from industrialism to informationalism is
not the historical equivalent of the transition from agricultural to industrial economies, and cannot be equated to the emergence of the
service economy. There are informational agriculture, informational
manufacturing, and informational service activities that produce and
distribute on the basis of information and knowledge embodied in the
work process by the increasing power of information technologies.
What has changed is not the kind of activities humankind is engaged
in, but its technological ability to use as a direct productive force what
distinguishes our species as a biological oddity: its superior capacity to
process symbols.

53   Harris (1987).
54   Katz (1987); Castells and Tyson (1988); Fajnzylber (1990); Kincaid and Portes (1994).

The Global Economy: Structure, Dynamics, and Genesis

The informational economy is global. A global economy is an historically new reality, distinct from a world economy.[55] A world economy – that is, an economy in which capital accumulation proceeds throughout the world – has existed in the West at least since the sixteenth century, as Fernand Braudel and Immanuel Wallerstein have taught us.[56] A global economy is something different: it is an economy with the capacity to work as a unit in real time, or chosen time, on a planetary scale. While capitalism is characterized by its relentless expansion, always trying to overcome limits of time and space, it was only in the late twentieth century that the world economy was able to become truly global on the basis of the new infrastructure provided by information and communication technologies, and with the decisive help of deregulation and liberalization policies implemented by governments and international institutions. Yet, not everything is global in the economy: in fact, most production, employment, and firms are, and will remain, local and regional. In the last two decades of the twentieth century, international trade grew faster than production, but the domestic sector of the economy still accounts for the large majority of GDP in most economies. Foreign direct investment grew even faster than trade in the 1990s, but still is a fraction of total direct investment. Yet, we can assert that there is a global economy because economies around the world depend on the performance of their globalized core. This globalized core includes financial markets, international trade, transnational production, and, to some extent, science and technology, and specialty labor. It is through these globalized, strategic components of the economy that the economic system is globally interconnected. Thus, I will define more precisely *the global economy as*

---

55 The best, and most comprehensive, analysis of globalization is Held et al. (1999). A key source of data and ideas is the 1999 United Nations' *Human Development Report* elaborated by UNDP (1999). A well-documented, journalistic report is *The New York Times* series "Global Contagion," published in February 1999: Kristoff (1999); Kristoff and Sanger (1999); Kristoff and WuDunn (1999); Kristoff and Wyatt (1999). Most data used in my analysis of economic globalization come from international institutions, such as the United Nations, the IMF, the World Bank, the World Trade Organization, and the OECD. Many of them are reported in the above-cited publications. For the sake of simplicity, I will not refer each figure to its specific source. This note should be considered to be a generic reference to data sources. I have also used in the general analysis underlying this section: Chesnais, (1994); Eichengreen, 1996; Estefania (1996); Hoogvelt (1997); Sachs (1998a, b); Schoettle and Grant (1998); Soros (1998); Friedmann (1999); Schiller (1999); Giddens and Hutton (2000).
56 Braudel (1967); Wallerstein (1974).

Table 2.6 Cross-border transactions in bonds and equities, 1970–1996
(percentage of GDP)

	1970	1975	1980	1985	1990	1996[a]
US	2.8	4.2	9.0	35.1	89.0	151.5
Japan	–	1.5	7.7	63.0	120.0	82.8
Germany	3.3	5.1	7.5	33.4	57.3	196.8
France	–	–	8.4[b]	21.4	53.6	229.2
Italy	–	0.9	1.1	4.0	26.6	435.4
UK	–	–	–	367.5	690.1	–
Canada	5.7	3.3	9.6	26.7	64.4	234.8

[a] January–September.
[b] 1982.
Source: IMF (1997: 60), compiled by Held et al. (1999: table 4.16)

*an economy whose core components have the institutional, organiza-
tional, and technological capacity to work as a unit in real time, or in
chosen time, on a planetary scale.* I shall review succinctly the key
features of this globality.

Global financial markets

Capital markets are globally interdependent, and this is not a small
matter in a capitalist economy.[57] Capital is managed around the clock
in globally integrated financial markets working in real time for the
first time in history: billion dollars worth of transactions take place in
seconds in the electronic circuits throughout the globe. New information systems and communication technologies allow capital to be
shuttled back and forth between economies in very short time, so that
capital, and therefore savings and investment, are interconnected worldwide, from banks to pension funds, stock exchange markets, and currency exchange. Thus, global financial flows have increased
dramatically in their volume, in their velocity, in their complexity, and
in their connectedness.

Table 2.6 provides a measure of the phenomenal growth and dimension of cross-border transactions of bonds and equities between
1970 and 1996 for major market economies: measured as a proportion of GDP, cross-border transactions increased by a factor of about

57   See Khoury and Ghosh (1987); Chesnais (1994); Heavey (1994); Shirref (1994); *The
Economist* (1995b); Canals (1997); Sachs (1998b, c); Soros (1998); Kristoff (1999); Kristoff
and Wyatt (1999); Picciotto and Mayne (1999); Giddens and Hutton (2000); Zaloom (forthcoming).

Table 2.7 Foreign assets and liabilities as a percentage of total assets and liabilities of commercial banks for selected countries, 1960–1997

	1960	1970	1980	1990	1997
France					
Assets	–	16.0	30.0	24.9	34.6
Liabilities	–	17.0	22.0	28.6	32.7
Germany					
Assets	2.4	8.7	9.7	16.3	18.2
Liabilities	4.7	9.0	12.2	13.1	20.6
Japan					
Assets	2.6	3.7	4.2	13.9	16.4
Liabilities	3.6	3.1	7.3	19.4	11.8
Sweden					
Assets	5.8	4.9	9.6	17.7	36.4
Liabilities	2.8	3.8	15.0	45.0	41.9
United Kingdom					
Assets	6.2	46.1	64.7	45.0	51.0
Liabilities	13.9	49.7	67.5	49.3	51.6
United States					
Assets	1.4	2.2	11.0	5.6	3.8
Liabilities	3.7	5.4	9.0	6.9	8.5

Source: Calculated from IMF, *International Financial Statistics Yearbook* (various years) by Held et al. (1999: table 4.17)

54 for the US, of 55 for Japan, and of almost 60 for Germany. To this trend in advanced economies, we should add the integration of so-called "emergent markets" (that is, developing countries and transition economies) in the circuits of global capital flows: total financial flows to developing countries increased by a factor of 7 between 1960 and 1996. The banking industry stepped up its internationalization in the 1990s (as shown in table 2.7). In 1996, while investors bought stocks and bonds from emerging markets for $50 billion, banks lent in these markets $76 billion. Acquisition of overseas stocks by investors in industrialized economies increased by a factor of 197 between 1970 and 1997. In the US, overseas investment by pension funds increased from less than 1 percent of their assets in 1980 to 17 percent in 1997. In the global economy, by 1995, mutual funds, pension funds, and institutional investors in general controlled $20 trillion; that is, about ten times more than in 1980, and an amount equivalent to about two-thirds of global GDP at that time. Between 1983 and 1995, calculating in average annual rates of change, while world real GDP grew by 3.4 percent, and world export volume increased by 6.0 percent, total issues of bonds and loans grew by 8.2 percent, and total stocks of

outstanding bonds and loans increased by 9.8 percent. As a result, in 1998, stocks of outstanding loans and bonds amounted to about 7.6 trillion US dollars, a figure equivalent to over one-quarter of global GDP.[58]

A critical development in financial globalization is the staggering volume of currency trading, which conditions the exchange rate between national currencies, decisively undermining governments' autonomy in monetary and fiscal policies. The daily turnover of currency markets around the world in 1998 reached 1.5 trillion US dollars, equivalent to more than 110 percent of the UK's GDP in 1998. This volume of currency trade represented an increase in the value of global currency trading by a factor of 8 between 1986 and 1998. This extraordinary increase was, by and large, unrelated to international trade. The ratio between the annual turnover of foreign exchange and the volume of world exports increased from 12:1 in 1979 to 60:1 in 1996, thus revealing the predominantly speculative nature of currency exchange.

The global interdependence of financial markets is the result of five main developments. The first factor is the deregulation of financial markets in most countries, and the liberalization of cross-border transactions. A turning point in this process of deregulation was the so-called "Big Bang" of the City of London on October 27, 1987. This new financial freedom allowed capital from all sources to be mobilized from anywhere to be invested anywhere. In the US, between 1980 and the late 1990s, investment by pension funds, mutual funds, and institutional investors increased by a factor of 10, so that in 1998 stock market capitalization in the US amounted to 140 percent of GDP.

The second element is the development of a technological infrastructure, which includes advanced telecommunications, interactive information systems, and powerful computers capable of the high-speed processing of models required to handle the complexity of transactions. The third factor of connectedness results from the nature of new financial products, such as derivatives (futures, options, swaps, and other complex products). Derivatives are synthetic securities which often combine the values of stocks, bonds, options, commodities, and currencies from various countries. They operate on the basis of mathematical models. They recombine value around the world and across time, thus generating market capitalization out of market capitalization. Some estimates put the market value of derivatives traded in 1997 at about $US 360 trillion, which would amount to 12 times the value of global GDP.[59] By linking together products traded in different mar-

58   Held et al. (1999: 203).
59   Kristoff and Wyatt (1999).

kets, derivatives link the performance of these markets to their product valuation in any market. If one of the components of a derivative (e.g. a currency) falls in value, the devaluation may be transmitted to other markets through the devaluation of the derivative, regardless of the performance of the market where the derivative is traded. However, this devaluation may be offset by the revaluation of another component of the derivative. The relative proportions, and timing, of movements of valuation and devaluation of various components are largely unpredictable. Because of this complexity of derivatives they increase volatility in the global financial networks.

A fourth source of integration of financial markets comprises speculative movements of financial flows, moving swiftly in and out of a given market, security, or currency, either to take advantage of differences in valuation or to avoid a loss, thus amplifying market trends, in both directions, and transmitting these movements to markets around the world.[60] In this new environment, financial organizations originally set up to counter the risk, such as hedge funds, have become a major tool of global integration, speculation, and, in the last resort, financial instability. Hedge funds, usually subject to loose regulation, and often located offshore from main financial markets, manage the money of large investors, including banks and institutional investors, in the hope of obtaining higher rates of return (at the price of higher risk) than those provided by the market within the constraints of a regulated environment. Hedge funds' capital and financial influence sky-rocketed in the 1990s. Between 1990 and 1997 their assets multiplied by 12, and in the late 1990s about 3,500 hedge funds were managing $US 200 billion, and using this capital to borrow – and bet – much larger sums.[61]

Fifth, market valuation firms, such as Standard & Poor, or Moody's, are also powerful elements of interconnection between financial markets. By rating securities, and sometimes entire national economies, according to global standards of accountability, they tend to assert common rules on markets around the world. Their ratings often trigger movements in certain markets (e.g. South Korea in 1997) which then diffuse to other markets.[62]

Since capital markets and currencies are interdependent, so are monetary policies and interest rates. And so are economies everywhere. Although major corporate centers provide the human resources and facilities necessary to manage an increasingly complex global financial

60 Soros (1998).
61 Kristoff and Wyatt (1999).
62 Kim (1998).

network,[63] it is in the information networks connecting such centers that the actual operations of capital take place. Capital flows become at the same time global and increasingly autonomous *vis-à-vis* the actual performance of economies.[64] Ultimately, it is the performance of capital in the globally interdependent financial markets that largely shapes the fate of economies at large. This performance is not entirely dependent on economic rules. Financial markets are markets, but so imperfect that they only partly respond to laws of supply and demand. Movements in financial markets are the result of a complex combination of market rules, business strategies, politically motivated policies, central banks' machinations, technocrats' ideology, crowd psychology, speculative maneuvering, and information turbulences of various origins.[65] The ensuing flows of capital, in and out of specific securities, and specific markets, are transmitted throughout the world at the speed of light, although the impact of these movements is processed specifically (and unpredictably) by each market. Daring financial investors try to ride the tiger, anticipating trends in their computer models, and betting on a variety of scenarios. So doing, they create capital out of capital, and increase nominal value exponentially (while periodically destroying some of this value during "market corrections"). The outcome of the process is the increasing concentration of value, and of value making, in the financial sphere, in a global network of capital flows managed by networks of information systems, and their ancillary services. The globalization of financial markets is the backbone of the new global economy.

Globalization of markets for goods and services: growth and transformation of international trade

International trade was, historically, the main link between national economies. However, its relative importance in the current process of globalization is less than that of financial integration, and that of internationalization of foreign direct investment and production. Yet trade is still a fundamental component of the new global economy.[66] International trade increased substantially in the last third of the twentieth century, both in volume, and as a percentage of GDP, for developed as well as for developing countries (see figure 2.3). For developed countries, the percentage of exports over GDP grew from 11.2 percent

63 Sassen (1991).
64 Chesnais (1994); Lee et al. (1994).
65 Soros (1998); Zaloom (forthcoming).
66 Tyson (1992); Hockman and Kostecki (1995); Krugman (1995); Held et al. (1999: 476–92).

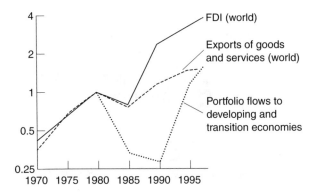

FDI (world)

Exports of goods
and services (world)

Portfolio flows to
developing and
transition economies

Figure 2.3 Growth in trade and capital flows, 1970–1995 (index
1980 = 1)
Source: Data from World Bank and UNCTAD, elaborated by UNDP (1999)

in 1913 to 23.1 percent in 1985, while the respective figure for imports was 12.4 percent in 1880–1900 to 21.7 percent in 1985. For non-oil exporting developing countries, the value of exports over GDP, in the late 1990s, amounted to about 20 percent. Focusing on specific countries, and comparing the value of exports over GDP in 1913 and in 1997, the US shows an increase from 4.1 to 11.4 percent, the UK, from 14.7 to 21 percent, Japan from 2.1 to 11 percent, France from 6.0 to 21.1 percent, and Germany from 12.2 to 23.7 percent. Overall, estimates of the proportion of world exports over world output in 1997 varied between 18.6 and 21.8 percent. In the United States, from the mid-1980s to the late 1990s, the share of exports plus imports in the gross domestic product increased from 18 to 24 percent.

The evolution of international trade in the last quarter of the twentieth century was characterized by four major trends: its sectoral transformation; its relative diversification, with a growing proportion of trade shifting to developing countries, albeit with great differences among developing countries; the interaction between liberalization of global trade and regionalization of the world economy; and the formation of a network of trade relations between firms, cutting across regions and countries. Together, these trends configure the trading dimension of the new global economy. Let us review each one of them.

Trade of manufactured goods represents the bulk of non-energy international trade, in sharp contrast to the predominance of primary commodities in earlier patterns of international trade. Since the 1960s, trade in manufactures has accounted for the majority of world trade,

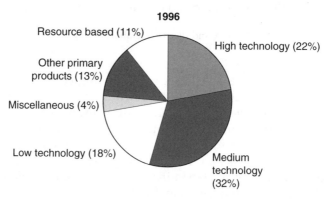

Figure 2.4 Goods in international trade by level of technological intensity, 1976/1996 (note that medium- and high-technology goods are those requiring intensive R&D as measured by R&D expenditure)
Source: World Bank, *World Development Report* (1998)

comprising three-quarters of all trade in the late 1990s. This sectoral transformation continues, with the growing importance of services in international trade, favored by international agreements liberalizing this trade. The construction of a transportation and telecommunications infrastructure is aiding the globalization of business services. By the mid-1990s the value of services trade was estimated at over 20 percent of total world trade.

There is a deeper transformation in the structure of trade: the knowledge component of goods and services becomes decisive in terms of value added. Thus, to the traditional trade imbalance between developed and developing economies, resulting from unequal exchange between valued manufactures and less valued primary commodities, a new form of imbalance is superimposed. This is the trade between high-

Table 2.8   Direction of world exports, 1965–1995 (percentage of world total)

	Between developed economies	Developed–developing	Between developing economies
1965	59.0	32.5	3.8
1970	62.1	30.6	3.3
1975	46.6	38.4	7.2
1980	44.8	39.0	9.0
1985	50.8	35.3	9.0
1990	55.3	33.4	9.6
1995	47.0	37.7	14.1

Totals do not sum to 100 due to trade with Comecon countries, countries not otherwise classified, and errors.
Source: Calculated from IMF, *Direction of Trade Statistics Yearbook* (various years) by Held et al. (1999: table 3.6)

technology and low-technology goods, and between high-knowledge and low-knowledge services, characterized by a pattern of uneven distribution of knowledge and technology between countries and regions around the world. From 1976 to 1996 the share of high- and medium-technology goods in global trade increased from about one-third to well above one-half (see figure 2.4). It follows that the outward orientation of an economy does not guarantee its development. It all depends on the value of what the economy is able to export. Thus, in one of the greatest paradoxes of new patterns of growth, Sub-Saharan Africa has a higher export/GDP ratio than that of developed economies: 29 percent of GDP in the 1990s. However, since these exports are concentrated in low-value primary commodities, the process of unequal exchange keeps African economies in their poverty, while small elites profit personally from a nationally unprofitable trade. Technological capacity, technological infrastructure, access to knowledge, and highly skilled human resources become critical sources of competitiveness in the new international division of labor.[67]

Alongside the worldwide expansion of international trade, there has been a trend toward relative diversification of the areas of trade (as shown in table 2.8). In 1965 exports between developed economies accounted for 59 percent of the total, but in 1995, the proportion had been reduced to 47 percent, while the corresponding figure for exports between developing economies increased from 3.8 to 14.1 percent. This broadening of the geographical basis of international trade must be qualified, however, by several considerations. First,

67   World Bank (1998).

developed economies continue to be the overwhelming partners in international trade: they have expanded their trade pattern toward newly industrializing economies, rather than being displaced by competition. Second, while the share of developing countries in manufacturing exports has substantially increased, from 6 percent in 1965 to 20 percent in 1995, this still leaves 80 percent for developed countries. Third, trade in high-value, high-technology products is overwhelmingly dominated by developed economies, and concentrated in intra-industry trade among developed economies. Fourth, the increasingly important trade in services is also skewed in favor of developed economies: in 1997, OECD countries accounted for 70.1 percent of total services exports, and for 66.8 percent of services imports. Fifth, manufacturing exports from developing countries are concentrated in a handful of newly industrialized, and industrializing countries, mainly in East Asia, while, during the 1990s, shares of world trade for Africa and the Middle East have stagnated, and Latin America's share has remained the same. However, China is not accounted for in the calculations of table 2.8 and its exports have increased substantially, at an annual average of about 10 percent between 1970 and 1997, so contributing to an increase in the overall share of developing countries in world exports well over the 20 percent mark. This still left OECD economies with 71 percent of the world's total exports of goods and services at the end of the twentieth century, while accounting for only 19 percent of the world's population.[68]

Thus, the new international division of labor, on the one hand, maintains the trade dominance of OECD countries, particularly in high-value trade, through technological deepening and trade in services. On the other hand, it opens up new channels of integration of newly industrializing economies in the patterns of international trade, but this integration is extremely uneven, and highly selective. It introduces a fundamental cleavage among countries, and regions, that were traditionally grouped under the vague notion of "the South."

Globalization versus regionalization?

In the 1980s and 1990s, the evolution of international trade was marked by the tension between two apparently contradictory trends: on the one hand, the growing liberalization of trade; on the other, a variety of governments' projects to set up trading blocs. The most important of these trading areas is the European Union, but the apparent trend toward regionalization of the world economy was present in other

68   UNDP (1999).

areas of the world, as exemplified by the North American Free Trade Agreement (NAFTA), MERCOSUR, and the Asian Pacific Economic Council (APEC). These trends, together with persistent protectionist practices throughout the world, mainly in East and South Asia, led a number of observers, including myself, to propose the notion of a regionalized global economy.[69] That is, a global system of trade between trading areas, with increasing homogenization of customs within the area, while maintaining trade barriers *vis-à-vis* the rest of the world. However, a closer look at the evidence, in the light of developments in the late 1990s, calls into question the regionalization thesis. Held and colleagues, after reviewing a number of studies, conclude that "the evidence suggests that trade regionalization is complementary, and has grown alongside, interregional trade."[70] Indeed, a study by Anderson and Norheim on world trade patterns since the 1930s shows an equally strong growth of trade both between and within regions. The intensity of intra-regional trade is in fact lower in Western Europe than in America or Asia, undermining the importance of institutionalization in reinforcing intra-regional trade.[71] Other studies suggest a rising propensity for extra-regional trade in America and Asia, and a fluctuating propensity in Europe.[72]

Developments in the 1990s compel us to re-examine the regionalization thesis more thoroughly. In 1999 the European Union became, for all practical purposes, one economy, with unified customs, a single currency, and a European Central Bank. The adoption of the euro by Britain and Sweden seemed to be a matter of time, to adjust to the requirements of their domestic politics. Thus, it seems inadequate to consider the European Union any longer as a trading bloc since intra-EU trade is not international, but interregional, similar to interregional trade within the United States. This does not imply that European states disappear, as I shall argue in volume III. But they have formed, together, a new form of state, the network state, one of whose key features is the sharing of a unified economy, not just a trading bloc.

Let us now consider the Asian Pacific. Frankel calculated that most of the growth in intra-Asian trade in the 1980s was a function of high rates of economic growth in the area, increasing its share in the world economy, compounded by geographical proximity.[73] Cohen and Guerrieri, in their revision of Frankel's analysis, differentiated two

69 Castells (1993); Cohen (1993).
70 Held et al. (1999: 168).
71 Anderson and Norheim (1993).
72 Held et al. (1999: 168).
73 Frankel (1991).

periods of intra-Asian trade: 1970–85, and 1985–92.[74] In the first period, Asian countries exported predominantly to the rest of the world, particularly to North America and Europe. Intra-regional imports in Asia increased steadily during this period. However, inside Asia, Japan posted significant trade surpluses *vis-à-vis* its neighbors. Thus, Japan ran a trade surplus with North America, Europe, and Asia, while the Asian countries compensated their deficit with Japan by building up an additional surplus with America and Europe. In the second period, intra-Asian trade grew substantially, from 32.5 percent of Asian exports in 1985 to 39.8 percent in 1992. Intra-regional imports reached 45.1 percent of all Asian imports. However, this aggregate figure hides an important asymmetry: Japan's imports from Asia decreased, while its exports to Asia increased, particularly in technology-intensive items. Asia's trade deficit with Japan substantially increased during the period. As in the first period, to offset their trade deficit with Japan, the Asian countries generated trade surpluses with the United States, and to a lesser extent with Europe. The conclusions of this analysis run against the notion of an integrated Asian Pacific region. This is because the internal dynamics of trade in the region, and the imbalance between Japan and the rest of Asia, have been sustained by continuously generating trade surpluses with the rest of the world, particularly with the United States. The growth of intra-Asian trade has not changed the fundamental dependency of the region *vis-à-vis* the performance of its exports in the world market, particularly in non-Asian OECD countries. The recession of the Japanese economy in the 1990s, and the Asian crisis of 1997–8, further reinforced this dependency on extra-regional markets. Faced with declining intra-regional demand, Asian economies betted their recovery on stepped-up export performance in markets outside the region to become even more competitive, with considerable success, particularly for companies in Taiwan, Singapore, and South Korea (see volume III, chapter 4). The addition of China as a major world exporter (particularly to the US market), and the increasing outward orientation of the Indian economy, definitely tip the balance in favor of a multi-directional pattern of trade in the Asian economies. As for APEC, it is merely a consulting association, working in close cooperation with the United States and with the World Trade Organization. APEC's most noted initiative, the Osaka declaration, proclaiming the goal of free trade around the Pacific by 2010, cannot be seen as a step toward regional integration, but rather as a project of full integration of Pacific countries in global trade. Furthermore, the institutional integration of the Asian

74   Cohen and Guerrieri (1995).

Pacific meets insurmountable geopolitical difficulties. The rise of China as a superpower, and the lasting memories of Japanese imperialism in World War II, make a model of institutional cooperation similar to the European Union unthinkable between the two giant economies of the region, and between them and their neighbors, thus excluding the possibility of a yen bloc or of an Asian Pacific customs union. In sum, what we observe is the growing integration of Asian Pacific trade in the global economy, rather than a Pacific intra-regional implosion.

Shifting to the Americas, NAFTA simply institutionalizes the already existing interpenetration of the three North American economies. The Canadian economy has been for a long time a region of the US economy. The meaningful change concerns Mexico, as the US succeeded in bringing down tariff barriers, mainly to the benefit of US firms on both sides of the border. But the liberalization of foreign trade and investment in Mexico was already underway in the 1980s, as exemplified by the *maquiladoras* program. If we add free movements of capital and currency, massive flows of Mexican labor across the border, and the formation of cross-border production networks in manufacturing and agriculture, what we observe is the formation of one economy, the North American economy, including the US, Canada, and Mexico, rather than the emergence of a trading bloc.[75] The Central American and Caribbean economies are, with the exception of Cuba for the time being, satellites of the NAFTA bloc, in historical continuity with their dependency on the United States.

MERCOSUR (formed by Brazil, Argentina, Uruguay, and Paraguay, with Bolivia and Chile in close association at the turn of the century) is a promising blueprint for the economic integration of South America. With a combined GDP of US$ 1.2 trillion in 1998, and a potential market of over 230 million people, it is indeed the one case that comes closest to the notion of a trading bloc. There is a gradual process of unification of customs inside MERCOSUR, leading to an intensification of intra-MERCOSUR trade. Possible future agreements with countries of the Andean Pact could expand the trading alliance to all of South America. There are, however, very serious obstacles to the consolidation of MERCOSUR. The most important is the need to coordinate monetary and fiscal policies, which ultimately would require the pegging of currencies of participating countries. Serious tensions which arose in 1999 between Brazil and Argentina showed the fragility of the agreement in the absence of a coordinated approach to financial integration in the global economy. The most meaningful aspect of MERCOSUR development is, in fact, that it signals the growing inde-

75 Tardanico and Rosenberg (2000).

pendence of South American economies *vis-à-vis* the United States. Indeed, in the 1990s, MERCOSUR's exports to the European Union outweighed exports to the United States. Together with growing European investment in South America (particularly from Spain), the consolidation of MERCOSUR could signal a trend toward a multi-directional integration of South America in the global economy.

While the projects of trading blocs either faded or evolved into full economic integration in the 1990s, the openness of global trade was boosted by a number of institutional steps toward its liberalization. After the successful conclusion of GATT's Uruguay Round by the Marrakesh Agreement in 1994, leading to a significant reduction of tariffs around the world, a new World Trade Organization (WTO) was created to act as watchdog of a liberal trade order and a mediator of trade disputes between trading partners. Multilateral agreements sponsored by the WTO have created a new framework for international trade, furthering global integration. In the late 1990s, on the initiative of the United States government, the WTO focused its activity on liberalizing trade in services, and on reaching an agreement on trade-related aspects of intellectual property rights (TRIPS). On both grounds, it signaled the strategic connection between the new stage of globalization and the informational economy.

So, on close examination, the configuration of the global economy at the turn of the century sharply departs from the regionalized structure that was hypothesized in the early 1990s. The European Union is one economy, not one region. Eastern Europe is in the process of becoming part of the European Union, and, for some time, it will be, essentially, an appendage of the EU. Russia will take a long time to recover from its devastating transition to wild capitalism, and when it will be finally able to trade with the global economy (beyond its current role of provider of primary commodities) will do so on its own terms. NAFTA and Central America are, in fact, extensions of the US economy. MERCOSUR is, for the time being, a work in progress, always in danger from the latest presidential mood in Brazil and Argentina. Chilean exports diversify all over the world. So probably do Colombian, Bolivian, and Peruvian exports, particularly if we were able to assess the value of their main export good (which is not coffee). Under these conditions, the traditional dependency of South American trade *vis-à-vis* the United States seems to be increasingly called into question. Consequently, a "region of the Americas" does not seem to exist, although there is a US/NAFTA entity, and, evolving independently, the project of MERCOSUR. There is no Asian Pacific region, although there is substantial trans-Pacific trade (with the US being at one end of it). China and India assert themselves as stand-alone, continental economies, establishing their own, independent connections with the networks of international trade. The Middle East continues to be kept in its limited role as oil supplier, with little diversification of its domestic economies. Northern Africa is in the process of being made a satellite of the European Union, as a deterrent against uncontrollable, and undesired immigration from impoverished countries. And Sub-Saharan Africa, with the important exception of South Africa, is being increasingly marginalized in the world economy, as I will analyze in volume III. Thus, after all, it seems that there is little regionalization of the global economy, beyond the customary pattern of trade agreements, and disputes, between the European Union, Japan, and the United States. Besides, the areas of influence of these three economic superpowers increasingly overlap. Japan and Europe make substantial in-roads into Latin America. The US intensifies its trade with both Asia and Europe. Japan expands its trade with Europe. And China and India are forcefully entering the global economy with a multiplicity of trade partners. In sum, the process of regionalization of the global economy has largely dissolved, in favor of a multi-layered, multi-networked structure of trade patterns, which cannot be apprehended by using the categories of countries as units of trade and competition.

Indeed, markets for goods and services are becoming increasingly globalized. But the actual trading units are not countries, but firms, and networks of firms. This does not mean that all firms sell worldwide. But it does mean that the strategic aim of firms, large and small, is to sell wherever they can throughout the world, either directly or via their linkage with networks that operate in the world market. And there are indeed, to a large extent thanks to new communication and transportation technologies, channels and opportunities to sell everywhere. This statement must be qualified, however, by the fact that domestic markets account for the largest share of GDP in most countries, and that in developing countries, informal economies, mainly aimed at local markets, constitute the bulk of urban employment. Also, some major economies, for instance Japan, still have important segments (for example, public works, retail trade) sheltered from worldwide competition by government protection and by cultural/institutional insulation.[76] And public services and government institutions throughout the world, accounting for between one-third and over a half of jobs in each country, are, and will be, by and large removed from international competition. Yet, the dominant segments and firms, the strategic cores of all economies, are deeply connected to the world

76 Tyson (1992).

market, and their fate is a function of their performance in such a market. Sectors and firms producing non-tradable goods and services cannot be understood in isolation from tradable sectors. The dynamism of domestic markets depends ultimately on the capacity of domestic firms and networks of firms to compete globally.[77] Furthermore, international trade can no longer be separated from transnational production processes in goods and services. Thus, intra-firm international trade may account for over one-third of total international trade.[78] And the internationalization of production, and finance, are among the most important sources of growth in the international trade of services.[79]

The debate over the regionalization of the global economy denotes, however, a very important matter: the role of governments and international institutions in the process of globalization. Networks of firms, trading in the global market, are only one part of the story. Equally important are the actions of public institutions in fostering, restraining, and shaping free trade, and in positioning governments to support those economic players whose interests they represent. Yet the complexity of interaction between government strategies and trade competition cannot be understood under the simplistic notions of regionalization and trading blocs. I shall propose some hints on this political–economic approach to globalization after reviewing another layer of its complexity: the networked internationalization of the core of the production process.

The internationalization of production: multinational corporations and international production networks

During the 1990s there was an accelerated process of internationalization of production, distribution, and management of goods and services. This process comprised three interrelated aspects: the growth of foreign direct investment, the decisive role of multinational corporations as producers in the global economy, and the formation of international production networks.

Foreign direct investment (FDI) increased by a factor of 4 in 1980–95, considerably faster than world output, and world trade (see figure 2.4). FDI doubled its share of world capital formation from 2 percent

---

77   Cohen (1990); BRIE (1992); Sandholtz et al. (1992); World Trade Organization (1997, 1998).
78   UNCTAD (1995).
79   Daniels (1993).

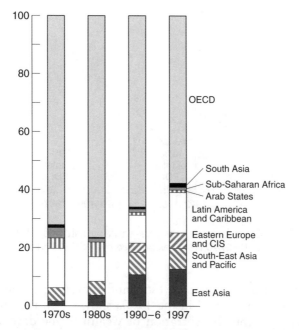

Figure 2.5 Foreign direct investment (as percentage of total FDI)
Source: Data from UNCTAD (1999) elaborated by UNDP (1999)

in the 1980s to 4 percent in the mid-1990s. In the late 1990s, FDI continued to increase at about the same rate as in the early 1990s. Most of FDI originates in a few OECD countries, although US domination in FDI outflows is on the decline (in spite of its much higher volume): US share of global FDI fell from about 50 percent in the 1960s to about 25 percent in the 1990s. Other major investors are headquartered in Japan, Germany, the UK, France, The Netherlands, Sweden, and Switzerland. Most FDI stocks are concentrated in developed economies, in contrast with earlier historical periods, and this concentration grew over time: in 1960, developed economies accounted for two-thirds of FDI stocks; in the late 1990s, their share had grown to three-quarters. However, the pattern of FDI flows (as opposed to stocks) is increasingly diversified, with developing countries receiving a growing share of this investment, although still significantly less than developed economies (see figure 2.5). Some studies show that FDI flows, in the late 1980s, were less concentrated than international trade. In the 1990s developing countries increased their share of outward FDI flows, although they still accounted for less than 10 percent of FDI stocks. However, a smaller share of world FDI still represents a sig-

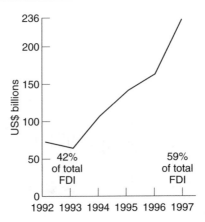

Figure 2.6   Cross-border mergers and acquisitions, 1992–1997
Source: Data from UNCTAD (1998) elaborated by UNDP (1999)

nificant share of total direct investment for developing economies. Thus, overall, patterns of FDI in the 1990s showed, on the one hand, the persistence of the concentration of wealth in the developed economies; on the other hand, the increasing diversification of productive investment following the internationalization of production.[80]

FDI is associated with the expansion of multinational corporations as major producers of the global economy. FDI frequently takes the form of mergers and acquisitions in the developed economies and, increasingly, in the developing world as well. Annual cross-borders of mergers and acquisitions jumped from 42 percent of total FDI in 1992 to 59 percent of FDI in 1997, reaching a total value of US$ 236 billion (see figure 2.6). Multinational corporations (MNCs) are the main source of FDI. But FDI accounts for only 25 percent of investment in international production. MNCs' foreign subsidiaries finance their investments from a variety of sources, including borrowing in local and international markets, subsidies from governments, and co-financing from local firms. MNCs, and their linked production networks, are the vector of internationalization of production, of which the expansion of FDI is just one manifestation. Indeed, the expansion of world trade is, by and large, the result of MNC's production, since they account for about two-thirds of total world trade, including about one-third of world trade which takes place between branches of the same corporation. If networks of firms linked to a given MNC were included in the calculation, the proportion of intra-networked firm trade

80   IMF (1997); UNDP (1999).

Table 2.9 Parent corporations and foreign affiliates by area and country, latest available year (number)

Area/economy	Parent corporations based in country	Foreign affiliates located in economy[a]
Developed countries	36,380	93,628
Western Europe	26,161	61,902
European Union	22,111	54,862
Japan	3,967[b]	3,405[c]
United States	3,470[d]	18,608[e]
Developing countries	7,932	129,771
Africa	30	134
Latin America and the Caribbean	1,099	24,267
South, East and South-East Asia	6,242	99,522
West Asia	449	1,948
Central and Eastern Europe	196	53,260
World 1997	44,508	276,659
World 1998	53,000	450,000

The data can vary significantly from preceding years, as data become available for countries not covered before, as definitions change, or as older data are updated.
[a] Represents the number of foreign affiliates in the economy shown, as defined by it.
[b] The number of parent companies not including finance, insurance, and real-estate industries in March 1995 (3,695) plus the number of parent companies in finance, insurance, and real-estate industries in December 1992 (272).
[c] The number of foreign affiliates not including finance, insurance, and real-estate industries in March 1995 (3,121) plus the number of foreign affiliates, insurance, and real-estate industries in November 1995 (284).
[d] Represents a total of 2,658 non-bank parent companies in 1994 and 89 bank parent companies in 1989 with at least one foreign affiliate whose assets, sales or net income exceeded $3 million, and 723 non-bank and bank parent companies in 1989 whose affiliate(s) had assets, sales, and net income under $3 million.
[e] Represents a total of 12,523 bank and non-bank affiliates in 1994 whose assets, sales, and net income exceeded $1 million, and 5,551 bank and non-bank affiliates in 1992 with assets, sales, and net income under $1 million, and 534 United States affiliates that are depository institutions. Each affiliate represents a fully consolidated United States business enterprise, which may consist of a number of individual companies.
Source: UNCTAD (1997, 1998), compiled by Held et al. (1999: table 5.3)

would considerably increase. Thus, a large share of what we measure as international trade is, in fact, a measure of cross-border production within the same production unit. In 1998, there were about 53,000 MNCs, with 450,000 foreign subsidiaries, and global sales of $9.5 trillion dollars (which exceeded the volume of world trade). They accounted for 20–30 percent of total world output, and between 66 and 70 percent of world trade (depending on various estimates) (see table 2.9). The sectoral composition of MNCs experienced a substantial transformation in the second half of the twentieth century. Until the

1950s, most FDI was concentrated in the primary sector. But by 1970, FDI in the primary sector accounted for only 22.7 percent of total FDI, in contrast to 45.2 percent in the secondary sector, and 31.4 percent in the tertiary sector. In 1994, a new structure of investment could be perceived, as FDI in services accounted for the majority of FDI (53.6 percent), while the primary sector was down to 8.7 percent, and manufacturing's share had shrunk to 37.4 percent. Even so, MNCs account for the majority of world's manufacturing exports. With the liberalization of trade in services, and the conclusion of the TRIPS agreement protecting intellectual property rights, MNCs' dominance in the international trade of services, and particularly of advanced business services, seems to be guaranteed.[81] As with manufacturing, increase in trade in services in fact reflects the expansion of international production of goods and services, since multinationals and their subsidiaries need the infrastructure of services required to operate globally.

While there is no doubt that multinationals constitute the core of internationalized production, and thus a fundamental dimension of the globalization process, it is less clear what they exactly are.[82] A number of analysts question their multinational character, arguing that they are nation-based corporations with a global reach. Multinational corporations are overwhelmingly based in OECD countries. Yet, on the other hand, in 1997 there were 7,932 multinational corporations based in developing countries, up from 3,800 in the late 1980s, thus representing about 18 percent of the total number for 1997 (which was 44,508). Furthermore, if we calculate, on the basis of table 2.9, for 1997 values, a simple ratio between parent corporations located in a given area of the world and foreign affiliates located in this area, we obtain some interesting observations. To be sure, the ratio is 38.9 for developed economies in contrast to 6.1 for developing countries, illustrating the asymmetrical distribution of global productive power, a rough measure of economic dependency. But most revealing is the comparison of ratios between different developed areas. Japan (with a whopping 116.5 ratio) shows its asymmetrical integration in global production networks. On the other hand, the US, with an 18.7 ratio, appears to be deeply penetrated by foreign companies. Western Europe is in between these two marks, with a 40.3 ratio, displaying the highest number of home-based parent corporations, but, at the same time, being also the location of 61,900 foreign affiliates (in contrast to

81   UNDP (1999).
82   Reich (1991); Carnoy (1993); Dunning (1993); UNCTAD (1993, 1994, 1995, 1997); Graham (1996); Dicken (1998); Held et al. (1999: 236–82).

18,600 for the US). This reciprocal penetration of advanced economies is confirmed by the fact that inward stocks of foreign direct investment in the most advanced economies grew substantially in the 1990s. In other words, the US and Western European companies have increasing numbers of subsidiaries in each other's territories; Japanese companies have extended their multilocational pattern around the world, while Japan remains much less permeable to foreign subsidiaries than other areas of the world; multinationals based in developing countries are making inroads into the global production system, as yet on a limited scale. OECD-based corporations are present all over the developing world: in the late 1990s, MNCs accounted for about 30 percent of domestic manufacturing in Latin America, between 20 and 30 percent of total private output in China, 40 percent of value added in manufacturing in Malaysia, and 70 percent in Singapore – but only 10 percent of Korean, 15 percent of Hong Kong, and 20 percent of Taiwanese manufacturing output.

How national are these multinational corporations? There is a persistent mark of their national matrix in their top personnel, in the company's culture, and in the privileged relationship to the government of their original birthplace.[83] However, a number of factors work toward the increasingly multinational character of these corporations. Sales and earnings of foreign affiliates account for a substantial proportion of total earnings for each corporation, particularly for US companies. High-level personnel are often recruited with their familiarity with each specific environment in mind. And the best talent is promoted within the corporate chain of command, regardless of national origin, thus contributing to an increasingly multicultural mix in the higher echelons. Business and political contacts are still crucial, but they are specific to the national context where the corporation operates. Thus, the greater the extent of a company's globalization, the greater the spectrum of its business contacts and political connections, according to conditions in each country. In this sense, they are multinational rather than transnational corporations. That is, they have multiple national allegiances, rather than being indifferent to nationality and national contexts.[84]

However, the critical trend in the evolution of global production in the 1990s is the organizational transformation of the production process, including the transformation of multinational corporations themselves. Global production of goods and services, increasingly, is not

83 Cohen (1990); Porter (1990).
84 Imai (1990a, b); Dunning (1993); Howell and Woods (1993); Strange (1996); Dicken (1998).

performed by multinational corporations, but by transnational production networks, of which multinational corporations are an essential component, yet a component which could not operate without the rest of the network.[85] I shall analyze in detail this organizational transformation in chapter 3 of this volume. But I must refer to the matter here to provide an accurate account of the structure and process of the new, global economy.

Besides multinational corporations, small and medium firms in many countries – with the US (e.g. Silicon Valley), Hong Kong, Taiwan, and northern Italy hosting the most prominent examples – have formed cooperative networks, enabling themselves to be competitive in the globalized production system. These networks have connected with multinational corporations, becoming reciprocal subcontractors. Most often, networks of small/medium businesses become subcontractors of one or several large corporations. But there are also frequent cases of these networks setting up agreements with multinational companies to obtain market access, technology, management skills, or brand name. Many of these networks of small and medium businesses are transnational themselves, through agreements that operate across borders, as exemplified by the Taiwanese and Israeli computer industries extending their networks to Silicon Valley.[86]

Furthermore, as I will argue in chapter 3, multinational corporations are increasingly decentralized internal networks, organized in semi-autonomous units, according to countries, markets, processes, and products. Each one of these units links up with other semi-autonomous units of other multinationals, in the form of *ad hoc* strategic alliances. And each one of these alliances (in fact, networks) is a node of ancillary networks of small and medium firms. These networks of production networks have a transnational geography, which is not undifferentiated: each productive function finds the proper location (in terms of resources, cost, quality, and market access) and/or links up with a new firm in the network which happens to be in the proper location.

Thus, dominant segments of most production sectors (either for goods or for services) are organized worldwide in their actual operating procedures, forming what Robert Reich labeled "the global web."[87] The production process incorporates components produced in many different locations by different firms, and assembled for specific pur-

---

85   Henderson (1989); Coriat (1990); Gereffi and Wyman (1990); Sengenberger and Campbell (1992); Gereffi (1993); Borrus and Zysman (1997); Dunning (1997); Ernst (1997); Held et al. (1999: 259–70).
86   Adler (1999); Saxenian (1999).
87   Reich (1991).

poses and specific markets in a new form of production and commer-cialization: high-volume, flexible, customized production. Such a web does not correspond to the simplistic notion of a global corporation obtaining its supplies from different units around the world. The new production system relies on a combination of strategic alliances and *ad hoc* cooperation projects between corporations, decentralized units of each major corporation, and networks of small and medium enter-prises connecting among themselves and/or with large corporations or networks of corporations. These trans-border production networks operate under two main configurations: in Gereffi's terminology, pro-ducer-driven commodity chains (in industries such as automobiles, computers, aircraft, electrical machinery), and buyer-driven commod-ity chains (in industries such as garment, footwear, toys, housewares).[88] What is fundamental in this web-like industrial structure is that it is territorially spread throughout the world, and its geometry keeps chang-ing, as a whole and for each individual unit. In such a structure, the most important element for a successful managerial strategy is to pos-ition a firm (or a given industrial project) in the web in such a way as to gain competitive advantage for its relative position. Thus, the struc-ture tends to reproduce itself and to keep expanding as competition goes on, so deepening the global character of the economy. For the firm to operate in such a variable geometry of production and distri-bution a very flexible form of management is required, a form that is dependent on the flexibility of the firm itself and on the access to com-munication and production technologies suited to this flexibility (see chapter 3). For instance, to be able to assemble parts produced from very distant sources, it is necessary to have, on the one hand, a micro-electronics-based precision quality in the fabrication process, so that the parts are compatible to the smallest detail of specification; and, on the other, a computer-based flexibility enabling the factory to pro-gram production runs according to the volume and customized charac-teristics required by each order. In addition, the management of inventories will depend on the existence of an adequate network of trained suppliers, whose performance was enhanced in the past dec-ade by new technological capability to adjust demand and supply on-line. Thus, the new international division of labor is increasingly intra-firm. Or, more precisely, intra-networks of firms. These trans-national production networks, anchored by multinational corpora-tions, unevenly distributed across the planet, shape the pattern of global production, and, ultimately, the pattern of international trade.

88   Gereffi (1999).

Informational production and selective globalization of science and technology

Productivity and competitiveness in informational production are based on the generation of knowledge and information processing. Knowledge generation and technological capacity are key tools for competition between firms, organizations of all kinds, and, ultimately, countries.[89] Thus, the geography of science and technology should have a major impact on the sites and networks of the global economy. Indeed, we observe an extraordinary concentration of science and technology in a small number of OECD countries. In 1993, ten countries accounted for 84 percent of global R&D, and controlled 95 percent of the US patents of the past two decades. By the late 1990s, the fifth of the world's people living in the high-income countries had at their disposal 74 percent of telephone lines, and accounted for over 93 percent of Internet users.[90] This technological domination would run against the idea of a knowledge-based global economy, except under the form of a hierarchical division of labor between knowledge-based producers, located in a few "global cities and regions," and the rest of the world, made up of technologically dependent economies. Yet patterns of technological interdependence are more complex than the statistics of geographical inequality would suggest.

First of all, basic research, the ultimate source of knowledge, is located, in overwhelming proportion, in research universities and in the public research system around the world (such as Germany's Max Planck; France's CNRS; Russia's Academy of Sciences; China's Academia Sinica, and in the US, institutions such as the National Institute of Health, major hospitals, and research programs sponsored by institutions such as the National Science Foundation, and the Defense Department's DARPA). This means that, with the important exception of military-related research, the basic research system is open and accessible. Indeed, in the US, in the 1990s, over 50 percent of PhD degrees in science and engineering were conferred upon foreign nationals. About 47 percent of these foreign PhD holders ended up staying in the US, but this is a matter of the inability of their countries of origin to attract them, rather than an indication of the closed nature of the science system (thus, 88 percent of PhD students from China and 79 percent from India stayed in the US, but only 13 percent from Japan and 11 percent from South Korea).[91] Furthermore, the academic

89   Freeman (1982); Dosi et al. (1988b); Foray and Freeman (1992); World Bank (1998).
90   Sachs (1999); UNDP (1999).
91   Saxenian (1999).

research system is global. It relies on relentless communication between scientists around the world. The scientific community has always been to a large extent an international, if not global, community of scholars, in the West since the times of European scholasticism. Science is organized in specific fields of research, structured around networks of researchers who interact through publications, conferences, seminars, and academic associations. But, in addition, contemporary science is characterized by on-line communication as a permanent feature of its endeavor. Indeed, the Internet was born from the perverse coupling of the military and "big science," and its development until the early 1980s was, by and large, confined to networks of scientific communication. With the spread of the Internet in the 1990s, and the acceleration of the speed and scope of scientific discovery, the Internet and electronic mail have contributed to the formation of a global scientific system. In this scientific community there is certainly a bias in favor of dominant countries and institutions, as English is the international language, and US and Western European science institutions overwhelmingly dominate access to publications, research funds, and prestigious appointments. However, within these limits, there is a global network of science, which, albeit asymmetrical, ensures communication, and diffusion of findings and knowledge. Indeed, those academic systems, such as the Soviet Union, which forbade communication in some fields of research (e.g. information technology) paid the heavy penalty of insurmountable retardation. Scientific research in our time is either global or ceases to be scientific. Yet, while science is global, the practice of science is skewed toward issues defined by advanced countries, as Jeffrey Sachs has pointed out.[92] Most research findings end up diffusing throughout planetary networks of scientific interaction, but there is a fundamental asymmetry in the kind of issues taken up by research. Problems which are critical for developing countries, but offer little general, scientific interest, or do not have a promising, solvent market, are neglected in research programs of dominant countries. For instance, an effective malaria vaccine could save the lives of tens of millions of people, particularly children, but there have been few resources dedicated to a sustained effort toward finding it, or to diffuse worldwide the results of promising treatments, usually sponsored by the World Health Organization. AIDS medicines developed in the West are too expensive to be used in Africa, while about 95 percent of HIV cases are in the developing world. The business strategies of multinational pharmaceutical companies have repeatedly blocked attempts to produce some of these drugs cheaply, or

92   Sachs (1999).

to find alternative drugs, as they control the patents on which most research is based. Therefore, science is global, but it also reproduces in its internal dynamics the process of exclusion of a significant proportion of people, by not treating their specific problems, or by not treating them in terms which could yield results leading to improvement in their living conditions.

Economic development and competitive performance are not predicated on basic research, but on the connection between basic and applied research (the R&D system), and their diffusion throughout organizations and individuals. Advanced academic research and a good educational system are necessary but not sufficient conditions for countries, firms, and individuals to enter the informational paradigm. Thus, the selective globalization of science does not spur globalization of technology. Global technological development needs the connection between science, technology, and the business sector, as well as with national and international policies.[93] Mechanisms of diffusion do exist, albeit with their own biases and constraints. Multinational corporations and their production networks are, at the same time, instruments of technological domination, and channels of selective technological diffusion.[94] Multinational corporations account for the overwhelming majority of non-public R&D, and they use this knowledge as a key asset for competition, market penetration, and government support. On the other hand, because of the increasing cost, and strategic importance, of R&D, corporations engage in cooperative research efforts with other corporations, with universities, and with public research institutions (e.g. hospitals in bio-medical research) around the world. So doing, they contribute to create, and shape, a horizontal network of R&D that permeates sectors and countries. Furthermore, for transborder production networks to operate efficiently, multinational corporations must share some of their know-how with their partners, enabling small and medium businesses to improve their own technology, and, in the last analysis, their capacity to develop a learning curve.[95] There is some evidence of the positive impact of the presence of foreign affiliates of multinational corporations in the production system of OECD countries on the technological advancement and productivity of these countries.[96] After surveying studies on this matter, Held and colleagues concluded that "Although systematic evidence is lacking, research suggests that over time the globalization of production involves a progressive decoupling of national economic performance

93 Foray (1999).
94 Archibugi and Michie (1997).
95 Geroski (1995); Tuomi (1999).
96 OECD (1994d).

from that of home-based MNCs. Further, this process appears to be pronounced for high-technology industries, where the profits from innovation might be expected to be highest."[97] This would imply that national policies supporting high-technology development in the most advanced countries do not necessarily succeed in securing comparative advantage for the country. On the other hand, for developing, and newly industrializing countries, national policies are necessary to enable local labor and local firms to enter into cooperation with transnational production networks and to compete in the world market. This was indeed the case for Asian newly industrializing countries, where governments' technology policies were a decisive developmental tool (volume III, chapter 4). The World Bank's 1998 *World Development Report* concluded that, under conditions of an improving technological infrastructure and education system, a process of global diffusion of technology could be observed in the 1990s, although within the limits of a highly selective pattern of inclusion/exclusion, as I will analyze below.

Once the technological connection is assured, the process of technology generation and diffusion becomes organized around transnational production networks, largely independent of government policy. However, the role of governments remains essential in providing the human resources (that is, education at all levels), and technological infrastructure (particularly, accessible, low-cost, high-quality communication and information systems).

To understand how and why technology diffuses in the global economy it is important to consider the character of new, information-based technologies. Because they are essentially based in knowledge stored/developed in human minds, they have extraordinary potential for diffusion beyond their source, provided that they find the technological infrastructure, organizational environment, and human resources to be assimilated and developed through the process of learning by doing.[98] These are quite demanding conditions. However, they do not preclude catch-up processes for latecomers, if these "latecomers" quickly develop the proper environment. This is exactly what happened in the 1960s and 1970s in Japan, in the 1980s in the Asian Pacific, and, to a lesser extent, in the 1990s in Brazil and Chile. But the global experience of the 1990s suggests a different path of technological development. As soon as firms and individuals around the world accessed the new technological system (be it by technology transfer or endogenous adoption of technological know-how), they hooked up

97   Held et al. (1999: 281).
98   Mowery and Rosenberg (1998).

with producers and markets where they could use their knowledge and market their products. Their projection went beyond their national base, thus reinforcing the multinational corporations-based production networks, while, at the same time, these firms and individuals learned through their connections with these networks, and developed their own competitive strategies. So, there has been, at the same time, a process of concentration of technological know-how in transnational production networks, and a much broader diffusion of this know-how around the world, as the geography of trans-border production networks becomes increasingly complex.

I will illustrate this analysis with developments in Silicon Valley in the late 1990s. Seizing new opportunities of innovation spurred by the Internet revolution, Silicon Valley increased its technological leadership in information technology *vis-à-vis* the rest of the world. But Silicon Valley in 2000 is, socially and ethnically, a totally different Silicon Valley from what it was in the 1970s. Anna Lee Saxenian, the leading analyst of Silicon Valley, has shown, in her 1999 study the decisive role of immigrant entrepreneurs in the new make-up of this high-tech node. According to Saxenian:

> Recent research suggests that the "brain drain" may be giving way to a process of "brain circulation," as talented immigrants who study and work in the US return to their home countries to take advantage of promising opportunities there. And advances in transportation and communication technologies mean that even when these skilled immigrants choose not to return home, they still play a critical role as middlemen linking businesses in the United States to those in geographically distant regions.[99]

Saxenian's study shows that as early as 1990, 30 percent of the high-technology work force in Silicon Valley was foreign-born, mainly concentrated in professional occupations. As a new wave of innovation took place in the second half of the 1990s, thousands of new information technology companies were created, many of them by foreign entrepreneurs. Chinese and Indian executives were running at least 25 percent of companies started in Silicon Valley between 1980 and 1998, and 29 percent of companies started between 1995 and 1998. These high-technology networks of ethnic entrepreneurs work both ways:

> As Silicon Valley's skilled Chinese and Indian immigrants create social and economic links to their home countries, they simultaneously open the markets, manufacturing and technical skills in growing regions of

99 Saxenian (1999: 3).

Asia to the broader business community in California. Firms now increasingly turn to India for software programming talent. Meanwhile, California's complex of technology-related sectors increasingly relies on Taiwan's speedy and flexible infrastructure for manufacturing semiconductors and PCs, as well as their fast-growing markets for advanced technology components.[100]

The California connection is not limited to Asia. Two of Saxenian's students have shown a similarly powerful connection between Silicon Valley and the booming Israeli software industry, and a significant, if still small, presence of Mexican engineers in Silicon Valley.[101] Thus, Silicon Valley expanded on the basis of the technological and business networks it spun around the world. In return, the firms created around these networks attracted talent from everywhere (but primarily from India and China – in just proportion of the world population), who ultimately transformed Silicon Valley itself, and furthered the technology connection with their countries of origin. Granted, Silicon Valley is a very special case because of its pre-eminence in information technology innovation. Yet, it is likely that studies in other high-technology regions around the world will show a similar mechanism, as networks reinforce themselves, cutting across national borders, and attracting embodied know-how, which is the most significant process of technology transfer and innovation in the Information Age.

In sum, while there is still a concentration of the stock of science and technology in a few countries, and regions, the flows of technological know-how increasingly diffuse around the world, albeit in a highly selective pattern. They are concentrated in decentralized, multidirectional production networks, which link up with university and research resources around the world. This pattern of technology generation and technology transfer contributes decisively to globalization, as it closely mirrors the structure and dynamics of transnational production networks, adding new nodes to these networks. The uneven development of science and technology de-localizes the logic of informational production from its country basis, and shifts it to multilocational, global networks.[102]

---

100   Saxenian (1999: 71).
101   Alarcon (1998); Adler (1999).
102   The analysis of global networks of innovative milieux, as exemplified by Silicon Valley, was pioneered by the late Richard Gordon; see Gordon (1994). For a collective discussion of Gordon's important intellectual insights, see the special issue "Competition and Change" of the *Journal of Global Political Economy* (May, 1998).

Global labor?

If labor is the decisive production factor in the informational economy, and if production and distribution are increasingly organized on a global basis, it would seem that we should witness a parallel process of globalization of labor. However, matters are far more complicated. For reasons of coherence in the structure of this volume, I will deal extensively with this issue in chapter 4, when analyzing the transformation of work and employment in the network society. None the less, to complete the overview of the main components of globalization, I will anticipate the main conclusions here, taking the liberty of referring the reader to the relevant section in chapter 4.

There is, increasingly, a process of globalization of specialty labor. That is, not only highly skilled labor, but labor which becomes in exceptionally high demand around the world and, therefore, will not follow the usual rules in terms of immigration laws, wages, or working conditions. This is the case for high-level professional labor: top business managers, financial analysts, advanced services consultants, scientists and engineers, computer programmers, biotechnologists, and the like. But it is also the case for artists, designers, performers, sports stars, spiritual gurus, political consultants, and professional criminals. Anyone with the capacity to generate exceptional value added in any market enjoys the chance to shop around the globe – and to be shopped around, as well. This fraction of specialty labor does not add up to tens of millions of people, but it is decisive for the performance of business networks, of media networks, and of political networks, so that, overall, the market for most valuable labor is indeed becoming globalized.

On the other hand, for the huddled masses of the world, for those without exceptional skills, but with the stamina, or the desperation, to improve their living conditions, and to fight for their children's future, the record is mixed. By the end of the twentieth century an estimated 130–145 million people were living outside their countries, up from 84 million in 1975. Since these figures refer to legally recorded migration, the high number of undocumented immigrants would probably add many millions. Still, the total number of immigrants amounts to only a small fraction of the global labor force. A significant proportion of these migrants were in Africa and in the Middle East (some calculations put it at about 40 million migrants in 1993). In the 1990s there was a substantial increase of immigration in the United States, in Canada, in Australia, and, to a lesser extent, in Western Europe. There were also hundreds of thousands of new immigrants in countries which had little immigration until recently, as in the case of Japan.[103] A substantial proportion of this immigration is undocumented. However, the level of immigration in most Western countries does not exceed historical levels, in proportion to the native population. Thus, it seems that, together with increasing flows of immigration, what is really happening, and triggering xenophobic reactions, is the transformation of the ethnic make-up of Western societies. This is particularly the case in Western Europe, where many of the so-called immigrants were in fact born in their country of "immigration," but were being kept, in the late 1990s, as second-class citizens by barriers to naturalization: the situation of Turks in Germany, and of Koreans in Japan are examples of the use of the "immigrant" label as a code word for discriminated minorities. This trend toward multi-ethnicity in both North America and Western Europe will accelerate in the twenty-first century as a result of the lower birth rate of the native population, and as new waves of immigration are triggered by the growing imbalance between rich and poor countries.

A significant proportion of international migration is the result of wars and catastrophes, which displaced about 24 million refugees in the 1990s, particularly in Africa. While this trend is not necessarily related to globalization of labor, it does move millions of people around the world, in the wake of the globalization of human misery. Thus, as the 1999 United Nations *Human Development Report* states, "the global labour market is increasingly integrated for the highly skilled – corporate executives, scientists, entertainers, and the many others who form the global professional elite – with high mobility and wages. But the market for unskilled labour is highly restricted by national barriers."[104] While capital is global, and core production networks are increasingly globalized, the bulk of labor is local. Only an elite specialty labor force, of great strategic importance, is truly globalized.

However, beyond the actual movements of people across borders, there is a growing interconnection between workers in the country where they work, and the rest of the world, through global flows of production, money (remittances), information, and culture. The establishment of global production networks affects workers around the world. Migrants send their money home. Lucky entrepreneurs in their country of immigration often become middlemen between their country of origin and their country of residence. Networks of family, friends, and acquaintances grow over time, and advanced communication and transportation systems allow millions to live in-between countries.

103   Campbell (1994); Stalker (1994, 1997); Massey et al. (1999); UNDP (1999).
104   UNDP (1999: 2).

Thus, the study of "transnationalism from below," in the terminology of the leading researchers in this area, Michael P. Smith and Luis E. Guarnizo,[105] reveals a global networking of labor that goes beyond the simplistic notion of a global labor force – which, in strict analytical sense, does not exist. In sum, while most labor is not globalized, throughout the world, there is increasing migration, increasing multiethnicity in most developed societies, increasing international population displacement, and the emergence of a multilayered set of connections between millions of people across borders and across cultures.

The geometry of the global economy: segments and networks

An additional qualification is essential in defining the contours of the global economy: it is not a planetary economy, albeit it has a planetary reach. In other words, the global economy does not embrace all economic processes in the planet, it does not include all territories, and it does not include all people in its workings, although it does affect directly or indirectly the livelihood of all humankind. While its effects reach out to the whole planet, its actual operation and structure concern only segments of economic sectors, countries, and regions, in proportions that vary according to the particular position of a sector, country, or region in the international division of labor.

In the midst of a substantial expansion of international trade, the share of less-developed countries in the value of world exports fell from 31.1 percent in 1950 to 21.2 percent in 1990. While the share of OECD countries in world exports of goods and services declined between the 1970s and 1996, it still counted for over two-thirds of total exports in the late 1990s (see figure 2.7). Most international trade takes place within the OECD area. Foreign direct investment follows a similar pattern. While the share of OECD countries over total FDI is significantly lower than in the 1970s, it still accounts for almost 60 percent. In 1997, FDI reached $400 billion, a seven-fold increase over the level of 1970, but 58 percent went to advanced industrial economies, 37 percent to developing countries, and 5 percent to the transition economies of Eastern Europe. Furthermore, FDI in developing countries, while rising substantially in the 1990s, is heavily concentrated in a few markets: 80 percent went to 20 countries, with the lion's share belonging to China, and, far behind, Brazil and Mexico. A similar pattern of selective globalization emerges in financial markets.

105   Smith and Guarnizo (1998).

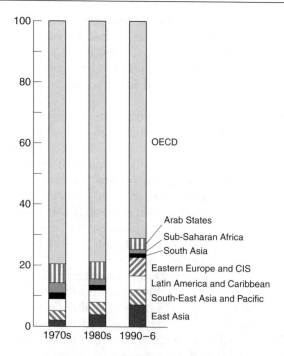

Figure 2.7 Export shares (percentage of total exports of goods and services)
Source: Data from World Bank (1999) elaborated by UNDP (1999)

In 1996, 94 percent of the portfolio and other short-term capital flow to developing countries and transitional economies went to just 20 countries. Only 25 developing countries have access to private markets for bonds, commercial bank loans, and equity. In spite of all the talk about emergent markets in global finance, in 1998 they only accounted for 7 percent of total market capitalization value, while representing 85 percent of the world's population.[106] As for production, in 1988, OECD countries, together with the four Asian tigers, accounted for 72.8 percent of world manufactures, a proportion that declined only slightly in the 1990s. The concentration is even greater in high-value production: in 1990, the G-7 countries accounted for 90 percent of high-technology manufacturing, and were holding 80.4 percent of global computing power.[107] Data collected by UNESCO in 1990 indi-

106 Data are from UNDP (1999); see also Sengenberger and Campbell (1994); Hoogvelt (1997); Duarte (1998); PNUD (1998a, b); UNISDR (1998); World Bank (1998); Dupas (1999).
107 CEPII (1992).

cated that scientific and technical manpower resources, in proportion to the population, were 15 times higher in North America than the average level for developing countries. R&D expenditures in North America represented over 42 percent of the world's total, while expenditures in Latin America and Africa together amounted to less than 1 percent of the same total.[108]

In sum, the global economy is characterized by a fundamental asymmetry between countries, in terms of their level of integration, competitive potential, and share of benefits from economic growth. This differentiation extends to regions within each country, as shown by Allen Scott in his investigation of new patterns of uneven regional development.[109] The consequence of this concentration of resources, dynamism, and wealth in certain territories is the increasing segmentation of the world population, following the segmentation of the global economy, and ultimately leading to global trends of increasing inequality and social exclusion.

This pattern of segmentation is characterized by a double movement: on the one hand, valuable segments of territories and people are linked in the global networks of value making and wealth appropriation. On the other hand, everything, and everyone, which does not have value, according to what is valued in the networks, or ceases to have value, is switched off the networks, and ultimately discarded. Positions in the networks can be transformed over time, by revaluation or devaluation. This places countries, regions, and populations constantly on the move, which is tantamount to structurally induced instability. For instance, in the late 1980s and throughout the 1990s, the dynamic centers of developing Asian economies, such as Thailand, the Philippines, and Indonesia, were connected to multinational production/trade networks, and global financial markets. The financial crisis of 1997–8 destroyed much of the newly acquired wealth of these countries. By the end of 1999, the Asian economies seemed to be on their path to recovery. But a substantial part of manufacturing, of the property market, and of the banking industry of these countries, and a large proportion of formal employment, had been wiped out by the crisis. Poverty and unemployment sky-rocketed. In Indonesia a process of de-industrialization, and de-urbanization took place, as millions of people returned to the countryside, looking for survival (see volume III, chapter 4). The fall-out of the Asian crisis, of the Mexican crisis, of the Brazilian crisis, of the Russian crisis, shows the destructive power of volatility in the global economy. The new economic

---

108   US National Science Board (1991).
109   Scott (1998).

system is at the same time highly dynamic, highly selective, highly exclusionary, and highly unstable in its boundaries. Powered by new communication and information technologies, networks of capital, production, and trade are able to identify sources of value making anywhere in the world, and link them up. However, while dominant segments of all national economies are linked into the global web, segments of countries, regions, economic sectors, and local societies are disconnected from the processes of accumulation and consumption that characterize the informational, global economy. I do not pretend that these "marginal" sectors are not socially connected to the rest of the system, since there is no such thing as a social vacuum. But their social and economic logic is based upon mechanisms clearly distinct from those of the informational economy. While the informational economy shapes the entire planet, and in this sense it is indeed global, most people in the planet do not work for or buy from the informational, global economy. Yet all economic and social processes do relate to the structurally dominant logic of such an economy. How and why such a connection is operated, and who and what is connected and disconnected over time, are fundamental features of our societies which require specific, careful analysis (see volume III, chapter 2).

The political economy of globalization: capitalist restructuring, information technology, and state policies

A global economy, in the precise sense defined in this chapter, emerged in the last years of the twentieth century.[110] It resulted from the restructuring of firms and financial markets in the wake of the 1970s' crisis. It expanded by using new information and communication technologies. It was made possible, and by and large induced, by deliberate government policies. The global economy was not created by markets, but by the interaction between markets and governments and international financial institutions acting on behalf of markets – or of their notion of what markets ought to be.

Business strategies to increase productivity, and to enhance profitability, included the search for new markets, and the internationalization of production. New, high-technology manufacturing industries were, from the outset, characterized by their international division of

---

110   For an empirical account of the process of globalization in different areas of the world during the 1980s and early 1990s, I refer the reader to the first edition of this volume, *The Rise of the Network Society* (1996), chapter 2, section on "The Newest International Division of Labor", pp. 106–50. This section has been deleted in the current edition in order to sharpen the analytical focus of this chapter.

labor (see chapter 6). The stepped-up presence of American multinational corporations in Europe and Asia set up a new trend of multilocational production, which contributed to the expansion of international trade. In the 1980s, this strategy was followed by European and Japanese multinationals as well, establishing a web of transnational production networks. Firms from Japan, and from the newly industrializing countries in the Asian Pacific, based their hypergrowth on exports to the US and, to a lesser extent, European markets (see volume III, chapter 4). So doing, they contributed to stimulating competition in international trade, when both the US and the European Community took measures to respond to the Pacific challenge to their previously uncontested economic hegemony. The European Community extended its membership to southern and northern Europe, and accelerated its process of economic integration to expand its internal market, while presenting a united customs front *vis-à-vis* Japanese and American competitors. The US, building on its superior technology and business flexibility, increased its pressures for trade liberalization and open markets, while keeping, as a bargaining chip, its own protectionist barriers.

Capital markets increased their global circulation on the basis of the eurodollars market, largely created to allow US multinationals to lend and borrow outside the US, circumventing American regulations. Financial flows substantially expanded in the 1970s to recycle the petrodollars from OPEC countries and oil companies. Since in the 1970s most OECD economies were in a downturn, a substantial share of loans went to developing countries, often without proper lending controls, thus prompting, at the same time, the global expansion of financial markets, and the debt crisis that strangled economies in Latin America and Africa during the 1980s. The subsequent restructuring of financial markets around the world, led to an explosion of cross-border financial flows, global investments of financial institutions, and to a fully fledged internationalization of banking activity, as documented above. In 1985, the World Bank, failing to attract private investment in "Third World markets," coined a new term: "emerging markets." It signaled a new era of financial integration around the planet, as investors from everywhere sought opportunities of high return, discounting the high risk in the hope of government support in case of crisis for banks and currencies. The seeds of the 1990s' financial crises in Mexico, Asia, Russia, Brazil, and beyond were planted.

Fully fledged economic globalization could proceed only on the basis of new information and communication technologies. Advanced computer systems allowed new, powerful mathematical models to manage complex financial products, and to perform transactions at high speed. Sophisticated telecommunication systems linked up in real time financial centers around the globe. On-line management allowed firms to operate across the country, and across the world. Micro-electronics-based production made possible standardization of components, and customization of the final product in high volume, flexible production, organized in an international assembly line. Transnational production networks of goods and services relied on an interactive system of communication, and transmission of information to ensure feedback loops, and to set up coordination of decentralized production and distribution. Information technology was crucial to operate a world wide web of fast, high-capacity transportation of goods and people, established by air transportation, trans-oceanic shipping lines, railways, and highways. Multi-modal container cargo was made efficient by information systems that would track and program merchandise and routing, as well as by automated systems of loading/unloading. A vast system of airlines and high-speed trains, airport VIP lounges and business services, supported firms in hubs around the world; Internet-equipped international hotels, and cosmopolitan entertainment, provided the infrastructure for managerial mobility. And, in the late 1990s, the Internet became the technological backbone of the new type of global business firm, the network enterprise (see chapter 3).

Yet, neither technology nor business could have developed the global economy on its own. The decisive agents in setting up a new, global economy were governments, and, particularly, the governments of the wealthiest countries, the G-7, and their ancillary international institutions, the International Monetary Fund, the World Bank, and the World Trade Organization. Three interrelated policies created the foundations for globalization: deregulation of domestic economic activity (starting with financial markets); liberalization of international trade and investment; and privatization of publicly controlled com-panies (often sold to foreign investors). These policies began in the United States in the mid-1970s, and in Britain in the early 1980s, spread throughout the European Union in the 1980s, and became the dominant policy in most countries in the world, and the common standard in the international economic system, in the 1990s.[111]

How and why it happened is a matter for historians. Yet, a few remarks on the genesis of the global economy could help to understand its contours in the twenty-first century. Although some important measures were adopted in the 1970s (for example, in the US cross-border capital controls were abolished, for all practical purposes,

111 See Hutton (1995); Zaldivar (1995); Estefania (1996); Hill (1996); Hoogvelt (1997); Yergin and Stanislaw (1998); UNDP (1999).

in 1974), there were two distinctive periods of government-led globalization. To simplify, I will differentiate between the 1980s and the 1990s. In the 1980s, the simultaneous arrival to power of staunch conservative, ideological free-marketeers in the United States (Reagan, elected in 1980) and in the UK (Thatcher, elected in 1979) signaled a turning point. In the US it was not unexpected. In my analysis of the impact of the 1970s' economic crisis on American policy, published in 1976,[112] I proposed as one likely alternative the development of supply-side economics, and I gave it a name, for the purpose of illustration: the Reagan policy. Both administrations pushed hard for deregulation and liberalization of finance and investment, and, in Britain, for privatization of publicly owned companies, setting the precedent for the rest of the world. The most immediate impact was felt in financial trade. In the US, the options market established in Chicago in 1972 expanded rapidly, and ultimately developed into a multiproduct derivatives market. Britain abolished exchange controls in 1980, and the second financial futures exchange market, after Chicago, was established in London in 1982. France followed, setting up its own futures exchange, MATIF, in 1986. Germany remained more cautious about financial deregulation, although cross-border capital controls were eliminated in 1981. The Asian financial markets, particularly Hong Kong and Singapore, took advantage of their loosely regulated environment to attract financial transactions, winning market shares over a more regulated Tokyo stock-exchange market. The full deregulation of financial markets in the City of London in October 1987 opened a new era of financial globalization, in spite (or because?) of the simultaneous October 1987 crash in the New York stock exchange. Yet, the first round of supply-side economic policies did not work entirely to the expectations of their ideologues in the US and Britain because of a basic, internal contradiction in their position: they were, at the same time, nationalists and globalizers. In principle, these two positions are not contradictory under the condition of imperialist policies – and, indeed, that was the case of Victorian England which is often presented as an historical example of earlier globalization. But this time the conditions were different: in a multi-centered international economy operated by transnational production networks, and with people in core societies reluctant to die for the glory of their governments, the contradiction became insurmountable, as the leading political figures, Reagan and Thatcher, came to realize. Vowing to reduce the budget deficit, Reagan actually created the largest federal deficit in peacetime history, as a result of his commitment to a huge

112   Castells (1976).

military build-up, while cutting taxes for the rich. Open to international markets but not to Europe, Thatcher was faced with the choice of adopting the European version of globalization – that is, a unified European economy with a single currency – or retreating to fortress Britain without the power to impose its will on the world. She was never given the chance to make the choice (although she was clearly leaning toward isolationism). Her own party, convinced of the historical necessity of the European Union, and fed up with the Iron Lady, forced her into early retirement in 1990. Furthermore, both in the US and in the UK, the conservative obsession with rolling back the welfare state was met with fierce social and political resistance, as well as with the realities of historical inertia, and the basic needs of society. Thus, while Reagan succeeded in taking away breakfast from thousands of children, and Thatcher jeopardized the traditional quality of the British university system, overall, the bulk of the welfare state remained in place, albeit limited in its expansion. However, both the British and the US economy turned around in terms of profitability and productivity, and international trade, investment, and finance expanded dramatically as firms took advantage of new opportunities offered by the disarray of organized labor, and by deregulation of business activity.

On the European mainland, a political watershed was the misadventure of the first Mitterrand socialist administration, elected in 1981. Ignorant of elementary economics, Mitterrand the politician thought that he could reduce working time, increase wages and social benefits, and tax companies, in a quasi-integrated European economy, without suffering the backlash of currency markets. His government was forced to devalue the franc, and two years later it made a complete u-turn in economic policies, modeling itself on the example of German monetary stability. This French affair heavily influenced the cautious economic policy of the new Spanish socialist government, elected in October 1982, which opted for deregulation, and controlled liberalization, thus moving toward the middle ground of new economic policy. Indeed, Felipe Gonzalez and Helmut Kohl became strong allies in the building of a unified Europe around the principles of a liberal economy – tempered with compassion and a social market economy. Slowly but surely this middle ground (which later Giddens would theorize as "the third way") won over most of European public opinion, and governments. By the turn of the century, 13 of the 15 countries of the European Union were governed by social democratic governments which, with different ideological labels, were supportive of this pragmatic strategy.[113]

113   Giddens (1998).

Yet, it was in the 1990s that the institutions and rules of globalization were set up, and expanded throughout the planet. Indeed, as Ankie
Hoogvelt writes, "the sceptics in the globalization debate make rather
much of the continuing, indeed in some cases apparently enhanced,
exercise of sovereignty and regulation by national governments. And
yet, much of this regulation amounts in effect to no more than regulation for globalization."[114]

The mechanism to bring in the globalization process to most countries in the world was simple: political pressure either through direct
government action or through imposition by the IMF/World Bank/
World Trade Organization. Only after economies were liberalized
would global capital flow in. The Clinton administration was in fact
the true political globalizer, particularly under the leadership of Robert
Rubin, former chairman of Goldman & Sachs, and a Wall Street hand.
To be sure, Clinton built on the foundations provided by Reagan, but
he took the whole project much further, making the opening of markets for goods, services, and capital a paramount priority in his administration. In a remarkable report, *The New York Times* documented
in 1999 the all-out effort of the Clinton team in this direction, putting
direct pressure on governments around the world, and instructing the
IMF to pursue this strategy in the strictest possible terms.[115] The goal
was the unification of all economies around a set of homogeneous
rules of the game, so that capital, goods, and services could flow in
and out, as determined by the judgment of the markets. As in the best
of Smithian worlds, everybody would end up benefiting from it, so
that global capitalism, powered by information technology, would become the magic formula, ultimately uniting prosperity, democracy and,
down the line, a reasonable level of inequality, and reduced poverty.

The success of this strategy around the world can be predicated on
its starting-point: economic crises were pervasive in many areas. In
most Latin American and African countries the first round of the globalization of finance in the 1980s had devastated economies by imposing austerity policies to service the debt. Russia and Eastern Europe
had just begun an arduous transition to the market economy, which
meant, by and large, their economic collapse at the outset.[116] Later on,
the Asian crisis of 1997–8 turned the Pacific economies upside down –
often undermining their developmental states. In most cases, after such
crises, the IMF and the World Bank came to the rescue, but on the
condition that governments would accept the IMF's prescriptions for

114 Hoogvelt (1997: 131).
115 Kristoff and Sanger (1999).
116 Castells and Kiselyova (1998).

economic health. These policy recommendations (in fact, impositions) were based on pre-packaged adjustment policies, astonishingly similar to each other, whatever each country's specific conditions; they were, in fact, mass produced by orthodox neoclassical economists, mainly from the University of Chicago, Harvard, and MIT. By the end of the 1990s, the IMF was operating and advising adjustment policies in over 80 countries around the world. Even the large economies of very important countries, such as Russia, Mexico, Indonesia, or Brazil, were dependent on the IMF's approval for their policies. Most of the developing world, as well as the transition economies, became an economic protectorate under the IMF – which ultimately meant the US Treasury Department. The power of the IMF was not so much financial as symbolic. The IMF's help was often in the form of virtual money; that is, a line of credit on which governments could draw in case of financial emergency. Credit given by the IMF meant credibility for global financial investors. And withdrawal of the IMF's confidence meant, for a given country, becoming a financial pariah. Such was the logic: if a country decided to stay out of the system (for example, Alan Garcia's Peru in the 1980s) it was punished with financial ostracism – and it collapsed, so verifying the IMF's self-fulfilling prophecy. So, few countries dared to resist this conditional "welcome to the club," in contrast to the alternative of isolation from global flows of capital, technology, and trade.

A similar logic in international trade was implemented through the World Trade Organization, established in 1994. For countries opting for an outward development strategy, such as the continental economies of China and India, access to affluent markets was essential. But to obtain this access, they had to adhere to the rules of international trade. Adherence to the rules meant, by and large, gradually dismantling protection for industries that were uncompetitive because of their late coming into international competition. But rejection of the rules was sanctioned with stiff tariffs in affluent markets, thus shutting off the chance of development by winning market shares in the markets where wealth is concentrated. Thus, the UNDP's 1999 report states:

> Ever-growing numbers of developing countries adopted an open trade approach, shifting away from import substitution policies. By 1997 India had reduced its tariffs from an average of 82% in 1990 to 30%, Brazil from 25% in 1991 to 12%, and China from 43% in 1992 to 18%. Driven by technocrats, the changes were strongly supported by International Monetary Fund and World Bank financing as part of comprehensive economic reform and liberalization packages. Conditions of membership in the WTO and the OECD were important incentives. Country after country undertook deep unilateral liberalization, not just

in trade but in foreign direct investment. In 1991, for example, 35 countries introduced changes in 82 regulatory regimes, in 80 of them moving to liberalize or promote foreign direct investment. In 1995 the pace accelerated, with even more countries – 65 – changing regimes, most continuing the trend of liberalization.[117]

In November 1999, China reached a trade agreement with the United States, to liberalize its trade and investment regulations, thus opening the way for China's membership of the WTO, and bringing China closer to the rules of the global capitalist regime.

The more countries join the club, the more difficult it is for those outside the liberal economic regime to go their own way. So, in the last resort, locked-in trajectories of integration in the global economy, with its homogeneous rules, amplify the network, and the networking possibilities for its members, while increasing the cost of being outside the network. This self-expanding logic, induced and enacted by governments and international finance and trade institutions, ended up linking the dynamic segments of most countries in the world in an open, global economy.

Why did governments engage in this dramatic push for globalization, thus undermining their own sovereign power? If we reject dogmatic interpretations that would reduce governments to the role of being "the executive committee of the bourgeoisie," the matter is rather complex. It requires differentiating between four levels of explanation: the perceived strategic interests of a given nation-state; the ideological context; the political interests of the leadership; and the personal interests of people in office.

Concerning the interests of the state, the answer varies for each state. The answer is clear for the main globalizer, the US government: an open, integrated global economy works to the advantage of American firms, and American-based firms, thus of the American economy. This is because of the technological advantage, and superior managerial flexibility, that the US enjoys *vis-à-vis* the rest of the world. Together with the long-time presence of American multinationals around the world, and with American hegemonic presence in the international institutions of trade and finance, globalization is tantamount to increased economic prosperity for the US, although certainly not for all firms, and not for all people on American soil. This American economic interest is something that Clinton and his economic team, particularly Rubin, Summers, and Tyson, understood well. They worked hard to bring the liberal trade gospel to the world, applying US economic and political muscle when necessary.

117   UNDP (1999: 28).

For European governments, the Maastricht Treaty, committing them to economic convergence, and true unification by 1999, was their specific form of adopting globalization. It was perceived as the only way for each government to compete in a world increasingly dominated by American technology, Asian manufacturing, and global financial flows which had wiped out European monetary stability in 1992. Engaging global competition from the strength of the European Union appeared to be the only chance of saving European autonomy, while prospering in the new world. Japan adapted only reluctantly, but, forced by a serious, lasting recession, and a deep financial crisis, by the late 1990s introduced a series of reforms that would gradually open up the Japanese economy, and would align its financial rules on global standards (see volume III, chapter 4). China and India saw in the opening of world trade the opportunity to engage in a development process, and to build the technological and economic basis for renewed national power. The price to pay was a cautious opening to foreign trade and investment, thus linking their fate to global capitalism. For industrializing countries around the world, most of them with recent experience of economic crisis and hyperinflation, the new model of public policy held the promise of a new departure, and the significant incentive of support from major world powers. For the reformers who came to power in the transition economies in Eastern Europe, liberalization was tantamount to a definitive break with the communist past. And for many developing countries around the world, they did not even have to figure out their strategic interests: the IMF and the World Bank decided for them, as the price to repair their run down economies.

States' interests are always perceived within an ideological framework. And the framework of the 1990s was constituted around the collapse of statism, and the crisis of legitimacy suffered by welfarism and government control during the 1980s. Even in the Asian Pacific countries the developmental state suffered a crisis of legitimacy when it became an obstacle for democracy. Neo-liberal ideologues (called "neo-conservatives" in the US) came out of their closet around the world, and were joined in their crusade by new converts, striving to deny their Marxist past, from French *nouveaux philosophes* to brilliant Latin American novelists. When neo-liberalism, as the new ideology came to be known, spilled over its narrow-minded Reagan/Thatcher mold, to cast itself in a variety of expressions adapted to specific cultures, it quickly established a new ideological hegemony. In the early 1990s it came to constitute what Ignacio Ramonet labeled as *"la pensée unique"* ("the only thinking"). While the actual ideological debate was considerably richer, on the surface it did appear as if political establishments around the world had adopted a common intellectual ground: an intellectual current not necessarily inspired by Von Hayek and Fukuyama, but certainly tributary of Adam Smith and Stuart Mill. In this context, free markets were expected to operate economic and institutional miracles, particularly when coupled with the new technological wonders promised by futurologists.

The political interest of new leaders coming to government in the late 1980s and early 1990s favored the globalization option. By political interest, I mean to be elected to government, and to stay in it. In most instances, new leaders were elected as a result of a declining, or sometimes collapsing, economy, and they consolidated their power by substantially improving the country's economic performance. This was the case for Clinton in 1992 (or, at least, so said flawed economic statistics, to George Bush's dismay). His successful presidential campaign was built around the motto "It's the economy, stupid!", and the key strategy of Clinton's economic policy was for further deregulation and liberalization, domestically and internationally, as exemplified by the approval of NAFTA in 1993. While Clinton's policy cannot really be credited as the cause of the outstanding performance of the US economy in the 1990s, Clinton and his team helped the dynamism of the new economy by getting out of the way of private business, and by using US influence to open markets around the world.

Cardoso was unexpectedly elected president of Brazil in 1994, on the basis of his successful monetary stabilization Plan Real, which he implemented as Finance Minister, breaking the back of inflation for the first time ever. To keep inflation under control he had to integrate Brazil into the global economy, facilitating the competitiveness of Brazilian firms. This goal, in turn, required financial stabilization. Similar developments took place in Mexico, with Salinas and Zedillo, economic reformers within the PRI; with Menem in Argentina, reversing the traditional nationalism of his Peronist party; with Fujimori in Peru, out of nowhere; with the new democratic government in Chile; and, much earlier, with Rajiv Gandhi in India, with Deng Xiao Ping, and later Jiang Zemin and Zhu-Rongji in China, and with Felipe Gonzalez in Spain.

In Russia, Yeltsin and his endless succession of economic teams, played as their only card the integration of Russia into global capitalism, and they surrendered their economic sovereignty to the IMF, and to Western governments. In Western Europe, in the 1990s, the adjustment policies imposed by the Maastricht Treaty exhausted the political capital of incumbent governments, and opened the way for a new wave of economic reform. Blair in Britain, Romano Prodi and the Partito Democratico di Sinistra in Italy, and Schroeder in Germany, all betted on improving the economy, and fighting unemployment, by furthering liberal economic policies, tempered with innovative social policies. Jospin in France followed a pragmatic policy, without the ideological themes of liberalism, but with a *de facto* convergence with market-oriented European Union policies. The ironic twist of political history is that the reformers who enacted globalization, all over the world, came mostly from the left, breaking with their past as supporters of government control of the economy. It would be a mistake to consider this a proof of political opportunism. It was, rather, realism about new economic and technological developments, and a sense of the quickest way to take economies out of their relative stagnation.

Once the option for the liberalization/globalization of the economy was taken, political leaders were compelled to find the appropriate personnel to manage these post-Keynesian economic policies, often far removed from the traditional orientations of pro-government, left-wing policies. Thus, Felipe Gonzalez, coming to power in October 1982, in the midst of a grave economic and social crisis, appointed as Super-Minister of Economy one of the few socialists with personal entry into the conservative circles of Spanish high finance. The subsequent appointments of the appointee configured an entirely new class of neo-liberal technocrat throughout the Spanish socialist government, some of them recruited from IMF circles. In another example of this process, Brazil's President Cardoso, when faced by a monetary crisis running out of control in January 1999, fired two different presidents of Brazil's Central Bank in two weeks, and ended up appointing the Brazilian financier who used to manage the Soros hedge fund for Brazil, counting on his ability to deal with speculators in global financial markets. He in fact succeeded in calming down the financial turmoil, at least for a while. My argument is not that the financial world controls governments. It is in fact the contrary. For governments to manage economies in the new global context, they need personnel embodying the knowledge of daily survival in this brave new economic world. To do their job, these economic experts need additional personnel, who share similar skills, language, and values. Because they have the access codes to the management of the new economy, their power grows disproportionately to their actual political appeal. Therefore, they establish a symbiotic relationship with political leaders who come to power because of their appeal to voters. Together they work to improve their fate through their performance in global competition – in the hope that this will also benefit their shareholders, as citizens have come to be known.

There is a fourth layer of explanation concerning the fatal attraction of governments to economic globalization: the personal interests of people in positions of decision-making power. In general, this is

not, by any means, the most important factor in explaining government policies toward globalization. And it is a negligible factor in some
instances of high levels of government that I have been able to observe
personally – for instance, in the Brazilian presidency in 1994–9. Yet,
the personal vested interests of political leaders and/or their high-rank-
ing personnel in the globalization process have exercised considerable
influence in the speed and shape of globalization. These personal interests take, primarily, the form of increasing personal wealth obtained
by two main channels. The first consists of the financial rewards, and
lucrative appointments on leaving office, gained as a result of the network of contacts they have established and/or as appreciation of decisions which helped business deals. The second channel is, more
blatantly, corruption in its different forms: bribes, taking advantage
of insider knowledge on financial deals and real-estate acquisitions,
participation in business ventures in exchange for political favors, and
the like. Certainly, the personal business interests of political personnel (legal or illegal) are a very old story, probably a constant of politics
in recorded history. Yet, my argument here is more specific: it favors
pro-globalization policies because it opens up a whole new world of
opportunity. In many developing countries, it is in fact the only game
in town, since access to the country is the main asset controlled by the
political elites, enabling them to participate in the global networks of
wealth. For instance, the catastrophic management of the Russian economic transition cannot be understood without considering its over-
arching logic: the formation of a government-protected financial
oligarchy, which rewarded personally many of the leading Russian
liberal reformers (and decisively helped to re-elect Yeltsin in 1996), in
exchange for the privilege of being the intermediaries between the
Russian riches and global trade and investment – while the IMF was
blinding itself to the matter, and using Western taxpayers' money to
feed this liberal oligarchy with billions of dollars. Similar stories can
be documented throughout Asia, Africa, and Latin America. But they
are not absent either in North America and Western Europe. For instance, in 1999 a few weeks after the entire European Commission
was forced to resign by the European Parliament, under strong sus-
picion of petty wrong-doing, the still-acting Commissioner for Telecommunications, Mr Bangemann, was appointed by Spanish Telefonica
to a special consultant position in the company. While there were no
explicit accusations of corruption, European public opinion was
shocked to learn of the appointment of Mr Bangemann by a company
which had greatly benefited from the deregulation of European telecommunications accomplished under Bangemann's tenure. These examples simply illustrate an important analytical point: political

decisions cannot be understood in a personal and social vacuum. They are made by people who, besides representing governments, and holding political interests, have a personal interest in a process of globalization that has become an extraordinary source of potential wealth for the world's elites.

So, the global economy was politically constituted. Restructuring of business firms, and new information technologies, while being at the source of globalizing trends, could not have evolved, by themselves, toward a networked, global economy without policies of de-regulation, privatization, and liberalization of trade and investment. These policies were decided and enacted by governments around the world, and by international economic institutions. A political economy perspective is necessary to understand the triumph of markets over governments: governments themselves called for such a victory, in a historic death-wish. They did so to preserve/enhance the interests of their states, within the context of the emergence of a new economy, and in the new ideological environment that resulted from the collapse of statism, the crisis of welfarism, and the contradictions of the developmental state. In acting resolutely for globalization (sometimes hoping for a human face) political leaders also pursued their political interests, and often their personal interests, within various degrees of decency. Yet, the fact that the global economy was politically induced at its onset does not mean that it can be politically undone, in its main tenets. At least, not that easily. This is because the global economy is now a network of interconnected segments of economies, which play, together, a decisive role in the economy of each country – and of many people. Once such a network is constituted, any node that disconnects itself is simply bypassed, and resources (capital, information, technology, goods, services, skilled labor) continue to flow in the rest of the network. Any individual decoupling from the global economy implies a staggering cost: the devastation of the economy in the short term, and the closing of access to sources of growth. Thus, within the value system of productivism/consumerism, there is no individual alternative for countries, firms, or people. Barring a catastrophic meltdown of the financial market, or opting out by people following completely different values, the process of globalization is set, and it accelerates over time. Once the global economy has been constituted, it is a fundamental feature of the new economy.

The New Economy

The new economy emerged in a given time, the 1990s, a given space, the United States, and around/from specific industries, mainly information technology and finance, with biotechnology looming on the horizon.[118] It was in the late 1990s that the seeds of the information technology revolution, planted in the 1970s, seemed to come to fruition in a wave of new processes and new products, spurring productivity growth and stimulating economic competition. Each technological revolution has its own tempo for its diffusion in social and economic structures. For reasons that historians will determine, this particular technological revolution appeared to require about a quarter of a century to retool the world – a much shorter span than its predecessors.

Why the United States? It seems to have resulted from a combination of technological, economic, cultural, and institutional factors, all reinforcing each other. The US, and most specifically California, has been the birth place of most revolutionary breakthroughs in information technology, and the place where entire industries spun off from these innovations, as documented in chapter 1. Economically, the size of the US market, and its dominant position in global networks of capital and commodities around the world, provided breathing space for technologically innovative industries, allowing them quickly to find market opportunities, attract capital investment, and recruit talent from around the world. Culturally, entrepreneurialism, individualism, flexibility, and multi-ethnicity were key ingredients of both the new industries and the United States. Institutionally, capitalist restructuring, in the form of deregulation and liberalization of economic activities, took place earlier and faster in the US than in the rest of the world, facilitating capital mobility, diffusing innovation from the public research sector (for example, the Internet from the Department of Defense, biotechnology from public health institutes and non-profit hospitals), and breaking up key monopolies (for example, the divestiture of ATT in telecommunications in 1984).

The new economy took shape first in two key industries which not only innovated in products and processes, but applied these inventions to themselves, thus spurring growth and productivity, and, through competition, diffusing a new business model throughout much of the economy. These industries were (and will be for a long time) information technology and finance. In the United States, the information technology industries led the charge in the 1990s (see figure 2.8).[119] Between 1995 and 1998, the information technology sector, accounting for only about 8 percent of America's GDP, contributed,

118   Data presented in this section are from standard statistical sources, and have been published in the business press. Thus, they are in the public domain and I do not consider it necessary to provide detailed sources for each figure, except when the relevance of the figure requires it to be linked to a specific reference.

119   Mandel (1999a, b).

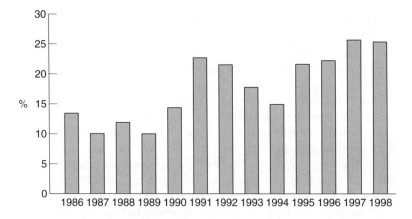

Figure 2.8 Share of growth from high-tech sector in the United States, 1986–1998 (figures are fourth quarter to fourth quarter, except for 1998. High-tech spending primarily includes business and consumer spending in information technology hardware and consumer spending in telephone service, adjusted for exports and imports of information technology equipment)
Source: Data from US Commerce Department elaborated by Mandel (1999b)

on average, 35 percent of GDP growth. Value added per worker in information technology-producing industries grew at an annual average of 10.4 percent in the 1990s, about five times the growth rate in the economy as a whole.[120] Projections from the Commerce Department[121] indicate that by 2006 almost 50 percent of the American labor force will be employed in industries which are either producers or big users of information technology.

At the heart of new information technology industries are, and will increasingly be in the twenty-first century, the Internet-related firms.[122] First, because of their potential dramatic influence on the way business is conducted. An often-cited projection by Forrester Research in 1998 put the expected value of electronic business transactions in 2003 at about $1.3 trillion, up from $43 billion in 1998. But, secondly, the Internet industry has also become a major force on its own ground because of its exponential growth in revenues, employment, and market capitalization value. In 1998–9 the Internet industry's revenue grew at an average rate of 68 percent, reaching by the end of 1999 a total

120 *The Economist* (1999a).
121 US Commerce Department (1999a).
122 Tapscott (1998).

revenue over $500 billion, well in excess of the revenue of major industries such as telecommunications ($300 billion) and airlines ($355 billion). Extrapolating the same rate of growth (a plausible hypothesis, unless there is a major financial crisis), the Internet-related industries in the US would generate in excess of $1.2 trillion in revenue in 2002. At that level they would reach the amount of revenue generated by the mammoth health-care industry, although still probably short of the revenue generated in the global criminal economy (see volume III, chapter 3) – a reminder that puts our model of progress into perspective.

A close-up of this Internet industry will help in specifying the contours of the new economy. In 1999 the US Internet-related industry could be classified in four layers, according to the useful typology proposed by the University of Texas–Austin's Center for Research in Electronic Commerce (CREC) in its on-line report of October 1999.[123] All data are for the first quarter of 1999, and annual growth rates are calculated over the first quarter of 1998. The first layer comprises companies which provide the Internet infrastructure; that is, telecommunications companies, Internet service providers, Internet backbone carriers, companies providing final access, and manufacturers of end-user networking equipment. Examples of companies in this layer are Compaq, Qwest, Corning, Mindspring (some of which may have been merged, or gone under, by the time you read this). This layer collected, in the quarter, $40 billion in revenue, and was growing annually at 50 percent in revenue, and 39 percent in employment. It posted the highest revenue per employee in the industry, at $61,136. The top ten companies accounted for 44 percent of the revenue.

The second layer is formed by firms developing the Internet infrastructure applications; that is, software products and services for web transactions. This layer also includes consulting and service companies designing, building, and maintaining web sites, including portals, e-commerce sites, and audio and video delivery sites. Among the companies in this layer are Oracle, Microsoft, Netscape, and Adobe (but remember this refers only to the Internet-related business of these companies, not to software in general). The quarterly revenue of this layer was about $20 billion, with an annual growth of 61 percent in revenue and 38 percent in employment. Total employment in 1999 was over 560,000 employees (although not all of them, in this case, were working on Internet-related business). Revenue per employee was at almost $40,000. The top ten companies in this layer were all among the largest software producing and consulting companies, and accounted for 43 percent of the layer's revenue.

123   CREC (1999a).

The third layer includes a new kind of company: companies which do not directly generate revenue from business transactions, but from advertising, membership fees, and commissions, in exchange for which they provide free services over the web. Some of these companies are web content providers, others are market intermediaries. They include media, brokerage firms, resellers, portals, and other intermediaries. Among these companies are some famous names, in spite of their short history: Yahoo!, E-Bay, and E*Trade. Although the smallest segment of the industry, at about $17 billion revenue, they were growing fast in 1999, at 52 percent in revenue and 25 percent in employment, and they were major employers, with over half a million employees in late 1999. Revenue per employee was the lowest in the industry, at $37,500, and the industry was less concentrated, with the top ten representing 23 percent of the revenue.

The fourth layer may represent the future of the Internet industry as viewed from 1999. These are companies conducting web-based economic transactions, such as Amazon, E-toys, Dell-Direct World, or The Street.com: their kind of trade is what is usually labeled as e-commerce. This segment grew in 1998–9 by 127 percent in revenue and by 78 percent in employment, with quarterly revenues of $37.5 billion. On the basis of the compounded growth rate, this projected to an annualized revenue of $170 billion in 1999. The greatest proportion of fourth layer revenue was still concentrated among computer companies. However, the top ten companies in the layer accounted for only 32 percent of revenue, in contrast to the more capital-intensive layers one and two. E-tailers, banks, and financial firms were entering this layer of the industry in large numbers.

As for the impact of the Internet industries on the economy as a whole, Internet-related jobs in the US increased from 1.6 million in the first quarter of 1998 to 2.3 million in the first quarter of 1999. E-commerce represented the fastest growing sector. The speed of development of the new industry was without precedent: one-third of the 3,400 companies surveyed in 1999 did not exist in 1996. These new companies added by themselves over 300,000 jobs. The proportion of Internet-derived revenues over total corporate revenues increased from 10 percent in 1998 to 14 percent in 1999. The growth of revenue in Internet industries in 1999 was projected to account for $200 billion – this in contrast to total growth in revenue in the US economy of about $340 billion.[124] By the turn of the century, the Internet economy, and the information technology industries, had become the core of the US economy – not only qualitatively but quantitatively.

124   CREC (1999b).

The stock market appeared to recognize this trend. Market capitalization value of Internet companies sky-rocketed. Thus, in 1999, the 294 companies doing the most business on the Internet had an average market capitalization value of $18 billion. That was 30 times the average market capitalization value for the 5,068 companies listed on Nasdaq, the high-technology stock market. In January 1999 a telling journalistic report compared the market capitalization value of some of these Internet-based companies with the value of some legendary names of the industrial era.[125] As an illustration of the argument presented here it is worthwhile to report some of these comparisons. Thus, America On-Line, employing 10,000 workers, and with earnings of $68 million in the fourth quarter of 1998, was valued at $66.4 billion, almost doubling the total value of General Motor's stock ($34.4 billion), in spite of the fact that General Motors employed 600,000 workers and could post quarterly earnings in excess of $800 million. Yahoo!, employing 673 people was valued at $33.9 billion, in spite of meager quarterly earnings of $16.7 million, in contrast to Boeing, employing 230,000 workers, with quarterly earnings of $347 million, yet only slightly more valued than Yahoo!, with a market capitalization of $35.8 billion. Just a mirage from a financial bubble? In fact, it is a more complex development. While many Internet stocks were (and are) wildly overvalued, and submitted to periodic stock market corrections, the overall trend in valuation seems to respond to a rational expectation of the new sources of economic growth. Furthermore, by so doing, investors attract attention to the potential of Internet companies, inducing new capital investment, both in venture capital and in stocks. As a result, the industry is flushed with cash, thus enjoying ample opportunity for innovation and entrepreneurship. Therefore, even if there would have been (and may still be) a bubble, it was (and it is) a productive one, spurring economic growth in the "real" Internet economy, before bursting, thus partly undoing the side-effects of its speculative spiral. Which leads me to the second major source of transformation of the economy: the finance industry itself.

The financial world was transformed in the 1990s by institutional change and technological innovation. For the sake of clarity I will distinguish several key developments which, in real life, are intertwined. The roots of the transformation of finance are to be found in the deregulation of the industry and the liberalization of domestic and international financial transactions throughout the 1980s and 1990s, first in the US and the UK, then, gradually, in most of the world.[126] The

---

125   Barboza (1999a).
126   Estefania (1996); Soros (1998); Friedmann (1999).

process culminated in November 1999 when President Clinton abolished the institutional barriers to consolidation between different segments of the finance industry legislated in the 1930s and 1940s to prevent the kind of financial crises that led to the Great Depression of 1929. From 2000 onwards, banks, securities firms, and insurance companies in the United States can operate jointly or even merge operations in a single financial firm. For a number of years, the proliferation of offshore banking and investment firms, for instance hedge funds, had already bypassed many of the financial constraints. And megamergers, such as the one between CitiCorp and Travelers, had made a mockery of regulations. Yet, by making official the hands-off policy of the federal regulator, the US signaled the freedom for private companies to manage money and securities in any way the market would bear, with no other limits than those established by the law and the courts relating to trade in general.

The finance industry took advantage of this newfound freedom to reinvent itself organizationally and technologically. On the one hand, throughout the world major mergers between financial firms led to the consolidation of the industry in a few mega-groups, capable of a global reach, covering a wide range of financial activities, in an increasingly integrated manner (for example, one-stop financial shop for retail customers and investors). On the other hand, information technology qualitatively changed the way financial transactions were conducted. Powerful computers, and advanced mathematical models, allowed for sophisticated designing, tracking, and forecasting of increasingly complex financial products, operating both in real time and in future time. Electronic communication networks and the widespread use of the Internet revolutionized financial trade between firms, between investors and firms, between sellers and buyers, and, ultimately, the stock exchange markets.[127]

One major consequence of the transformation of finance was the global integration of financial markets, as analyzed above in this chapter. Another major development was the process of financial disintermediation; that is, the direct relationships between investors and securities markets, bypassing traditional brokerage firms, on the basis of electronic communication networks (ECNs). While Internet technology was crucial in allowing this trend to happen, a major institutional change made possible electronic trading. This was the creation of Nasdaq in 1971, as an electronic marketplace built on computer networks, without a central trading floor. New rules, aimed at encouraging electronic trading in the 1990s, allowed ECNs to post orders

127   Canals (1997); Zaloom (forthcoming).

from their clients on Nasdaq's system, and receive a commission when the order was filled. A large number of individual investors entered the stock market on their own, using the power of technology. The so-called day-traders, whose favorite investment targets were stocks of Internet companies, were the ones who really popularized electronic trading. They are called day-traders because they usually cash out at the end of the day, since they operate on small margins of change in the valuation of securities, and do not have financial reserves. Thus, they stay until they make a sufficient profit, by buying and selling on very short-term transactions – or until they have had enough losses for the day.[128] According to the Securities Exchange Commission, on-line trading grew from less than 100,000 trades a day in mid-1996 to over half a million a day by the end of 1999. In 1999, in the US, electronic trading was used in about 25 percent of transactions by individual investors. Many firms, including some large Wall Street brokers, re-positioned themselves in the new technological world, setting up private electronic trading networks, such as Instinet. These networks were not subjected to the same regulations as Nasdaq or the New York Stock Exchange. For instance, they allow investors to trade anonymously. Brokerage firms, led by Charles Schwab & Co., actively entered electronic trade: in 1998, 14 percent of all equity trades in the US were on-line, a 50 percent increase over 1997. The on-line brokerage industry in the US in 1999 had about 9.7 million accounts, three times the number in 1997, with customers' assets of nearly half a trillion dollars – a figure that is likely to be dwarfed in the early twenty-first century.

Electronic trading quickly spread from stocks to bonds. In November 1999, the city of Pittsburgh used the opportunity of electronic disintermediation to offer $55 million worth of municipal bonds directly to institutional investors over the Internet, thus bypassing Wall Street. This was the first time municipal bonds were directly sold electronically. The entry of electronic trading into the $13.7 trillion bond market is likely to change financial markets even further. Indeed, while in 1995 only 0.6 percent of US bonds were electronically traded, the projected share of electronic trading for 2001 is 37 percent, with the share of electronic trading for US government bonds reaching even higher, at 55 percent.[129]

Stock exchange markets around the world moved toward electronic trading in the second half of the 1990s. The German bond futures market is controlled by Eurex, an electronic network formed in 1990

---

128   Klam (1999).
129   Gutner (1999).

by the merger of German and Swiss derivatives exchange markets. The French futures exchange market (MATIF) moved entirely to electronic trading in 1998, and so later did London's LIFFE. In late 1999, the New York Stock Exchange was preparing to set up its own electronic trading system. And the venerable Chicago Board of Trade was in turmoil, with its leadership fighting over how to adapt to the new technological medium after it had to concede its position as the world's largest futures and options exchange market to Eurex.[130]

Why does the technology of transactions matter? How does it affect the finance industry? It reduces transaction costs (as much as 50 percent in the late 1990s in the US), thus attracting a much broader pool of individual investors, and reducing the cost of active trading. It also opens up investment opportunities to millions of individual investors, assessing value and seizing chances on the basis of on-line information. The consequences are threefold. First, there is a substantial increase in the amount of value traded, both because it mobilizes savings in search of higher returns, and because it considerably accelerates the rate of turnover of capital. Second, information, and thus information turbulences, become critical in affecting movements of capital, and thus value of securities. Third, financial volatility grows exponentially because investment patterns become highly decentralized, investors go in and out of securities, and market trends trigger quasi-immediate reactions. Moreover, the decline of central marketplaces, and the looser regulation of electronic trading, make it difficult to track capital movements. Growing secrecy of investment attracts large pools of capital. But small investors, while able to access information on-line, do not have the same access to non-public information that large companies or institutional investors have. As they have less than perfect information, individual investors have to react quickly to indirect signs of changes in the value of securities, thus increasing market instability. Thus, in the electronic financial market there are many more investors with a wide range of strategies to counter uncertainty, using speed and flexibility to compensate for lower levels of information. The overall outcome is greater complexity and greater volatility in the market.

The openness and dynamism of financial markets, and their global integration, attract increasing amounts of capital from all sources, and from around the world. Their new technological infrastructure allows the design of new financial products which create value out of the trade in securities. The securitization of all potential sources of value is the keystone of the new finance industry. Almost everything can become a security, and be traded in the financial market. Therefore,

130   Barboza (1999b).

financial markets constitute the strategic, dominant network of the new economy. It is in the financial marketplace where, in the last resort, the market assigns value to any economic activity – as represented by its stocks, bonds, or any kind of security (including derivatives). The value of companies, and thus their capacity to attract investors (or to fend off hostile takeovers), depends on the judgment of the financial market. How is this judgment formed? What are the underlying criteria for market valuation? This is one of the most complex matters in the economics of the new economy, and, certainly, a matter without consensus among financial experts. And yet, this is the cornerstone of the political economy for the Information Age. Because only if we know how value is assigned to economic activity can we understand the sources of investment, growth, and stagnation. Moreover, the value judgment on the performance of any given economic system (informational capitalism in our case) will largely depend on the criteria found to be the standards to judge what is value. I will certainly disappoint the reader by not even trying to answer this critical question: we simply do not have enough reliable information to assess it rigorously. However, I will risk a few thoughts that may contribute to indicating the path of inquiry.

We know that capitalism is based on the relentless search for profit. Thus, the answer to the above-formulated question should be simple: the market will value stocks, and other securities, according to how profitable a firm or economic activity is. However, in this turn-of-the-millennium capitalism, this is simply not the case. The most often cited example is that of Internet-related companies, with little or no profits, yet posting phenomenal increases in the growth of value of their stocks (see above). True, many start-up companies fail, taking their investors down with them. But both the entrepreneurs, and their investors, often have other options, so that failure translates into catastrophe for only a minority of investors: after all, the turnover of ownership for most companies' shares in the late 1990s in America was about 100 percent; that is, shareholders on average own a share for less than a year – thus making losses a matter of bad timing rather than bad judgment on the company. To be sure, in the long term, and for the economy as a whole, growth certainly requires profit to fuel investment. And the market does use profit yields as one of its standards to increase valuation. But, overall, valuation of a given security does not directly relate to the issuing company's profitability in the short term. A strong indication of this sense is the absence of relationship between the distribution of dividends and the growth of value of stocks. The proportion of American companies paying dividends dwindled in the 1990s, until reaching only about 20 percent of all companies (see figure 2.9).

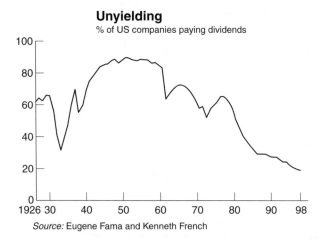

Unyielding
% of US companies paying dividends

Source: Eugene Fama and Kenneth French

Figure 2.9 Declining dividends payments
Source: The Economist (1999b)

Even among highly profitable companies, only 32 percent paid dividends, against almost two-thirds in the 1970s. According to an academic study by Eugene Fama and Kenneth French, part of the explanation for this change in corporate behavior seems to be related to the entry into the financial markets of new companies, mainly in the high-technology sector, using the opportunities of listing provided by Nasdaq. From an average new listings of 115 companies per year in the 1970s, they increased in the 1990s to over 460 a year, 85 percent of them in Nasdaq. In the mid-1990s while publicly traded corporations as a whole made returns on equity of about 11 percent, the figure for newly listed companies was about 3 percent. Indeed, in 1997, just about 50 percent of the newly listed companies made any profits at all.[131]

So, while profits and dividends are still among the criteria to value a company in the stock market, they do not seem to be the overriding factor. What is then? Two illustrations may help to elaborate a tentative hypothesis.

Exhibit one: In the high-flying American economy of the late 1990s, the top ten growth stocks in 1995–9 were all related to the information technology business sector, be it in computers, chips, software, Internet equipment, data storage, or electronic brokerage (see table

131 *The Economist* (1999b).

Table 2.10   Stocks valuation, 1995–1999: the Standard & Poor 500's top growth stocks

Company	% Increase[a]
Dell Computers	9,402
Cisco Systems	2,356
Sun Microsystems	2,304
Qualcomm	1,646
Charles Schwab	1,634
EMC Corporation	1,233
Microsoft	1,168
Tellabs	1,036
Solectron	926
Intel	900

[a] Percentage increase in total return for the five years ended August 31, 1999.
Source: Bloomberg Financial Markets, compiled by *Business Week*

2.10). While these companies were profitable (particularly Microsoft), they were not top performers in terms of traditional calculations of profitability, in comparison with companies in other industries. It was not their profit performance that could explain the revaluation of their stocks in excess of 1,000 percent or 2,000 percent, or even 9,000 percent in five years. Their common feature is sharing the attributes of the new economy: their key role as producers and/or users of new information technology, networking organization, innovation-driven business, very high rates of investment in R&D and/or computer-related equipment. And, not forgetting that they were all glamorous companies in terms of their image as trend-setters in the new business world.

Exhibit two: In January 1999, Amazon.com's stock was valued in excess of $25 billion. Not bad for a three-year-old company, whose quarterly earnings were just about $45 million, and which still had to show a profit. At approximately the same time, the total value of the entire Russian stock market was less than half of this figure, at $12 billion in total. Admittedly, this was a low point for Russian stocks (albeit still higher than in the immediate aftermath of the August 1998 devaluation crisis). But even so, the fact that Amazon, a medium-sized Internet company, could be valued more than twice the entire Russian economy is a meaningful observation. Because, after all, several of the Russian companies included in this evaluation were quite profitable, as the tens of billions of dollars in capital exported from Russia by some of these companies seem to indicate. To be sure, market capitalization is not money in your pocket, because if you try to cash it you destroy the value of the very stocks you are selling. This is precisely the point of the observation: in the new financial world whatever makes market value only lasts as long as this value remains in the market.

Reflecting on these examples a plausible hypothesis emerges. Two key factors appear to be at work in the valuation process: trust and expectations. If there is no trust in the institutional environment in which value making operates, no performance in profits, technology, or use value (for example, energy resources) will translate into financial value. On the other hand, if there is trust in the institutions underlying the market, then expectations of the potential future value of a future stock will increase its value. In the case of Russia, neither trust nor expectations were inducers of value in 1999. In the case of Amazon, in spite of losing money, the institutional environment of the new economy (essentially characterized by deregulation and disintermediation) had won the approval and trust of investors. And expectations were high on the ability of the on-line selling pioneer to move into e-commerce beyond books. This is why, for firms that bring together a "new economy" flavor with traditional virtues in profit-making and corporate respectability, the rewards are the highest, as shown in Exhibit one.

But how are expectations created? It seems to be partly a subjective process, made up of a vague vision of the future, some insider knowledge distributed on-line by financial gurus and economic "whispers" from specialized firms (such as Whisper.com), conscious image-making, and herd behavior. All this stirred up by information turbulences, generated by geopolitical or economic events (or by their interpretation), by valuations from respected firms, by announcements from the US Federal Reserve Board, or, simply, by personal moods from key players, such as the chairmen of Central Banks or Ministers of Finance. This is not to say that all valuation is subjective. But the performance of companies, supply and demand, macro-economic indicators, interact with various sources of information in an increasingly unpredictable pattern, where valuation may be ultimately decided by random combinations of a multiplicity of factors recombining at increasing levels of complexity, as the speed and volume of transactions continues to accelerate.

This is why, in the last resort, real world economic calculations (meaning decisions on how to invest your money) are not made in terms of profitability but in terms of expected growth of financial value. Expected growth value is the rule of thumb for investment in the new economy. This is equally the case for individual investors in electronic trading, for institutional investors in global financial markets or for innovative start-ups expecting to cash in their effort by an early IPO

(initial public offering) or by becoming attractive enough to be gob-
bled up by a bigger fish in the pond – at a price.

Indeed, we should remember that the concept of profit (now apparently insufficient, although still necessary, to explain investment and
value in the new economy) has always been the noble version of a
deeper, more fundamental human instinct: greed. It looks like greed is
now expressed more directly in value creation through the expecta-
tion of higher value – thus changing the rules of the game without
changing the nature of the game. This is not speculation. Or else, all
capitalism is speculative. Because within the logic of capitalism, creation of value does not need to be embodied in material production.
Everything goes, within the rule of law, as long as a *monetized* surplus
is generated, and appropriated by the investor. How and why this
monetized surplus is generated is a matter of context and opportunity.
This general statement about capitalism is particularly important when
we reach a point in historical development when food and consumer
goods are increasingly produced by machines – at a fraction of the
cost of, say, movies or higher education. There is a growing decoupling
between material production, in the old sense of the industrial era,
and value making. Value making, under informational capitalism, is
essentially a product of the financial market. But to reach the financial
market, and to vie for higher value in it, firms, institutions, and individuals have to go through the hard labor of innovating, producing,
managing, and image-making in goods and services. Thus, while the
whirlwind of factors entering in the valuation process are ultimately
expressed in financial value (always uncertain), throughout the process of reaching this critical judgment, managers and workers (that is,
people) end up producing and consuming our material world – including the images that shape it and make it. The new economy brings
information technology and the technology of information together in
the creation of value out of our belief in the value we create.

There is an additional, essential component of the new economy:
networking. The organizational transformation of the economy, as
well as of society at large, are, as in past periods of historical transition, a necessary condition for institutional restructuring and technological innovation to usher in a new world. I will examine this matter in some detail in the next chapter. But before undertaking a new
stage of our analytical trip, I will recast the argument presented in this
chapter. In sum, what is the new economy?

The new economy is certainly, for the time being, a capitalist economy. Indeed, for the first time in history, the whole planet is capitalist or dependent on its connection to global capitalist networks. But
this is a new brand of capitalism, technologically, organizationally,

and institutionally distinct from both classical (*laissez-faire*) capitalism and Keynesian capitalism.

As the empirical record (in spite of all the measurement problems) seems to indicate at the turn of the millennium, the new economy is/ will be predicated on a surge in productivity growth resulting from the ability to use new information technology in powering a knowledge-based production system. For new sources of productivity to dynamize the economy it is, however, necessary to ensure the diffusion of networking forms of organization and management throughout the economy – and networks are indeed spreading throughout the entire economy, phasing out, through competition, previous, rigid forms of business organization. In addition, the dramatic expansion of the productive base requires an equivalent broadening of markets, as well as new sources of capital and labor. Globalization, by dramatically expanding markets and tapping into new sources of capital and skilled labor, is an indispensable feature of the new economy.

Each one of these two processes – that is, network-based productivity growth, and network-based globalization – are spearheaded by a specific industry: the information technology industry, increasingly organized around the Internet, as the source of new technologies and managerial know-how for the whole economy; and the finance industry as the driving force in the formation of an electronically connected global financial market, the ultimate source of investment and value making for the whole economy. As the twenty-first century progresses, the biology revolution is likely to join the information technology industry in creating new business, in stimulating productivity (particularly in health care and in agriculture), and in revolutionizing labor, adding to the virtuous circle of innovation and value generation in the new economy.

Under conditions of high productivity, technological innovation, networking, and globalization, the new economy seems to be able to induce a sustained period of high economic growth, low inflation, and low unemployment in those economies able to fully transform themselves into this new mode of development. However, the new economy is not without flaws nor without dangers. On the one hand, its expansion is highly uneven, throughout the planet, and within countries, as argued above in this chapter, and as it will be documented in this book (volume I, chapter 4; volume III, chapter 2). The new economy affects everywhere and everybody but is inclusive and exclusionary at the same time, the boundaries of inclusion varying for every society, depending on institutions, politics, and policies. On the other hand, systemic financial volatility brings with it the possibility of recurrent financial crises with devastating effects on economies and societies.

While the new economy originated mainly in the United States, it is spreading fast into Europe, Japan, the Asian Pacific, and in selected developing areas around the world, inducing restructuring, prosperity, and crisis, in a process perceived under the label of globalization – and often feared and opposed by many people. In fact, this process, in the diversity of its manifestations, expresses a major structural change, as economies and societies find their specific ways to engage in the transition to a new mode of development, informationalism, of which networking is a critical attribute. Thus, I now turn to analyze the emergence of networks as the quintessential form of the new economy.

3

The Network Enterprise: the Culture, Institutions, and Organizations of the Informational Economy

The informational economy, as with all historically distinctive forms of production, is characterized by its specific culture and institutions. Yet culture, in this analytical framework, should not be considered as a set of values and beliefs linked to a particular society. What characterizes the development of the informational, global economy is precisely its emergence in very different cultural/national contexts: in North America, in Western Europe, in Japan, in the "China circle," in Russia, in Latin America, as well as its planetary reach, affecting all countries, and leading to a multicultural framework of reference. Indeed, the attempts to propose a theory of "cultural economics" to account for new development processes on the basis of philosophies and mentalities (such as Confucianism), particularly in the Asian Pacific,[1] have not resisted the scrutiny of empirical research.[2] But the diversity of cultural contexts where the informational economy emerges and evolves does not preclude the existence of a common matrix of organizational forms in the processes of production, consumption, and distribution. Without such organizational arrangements, technological change, state policies, and firms' strategies would not be able to come together in a new economic system. I contend, along with a growing number of scholars, that cultures manifest themselves fundamentally through their

---

1 Berger (1987); Berger and Hsiao (1988).
2 Hamilton and Biggart (1988); Clegg (1990); Biggart (1991); Janelli (1993); Whitley (1993).

embeddedness in institutions and organizations.[3] By organizations I understand specific systems of means oriented to the performance of specific goals. By institutions I understand organizations invested with the necessary authority to perform some specific tasks on behalf of society as a whole. The culture that matters for the constitution and development of a given economic system is the one that materializes in organizational logics, using Nicole Biggart's concept: "By organizational logics I mean a legitimating principle that is elaborated in an array of derivative social practices. In other words, organizational logics are the ideational bases for institutionalized authority relations."[4]

My thesis is that the rise of the informational, global economy is characterized by the development of a new organizational logic which is related to the current process of technological change, but not dependent upon it. It is the convergence and interaction between a new technological paradigm and a new organizational logic that constitutes the historical foundation of the informational economy. However, this organizational logic manifests itself under different forms in various cultural and institutional contexts. Thus, in this chapter I shall try to account at the same time for the commonality of organizational arrangements in the informational economy, and for their contextual variety. In addition, I shall examine the genesis of this new organizational form and the conditions of its interaction with the new technological paradigm.

Organizational Trajectories in the Restructuring of Capitalism and in the Transition from Industrialism to Informationalism

The economic restructuring of the 1980s induced a number of reorganizing strategies in business firms.[5] Some analysts, particularly Piore and Sabel, argue that the economic crisis of the 1970s resulted from the exhaustion of the mass-production system, constituting a "second industrial divide" in the history of capitalism.[6] For others, such as Storper and Harrison,[7] the diffusion of new organizational forms, some of which had already been practiced in some countries or firms for many years, was the response to the crisis of profitability in the pro-

---

3 Granovetter (1985); Clegg (1992); Evans (1995).
4 Biggart (1992: 49).
5 Williamson (1985); Sengenberger and Campbell (1992); Harrison (1994).
6 Piore and Sabel (1984).
7 Harrison (1994).

cess of capital accumulation. Others, like Coriat[8] suggest a long-term evolution from "Fordism" to "post-Fordism," as an expression of a "grand transition," the historical transformation of the relationships between, on the one hand, production and productivity, and, on the other hand, consumption and competition. Still others, like Tuomi,[9] emphasize organizational intelligence, organizational learning, and knowledge management as the key elements of new business organizations in the Information Age. But in spite of the diversity of approaches there is coincidence in five fundamental points of the analysis:

1 Whatever the causes and the genesis of the organizational transformation, there was from the mid-1970s onwards a major divide (industrial or otherwise) in the organization of production and markets in the global economy.
2 Organizational changes interacted with the diffusion of information technology but by and large were independent, and in general preceded the diffusion of information technologies in business firms.
3 The fundamental goal of organizational changes, in various forms, was to cope with the uncertainty caused by the fast pace of change in the economic, institutional, and technological environment of the firm by enhancing flexibility in production, management, and marketing.
4 Many organizational changes were aimed at redefining labor processes and employment practices, introducing the model of "lean production" with the objective of saving labor, by the automation of jobs, elimination of tasks, and suppression of managerial layers.
5 Knowledge management and information processing are essential to the performance of organizations operating in the informational, global economy.

However, sweeping interpretations of major organizational changes in the past two decades display an excessive tendency to merge in one single evolutionary trend various processes of change that are in fact different, albeit interrelated. In a parallel analysis to the notion of technological trajectories,[10] I propose to consider the development of different organizational trajectories, namely specific arrangements of systems of means oriented toward increasing productivity and competitiveness in the new technological paradigm and in the new global

8   Coriat (1990).
9   Tuomi (1999).
10 Dosi (1988).

economy. In most cases, these trajectories evolved from industrial organizational forms, such as the vertically integrated corporation and
the independent small business firm, which had become unable to perform their tasks under the new structural conditions of production
and markets, a trend that became fully apparent in the crisis of the
1970s. In other cultural contexts, new organizational forms emerged
from pre-existing ones that had been pushed aside by the classical
model of industrial organization, to find new life in the requirements
of the new economy and in the possibilities offered by new technologies. Several organizational trends evolved from the process of capitalist restructuring and industrial transition. They must be considered
separately before proposing their potential convergence in a new kind
of organizational paradigm.

From mass production to flexible production

The first, and broader, trend of organizational evolution that has been
identified, particularly in the pioneering work of Piore and Sabel, is
the transition from mass production to flexible production, or from
"Fordism" to "post-Fordism" in Coriat's formulation. The mass-
production model was based on productivity gains obtained by economies of scale in an assembly-line-based, mechanized process of production of a standardized product, under the conditions of control of
a large market by a *specific organizational form: the large corporation
structured on the principles of vertical integration, and institutionalized social and technical division of labor.* These principles were embedded in the management methods known as "Taylorism" and
"scientific organization of work," methods adopted as guidelines by
both Henry Ford and Lenin.

When demand became unpredictable in quantity and quality, when
markets were diversified worldwide and thereby difficult to control,
and when the pace of technological change made obsolete single-
purpose production equipment, the mass-production system became
too rigid and too costly for the characteristics of the new economy. A
tentative answer to overcome such rigidity was the flexible production system. It has been practiced and theorized in two different forms:
first, as flexible specialization, in the formulation of Piore and Sabel,
on the basis of the experience of the northern Italian industrial districts, when "production accommodates to ceaseless change without
pretending to control it"[11] in a pattern of industrial craft, or customized production. Similar practices have been observed by researchers

11   Piore and Sabel (1984: 17).

in firms performing advanced services, such as banking.[12]

Yet industrial management practice in the 1980s and 1990s introduced another form of flexibility: dynamic flexibility in the formulation of Coriat, or high-volume flexible production in the formula proposed by Cohen and Zysman, also shown by Baran to characterize the transformation of the insurance industry.[13] High-volume flexible production systems, usually linked to a situation of growing demand for a given product, combine high-volume production, permitting economies of scale, and customized, reprogrammable production systems, capturing economies of scope. New technologies allow for the transformation of assembly lines characteristic of the large corporation into easy-to-program production units that can be sensitive to variations in the market (product flexibility) and in the changes of technological inputs (process flexibility).

Small business and the crisis of the large corporation: myth and reality

A second, distinct trend, emphasized by analysts in recent years, is *the crisis of the large corporation, and the resilience of small and medium firms as agents of innovation and sources of job creation.*[14] For some observers, the crisis of the corporation is the necessary consequence of the crisis of standardized mass production, while the revival of customized, craft production and flexible specialization is better enacted by small businesses.[15] Bennett Harrison has written a devastating empirical critique of this thesis.[16] According to his analysis, based on data from the United States, Western Europe, and Japan, large corporations have continued to concentrate a growing proportion of capital and markets in all major economies; their share of employment has not changed in the past decade, except in the UK; small and medium firms remain by and large under the financial, commercial, and technological control of large corporations; he also contends that small businesses are less technologically advanced, and less able to innovate technologically in process and in product than larger firms. Furthermore, on the basis of the work of a number of Italian researchers (Bianchi and Belussi, particularly) he shows how the archetype of flexible specialization, the Italian firms in the industrial districts of Emilia-Romagna during the early 1990s, went through a series of mergers,

---

12 Hirschhorn (1985); Bettinger (1991); Daniels (1993).
13 Baran (1985); Cohen and Zysman (1987); Coriat (1990: 165).
14 Weiss (1988); Clegg (1990); Sengenberger et al. (1990).
15 Piore and Sabel (1984); Birch (1987); Lorenz (1988).
16 Harrison (1994).

and either came under the control of large corporations or became large corporations themselves (for example, Benetton), or else were unable to keep up with the pace of competition if they remained small and fragmented, as in the Prato district.

Some of these statements are controversial. The work by other researchers points to somewhat different conclusions.[17] For instance, the study by Schiatarella on Italian small firms suggests that small businesses have outperformed large firms in job creation, profit margins, investment per capita, technological change, productivity, and value added. Friedman's study on Japanese industrial structure even pretends that it is precisely this dense network of small and medium subcontracting enterprises that lies at the root of Japanese competitiveness. Also, the calculations of Michael Teitz and collaborators, years ago, on California's small businesses pointed to the enduring vitality and critical economic role of small businesses.[18]

In fact, we must separate the argument concerning the shift of economic power and technological capability from the large corporation to small firms (a trend that, as Harrison argues, does not seem to be supported by empirical evidence) from the argument referring to the decline of the large, vertically integrated corporation as an organizational model. Indeed, Piore and Sabel foresaw the possibility of survival of the corporate model through what they called "multinational Keynesianism;" that is, the expansion and conquest of world markets by corporate conglomerates, counting on growing demand from a rapidly industrializing world. But to do so, corporations did have to change their organizational structures. Some of the changes implied the growing use of subcontracting to small and medium businesses, whose vitality and flexibility allowed gains in productivity and efficiency for large corporations, as well as for the economy as a whole.[19]

Thus, at the same time, it is true that small and medium businesses appear to be forms of organization well adapted to the flexible production system of the informational economy, and it is also true that their renewed dynamism comes under the control of large corporations that remain at the center of the structure of economic power in the new global economy. We are not witnessing the demise of powerful, large corporations, but we are indeed observing the crisis of the traditional corporate model of organization based on vertical integration, and hierarchical, functional management: the "staff and line" system of strict technical and social division of labor within the firm.

---

17   Weiss (1988, 1992).
18   Teitz et al. (1981); Schiatarella (1984); Friedman (1988).
19   Gereffi (1993).

"Toyotism": management–worker cooperation, multifunctional labor, total quality control, and reduction of uncertainty

A third development concerns *new methods of management*, most of them originating in Japanese firms,[20] although in some cases they were experimented with within other contexts, for example in Volvo's Kalmar complex in Sweden.[21] The substantial success in productivity and competitiveness obtained by Japanese automobile firms has been attributed to a large extent to this managerial revolution, so that in the business literature "Toyotism" is opposed to "Fordism" as the new winning formula adapted to the global economy and to the flexible production system.[22] The original Japanese model has been widely imitated by other companies, as well as transplanted by Japanese firms to their foreign locations, often leading to a substantial improvement in the performance of these firms *vis-à-vis* the traditional industrial system.[23] Some elements of this model are well known:[24] the *kan-ban* (or "just in time") system of supplies, by which inventories are eliminated or reduced substantially through delivery from the suppliers to the production site at the exact required time and with the characteristics specified for the production line; "total quality control" of products in the production process, aiming at near-zero defects and best use of resources; workers' involvement in the production process, by using teamwork, decentralized initiative, greater autonomy of decision on the shopfloor, rewards for team performance, and a flat management hierarchy with few status symbols in the daily life of the firm.

Culture may have been important in generating "Toyotism" (particularly the consensus-building, cooperative model of teamwork) but it is certainly not a determinant for its implementation. The model works equally well in Japanese firms in Europe, and in the United States, and several of its elements have been successfully adopted by American (GM-Saturn) or German (Volkswagen) factories. Indeed, the model was perfected by Toyota engineers over a period of 20 years, after its first, limited introduction in 1948. To be able to generalize the method to the whole factory system, Japanese engineers studied the control procedures used in American supermarkets to assess stock on their shelves, so it could be argued that "just in time" is to some extent

20 Coriat (1990); Nonaka (1990); Durlabhji and Marks (1993).
21 Sandkull (1992).
22 McMillan (1984); Cusumano (1985).
23 Wilkinson et al. (1992).
24 Dohse et al. (1985); Aoki (1988); Coriat (1990).

an American mass-production method, adapted to flexible management by using the specificity of Japanese firms, particularly the cooperative relationship between management and workers.

The stability and complementarity of relationships between the core firm and the suppliers' network are extremely important for the implementation of this model: Toyota maintains in Japan a three-tier network of suppliers embracing thousands of firms of different sizes.[25] Most of the markets for most of the firms are captive markets for Toyota, and the same can be said for other major firms. How different is this from the structure of divisions and departments in a vertically integrated corporation? Most of the key suppliers are in fact controlled or influenced by financial, commercial or technological undertakings, belonging either to the parent firm or to the overarching *keiretsu*. Under such conditions, are we not observing a system of planned production under the premise of relative market control by the large corporation? Thus, what is important in this model is the vertical disintegration of production along a network of firms, a process that substitutes for the vertical integration of departments within the same corporate structure. The network allows for greater differentiation of the labor and capital components of the production unit, and probably builds in greater incentives and stepped-up responsibility, without necessarily altering the pattern of concentration of industrial power and technological innovation.

The performance of the model relies also on the absence of major disruptions in the overall process of production and distribution. Or, to put it in other words, it is based on the assumption of the "five zeros": zero defect in the parts; zero mischief in the machines; zero inventory; zero delay; zero paperwork. Such performances can only be predicated on the basis of an absence of work stoppages and total control over labor, on entirely reliable suppliers, and on adequately predicted markets. *"Toyotism" is a management system designed to reduce uncertainty rather than to encourage adaptability.* The flexibility is in the process, not in the product. Thus, some analysts have suggested that it could be considered as an extension of "Fordism,"[26] keeping the same principles of mass production, yet organizing the production process on the basis of human initiative and feedback capacity to eliminate waste (of time, work, and resources) while maintaining the characteristics of output close to the business plan. Is this really a management system well fitted to a global economy in constant swirl? Or, as Stephen Cohen has expressed it to me, "Is it too late for 'just in time'?"

25   Friedman (1988); Weiss (1992).
26   Tetsuro and Steven (1994).

In fact, the truly distinctive character of Toyotism, as distinct from Fordism, does not concern relationships between firms, but between management and workers. As Coriat argued, in the international seminar convened in Tokyo to debate the question "Is Japanese Management Post-Fordism?," in fact, "it is neither pre- nor post-Fordist, but an original and new way of managing the labor process: the central and distinctive feature of the Japanese path was to de-specialize the professional workers and, instead of scattering them, to turn them into multi-functional specialists."[27] A distinguished Japanese economist, Aoki, also emphasizes labor organization as the key to the success of Japanese firms:

> The main difference between the American firm and the Japanese firm may be summarized as follows: the American firm emphasizes efficiency attained through fine specialization and sharp job demarcation, whereas the Japanese firm emphasizes the capability of the workers' group to cope with local emergencies autonomously, which is developed through learning by doing and sharing knowledge on the shopfloor.[28]

Indeed, some of the most important organizational mechanisms underlying productivity growth in Japanese firms seem to have been overlooked by Western experts of management. Thus, Ikujiro Nonaka,[29] on the basis of his studies of major Japanese companies, has proposed a simple, elegant model to account for the generation of knowledge in the firm. What he labels "the knowledge-creating company" is based on the organizational interaction between "explicit knowledge" and "tacit knowledge" at the source of innovation. He argues that much of the knowledge accumulated in the firm comes from experience, and cannot be communicated by workers under excessively formalized management procedures. And yet the sources of innovation multiply when organizations are able to establish bridges to transfer tacit into explicit knowledge, explicit into tacit knowledge, tacit into tacit, and explicit into explicit. By so doing, not only is worker experience communicated and amplified to increase the formal body of knowledge in the company, but also knowledge generated in the outside world can be incorporated into the tacit habits of workers, enabling them to work out their own uses and to improve on the standard procedures. In an economic system where innovation is critical, the organizational ability to increase its sources from all forms of knowledge becomes the foundation of the innovative firm. This organizational process,

27   Coriat (1994: 182).
28   Aoki (1988: 16).
29   Nonaka (1991); Nonaka and Takeuchi (1994).

however, requires the full participation of workers in the innovation process, so that they do not keep their tacit knowledge solely for their own benefit. It also requires stability of the labor force in the company, because only then does it become rational for the individual to transfer his/her knowledge to the company, and for the company to diffuse explicit knowledge among its workers. Thus, this apparently simple mechanism, the dramatic effects of which in enhancing productivity and quality are shown in a number of case studies, in fact engages a profound transformation of management–labor relationships. Although information technology does not play a prominent role in Nonaka's "explicit analysis," in our personal conversations we shared the thought that on-line communication and computerized storage capacity have become powerful tools in developing the complexity of organizational links between tacit and explicit knowledge. Yet this form of innovation preceded the development of information technologies, and was, in fact, for the past two decades "tacit knowledge" of Japanese management, removed from the observation of foreign managerial experts, but truly decisive in improving the performance of the Japanese firms.

Inter-firm networking

Let us now turn to consider two other forms of organizational flexibility in the international experience, characterized by inter-firm linkages. These are *the multidirectional network model enacted by small and medium businesses* and *the licensing–subcontracting model of production under an umbrella corporation.* I shall briefly describe these two distinct organizational models which have played a considerable role in the economic growth of several countries in the past two decades.

Small and medium enterprises, as I have said, in concurrence with Bennett Harrison's argument, are often under the control of subcontracting arrangements or financial/technological domination by large corporations. Yet they also frequently take the initiative in establishing networking relationships with several large firms and/or with other small and medium enterprises, finding market niches and cooperative ventures. Besides the classical example of the Italian industrial districts, a good case in point is represented by Hong Kong's manufacturing firms. As I argued in my book on Hong Kong, on the basis of work by Victor Sit and other researchers of the Hong Kong scene,[30] its export success was based, for a long period between the late 1950s and the early 1980s, on domestic small business networks competing

30   Sit et al. (1979); Sit and Wong (1988); Castells et al. (1990).

in the world economy. Over 85 percent of Hong Kong manufacturing exports up to the early 1980s originated from Chinese family-based firms, of which 41 percent were small enterprises employing fewer than 50 workers. In most cases they did not subcontract to larger firms, but exported through the network of Hong Kong's import–export firms – also small, also Chinese, and also family-based – which numbered 14,000 in the late 1970s. Networks of production and distribution formed, disappeared, and reformed on the basis of variations in the world market, through the signals transmitted by flexible intermediaries often using a network of "commercial spies" in the main world markets. Very often the same person would be entrepreneur or salaried worker at different points in time, according to the circumstances of the business cycle and his own family needs.

Taiwan's exports during the 1960s came also mainly from a similar small and medium enterprise system, although in this case the traditional Japanese trading companies were the main intermediaries.[31] Granted, as Hong Kong prospered, many of the small enterprises merged, refinanced, and grew bigger, sometimes linking up with large department stores or manufacturers in Europe and America, to become their surrogate producers.[32] Yet, by then, medium–large businesses subcontracted much of their own production to firms (small, medium, and large) across the Chinese border in the Pearl River Delta. By the mid-1990s, somewhere between six and ten million workers, depending upon the estimates used, were involved in Guandong province in these subcontracting production networks.

Taiwanese companies took an even more complex circuit. In order to produce in China, taking advantage of low labor costs, social control, and China's export quotas, they set up intermediary firms in Hong Kong. These firms linked up with local governments in Guandong and Fujian provinces, setting up manufacturing subsidiaries in China.[33] These subsidiaries put out work to small shops and homes in the surrounding villages. The flexibility of such a system allowed it to capture cost advantages in different locations, to diffuse technology throughout the system, to benefit from various supports from various governments, and to use several countries as export platforms.

In a very different context, Ybarra found a similar networking production pattern among small and medium footwear, textile, and toy-making enterprises in the Valencia region of Spain.[34] There are

31 Gold (1986).
32 Gereffi (1999).
33 Hsing (1996).
34 Ybarra (1989).

numerous examples of such horizontal networks of enterprises in other countries and industries, as reported in the specialized literature.[35]

A different kind of production network is the one exemplified by the so-called "Benetton model," the object of much commentary in the business world, as well as of some limited but revealing research, particularly that of Fiorenza Belussi and of Bennett Harrison.[36] The Italian knitwear firm, a multinational enterprise grown from a small family business in the Veneto region, operates on the basis of licensing commercial franchises, reaching about 5,000 stores in the whole world, for the exclusive distribution of its products under the strictest control of the core firm. On-line feedback is received by the center from all distribution points, triggering resupply of stock, as well as defining market trends in shapes and colors. The network model is also effective at the production level by putting out work to small firms and homes in Italy and other Mediterranean countries, such as Turkey. This type of network organization is an intermediate form of arrangement between vertical disintegration through the subcontracting arrangements of a large firm and the horizontal networks of small businesses. It is a horizontal network, but based on a set of core–periphery relationships, both on the supply and on the demand side of the process. Similar forms of horizontal business networks integrated vertically by financial control have been shown to characterize direct sales operations in America, as researched by Nicole Biggart, and to inform the decentralized structure of many business consulting firms in France, organized under an umbrella of quality control.[37]

Corporate strategic alliances

A sixth organizational pattern emerging in recent years refers to *the intertwining of large corporations* in what has come to be known as strategic alliances.[38] Such alliances are very different from the traditional forms of cartels and other oligopolistic agreements because they concern specific times, markets, products, and processes, and they do not exclude competition in all the areas (the majority) not covered by the agreements.[39] They have been particularly relevant in high-technology industries, as the cost of R&D has sky-rocketed and access to privileged information has become increasingly difficult in an in-

35   Powell (1990).
36   Belussi (1992); Harrison (1994).
37   Leo and Philippe (1989); Biggart (1990b).
38   Imai (1980); Gerlach (1992); Cohen and Borrus (1995b); Ernst (1995).
39   Dunning (1993).

dustry where innovation is the main competitive weapon.[40] Access to markets and capital resources is often exchanged for technology and manufacturing skills; in other cases joint efforts by two or more companies are undertaken to develop a new product or refine a new technology, often under the sponsorship of governments or public agencies. In Europe, the European Union has even forced companies from different countries to cooperate as a condition of receiving subsidies, as was the case with Philips, Thomson-SGS, and Siemens in the microelectronics JESSI program. Small and medium firms receive European Union and EUREKA program support for R&D on the basis of establishing joint ventures between firms of more than one country.[41] The structure of high-technology industries in the world is an increasingly complex web of alliances, agreements, and joint ventures in which most large corporations are interlinked. Such linkages do not preclude stepped-up competition. Rather, strategic alliances are decisive instruments in this competition, with today's partners becoming tomorrow's foes, while collaboration in a given market is in sharp contrast to the ferocious struggle for market share in another region of the world.[42] Furthermore, because large corporations are the tip of the pyramid of a vast network of subcontracting arrangements, their patterns of alliance and competition involve also their subcontractors. Often, practices such as securing supplies from subcontracting firms or barring access to a network are competitive weapons used by firms. Reciprocally, subcontractors use whatever margin of freedom they have to diversify their clients and hedge their bets, while absorbing technology and information for their own use. This is why proprietary information and technological copyright are so critical in the new global economy.

In sum, the large corporation in such an economy is not, and will no longer be, self-contained and self-sufficient. The arrogance of the IBMs, the Philips, or the Mitsuis of the world has become a matter of cultural history.[43] Their actual operations are conducted with other firms: not only with the hundreds or thousands of subcontracting and ancillary enterprises, but with the dozens of relatively equal partners with whom they cooperate and compete at the same time in this new brave economic world where friends and foes are the same.

40   Van Tulder and Junne (1988); Ernst and O'Connor (1992); Ernst (1995).
41   Baranano (1994).
42   Mowery (1988).
43   Bennett (1990).

The horizontal corporation and global business networks

The corporation itself has changed its organizational model to adapt to the conditions of unpredictability ushered in by rapid economic and technological change.[44] *The main shift can be characterized as the shift from vertical bureaucracies to the horizontal corporation.* The horizontal corporation seems to be characterized by seven main trends: organization around process, not task; a flat hierarchy; team management; measuring performance by customer satisfaction; rewards based on team performance; maximization of contacts with suppliers and customers; information, training, and retraining of employees at all levels.[45] This transformation of the corporate model, particularly visible in the 1990s in some leading American companies (such as ATT), follows the realization of the limits of the "lean production" model attempted in the 1980s. This "lean model" (justifiably called by its critics "lean and mean") was fundamentally predicated on labor savings, by using a combination of automation, computerized worker control, "putting out" work, and retrenchment of production. In its most extreme manifestation, it created what has been labeled the "hollow corporation;" that is, a business specialized in intermediation between financing, production, and market sales, on the basis of an established trade mark or industrial image. A direct expression of capitalist restructuring to overcome the crisis of profitability of the 1970s, the "lean production" model reduced costs but also perpetuated obsolete organizational structures rooted in the logic of the mass-production model under the conditions of oligopolistic market control. To maneuver in the new global economy, characterized by an endless flurry of new competitors using new technologies and cost-cutting capabilities, the large corporations had to become primarily more effective rather than more thrifty. The networking strategies added flexibility to the system, but they did not solve the problem of adaptability for the corporation. To be able to internalize the benefits of network flexibility the corporation had to become a network itself and dynamize each element of its internal structure: this is in essence the meaning and the purpose of the "horizontal corporation" model, often extended in the decentralization of its units and in the growing autonomy given to each of these units, even allowing them to compete against each other, albeit within a common overall strategy.[46]

44 Drucker (1988).
45 *Business Week* (1993a, 1995a).
46 Goodman et al. (1990).

Ken'ichi Imai is probably the organizational analyst who has gone the furthest in proposing and documenting the thesis of the transformation of corporations into networks.[47] On the basis of his studies of Japanese and American multinational corporations, he argues that the process of internationalization of business activity has proceeded along three different strategies for firms. The first, and most traditional, refers to a multi-domestic market strategy for companies investing abroad from their national platform. The second targets the global market, and organizes different company functions in different locations, which are integrated within an articulated, global strategy. The third strategy, characteristic of the most advanced economic and technological stage, is based on cross-border networks. Under this strategy, on the one hand, companies relate to a variety of domestic markets; on the other hand, there is an exchange of information between these various markets. Rather than controlling markets from the outside, companies try to integrate their market shares and market information across borders. Thus, in the old strategy, foreign direct investment aimed at taking control. Under the most recent strategy, investment is geared toward the construction of a set of relationships between companies in different institutional environments. Global competition is greatly helped by "on the spot information" from each market, so that designing strategy in a top-down approach will invite failure in a constantly changing environment and with highly diverse market dynamics. Information coming from specific time and space is the crucial factor. Information technology allows simultaneously for the decentralized retrieval of such information and for its integration into a flexible system of strategy-making. This cross-border structure allows small and medium businesses to link up with major corporations, forming networks that are able to innovate and adapt relentlessly. Thus, *the actual operating unit becomes the business project, enacted by a network*, rather than individual companies or formal groupings of companies. Business projects are implemented in fields of activity, which can be product lines, organizational tasks, or territorial areas. Appropriate information is critical to companies' performance. And the most important information, under new economic conditions, is that processed between companies, on the basis of experience received from each field. Information circulates through networks: networks between companies, networks within companies, personal networks, and computer networks. New information technologies are decisive in allowing such a flexible, adaptive model to actually work. For Imai, this cross-border network model is at the root of the competitiveness of Japanese firms.

47   Imai (1990a).

Provided the large corporation can reform itself, transforming its organization into an articulated network of multifunctional decision-making centers, it could actually be a superior form of management in the new economy. The reason for this is that the most important management problem in a highly decentralized, extremely flexible structure is the correction of what organizational theorist Guy Benveniste calls "articulation errors." I agree with his definition: "Articulation errors are the partial or total lack of fit between what is wanted and what is available."[48] With the increasing interconnectedness and extreme decentralization of processes in the global economy, articulation errors become more difficult to avoid, and their micro- and macro-economic impacts have greater intensity. The flexible production model, in its different forms, maximizes the response of economic agents and units to a fast-changing environment. But it also increases the difficulty of controlling and correcting articulation errors. Large corporations, with adequate levels of information and resources, can handle such errors better than fragmented, decentralized networks, provided that they use adaptability on top of flexibility. This implies the capacity of the corporation to restructure itself, not simply by eliminating redundancy, but by allocating reprogramming capabilities to all its sensors while reintegrating the over-arching logic of the corporate system into a decision-making center, working on-line with the networked units in real time. Many of the debates and experiments concerning the transformation of large-scale organizations, be they private or public, business-oriented or mission-oriented, are attempts to combine flexibility and coordination capabilities, to ensure both innovation and continuity in a fast-changing environment. The "horizontal corporation" is a dynamic and strategically planned network of self-programmed, self-directed units based on decentralization, participation, and coordination.

The crisis of the vertical corporation model and the rise of business networks

These different trends in the organizational transformation of the informational economy are relatively independent of each other. The formation of subcontracting networks centered on large enterprises is a different phenomenon from the formation of horizontal networks of small and medium businesses. The web-like structure of strategic alliances between large corporations is different from the shift toward the horizontal corporation. Workers' involvement in the pro-

48   Benveniste (1994: 74).

duction process is not necessarily reduced to the Japanese model based also on *kan-ban* and total quality control. These various trends interact with each other, influence each other, but they all are different dimensions of a fundamental process: the process of disintegration of the organizational model of vertical, rational bureaucracies, characteristic of the large corporation under the conditions of standardized mass production and oligopolistic markets.[49] The historic timing of these various trends is also different, and the time sequence of their diffusion is extremely important to the understanding of their social and economic meaning. For instance, *kan-ban* originated in Japan in 1948, and was designed by Ono Taiichi, a former labor union staff member, who became a Toyota manager.[50] "Toyotism" was gradually adopted by Japanese automobile firms at an historical moment (the 1960s) when they did not yet represent a competitive threat to the rest of the world.[51] "Toyotism" was able to develop by taking advantage of two specific mechanisms historically available to Toyota: its control over labor and its total control over a huge network of suppliers which were external to the firm but internal to the *keiretsu*. When in the 1990s Toyota had to offshore some of its production, it was not always possible to reproduce the *kan-ban* model (it was not in the symbolic NUMMI plant of Toyota–GM in Fremont, California). Thus "Toyotism" is a transitional model between standardized, mass production and a more efficient work organization characterized by the introduction of craft practices, as well as by workers' and suppliers' involvement, in an assembly-line-based, industrial model.

Thus, what emerges from the observation of major organizational changes in the last two decades of the twentieth century is not a new, "one best way" of production, but the crisis of an old, powerful but excessively rigid model associated with the large, vertical corporation, and with oligopolistic control over markets. A variety of models and organizational arrangements emerged from this crisis, prospering or failing according to their adaptability to various institutional contexts and competitive structures. As Piore and Sabel conclude in their book, "Whether our economy is based on mass production or on flexible specialization are open questions. The answers will depend in part on the capacity of nations and social classes to envision the future that they want."[52] Yet recent historical experience has already provided some of the answers concerning the new organizational forms of the

---

49   Vaill (1990).
50   Cusumano (1985).
51   McMillan (1984).
52   Piore and Sabel (1984: 308).

informational economy.[53] Under different organizational arrangements, and through diverse cultural expressions, they are all based on networks. *Networks are the fundamental stuff of which new organizations are and will be made.* And they are able to form and expand all over the main streets and back alleys of the global economy because of their reliance on the information power provided by the new technological paradigm.

Networking the networks: the Cisco model

Every period of organizational transformation has its archetypical expression. Ford Motor Company became the symbol of the industrial era of standardized production and mass consumption – to the point of inspiring the concept of "Fordism," a favorite of political economists in the 1980s. It may well be that the business model of the Internet-based economy will be epitomized by Cisco Systems.[54] Or, rather, by the "global networked business model" that Cisco Systems proposes as the expression of its business organization and strategy. In the company's own formulation, this business model is based on three core assumptions:

> the relationships a company maintains with its key constituencies can be as much of a competitive differentiator as its core products or services; the manner in which a company shares information and systems is a critical element in the strength of its relationships; being connected is no longer adequate: business relationships and the communications that support them must exist in a "networked" fabric. The global networked business model opens the corporate information infrastructure to all key constituencies, leveraging the network for competitive advantage.[55]

Let us examine what this actually means in practice.

Cisco Systems (a universally known firm in the Internet industry) is a company based in San Jose, California, which provides the switchers and routers that direct data around communication networks. It is the leader of Internet backbone equipment, having supplied in 1999 about 80 percent of such equipment sold around the world. In 1999, 55 percent of its sales went to corporate networks, but the company was

53   Tuomi (1999).
54   This section is based on business reports, both in print and on-line, particularly from *Business Week* and *The Wall Street Journal*, as well as on company documents published on their web sites. I do not consider it necessary to provide specific references, except when I cite excerpts from documents. On Cisco Systems I also relied on a research seminar paper by my graduate student Abbie Hoffman (1999). See also Hartman and Sifonis (2000).
55   Cisco Systems (1999: 1–2).

increasing its market share in network equipment and support for small and medium businesses, Internet service providers, and consumer networking. At the turn of the century it was trying to expand beyond Internet communications equipment, and enter forcefully the telephone networks industry, betting on its ability to produce networking equipment for new transmission technologies able to carry through the same wire data, voice, and video. A company created in 1985 by a couple of Stanford professors (who later left the company) with a $2 million investment from a venture capitalist, it shipped its first product in 1986, and went public in 1990. Its annual revenues in that year were $69 million. By fiscal 1999, its revenues had climbed to $12.2 billion, with $2.55 billion annual earnings. The value of its stock grew by 2,356 percent between 1995 and 1999, to reach a market capitalization value of $220 billion, the fifth highest in the world and about four times the market capitalization value of General Motors at that time. The extraordinary success of Cisco Systems in little more than a decade is partly due to its good timing: it provided the plumbing systems for the Internet at the time that the Internet exploded. But other companies were also in the trade, some of them backed by major corporations; others, smaller, were clearly ahead of Cisco in technological innovation. Indeed, as soon as it had the cash (or the equity value), Cisco went into a frenzy of acquisitions of innovative start-ups to incorporate talent and technology on top of its own resources (13 percent of revenues spent in R&D). Thus, in August 1999, Cisco paid $6.9 billion for Cerent, a promising California start-up with only $10 million in annual sales. The consensus in business circles, including Cisco's own perception, was that the business model pioneered by the company was the key to its productivity, profitability, and competitiveness. Cisco applied to itself the networking logic it was selling to its customers. It organized in/around the Net all relationships with its customers, its suppliers, its partners and its employees, and, through excellent engineering, design, and software, it automated much of the interaction. By building a network of suppliers on-line, Cisco was able to cut its own manufacturing to the bone. In fact, by 1999 it only owned two production facilities out of the 30 plants producing Cisco gears, and employed worldwide a mere 23,500 employees (about half of them in San Jose), most of whom were engineers, researchers, business managers, and salespersons. The core of Cisco Systems operation is its web site. Prospective customers find a number of options on different product lines that they can specify to their convenience. Cisco engineers update the site on a day-to-day basis. If necessary, on-line advice and support is provided, at a higher price. Only major contracts are dealt with in person. Once the customer's order is specified, it is automatically transferred to the network of suppliers, also connected on-line. Manufacturers ship their products directly to the customers. In 1999, Cisco was handling 83 percent of its orders over the web, as well as 80 percent of customer-service issues. By so doing, Cisco saved an estimated $500 million a year in 1997–9. In addition, over 50 percent of the orders placed by customers flow over the Net to Cisco's contractors, who serve them directly. Cisco simply gets the payment. For what? Well, for R&D, technology, design, engineering, information, technical support, and business savvy in building a reliable network of suppliers, and in marketing to customers. This is a manufacturing company (indeed, the largest in the world in terms of market capitalization value in 2000) which does almost no manufacturing, and may do none by the time you read this. Cisco's networking also extends to its employees. The Cisco Employee Connection is an Intranet that provides instant communication to over 10,000 employees around the globe. From joint engineering to marketing and training, information flows freely and instantly around the network according to the needs of each department and employee. As a result, in 1999, revenues per employee at Cisco were $650,000 in contrast to the average of $396,000 for the S&P 500 companies, and to $253,000 per employee in Lucent Technologies, a major corporation producing telephone networking equipment. Cisco engaged also in strategic alliances with major companies in various areas of business: service providers, such as US West and Alcatel; servers, such as Intel, Hewlett Packard and Microsoft; Internet appliance companies, such as Microsoft and Intel; and systems integrators, such as KPMG and EDS. In all these cases, the organizational networking in joint business projects takes the form of shared information sources, and on-line interaction which gives rise to business cooperation with each partner. By networking its operation internally and externally, using the equipment it designs and sells, Cisco Systems epitomizes the virtuous circle of the information technology revolution: the use of information technologies to enhance the technology of information, on the basis of organizational networking powered by information networks.

Although I chose to focus on Cisco Systems because it is, probably, the most self-conscious model of the networking form of organization, it is not an isolated example. It is, rather, a trend-setter. Indeed, some observers would argue that the pioneer in business on-line networking was Dell Computers, which became one of the leaders in the PC industry, and the most profitable company in the computer industry in the 1990s, not so much on the basis of distinctive technology as on its innovative business model. As Cisco, Dell takes orders on-line, using a web site built with advanced software which allows its clients to customize their product. In 1999, the company was selling $30 million a day, and expecting its on-line business revenues to represent 50 percent of total revenue by 2000. Dell also relies heavily on a network of suppliers which receive orders on-line and supply directly to Dell's buyers. Overall, about 50 percent of Dell's orders are processed through the web, without direct contact with Dell's managers. Productivity and competitiveness, resulting from its early adoption of an integral networking model, led Dell to a revaluation of its stock by a staggering 9,400 percent between 1995 and 1999.

Hewlett Packard, a legendary name in the computer industry, was moving in the late 1990s toward becoming an on-line service company. Instead of selling computers, it was proposing to its clients to provide the computer power of its powerful computers over the network, for a monthly fee. Or, for e-commerce sites, to charge a percentage for the customer's transaction revenues. Thus, the Hewlett Packard network of business would work as follows: Hewlett Packard would design top-of-the-range computers which would be produced by manufacturing suppliers around the world and Hewlett Packard would keep the computers for itself, then sell their operation on-line to companies in need of computer power. The network between manufacturing, computing, and the uses of computing becomes the actual operating unit, with different firms making business out of different steps in the process, on the basis of their cooperation.

The Cisco model is not confined to the Internet economy, or for that matter to the information technology industry. It diffused rapidly in the 1990s to areas as diverse as agricultural machinery (e.g. John Deere); grocery shopping, combining on-line grocery delivery (by the Webvan Group Inc.) with warehousing logistics (provided by the Bechtel Group); automobile production (e.g. Renault); energy (e.g. Houston's Altra Energy Technologies, accounting for 40 percent of natural gas liquids sales); automobile sales (e.g. Microsoft as a major force in on-line automobile sales dealing, actually threatening traditional car dealers' business); business consulting services (e.g. Global Business Networks, a California firm specializing in scenario planning and corporate strategy); or even higher education (e.g. Duke University's business school started in 1999 a global MBA program conducted both on-line, and through physical interaction on four campuses around the world with faculty and students rotating locations, while maintaining their networked connection for the duration of the program). Manufacturing is likely to be entirely transformed in its operation: thus, in a conference in Seattle in September 1999, I listened to one of the vice-presidents of Microsoft introducing the technology that would enable on-line, customized production and sale of automobiles.

In this way, prospective buyers could customize their preferences before the car was actually manufactured, similar to Dell's customers with PCs. The factory (actually a network of factories) would receive the order, then proceed to produce and deliver the automobile directly to the client – within a week of receipt of the customized order, according to the presentation at the conference. "Just in time on your time" may be the new management–customer relationship already emerging in the automobile industry.

The global networked business model, pioneered by Cisco, seems to have become, at the turn of the century, the predominant model for the most successful competitors in most industries around the world.

Information Technology and the Network Enterprise

The new organizational trajectories I have described were not the mechanical consequence of technological change. Some of them preceded the rise of new information technologies. For instance, as mentioned, the *kan-ban* system was first introduced in Toyota in 1948, and its implementation did not require on-line electronic linkages. Instructions and information were written on standardized cards posted at different working points, and exchanged between suppliers and factory operators.[56] Most of the methods to involve workers, experimented with by Japanese, Swedish, and American companies, required a change of mentality rather than a change of machinery.[57] The most important obstacle in adapting the vertical corporation to the flexibility requirements of the global economy was the rigidity of traditional corporate cultures. Furthermore, at the moment of its massive diffusion, in the 1980s, information technology was supposed to be the magic tool to reform and change the industrial corporation.[58] But its introduction in the absence of fundamental organizational change in fact aggravated the problems of bureaucratization and rigidity. Computerized controls are even more paralyzing than traditional face-to-face chains of command in which there was still place for some form of implicit bargaining.[59] In the 1980s in America, more often than not, new technology was viewed as a labor-saving device and as an opportunity to take control of labor, not as an instrument of organizational change.[60]

56 McMillan (1984); Cusumano (1985).
57 Dodgson (1989).
58 Harrington (1991); Kotter and Heskett (1992).
59 Hirschhorn (1985); Mowshowitz (1986).
60 Shaiken (1985).

Thus, organizational change happened, independently of technological change, as a response to the need to cope with a constantly changing operational environment.[61] Yet, once it started to take place, the feasibility of organizational change was extraordinarily enhanced by new information technologies. As Boyett and Conn write, "The ability of large American companies to reconfigure themselves to look and act like small businesses can, at least in part, be attributed to the development of new technology that makes whole layers of managers and their staffs unnecessary."[62] The ability of small and medium businesses to link up in networks among themselves and with large corporations also became dependent on the availability of new technologies, once the networks' horizon (if not their daily operations) became global.[63] True, Chinese business had been based on networks of trust and cooperation for centuries. But when in the 1980s they stretched out across the Pacific, from Tachung to Fukien, from Hong Kong to Guandong, from Jakarta to Bangkok, from Hsinchu to Mountain View, from Singapore to Shanghai, from Hong Kong to Vancouver, and, above all, from Taipei and Hong Kong to Guangzhou and Shanghai, only reliance on new communication and information technologies allowed them to work on a continuing basis, once the family, regional, and personal codes established the basis for the rules of the game to be followed up in their computers.

The complexity of the web of strategic alliances, of subcontracting agreements, and of decentralized decision-making for large firms would have been simply impossible to manage without the development of computer networks;[64] more specifically, without powerful microprocessors installed in desktop computers linked up via digitally switched telecommunication networks. This is a case in which organizational change induced to some extent the technological trajectory. If the large, vertical corporations had been able to continue to operate successfully in the new economy, the crisis of IBM, Digital, Fujitsu, and of the mainframe computer industry in general might not have happened. It was because of the networking needs of new organizations, large and small, that personal computers and computer networking underwent an explosive diffusion. And because of the massive need for the flexible, interactive manipulation of computers, software became the most dynamic segment of the industry and the information-producing activity that is likely to shape processes of production and management in the future. On the other hand, it was because of the availability of

61   Cohendet and Llerena (1989).
62   Boyett and Conn (1991: 23).
63   Shapira (1990); Hsing (1996).
64   Whightman (1987).

these technologies (due to the stubbornness of innovators in Silicon Valley resisting the "1984" model of informatics) that networking became the key for organizational flexibility and business performance.[65]

Bar and Borrus have shown, in a stream of important research papers, that information networking technology jumped by a quantum leap in the early 1990s, due to the convergence of three trends: digitization of the telecommunications network, development of broadband transmission, and a dramatic increase in the performance of computers connected by the network, performance which was in turn determined by technological breakthrough in micro-electronics and software. Then, computer interactive systems, which had been limited until then to local area networks, became operational in wide area networks, and the computer paradigm shifted from the mere linkage between computers to "cooperative computing," regardless of the location of the interacting partners. Qualitative advances in information technology, not available until the 1990s, allowed the emergence of fully interactive, computer-based, flexible processes of management, production, and distribution, involving simultaneous cooperation between different firms and units of such firms.[66]

In the late 1990s, the fast development of network technologies, and advanced software, were essential in the implementation and diffusion of what I have labeled the Cisco model. For instance, in the mid-1990s, large companies were using a technology called EDI (electronic data interchange) to communicate with customers and suppliers electronically, thus eliminating paperwork and intermediate steps. However, the technology was expensive, complex to set up and use, and rigid, requiring strict formatting of electronic documents such as invoices and purchase orders. With the generalization of the Internet, Intranets, and Extranets, on the basis of broad-band, fast communication networks, companies, large and small, could easily relate with each other, and with their client, in a flexible, interactive pattern. As a result, everybody was technologically able to adopt the networking form of organization, provided the firm was capable of managerial innovation.[67]

On the other hand, Dieter Ernst has shown that the convergence between organizational requirements and technological change has established networking as the fundamental form of competition in the new, global economy. Barriers to entry in the most advanced indus-

---

65 Fulk and Steinfield (1990); *Business Week* (1996).
66 Bar and Borrus (1993).
67 *Business Week* (1998).

tries, such as electronics or automobiles, have sky-rocketed, making it extremely difficult for new competitors to enter the market by themselves, and even hampering large corporations' ability to open up new product lines or to innovate their own processes in accordance with the pace of technological change.[68] Thus, cooperation and networking offer the only possibility of sharing costs, and risks, as well as keeping up with constantly renewed information. Yet networks also act as gatekeepers. Inside the networks, new possibilities are relentlessly created. Outside the networks, survival is increasingly difficult. Under the conditions of fast technological change, networks, not firms, have become the actual operating unit. In other words, through the interaction between organizational crisis and change and new information technologies a new organizational form has emerged as characteristic of the informational, global economy: *the network enterprise.*

To define more precisely the network enterprise, I need to recall my definition of organization: a system of means structured around the purpose of achieving specific goals. I would add a second analytical distinction, adapted (in a personal version) from Alain Touraine's theory.[69] In a dynamic, evolutionary perspective there is a fundamental difference between two types of organizations: organizations for which the reproduction of their system of means becomes their main organizational goal; and organizations in which goals, and the change of goals, shape and endlessly reshape the structure of means. I call the first type of organizations bureaucracies; the second type, enterprises.

On the basis of these conceptual distinctions, I propose what I believe to be a potentially useful (non-nominalist) definition of the network enterprise: *that specific form of enterprise whose system of means is constituted by the intersection of segments of autonomous systems of goals.* Thus, the components of the network are both autonomous and dependent *vis-à-vis* the network, and may be a part of other networks, and therefore of other systems of means aimed at other goals. The performance of a given network will then depend on two fundamental attributes of the network: its *connectedness*, that is, its structural ability to facilitate noise-free communication between its components; and its *consistency*, that is, the extent to which there is a sharing of interests between the network's goals and the goals of its components.

Why is the network enterprise the organizational form of the informational, global economy? One easy answer would be predicated on an empiricist approach: it is what has emerged in the formative period

68   Ernst (1994b).
69   Touraine (1959).

of the new economy, and it is what seems to be performing. But it is intellectually more satisfying to understand that this performance seems to be in accordance with the characteristics of the informational economy: the successful organizations are those able to generate knowledge and process information efficiently; to adapt to the variable geometry of the global economy; to be flexible enough to change their means as rapidly as goals change, under the impact of fast cultural, technological, and institutional change; and to innovate, as innovation becomes the key competitive weapon.[70] These characteristics are indeed features of the new economic system we have analyzed in the preceding chapter. In this sense, *the network enterprise makes material the culture of the informational, global economy: it transforms signals into commodities by processing knowledge.*

Culture, Institutions, and Economic Organization: East Asian Business Networks

Forms of economic organization do not develop in a social vacuum: they are rooted in cultures and institutions. Each society tends to generate its own organizational arrangements. The more a society is historically distinct, the more it evolves in isolation from other societies, and the more its organizational forms are specific. However, when technology broadens the scope of economic activity, and when business systems interact on a global scale, organizational forms diffuse, borrow from each other, and create a mixture that responds to largely common patterns of production and competition, while adapting to the specific social environments in which they operate.[71] This is tantamount to saying that the "market logic" is so deeply mediated by organizations, culture, and institutions that economic agents daring to follow an abstract market logic, as dictated by neoclassical economics orthodoxy, would be at a loss.[72] Most firms do not follow such logic. Some governments do, out of ideology, and they end up losing control over their economies (for example, the Reagan administration in the US in the 1980s, or the Spanish socialist government in the early 1990s). In other words, market mechanisms change over history and work through a variety of organizational forms. The critical question is then: what are the sources of market specificity? And such a question can only be answered by comparative studies of economic organization.

70 Tuomi (1999).
71 Hamilton (1991).
72 Abolaffia and Biggart (1991).

A major stream of research in comparative organizational theory has shown the fundamental differences in firms' organization and behavior in contexts very different from the traditional Anglo-Saxon pattern embedded in property rights, individualism, and separation between state and enterprises.[73] The focus of much of this research has been on the East Asian economies, an obvious choice because of the astounding performance of such economies in the 1970s and 1980s. The findings of organizational research on East Asian economies are important for a general theory of economic organization, for two reasons.

First, it can be shown that patterns of business organization in East Asian societies are produced by the interplay of culture, history, and institutions, with the latter being the fundamental factor in the formation of specific business systems. Furthermore, as expected in the institutionalist theory of economics, such patterns present common trends, linked to cultural similarity, as well as very distinct features that can be traced to major differences in institutions, as a result of specific historical processes.

Secondly, the fundamental common trend of East Asian business systems is that they are based on networks, albeit on different forms of networks. The building block of such systems is not the firm or the individual entrepreneur, but networks or business groups of different kinds, in a pattern that, with all its variations, tends to fit with the organizational form that I have characterized as the network enterprise. But Asian business networks have performed unevenly, as the new economy unfolded, and globalization accelerated. Thus, in order to assess their relationship to the model of network enterprise emerging in the West we need to consider, simultaneously, the historical specificity of cultures, the historical trajectories of institutions, the structural requisites of the informational paradigm, and the forms of competition in the global economy. It is in the interplay of these different social domains that we can find some tentative answers about "the spirit of informationalism."

A typology of East Asian business networks

Let us first set forth the record on the formation, structure, and dynamics of East Asian business networks. Fortunately, this is a subject that has received sufficient attention in social research,[74] and in which I can rely on the systematic efforts of comparative analysis and

73 Clegg and Redding (1990).
74 Whitley (1993).

theorization by the leading social scientists in this field, Nicole Woolsey Biggart and Gary Hamilton,[75] in addition to my own research work in the Asian Pacific between 1983 and 1995.

The organized network of independent firms is the prevailing form of economic activity in the market economies of East Asia. There are three distinctive, basic types of network, each one of them characterizing Japanese, Korean, and Chinese businesses.[76]

Japan

In Japan, business groups are organized around networks of firms that mutually own each other (*kabushiki mochiai*), and whose main companies are run by managers. There are two sub-types of these networks:[77]

1 Horizontal networks based on intermarket linkages among large firms (*kigyo shudan*). These networks reach out across a variety of economic sectors. Some of them are the heirs of the *zaibatsu*, the giant conglomerates that led Japanese industrialization and trade before the Second World War, prior to their formal (and ineffective) dissolution during the American occupation. The three largest old networks are Mitsui, Mitsubishi, and Sumitomo. After the war three new networks were formed around major banks: Fuyo, Dao-ichi Kangin, and Sanwa. Each one of the networks has its own sources of financing, and competes in all main sectors of activity.

2 Vertical networks (*keiretsu*), built around a *kaisha*, or large specialized industrial corporation, comprising hundreds, and even thousands, of suppliers and their related subsidiaries. Main *keiretsu* are those centered around Toyota, Nissan, Hitachi, Matsushita, Toshiba, Tokai Bank, and Industrial Bank of Japan.

These stable business groups practically control the core of the Japanese economy, organizing a dense network of mutual obligations, financial interdependency, market agreements, personnel transfer, and information sharing. A critical component of the system is the general trading company (*sogo shosha*) for each network, which acts as a general intermediary between suppliers and consumers, and adjusts in-

---

75 Hamilton and Biggart (1988); Biggart (1991); Hamilton (1991); Biggart and Hamilton (1992).
76 Hamilton et al. (1990).
77 Imai and Yonekura (1991); Gerlach (1992); Whitley (1993).

puts and outputs.[78] It is the system integrator. Such a business organization works as a flexible unit in the competitive market, allocating resources to each member of the network as it sees fit. This also makes it extremely difficult for any external firm to penetrate markets. This specific economic organization explains to a large extent the problems that foreign firms meet in penetrating the Japanese market, since all operations must be established anew, and suppliers refuse to serve other customers unless their parent *kaisha* agrees to the deal.[79]

Labor practices and work organization reflect this hierarchical network structure.[80] At the core, large companies offer their workers lifetime employment, reward systems based on seniority, and cooperation with firm-based unions. Teamwork and autonomy of task performance is the rule, counting on workers' commitment to the prosperity of their company. Management is involved at the shopfloor level, and they share facilities and working conditions with manual workers. Consensus-building is sought through a number of procedures, from the organization of work to symbolic action such as the singing of a corporate anthem to start the day.[81]

On the other hand, the more that firms are in the periphery of the network, the more labor is considered expendable and exchangeable, most of it being accounted for by temporary workers and part-time employees (see chapter 4). Women and poorly educated young people are the bulk of such peripheral labor.[82] Thus, networked business groups lead both to flexible cooperation and to highly segmented labor markets that induce a dual social structure, mainly organized along gender lines. Only the relative stability of the patriarchal Japanese family integrates both ends of the social structure, downplaying the trends toward a polarized society – but only for as long as Japanese women can be kept in subservience, both at home and at work.[83]

Korea

The Korean networks (*chaebol*), although historically inspired by the Japanese *zaibatsu*, are far more hierarchical than their Japanese counterparts.[84] Their main distinctive trend is that all firms in the network are controlled by a central holding company owned by an individual

78 Yoshino and Lifson (1986).
79 Abegglen and Stalk (1985).
80 Clark (1979); Koike (1988); Durlabhji and Marks (1993).
81 Kuwahara (1989).
82 Jacoby (1979); Shinotsuka (1994).
83 Chizuko (1987, 1988); Seki (1988).
84 Steers et al. (1989).

and his family.[85] In addition, the central holding company is backed by government banks and by government-controlled trading companies. The founding family keeps tight control by appointing members of the family, regional acquaintances, and close friends to top managerial posts throughout the *chaebol*.[86] Small and medium businesses play a minor role, unlike in the Japanese *keiretsu*. Most of the firms of the *chaebol* are relatively sizeable, and they work under the coordinated initiative of the top, centralized management of the *chaebol*, often reproducing the military style that their government backers brought to it, particularly after 1961. *Chaebol* are multi-sectoral, and their managers are transferred from one sector of activity to another, thus ensuring unity of strategy, and cross-fertilization of experience. The four largest Korean *chaebol* (Hyundai, Samsung, Lucky Gold Star, and Daewoo) figure today among the world's largest economic conglomerates, and together accounted in 1985 for 45 percent of all South Korean gross domestic product. *Chaebol* are largely self-sufficient entities, only dependent on government. Most contractual relations are internal to the *chaebol*, and subcontracting plays a minor role. Markets are shaped by the state, and developed by competition between *chaebol*.[87] Mutual obligation networks external to the *chaebol* are rare. Internal *chaebol* relations are a matter of discipline down the network, rather than of cooperation and reciprocity.

Labor policies and practices also fit this authoritarian pattern. There is, as in Japan, a sharp segmentation of labor markets between core workers and temporary workers, depending on the centrality of the firm in the *chaebol*.[88] Women play a much reduced role, since patriarchalism is even more intense in Korea than in Japan,[89] and men are reluctant to let women work outside the household. But core workers do not receive the same kind of commitment to long-term employment and working conditions from their firms.[90] Nor are they expected to commit themselves by taking the initiative. They are mainly supposed to fulfill the orders they receive. Unions were state-controlled and were kept subservient for a long period. When in the 1980s democracy made substantial gains in Korea, the unions' growing independence was met with confrontational tactics from *chaebol* leaders, giving rise to a highly conflictual pattern of industrial relations,[91] a

85 Biggart (1990a).
86 Yoo and Lee (1987).
87 Kim (1989).
88 Wilkinson (1988).
89 Gelb and Lief Palley (1994).
90 Park (1992).
91 Koo and Kim (1992).

trend that belies the racist ideology about Asian labor's supposedly obedient attitude, sometimes mistakenly attributed to Confucianism.

However, while distrust of workers is the rule, trust is a fundamental feature between different levels of management in the Korean networks, to the point that this trust is mainly embedded in kinship relationships: in 1978, 13.5 percent of the directors of the largest 100 *chaebol* were part of the owner's family, and they were in control of 21 percent of top management positions.[92] Additional managerial positions are generally held by persons trusted by the owner's family on the basis of direct knowledge, enforced by mechanisms of social control (local social networks, family networks, school networks). However, the interests of the *chaebol* are paramount, even in relation to the family. If there is a contradiction between the two, government makes sure that the *chaebol*'s interests, not individuals' or families' concerns, prevail.[93]

China

The Chinese business organization is based on family firms (*jiazuqiye*), and cross-sectoral, business networks (*jituanqiye*), often controlled by one family. Although most of the detailed research available concerns the formation and development of business networks in Taiwan,[94] empirical evidence, as well as my personal knowledge, allow for an extrapolation of such a pattern to Hong Kong and to overseas Chinese communities in South-East Asia.[95] Interestingly enough, similar networks seem to be at work in the fast process of market-driven industrialization in south China, if we extend the networks' reach to include among them the officials of local government.[96]

The key component of Chinese business organization is the family.[97] Firms are family property, and the dominant value concerns the family, not the firm. When the firm prospers, so does the family. Thus, after enough wealth has been accumulated, it is divided among family members who invest in other businesses, most often unrelated to the activity of the original firm. Sometimes, the pattern of creation of new businesses, as the family increases its wealth, is intragenerational. But if this does not happen in the life of the founder of the firm, it will after his death. This is because, unlike in Japan and Korea, the family

---

92 Shin and Chin (1989).
93 Amsdem (1989); Evans (1995).
94 Hamilton and Kao (1990).
95 Sit and Wong (1988); Yoshihara (1988).
96 Hamilton (1991); Hsing (1994).
97 Greenhalgh (1988).

system is based on patrilineage and equal inheritance among the sons, and thus each son will receive his share of the family assets, to start a business of his own. Wong, for instance, considers that successful Chinese businesses go through four phases in three generations: emergent, centralized, segmented, and disintegrative, after which the cycle starts all over again.[98] In spite of frequent intra-family rivalries, personal trust is still the basis for business deals, beyond and aside from legal-contractual rules. Thus, families prosper by creating new firms in any sector of activity deemed profitable. Family-based firms are linked by subcontracting arrangements, exchange of investment, sharing of stock. Firms are specialized in their trade, families are diversified in their investments. Connections between firms are highly personalized, fluid, and changeable, unlike the long-term commitment patterns of Japanese networks. Sources of finance tend to be informal (family savings, loans from trusted friends, revolving credit associations, or other forms of informal lending, such as Taiwan's "curb market").[99]

In such a structure, management is highly centralized and authoritarian. Middle management, not being part of the family, is considered only as a transmission belt; and workers' loyalty is not expected, since the workers' ideal is to start their own businesses, and thus they are suspect as future competitors. Commitments are short term, which undermines long-range planning strategies. On the other hand, the extreme decentralization and flexibility of such a system allows for fast adjustments to new products, new processes, and new markets. Through alliances between families, and their corresponding networks, capital turnover is accelerated, and allocation of resources is optimized.

The weak point in these small-scale Chinese business networks is their inability to undertake major strategic transformations, requiring for instance R&D investment, knowledge of world markets, large-scale technological modernization, or offshoring of production. I shall argue below, unlike some observers of Chinese business, that the state, particularly in Taiwan but also in other contexts, such as Hong Kong and certainly in China, has provided this critical strategic backing for Chinese networks to prosper in the informational, global economy beyond their profitable, but limited, local horizon. The ideology of entrepreneurial familism, rooted in an ancestral distrust of the state in southern China, cannot be taken at face value, even if it shapes, to a large extent, the behavior of Chinese businessmen.

Entrepreneurial familism is only part of the success story of Chinese

---

98   Wong (1985).
99   Hamilton and Biggart (1988).

business networks, albeit the substantial one. Another element is the Chinese version of the developmental state, in Taiwan, Hong Kong, or China. Under different forms, the state, after so many historic failures, had the intelligence finally to find the formula to support Chinese entrepreneurialism, based on familistic, trustworthy, information relationships, without suffocating its autonomy, once it became clear that the lasting glory of Chinese civilization was in fact dependent upon the relentless vitality of selfishly bustling families. It is probably not by accident that the convergence between families and the state occurred in Chinese culture at the dawn of the informational, global age, when power and wealth depend more on network flexibility than on bureaucratic might.

Culture, organizations, and institutions: Asian business networks and the developmental state

Thus, East Asian economic organization is based on business networks, both formal and informal. But there are considerable differences between the three cultural areas where these networks have arisen. As Nicole Biggart and Gary Hamilton put it, within the network Japanese firms enact a communitarian logic, Korean firms a patrimonial logic, and Taiwanese firms a patrilineal logic.[100]

Both the similarities and differences of East Asian business networks can be traced back to the cultural and institutional characteristics of these societies. The three cultures intermixed over centuries, and were deeply permeated by philosophical/religious values of Confucianism and Buddhism, in their various national patterns.[101] Their relative isolation from other areas of the world until the nineteenth century reinforced their specificity. The basic social unit is the family, not the individual. Loyalty is due to the family, and contractual obligations to other individuals are subordinated to familistic "natural law." Education is of central value, both for social betterment and for personal enhancement. Trust and reputation, within a given network of obligation, are the most valued qualities, and the most severely sanctioned rule in case of failure.[102]

Although the shaping of organizational forms by cultural attributes is sometimes too indeterminate an argument, because of its lack of specificity, it would seem that the commonality of network forms in East Asia can be related to these common cultural trends. If the unit of

---

100   Hamilton and Biggart (1988).
101   Whitley (1993).
102   Willmott (1972); Baker (1979).

economic transaction is not the individual, property rights take second place to family rights. And if the hierarchy of obligations is structured along mutual trust, stable networks have to be established on the basis of such trust, while agents external to these networks will not be treated equally in the marketplace.

But if culture fosters the commonality of network business patterns, institutions seem to account for their substantial differences while, at the same time, reinforcing their networking logic. The fundamental difference between the three cultures concerns the role of the state, both historically and in the process of industrialization. In all cases, the state pre-empted civil society: merchant and industrial elites came under the guidance, alternatively benevolent and repressive, of the state. But in each case, the state was historically different and played a different role. At this point in the argument, I must set a distinction between the role of the state in history and the performance of the contemporary, developmental state.[103]

In recent history, the substantial difference was between the Japanese state[104] and the Chinese state.[105] The Japanese state not only molded Japan, but also Korea and Taiwan under its colonial domination.[106] Since the Meiji period it was an agent of authoritarian modernization, but working through, and with, clan-based business groups (the *zaibatsu*), some of which (Mitsui, for instance) can be traced back to merchant houses linked to powerful feudal lords.[107] The Japanese imperial state set up a modern, insulated technocracy which sharpened its skills in the preparation of the Japanese war machine (the immediate ancestor of MITI was the Ministry of Munitions, core of the Japanese military industry).[108] It is only when we introduce this particular institutional setting that we understand the precise workings of culture on organizations. For instance, Hamilton and Biggart show the institutional background of the cultural explanation usually provided for Japanese consensus-building in the work process through the notion of *Wa* or harmony. *Wa* searches for the integration of the world order, through the subordination of the individual to group practices. But Biggart and Hamilton refuse to accept the direct determination of Japanese management practices as the cultural expression of *Wa*. They argue that such organizational arrangements result from an industrial system, fostered and enforced by the state, which finds support for its

103   Wade (1990); Biggart (1991); Whitley (1993).
104   Beasley (1990); Johnson (1995).
105   Feuerwerker (1984).
106   Amsdem (1979, 1985, 1989, 1992).
107   Norman (1940).
108   Johnson (1982).

implementation in the elements of traditional culture, the building materials with which institutions work to produce organizations. As they write, citing Sayle, "the Japanese government does not stand apart from or over the community: it is rather the place where *Wa* deals are negotiated."[109] Thus, business groups in Japan, as was historically the case in the areas of Japanese influence, tend to be organized vertically, around a core corporation with direct access to the state.

The Chinese state had a very different relationship to business, and particularly to business in southern China, the fundamental source of Chinese entrepreneurialism. Both in the last decades of the imperial state and in the brief period of the Kuomintang state in China, business was at the same time abused and solicited, seen as a source of income rather than as an engine of wealth. This led, on the one hand, to the harmful practices of excessive taxation and lack of support for industrialization; on the other hand, to favoritism for some business groups, thus breaking the rules of competition. Reactions to this state of affairs led Chinese business to stay away from the state as much as possible, building on a secular fear imposed on southern entrepreneurial Chinese by their northern conquerors. Such a distance from the state emphasized the role of family, as well as local and regional connections, in setting up business transactions, a trend that Hamilton shows can be dated back to the Qin dynasty.[110]

Without a reliable state enforcing property rights, you do not need to be Confucian in order to place your trust in kin rather than in a legal contract on paper. Significantly enough, it was the active involvement of the state in the West in enforcing property rights, as North has shown,[111] and not the lack of state intervention, that became the critical factor in organizing economic activity along market transactions between free individual agents. When the state did not act to create the market, as in China, families did it on their own, bypassing the state and embedding market mechanisms in socially constructed networks.

But the dynamic configuration of East Asian business networks, able to take on the global economy, came in the second half of the twentieth century, under the decisive impulse of what Chalmers Johnson has labeled the developmental state.[112] To extend this fundamental concept, which originated in Johnson's study of the role of MITI in the Japanese economy, to the broader experience of East Asian industrialization, I used in my own work a somewhat modified definition of

109 Hamilton and Biggart (1988: 72).
110 Hamilton (1984, 1985).
111 North (1981).
112 Johnson (1982, 1995).

the developmental state.[113] A state is developmental when it establishes as its principle of legitimacy its ability to promote and sustain development, understanding by development the combination of steady high rates of economic growth and structural change in the economic system, both domestically and in its relationship to the international economy. This definition is misleading, however, unless we specify the meaning of legitimacy in a given historical context. Most political theorists remain prisoners of an ethnocentric conception of legitimacy, related to the democratic state. But not all states have attempted to ground their legitimacy on the consensus of the civil society. The legitimacy principle may be exercised on behalf of the society-as-it-is (in the case of the democratic state), or on behalf of a societal project carried on by the state, as self-proclaimed interpreter of the "historical needs" of the society (the state as social "vanguard," in the Leninist tradition). When such a societal project involves a fundamental transformation of the social order, I refer to it as a revolutionary state, based on revolutionary legitimacy, regardless of the degree of internalization of such legitimacy by its subjects, for example the Communist party state. When the societal project carried forward by the state respects the broader parameters of social order (although not necessarily of a specific social structure, for example an agrarian society), I consider it to be a developmental state. The historical expression of this societal project in East Asia took the form of the affirmation of national identity, and national culture, building or rebuilding the nation as a force in the world, in this case by means of economic competitiveness and socioeconomic improvement. Ultimately, for the developmental state economic development is not a goal, but a means: the means of implementing a nationalist project, superseding a situation of material destruction and political defeat after a major war, or, in the case of Hong Kong and Singapore, after the severance of their ties with their economic and cultural environment (communist China, independent Malaysia). Along with a number of researchers,[114] I have empirically argued in several publications that at the roots of the rise of Asian Pacific economies lies the nationalist project of the developmental state. This is now generally acknowledged in the case of Japan, Korea, and Singapore. There is some debate on the matter in the case of Taiwan, although it does seem to fit the model.[115] And I raised a few eyebrows

---

113   Castells (1992). Chalmers Johnson, in his latest book (1995) converged on my redefinition of the developmental state, accepting it as a further refinement of his theory, which it is.
114   Johnson (1982, 1985, 1987, 1995); Gold (1986); Deyo (1987); Amsdem (1989, 1992); Wade (1990); Appelbaum and Henderson (1992); Evans (1995).
115   Amsdem (1985); Gold (1986).

when I extended the analysis to Hong Kong, albeit with due specifications.[116]

I cannot go into the empirical detail of this debate in the framework of this text. It would take the analysis of Asian business too far away from the focus of this chapter, namely the emergence of the network enterprise as the prevailing organizational form in the information economy. But it is possible and useful for the sake of the argument to show the correspondence between the characteristics of state intervention in each East Asian context and the variety of network forms of business organization.

In Japan, government guided economic development by advising business on product lines, export markets, technology, and work organization.[117] It backed its guidance with powerful financial and fiscal measures, as well as with selective support for strategic R&D programs. At the core of government industrial policy was the activity of the Ministry of International Trade and Industry (MITI), which periodically elaborated "visions" for Japan's development trajectory, and set up the industrial policy measures necessary to implement the desirable course along this trajectory. The crucial mechanism in ensuring that private business broadly follows government policies relied on financing. Japanese corporations are highly dependent on bank loans. Credit is channeled to the banks of each major business network by the Central Bank of Japan, under instructions from the Finance Ministry, in coordination with the MITI. Indeed, while the MITI took responsibility for strategic planning, real power in the Japanese government always lay with the Finance Ministry. Furthermore, much of the lending funds comes from postal savings, a massive supply of available finance controlled by the Ministry of Posts and Telecommunications. The MITI targeted specific industries for their competitive potential, and provided a number of incentives, such as tax breaks, subsidies, market and technology information, and support for R&D and personnel training. Until the 1980s, the MITI also enforced protectionist measures, insulating specific industries from world competition during their nurturing period. Such long-standing practices have created a protectionist inertia that survives to some extent after the formal abolition of restrictions on free trade.

Government economic intervention in Japan is organized around the autonomy of the state *vis-à-vis* business, and to a large extent *vis-à-vis* the political party system, although the conservative Liberal Democratic party ruled uncontested until 1993. Recruitment of the top-level

---

116   Castells et al. (1990).
117   Johnson (1982, 1995); Johnson et al. (1989); Gerlach (1992).

bureaucracy on the basis of merit, most often from Tokyo University graduates and particularly from the Law School, and always from elite universities (Kyoto, Hitotsubashi, Keio, and so on), ensures a tight social network of highly professional, well-trained, and largely apolitical technocrats, who constitute the actual ruling elite of contemporary Japan. Furthermore, only about 1 percent of these high-level bureaucrats reach the top of the hierarchy. The others in the later stage of their career take well-paid jobs either in para-public-sector institutions, in corporate business, or in mainstream political parties, thus ensuring the diffusion of the values of the bureaucratic elite among the political and economic agents who are in charge of implementing the government's strategic vision of Japan's national interests.

This form of state intervention, based on consensus, strategic planning, and advice, largely determines the organization of Japanese business in networks, and the particular structure of such networks. Without a centralized planning mechanism to allocate resources, Japan's industrial policy can only be effective if business itself is tightly organized in hierarchical networks that can carry out the guidelines issued by the MITI. Such coordinating mechanisms have very concrete expressions. One of them is the *shacho-kai*, or monthly meetings, which bring together the presidents of the core companies of a major intermarket network. These meetings are occasions for building social cohesion in the networks, in addition to carrying out the directives that are signaled by the government's formal or informal communications. The actual structure of the network also reflects the type of government intervention: financial dependency on government-approved loans gives a strategic role to the main bank (or banks) of the network; international trade restrictions and incentives are channeled through the general trading company of each network which works as a system integrator, both between the members of the network and between the network and the MITI. Thus, for a firm to break the discipline of the government's industrial policy is tantamount to excluding itself from the network, being cut off from access to financing, technology, and import–export licensing. Japan's strategic planning and the centralized network structure of Japanese business are but two faces of the same model of economic organization.

The connection between government policy and business organization was even more evident in the case of the Republic of Korea.[118] Yet it is important to notice that the developmental state in Korea was not characteristic of Korea during the 1950s. After the war, Syngman Rhee's dictatorship was a corrupt regime, playing simply the role of a vassal

---

118   Jones and Sakong (1980); Lim (1982); Jacobs (1985); Amsdem (1989); Evans (1995).

government of the United States. It was the nationalistic project of the Park Chung Hee regime, after the 1961 military coup, that set up the bases for a state-led process of industrialization and competition in the world economy, enacted by Korean business on behalf of the interests of the nation and under the strict guidance of the state. The Park government aimed at creating the equivalent of the Japanese *zaibatsu*, on the basis of existing large Korean companies. But because the resulting networks were forced into existence by the state they were even more centralized and authoritarian than their Japanese predecessors. To achieve its design, the Korean government closed the domestic market to international competition and practiced an import-substitution policy. As soon as Korean firms started to operate, it targeted the enhancement of their competitiveness, and favored an export-oriented strategy along a trajectory of increasingly capital- and technology-intensive industries, with specific goals outlined in five-year economic plans established by the Economic Planning Board, the brain and engine of Korea's economic miracle. In the vision of the Korean military, to be competitive Korean firms had to be concentrated in large conglomerates. They were forced to do so by government control of the banking system, and of the export–import licenses. Both credit and licenses were selectively given to firms on condition of joining a *chaebol*, since government privileges were accorded to the central firm (owned by a family) in the *chaebol*. Business was also explicitly requested to finance the government's political activities, as well as to pay in cash for any special favors obtained from top-level bureaucrats, generally military officers. To enforce strict business discipline, the Park government did not relinquish control over the banking system. Thus, unlike in Japan, Korean *chaebol* were not financially independent until the 1980s. Labor policies were also shaped by military-induced authoritarianism, with the unions being directly under government control to make sure that they would be purged of any communist influence. These labor policies led to the ferocious repression of any independent labor organization, thus destroying the possibility of consensus-building in the work process of Korean industry.[119] The military state origin of *chaebol* was certainly more influential in shaping the authoritarian and patrilineal character of Korean business networks than the Confucian tradition of rural Korea.[120]

The interaction between state and business is far more complex in the case of Chinese family firms, rooted in centuries-old distrust of government interference. And yet government planning and policy have

119   Kim (1987).
120   Janelli (1993).

been a decisive factor in Taiwan's economic development.[121] Not only does Taiwan have the largest public enterprise sector of the capitalist Asian Pacific (amounting to about 25 percent of GDP up to the late 1970s), but government guidance was formalized in successive four-year economic plans. As in Korea, control of banks and of export–import licenses were the main instruments for the implementation of government economic policy, also based on the combination of an import-substitution policy and export-oriented industrialization. Yet, unlike in Korea, Chinese firms did not depend primarily on bank credits but, as mentioned above, relied on family savings, credit cooperatives, and informal capital markets, largely autonomous from the government. Thus, small and medium-sized enterprises thrived on their own, and established the horizontal, family-based networks I have described. The intelligence of the KMT state, having learned from its historical mistakes in 1930s' Shanghai, was to build on the foundations of these dynamic networks of small enterprises, many of them in the rural fringes of the metropolitan areas, sharing farming and craft industrial production. However, it is doubtful that these small enterprises would have been able to compete on the world market without critical, strategic support from the state. Such support took three main forms: (a) subsidized health and education, public infrastructure, and income redistribution, on the basis of a radical agrarian reform; (b) attraction of foreign capital, via tax incentives, and the establishment of the first export-processing zones in the world, thus ensuring linkages, subcontracting and enhancement of quality standards for Taiwanese firms and workers that came into contact with foreign companies; (c) decisive government support for R&D, technology transfer, and diffusion. This latter point was particularly critical to enable Taiwanese firms to climb up the ladder of the technological division of labor. For instance, the process of diffusion of advanced electronics technology, at the origin of the expansion of the most dynamic sector of Taiwan's industry in the 1980s, PC clone manufacturing, was directly organized by the government in the 1960s.[122] The government acquired the license for chip design technology from RCA, together with the training of Chinese engineers by the American company. Relying on these engineers, the government created a public research center, ETRI, which kept up to date with developments in the world's electronic technology, emphasizing its commercial applications. Under government directives, ETRI organized enterprise seminars to diffuse, at no cost, the technology it was generating among Taiwanese

121   Amsdem (1979, 1985); Chen (1979); Kuo (1983); Gold (1986).
122   Chen (1979); Lin et al. (1980); Wong (1988); Castells et al. (1990).

small firms. Furthermore, ETRI engineers were encouraged to leave the institute after a few years, and were provided with government funding and technology support to start up their own businesses. Thus, although in more traditional industries government support in Taiwan was more indirect than in South Korea or Japan, what is characteristic is that productive interaction was found between government and business networks: networks continued to be family-based and relatively small in the size of their firms (although there are also major industrial groups in Taiwan; for example, Tatung); but government policies assumed the coordinating and strategic planning functions when it was necessary for such networks to broaden and upgrade the scope of their activities in products, processes, and markets.

The story is more complex in the case of Hong Kong, but the outcome is not too dissimilar.[123] The basis of the export-oriented industrial structure of Hong Kong was made from small and medium businesses which originated mainly from family savings, starting with 21 industrialists' families who emigrated from Shanghai after the communist revolution. But the colonial government aimed at making Hong Kong into a showcase for the successful implementation of British benevolent colonialism, and in the process also tried to make the Territory self-sufficient in its finances in order to put off pressures for decolonization from the Labour party back home. To do so behind the ideological screen of "positive non-intervention" (eagerly consumed by the Milton Friedmans of the world), the Hong Kong "cadets," career civil servants from the British Colonial Service, introduced an active developmental policy, half by design, half by accident.[124] They strictly controlled the distribution of textile and garment export quotas among firms, allocating them on the basis of their knowledge of competitive capabilities. They built a network of government institutions (productivity center, trade council, and so on) to diffuse information about markets, technology, management, and other critical matters throughout the networks of small enterprises, thus accomplishing the coordinating and strategic functions without which such networks would never have been able to tap into the markets of the US and of Commonwealth countries. They built the largest public housing program in the world in terms of the proportion of the population housed in its premises (later it became second to Singapore, after Singapore had imitated the formula). Not only were there thousands of factories in high-rise buildings (called "flatted factories") paying low rents as an integral part of the public housing program, but

123 Castells (1989c); Castells and Hall (1994).
124 Lethbridge (1978); Mushkat (1982); Miners (1986).

the subsidy of the program substantially lowered labor costs, and the safety net it provided made it possible for workers to venture into starting their own businesses without excessive risk (seven starts on average before succeeding). In Taiwan, the rural dwelling and the family plot of land, resulting from the persistence of farming in the industrial areas, was the safety mechanism that allowed for movement back and forth between self-employment and salaried employment.[125] In Hong Kong, the functional equivalent was the public housing program. In both cases, networks of small businesses could emerge, disappear, and re-emerge under a different form because there was a safety net provided by family solidarity and a peculiar colonial version of the welfare state.[126]

A similar form of linkage between supportive government and family-based business networks seemed to be emerging in the process of export-oriented industrialization in southern China in the 1990s.[127] On the one hand, Hong Kong and Taiwanese manufacturers tapped into the regional networks of their villages of origin in Guandong and Fukien provinces to create subsidiaries and to establish subcontractors, in order to offshore the low end of their manufacturing production (for example, in shoes, plastics, or consumer electronics). On the other hand, such production networks can only exist on the basis of the support of provincial and local governments, which provide the necessary infrastructure, enforce labor discipline, and act as intermediaries between management, labor, and export firms. As Hsing writes in concluding her pioneering effort of research into Taiwanese manufacturing investment in southern China:

> The new pattern of foreign direct investment in the rapidly industrializing regions of China is characterized by the dominant role played by small and medium-sized investors and their collaboration with low-level local authorities in new production sites. The institutional basis that maintains and enhances the flexibility of their operations is a network form of production and marketing organizations, as well as the increasing autonomy of the local governments. Of equal importance, the cultural affinity of overseas investors and their local agents, including local officials and local workers, facilitates a much smoother and faster process of establishing transnational production networks.[128]

Thus, the form of Chinese business networks is also a function of the indirect, subtle, yet real and effective form of state intervention in the

125   Chin (1988).
126   Schiffer (1983).
127   Hamilton (1991); Hsing (1994, 1996).
128   Hsing (1996: 307).

process of economic development in various contexts. However, a process of historical transformation may be underway, as Chinese business networks have grown extraordinarily in wealth, influence, and global reach. Interestingly enough, they continue to be family-based, and their interlocking seems to reproduce the early forms of networking between small entrepreneurs. But they are certainly powerful enough to bypass directives from government in Taiwan, in Hong Kong, and for that matter, in other South-East Asian countries, with the exception of the strong Singaporean state. Chinese business networks, while keeping in essence their organizational structure and cultural dynamics, appear to have reached a qualitatively larger size, one that allows them finally to be set free from the state.[129] But such a perception might be an illusion linked to a period of historical transition because what is looming on the horizon is the gradual linkage between powerful Chinese business networks and the multilayered structure of the mainland Chinese state. Indeed, the most profitable investments of Chinese businesses are already taking place in China. When and if such linkage takes place, the autonomy of Chinese business networks will be tested, as will be the ability of a developmental state constructed by a communist party to evolve into a form of government able to steer without subduing the flexible, family-based, network enterprises. If such convergence takes place, the world's economic landscape will be transformed.

Thus, observation of East Asian business networks shows the cultural and institutional sources of such organizational forms, both in their common features and in their significant differences. Let us now return to the general analytical implications of this conclusion. Are such networking forms of economic organization able to develop in other cultural/institutional contexts? How does contextual variation influence their morphology and performance? What is common to the new rules of the game in the informational, global economy, and what is specific to particular social systems (for example, East Asian business systems, the "Anglo-Saxon model," the "French model," the "northern Italian model," and so on)? And the most important question of all: how will the organizational forms of the late industrial economy, such as the large multi-unit corporation, interact with the emerging network enterprise in its various manifestations?

129   Mackie (1992a, b).

Multinational Enterprises, Transnational Corporations, and International Networks

The analysis of East Asian business networks shows the institutional/ cultural production of organizational forms. But it also shows the limits of the market-driven theory of business organizations, ethnocentrically rooted in the Anglo-Saxon experience. Thus, Williamson's influential interpretation[130] of the emergence of the large corporation as the best way to reduce uncertainty and minimize transaction costs, by internalizing transactions within the corporation, simply does not hold when confronted with the empirical evidence of the spectacular process of capitalist development that took place in the Asian Pacific between the mid-1960s and the early 1990s, based on networks external to the corporation.[131]

Similarly, the process of economic globalization based on network formation seems also to contradict the classical analysis by Chandler[132] that attributes the rise of the large multi-unit corporation to the growing size of the market, and to the availability of communications technology that enables the large firm to take hold on such a broad market, thus reaping economies of scale and scope, and internalizing them within the firm. Chandler extended his historical analysis of the expansion of the large firm in the US market to the rise of the multinational enterprise as a response to the globalization of the economy, this time by using enhanced information technologies.[133] In most of the literature of the past 20 years it seems as if the multinational enterprise, with its divisional, centralized structure, was the organizational expression of the new, global economy.[134] The only debate on the matter was between those who argued for the persistence of the national roots of the multinational enterprise,[135] and those who considered the new forms of enterprise as truly transnational corporations, having superseded in their vision, interests, and commitments any particular country, regardless of their historical origin.[136] Yet empirical analyses of the structure and practice of large corporations with a global scope appear to show that both visions are outdated and should be replaced by the emergence of international networks of firms, and of subunits

---

130   Williamson (1985).
131   Hamilton and Biggart (1988).
132   Chandler (1977).
133   Chandler (1986).
134   Enderwick (1989); De Anne (1990); Dunning (1993).
135   Ghoshal and Westney (1993).
136   Ohmae (1990).

of firms, as the basic organizational form of the informational, global economy. Dieter Ernst has summarized a substantial amount of available evidence concerning the formation of inter-firm networks in the global economy, and considers that most economic activity in leading industries is organized around five different types of networks (electronics and automobiles being the most advanced industries in the diffusion of this organizational pattern). These five types of networks are:

1 *Supplier networks* which are defined to include subcontracting, OEM (original equipment manufacturing) and ODM (original design manufacturing) arrangements between a client (the "focal company") and its suppliers of intermediate production inputs.
2 *Producer networks* which are defined to include all co-production arrangements that enable competing producers to pool their production capacities, financial, and human resources in order to broaden their product portfolios and geographic coverage.
3 *Customer networks* which are defined as the forward linkages of manufacturing companies with distributors, marketing channels, value-added resellers and end-users, either in the major export markets or in domestic markets.
4 *Standard coalitions* which are initiated by potential global standard setters with the explicit purpose of locking-in as many firms as possible into their proprietary product or interface standards.
5 *Technology cooperation networks* which facilitate the acquisition of product design and production technology, enable joint production and process development, and permit generic scientific knowledge and R&D to be shared.[137]

However, the formation of these networks does not imply the demise of the multinational enterprise. Ernst, concurring with a number of observers on this matter,[138] considers that networks are either centered on a major multinational enterprise or are formed on the basis of alliances and cooperation between such enterprises. Cooperative networks of small and medium enterprises do exist (for example, in Italy and in East Asia), but they play a minor role in the global economy, at least in the key industries. Oligopolistic concentration seems to have been maintained or increased in most sectors of major industries, not only in spite of but because of the networked form of organization. This is because entry into the strategic networks requires either considerable

137 Ernst (1994b: 5–6).
138 Harrison (1994).

resources (financial, technological, market share) or an alliance with a major player in the network.

Multinational enterprises seem to be still highly dependent on their national basis. The idea of transnational corporations being "citizens of the world economy" does not seem to hold. Yet the networks formed by multinational corporations do transcend national boundaries, identities, and interests.[139] My hypothesis is that, as the process of globalization progresses, organizational forms evolve from *multinational enterprises* to *international networks*, actually bypassing the so-called "transnationals" that belong more to the world of mythical representation (or self-serving image-making by management consultants) than to the institutionally bounded realities of the world economy.

Furthermore, as mentioned above, multinational enterprises are not only engaged in networking, but are increasingly organized themselves in decentralized networks. Ghoshal and Bartlett, after summarizing evidence on the transformation of multinational corporations, define the contemporary multinational as "an inter-organizational network," or, more precisely, as "a network that is embedded within an external network."[140] This approach is critical to our understanding because, so the argument goes, the characteristics of the institutional environments where the various components of the corporation are located actually shape the structure and dynamics of the corporation's internal network. Thus, multinational corporations are indeed the power-holders of wealth and technology in the global economy, since most networks are structured around such corporations. But at the same time, they are internally differentiated in decentralized networks, and externally dependent on their membership in a complex, changing structure of interlocked networks, cross-border networks in Imai's formulation.[141] Besides, each one of the components of these networks, internal and external, is embedded in specific cultural/institutional environments (nations, regions, locales) that affect the network in varying degrees. Overall, the networks are asymmetrical, but each single element of the network can hardly survive by itself or impose its diktat. The logic of the network is more powerful than the powers in the network. The management of uncertainty becomes critical in a situation of asymmetrical interdependency.

Why are networks central in the new economic competition? Ernst argues that two factors are foremost sources in this process of organizational transformation: globalization of markets and inputs; and dramatic technological change that makes equipment constantly obsolete

---

139   Imai (1990a).
140   Ghoshal and Bartlett (1993: 81).
141   Imai (1990a).

and forces firms to be relentlessly updated with information on processes and products. In such a context, cooperation is not only a way of sharing costs and resources, but also an insurance policy against a bad technological decision: the consequences of such a decision would also be suffered by the competitors since networks are ubiquitous and intertwined.

Interestingly enough, Ernst's explanation for the emergence of the international network enterprise echoes the argument of market theorists, which I have tried to personalize in Chandler for the classics, and in Williamson for the new wave of neoclassical economists. Market characteristics and technology are suggested to be the key variables. However, in Ernst's analysis, the organizational effects are exactly the opposite of those expected by the traditional economic theory: while market size was supposed to induce the formation of the vertical, multi-unit corporation, the globalization of competition dissolves the large corporation in a web of multidirectional networks, which become the actual operating unit. The increase of transaction costs, because of added technological complexity, does not result in the internalization of transactions within the corporation but in the externalization of transactions and sharing of costs throughout the network, obviously increasing uncertainty, but also making possible the spreading and sharing of uncertainty. Thus, either the mainstream explanation of business organization, based on neoclassical market theory, is wrong, or else available evidence on the emergence of business networks is faulty. I am inclined to think the former.

Thus, the network enterprise, a predominant form of business organization in East Asia, seems to be flourishing in various institutional/cultural contexts, in Europe,[142] as in the United States,[143] while the large, multi-unit corporation, hierarchically organized around vertical lines of command seems to be ill-adapted to the informational, global economy. Globalization and informationalization seem to be structurally related to networking and flexibility. Does this trend mean that we are shifting to an Asian model of development which would replace the Anglo-Saxon model of the classical corporation? I do not think so, in spite of the diffusion of work and management practices across countries. Cultures and institutions continue to shape the organizational requirements of the new economy, in an interaction between the logic of production, the changing technological basis, and the institutional features of the social environment. A survey of business cultures in Europe shows the variation within Europe of

142 Danton de Rouffignac (1991).
143 Bower (1987); Harrison (1994).

organizational patterns, particularly *vis-à-vis* the relationships between governments and firms.[144] The architecture and composition of business networks being formed around the world are influenced by the national characteristics of societies where such networks are embedded. For instance, the content and strategies of electronic firms in Europe are highly contingent on the policies of the European Union, regarding the reduction of technological dependency on Japan and the US. But, on the other hand, the alliance of Siemens with IBM and Toshiba in micro-electronics is dictated by technological imperatives. The formation of high-technology networks around defense programs in the US is an institutional characteristic of American industry, and one that tends to exclude foreign partnership. The gradual incorporation of northern Italian industrial districts by major Italian firms was favored by agreements between government, large firms, and labor unions concerning the convenience of stabilizing and consolidating the productive base formed during the 1970s, with the support of regional governments that were dominated by left-wing parties. In other words, the network enterprise is increasingly international (not transnational), and its conduct will result from the managed interaction between the global strategy of the network and the nationally/regionally rooted interests of its components. Since most multinational firms participate in a variety of networks depending on products, processes, and countries, the new economy cannot be characterized as being centered any longer on multinational corporations, even if they continue to exercise jointly oligopolistic control over most markets. This is because corporations have transformed themselves into a web of multiple networks embedded in a multiplicity of institutional environments. Power still exists, but it is randomly exercised. Markets still trade, but purely economic calculations are hampered by their dependency on unsolvable equations overdetermined by too many variables. The market's hand which institutional economists tried to make visible has returned to invisibility. But this time, its structural logic is not only governed by supply and demand but also influenced by hidden strategies and untold discoveries played out in the global information networks.

The Spirit of Informationalism

Max Weber's classic essay on *The Protestant Ethic and the Spirit of Capitalism,* originally published in 1904–5,[145] still remains the meth-

---

144 Randlesome et al. (1990).
145 Weber (1958).

odological cornerstone of any theoretical attempt at grasping the essence of cultural/institutional transformations which in history usher in a new paradigm of economic organization. His substantive analysis of the roots of capitalist development has certainly been challenged by historians, who have pointed to alternative historical configurations that sustained capitalism as effectively as the Anglo-Saxon culture did, albeit in different institutional forms. Furthermore, the focus of this chapter is not so much on capitalism, which is alive and well in spite of its social contradictions, as on informationalism, a new mode of development that alters, but does not replace, the dominant mode of production. Yet the theoretical principles proposed by Max Weber almost a century ago still provide a useful guideline to make sense of the series of analyses and observations I have presented in this chapter, bringing them together to highlight the new cultural/institutional configuration underlying the organizational forms of economic life. In homage to one of sociology's founding fathers, I shall call this configuration "the spirit of informationalism."

Where to start? How to proceed? Let us read Weber again:

> The spirit of capitalism. What is to be understood by it? . . . If any object can be found to which this term can be applied with any understandable meaning, it can only be an historical individual, i.e. a complex of elements associated in historical reality which we unite into a conceptual whole from the standpoint of their cultural significance. Such an historical concept, however, since it refers in its content to a phenomenon significant for its unique individuality . . . must be gradually put together out of the individual parts which are taken from historical reality to make it up. Thus the final and definitive concept cannot stand at the beginning of the investigation, but must come at the end.[146]

We are at the end, at least of this chapter. What are the elements of historical reality we have uncovered as being associated in the new organizational paradigm? And how can we unite them in a conceptual whole of historical significance?

They are, first of all, *business networks*, under different forms, in different contexts, and from different cultural expressions. Family-based networks in Chinese societies and northern Italy; entrepreneurial networks emerging from technological seedbeds in the milieux of innovation, as in Silicon Valley; hierarchical, communal networks of the Japanese *keiretsu* type; organizational networks of decentralized corporate units from former vertically integrated corporations forced to adapt to the realities of the time; business networks made up of

146 Weber (1958: 47).

customers and suppliers of a given company, inserted in a broader web of networks formed around other networked companies; and cross-border networks resulting from strategic alliances between firms, and their ancillary support networks.

There are also *technological tools*: new telecommunication networks; new, powerful desktop computers; ubiquitous computing devices connected to powerful servers; new, adaptive, self-evolving software; new, mobile communication devices that extend on-line linkages to any space at any time; new workers and managers, connected to each other around tasks and performance, able to speak the same language, the digital language.

There is *global competition*, forcing constant redefinitions of products, processes, markets, and economic inputs, including capital and information.

And there is, as always, *the state*: developmental in the take-off stage of the new economy, as in East Asia; agent of incorporation when economic institutions have to be rebuilt, as in the process of European unification; coordinating when territorially based networks need the nurturing support of local or regional governments to generate synergistic effects that will set up milieux of innovation; and mission-oriented messenger when it steers a national economy, or the world economic order, into a new historical course, scripted in the technology but not fulfilled in the business practice, as in the US government's design to build the twenty-first century's information superhighway, or to impose a liberal world trade order. All these elements come together to give rise to the network enterprise.

The *emergence and consolidation of the network enterprise*, in all its different manifestations, may well be the answer to the "productivity enigma" that cast such a long shadow on my analysis of the informational economy in the preceding chapter. Because, as Bar and Borrus argue in their study on the future of networking:

> One reason Information Technology investments have not translated into higher productivity is that they have primarily served to automate existing tasks. They often automate inefficient ways of doing things. Realizing the potential of Information Technology requires substantial re-organization. The ability to re-organize tasks as they become automated rests largely on the availability of a coherent infrastructure, i.e. a flexible network able to interconnect the various computer-based business activities.

They go on to establish a historical parallel with the impact of decentralization of small electrical generators to the shopfloor of industrial factories, to conclude "These decentralized computers are only now

[1993] being interconnected, so as to allow and support re-organization. Where this has been effectively accomplished, there are corresponding gains in productivity."[147]

Yet, while all these elements are ingredients of the new developmental paradigm, they still lack the cultural glue that brings them together. Because, as Max Weber wrote:

> The capitalism of today, which has come to dominate economic life, educates and selects the economic subjects which it needs through a process of economic survival of the fittest. But here one can easily see the limits of the concept of selection as a means of historical explanation. In order that a manner of life so well adapted to the peculiarities of capitalism could be selected at all, i.e. should come to dominate others, it had to originate somewhere, and not in isolated individuals alone, but as a way of life common to a whole group of men. This origin is what really needs explanation . . . In the country of Benjamin Franklin's birth . . . the spirit of capitalism was present before the capitalistic order.

And he adds:

> The fact to be explained historically is that in the most highly capitalistic centre of that time, in Florence of the fourteenth and fifteenth centuries, the money and capital market of all the great political Powers, this attitude [Benjamin Franklin's defense of profit-searching] was considered ethically unjustifiable, or at best to be tolerated. But in the backwoods small bourgeois circumstances of Pennsylvania in the eighteenth century, where business threatened for simple lack of money to fall back into barter, where there was hardly a sign of large enterprise, where only the earliest beginnings of banking were to be found, the same thing was considered the essence of moral conduct, even commanded in the name of duty. To speak here of a reflection of material conditions in the ideal superstructure would be patent nonsense. What was the background of ideas which could account for the sort of activity apparently directed toward profit alone as a calling toward which the individual feels himself to have an ethical obligation? For it was this idea which gave the way of life of the new entrepreneur its ethical foundation and justification.[148]

What is the ethical foundation of informationalism? And does it need an ethical foundation at all? I should remind the patient reader that in the historical period of the rise of informationalism, capitalism, albeit in new, profoundly modified forms *vis-à-vis* the time of

147　Bar and Borrus (1993: 6).
148　Weber (1958: 55, 75).

Weber's writing, is still operating as the dominant economic form. Thus, the corporate ethos of accumulation, the renewed appeal of consumerism, are driving cultural forms in the organizations of informationalism. Additionally, the state and the affirmation of national/cultural collective identity have been shown to muster decisive force in the arena of global competition. Families, in their complexity, continue to thrive and reproduce by the means of economic competition, accumulation, and heritage. But while all these elements seem to account, together, for the cultural sustainment of renewed capitalist competition, they do not seem to be specific enough to distinguish the new agent of such capitalist competition: the network enterprise.

For the first time in history, the basic unit of economic organization is not a subject, be it individual (such as the entrepreneur, or the entrepreneurial family) or collective (such as the capitalist class, the corporation, the state). As I have tried to show, *the unit is the network*, made up of a variety of subjects and organizations, relentlessly modified as networks adapt to supportive environments and market structures. What glues together these networks? Are they purely instrumental, accidental alliances? It may be so for particular networks, but the networking form of organization must have a cultural dimension of its own. Otherwise, economic activity would be performed in a social/cultural vacuum, a statement that can be sustained by some ultra-rationalist economists, but that is fully belied by the historical record. What is, then, this *"ethical foundation of the network enterprise"* this *"spirit of informationalism?"*

It is certainly not a new culture, in the traditional sense of a system of values, because the multiplicity of subjects in the network and the diversity of networks reject such a unifying "network culture." Nor is it a set of institutions because we have observed the diverse development of the network enterprise in a variety of institutional environments, to the point of being shaped by such environments into a broad range of forms. But there is indeed a common cultural code in the diverse workings of the network enterprise. It is made of many cultures, many values, many projects, which cross through the minds and inform the strategies of the various participants in the networks, changing at the same pace as the network's members, and following the organizational and cultural transformation of the units of the network. It is a culture, indeed, but a culture of the ephemeral, a culture of each strategic decision, a patchwork of experiences and interests, rather than a charter of rights and obligations. It is a *multi-faceted, virtual culture*, as in the visual experiences created by computers in cyberspace by rearranging reality. It is not a fantasy, it is a material force because it informs, and enforces, powerful economic decisions at every moment in the life of the network. But it does not stay long: it goes into the computer's memory as raw material of past successes and failures. The network enterprise learns to live within this virtual culture. Any attempt at crystallizing the position in the network as a cultural code in a particular time and space sentences the network to obsolescence, since it becomes too rigid for the variable geometry required by informationalism. The "spirit of informationalism" is the culture of "creative destruction" accelerated to the speed of the opto-electronic circuits that process its signals. Schumpeter meets Weber in the cyberspace of the network enterprise.

As for the potential social consequences of this new economic history, the voice of the master resonates with force 100 years later:

> The modern economic order . . . is now bound to the technical and economic conditions of machine production which today determine the lives of all individuals who are born into this mechanism, not only those directly concerned with economic acquisition, with irresistible force . . . The care for external goods should only lie on the shoulders of the "saint like a light cloak, which can be thrown aside at any moment." But fate decreed that the cloak should become an iron cage . . . Today the spirit of religious asceticism . . . has escaped from the cage. But victorious capitalism, since it rests on mechanical foundations, needs its support no longer . . . No one knows who will live in this cage in the future, or whether at the end of this tremendous development, entirely new prophets will arise, or there will be a great rebirth of old ideas, or, if neither, mechanized petrification, embellished with a sort of convulsive self-importance. For of the last stage of this cultural development, it might well be truly said: "Specialists without spirit, sensualists without heart; this nullity imagines that it has attained a level of civilization never before achieved."[149]

---

149 Weber (1958: 180–2).

4

The Transformation of Work and Employment: Networkers, Jobless, and Flex-timers[1]

The process of work is at the core of social structure. The technological and managerial transformation of labor, and of production relationships, in and around the emerging network enterprise is the main lever by which the informational paradigm and the process of globalization affect society at large. In this chapter I shall analyze this transformation on the basis of available evidence, while attempting to make sense of contradictory trends observed in the changes of work and employment patterns over the past decades. I shall first address the classic question of secular transformation of employment structure that underlies theories of post-industrialism, by analyzing its evolution in the main capitalist countries between 1920 and 2005. Next, to reach beyond the borders of OECD countries, I shall consider the arguments on the emergence of a global labor force. I shall then turn to analyze the specific impact of new information technologies on the process of work itself, and on the level of employment, trying to assess the widespread fear of a jobless society. Finally, I shall treat the potential impacts of the transformation of work and employment on the social structure by focusing on processes of social polarization that have been associated with the emergence of the informational para-

1 I would like to acknowledge the significant input to this chapter of Martin Carnoy and Harley Shaiken. I have also relied extensively on data and material provided by the International Institute of Labour Studies, International Labour Office. For this, I am particularly grateful to Padmanabha Gopinath and Gerry Rodgers.

digm. In fact, I shall suggest an alternative hypothesis that, while acknowledging these trends, will place them in the broader framework of a more fundamental transformation: the individualization of work and the fragmentation of societies.[2] Along such an intellectual itinerary, I shall use data and research findings from a flurry of monographs, simulation models, and standard statistics that have treated these questions with minute attention over many years in many countries. Yet the purpose of my inquiry, as for this book in general, is analytical: it aims at raising new questions rather than answering old concerns.

The Historical Evolution of Employment and Occupational Structure in Advanced Capitalist Countries: the G-7, 1920–2005

In any process of historical transition one of the most direct expressions of systemic change is the transformation of employment and occupational structure. Indeed, theories of post-industrialism and informationalism use as the strongest empirical evidence for the change in historical course the coming into being of a new social structure, characterized by the shift from goods to services, by the rise of managerial and professional occupations, by the demise of agricultural and manufacturing jobs, and by the growing information content of work in the most advanced economies. Implicit in much of these formulations is a sort of natural law of economies and societies, which should follow a single path along a trajectory of modernity in which American society has led the way.

I take a different approach. I contend that while there is a common trend in the unfolding of the employment structure characteristic of informational societies, there is also an historical variation in employment patterns according to specific institutions, culture, and political environments. In order to assess both the commonality and the variation of employment structures in the informational paradigm I have examined the evolution of employment structure between 1920 and 1990 for the major capitalist countries that constitute the core of the global economy, the so-called G-7 countries. All of them are in an

2 To understand the transformation of work in the informational paradigm it is necessary to root this analysis in a comparative and historical perspective. For this, I have relied on what I consider to be the best available source of ideas and research on the matter: Pahl (1988). The central thesis of this chapter on the transition toward individualization of work, inducing potentially fragmented societies, is also related, although from a very different analytical perspective, to an important book that builds on Polanyi's theory, and relies on empirical analysis of Italian social structure: Mingione (1991).

advanced stage of transition to the informational society, thus can be used to observe the emergence of new employment patterns. They also represent very distinct cultures and institutional systems, allowing us to examine historical variety. In conducting this analysis I am not implying that all other societies, at different levels of development, will conform to one or another of the historical trajectories represented by these countries. As I have argued in the general introduction to this book, the new, informational paradigm interacts with history, institutions, levels of development, and position in the global system of interaction along the lines of different networks. The analysis presented in the following pages has a more precise purpose: to unveil the interaction between technology, economy, and institutions in the patterning of employment and occupation, in the process of transition between agricultural, industrial, and informational modes of development.

By differentiating the internal composition of service employment, and by analyzing the differential evolution of the employment and occupational structure in each one of the seven countries (United States, Japan, Germany, France, Italy, the United Kingdom, and Canada) between *circa* 1920 and *circa* 1990, the analysis presented here introduces an empirically grounded discussion of the cultural/institutional diversity of the informational society. To proceed in such a direction, I shall introduce the analytical issues researched in this section, define the concepts, and describe briefly the methodology I have used in this study. [3]

Post-industrialism, the service economy, and the informational society

The classical theory of post-industrialism combined three statements and predictions which ought to be analytically differentiated:[4]

1 The source of productivity and growth lies in the generation of knowledge, extended to all realms of economic activity through information processing.
2 Economic activity would shift from goods production to services delivery. The demise of agricultural employment would be followed by the irreversible decline of manufacturing jobs, to the benefit of service jobs which would ultimately form the overwhelming pro-

---

3   The analysis of the evolution of employment structure in the G-7 countries was conducted with considerable help from Dr Yuko Aoyama, formerly my research assistant at Berkeley, particularly for the construction of the international, comparative database on which this analysis is grounded.
4   Bell (1976); Dordick and Wang (1993).

portion of employment. The more advanced an economy, the more its employment and its production would be focused on services.

3   The new economy would increase the importance of occupations with a high information and knowledge content in their activity. Managerial, professional, and technical occupations would grow faster than any other occupational position and would constitute the core of the new social structure.

Although various interpretations would extend the theory of post-industrialism in different versions to the realm of social classes, politics, and culture, the preceding three interrelated statements anchor the theory at the level of the social structure, the level where, in Bell's thinking, the theory belongs. Each one of these major assertions deserves qualification. In addition, the historical linkage between the three processes has still to be submitted to empirical verification.

First, as I argued in chapter 2, knowledge and information seem indeed to be major sources of productivity and growth in advanced societies. However, as we also saw above, it is important to notice that theories of post-industrialism based their original assertion on research by Solow and by Kendrick, both referring to the first half of the twentieth century in America, at the height of the industrial era. This is to say that the knowledge base of productivity growth was a feature of the industrial economy when manufacturing employment was at its peak in the most advanced countries. Thus, although the late twentieth-century economies were clearly different from the pre-World War II economies, the feature that distinguishes these two types of economy does not seem to be rooted primarily in the source of their productivity growth. *The appropriate distinction is not between an industrial and a post-industrial economy, but between two forms of knowledge-based industrial, agricultural, and services production.* As I have argued in the opening chapters of this book, what is most distinctive, in historical terms, between the economic structures of the first half and of the second half of the twentieth century is the revolution in information technology, and its diffusion in all spheres of social and economic activity, including its contribution to providing the infrastructure for the formation of a global economy. Therefore, I propose to shift the analytical emphasis from *post-industrialism* (a relevant question of social forecasting still without an answer at the moment of its formulation) to *informationalism*. In this perspective, societies will be informational, not because they fit into a particular model of social structure, but because they organize their production system around the principles of maximizing knowledge-based productivity through the development and diffusion of information technologies, and by fulfilling the prerequisites for their utilization (primarily human resources and communications infrastructure).

The second criterion of post-industrialist theory by which to consider a society as post-industrial concerns the shift to service activities and the demise of manufacturing. It is an obvious fact that most employment in advanced economies is in services, and that the service sector accounts for the largest contribution to GNP. Yet it does not follow that manufacturing industries are disappearing or that the structure and dynamics of manufacturing activity are indifferent to the health of a service economy. Cohen and Zysman,[5] among others, have forcefully argued that many services depend on their direct linkage to manufacturing, and that manufacturing activity (distinct from manufacturing employment) is critical to the productivity and competitiveness of the economy. For the United States, Cohen and Zysman estimate that 24 percent of GNP comes from the value added by manufacturing firms, and another 25 percent of GNP comes from the contribution of services directly linked to manufacturing. Thus, they argue that the post-industrial economy is a "myth," and that we are in fact in a different kind of industrial economy. Much of the confusion comes from the artificial separation between advanced economies and developing economies which, under the conditions of globalization, are in fact part of the same productive structure. Thus, while analysts were proclaiming the de-industrialization of America, or of Europe in the 1980s, they simply overlooked what was happening in the rest of the world. And what was happening was that, according to studies from the ILO,[6] global manufacturing employment was at its highest point in 1989, having increased by 72 percent between 1963 and 1989. The trend continued in the 1990s. Between 1970 and 1997, while manufacturing jobs declined slightly in the US (from 19,367 million to 18,657 million), and substantially in the European Union (from 38,400 to 29,919), they actually increased in Japan, and were multiplied by a factor of between 1.5 and 4 in major industrializing countries, so that, overall, new manufacturing jobs elsewhere largely exceeded the losses in the developed world.

Furthermore, the notion of "services" is often considered to be ambiguous at best, misleading at worst.[7] In employment statistics, it has been used as a residual notion that embraces all that is not agriculture, mining, construction, utilities, or manufacturing. Thus, the category of services includes activities of all kinds, historically originated from

5 Cohen and Zysman (1987).
6 Wieczorek (1995).
7 Castells (1976a); Stanback (1979); Gershuny and Miles (1983); De Bandt (1985); Cohen and Zysman (1987); Daniels (1993).

various social structures and productive systems. The only common feature of these service activities is what they are not. Attempts at defining services by some intrinsic characteristics, such as their "intangibility," opposed to the "materiality" of goods, have been definitely voided of meaning by the evolution of the informational economy. Computer software, video production, micro-electronics design, biotechnology-based agriculture, and many other critical processes characteristic of advanced economies, merge inextricably their information content with the material support of the product, making it impossible to distinguish the boundaries between "goods" and "services." To understand the new type of economy and social structure, we must start by characterizing different types of "services" in order to establish clear distinctions between them. In understanding the informational economy, each one of the specific categories of services becomes as important a distinction as was the old borderline between manufacturing and services in the preceding type of industrial economy. As economies become more complex, we must diversify the concepts through which we categorize economic activities, and ultimately abandon Colin Clark's old paradigm based on the distinction between primary, secondary, and tertiary sectors. Such a distinction has become an epistemological obstacle to the understanding of our societies.

The third major prediction of the original theory of post-industrialism refers to the expansion of information-rich occupations, such as managerial, professional, and technical positions, as the core of the new occupational structure. This prediction also requires qualification. A number of analysts have argued that this trend is not the only characteristic of the new occupational structure. Simultaneous to this trend there is also the growth of low-end, unskilled, service occupations. These low-skilled jobs, despite their slower growth rate, may represent a substantial proportion of the post-industrial social structure in terms of their absolute numbers. In other words, advanced, informational societies could also be characterized by an increasingly polarized social structure, where the top and the bottom increase their share at the expense of the middle.[8] In addition, there is a widespread challenge in the literature to the notion that knowledge, science, and expertise are the critical components in most of the managerial/professional occupations. A harder, closer look must be taken at the actual content of such general statistical classifications before we jump to characterizing our future as the republic of the learned elite.

Yet the most important argument against a simplistic version of

---

8 Kuttner (1983); Rumberger and Levin (1984); Bluestone and Harrison (1988); Sayer and Walker (1992); Leal (1993).

post-industrialism is the critique of the assumption according to which the three features we have examined coalesce in historical evolution, and that this evolution leads to a single model of the informational society. This analytical construct is in fact similar to the formulation of the concept of capitalism by classical political economists (from Adam Smith to Marx), exclusively based on the experience of English industrialization, only to find continuous "exceptions" to the pattern throughout the diversity of economic and social experience in the world. Only if we start from the analytical separation between the structural logic of the production system of the informational society and its social structure can we observe empirically if a specific techno-economic paradigm induces a specific social structure and to what extent. And only if we open up the cultural and institutional scope of our observation can we separate what belongs to the structure of the informational society (as expressing a new mode of development) from what is specific to the historical trajectory of a given country. To make some tentative steps in such a direction, I have compiled and made somewhat comparable basic statistics for the seven largest market economies in the world, the so-called G-7 countries. Thus I can compare, with reasonable approximation, the evolution of their employment and occupational structure over the past 70 years. I have also considered some employment projections for Japan and the United States through the early twenty-first century. The empirical core of this analysis consists in an attempt at differentiating between various service activities. To do so, I have followed the well-known typology of service employment constructed by Singelmann more than 20 years ago.[9] Singelmann's conceptualization is not without flaws, but has a fundamental merit: it is well adapted to the usual statistical categories, as shown in Singelmann's own doctoral dissertation which analyzed the change of employment structure in various countries between 1920 and 1970. Since the main purpose of this book is analytical I decided to build on Singelmann's work, to compare the 1970–90 period with his findings for the 1920–79 period. Thus, I constructed a similar typology of sectoral employment, and processed the statistics of the G-7 countries along roughly comparable categories, extending Singelmann's analysis to the critical period of development of informational societies, from the 1970s onwards. Because I cannot ensure the absolute equivalence of my decisions in classifying activities with those taken earlier by Singelmann, I present our data separately for the two periods: they must not be read as a statistical series, but as two distinct statistical trends made roughly equivalent in terms of the analytical

9   Singelmann (1978).

categories used to compile the data. I did find considerable method-ological difficulties in establishing equivalent categories among different countries. The appendix to this chapter provides details of the procedures followed in building this database. In analyzing these data I have used the simplest statistical procedures, always trying to show the actual trends in the social structure, rather than using analytical methods that would be unnecessarily sophisticated for the current level of elaboration of the database. I have opted for using descriptive statistics that would simply suggest lines of new theoretical understanding.

By adopting Singelmann's categories of service activities I have embraced a structuralist view of employment, dividing it up according to the place of the activity in the chain of linkages that starts from the production process. Thus, distributive services refer both to communication and transportation activities, as well as to commercial distribution networks (wholesale and retail). Producer services refer more directly to those services that appear to be critical inputs in the economy, although they also include auxiliary services to business which may not be necessarily highly skilled. Social services include a whole realm of government activities, as well as collective consumption-related jobs. Personal services are those related to individual consumption, from entertainment to eating and drinking places. Although these distinctions are admittedly broad, they do allow us to think differentially about the evolution of the employment structure across countries, at least with greater analytical depth than the usual statistical accounts. I have also tried to establish a difference between the services/goods dichotomy and the classification of employment between information-processing and goods-handling activities, since each one of these distinctions belongs to a different approach in the analysis of social structure. To do so, I built two elementary indexes of service-delivery employment/goods-producing employment, and of information-processing employment/goods-handling employment, and calculated these indexes for the countries and periods under consideration. Finally, I also calculated a simplified typology of occupations across countries, building the various countries' categories around those used by American and Japanese statistics. Although I have serious concerns about the definitions of such occupational categories which mix, in fact, occupational positions and types of activities, using standard statistics that are widely available gives us the opportunity of looking at the evolution of occupational structures in roughly comparative terms. The purpose of this exercise is to recast the sociological analysis of informational societies by assessing in a comparative framework the differences in the evolution of their employment structure as a fundamental indicator for both their commonality and their diversity.

The transformation of employment structure, 1920–1970 and 1970–1990

The analysis of the evolution of employment structure in the G-7 countries must start from the distinction between two periods that, by sheer luck, match our two different databases: *circa* 1920–70 and *circa* 1970–90. *The major analytical distinction between the two periods stems from the fact that during the first period the societies under consideration became post-agricultural, while in the second period they became post-industrial.* I understand obviously by such terms the massive decline of agricultural employment in the first case and the rapid decline of manufacturing employment in the second period. Indeed, *all G-7 countries maintained or increased (in some cases substantially) the percentage of their employment in transformative activities and in manufacturing between 1920 and 1970.* Thus, if we exclude construction and utilities in order to have a sharper view of the manufacturing labor force, England and Wales decreased only slightly the level of their manufacturing labor force from 36.8 percent in 1921 to 34.9 percent in 1971; the United States increased manufacturing employment from 24.5 percent in 1930 to 25.9 percent in 1970; Canada from 17.0 percent in 1921 to 22.0 percent in 1971; Japan saw a dramatic increase in manufacturing from 16.6 percent in 1920 to 26.0 percent in 1970; Germany (although with a different national territory) increased its manufacturing labor force from 33 to 40.2 percent; France, from 26.4 to 28.1 percent; and Italy, from 19.9 to 27.4 percent. Thus, as Singelmann argues, the shift in the structure of employment in this half-century (1920–70) was from agriculture to services and construction, not out of manufacturing.

The story is a very different one in the 1970–90 period, when the process of economic restructuring and technological transformation which took place during these two decades led to a reduction of manufacturing employment in all countries (see tables 4.1–4.14 in Appendix A). However, while this trend was general, the shrinkage of manufacturing employment was uneven, clearly indicating the fundamental variety of social structures according to differences in economic policies and in firms' strategies. Thus, while the United Kingdom, the United States, and Italy experienced rapid de-industrialization (reducing the share of their manufacturing employment in 1970–90 from 38.7 to 22.5 percent; from 25.9 to 17.5 percent; from 27.3 to 21.8 percent, respectively), Japan and Germany reduced their share of manufacturing labor force moderately: from 26.0 to 23.6 percent in the case of Japan, and from 38.6 percent to a still rather high level of 32.2

percent in 1987 in the case of Germany. Canada and France occupy an intermediate position, reducing manufacturing employment from 19.7 percent (in 1971) to 14.9 percent, and from 27.7 to 21.3 percent, respectively.

In fact, England and Wales had already become a post-agricultural society in 1921, with only 7.1 percent of their labor force in agriculture. The United States, Germany, and Canada still had a sizeable agricultural population (from a quarter to a third of total employment), and Japan, Italy, and France were, by and large, societies dominated by agricultural and commercial occupations. From this differential starting-point in the historical period under study, trends converged toward an employment structure characterized by simultaneous growth of manufacturing and services at the expense of agriculture. Such a convergence is explained by very rapid processes of industrialization in Germany, Japan, Italy, and France, which distributed the surplus of agricultural population between manufacturing and services.

Thus, if we calculate the employment ratio of services to industry (our indicator of the "service economy"), it shows only a moderate increase for most countries between 1920 and 1970. Only the United States (change from 1.1 to 2.0) and Canada (1.3 to 2.0) witnessed a significant increase in the relative proportion of service employment during the period that I call post-agricultural. In this sense, it is true that the United States was the standard-bearer of the employment structure characteristic of the service economy. Thus, when the trend toward service employment accelerated and generalized in the post-industrial period, the United States and Canada increased even more their service predominance, with indexes of 3.0 and 3.3 respectively. All other countries followed the same tendency, but at different speeds, thus reaching different levels of de-industrialization. While the United Kingdom, France, and Italy seem to be on the same path, North America, Japan, and Germany clearly stand out as strong industrial economies, with lower rates of increase in service employment, and lower service to industry employment ratios: 1.8 and 1.4 respectively in 1987–90. This is a fundamental observation that deserves careful discussion below. Yet, as a trend, in the 1990s the majority of the population in all G-7 countries was employed in services. Is employment also concentrating on information processing? Our ratio of information-processing to goods-handling employment provides some interesting clues for the analysis. First, we must put aside Japan for further consideration.

For all other countries there has been a trend toward a higher percentage of information-processing employment. Although Italy and

Germany had no or only slow increase in 1920–70, their share of information employment grew considerably in the 1980s and 1990s. The United States holds the highest information employment ratio among the seven countries, but the United Kingdom, Canada, and France are almost at the same level. Thus, the trend toward information processing is clearly not a distinctive feature of the United States: the American employment structure is more clearly set apart from the others as a "service economy" than as an "information economy." Germany and Italy have a significantly lower rate of information employment, but they have doubled it in the past two decades, thus displaying the same trend.

The data on Japan are most interesting. They show only a moderate increase in information employment in 50 years (from 0.3 to 0.4), and an even slower increase in the past 20 years, from 0.4 to 0.5. Thus, what is probably the society which puts the strongest emphasis on information technologies, and in which high technology plays a most significant role in productivity and competitiveness, also appears to have the lowest level of information-processing employment, and the lowest rate of progression of such employment. The expansion of information employment and the development of an "information society" (*johoka shakai*, in the Japanese concept) seem to be different, although interrelated, processes. It is indeed interesting, and problematic for some interpretations of post-industrialism, that Japan and Germany, the two most competitive economies among major economies in the 1970s and 1980s, are those with the strongest manufacturing employment, the lowest service to industry employment ratio, the lowest information to goods employment ratio, and, for Japan (which has experienced the fastest productivity growth), the lowest rate of increase in information employment throughout the century. I suggest the idea that information processing is most productive when it is embedded in material production or in the handling of goods, instead of being disjointed in a stepped-up technical division of labor. After all, most automation refers precisely to the integration of information processing in goods handling.

This hypothesis may also help to interpret another important observation: none of the seven countries had a ratio of information employment over 1 in 1990, and only the United States was approaching that threshold. Thus, if information is a critical component in the functioning of the economy and in the organization of society, it does not follow that most jobs are or will be in information processing. The march toward information employment is proceeding at a significantly slower pace, and reaching much lower levels, than the trend toward service employment. Thus, to understand the actual profile of the transformation of employment in advanced societies we must now turn to the differential evolution of each type of service in the G-7 countries.

To do so, I shall first comment on the evolution of each category of service in each country; then I shall compare the relative importance of each type of service *vis-à-vis* each other in each country; finally, I shall consider the trends of evolution of employment in those services that have been identified in the literature as characteristic of "post-industrial" societies. In proceeding with this analysis I must remind the reader that the further we go into the fine-grain analysis of specific categories of employment, the less solid the database becomes. The inability to obtain reliable data for some categories, countries, and periods will make it difficult to be systematic in our analysis across the board. Yet the observation of the tables presented here still suggests that there are some features that merit closer analysis and further elaboration on country-specific databases.

Let us start with *producer services*. They are considered in the literature to be the strategic services of the new economy, the providers of information and support for the increase in the productivity and efficiency of firms. Thus, their expansion should go hand in hand with the increasing sophistication and productivity of the economy. Indeed, we observe throughout the two periods (1920–1970, 1970–1990) a significant expansion of employment in these activities in all countries. For instance, in the United Kingdom employment in producer services shot up from 5 percent in 1970 to 12 percent in 1990; in the United States, for the same period, from 8.2 to 14 percent; in France, it doubled, from 5 to 10 percent. It is significant that Japan increased dramatically its producer services employment between 1921 (0.8 percent) and 1970 (5.1 percent), most of this increase taking place during the 1960s, the moment when the Japanese economy internationalized its scope. On the other hand, focusing on 1970–90 on a different database, the increase of Japanese employment in producer services between 1971 and 1990 (from 4.8 to 9.6 percent), while substantial, still leaves Japan in the lower tier of employment in producer services among the advanced economies. This could suggest that a significant proportion of producer services are internalized in Japan in manufacturing companies, which could appear to be a more efficient formula, if we consider the competitiveness and productivity of the Japanese economy.

This hypothesis receives additional support from the observation of data concerning Germany. While increasing significantly the share of employment in producer services from 4.5 percent in 1970 to 7.3 percent in 1987, Germany still displays the lowest level of producer services employment of the G-7 countries. This could imply a great degree of internalization of service activities in German firms. If these data were confirmed, we must emphasize that the two most dynamic economies (Japan and Germany) have also the lowest rate of employment in producer services, while it is obvious that their firms do use such services in great amount, yet probably with a different organizational structure that links up more closely producer services to the production process.

While it is evident that producer services are strategically crucial in an advanced economy, they still do not represent a substantial proportion of employment in most advanced countries, in spite of their rapid rate of growth in several of them. With the unknown position of Italy, the proportion of employment varies between 7.3 and 14 percent in the other countries, of course putting them well ahead of agriculture, but far behind in manufacturing. The battalions of professionals and managers have indeed swelled the ranks of employment in advanced economies, but not always, and not predominantly, in the visible spots of the management of capital and the control of information. It seems that the expansion of producer services is linked to the processes of vertical disintegration and outsourcing that characterize the informational corporation.

Social services form the second employment category which, according to the post-industrial literature, should characterize the new society. And indeed it does. With, again, the exception of Japan, employment in social services represents between one-fifth and one-quarter of total employment in the G-7 countries. But the interesting observation here is that the major increase in social services took place during the roaring sixties, actually linking their expansion with the impact of social movements rather than with the advent of post-industrialism. Indeed, the United States, Canada, and France had very moderate rates of growth of employment in social services in the 1970–90 period, while in Germany, Japan, and Britain it grew at a robust rate.

Overall, it would seem that the expansion of the welfare state has been a secular trend since the beginning of the century, with moments of acceleration in periods that vary for each society, and a tendency to slow down in the 1980s. Japan is the exception because it appears to be catching up. It maintained a very low level of employment in social services until 1970, probably linked to a greater decentralization of social support both by the firm and the family. Then, when Japan became a major industrial power, and when more traditional forms of support could not be maintained, Japan engaged in forms of social redistribution similar to the other advanced economies, providing services and creating jobs in the social services sector. Overall, we can say that although the expansion of social services employment at a very high level is a feature of all advanced societies, the pace of such expansion seems to be directly dependent on the relationship between the state and society, rather than on the stage of development of the economy. Indeed, the expansion of social services employment (except in Japan) is more characteristic of the 1950–70 period than of the 1970–90 period, at the dawn of the informational society.

Distributive services combine transportation and communication, relational activities of all advanced economies, with wholesale and retail trade, the supposedly typical service activities of less industrialized societies. Is employment declining in these low-productivity, labor-intensive activities, as the economy progresses toward the automation of work, and toward the modernization of commercial shops? In fact, employment in distributive services remains at a very high level in advanced societies, also oscillating between one-fifth and one-quarter of total employment, with the exception of Germany, which stood at 17.7 percent in 1987. This level of employment is substantially higher than that of 1920, and has only declined slightly in the past 20 years in the United States (from 22.4 to 20.6 percent). Thus employment in distributive services is roughly double that in producer services, considered typical of advanced economies. Japan, Canada, and France increased the share of such employment in the 1970–90 period. About half of employment in distributive services in the G-7 countries corresponds to retail services, although it is often impossible to differentiate the data between wholesale and retail trade. Overall, retail employment has not significantly declined over a 70-year period. In the United States, for instance, it grew from 1.8 percent in 1940 to 12.8 percent in 1970, later declining slightly from 12.9 percent in 1970 to 11.7 percent in 1991. Japan had increased retail employment from 8.9 percent in 1960 to 11.2 percent in 1990, and Germany, while having a lower level of employment in such activity (8.6 percent in 1987) had actually increased it over its 1970 figure. Thus, there is a large sector of employment still engaged in distribution, as the movements of the employment structure are in fact very slow in the so-called service activities.

Personal services are viewed, at the same time, as the remnants of a proto-industrial structure, and as the expression (at least for some of them) of the social dualism that, according to observers, characterizes the informational society. Here also, the observation of the long-term evolution in the seven countries invites the introduction of a word of caution. They continued to represent a sizeable proportion of employment in 1990: with the exception of Germany (6.3 percent in 1987), they vary in the range between 9.7 and 14.1 percent, that is roughly equivalent to the quintessential post-industrialist producer services. Overall, they had increased their share since 1970. Focusing on the famous/infamous "eating and drinking places" jobs, a favorite theme of the literature critical of post-industrialism, we do find a significant expansion of such jobs in the past two decades, particularly in the United Kingdom and in Canada, although the data often mix restaurants and bars with hotel employment which could also be considered as characteristic of the "leisure society." In the United States, eating and drinking places employment stood at 4.9 percent of total employment in 1991 (up from 3.2 percent in 1970), which is about twice the size of agricultural employment, but still less than we are asked to believe by the essays elaborating on the notion of the "hamburger society." The main remark to be made on employment in personal services is that it is not fading away in the advanced economies, thus providing ground for the argument that the changes in the social/economic structure concern more the type of services and the type of jobs than the activities themselves.

Let us try now to evaluate some of the traditional theses on post-industrialism in the light of the evolution of employment structure since 1970, more or less at the moment when Touraine, Bell, Richta, and other early theorists of the new, information society were publishing their analyses. In terms of activity, producer services and social services were considered to be typical of post-industrial economies, both as sources of productivity and as responses to social demands and changing values. If we aggregate employment in producer services and social services, we do observe a substantial increase in what could be labeled the "post-industrial services category" in all countries between 1970 and 1990: from 22.8 to 39.2 percent in the United Kingdom; from 30.2 to 39.5 percent in the United States; from 28.6 to 33.8 percent in Canada; from 15.1 to 24.0 percent in Japan, from 20.2 to 31.7 percent in Germany; from 21.1 to 29.5 percent in France (Italian data in our database do not allow any serious evaluation of this trend). Thus, the trend is there, but it is uneven since it starts from a very different base in 1970: the Anglo-Saxon countries had already developed a strong basis in advanced services employment, while Japan, Germany, and France kept much higher employment in manufacturing, as well as in agriculture. Thus, we observe two different paths in the expansion of "post-industrial" services' employment: one, the Anglo-Saxon model, which shifts from manufacturing to advanced services, maintaining employment in the traditional services; the other, the Japanese/German model, which both expands advanced services and preserves a manufacturing basis, while internalizing some of the service activities in the industrial sector. France is in-between, although leaning toward the Anglo-Saxon model.

In sum, the evolution of employment during what we called the "post-industrial" period (1970–90) shows, at the same time, a general pattern of shifting away from manufacturing jobs, and two different paths regarding manufacturing activity: the first amounts to a rapid phasing out of manufacturing, coupled with a strong expansion of employment in producer services (in rate) and in social services (in size), while other service activities are still kept as sources of employment. A second, different path more closely links manufacturing and producer services, more cautiously increases social services employment, and maintains distributive services. The variation within this second path is between Japan, with a greater agricultural and retail trade population, and Germany with a significantly higher manufacturing employment.

In the process of transformation of the employment structure there is no disappearance of any major service category with the exception of domestic service as compared to 1920. What happens is an increasing diversity of activities, and the emergence of a set of linkages between different activities that makes the employment categories obsolete. Indeed, a postmanufacturing employment structure emerged in the last quarter of the twentieth century, but there was a great deal of variation in the emerging structures of various countries, and it does not seem that great productivity, social stability, and international competitiveness were directly associated with the highest degree of service-related or information-processing jobs. On the contrary, those societies in the G-7 group that have been at the forefront of economic progress and social stability in recent years (Japan and Germany) seem to have developed a more efficient linkage system between manufacturing, producer services, social services, and distributive services than Anglo-Saxon societies, with France and Italy being at the crossroads between the two paths. In all of these societies, informationalization seems to be more decisive than information processing.

Thus, when societies massively destroy manufacturing jobs in a short period of time, instead of gradually phasing the industrial transformation, it is not necessarily because they are more advanced, but because they follow specific policies and strategies that are based in their cultural, social, and political backdrop. And the options taken to conduct the transformation of the national economy and of the labor force have profound consequences for the evolution of the occupational structure that provides the foundations for the new class system of the informational society.

The new occupational structure

A major statement of theories on post-industrialism is that people, besides being engaged in different activities, also hold new positions in the occupational structure. By and large, it was predicted that as we move into what we call the informational society we would observe the increasing importance of managerial, professional, and technical positions, a decreasing proportion of workers in the craft and operator positions, and a swelling in the numbers of clerical and sales workers. In addition, the "left-wing" version of post-industrialism points to the growing importance of semi-skilled (often unskilled) service occupations as a counterpart to the growth of professional jobs.

To examine the accuracy of such predictions in the evolution of the G-7 countries over the past 40 years is not an easy task, both because the statistical categories do not always correspond exactly across countries and because dates for the various available statistics do not always coincide. Thus, in spite of our methodological efforts to clean up the data, our analysis on this point remains rather tentative, and should be taken only as a first empirical approach to suggest lines of analysis on the evolution of the social structure.

First, let us start with the *diversity of the occupational profiles across societies*. Table 4.15 in Appendix A brings together the distribution of the labor force in the main occupational categories for each country at the time of the latest available statistical information when we conducted this study (1992–3). The first and most important conclusion of our observation is that there are very strong differences between the occupational structures of societies equally entitled to be considered as informational. Thus, if we take the category that groups managers, professionals, and technicians, the epitome of the informational occupations, it was indeed very strong in the United States and in Canada, amounting to almost one-third of the labor force in the early 1990s. But in early 1990s Japan it was only 14.9 percent. And in France and Germany in 1989 it was only at about one-quarter of all labor. On the other hand, while crafts and operators have substantially dwindled down in North America, they still represented 31.8 percent of the labor force of Japan, and they were over 27 percent in both France and Germany. Similarly, sales workers were not a major category in France (3.8 percent) but they were still important in the United States (11.9 percent) and truly significant in Japan (15.1 percent). Japan had a very low proportion of managers (only 3.8 percent) in 1990, compared to 12.8 percent in the United States, which could be an indicator of a much more hierarchical structure. France's distinctive feature was the strong component of technicians in the higher professional groups (12.4 percent of all labor force), in contrast to Germany's 8.7 percent. On the other hand, Germany had many more jobs than France in the "professionals" category: 13.9 against 6.0 percent.

Another factor of diversity is the variation in the proportion of semi-skilled service workers: it was significant in the United States, Canada, and Germany, much lower in Japan and France, precisely the countries that, together with Italy, have preserved somewhat more sizeable traditional agricultural and commercial activities.

Overall, *Japan and the United States represent the opposite ends of the comparison, and their contrast emphasizes the need to recast the theory of post-industrialism and informationalism.* The data on the United States fit well with the predominant model in the literature, very simply because the "model" was but a theorization of the evolution of the US employment structure. Meanwhile, Japan appears to combine an increase in the professional occupations with the persistence of a strong craft labor force, linked to the industrial era, and with the durability of the agricultural labor force and of sales workers that witness the continuity, under new forms, of the occupations characteristic of the pre-industrial era. The US model progresses into informationalism by substituting new occupations for the old ones. The Japanese model does equally progress into informationalism but following a different route: by increasing some of the required new occupations while redefining the content of occupations of a previous era, yet phasing out those positions that become an obstacle to increased productivity (particularly in agriculture). In between these two "models," Germany and France combine elements of both: they are closer to the United States in terms of the professional/managerial occupations, but closer to Japan in the slower decline of craft/operators jobs.

The second major observation refers, in spite of the diversity we have shown, to the existence of a common trend toward the increase of the relative weight of the most clearly informational occupation (managers, professionals, and technicians), as well as of the overall "white-collar" occupations (including sales and clerical workers). Having first established my call for diversity I also want to give empirical credit to the notion that there is indeed a tendency toward a greater informational content in the occupational structure of advanced societies, in spite of their diverse cultural/political system, and in spite also of the different historical moments of their processes of industrialization.

To observe such a common trend, we must concentrate on the growth of each occupation in each country over time. Let us compare for instance (see tables 4.16–4.21 in Appendix A) the evolution of four critical groups of occupations: craft/operators; technicians, professionals, and managers; sales and clerical workers; farm workers and managers. Calculating the rates of change in share of each occupation and group of occupations, we observe some general trends and some critical differences. The share of the managerial/professional/technical occupations showed strong growth in all countries except France. Crafts and operators declined substantially in the United States, the United Kingdom, and Canada, and moderately in Germany, France, and Japan. Sales and clericals increased moderately their share in the United Kingdom and France and strongly in the four other countries. Farm workers and managers declined substantially in all countries. And semi-skilled service and transportation workers presented clearly different trends: they increased their share strongly in the United States and in the United Kingdom; they increased moderately in France; they declined or stabilized in Japan and Germany.

Of all countries considered, Japan was the one that most dramatically upgraded its occupational structure, increasing its share of managers by 46.2 percent in a 20-year period, and the share of its professional/technical labor force by 91.4 percent. The United Kingdom also increased the share of its managers by 96.3 percent, although the increase of its professional/technical workers was much more moderate (5.2 percent). Thus, we observe a great diversity of rates of change in the share of its occupational group in the overall employment structure. There is diversity in rates because there is some degree of convergence toward a relatively similar occupational structure. At the same time, the differences in management style and in the importance of manufacturing in each country also introduce some variation in the process of change.

Overall, the tendency toward a predominantly white-collar labor force skewed toward its higher tier seems to be the general trend (in the United States in 1991, 57.3 percent of the labor force were white collar), with the exceptions of Japan and Germany, whose white-collar labor force still does not exceed 50 percent of total employment. However, even in Japan and Germany, the rates of growth of the informational occupations have been the highest among the various occupational positions; thus, as a trend Japan will count increasingly on a substantial professional labor force, although still holding on to a broader craft and commercial basis than in other societies.

Thirdly, *the widespread argument concerning the increasing polarization of the occupational structure of informational society does not seem to fit with this data set*, if by polarization we mean the simultaneous expansion in equivalent terms of the top and bottom of the occupational scale. If such were the case the managerial–professional–

technical labor force and the semi-skilled service and transport workers would be expanding at similar rates and in similar numbers. Such
is clearly not the case. In the United States, semi-skilled service workers have indeed increased their share in the occupational structure but
at a lower rate than the managerial/professional labor force, and they
only represented 13.7 percent of the labor force in 1991. By contrast,
managers, at the top of the scale, increased their share between 1950
and 1991 at a rate much higher than that of the semi-skilled service
workers, increasing their number to 12.8 percent of the labor force in
1991, almost at the same level as that of semi-skilled service workers.
Even if we add semi-skilled transportation workers, we still reach a
mere 17.9 percent of the labor force in 1991, in sharp contrast with
the 29.7 percent of the top managerial–professional–technical category.
Of course, many jobs among clerical and sales workers, as well as
among operators, are also semi-skilled, so that we cannot truly assess
the evolution of the occupational structure in terms of skills. Additionally, we know from other sources that *there has been a polarization of income distribution in the United States and in other countries
in the past two decades.*[10] However, here I am objecting to the popular
image of the informational economy as providing an increasing number
of low-level service jobs at a disproportionately higher rate than the
rate of increase in the share of the professional/technical component
of the labor force. According to this database, this is simply not the
case. In the United Kingdom there was, however, a substantial increase in such semi-skilled service jobs between 1961 and 1981, but,
even here, the share of the higher occupational level increased faster.
In Canada, semi-skilled service workers also increased their share substantially to reach 13.7 percent in 1992 but managerial–professional–
technical jobs progressed even more, almost doubling their representation to account for 30.6 percent of the labor force in 1992. A
similar pattern can be found in Germany: low-end service jobs remained relatively stable and well below the progression in rate and in
size of the upper occupational tier. France, while increasing substantially such service jobs during the 1980s, still counted them only as 7.2
percent of the labor force in 1989. As for Japan, semi-skilled service
jobs experienced a slow growth, from 5.4 percent in 1955 to a modest
8.6 percent in 1990.

Thus, while there are certainly signs of social and economic polarization in advanced societies, they do not take the form of divergent
paths in the occupational structure, but of different positions of similar occupations across sectors and between firms. Sectoral, territorial,

10   Esping-Andersen (1993); Mishel and Bernstein (1994).

firm-specific, and gender/ethnic/age characteristics are clearer sources of social polarization than occupational differentiation *per se*. Informational societies are certainly unequal societies, but inequalities stem less from their relatively upgraded occupational structure than from the exclusions and discriminations that take place in and around the labor force.

Finally, a view of the transformation of the labor force in advanced societies must also consider the *evolution of its employment status*. Again, the data challenge predominant views of post-industrialism, exclusively based on the American experience. Thus, the hypothesis of the fading away of self-employment in mature, informational economies is somewhat supported by the US experience, where the percentage of self-employment in the total labor force declined from 17.6 percent in 1950 to 8.8 percent in 1991 *although it has been almost at a standstill for the past 20 years*. But other countries present different patterns. Germany declined at a slow, steady pace, from 13.8 percent in 1955 to 9.5 percent in 1975, then to 8.9 percent in 1989. France maintained its share of self-employment in the labor force between 1977 and 1987 (12.8 and 12.7 percent respectively). Italy, while being the fifth largest market economy in the world, still retained 24.8 percent of its labor force in self-employment in 1989. Japan, while experiencing a decline in self-employment from 19.2 percent in 1970 to 14.1 percent in 1990, still has a significant level of such autonomous employment, to which we must add 8.3 percent of family workers, which places almost one-quarter of the Japanese labor force outside salaried work. As for Canada and the United Kingdom, they have reversed the supposed secular pattern of corporatization of employment in the past 20 years, as Canada increased the proportion of self-employed in its population from 8.4 percent in 1970 to 9.7 percent in 1992, and the United Kingdom increased the share of self-employment and family workers in the labor force from 7.6 percent in 1969 to 13.0 percent in 1989: a trend that has continued in the 1990s, as I shall show later in this chapter.

Granted, the majority of the labor force in the advanced economies is under salaried conditions. But the diversity of the levels, the unevenness of the process, and the reversal of the trend in some cases calls for a differential view of the patterns of evolution of the occupational structure. We could even formulate the hypothesis that as networking and flexibility become characteristic of the new industrial organization, and as new technologies make it possible for small business to find market niches, we witness a resurgence of self-employment and mixed employment status. Thus, the occupational profile of the informational societies, as they emerge historically, will be far more diverse than that imagined by the quasi-naturalistic vision of post-industrial theories biased by an American ethnocentrism which did not fully represent even the American experience.

The maturing of the informational society: employment projections into the twenty-first century

The informational society, in its historically diverse manifestations, began to take shape in the twilight of the twentieth century. Thus, an analytical clue for its future direction and mature profile could be provided by employment and occupational projections that forecast the social structure of advanced societies into the early years of the twenty-first century. Such projections are always subject to a number of economic, technological, and institutional assumptions that are hardly established on solid ground. Thus, the status of the data that I shall be using in this section is even more tentative than the analysis of the employment trends up to 1990. Yet, by using reliable sources, such as the US Bureau of Labor Statistics, the Japanese Ministry of Labor, and government data compiled by OECD, and by keeping in mind the approximative nature of the exercise, we may be able to generate some hypotheses on the future path of informational employment.

My analysis of employment projections will be mainly focused on the United States and Japan because I want to keep within limits the empirical complexity of the study in order to be able to focus on the main argument of my analysis.[11] Thus, by pinpointing the United States and Japan, which appear to be two different models of the informational society, I can better assess the hypotheses on the convergence and/or divergence of the informational society's employment and occupational structure.

For the United States, the US Bureau of Labor Statistics (BLS) published in 1991–3 a series of studies, updated in 1994,[12] that together offer a meaningful overview of the evolution of employment and occupational structure between 1990–2 and 2005. To simplify the analysis, I shall refer to the "moderative alternative projection" of the three scenarios considered by the Bureau.

The American economy is projected to create over 26 million jobs between 1992 and 2005. That is a total increase of 22 percent, slightly

11 For employment projections concerning other OECD countries, see OECD (1994a: 71–100).
12 See Carey and Franklin (1991); Kutscher (1991); Silvestri and Lukasiewicz (1991); Braddock (1992); Bureau of Labor Statistics (1994).

higher than the increase in the previous 13-year period, 1979–92. The most apparent features in the projections are the continuation of the trend toward the decline of agricultural and manufacturing jobs, which in 1990–2005 would decline, respectively, at an average annual rate of −0.4 and −0.2. However, manufacturing output would continue to grow at a slightly higher rate than the economy as a whole, at 2.3 percent per year. Thus the differential growth rate between employment and output in manufacturing and in services shows a substantial gap in labor productivity in favor of manufacturing, in spite of the introduction of new technologies in information-processing activities. Higher than average manufacturing productivity continues to be the key to sustained economic growth able to provide jobs for all other sectors in the economy.

An interesting observation comes from the fact that, although employment in agriculture would decline, to a low 2.5 percent of total employment, agriculture-related *occupations* are expected to grow: this is because, while farmers are expected to decrease by 231,000, an increase of 311,000 jobs for gardeners and groundskeepers is expected: the surpassing of farming jobs by urban-oriented agricultural service jobs underlines how far informational societies have come in their post-agricultural status.

Although only 1 million of the projected 26.4 million new jobs are expected to be created in the goods-producing industries, decline in manufacturing employment is expected to slow down, and some occupational categories in manufacturing, such as precision production, craft, and repair, are actually expected to increase. Yet the bulk of new job growth in the United States is expected to take place in "service activities." About half of such growth is expected to be contributed by the so-called "services division," whose main components are *health services* and *business services*. Business services, which were the fastest-growing service sector in 1975–90, will continue to be at the top of the expansion through 2005, although with a slower growth rate of about 2.5 percent per year. One should be aware, though, that not all business services are knowledge intensive: an important component of them are computer data-processing jobs, but *in the 1975– 90 period the fastest growing activity was personnel supply services, linked to the increase of temporary work and of contracting-out services by firms.* Other fast-growing services in the coming years are expected to be legal services (particularly para-legal), engineering and architectural services, and educational services (private schools). In the BLS categories, finance, insurance, and real estate (FIRE) are not included in business services. Thus, to the strong growth in business services we must add the moderate but steady growth projected for this FIRE category, expected to be at about 1.3 percent per year, to reach 6.1 percent of total employment by 2005. When comparing these data with my analysis of "producer services" in the preceding sections, both business services and FIRE should be taken into consideration.

Health services will be among the fastest growing activities, at a rate twice as fast as its own increase for the 1975–90 period. By 2005, health services are projected to account for 11.5 million jobs, that is 8.7 percent of all non-farm wage and salary employment. To put this figure into perspective, the comparable number for all manufacturing employment in 2005 is projected to be 14 percent of the labor force. Home health-care services, particularly for the elderly, will be the fastest growing activity.

Retail trade, growing at a healthy 1.6 percent average annual rate, and starting from a high level in absolute numbers of jobs, represents the third major source of potential new growth, with 5.1 million new jobs. Within this sector, eating and drinking places will account for 42 percent of total jobs in retail in 2005. State and local government jobs will also add to employment in sizeable numbers, rising from 15.2 million in 1990 to 18.3 million by 2005. More than half of this increase is expected to take place in education. Thus, overall, the projected employment structure for the United States closely fits the original blueprint for the informational society:

- agricultural jobs are being phased out;
- manufacturing employment will continue to decline, although at a lower pace, being reduced to a hard core of the craft and engineering workforce. Most of the employment impact of manufacturing production will be transferred to services for manufacturing;
- producer services, as well as health and education, lead employment growth in terms of rate, also becoming increasingly important in terms of absolute numbers;
- retail jobs and service jobs continue to swell the ranks of low-skilled activities of the new economy.

If we now turn to examine the projected occupational structure, at first sight the hypothesis of informationalism seems to be confirmed: the fastest-growing rates among occupational groups are those of professionals (32.3 percent for the period) and technicians (36.9 percent). But "service occupations," mostly semi-skilled, are also growing fast (29.2 percent) and they will still represent 16.9 percent of the occupational structure in 2005. Altogether, managers, professionals, and technicians will increase their share of total occupational employment from

24.5 percent in 1990 to 28.9 percent in 2005. Sales and clerical workers, taken as a group, will remain stable at about 28.8 percent of total employment. Craft workers will actually increase their share, confirming the tendency to stabilize a hard core of manual workers around craft skills.

Let us examine more closely this argument: is the future informational society characterized by an increasing polarization of occupational structure? In the case of the United States, the Bureau of Labor Statistics included in its projections an analysis of the educational level required for the 30 occupations that were expected to grow most rapidly and for the 30 occupations that were expected to decline fastest between 1990 and 2005. The analysis considered both the rate of growth or decline of the occupations and their variation in absolute numbers. The conclusion of the authors of the study is that "in general, a majority of the [growing] occupations require education or training beyond high school. In fact, more than 2 out of 3 of the 30 fastest growing occupations, and nearly half of the 30 with the largest number of jobs added had a majority of workers with education or training beyond high school in 1990."[13] The largest job declines, on the other hand, are expected in manufacturing industries, and in some clerical jobs that will be swept away by office automation, generally in the lower tier of skills. Yet at the aggregate level of new jobs being created in the 1992–2005 period Silvestri foresees only modest changes in the distribution of the educational level of the labor force.[14] The proportion of workers who are college graduates is projected to increase by 1.4 percentage points, and the proportion of those with some college education will increase slightly. Conversely, the proportion of high school graduates decreases by 1 percentage point and the proportion of the lowest educated decreases slightly. Thus, some trends point to an upgrading of the occupational structure, in line with the predictions of post-industrial theory. However, on the other hand, the fact that high-skill occupations tend to grow faster does not mean that society at large necessarily avoids polarization and dualism, because of the relative weight of unskilled jobs when they are counted in absolute numbers. BLS projections for 1992–2005 show that the shares of employment for professionals and for service workers are expected to increase approximately by the same amount, about 1.8 and 1.5 percentage points respectively. Since these two groups account together for about half of total job growth, in absolute numbers they do tend to concentrate jobs at both ends of the occupational ladder: 6.2 million

13   Silvestri and Lukasiewicz (1991: 82).
14   Silvestri (1993).

new professional workers, and 6.5 million new service workers, whose earnings in 1992 were about 40 percent below the average for all occupational groups. As Silvestri writes, "part of the reason [for lower earnings of service workers] is that almost a third of these employees had less than a high school education and twice as many worked part-time than the average for all workers."[15] Trying to provide a synthetic vision of projected changes in the occupational structure, I calculated a simplified stratification model on the basis of the detailed data provided by another study by Silvestri concerning distribution of employment by occupation, education, and earnings, for 1992 (actual data) and 2005 (projection).[16] Using median weekly earnings as a most direct indicator of social stratification, I constructed four social groups: upper class (managers and professionals); middle class (technicians and craft workers); lower middle class (sales, clerical, and operators); and lower class (service occupations and agricultural workers). Recalculating Silvestri's data under these categories, I found for the upper class an increase in its share of employment from 23.7 percent in 1992 to 25.3 percent in 2005 (+1.6); a slight decline for the middle class, from 14.7 to 14.3 percent (−0.3); a decline for the lower middle class, from 42.7 percent to 40.0 percent (−2.7); and an increase for the lower class, from 18.9 to 20 percent (+1.1). Two facts deserve comment: on the one hand, there is at the same time relative upgrading of the stratification system and a moderate trend toward occupational polarization. This is because there are simultaneous increases at both the top and the bottom of the social ladder, although the increase at the top is of greater magnitude.

Let us now turn to examine the projections on the Japanese employment and occupational structure. We have two projections, both from the Ministry of Labor. One of them, published in 1991, projects (on the basis of the 1980–85 data) to 1989, 1995, and 2000. The other, published in 1987, projects to 1990, 1995, 2000, and 2005. Both project the employment structure by industry and occupational structure. I have chosen to elaborate on the basis of the 1987 projection because, while being equally reliable, it is more detailed in its breakdown by industries and reaches out to 2005.[17]

The most significant feature of these projections is the slow decline of manufacturing employment in Japan in spite of the acceleration of the transformation of Japan into an informational society. In the 1987 statistical projection, manufacturing employment stood at 25.9

15   Silvestri (1993: 85).
16   Silvestri (1993: table 9).
17   Ministry of Labor (1991).

percent in 1985 and was projected to remain at 23.9 percent of total employment in 2005. As a reminder, in the US projection, manufacturing employment was expected to decline from 17.5 percent in 1990 to 14 percent in 2005, a much sharper decline from a substantially lower base. Japan achieves this relative stability of manufacturing jobs by compensating declines in the traditional sectors with actual increases in the newest sectors. Thus, while employment in textiles will decline from 1.6 percent in 1985 to 1.1 percent in 2005, in the same period employment in electrical machinery will increase from 4.1 to 4.9 percent. Metalworkers will decline substantially, but jobs in the food processing industry will jump from 2.4 to 3.5 percent.

Overall, the most spectacular increase in employment in Japan is projected to be in business services (from 3.3 percent in 1985 to 8.1 percent in 2005), thus showing the increasing role of information-intensive activities in the Japanese economy. However, the employment share of activities in financial, insurance and real estate is projected to remain stable for the 20-year period of the projection. Coupled with the preceding observation, this seems to imply that these rapidly growing business services are, mainly, services to manufacturing and to other services; that is, services which input knowledge and information into production. Health services are projected to grow slightly, and education employment is expected to remain at the same share as in 1985. On the other hand, agricultural employment is expected to decline sharply, from 9.1 percent in 1985 to 3.9 percent in 2005, as if Japan had finally assumed its transition to the post-agricultural (not post-industrial) age. In general terms, with the exception of business services and agriculture, the Japanese employment structure is projected to remain remarkably stable, verifying again this gradual transition to the informational paradigm, reworking the content of existing jobs into the new paradigm without necessarily phasing out such jobs.

As for the occupational structure, the most substantial change projected is an increase in the share of professional and technical occupations, which will grow from 10.5 percent in 1985 to a staggering 17 percent in 2005. On the other hand, managerial occupations, while growing significantly in their share, will grow at a slower rate, and will still represent less than 6 percent of total employment in 2005. This will confirm the tendency toward the reproduction of the lean hierarchical structure of Japanese organizations with power concentrated in the hands of a few managers. The data also seem to indicate the increase in the professionalization of middle-level workers and the specialization of tasks in information processing and knowledge generation. Crafts and operators are expected to decline, but will still represent over one-quarter of the labor force in 2005, about 3 percentage points ahead of the corresponding occupational categories for the United States at the same date. Clerical workers are also expected to increase at a moderate rate, while farming occupations will be reduced by about two-thirds in relation to their 1985 level.

Thus, the projections of the employment structure of the United States and Japan seem to continue the trends observed for the 1970–90 period. These are clearly two different employment and occupational structures corresponding to two societies which can be equally labeled informational in terms of their socio-technical paradigm of production, yet with clearly distinct performances in productivity growth, economic competitiveness, and social cohesion. While the United States appears to be emphasizing its tendency to move away from manufacturing jobs, and to concentrate in both producer and social services, Japan is maintaining a more balanced structure, with a strong manufacturing sector and a wide cushion of retail service activities. Japanese emphasis on business services is significantly less concentrated in finance and real estate, and the expansion of employment in social services is also more limited. The projections of the occupational structure confirm different styles of management, with Japanese organizations establishing cooperative structures at the shopfloor and office level while at the same time continuing to concentrate decision-making into a leaner managerial rank. Overall, the general hypothesis of diverse paths to the informational paradigm within a common pattern of employment structure seems to be confirmed by the limited test offered by the projections presented here.

Summing up: the evolution of employment structure and its implications for a comparative analysis of the informational society

The historical evolution of employment structure, at the roots of social structure, has been dominated by the secular trend toward the increasing productivity of human labor. As technological and organizational innovations have allowed men and women to put out more and better product with less effort and resources, work and workers have shifted from direct production to indirect production, from cultivation, extraction, and fabrication to consumption services and management work, and from a narrow range of economic activities to an increasingly diverse occupational universe.

But the tale of human creativity and economic progress throughout history has been often told in simplistic terms, thus obscuring the understanding not only of our past but of our future. The usual version of this process of historical transition as a shift from agriculture, to industry, then to services, as an explanatory framework for the current transformation of our societies, presents three fundamental flaws:

1　It assumes homogeneity between the transition from agriculture to industry and that from industry to services, overlooking the ambiguity and internal diversity of the activities included under the label of "services."

2　It does not pay enough attention to the truly revolutionary nature of new information technologies, which, by allowing a direct, online linkage between different types of activity in the same process of production, management, and distribution, establish a close, structural connection between spheres of work and employment artificially separated by obsolete statistical categories.

3　It forgets the cultural, historical, and institutional diversity of advanced societies, as well as the fact that they are interdependent in a global economy. Thus, the shift to the socio-technical paradigm of informational production takes place along different lines, determined by the trajectory of each society and by the interaction between these various trajectories. It follows a diversity of employment/occupational structures within the common paradigm of the informational society.

Our empirical observation of the evolution of employment in the G-7 countries shows some fundamental common features which seem indeed to be characteristic of informational societies:

- the phasing out of agricultural employment;
- the steady decline of traditional manufacturing employment;
- the rise of both producer services and social services, with the emphasis on business services in the first category, and health services in the second group;
- the increasing diversification of service activities as sources of jobs;
- the rapid rise of managerial, professional, and technical jobs;
- the formation of a "white-collar" proletariat, made up of clerical and sales workers;
- the relative stability of a substantial share of employment in retail trade;
- the simultaneous increase of the upper and lower levels of the occupational structure;
- the relative upgrading of the occupational structure over time, with an increasing share of those occupations that require higher skills and advanced education proportionally higher than the increase of the lower-level categories.

It does not follow that societies at large are upgraded in their skills, education, or income status, nor in their stratification system. The impact of a somewhat upgraded employment structure into the social structure will depend on the ability of the institutions to incorporate the labor demand into the labor force and to reward workers proportionally to their skills. On the other hand, the analysis of the differential evolution of the G-7 countries clearly shows some variation in their employment and occupational structures. At the risk of oversimplifying, we can propose the hypothesis of two different informational models:

1 The *service economy model*, represented by the United States, the United Kingdom, and Canada. It is characterized by a decline in the share of manufacturing employment in overall employment after 1970, as the pace toward informationalism accelerated. Having already eliminated almost all agricultural employment, this model emphasizes an entirely new employment structure where the differentiation among various service activities becomes the key element to analyze social structure. This model emphasizes capital management services over producer services, and keeps expanding the social service sector because of a dramatic rise in health-care jobs and, to a lesser extent, in education employment. It is also characterized by the expansion of the managerial category which includes a considerable number of middle managers.

2 The *industrial production model*, clearly represented by Japan and to a considerable extent by Germany, which, while reducing also the share of their manufacturing employment, continues to keep it at a relatively high level (around one-quarter of the labor force) in a much more gradual movement that allows for the restructuring of manufacturing activities into the new socio-technical paradigm. Indeed, this model reduces manufacturing jobs while reinforcing manufacturing activity. Partly as a reflection of this orientation, producer services are much more important than financial services, and they seem to be more directly linked to manufacturing firms. This is not to say that financial activities are not important in Japan and Germany: after all, eight of the world's ten largest banks are Japanese. Yet, while financial services are indeed important and have increased their share in both countries, the bulk of service growth is in services to companies, and in social services. However, Japan is also specific in showing a significantly lower level of employment in social services than other informational societies. This is probably linked to the structure of the Japanese family and to the internalization of some social services into the

structure of the firms: a cultural and institutional analysis of the variegations of employment structure seems to be a necessity to account for the diversity of informational societies.

In between, France seems to be leaning toward the service economy model, but maintaining a relatively strong manufacturing basis and emphasizing both producer and social services. The close linkage between the French and the German economies in the European Union is probably creating a division of labor between management and manufacturing activities that could ultimately benefit the German component of the emerging European economy. Italy characterizes itself as keeping almost one-quarter of employment in self-employed status, perhaps introducing a third model that would emphasize a different organizational arrangement, based on networks of small and medium businesses adapted to the changing conditions of the global economy, thus laying the ground for an interesting transition from proto-industrialism to proto-informationalism.

The different expressions of such models in each one of the G-7 countries are dependent upon their position in the global economy. In other words, for a country to be focused on the service economy model means that other countries are exercising their role as industrial production economies. The implicit assumption of post-industrial theory that the advanced countries would be service economies and the less advanced countries would specialize in agriculture and manufacturing has been rejected by historical experience. Throughout the world, many economies are quasi-subsistence economies, while agricultural and industrial activities that thrive outside the informational core do so on the basis of their close connection to the global economy, dominated by the G-7 countries. Thus, the employment structure of the United States and of Japan reflect their different forms of articulation to the global economy, and not just their degree of advancement in the informational scale. The fact that there is a lower proportion of manufacturing jobs or a higher proportion of managers in the United States is partly due to the offshoring of manufacturing jobs by US firms, and to the concentration of management and information-processing activities in the United States at the expense of production activities generated in other countries by US consumption of these countries' products.

Furthermore, different modes of articulation to the global economy are not only due to different institutional environments and economic trajectories, but to different government policies and firms' strategies. Thus, the observed trends can be reversed. If policies and strategies can modify the service and industrial mix of a given economy it means that the variations of the informational paradigm are as important as its basic structure. It is a socially open, politically managed paradigm, whose main common feature is technological.

As economies rapidly evolve toward their integration and interpenetration, the resulting employment structure will largely reflect the position of each country and region in the interdependent, global structure of production, distribution, and management. Thus, the artificial separation of social structures by institutional boundaries of different nations (the United States, Japan, Germany, and so on) limits the interest of analyzing the occupational structure of the informational society in a given country in isolation from what happens in another country whose economy is so closely interrelated. If Japanese manufacturers produce many of the cars consumed by the American market and many of the chips consumed in Europe, we are not just witnessing the demise of American or British manufacturing, but the impact on the employment structure of each country of the division of labor among different types of informational societies.

The implications of such an observation for the theory of informationalism are far-reaching: the unit of analysis to comprehend the new society will necessarily have to change. The focus of the theory must shift to a comparative paradigm able to explain at the same time the sharing of technology, the interdependence of the economy, and the variations of history in the determination of an employment structure spread across national boundaries.

Is There a Global Labor Force?

If there is a global economy, there should be a global labor market and a global labor force.[18] Yet, as with many such obvious statements, taken in its literal sense it is empirically wrong and analytically misleading. While capital flows freely in the electronic circuits of global financial networks, labor is still highly constrained, and will be for the foreseeable future, by institutions, culture, borders, police, and xenophobia. However, international migrations are on the rise, in a long-term trend that contributes to transforming the labor force, although in terms more complex than those presented by the notion of a global labor market.

Let us examine the empirical trends. A 1993 ILO estimate put at about 1.5 percent of the global labor force (that is, 80 million immigrant workers) the number of persons working outside their country, with half of them concentrated in Sub-Saharan Africa and the Middle

18   Johnston (1991).

East.[19] This seems to underestimate the extent of global migration, particularly taking into consideration the acceleration of migration in the 1990s. In a comprehensive study of migration dynamics on the global scale, the leading expert on the matter, Douglas Massey and his co-authors have shown the intensification of labor mobility in all regions of the world, and in most countries.[20] However, trends vary in time and space. In the European Union, the proportion of foreign population increased from 3.1 percent in 1982 to 4.5 percent in 1990 (see table 4.22 in Appendix A), but while it increased significantly in Germany, Austria, and Italy, the proportion of foreign-born residents actually decreased in the UK and in France. Concerning mobility within the European Union, in spite of the free movement of their citizens in the member countries, only 2 percent of their nationals worked in another European Union country in 1993, a proportion unchanged for ten years.[21] The percentage of foreign labor in the total labor force in Britain was 6.5 percent in 1975, and 4.5 percent in 1985–7; in France, it went down from 8.5 to 6.9 percent; in Sweden from 6 to 4.9 percent; and in Switzerland from 24 to 18.2 percent.[22] In the early 1990s, because of social disruption in Eastern Europe (mainly in Yugoslavia), political asylum increased the number of immigrants, particularly in Germany. Overall, in the European Union it was estimated that in the early 1990s the total foreign population of non-European citizens amounted to about 13 million, of which about one-quarter was undocumented.[23] The proportion of foreigners in the total population, for the five largest countries of the European Union in 1994, only surpassed 5 percent in Germany; it was actually lower than in 1986 in France; and it was only slightly over the 1986 level in the UK.[24] The situation changed in the late 1990s, as Eastern European migrations intensified in Germany, Austria, Switzerland, and Italy, and African migrants made their way into southern Europe. A relatively new phenomenon was massive illegal immigration particularly from Eastern Europe, often organized by criminal smuggler rings, and including thousands of enslaved women for the profitable prostitution traffic in the civilized Western European countries. In 1999 the number of illegal immigrants into the European Union was estimated at about 500,000 per year, with their main points of destination being Germany, Austria, Switzerland, and Italy (see volume III, chapter 3). Be-

19 Campbell (1994).
20 Massey et al. (1999).
21 *Newsweek* (1993).
22 Sources collected and elaborated by Soysal (1994: 23); see also Stalker (1994).
23 Soysal (1994: 22).
24 *The Economist* (Feb 20, 1999: 45).

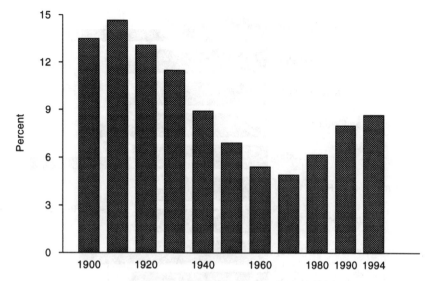

Figure 4.1 Percentage of the United States' population that is foreign-born, 1900–1994
Source: US Bureau of the Census

cause of its restrictive naturalization laws, Germany reached the level of about 10 percent of foreigners in its population, to which should be added undocumented residents. As for the United States, where a significant new wave of immigration did indeed occur during the 1980s and 1990s (about 1 million new immigrants per year in the 1990s), it was always an immigrant society, and current trends are in a line of long-term, historical continuity (see figure 4.1).[25] What has changed, in both contexts, is the ethnic and cultural composition of immigration, with a decreasing proportion of immigrants of European stock in America, and with a higher proportion of African, Asian, and Muslim immigrants in European countries. What is also happening is that because of differential birth rates between the native population and the residents and citizens of immigrant origin, affluent societies are becoming more ethnically diverse (figure 4.2). The visibility of immigrant workers, and their descendants, has increased because of their concentration in the largest metropolitan areas and in a few regions.[26] As a result of both features, in the 1990s ethnicity and cultural diversity became a major social problem in Europe, a new issue in Japan,

25 Borjas et al. (1991); Bouvier and Grant (1994); Stalker (1994).
26 Machimura (1994); Stalker (1994).

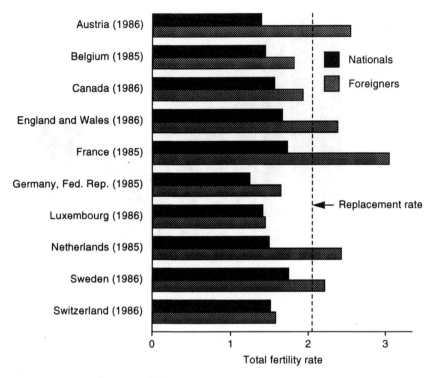

Figure 4.2 Total fertility rates for nationals and foreigners in selected OECD countries
Source: SOPEMI/OECD, elaborated by Stalker (1994)

and continued to be, as they always were, at the top of the American agenda. Massey and his co-authors have also shown the growing role of migrations in Asia, Africa, the Middle East, and Latin America. Overall, the UNDP's *Human Development Report* estimated in 1999 that worldwide there were between 130 and 145 million legal immigrant workers, up from 84 million in 1975, to which many more millions of undocumented workers should be added.[27] Yet, this is still a small fraction of the global labor force, and while immigrant workers are an increasingly important component in the labor market of many countries, particularly in the United States, Canada, Australia, Switzerland, and Germany, this does not mean that the labor force has become global. There is indeed a global market for a tiny fraction of the labor force, concerning the highest-skilled professionals in innovative

27 UNDP (1999).

R&D, cutting-edge engineering, financial management, advanced business services, and entertainment, who shift and commute between nodes of the global networks that control the planet.[28] Yet while this integration of the best talent in the global networks is critical for the commanding heights of the informational economy, the overwhelming proportion of labor, in developed as well as in developing countries, remains largely nation-bound. Indeed, for two-thirds of workers in the world, employment still means agricultural employment, rooted in the fields, usually in their region.[29] Thus, in the strictest sense, with the exception of the highest level of knowledge generators/symbol manipulators (whom I call below the *networkers*, *commanders*, and *innovators*), there is not, and will not be in the foreseeable future, a unified global labor market, in spite of emigration flows to OECD countries, to the Arabian peninsula, and to the metropolitan centers in the Asian Pacific. More important for movements of people are massive displacements of population because of war and hunger.

However, there is an historical tendency toward increasing interdependence of the labor force on a global scale, through three mechanisms: global employment in the multinational corporations and their associated cross-border networks; impacts of international trade on employment and labor conditions, both in the North and in the South; and effects of global competition and of the new mode of flexible management on each country's labor force. In each case, information technology is the indispensable medium for the linkages between different segments of the labor force across national boundaries.

As stated in chapter 2, foreign direct investment has become the driving force of globalization, more significant than trade as a conductor of trans-border interdependence.[30] The most significant agents of the new pattern of foreign direct investment are multinational corporations and their associated networks: together they organize the core labor force in the global economy. The number of multinational firms increased from 7,000 in 1970 to 37,000 in 1993, with 150,000 affiliates around the world, and to 53,000 with 415,00 affiliates in 1998. Although they employed directly "only" 70 million workers in 1993, these workers produced one-third of the world's total private output. The global value of their sales in 1992 was US$5,500 billion, a figure 25 percent greater than the total value of world trade. The labor force located in different countries depends on the division of labor between distinct functions and strategies of these multinational networks. Thus, most of the labor

28   Johnston (1991).
29   ILO (1994).
30   Tyson et al. (1988); Bailey et al. (1993); UNCTAD (1993, 1994).

force does not circulate in the network, but becomes dependent on the function, evolution, and behavior of other segments in the network. This results in a process of hierarchical, segmented interdependence of the labor force, under the impulse of relentless movements by firms in the circuits of their global network.

The second major mechanism of global labor interdependence concerns the impacts of trade on employment, both in the North and in the South.[31] On the one hand, the combination of North-bound exports, foreign direct investment, and growth of domestic markets in the South has triggered a gigantic wave of industrialization in some developing countries.[32] Simply accounting for the direct impact of trade, Wood[33] estimates that between 1960 and 1990 20 million manufacturing jobs have been created in the South. In Guandong province's Pearl River Delta alone, between 5 and 6 million workers were hired in factories in semi-rural areas between the mid-1980s and the mid-1990s.[34] But while there is agreement on the significance of the new process of industrialization triggered in Asia and Latin America by the new outward orientation of developing economies, an intense debate has raged on the actual impact of trade on employment and labor conditions in OECD countries. The White Paper of the Commission of European Communities (1994) considered global competition to be a significant factor in the rise of unemployment in Europe. In sharp contrast, the 1994 employment study of the OECD secretariat rejects this relationship, arguing that imports from industrializing countries account for only 1.5 percent of total demand in the OECD area. Some noted economists, such as Paul Krugman and Robert Lawrence,[35] have proposed empirical analyses according to which the impact of trade on employment and wages in the United States is very small. Yet their analysis has been submitted to serious criticism, both methodological and substantive, by Cohen, Sachs and Shatz, and Mishel and Bernstein, among others.[36] Indeed, the complexity of the new global economy is not easily captured by traditional trade and employment statistics. UNCTAD and the ILO estimate that intra-firm trade represents the equivalent of about 32 percent of world trade. Such exchanges do not take place through the market, but are internalized (through ownership) or quasi-internalized (through networks).[37] It is this kind of trade

---

31   Mishel and Bernstein (1993); Rothstein (1993).
32   Patel (1992); ILO (1993, 1994); Singh (1994).
33   Wood (1994).
34   Kwok and So (1995).
35   Krugman (1994a); Krugman and Lawrence (1994).
36   See, for instance, Cohen (1994); Mishel and Bernstein (1994).
37   Bailey et al. (1993); UNCTAD (1993); Campbell (1994).

that affects the labor force in OECD countries most directly. Subcontracting of services by companies around the globe, using telecommunications linkages, further integrates the labor force without displacing it or trading its output. But even using standard trade statistics, it seems that the impact of trade on the labor force has been underestimated by some economic analyses. Perhaps a balanced view of this matter is the empirical study by Adrian Wood on the impact of trade on employment and inequality between 1960 and 1990.[38] According to his calculations (which revise, on the basis of a sound methodological critique, usual estimates), skilled workers in the North greatly benefited from global trade on two grounds: first, they took advantage of higher economic growth brought about by increased trade; secondly, the new international division of labor gave their firms, and themselves, a comparative advantage in higher value-added products and processes. On the other hand, unskilled workers in the North suffered considerably because of the competition with producers in lower-cost areas. Wood estimates that overall demand for unskilled labor was reduced by 20 percent. When government and firms could not change the conditions of labor contracts, as in the European Union, unskilled labor became too costly with reference to commodities traded with newly industrializing countries. Unemployment of unskilled labor followed, which was, by comparative standards, too expensive for its low skills. Because skilled workers, by contrast, were still in demand, wage inequality surged in the OECD area.

Yet the new international division of labor theory that underlies the analyses of the differential impact of trade and globalization on the labor force relies on an assumption that has been questioned by empirical observation of production processes in newly industrializing areas, namely the persistence of a productivity gap between workers and factories in the South and the North. The pioneering research by Harley Shaiken on American automobile and computer plants and on Japanese consumer electronic plants in northern Mexico shows that the productivity of Mexican workers and factories is comparable to that of American plants.[39] Mexican production lines are not at a lower technological level than those in the United States either in process (CAM manufacturing) or products (engines, computers), yet they operate at a fraction of the cost north of the Rio Grande. In another typical example of new labor interdependence, Bombay and Bangalore have become major subcontractors of software for companies around the globe, using the work of thousands of highly skilled Indian engin-

38   Wood (1994).
39   Shaiken (1990).

eers and computer scientists who receive about 20 percent of the wage paid in the United States for similar jobs.[40] Similar trends were taking place in finance and business services in Singapore, Hong Kong, and Taipei.[41] In sum, the more the process of economic globalization deepens, the more the interpenetration of networks of production and management expands across borders, and the closer the links become between the conditions of the labor force in different countries, placed at different levels of wages and social protection, but decreasingly distinct in terms of skills and technology.

Thus, a wide range of opportunities opens up for companies in advanced capitalist countries, concerning their strategies toward labor, both skilled and unskilled. They can:

- downsize the firm, keeping the indispensable highly skilled labor force in the North, and importing inputs from low-cost areas; or,
- subcontract part of the work to their transnational establishments and to the auxiliary networks whose production can be internalized in the network enterprise system; or,
- use temporary labor, part-time workers, or informal firms as suppliers in the home country; or,
- automate or relocate tasks and functions for which the standard labor market prices are considered too high *vis-à-vis* alternative formulae; or,
- obtain from their labor force, including the core labor force, acquiescence to more stringent conditions of work and pay as a condition for the continuation of their jobs, thus reversing social contracts established under circumstances more favorable for labor.

In the real world, this range of possibilities translates into the actual use of all of them, depending upon firms, countries, and periods of time. Thus, although global competition may not affect directly the majority of the labor force in OECD countries, its indirect effects entirely transform the condition of labor and labor institutions everywhere.[42] Furthermore, the alignment of labor conditions across countries does not take place only because of competition from low-cost areas: it also forces Europe, America, and Japan to converge. The pressures toward greater flexibility of the labor market and toward the reversal of the welfare state in Western Europe come less from the pressures derived from East Asia than from the comparison with the

40   Balaji (1994).
41   Tan and Kapur (1986); Fouquin et al. (1992); Kwok and So (1995).
42   Rothstein (1994); Sengenberger and Campbell (1994).

United States.[43] It will become increasingly difficult for Japanese firms to continue life employment practices for the privileged 30 percent of its labor force if they have to compete in an open economy with American companies practicing flexible employment (see chapter 3).[44] Lean production, downsizing, restructuring, consolidation, and flexible management practices are induced and made possible by the intertwined impact of economic globalization and diffusion of information technologies. The indirect effects of such tendencies on the conditions of labor in all countries are far more important than the measurable impact of international trade or cross-border direct employment.

Thus, while there is not a unified global labor market, and therefore not a global labor force, there is indeed global interdependence of the labor force in the informational economy. Such interdependence is characterized by the hierarchical segmentation of labor not between countries but across borders.

The new model of global production and management is tantamount to the simultaneous integration of work process and disintegration of the workforce. This model is not the inevitable consequence of the informational paradigm but the result of an economic and political choice made by governments and companies selecting the "low road" in the process of transition to the new, informational economy, mainly using productivity increases for short-term profitability. These policies contrast sharply, in fact, with the possibilities of work enhancement and sustained, high productivity opened up by the transformation of the work process under the informational paradigm.

The Work Process in the Informational Paradigm

The maturation of the information technology revolution in the 1990s has transformed the work process, introducing new forms of social and technical division of labor. It took the 1980s for micro-electronics-based machinery to fully penetrate manufacturing, and it was only in the 1990s that networked computers widely diffused throughout the information-processing activities at the core of the so-called services sector. By the mid-1990s the new informational paradigm, associated with the emergence of the network enterprise, was well in place and set for its unfolding.[45]

There is an old and honorable tradition of sociological and organ-

---

43   Navarro (1994b).
44   NIKKEIREN (1993); Joussaud (1994).
45   For a documented view of developments in the diffusion of information technology in the workplace up to 1995, see *Business Week* (1994a, 1995a).

izational research on the relationship between technology and work.[46] Thus, we know that technology *per se* is not the cause of the work arrangements to be found in the workplace. Management decisions, systems of industrial relations, cultural and institutional environments, and government policies are such fundamental sources of labor practices and production organization that the impact of technology can only be understood in complex interaction within a social system comprising all these elements. Furthermore, the process of capitalist restructuring decisively marked the forms and outcomes of introducing information technologies into the work process.[47] The means and ways of this restructuring were also diverse depending upon countries' technological capability, political culture, and labor traditions. Thus, the new informational paradigm of work and labor is not a neat model but a messy quilt, woven from the historical interaction between technological change, industrial relations policy, and conflictive social action. To find patterns of regularity behind this confusing scene, we must have the patience to abstract successive layers of social causation, to first deconstruct, then reconstruct the emerging pattern of work, workers, and labor organization that characterize the new, informational society.

Let us start with information technology. Mechanization first, automation later, have been transforming human labor for decades, always triggering similar debates around issues of workers' displacement, deskilling versus reskilling, productivity versus alienation, management control versus labor autonomy.[48] To follow a French *"filière"* of analysis over the past half-century, Georges Friedmann criticized *"le travail en miettes"* (piecemeal work) of the Taylorist factory; Pierre Naville denounced the alienation of workers under mechanization; Alain Touraine, on the basis of his pioneering sociological study in the late 1940s on the technological transformation of Renault factories, proposed his typology of work processes as A/B/C (craft, assembly line, and innovation work); Serge Mallet announced the birth of "a new working class" focused on the capacity to manage and operate advanced technology; and Benjamin Coriat analyzed the emergence of a post-Fordist model in the labor process, on the basis of linking up flexibility and integration in a new model of relationships between production and consumption. At the end of this intellectual itinerary, impressive on many grounds, one fundamental idea emerges: automation, which received its full meaning only with the deployment of

---

46 For a review of relevant literature, see Child (1986); see also Burawoy (1979); Noble (1984); Buitelaar (1988); Appelbaum and Schettkat (1990).
47 Shaiken (1985); Castano (1994a).
48 Hirschhorn (1984).

information technology, increases dramatically the importance of human brain input into the work process.[49] While automated machinery, and later computers, have indeed been used for transforming workers into second-order robots, as Braverman argued,[50] this is not the corollary of technology, but of a social organization of labor that stalled (and still does) the full utilization of the productive capacity generated by the new technologies. As Harley Shaiken, Maryellen Kelley, Larry Hirschhorn, Shoshana Zuboff, Paul Osterman, and others have shown in their empirical work, the broader and deeper the diffusion of advanced information technology in factories and offices, the greater the need for an autonomous, educated worker able and willing to program and decide entire sequences of work.[51] Notwithstanding the formidable obstacles of authoritarian management and exploitative capitalism, information technologies call for greater freedom for better-informed workers to deliver the full promise of their productivity potential. The networker is the necessary agent of the network enterprise made possible by new information technologies.

In the 1990s several factors accelerated the transformation of the work process: computer technology, network technologies, the Internet, and its applications, progressing by quantum leaps, became increasingly cheaper and better, thus being affordable and manageable on a large scale; global competition triggered a technology/management race between companies all over the world; organizations evolved and adopted new shapes that were generally based on flexibility and networking; managers, and their consultants, finally understood the potential of new technology and how to use it, although more often than not they constrained such potential within the limits of the old set of organizational goals (such as a short-term increase of profits calculated on a quarterly basis).

The massive diffusion of information technologies has caused rather similar effects in factories, offices, and service organizations.[52] These effects are not, as was forecast, the shift toward indirect work at the expense of direct work which would become automated. On the contrary, the role of direct work has increased because information technology has empowered the direct worker at the shopfloor level (be it in the process of testing chips or underwriting insurance policies). What *tends* to disappear through integral automation are the routine,

49   Touraine (1955); Friedmann (1956); Friedmann and Naville (1961); Mallet (1963); Pfeffer (1998); Coriat (1990).
50   Braverman (1973).
51   Hirschhorn (1984); Japan Institute of Labour (1985); Shaiken (1985, 1993); Kelley (1986, 1990); Zuboff (1988); Osterman (1999). For a discussion of the literature, see Adler (1992); for a comparative approach, see Ozaki et al. (1992).
52   Quinn (1988); Bushnell (1994).

repetitive tasks that can be precoded and programmed for their execution by machines. It is the Taylorist assembly line that becomes an historic relic (although it is still the harsh reality for millions of workers in the industrializing world). It should not be surprising that information technologies do precisely that: replace work that can be encoded in a programmable sequence and enhance work that requires analysis, decision, and reprogramming capabilities in real time at a level that only the human brain can master. Every other activity, given the extraordinary rate of progress in information technology and its constant lowering in price per information unit, is potentially susceptible to automation, and thus the labor engaged in it is expendable (although workers as such are not, depending upon their social organization and political capacity).

The informational work process is determined by the characteristics of the informational production process. Keeping in mind the analyses presented in previous chapters on the informational, global economy, and on the network enterprise as its organizational form, this process can be summarized as follows:

1   Value added is mainly generated by innovation, both of process and products. New designs of chips, new software-writing, largely condition the fate of the electronics industry. The invention of new financial products (for example, the creation of the "derivatives market" on the stock exchanges during the late 1980s) are at the roots of the boom (however risky) of financial services, and of the prosperity (or collapse) of financial firms, and of their clients.
2   Innovation is itself dependent upon two conditions: research potential and specification capability. That is, new knowledge has to be discovered, then applied to specific purposes in a given organizational/institutional context. Custom design was critical for micro-electronics in the 1990s; instant reaction to macro-economic changes is fundamental in managing the volatile financial products created in the global market.
3   Task execution is more efficient when it is able to adapt higher-level instructions to their specific application, and when it can generate feedback effects into the system. An optimum combination of worker/machine in the execution of tasks is set to automate all standard procedures, and to reserve human potential for adaptation and feedback effects.
4   Most production activity takes place in organizations. Since the two main features of the predominant organizational form (the network enterprise) are internal adaptability and external flexibility, the two key features for the work process will be: the ability to

generate flexible strategic decision-making; and the capacity to achieve organizational integration between all elements of the production process.

5   Information technology becomes the critical ingredient of the process of work as described because:

- it largely determines innovation capability;
- it makes possible the correction of errors and generation of feedback effects at the level of execution;
- it provides the infrastructure for flexibility and adaptability throughout the management of the production process.

This specific production process introduces a *new division of labor* that characterizes the emerging informational paradigm. The new division of labor can be better understood by presenting a typology constructed around three dimensions. *The first dimension refers to the actual tasks performed in a given work process. The second dimension concerns the relationship between a given organization and its environment, including other organizations. The third dimension considers the relationship between managers and employees in a given organization or network. I call the first dimension value-making, the second dimension relation-making, and the third dimension decision-making.*

In terms of *value-making*, in a production process organized around information technology (be it goods production or service delivery), the following fundamental tasks, and their corresponding workers, can be distinguished:

- strategic decision-making and planning by the *commanders*;
- innovation in products and process by the *researchers*;
- adaptation, packaging, and targeting of innovation by the *designers*;
- management of the relationships between the decision, innovation, design, and execution, taking into consideration the means available to the organization to achieve the stated goals, by the *integrators*;
- execution of tasks under their own initiative and understanding by the *operators*;
- execution of ancillary, preprogrammed tasks that have not been, or cannot be, automated, by what I dare to call the *"operated"* (or human robots).

This typology must be combined with another referring to the need and capacity of each task (and its performer) to link up with other workers in real time, be it within the same organization or in the overall system of the network enterprise. According to this relational capacity we may distinguish between three fundamental positions:

- the *networkers*, who set up connections on their initiative (for example, joint engineering with other departments of companies), and navigate the routes of the network enterprise;
- the *networked*, workers who are on-line but without deciding when, how, why, or with whom;
- the *switched-off* workers, tied to their own specific tasks, defined by non-interactive, one-way instructions.

Finally, in terms of the capacity to input the *decision-making process* we can differentiate between:

- the *deciders*, who make the decision in the last resort;
- the *participants*, who are involved in decision-making;
- the *executants*, who merely implement decisions.

The three typologies do not coincide, and the difference in the relational dimension or in the decision-making process can occur, and indeed does in practice, at all levels of the value-making structure.

This construction is not an ideal type of organization, or some futuristic scenario. It is a synthetic representation of what seems to be emerging as the main task-performing positions in the informational work process, according to empirical studies on the transformation of work and organizations under the impact of information technologies.[53] Yet my argument is certainly not that all or most work processes and workers in our society can be reduced to these typologies. Archaic forms of socio-technical organization do survive, and will for a long, long time remain in many countries, in the same way as pre-industrial, handicraft forms of production were combined with mechanization of industrial production for an extended historical period. But it is critical to distinguish the complex and diverse forms of work and workers in our observation from the emerging patterns of production and management that, because they are rooted in a dynamic socio-technical system, will tend to become dominant through the dynamics of competition and demonstration effects. My hypothesis is

53   See, among others, Hartmann (1987); Wall et al. (1987); Buitelaar (1988); Hyman and Streeck (1988); ILO (1988); Carnoy (1989); Mowery and Henderson (1989); Wood (1989); Dean et al. (1992); Rees (1992); Tuomi (1999).

that the work organization sketched in this analytical scheme represents the emerging informational work paradigm. I shall illustrate this emerging paradigm by referring briefly to some case studies on the impacts of computer-aided manufacturing and office automation on work, in order to make somewhat concrete the analytical construction I have proposed.

Thus, Harley Shaiken in 1994 studied the practice of so-called "high performance work organization" in two up-to-date American automobile factories: the GM–Saturn complex on the outskirts of Nashville, Tennessee, and the Chrysler Jefferson North Plant on the east side of Detroit.[54] Both are cases of successful, highly productive organizations which have integrated the most advanced computer-based machinery in their operation, and have simultaneously transformed the organization of work and management. While acknowledging differences between the two plants, Shaiken points to the critical factors accounting for high performance in both of them, on the basis of new technological tools. The first is the high level of skills of an experienced industrial labor force, whose knowledge of production and products was critical to modifying a complex process when necessary. In order to develop these skills, at the heart of the new work system there is regular work training on special courses outside the plant and on the job. Saturn workers spend 5 percent of their annual working time in training sessions, most of them in the work development center, a facility adjacent to the plant.

The second factor fostering high performance is increased worker autonomy, as compared to other factories, allowing for shopfloor co-operation, quality circles, and feedback from workers in real time during the production process. Both plants organize production in work teams, with a flat occupational classification system. Saturn had eliminated the position of first line supervisor, and Chrysler was moving in the same direction. Workers are able to work with considerable freedom, and are encouraged to increase formal interaction in the performance of their tasks.

Workers' involvement in the upgraded process is dependent on two conditions that were met in both factories: job security and labor union participation in negotiating and implementing the reorganization of work. The building of the new Chrysler plant in Detroit was preceded by a "modern operating agreement," emphasizing managerial flexibility and workers' input. Of course, this is not an ideal world, exempt from social conflicts. Shaiken observed the existence of tensions, and potential sources of labor disputes, between labor and

54 Shaiken (personal communications, 1994, 1995); see also Shaiken (1995).

management, as well as between the local union (increasingly behaving as a factory union, in the case of Saturn), and the United Auto Workers leadership. Yet the nature of the informational work process calls for cooperation, teamwork, workers' autonomy and responsibility, without which new technologies cannot be used to their full potential. The networked character of informational production permeates the whole firm, and requires constant interaction and processing of information between workers, between workers and management, and between humans and machines.

As for office automation, it has gone through three different phases, largely determined by available technology.[55] In the first phase, characteristic of the 1960s and 1970s, mainframe computers were used for batch processing of data; centralized computing by specialists in data-processing centers formed the basis of a system characterized by the rigidity and hierarchical control of information flows; data entry operations required substantial efforts since the goal of the system was the accumulation of large amounts of information in a central memory; work was standardized, routinized, and, in essence, deskilled for the majority of clerical workers, in a process analyzed, and denounced, by Braverman in his classic study.[56] The following stages of automation, however, were substantially different. The second phase, in the early 1980s, was characterized by the emphasis on the use of microcomputers by the employees in charge of the actual work process; although they were supported by centralized databases, they interacted directly in the process of generating information, although often requiring the support of computer experts. By the mid-1980s, the combination of advances in telecommunications, and the development of microcomputers, led to the formation of networks of workstations and literally revolutionized office work, although the organizational changes required for the full use of new technology delayed the widespread diffusion of the new model of automation until the 1990s. In this third phase of automation, office systems were integrated and networked, with multiple microcomputers interacting among themselves and with mainframes, forming an interactive web that is capable of processing information, communicating, and making decisions in real time.[57] Interactive information systems, not just computers, are the basis of the automated office, and of the so-called "alternative officing" or "virtual offices," networking tasks performed in distant locations. There might be a fourth phase of office automation brewing up in the tech-

55   Zuboff (1988); Dy (1990).
56   Braverman (1973).
57   Strassman (1985).

nological cauldrons of the turn of the century: the mobile office, performed by individual workers provided with portable, powerful information processing/transmitting devices.[58] If it does develop, as seems likely, it will enhance the organizational logic I have described under the concept of the network enterprise, and it will deepen the process of transformation of work and workers along the lines proposed in this chapter.

The effects of these technological changes on office work are not yet fully identified, because empirical studies, and their interpretation, are running behind the fast process of technological change. However, during the 1980s, a number of doctoral students at Berkeley, whose work I followed and supervised, were able to produce a number of detailed monographs documenting the trends of change that seem to be confirmed by the evolution in the 1990s.[59] Particularly revealing was the doctoral dissertation by Barbara Baran on the impact of office automation on the work process in some large insurance companies in the United States.[60] Her work, as well as other sources, showed a tendency for firms to automate the lower end of clerical jobs, those routine tasks that, because they can be reduced to a number of standard steps, can be easily programmed. Also, data entry was decentralized, gathering the information and entering it into the system as close as possible to the source. For instance, sales accounting is now linked to scanning and storage at the cashier's point-of-sale machine. ATMs (automated teller machines) constantly update bank accounts. Insurance claims are directly stored in memory with regard to all elements that do not call for a business judgment, and so on. The net result of these trends is the possibility of eliminating most mechanical, routine clerical work. On the other hand, higher-level operations are concentrated in the hands of skilled clerical workers and professionals, who make decisions on the basis of the information they have stored in their computer files. So, while at the bottom of the process there is increasing routinization (and thus automation), at the middle level there is reintegration of several tasks into an informed decision-making operation, generally processed, evaluated, and performed by a team made up of clerical workers with increasing autonomy in making decisions. In a more advanced stage of this process of reintegration of tasks, middle managers' supervision also disappears, and controls and safety procedures are standardized in the computer. The critical linkage then

---

58 Thach and Woodman (1994).
59 Particularly, I relied on work performed for their doctoral dissertations at Berkeley by Lionel Nicol (1985), Carol Parsons (1987), Barbara Baran (1989), Penny Gurstein (1990), and Lisa Bornstein (1993).
60 Baran (1989).

becomes the one between professionals, evaluating and making decisions on important matters, and informed clerks making decisions on day-to-day operations on the basis of their computer files and their networking capabilities. Thus the third phase of office automation, instead of simply rationalizing the task (as was the case in batch-processing automation) rationalizes the process, because the technology allows the integration of information from many different sources and its redistribution, once processed, to different, decentralized units of execution. So, instead of automating discrete tasks (such as typing, calculating), the new system rationalizes an entire procedure (for example, new business insurance, claims processing, underwriting), and then integrates various procedures by product lines or segmented markets. Workers are then functionally reintegrated instead of being organizationally distributed.

A similar trend has been observed by Hirschhorn in his analyses of American banks, and by Castano in her study of Spanish banking.[61] While routine operations have been increasingly automated (ATMs, telephone information services, electronic banking), the remaining bank clerks are increasingly working as sales persons, to sell financial services to customers, and as controllers of the repayment of the money they sell. In the United States the federal government plans to automate tax and social security payments by the end of the century, thus extending a similar change of the work process to public sector agencies.

However, the emergence of the informational paradigm in the work process does not tell the whole story of labor and workers in our societies. The social context, and particularly the relationship between capital and labor according to specific decisions by the management of firms, drastically affects the actual shape of the work process and the consequences of the change for workers. This was particularly true during the 1980s when the acceleration of technological change went hand in hand with the process of capitalist restructuring, as I have argued above. Thus, the classic study by Watanabe [62] on the impact of the introduction of robots into the automobile industry in Japan, the United States, France, and Italy, showed substantially different impacts of a similar technology in the same industry: in the United States and Italy, workers were displaced, because the main goal of introducing new technology was to reduce labor costs; in France, job loss was lower than in the two other countries because of government policies to cushion the social impacts of modernization; and in Japan, where

61 Hirschhorn (1985); Castano (1991).
62 Watanabe (1986).

companies were committed to life-tenured employment, employment actually increased, and productivity shot up, as a result of retraining and higher teamwork effort which increased the competitiveness of firms and took market share away from their American counterparts.

Studies conducted on the interaction between technological change and capitalist restructuring during the 1980s also showed that more often than not technologies were introduced, first of all, to save labor, to subdue unions, and to trim costs, rather than to improve quality or to enhance productivity by means other than downsizing. Thus, another of my former students, Carol Parsons, studied in her Berkeley doctoral dissertation the socio-technological restructuring of metalworking and garment industries in America.[63] In the metalworking sector, among the firms surveyed by Parsons, the most-often cited purpose for the introduction of technology was the reduction of direct labor. Furthermore, instead of retooling their factories, firms often closed plants that were unionized and opened new ones, generally without a union, even if firms did not change region for their new location. As a result of the restructuring process, employment fell substantially in all metalworking industries, with the exception of office equipment. In addition, production workers saw their relative numbers reduced vis-à-vis managers and professionals. Within production workers there was a polarization between craft workers and unskilled laborers, with assembly-line workers being substantially squeezed by automation. A similar development was observed by Parsons in the garment industry in relation to the introduction of micro-electronics-based technology. Direct production workforce was rapidly being phased out, and the industry was becoming a dispatching center connecting the demand of the American market with manufacturing suppliers all over the world. The net result was a bipolar labor force composed of highly skilled designers and telecommunicating sales managers on the one hand, and low-skilled, low-paid manufacturing workers, located either offshore or in American, often illegal, domestic sweatshops. This is a strikingly similar model to the one I described in chapter 3 for Benetton, the worldwide knitwear networked firm, considered to be the epitome of flexible production.

Eileen Appelbaum[64] found similar trends in the insurance industry, whose dramatic technological changes I have described above on the basis of Barbara Baran's work. Indeed, the story concerning technological innovation, organizational change, and work reintegration in the insurance industry must be completed with the observation of

63   Parsons (1987).
64   Appelbaum (1984).

massive layoffs and underpayment of skilled work in the same industry. Appelbaum links the process of rapid technological change in the insurance industry to the impact of deregulation and global competition in the financial markets. As a result, it became critical to ensure the mobility of capital and the versatility of labor. Labor was both trimmed and reskilled. Unskilled data entry jobs, where ethnic minority women were concentrated, were projected to be all but eliminated by automation by the end of the century. On the other hand, the remaining clerical positions were reskilled, by integrating tasks into multi-skilled, multi-functional jobs susceptible to greater flexibility and adaptation to the changing needs of an increasingly diversified industry. Professional jobs were also polarized between less-skilled tasks, taken on by upgraded clerical workers, and highly specialized tasks that generally required college education. These occupational changes were specified by gender, class, and race: while machines mainly replaced ethnic minority, less-educated women at the bottom of the scale, educated, mainly white women began replacing white men in the lower professional positions, yet for lower pay and reduced career prospects than those which men used to have. Multi-skilling of jobs and individualization of responsibility were often accompanied by ideologically tailored new titles (for example, "assistant manager" instead of "secretary"), thus enhancing the potential for commitment of clerical workers without correspondingly increasing their professional rewards.

Thus, new information technology is redefining work processes, and workers, and therefore employment and occupational structure. While a substantial number of jobs are being upgraded in skills, and sometimes in wages and working conditions in the most dynamic sectors, a large number of jobs are being phased out by automation in both manufacturing and services. These are generally jobs that are not skilled enough to escape to automation but are expensive enough to be worth the investment in technology to replace them. Increasing educational qualifications, either general or specialized, required in the reskilled positions of the occupational structure further segregate the labor force on the basis of education, itself a highly segregated system because it roughly corresponds institutionally to a segregated residential structure. Downgraded labor, particularly in the entry positions for a new generation of workers made up of women, ethnic minorities, immigrants, and young people, is concentrated in low-skill, low-paid activities, as well as in temporary work and/or miscellaneous services. The resulting bifurcation of work patterns and polarization of labor is not the necessary result of technological progress or of inexorable evolutionary trends (for example, the rise of the "post-industrial society" or of the "service economy"). It is socially determined and managerially designed in the process of the capitalist restructuring taking place at the shopfloor level, within the framework and with the help of the process of technological change at the roots of the informational paradigm. Under these conditions, work, employment, and occupations are transformed, and the very notion of work and working time may be changed for ever.

The Effects of Information Technology on Employment: Toward a Jobless Society?

The diffusion of information technology in factories, offices, and services has reignited a centuries-old fear by workers of being displaced by machines, thus becoming irrelevant for the productivist logic that still dominates our social organization. While the Information Age version of the Luddite movement that terrorized English industrialists in 1811 has not appeared yet, increasing unemployment in Western Europe in the 1980s and 1990s prompted questions about the potential disruption of labor markets, and therefore of the whole social structure, by the massive impact of labor-saving technologies.

The debate on this question has raged over the past decade, and is far from generating a clear-cut answer.[65] On the one hand, it is argued that historical experience shows the secular transfer from one kind of activity to another as technological progress replaces labor with more efficient tools of production.[66] Thus, in Britain, between 1780 and 1988 the agricultural labor force was reduced by half in absolute numbers, and fell from 50 to 2.2 percent of the total labor force; yet productivity per capita increased by a factor of 68, and the increase in productivity allowed for the investment of capital and labor in manufacturing, then in services, so as to employ an increasing population. The extraordinary rate of technological change in the American economy during the twentieth century also massively displaced labor from agriculture, but the number of total jobs created by the US economy climbed from about 27 million in 1900 to 133 million in 1999. On this view, most traditional manufacturing jobs will know the same fate as agricultural jobs, but new jobs are being created, and will be created, in high-technology manufacturing (see table 4.23 in Appendix A) and, more significantly, in "services."[67] As evidence of

65   For a balanced and thorough analysis of unemployment trends in the 1980s and 1990s, see Freeman and Soete (1994).
66   Jones (1982); Lawrence (1984); Cyert and Mowery (1987); Hinrichs et al. (1991); Bosch et al. (1994); Commission of the European Communities (1994); OECD (1994b).
67   OECD (1994b).

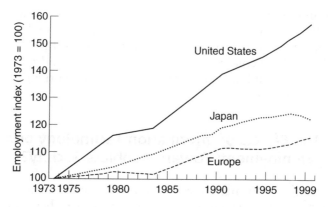

Figure 4.3 Index of employment growth by region, 1973–1999
Source: Data from OECD, compiled and elaborated by Carnoy (2000)

the continuity of this technical trend, it is easy to point to the experience of the most technologically advanced industrial economies, Japan and the United States: they are precisely the ones which created most jobs during the 1980s and 1990s.[68] According to the 1994 White Paper of the European Commission on *Growth, Competitiveness, and Employment*, between 1970 and 1992, the US economy grew in real terms by 70 percent, and employment by 49 percent. Japan's economy grew by 173 percent, and its employment by 25 percent, while the European Community's economy grew by 81 percent, but with an employment increase of only 9 percent.[69] And what the Commission does not say is that almost all of this new employment was created by the public sector: private employment creation in the European Community remained at a standstill during the 1980s. In the 1990s, the gap in employment creation between Europe, on the one hand, and the US, and Japan increased (see figure 4.3). Indeed, between 1975 and 1999 the United States created about 48 million new jobs and Japan 10 million. On the other hand, the European Union created only 11 million new jobs in these 24 years, and most of them, until the late 1990s, were in the public sector. Furthermore, between January 1, 1993 and January 1, 2000, the United States created over 20 million new jobs, while the absolute number of jobs in the European Union declined between 1990 and 1996. Moreover, employment started to grow in Europe in 1997–9, at the time when European countries stepped up the diffusion of information technologies in their firms, while pro-

68 OECD *Employment Outlook* (various years).
69 Commission of the European Communities (1994: 141).

ceeding with reforms in those institutional aspects of the labor market that were stalling job creation. In October 1999, for the first time in the decade, the unemployment rate in the European Union as a whole went below the 10 percent mark. Growth employment performance was in fact highly differentiated between European countries: in fact, in 1999, double-digit unemployment existed only in Spain, Italy, France, Germany, Finland, and Belgium, while the other European countries had unemployment rates below 8 percent, and some of them (The Netherlands, Switzerland, Norway) had unemployment rates lower than the United States. The skills profile of the new jobs created was, on average, of a higher level than that of the average skills of the overall labor force. Thus, for the United States, table 4.24 (in Appendix A), elaborated by Martin Carnoy, shows that the proportion of high-wage jobs increased from 24.6 percent in 1960 to 33 percent in 1998, a far greater increase than the often publicized growth of jobs at the bottom of the scale, which went up from 31.6 to 32.4 percent, confirming the decline of the middle, but mainly to the benefit of the top of the occupational scale. A study conducted in 1999 by the US Labor Department on the profile of new jobs created in the 1990s found that a great majority of the new jobs were in occupations that paid more than the national median wage of $13 an hour.[70] According to an OECD study, the variation in percentage in net job creation in 1980–95 for OECD countries, was of 3.3 percent in high-technology sectors, of −8.2 percent in medium-technology sectors, and of −10.9 percent in low-technology sectors.[71] Looking into the future, the 1997 Tregouet report, commissioned by the French Senate's Commission of Finance concluded that "as the information society gains strength, half of the occupations needing to be filled 20 years from now do not yet exist; they will essentially involve adding knowledge and information."[72]

A fundamental feature characterizing the new labor market of the past two decades is the massive incorporation of women into paid work: the rate of participation of women in the labor force for ages 15–64 increased from 51.1 percent in 1973 to 70.7 percent in 1998, for the United States; from 53.2 to 67.8 percent for the UK; from 50.1 to 60.8 percent for France; from 54 to 59.8 percent for Japan; from 50.3 to 60.9 percent for Germany; from 33.4 to 48.7 percent for Spain; from 33.7 to 43.9 percent for Italy; from 63.6 to 69.7 percent for Finland; and from 62.6 to 75.5 percent for Sweden, the country with the largest women's labor force participation rate in the

70 *The New York Times* (December 4, 1999: B14).
71 OECD (1997: 34).
72 Cited by Saussois (1998: 4).

world.[73] Yet the pressure of this substantial increase in labor supply did not create high unemployment in the US and Japan as it did *in some* Western European countries. The US, in the midst of a dramatic technological retooling, registered in November 1999 its lowest unemployment rate in 30 years at 4.1 percent. Japan, in spite of a prolonged recession in the 1990s, was still keeping its unemployment rate below 5 percent, while modifying its traditional pattern of labor relations, as I will discuss below. And The Netherlands, a technologically advanced economy, after modifying its labor institutions, reduced its unemployment rate to about 3 percent by the end of 1999.

Thus, all evidence points to the fact that high unemployment in developed countries was mainly a problem for some (but not all) European countries during the early stages of their transition to the new economy. This problem was mainly caused not by the introduction of new technologies, but by mistaken macro-economic policies and by an institutional environment that discouraged private job creation, while technological innovation and diffusion did not have a direct effect on job creation or destruction, at an aggregate level. Thus, Martin Carnoy elaborated tables 4.25 and 4.26 (see Appendix A) on the basis of OECD data, relating, for 21 countries, various indicators of information technology intensity with employment growth and unemployment in the mid-1990s. According to his calculations, there is no statistically significant relationship between technological diffusion and the evolution of employment in 1987–94. In fact, the only relationship (but not statistically significant) is between the level of IT spending per worker in 1994 and the unemployment rate. But the relationship is negative, indicating the possibility of a positive effect of technology on job creation.[74] As this, and other analyses indicate,[75] institutional variation seems to account for levels of unemployment, while effects of technological levels do not follow a consistent pattern. If any pattern did emerge from international data it would be in the opposite direction of Luddite predictions: higher technological level is generally associated with lower unemployment rate. Critics' objections, such as the argument of discouraged workers who are not counted in unemployment statistics, simply do not stand up to empirical scrutiny. A 1993 OECD study of discouraged workers between 1983 and 1991 evaluated these workers at about 1 percent of the labor force in 1991. When discouraged workers are added to unemployed workers, the unemployment rate in most OECD countries in 1991 would increase

73   OECD, *Employment Outlook* (various years).
74   Carnoy (2000: 2, 26).
75   Freeman and Soete (1994); OECD (1994c).

to about 8 percent. But, under the new calculations, the adjusted rate of unemployment would have fallen anyway in 1997 in the US, the UK, Japan, The Netherlands, Australia, and Canada; that is, the countries which were creating employment under new technological and organizational conditions.[76] But the definitive argument is to calculate the ratio between employment and the population at large for ages 15–64, the working age (see table 4.27). That is, everyone, discouraged or not, in prison or not, is counted in this way. If we proceed along these lines, between 1973 and 1998, in the United States the ratio of employed men over total male population went slightly down from 82.8 to 80.5 percent. But it sky-rocketed for women, climbing from 48 to 67.4 percent. On the other hand, it declined significantly for men in all European countries, in Canada, and Australia, while increasing for women in all countries, in some of them significantly (Canada), or meteorically (The Netherlands, from 28.6 to 59.4 percent). Japan stays in the middle with a clear decline of employment ratio for men, and a moderate increase for women. Thus, on the one hand, the US performance stands the test of the employment ratio/population evolution. On the other hand, what is really going on is a remarkable trend: the substitution of women for men in large segments of the labor market, under conditions, and with modalities, which will be analyzed more thoroughly in volume II, chapter 4.

Yet the prophets of mass unemployment, led by the honorable Club of Rome, argue that such calculations are based on a different historical experience that underestimates the radically new impacts of technologies, whose effects are universal and pervasive because they relate to information processing. Thus, so the argument goes, if manufacturing jobs go the way farmers did, there will not be enough service jobs to replace them because service jobs themselves are being rapidly automated and phased out. They predicted that because this trend was accelerating in the 1990s, mass unemployment would follow.[77] The obvious consequence of this analysis is that our societies would have to choose between massive unemployment, with its corollary, the sharp

---

76 Carnoy (2000: 2, 26).
77 King (1991); Aznar (1993); Aronowitz and Di Fazio (1994); Rifkin (1995). The most salient characteristic of all these writings announcing the jobless society is that they do not provide any consistent, rigorous evidence for their claims, relying on isolated press clippings, random examples of firms in some countries and sectors, and "commonsense" arguments on the "obvious" impact of computers on jobs. There is no serious analysis to explain, for instance, the high rate of job creation in the United States and Japan, as compared to Western Europe; and hardly any reference to the explosion of employment growth, particularly in manufacturing, in East and South-East Asia. Since most of these writers relate themselves to the "political left," their credibility must be challenged before their unfounded theses lead labor and the political left to a new dead end in the best tradition of ideological self-destructiveness.

division of society between the employed and the unemployed/occasional workers, or else a redefinition of work and employment, opening the way to a full restructuring of social organization and cultural values.

Given the importance of the matter, international institutions, governments, and researchers have made extraordinary efforts to assess the impact of new technologies. Dozens of technically sophisticated studies have been conducted in the past 20 years, particularly during the 1980s, when there was still hope that the data could provide the answer. Reading these studies reveals the difficulty of the search. It is obvious that introducing robots on to an assembly line reduces human working time for a given level of output. But it does not follow that this reduces employment for the firm or even for the industry. If the superior quality and productivity achieved by introducing electronic machinery increased competitiveness, both the firm and the industry would need to increase employment to supply the broader demand resulting from a larger market share. Thus, the question is raised at the level of the nation: the new growth strategy would imply increased competitiveness at the cost of reducing employment in some sectors, while using the surplus thus generated to invest and create jobs in other sectors, such as business services or environmental technology industries. In the last resort, the net employment results will depend on inter-nation competition. Trade theorists would then argue that there is no zero-sum game, since an expansion of global trade will benefit most of its partners by increasing overall demand. According to this line of argument, there would be a potential reduction of employment as a consequence of the diffusion of new information technologies only if:

- expansion in demand does not offset the increase in labor productivity; *and*
- there is no institutional reaction to such a mismatch by reducing working time, not jobs.

This second condition is particularly important. After all, the history of industrialization has shown a long-term increase in unemployment, production, productivity, real wages, profits, and demand, while significantly reducing working time, on the basis of progress in technology and management.[78] Why should it not be the case in the current stage of techno-economic transformation? Why would information technologies be more destructive for overall employment than mecha-

78   OECD (1994c).

nization or automation were during the earlier decades of the twentieth century? Let us check the empirical record.

Facing a plethora of studies on different countries and industries in the 1980s, the International Labour Office commissioned some literature reviews that would indicate the state of knowledge on the relationship between micro-electronics and employment in various contexts. Among these reviews two stand out as well documented and analytical: those by Raphael Kaplinsky[79] and by John Bessant.[80] Kaplinsky emphasized the need to distinguish the findings at eight different levels: process level, plant level, firm level, industry level, region level, sector level, national level, and meta level (meaning the discussion of differential effects related to alternative socio-technical paradigms). After reviewing the evidence for each one of these levels, he concluded:

> Insofar as the individual studies offer any clear statement on the issue, it would appear that the quantitative macro and micro studies are drawn to fundamentally different conclusions. Process and plant level investigations generally seem to point to a significant displacement of labour. On the other hand, national level simulations more often reach the conclusion that there is no significant employment problem on hand.[81]

Bessant dismisses as excessive what he calls the "repeated scares about automation and employment" that have been stated since the 1950s. Then, after closer examination of the study findings, he writes that "it became increasingly clear that the pattern of employment effects associated with microelectronics would vary widely." According to evidence reviewed by Bessant, on the one hand, micro-electronics displaces some jobs in some industries. But, on the other hand, it will also contribute to creating jobs, and it will also modify the characteristics of such jobs. The overall equation must take into consideration several elements at the same time:

> new employment generated by new product industries based on microelectronics; new employment in advanced technologies generated in existing industries; employment displaced by process changes in existing industries; employment displaced in industries whose products are being replaced by those based on microelectronics, such as telecommunications equipment; employment lost through a lack of overall competitiveness caused by non-adoption of microelectronics. All things

79   Kaplinsky (1986).
80   Bessant (1989).
81   Kaplinsky (1986: 153).

considered, across the whole spectrum the pattern is one of both losses and gains, with overall relatively small change in employment.[82]

Looking at studies of specific countries during the 1980s, the findings are somewhat contradictory although, overall, the same pattern of indetermination seems to emerge. In Japan, a 1985 study of the Japan Institute of Labour, concerning the employment and work effects of new electronic technologies in industries as diverse as automobiles, newspaper, electrical machinery, and software, concluded that "in any of the cases, the introduction of new technologies neither aimed at reducing the size of the work force in practice nor reduced it subsequently."[83]

In Germany, a major research effort, the so-called Meta Study, was commissioned by the Minister of Research and Technology during the 1980s to conduct both econometric and case-study research on the impacts of technological change on employment. Although the diversity of studies included in the research program does not allow a firm conclusion, the synthesis by its authors concluded that it is "the context" that counts for the variation in observed effects. In any case, technological innovation was understood to be an accelerating factor of existing trends in the labor market, rather than its cause. The study forecast that in the short term unskilled jobs would be displaced, although enhanced productivity would probably result in greater job creation in the long term.[84]

In the United States, Flynn analyzed 200 case studies of the employment impacts of process innovations between 1940 and 1982.[85] He concluded that, while process innovations in manufacturing eliminated high-skill jobs and helped to create low-skill jobs, the opposite was true for information processing in offices, where technological innovation suppressed low-skill jobs and created high-skill ones. Thus, according to Flynn, the effects of process innovation were variable, depending upon specific situations of industries and firms. At the industry level, again in the US, the analysis by Levy and co-workers of five industries showed different effects of technological innovation: in iron mining, coal mining, and aluminium, technological change increased output and resulted in higher employment levels; in steel and automobiles, on the other hand, growth of demand did not match reduction of labor per unit of output and job losses resulted.[86] Also in

82   Bessant (1989: 27, 28, 30).
83   Japan Institute of Labour (1985: 27).
84   Schettkat and Wagner (1990).
85   Flynn (1985).
86   Levy et al. (1984).

the United States, the analysis by Miller in the 1980s of the available evidence on the impact of industrial robotics concluded that most of the displaced workers would be reabsorbed into the labor force.[87]

In the UK, the study by Daniel on the employment impacts of technology in factories and offices concluded that there would be a negligible effect. Another study by the London Policy Studies Institute on a sample of 1,200 firms in France, Germany, and the UK estimated that, on average, for the three countries considered, the impact of microelectronics amounted to a job loss equivalent to, respectively, 0.5, 0.6, and 0.8 percent of annual decrease of employment in manufacturing.[88]

In the synthesis of studies directed by Watanabe on the impacts of robotization in the automobile industry in Japan, the United States, France, and Italy, the total job loss was estimated at between 2 and 3.5 percent, but with the additional caveat of the differential effects I mentioned above, namely the increase in employment in Japanese factories because of their use of micro-electronics to retrain workers and enhance competitiveness.[89] In the case of Brazil, Silva found no effect of technology on employment in the automobile industry, although employment varied considerably depending on the levels of output.[90]

In the study I directed on the impacts of new technologies on the Spanish economy in the early 1980s we found no statistical relationship between employment variation and technological level in the manufacturing and service sectors. Furthermore, a study within the same research program conducted by Cecilia Castano on the automobile and banking industry in Spain found a trend toward a positive association between the introduction of information technology and employment. An econometric study by Saez on the evolution of employment in Spain, by sector in the 1980s, also found a positive statistical relationship between technological modernization and employment gains, due to increased productivity and competitiveness.[91]

Studies commissioned by the International Labour Office on the UK, on the OECD as a whole, and on South Korea seem also to point to the lack of systematic links between information technology and employment.[92] The other variables in the equation (such as the countries' industrial mix, institutional contexts, place in the international division of labor, competitiveness, management policies, and so on) overwhelm, by and large, the specific impact of technology.

---

87 Office of Technology Assessment (1984, 1986); Miller (1989: 80).
88 Northcott (1986); Daniel (1987).
89 Watanabe (1987).
90 Cited in Watanabe (1987).
91 Castells et al. (1986); Saez et al. (1991); Castano (1994b).
92 Pyo (1986); Swann (1986); Ebel and Ulrich (1987).

Yet the argument has often been advanced that observed trends during the 1980s did not fully represent the extent of the employment impact of information technologies because their diffusion into the whole economy and society was still to come.[93] This forces us to venture on to the shaky ground of projections dealing with two uncertain variables (new information technologies and employment) and their even more uncertain relationship. Nevertheless, there have been a number of fairly sophisticated simulation models that have shed some light on the issues under discussion. One of them is the model built by Blazejczak, Eber, and Horn to evaluate the macro-economics impacts of investment in R&D in the West German economy between 1987 and 2000. They built three scenarios. Only under the most favorable circumstances does technological change increase employment by enhancing competitiveness. Indeed, they conclude that employment losses are imminent unless compensatory demand effects occur, and this demand cannot be generated only by better performance in international trade. Yet according to the projections in their model, "at the aggregate level demand effects do in fact compensate a relevant part of the predicted employment decrease."[94] Thus, it is likely that technological innovation will negatively affect employment in Germany, but at a rather moderate level. Here again, other elements such as macro-economic policies, competitiveness, and industrial relations seem to be much more important as factors determining the evolution of employment.

In the United States, the most widely cited simulation study was that performed in 1984 by Leontieff and Duchin to evaluate the impact of computers on employment for the period 1963–2000 using a dynamic input–output matrix of the US economy.[95] Focusing on their intermediate scenario, they found that 20 million fewer workers would

93   See, for instance, the apocalyptic prophecies of Adam Schaff (1992). It is surprising, to say the least, to see the credit given in the media to books such as Rifkin (1995), announcing "the end of work," published in a country, the United States, where between 1993 and 1996 over 8 million new jobs were created. A different matter is the quality of and pay for these jobs (although their skills profile was higher than that of overall employment structure). Work and employment are indeed being transformed, as this book tries to argue. But the number of paid jobs in the world, notwithstanding the Western European malaise, linked to institutional factors, is at its highest peak in history and going up. And rates of participation in the labor force by the adult population are increasing everywhere because of the unprecedented incorporation of women into the labor market. To ignore these elementary data is to ignore our society.

94   One of the most systematic efforts at forecasting the economic and employment effects of new technologies was the "Meta Study" conducted in Germany in the late 1980s. The main findings are presented in Matzner and Wagner (1990). See especially the chapter "Sectoral and Macroeconomic Impacts of Research and Development on Employment" in Blazejczak et al. (1990: 231).

95   Leontieff and Duchin (1985).

be required in relation to the number of workers that would have to be employed to achieve the same output while keeping the level of technology constant. This figure, according to their calculations, represented a drop of 11.7 percent in required labor. However, the impact is strongly differentiated among industries and occupations. Services, and particularly office activities, were predicted to suffer greater job losses than manufacturing as a result of massive diffusion of office automation. Clerical workers and managers would see their prospects of employment significantly reduced while those for professionals would increase substantially, and craftsmen and operatives would maintain their relative position in the labor force. The methodology of the Leontieff–Duchin study has, however, been strongly criticized because it relies on a number of assumptions which, on the basis of limited case studies, maximize the potential impact of computer automation while limiting technological change to computers. Indeed, from the vantage point of 2000, we can now assert the failure of Leontieff and Duchin's predictions. But this is not only an empirical observation. The failure was inscribed in the analytical model. As argued by Lawrence, the fundamental flaw in this, and other models, is that they assumed a fixed level of final demand and output.[96] This is precisely what past experience of technological innovation seems to reject as the most likely hypothesis.[97] If the economy does not grow, it is obvious that labor-saving technologies will reduce the amount of working time required. But in the past, rapid technological change has generally been associated with an expansionary trend that, by increasing demand and output, has generated the need for more working time in absolute terms, even if it represents less working time per unit of output. However, the key point in the new historical period is that in an internationally integrated economic system, expansion of demand and output will depend on the competitiveness of each economic unit and on their location in a given institutional setting (also called a nation). Since quality and production costs, the determinants of competitiveness, will largely depend on product and process innovation, it is likely that faster technological change for a given firm, industry, or national economy will result in a higher, not a lower, employment level. This is in line with the findings of Young and Lawson's study on the effect of technology on employment and output in US between 1972 and 1984.[98] In 44 of the 79 industries they examined, the labor-saving effects of new technologies were more than compensated for by

---

96   Lawrence (1984); Cyert and Mowery (1987).
97   Lawrence (1984); Landau and Rosenberg (1986); OECD (1994b).
98   Young and Lawson (1984).

higher final demand, so that, overall, employment expanded. At the level of national economies, studies on the newly industrialized countries of the Asian Pacific have also shown a dramatic increase in employment, particularly in manufacturing, following the technological upgrading of industries that enhanced their international competitiveness.[99]

In a more analytical vein, reflecting on the empirical findings in different European countries, the intellectual leader of the "regulation school," Robert Boyer, summarized his argument on the matter in several key points:[100]

1   All other variables being constant, technological change (measured by R&D density) improves productivity and obviously reduces the level of employment for any given demand.

2   However, productivity gains can be used to reduce relative prices, thus stimulating demand for a given product. If price elasticities are greater than one, a decline in price parallel to a rise in production will in fact enhance employment.

3   If prices are constant, productivity increases could be converted into real wage or profit increases. Consumption and/or investment will then be higher with stepped-up technological change. If price elasticities are high, employment losses will be compensated by extra demand from both old and new sectors.

4   Yet the critical matter is the right mix between process innovation and product innovation. If process innovation progresses faster, a decline in employment will occur, all other factors being equal. If product innovation leads the pace, then newly induced demand could result in higher employment.

The problem with such elegant economic analyses is always in the assumptions: all other factors are never equal. Boyer himself acknowledges this fact, and then examines the empirical fit of his model, observing, again, a wide range of variation between different industries and countries. While Boyer and Mistral found a negative relationship between productivity and employment for the OECD as a whole in the period 1980–86, a comparative analysis by Boyer on OECD countries identified three different patterns of employment in areas with similar levels of R&D density.[101]

99   Rodgers (1994).
100 Boyer (1990).
101 Boyer (1988b); Boyer and Mistral (1988).

1 In Japan an efficient model of mass production and consumption was able to sustain productivity growth and employment growth, on the basis of enhanced competitiveness.

2 In the United States, there was an impressive rate of job creation, but by concentrating on generating large numbers of low-wage, low-productivity jobs in traditional service activities.

3 In Western Europe, most economies entered a vicious circle: to cope with increased international competition, firms introduced labor-saving technologies, thus increasing output but leveling off the capacity to generate jobs, particularly in manufacturing. Technological innovation does *not* increase employment. Given the European characteristics of what Boyer calls "the mode of regulation" (for example, government economic policies and business strategies on labor and technology), innovation is likely to destroy employment in the European context. Yet innovation is increasingly required by competition.

In fact, the US experience of the 1980s is not representative of what happened in the 1990s, as I mentioned above. Nor was the Japanese experience. So, the necessary correction to Boyer and Mistral's dated study is that in the 1990s, while the largest European economies continued to lag in job creation until 1997, Japan kept a moderate growth of employment, and the US performed at an even higher level, increasing the number of jobs substantially while upgrading their quality – albeit at the price of stagnation of real average wages until 1996. In the late 1990s, after reforming its labor institutions, most European countries were also substantially reducing unemployment. Even Spain, the worse performer in job creation, reduced its unemployment rate from 22 percent in 1996 to 15.3 percent by the end of 1999, at the price of curtailing employment stability for most workers.

The employment study conducted by the OECD secretariat in 1994, after examining historical and current evidence on the relationship between technology and employment, concluded that:

> Detailed information, mainly from the manufacturing sector, provides evidence that technology is creating jobs. Since 1970 employment in high technology manufacturing has expanded, in sharp contrast to stagnation of medium and low technology sectors and job losses in low-skill manufacturing – at around 1% per year. Countries that have adapted best to new technologies and have shifted production and exports to rapidly growing high tech markets have tended to create more jobs. . . Japan realized a 4% increase in manufacturing employment in the 1970s and 1980s compared with a 1.5% increase in the US. Over the same period the European Community, where exports were increasingly spe-

cialized in relatively low-wage, low-tech industries, experienced a 20% drop in manufacturing employment.[102]

In sum, it seems, as a general trend, *that there is no systematic structural relationship between the diffusion of information technologies and the evolution of employment levels in the economy as a whole.* Jobs are being displaced and new jobs are being created, but the quantitative relationship between the losses and the gains varies among firms, industries, sectors, regions, and countries, depending upon competitiveness, firms' strategies, government policies, institutional environments, and relative position in the global economy. The specific outcome of the interaction between information technology and employment is largely dependent upon macro-economic factors, economic strategies, and sociopolitical contexts.[103]

The evolution of the level of employment is not a given, which would result from the combination of stable demographic data and a projected rate of diffusion of information technology. It will largely depend on socially determined decisions on the uses of technology, on immigration policy, on the evolution of the family, on the institutional distribution of working time in the life-cycle, and on the new system of industrial relations.

Thus, information technology *per se* does not cause unemployment, even if it obviously reduces working time per unit of output. But, under the informational paradigm, the kind of jobs change, in quantity, in quality, in the nature of the work being performed, and in the gender of who works where and how. Thus, a new production system requires a new labor force; those individuals and groups unable to acquire informational skills could be excluded from work or downgraded as workers. Also, because the informational economy is a global economy, widespread unemployment concentrated in some segments of the population (for example, French youth) and in some regions (such as Asturias) could indeed become a threat in the OECD area if global competition is unrestricted, and if the "mode of regulation" of capital–labor relations is not transformed.

The hardening of capitalist logic since the 1980s has fostered social polarization in spite of occupational upgrading. This tendency is not irreversible: it can be rectified by deliberate policies aimed at rebalancing the social structure. But left to themselves, the forces of unfettered competition in the informational paradigm will push employment and social structure toward dualization. Finally, the flexibility of labor

102 OECD (1994b: 32).
103 Carnoy (2000).

processes and labor markets induced by the network enterprise, and allowed by information technologies, profoundly affects the social relationships of production inherited from industrialism, introducing a new model of flexible work, and a new type of worker: the flex-timer.

Work and the Informational Divide: Flex-timers

Linda's new working life is not without its drawbacks. Chief among them is a constant cloud of anxiety about finding the next job. In some ways Linda feels isolated and vulnerable. Fearful of the stigma of having been laid off, for example, she doesn't want her last name to appear in this article.

But the freedom of being her own boss makes up for the insecurity. Linda gets to build her schedule around her son's. She gets to pick her own assignments. And she gets to be a pioneer of the new work force.

(*Newsweek*, June 14, 1993: 17)

I began to think that when I get older, if anyone asked what I have done with my life, all I could tell them about was work. I just decided that would have been a big waste, so I broke free.

(Yoshiko Kitani, a 30-year-old business graduate, after quitting her secure job at a Japanese publishing company in Yokohama in 1998, hiring herself out through temporary agencies)

In a job like this [a temp job] it takes a certain time to learn the programs and to get a feel for what you are doing. But by the time you feel you know what you are doing, because the rules are the way they are, your time is up.

(Yoshiko Kitani, 10 months later)[104]

A new specter haunts Europe (not America, and not so much Japan): the emergence of a jobless society under the impact of information technologies in factories, offices, and services. Yet, as is usually the case with specters in the electronic age, in close-up it appears to be more a matter of special effects than a terrifying reality. The lessons of history, current empirical evidence, employment projections in OECD countries, and economic theory do not support these fears in the long term, notwithstanding painful adjustments in the process of transition to the informational paradigm. Institutions and social organizations of work seem to play a greater role than technology in inducing job creation or destruction. However, if technology *per se* does not create

---

104   Reported by French (1999).

or destroy employment, it does profoundly transform the nature of work and the organization of production. The restructuring of firms and organizations, allowed by information technology and stimulated by global competition, is ushering in a fundamental transformation of work: *the individualization of labor in the labor process*. We are witnessing the reversal of the historical trend of salarization of work and socialization of production that was the dominant feature of the industrial era. The new social and economic organization based on information technologies aims at decentralizing management, individualizing work, and customizing markets, thereby segmenting work and fragmenting societies. New information technologies allow at the same time for the decentralization of work tasks and for their coordination in an interactive network of communication in real time, be it between continents or between floors of the same building. The emergence of lean production methods goes hand in hand with widespread business practices of subcontracting, outsourcing, offshoring, consulting, downsizing, and customizing.

Competition-induced, technology-driven trends toward flexibility underlie the current transformation of working arrangements. In his thorough examination of the emergence of flexible patterns of work, Martin Carnoy differentiates four elements in this transformation.

1 *Working time*: flexible work means work which is not constrained by the traditional pattern of 35–40 hours work per week in a full-time job.
2 *Job stability*: flexible work is task-oriented, and does not include a commitment to future employment.
3 *Location*: while the majority of workers still work regularly at the workplace of their company, an increasing proportion of workers work outside their workplace for part or all of their working time, whether at home, on the move, or in the location of a different company for whom the worker's company subcontracts.
4 *The social contract between employeer and employee*: the traditional contract is/was based on commitment by the employer to workers' well-defined rights, standardized level of compensation, options for training, social benefits, and a predictable career pattern (in some countries based on seniority), while, on the employee's side, it is/was expected that the employee would be loyal to the company, persevere in the job, and have a good disposition to work overtime if necessary – without compensation in the case of managers, with extra pay in the case of production workers.[105]

105 Carnoy (2000).

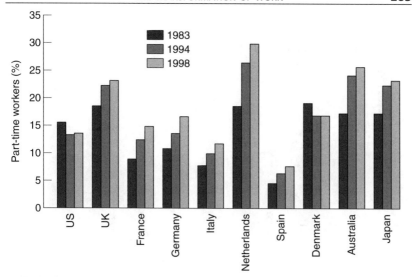

Figure 4.4 Part-time workers in employed labor force in OECD countries, 1983–1998
Source: Data from OECD, compiled and elaborated by Carnoy (2000)

This pattern of employment, that, together with Carnoy, I will call *standard*, is declining around the world, in favor of flexible work, which develops simultaneously along the four dimensions mentioned above. Let us first examine the trends for OECD countries for the 1980s and 1990s, on the basis of OECD data elaborated by Carnoy and displayed in figures 4.4–4.7. Between 1983 and 1998, part-time workers (the large majority of them, women) increased their numbers and their share significantly in all the countries analyzed except in the United States and in Denmark. They represented over 20 percent of the workforce in the UK, Australia, and Japan, and they reached over 30 percent in The Netherlands. The proportion of temporary workers increased in all countries analyzed, with the exception of The Netherlands. In the United States, temporary work was growing but remained at a very low level in 1994, an observation that I will examine in some detail. In Spain there was a substantial growth of temporary employment during the 1990s, to reach about one-third of the workforce in 1994.

Turning to self-employment, the data show a tendency to increase in the proportion of the labor force leaving salaried status in most countries between 1983 and 1993. Different data sources seem to indicate an accentuation of this trend in the late 1990s.[106] The trend was

106   Carnoy (2000); Gallie and Paugham (2000).

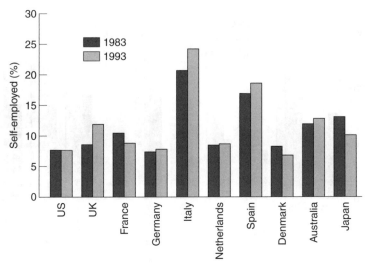

Figure 4.5   Self-employed workers in employed labor force in OECD countries, 1983–1993
Source: Data from OECD, compiled and elaborated by Carnoy (2000)

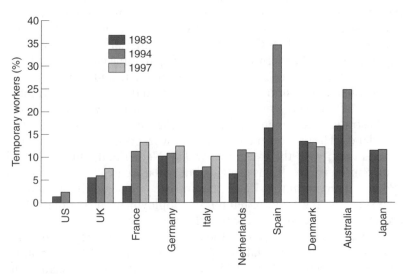

Figure 4.6   Temporary workers in employed labor force in OECD countries, 1983–1997
Source: Data from OECD, compiled and elaborated by Carnoy (2000)

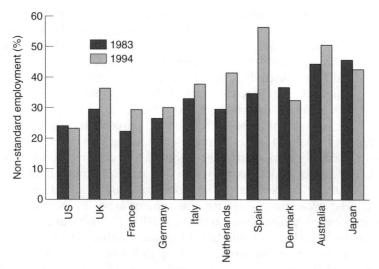

Figure 4.7 Non-standard forms of employment in employed labor force in OECD countries, 1983–1994
Source: Data from OECD, compiled and elaborated by Carnoy (2000)

particularly intense in Italy (reaching almost one-quarter of the labor force), and in the UK, while it was stable, at a low level, in the United States – a counter-intuitive finding, taking into consideration the image of American small business entrepreneurialism.

It appears that economies in various countries try different forms of flexibility in working arrangements, depending on their labor legislation, social security, and tax systems. Thus, it seems analytically useful to proceed, as Martin Carnoy did, combining different forms of non-standard employment in a single measure, while acknowledging partial overlapping of categories which, in any case, does not invalidate comparison between countries. The results, displayed in figure 4.7 show a significant increase in non-standard employment with the exception of Denmark and the United States. With Spain standing out as the least standardized country in employment patterns in the OECD, all countries under consideration, except the United States, have over 30 percent of their labor force employed in flexible working arrangements.

The US exception seems to indicate that when there is labor flexibility in the institutions of the country, non-standard forms of employment are not deemed necessary. This would be reflected in a lower average tenure in the job in the US than in other countries. Indeed, this is what in general terms, we observe: in 1995 the average number of years in the job in the United States was 7.4, in contrast to 8.3 for the UK, 10.4 for France, 10.8 for Germany, 11.6 for Italy, 11.3 for Japan, 9.6 for The Netherlands, and 9.1 for Spain (but still higher than Canada, 7.9, and Australia, 6.4)[107] Furthermore, in spite of the institutionally embedded labor flexibility, non-standard forms of employment are also significant in the United States. In 1990 self-employment accounted for 10.8 percent of the workforce, part-time for 16.9 percent, and "contract" or temporary work for about 2 percent, adding up to 29.7 percent of the labor force, although, again, categories overlap to some extent. According to a different estimate, the contingent workforce with no benefits, no job security, and no career amounted in the US in 1992 to about 25 percent of the labor force, up from 20 percent in 1982. The projections were for this type of labor to increase to 35 percent of the US labor force in the year 2000.[108] Mishel and co-workers, on the basis of data from the US Bureau of Labor Statistics, showed that employment in the temporary help industry in the US increased from 417,000 workers in 1982 to 2,646,000 in 1997 (see figure 4.8).[109] Furthermore, the Bureau of Labor Statistics estimated that between 1996 and 2006 temporary employment in the United States would grow by 50 percent. Outsourcing, facilitated by on-line transactions, concerns not just manufacturing but increasingly services. In a 1994 survey of 392 of America's fastest growing firms, 68 percent of them were subcontracting payroll services, 48 percent tax compliance services, 46 percent claim benefits administration, and the like.[110]

While the size of the US economy makes patterns of change difficult to observe until they reach a critical mass, the picture we obtain is very different when we look at California, the economic and technological powerhouse of America. In 1999, the Institute of Health Policy Studies of the University of California at San Francisco, in cooperation with the Field Institute, conducted a study on work arrangements and living conditions on a representative sample of California workers, the second survey of a three-year longitudinal study.[111] They defined "traditional jobs" as holding a single, full-time, day-shift job year round, as a permanent employee, paid by the firm for which the job is done, and not working from home or as an independent contractor – a definition very close to the one employed by Carnoy and myself. Under such a definition, 67 percent of California workers *did not* hold a traditional job. Adding the criterion of tenure, and calculating the proportion of

107   OECD, *Employment Outlook* (various years), compiled by Carnoy (2000).
108   Jost (1993).
109   Mishel et al. (1999).
110   Marshall (1994).
111   UCSF/Field Institute (1999).

Figure 4.8 Employment in the temporary help industry in the United States, 1982–1997
Source: Data from the US Bureau of Labor Statistics, elaborated by Mishel et al. (1999)

workers with traditional jobs with three or more years of tenure, the proportion of workers in these standard jobs shrinks to 22 percent (see figures 4.9 and 4.10). Incidentally, a measure of the disappearance of the traditional male-worker dominated household is that when we add to this percentage the criterion of only one wage earner in the house-hold, the proportion dwindles to 8 percent (7 percent male-headed, 1 percent female-headed). I must add, however, one correction. Since the notion of day-shift does not enter in my definition of non-traditional work, I obtained a recalculation of these data from the research team, deducting night-shift workers. Under the new calculations, with my restrictive definition, 57 percent, rather than 67 percent, is the propor-tion of workers in non-standard forms of employment. On the basis of the same survey we learn that only 49 percent of workers worked the traditional 35–40 hours a week, with about one-third of them working more than 45 hours, and 18 percent less than 35 hours. The median length of time with their current employer was four years, with 40 percent of the workers having less than two years in their current work; 25 percent of workers did not work year-round, while those who both worked year-round and worked a regular week of 35–40 hours were only 35 percent. The higher the professional level, the longer the work-ing time: while 29 percent of all workers worked over 40 hours a week, among those at the top of the salary scale ($60,000+), the proportion climbed to 58 percent. By and large, this is not a disgruntled lot: 59 percent of all workers reported increasing their earnings, and 39 per-cent either were promoted or moved to a better job.

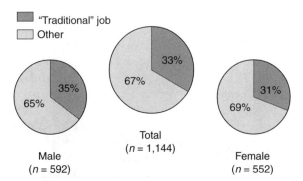

Figure 4.9 Percentage of working-age Californians employed in "traditional" jobs, 1999 ("traditional" is defined as holding a single, full-time, day-shift job year round, as a permanent employee, paid by the firm for which the work is done and not working from home or as an independent contractor)
Source: University of California, San Francisco and The Field Institute, 1999

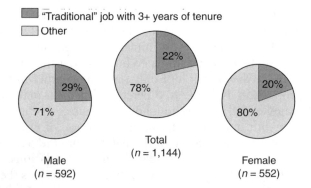

Figure 4.10 Distribution of working-age Californians by "traditional" job status and length of tenure in the job, 1999 ("traditional" job is as defined in figure 4.9)
Source: University of California, San Francisco and The Field Institute, 1999

The California model of flexible employment is even more distinct in Silicon Valley, the center of the new economy. Chris Benner has shown the emergence of a multiplicity of forms of flexible employment in the 1990s.[112] According to his estimates, between 1984 and 1997 in Santa Clara County (which is the heart of the so-called Silicon Valley), employment of temporary workers increased by 159 percent,

112 Benner (2000).

of part-time workers by 21 percent, of business services (a proxy for contracted services) by 152 percent, and self-employment by 53 percent. Thus he estimates that up to 80 percent of the net new jobs in the country during this period were in non-standard employment. He also estimates that the size of what he calls the "contingent labor force" as a proportion of the total labor force of Silicon Valley in 1997 could be evaluated at between 34 and 51 percent of the total labor force (depending upon the extent of double counting because of overlapping categories). Benner discovered the critical role of labor-market intermediaries in providing the flexible labor force for Silicon Valley. Not only traditional agencies, but all kinds of organizations, and institutions, including workers' guilds and the labor unions themselves (in the old tradition of the longshoremen union's hiring halls, translated into the information economy).[113]

The booming new economy in the United States was in fact facing a labor shortage at the turn of the century. To deal with it, companies, particularly in the high-technology and information sectors, were resorting to non-traditional incentives to retain their workers, including the distribution of stock options among their professional employees, a preferred form of compensation in the Internet start-up firms. Companies in all industries were also using an immigrant labor force on a large scale, both in highly skilled occupations and in unskilled jobs. And temporary employment, hired through labor intermediaries, was soaring in the United States as a whole. Just-in-time labor seems to be substituting for just-in-time supplies as the key resource of the informational economy.[114]

In the European context, an interesting close-up to detect emerging new patterns of work is the so-called Dutch model that provided a stellar performance in job creation and economic growth, without losing social protection, in the 1990s. Faced with rampant unemployment in the 1980s, the Dutch government, business, and labor reached a series of agreements to restructure the labor market. Under these agreements, labor unions consented to moderate wage increases in return for preserving core jobs in the industry. But in addition to this agreement (which is common in labor–business negotiations in all countries), the Dutch unions also agreed to the expansion, on the periphery of the labor force, of new, flexible forms of employment, mainly part-time work, and temporary contracts. The government also created programs to stimulate small business initiatives. The key element in this model, however is, that, unlike in the United States, part-timers

113 Benner et al. (1999).
114 *Business Week* (1999c).

and temporary workers are still fully protected under national health, disability, unemployment, and pension plans. And women, the main recipients of new, part-time jobs, can count on subsidized day care for their children. As a result of this strategy, the unemployment rate in The Netherlands, at a time of intense technological innovation, went down from an average 9 percent in the 1980s to 3 percent by the end of 1999. In macro-economic terms, The Netherlands enjoyed in the 1990s increased private investment, economic growth, employment growth, and moderate, but positive, wage growth. This model of negotiated flexibilization of labor markets and working conditions, together with a definition of institutional and fiscal responsibility in the social welfare systems, seems also to underlie the positive experience of balanced economic growth, with low unemployment, of Sweden, Denmark, and Norway.[115]

The mobility of labor concerns both unskilled and skilled workers. While a core labor force is still the norm in most firms, subcontracting and consulting is a fast-growing form of obtaining professional work. Not only the firm benefits from flexibility. Many professionals add to their main job (full- or part-time) consulting venues which help both their income and their bargaining power. The logic of this highly dynamic work system interacts with the labor institutions of each country: the greater the constraints to such flexibility, and the greater the bargaining power of the labor unions, the lesser will be the impact on wages and benefits, and the greater will be the difficulty for newcomers to enter the core labor force, thus limiting job creation.

While the social costs of flexibility can be high, a growing stream of research emphasizes the transformative value of new work arrangements for social life, and particularly for improved family relationships, and greater egalitarian patterns between genders.[116] A British researcher, P. Hewitt,[117] reports on the growing diversity of working formulae and schedules, and the potential offered by work-sharing between those currently employed full-time and those barely employed *within the same household*. Overall, *the traditional form of work, based on full-time employment, clear-cut occupational assignments, and a career pattern over the life-cycle is being slowly but surely eroded away.*

Japan is different, although not as much as observers usually think. Any analytical framework aimed at explaining new historical trends in the organization of work, and their impact on employment structure, must be able to account for "Japanese exceptionalism:" it is too

---

115   Carnoy (2000).
116   Bielenski (1994); for social problems associated with part-time work, see Warme et al. (1992); Carnoy (2000).
117   Hewitt (1993). This interesting study is pointedly cited by Freeman and Soete (1994).

important an exception to be left aside as an oddity for comparative theory. Therefore, let us consider the matter in some detail. At the end of 1999, in spite of a prolonged recession that halted Japanese growth for most of the 1990s, the Japanese unemployment rate, while reaching a record high level for the past two decades, was still below 5 percent. Indeed, the main concern of Japanese labor planners is the potential shortage of Japanese workers in the future, given the aging of the demographic structure and Japanese reluctance about foreign immigration.[118] Furthermore, the *chuki koyo* system, which provides assurance of long-term employment for the core labor force of large companies, while coming under increasing pressure, as I will show below, was still in place. Thus, it would seem that Japanese exceptionalism belies the general trend toward flexibility of the labor market and the individualization of work that characterizes the other informational, capitalist societies.[119] In fact, I would argue that while Japan has indeed created a highly original system of industrial relations and employment procedures, flexibility has been a structural trend of such a system for the past two decades, and it is increasing along with the transformation of the technological basis and occupational structure.[120]

The Japanese employment structure is characterized by extraordinary internal diversity, as well as by a complex pattern of fluid situations that resist generalization and standardization. The very definition of the *chuki koyo* system needs precision.[121] For most workers under this system it means simply that they can work until retirement in the same company, under normal circumstances, as a matter of custom, not of right. This employment practice is in fact limited to large companies (those with over 1,000 employees), and in most cases concerns only the male, core labor force. In addition to their regular workers, companies also employ at least three different kinds of workers: part-time workers, temporary workers, and workers sent to the company by another company, or by a recruiting agent ("dispatched workers"). None of these categories has job security, retirement benefits, or is entitled to receive the customary annual bonuses to reward productivity and commitment to the company. In addition, very often workers, particularly older men, are reallocated to other jobs in other companies within the same corporate group (*shukko*). This includes the practice of separating married men from their families (*tanshin-funin*) because of difficulties in finding housing and, most of all, because of

118   NIKKEIREN (1993).
119   Kumazawa and Yamada (1989).
120   Kuwahara (1989).
121   Inoki and Higuchi (1995).

the family's reluctance to relocate children to a different school in the middle of their education. *Tanshin-funin* is said to affect about 30 percent of managerial employees.[122] Nomura estimates that long-term job security in the same company applies only to about one-third of Japanese employees, including public sector employees.[123] Joussaud provides a similar estimate.[124] In addition, the incidence of job tenure varies widely, even for men, depending on age, level of qualification, and size of company. Table 4.28 (in Appendix A) provides an illustration of the profile of *chuki koyo* in 1991–2.

   The critical point in this labor market structure concerns the definition of part-time. According to the government's labor status definitions, "part-time" workers are those considered as such by the company.[125] In fact, they work almost full-time (6 hours a day, compared to 7.5 hours for regular workers), although the number of working days in a month is slightly less than for regular workers. Yet they receive, on average, about 60 percent of a regular worker's salary, and about 15 percent of the annual bonus. More importantly, they have no job security, so they are hired and fired according to the company's convenience. Part-timers and temporary workers provide the required labor flexibility. Their role has substantially increased since the 1970s, when the oil shock induced major economic restructuring in Japan. In the 1975–90 period, the number of part-time workers increased by 42.6 percent for male workers and by 253 percent for female workers. Indeed, women account for two-thirds of part-timers. Women are the skilled, adaptable workers who provide flexibility to Japanese labor management practices. This is in fact an old practice in Japanese industrialization. In 1872, the Meiji government recruited women to work in the nascent textile industry. A pioneer was Wada Ei, daughter of a samurai from Matsuhiro, who went to work in the Tomioka silk-reeling mill, learned the technology, and helped to train women in other mills. In 1899, women accounted for 70 percent of workers in spinning mills, and outnumbered male workers in the iron mills. However, at times of crisis women would be fired, while men would be kept as long as possible, emphasizing their role as the last-resort breadwinners of the family. In the past three decades, this historical pattern of gender-based division of labor has hardly changed, although a 1986 equal opportunity law corrected some of the most blatant legal discriminations. Women's participation in the labor force in 1990 featured a rate of 61.8 percent (compared to 90.2 percent for men),

122   Collective Author (1994).
123   Nomura (1994).
124   Joussaud (1994).
125   Collective Author (1994); Shinotsuka (1994).

lower than in the US, but similar to that of Western Europe. Yet their working status varies widely with age and marriage. Thus, 70 percent of the women who are hired in conditions roughly comparable with men (*sogoshoku*) are under 29 years of age, while 85 percent of part-timers are married. Women massively enter the labor force in their early twenties, stop working after marriage to raise their children, and return later to the labor force as part-timers. This structure of the occupational life-cycle is reinforced by the Japanese tax code, which makes it more advantageous for women to contribute in a relatively small proportion to the family income than to add a second salary. The stability of the Japanese patriarchal family, with a low rate of divorce and separation and strong intergenerational solidarity,[126] keeps men and women together in the same household, avoiding the polarization of social structure as the result of this obvious pattern of labor market dualism. Uneducated youth and elderly workers of small and medium companies are the other groups accounting for this segment of unstable employees, whose boundaries are difficult to establish because of the fluidity of labor status in Japanese networks of firms.[127] Figure 4.11 attempts to represent schematically the complexity of the Japanese labor market structure.

At the turn of the century, there were signs that the Japanese model of labor market was on its way to structural transformation. Shaken by recession, faced with renewed global competition, abroad and at home, and trying to catch up their technological lagging in network technologies, Japanese firms seemed to be ready to trim and select their labor. Young workers, particularly women, also seemed ready to adopt a new attitude towards companies whose loyalty did not seem any longer to be reliable. Companies were laying off workers, and replacing permanent jobs with temporary ones: millions of workers were part-time or temporary. The *chuki koyo* system was quickly becoming the status of just a fraction of the Japanese labor force. According to the Ministry of Labor, in 1997, 789,000 Japanese found their jobs through employment agencies. This concerned professionals as well as manual workers. Japan's leading job placement agency, Pasona, reported that since the beginning of the 1990s, the number of requests from companies to agencies of temporary labor increased from 100,000 to 1 million a year. Companies were putting pressure on the government to ease the rules that limited labor mobility for the core labor force. The government was slow to respond to these pressures, fearing threats to social stability. Thus, temporary agencies were forbidden to

126 Gelb and Lief Palley (1994).
127 Takenori and Higuchi (1995).

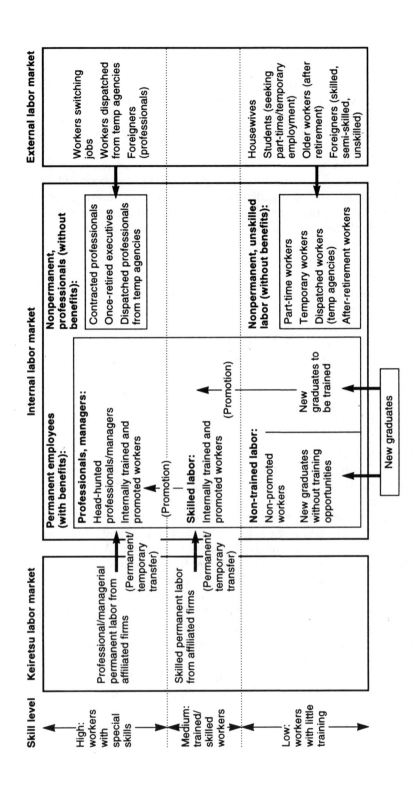

Figure 4.11 The Japanese labor market in the postwar period

Source: Elaborated by Yuko Aoyama, based on information from Japan's Economic Planning Agency, *Gaikokujin rodosha to shakai no shinro,* 1989, p. 99, figure 4.1

find a job for anyone within the first year of leaving the education system, and re-hiring in the same job was prohibited. On the other hand, in 1998, only one-third of the college graduates were able to find a full-time job in their first year in the labor market. The strategic planning institutions of government were increasingly aware of the need to move beyond the fiction of stable, tenured employment which was gradually becoming the exception rather than the rule. Thus in 1999, MITI issued a report advising companies, for the first time, to move toward non-tenured employment for most of their workers.[128]

Thus, it seems that Japan has been practicing for some time the dual labor market logic that is spreading in Western economies. By so doing, it has combined the benefits of the commitment of a core labor force with the flexibility of a peripheral labor market. The former has been essential because it has guaranteed social peace through cooperation between management and company unions; and because it has increased productivity by accumulating knowledge in the firm, and quickly assimilating new technologies. The latter has allowed for quick reaction to changes in labor demand, as well as to competitive pressures from offshored manufacturing in the 1980s. In the 1990s, figures for foreign immigration and day laborers started to rise, introducing additional choice and flexibility in the lower-skilled segments of the workforce. Altogether, Japanese firms seemed to be able to cope with competitive pressures by retraining their core labor force and adding technology, while multiplying their flexible labor, both in Japan and in their globalized production networks. However, since this labor practice relies essentially on the occupational subservience of highly educated Japanese women, which will not last for ever, I propose the hypothesis that it is just a matter of time until the hidden flexibility of the Japanese labor market diffuses to the core labor force, calling into question what has been the most stable and productive labor relations system of the late industrial era.[129]

Thus, overall, there is indeed a fundamental transformation of work, workers, and working organizations in our societies, but it cannot be apprehended in the traditional categories of obsolete debates over the "end of work" or the "deskilling of labor."[130] The prevailing model for labor in the new, information-based economy is that of a *core labor force*, formed by information-based managers and by those whom Reich calls "symbolic analysts," and a *disposable labor force* that can be automated and/or hired/fired/offshored, depending upon market

128 French (1999).
129 Kuwahara (1989); Whitaker (1990).
130 Rifkin (1995).

demand and labor costs. Furthermore, the networked form of business organization allows outsourcing and subcontracting as forms of externalizing labor in a flexible adaptation to market conditions. Analysts have rightly distinguished between various forms of flexibility in wages, geographical mobility, occupational status, contractual security, and task performance, among others.[131] Often all these forms are lumped together in a self-serving strategy to present as inevitable what is in fact a business or policy decision. Yet it is true that current technological trends foster all forms of flexibility, so that in the absence of specific agreements on stabilizing one or various dimensions of work, the system will evolve into multifaceted, generalized flexibility for workers and working conditions, both for highly skilled and unskilled workers. This transformation has shaken our institutions, inducing a crisis in the relationship between work and society.

Information Technology and the Restructuring of Capital–Labor Relations: Social Dualism or Fragmented Societies?

The diffusion of information technology in the economy does not directly induce unemployment. Instead, given the right institutional and organizational conditions, it seems to create more jobs in the long run. The transformation of management and work upgrades the occupational structure to a greater extent in that it increases the number of low-skill jobs. Increasing global trade and investment do not seem to be, by themselves, major causal factors in eliminating jobs and degrading work conditions in the North, while they contribute to creating millions of jobs in newly industrializing countries. And yet the process of historical transition toward an informational society and a global economy is characterized by the deterioration of living and working conditions for a significant proportion of labor.[132] This deterioration takes different forms in different contexts: the rise of unemployment in Europe; declining real wages (at least until 1996), increasing inequality, and job instability in the United States; underemployment and stepped-up segmentation of the labor force in Japan; informalization and downgrading of newly incorporated urban labor in industrializing countries; and increasing marginalization of the agricultural labor force in stagnant, underdeveloped economies. As argued above, these trends do not stem from the structural logic of the

---

131   Reich (1991); Freeman and Soete (1994).
132   Harrison (1994); ILO (1994).

informational paradigm, but are the result of the current restructuring of capital–labor relations, helped by the powerful tools provided by new information technologies, and facilitated by a new organizational form, the network enterprise. Furthermore, although the potential of information technologies could have provided for higher productivity, higher living standards, and higher employment simultaneously, once certain technological choices are in place, technological trajectories are "locked in,"[133] and the informational society could become at the same time (without the technological or historical necessity to be so) a dual society.

Alternative views prevailing in the OECD, IMF, and government circles in major Western countries have suggested that observed trends of rising unemployment, underemployment, income inequality, poverty, and social polarization are by and large the result of a skills mismatch, worsened by the lack of flexibility in the labor markets.[134] According to these views, while the occupational/employment structure is upgraded in terms of the educational content of the skills required for the informational jobs, the labor force is not up to the new tasks, either because of the low quality of the educational system or because of the inadequacy of this system to provide the new skills needed in the emerging occupational structure.[135]

In their report to the ILO's research institute, Carnoy and Fluitman have submitted this broadly accepted view to a devastating critique. After extensively reviewing the literature and evidence on the relationship between skills, employment, and wages in the OECD countries, they conclude that:

> Despite the apparent consensus around the supply-side, skill mismatch argument, the supporting evidence for it is extremely thin, especially in terms of improved education and more and better training solving either the problem of open unemployment (Europe) or the problem of wage distribution (US). It is much more convincing, we argue, that better education and more training could, in the longer run, contribute to higher productivity and economic growth rates.[136]

In the same sense, David Howell has shown for the US that while there has been an increasing demand for higher skills, this is not the cause of

133   Arthur (1989).
134   This is the view usually expressed by Alan Greenspan, chairman of the US Federal Reserve Board, and by the International Monetary Fund and other international expert circles. For an economic discourse articulating this thesis, see Krugman (1994a); and Krugman and Lawrence (1994).
135   Cappelli and Rogovsky (1994).
136   Carnoy and Fluitman (1994).

the substantial decline in average wages for American workers between 1973 and 1990 (a fall from a weekly wage of $327 to $265 in
1990, measured in 1982 dollars). Nor is the skill mix the source of
increasing income inequality. In his study with Wolff, Howell shows
that while the share of low-skilled workers in the US decreased across
industries, the share of low-wage workers increased in these same industries. Several studies also suggest that higher skills are in demand,
although not in shortage, but higher skills do not necessarily translate
into higher wages.[137] Thus, in the US, while decline in real wages was
more pronounced for the lowest-educated, salaries for the college-
educated also stagnated between 1987 and 1993.[138]

The direct consequence of economic restructuring in the United States
is that in the 1980s and the first half of the 1990s family income plum-
meted. Wages and living conditions continued to decline until 1996 in
spite of a strong economic recovery in 1993.[139] Furthermore, half a
century after Gunnar Myrdal pointed to the "American Dilemma,"
Martin Carnoy, in a powerful book, documented that racial discrimi-
nation continues to increase social inequality, contributing to mar-
ginalizing a large proportion of America's ethnic minorities.[140]
However, in 1996–2000, the sustained boom led by information technology and the new economy changed the trend, and increased average real wages at about 1.2 percent per year. And the rise in the
minimum wage in 1996 halted the long-term deterioration of their
income for the bottom 20 percent of Americans. The population below the poverty line decreased slightly, although over 20 percent of
American children were still living in poverty at the end of the century.
Income and assets inequality were at an all-time high. In 1995, the top
1 percent of American households earned 14.5 percent of total income, while the income share of the bottom 90 percent was 60.8 percent. The assets distribution was even more skewed: the top 1 percent
of households owned 38.5 percent of net worth, while the bottom 90
percent were left with 28.2 percent. Indeed, 18.5 percent of households had zero or negative net wealth. Much has been made of the
shareholders democracy in the new forms of capitalism, but table 4.29
shows the extreme concentration of stock ownership in 1995, even
when we include stock plans, mutual funds, individual retirement accounts, and other instruments of popular capitalism.

137   Howell and Wolff (1991); Mishel and Teixeira (1991); Howell (1994).
138   Center for Budget and Policy Priorities, Washington, DC, cited by *The New York
Times* (October 7, 1994: 9); see also Murphy and Welch (1993); Bernstein and Adler (1994).
139   Mishel and Bernstein (1994).
140   Carnoy (1994); for the persistence of racial inequality in the professional class in the
new economy companies, see Harper-Anderson (forthcoming).

While America is an extreme case of income inequality and declining real wages among the industrialized nations, its evolution is significant because it does represent the flexible labor market model at which most European nations, and certainly European firms, are aiming.[141] And the social consequences of such a trend are similar in Europe. Thus, in Greater London between 1979 and 1991 real disposable income of households in the lowest decile of income distribution declined by 14 percent, and the ratio of real income of the richest decile over the poorest almost doubled in the decade, from 5.6 to 10.2.[142] Poverty in the UK substantially increased during the 1980s and early 1990s.[143] And for other European countries, taking the incidence of child poverty as an indicator of the evolution of poverty, on the basis of data collected by Esping-Andersen, between 1980 and the mid-1990s child poverty increased by 30 percent in the US, by 145 percent in the UK, by 31 percent in France, and by 120 percent in Germany.[144] Inequality and poverty increased during the 1990s in the US, and in most of Europe.[145] I take the liberty of referring the reader to volume III, chapter 2, for a summary presentation of data and sources on inequality and poverty, both for the United States and for the world at large.

The new vulnerability of labor under conditions of unrestrained flexibility does not concern only the unskilled labor force. The core labor force, while better paid and more stable, is subjected to mobility by shortening the period of the working life in which professionals are recruited to the core of the enterprise. Martin Carnoy summarizes this trend:

> In the United States and in the OECD's other more flexible labor markets, downsizing is becoming a regular part of work life. Older workers are particularly vulnerable when firms "rationalize" their labor forces. Downsizing is largely a euphemism for reducing the number of "obsolete", higher-priced older employees, usually in their mid to late forties and early fifties, replacing them with younger, more recently educated, and lower-wage workers. Older workers, unlike their younger counterparts, suffer long periods of unemployment and sharp wage declines once re-employed ... Not only are the wages of young age cohorts decreasing, but the period of the average male worker's "prime" working life, defined by upward wage mobility, is becoming shorter. This is apparently true for college as well as high school graduates, which means

141 Sayer and Walker (1992).
142 Lee and Townsend (1993: 18–20).
143 Hutton (1995).
144 Esping-Anderson (1999).
145 Mishel et al. (1999); Bison and Esping-Anderson (2000).

that even well-educated (high skill) workers are now subject to this broader meaning of job insecurity: workers are not only subject to shorter job tenure but to flattening or even declining incomes as they hit middle age.[146]

The logic of this highly dynamic labor market model interacts with the specificity of labor institutions in each country. Thus, a study of German labor relationships shows that reduction of labor as a result of the introduction of computerized machinery in the 1980s was inversely related to the level of workers' protection provided by the unions in the industry. On the other hand, firms with high levels of protection were also those with the highest change in innovation. This study shows that there is not necessarily a conflict between upgrading the technological basis of the firm and keeping most of the workers, generally retraining them. These firms were also those with the highest level of unionization.[147] The study by Harley Shaiken on Japanese automobile companies in the United States, and on the Saturn automobile plant in Tennessee, reaches similar conclusions, showing the effectiveness of workers' input and unions' participation in the successful introduction of technological innovations, while limiting labor losses.[148]

This institutional variation is what explains the difference we have shown between the United States and the European Union. Social restructuring takes the form of pressuring wages and labor conditions in the US. In the European Union, where labor institutions defend better their historically conquered positions, the net result is increasing unemployment, because of limited entry to young workers and because of the early exit from the labor force for the oldest, or for those trapped in noncompetitive sectors and firms.[149] As for industrializing countries, they have been featuring for at least three decades a model of articulation between the formal and informal urban labor markets that is tantamount to the flexible forms diffused in the mature economies by the new technological/organizational paradigm.[150]

Why and how has this restructuring of the capital–labor relationship taken place at the dawn of the Information Age? It resulted from historical circumstances, technological opportunities, and economic imperatives. To reverse the profit squeeze without triggering inflation, national economies and private firms have acted on labor costs since

146   Carnoy (2000: 48).
147   Warnken and Ronning (1990).
148   Shaiken (1993, 1995).
149   Bosch (1995).
150   Portes et al. (1989); Gereffi (1993).

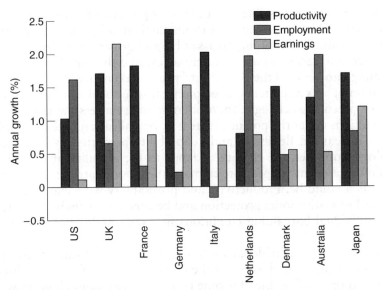

Figure 4.12 Annual growth of productivity, employment, and earnings in OECD countries, 1984–1998
Source: Data from OECD, compiled and elaborated by Carnoy (2000)

the early 1980s, either by increasing productivity without employment creation (main European economies) or by lowering the cost of a plethora of new jobs (US) (see figure 4.12). Labor unions, the main obstacle to one-sided restructuring strategy, were weakened by their inability to adapt to representing new kinds of workers (women, youth, immigrants), to acting in new workplaces (private sector offices, high-technology industries), and to functioning in the new forms of organization (the network enterprise on a global scale).[151] When necessary, politically induced offensive strategies helped the historical/structural trends working against the unions (for example, Reagan and the air traffic controllers, Thatcher and the coal miners). But even socialist governments in France and Spain went on changing the conditions of the labor market, thus weakening the unions, when the pressures of competition made it difficult to depart sharply from the new management rules of the global economy.

What made this historical redefinition of the relationship between

151   For assessments of the decline of traditional unionism under new economic/technological conditions, see Carnoy et al. (1993a); see also Gourevitch (1984); Adler and Suarez (1993).

capital and labor possible was the use of powerful information technologies and of organizational forms facilitated by the new technological medium. The ability to assemble and disperse labor on specific projects and tasks anywhere, anytime, created the possibility for the coming into being of the virtual enterprise as a functional entity. From then on, it was a matter of overcoming institutional resistance to the development of such logic, and/or of obtaining concessions from labor and unions under the potential threat of virtualization. The extraordinary increase in flexibility and adaptability permitted by new technologies opposed the rigidity of labor to the mobility of capital. It followed a relentless pressure to make the labor contribution as flexible as it could be. Productivity and profitability were enhanced, yet labor lost institutional protection and became increasingly dependent on individual bargaining conditions in a constantly changing labor market.

Society became divided, as it has been for most of human history, between winners and losers of the endless process of individualized, unequal bargaining. But this time there were few rules about how to win and how to lose. Skills were not enough, since the process of technological change accelerated its pace, constantly superseding the definition of appropriate skills. Membership of corporations, or even countries, ceased to have its privileges because stepped-up global competition kept redesigning the variable geometry of work and markets. Never was labor more central to the process of value-making. But never were the workers (regardless of their skills) more vulnerable to the organization, since they had become lean individuals, farmed out in a flexible network whose whereabouts were unknown to the network itself.

Thus, on the surface, societies were/are becoming dualized, with a substantial top and a substantial bottom growing at both ends of the occupational structure, so shrinking the middle, at a pace and in a proportion that depend upon each country's position in the international division of labor and on its political climate. But down in the deep of the nascent social structure, a more fundamental process has been triggered by informational work: the disaggregation of labor, ushering in the network society.

Appendix A:

Statistical Tables for Chapter 4

Table 4.1 United States: percentage distribution of employment by industrial sector and intermediate industry group, 1920–1991

Industry	(a) 1920–70						(b) 1970–91				
	1920	1930	1940	1950	1960	1970	1970	1980	1985	1990	1991
I Extractive	28.9	25.4	21.3	14.4	8.1	4.5	4.6	4.5	4.0	3.5	3.5
Agriculture	26.3	22.9	19.2	12.7	7.0	3.7	3.7	3.6	3.1	2.8	2.9
Mining	2.6	2.5	2.1	1.7	1.1	0.8	0.8	1.0	0.9	0.6	0.6
II Transformative	32.9	31.6	29.8	33.9	35.9	33.1	33.0	29.6	27.2	25.6	24.7
Constructive	<	6.5	4.7	6.2	6.2	5.8	6.0	6.2	6.5	6.5	6.1
Utilities	<	0.6	1.2	1.4	1.4	1.4	1.1	1.2	1.2	1.1	1.1
Manufacturing	<	24.5	23.9	26.2	28.3	25.9	25.9	22.2	19.5	18.0	17.5
Food	<	2.3	2.7	2.7	3.1	2.0	1.9	1.9	1.7	1.6	1.5
Textiles	<	4.2	2.0	2.2	3.3	3.0	1.3	0.8	0.7	0.6	0.6
Metal	<	7.7	2.9	3.6	3.9	3.3	3.1	2.7	2.0	1.8	1.7
Machinery	<	<	2.4	3.7	7.5	8.3	5.1	5.2	4.5	3.8	3.7
Chemical	<	1.3	1.5	1.7	1.8	1.6	1.5	1.6	1.3	1.3	1.3
Misc. mfg	<	9.0	11.8	12.3	8.7	7.7	12.9	10.0	9.4	8.9	8.6
III Distributive services	18.7	19.6	20.4	22.4	21.9	22.3	22.4	21.0	20.9	20.6	20.6
Transportation	7.6	6.0	4.9	5.3	4.4	3.9	3.9	3.7	3.5	3.5	3.6
Communication	<	1.0	0.9	1.2	1.3	1.5	1.5	1.5	1.5	1.3	1.4
Wholesale	11.1	12.6	2.7	3.5	3.6	4.1	4.0	3.9	4.1	3.9	4.0
Retail	<	<	11.8	12.3	12.5	12.8	12.9	11.9	11.9	11.8	11.7
IV Producer services	2.8	3.2	4.6	4.8	6.6	8.5	8.2	10.5	12.7	14.0	14.0
Banking	<	1.3	1.1	1.1	1.6	2.6	2.2	2.6	2.9	2.9	2.8
Insurance	<	1.1	1.2	1.4	1.7	1.8	1.8	1.9	1.9	2.1	2.1
Real estate	<	0.6	1.1	1.0	1.0	1.0	1.0	1.6	1.7	1.8	1.8

Engineering	<	–	1.3	0.2	0.3	0.4	0.4	0.6	0.7	0.7	0.7
Accounting	<	–	<	0.2	0.3	0.4	0.4	0.5	0.5	0.5	0.6
Misc. business serv.	<	0.1	<	0.6	1.2	1.8	1.8	2.6	4.0	4.9	5.0
Legal services	<	–	<	0.4	0.5	0.5	0.5	0.8	0.9	1.0	1.1
V Social services	8.7	9.2	10.0	12.4	16.3	21.9	22.0	23.7	23.6	24.9	25.5
Medical, health serv.	<	–	2.3	1.1	1.4	2.2	2.4	2.3	3.6	4.3	4.5
Hospital	<	–	<	1.8	2.7	3.7	3.7	5.3	4.0	4.0	4.1
Education	<	–	3.5	3.8	5.4	8.6	8.5	8.3	7.8	7.9	8.0
Welfare, relig. serv.	<	–	0.9	0.7	1.0	1.2	1.2	1.6	2.2	2.6	2.7
Nonprofit org.	<	–	<	0.3	0.4	0.4	0.4	0.5	0.4	0.4	0.4
Postal service	0.6	0.6	0.7	0.8	0.9	1.0	1.0	0.7	0.7	0.7	0.7
Government	2.2	2.2	2.6	3.7	4.3	4.6	4.5	4.7	4.7	4.8	4.8
Misc. social services	6.3	6.3	–	0.1	0.2	0.3	0.3	0.4	0.2	0.2	0.2
VI Personal services	8.2	11.2	14.0	12.1	11.3	10.0	10.0	10.5	11.7	11.5	11.7
Domestic serv.	<	6.5	5.3	3.2	3.1	1.7	1.7	1.3	1.2	0.9	0.9
Hotel	2.9	2.9	1.3	1.0	1.0	1.0	1.0	1.1	1.4	1.5	1.6
Eating, drinking places	<	<	2.5	3.0	2.9	3.3	3.2	4.4	4.9	4.8	4.9
Repair services	<	–	1.5	1.7	1.4	1.3	1.4	1.3	1.5	1.4	1.4
Laundry	<	–	1.0	1.2	1.0	0.8	0.8	0.4	0.4	0.5	0.4
Barber, beauty shops	<	0.9	–	–	0.8	0.9	0.9	0.7	0.8	0.7	0.7
Entertainment	<	0.9	0.9	1.0	0.8	0.8	0.8	1.0	1.2	1.3	1.3
Misc. personal serv.	<	–	1.6	1.2	0.4	0.3	0.3	0.3	0.4	0.4	0.4

^ Signifies that the figure is included in the above category.

The numbers may not add up due to rounding.

Sources: (a) Singelmann (1978); (b) 1970: Population Census; 1980–91: *Current Population Survey*, Bureau of Labor Statistics; Labor statistics: *Employment and Earnings* (various issues)

Table 4.2 Japan: percentage distribution of employment by industrial sector and intermediate industry group, 1920–1990

Industry	(a) 1920–70						(b) 1970–90			
	1920	1930	1940	1950	1960	1970	1970	1980	1985	1990
I Extractive	56.4	50.9	46.3	50.3	34.1	19.6	19.8	11.2	9.5	7.2
Agriculture	54.9	49.9	44.0	48.6	32.9	19.4	19.4	11.0	9.3	7.1
Mining	1.5	1.0	2.2	1.7	1.2	0.3	0.4	0.2	0.2	0.1
II Transformative	19.6	19.8	24.9	21.0	28.5	34.2	34.1	33.7	33.4	33.7
Construction	2.7	3.3	3.0	4.3	6.2	7.6	7.6	9.7	9.1	9.6
Utilities	0.3	0.4	0.4	0.6	0.6	0.6	0.6	0.6	0.6	0.6
Manufacturing	16.6	16.1	21.6	16.1	21.7	26.0	26.0	23.4	23.7	23.6
Food	2.0	1.8	1.4	2.2	2.1	2.1	2.1	2.1	2.2	2.3
Textiles	5.0	4.8	3.9	3.1	3.2	2.7	2.7	1.7	1.5	1.2
Metal	1.0	0.8	1.4	1.6	2.9	1.5	4.0	3.6	3.2	3.2
Machinery	0.4	0.7	2.9	1.6	3.1	4.9	5.0	4.6	5.9	5.9
Chemical	0.4	0.6	1.1	1.2	1.2	1.3	1.3	1.1	1.0	1.1
Misc. mfg	7.8	7.4	10.9	6.4	9.2	13.5	10.9	10.3	10.0	10.0
III Distributive services	12.4	15.6	15.2	14.6	18.6	22.5	22.4	25.1	24.8	24.3
Transportation	3.5	3.2	3.4	3.5	4.0	5.1	5.1	5.1	5.0	5.0
Communication	0.4	0.7	0.9	1.0	1.1	1.2	1.1	1.2	1.1	1.0
Wholesale	8.5	11.6	10.9	2.3	4.7	6.1	6.1	6.9	7.2	7.1
Retail	<	<	<	7.8	8.9	10.2	10.2	11.9	11.5	11.2
IV Producer services	0.8	0.9	1.2	1.5	2.9	5.1	4.8	7.5	8.6	9.6
Banking	0.4	0.5	0.6	0.7	1.2	1.4	1.4	2.8	3.0	1.9
Insurance	0.1	0.2	0.3	0.2	0.5	0.7	0.7	<	<	1.3
Real estate	–	–	0.1	0.0	0.2	0.5	0.5	0.8	0.8	1.1
Engineering	0.0	–	0.3	0.3	1.0	0.5	0.5	–	–	0.8

	1	2	3	4	5	6	7	8	9	10
Accounting	–	–	<	<	<	0.2	0.2	–	–	0.3
Misc. business serv.	0.2	0.2	<	<	<	1.7	1.4	3.9	4.8	4.0
Legal services	0.1	0.0	0.0	0.2	0.1	0.1	0.1	–	–	0.1
V Social services	4.9	5.5	6.0	7.2	8.3	10.1	10.3	12.9	13.5	14.3
Medical, health serv.	0.4	0.3	0.4	1.1	0.3	0.2	0.4	2.9	3.4	1.5
Hospital	0.3	0.5	0.7	<	1.3	1.8	1.8	<	<	2.2
Education	0.9	1.3	1.5	2.2	2.4	2.7	2.9	3.6	3.7	4.5
Welfare, relig. serv.	0.6	0.6	0.6	0.3	0.6	0.7	0.7	1.3	1.3	1.4
Nonprofit org.	0.1	–	0.7	0.2	0.2	0.5	1.0	1.1	1.1	1.1
Postal service	2.2	2.5	1.9	3.3	3.1	3.3	–	–	–	–
Government	<	<	<	<	<	<	3.4	3.6	–	3.4
Misc. social services	0.3	0.3	0.3	0.1	0.6	0.9	0.0	0.5	0.4	0.4
VI Personal services	5.7	7.3	6.3	5.3	7.6	8.5	8.5	9.6	10.1	10.2
Domestic serv.	2.5	2.7	2.2	0.8	0.7	0.3	0.3	0.1	0.1	0.1
Hotel	0.5	0.5	0.5	0.5	0.8	0.9	0.9	1.0	1.1	1.1
Eating, drinking places	1.4	2.4	1.8	1.1	2.2	3.1	3.0	4.1	4.3	4.1
Repair services	0.0	0.1	–	0.9	0.7	0.9	0.9	1.1	0.9	1.0
Laundry	0.1	0.2	0.2	0.2	0.4	0.5	0.5	1.6	1.7	0.6
Barber, beauty shops	0.5	0.7	0.6	0.6	1.1	1.1	1.1	<	<	1.1
Entertainment	0.4	0.3	0.8	0.5	0.7	0.7	0.8	0.9	1.0	1.3
Misc. personal serv.	0.2	0.3	0.3	0.7	1.0	1.0	1.0	0.9	0.9	0.9
Unclassifiable	–	–	–	–	–	–	–	–	–	0.6

^ Signifies that the figure is included in the category immediately above.
The numbers may not add up due to rounding.
Source: (a) Singelmann (1978); (b) Population Census, Bureau of Statistics

Table 4.3 Germany: percentage distribution of employment by industrial sector and intermediate industry group, 1925–1987

Industry	(a) 1925–70					(b) 1970–87	
	1925	1933	1950	1961	1970	1970	1987
I Extractive	33.5	31.5	16.1	9.0	5.1	8.7	4.1
Agriculture	30.9	29.1	12.9	6.8	3.8	7.5	3.2
Mining	2.6	2.4	3.2	2.2	1.3	1.2	0.9
II Transformative	38.9	36.3	47.3	51.3	49.0	47.1	40.3
Construction	5.3	6.1	9.3	8.5	8.0	7.7	7.1
Utilities	0.6	0.6	0.8	1.2	0.8	0.8	1.0
Manufacturing	33.0	31.6	37.1	41.6	40.2	38.6	32.2
Food	4.3	5.1	4.6	3.1	3.8	3.6	2.9
Textiles	3.7	3.5	3.5	5.1	2.2	2.4	1.1
Metal	3.7	4.5	2.3	3.7	3.7	4.7	4.3
Machinery	2.9	3.4	3.0	5.0	4.8	9.5	4.9
Chemical	1.1	1.1	1.7	2.4	2.7	2.4	2.7
Misc. mfg	17.3	14.0	22.0	22.3	23.0	16.0	16.2
III Distributive services	11.9	12.8	15.7	16.4	16.4	17.9	17.7
Transportation	4.0	4.2	5.1	4.5	3.9	5.4	5.9
Communication	–	–	–	0.5	–	<	<
Wholesale	7.9	8.6	10.6	3.9	4.4	4.2	3.2
Retail	<	<	<	7.5	8.6	8.2	8.6
IV Producer services	2.1	2.7	2.5	4.2	5.1	4.5	7.3
Banking	0.7	0.6	0.7	1.2	1.7	1.7	2.4
Insurance	0.4	0.6	0.8	0.7	1.0	0.9	1.0
Real estate	0.0	0.6	0.1	0.3	0.4	0.3	0.4
Engineering	0.1	0.1	0.2	0.4	0.6	0.6	0.7

Accounting	0.5	0.3	0.3	1.0	0.7	–	–
Misc. business serv.	^	^	^	^	^	0.9	2.8
Legal services	0.3	0.6	0.5	0.6	0.8	–	–
V Social services	6.0	6.8	11.1	12.5	17.4	15.7	24.3
Medical, health serv.	0.4	1.3	2.4	2.5	3.2	3.1	5.4
Hospital	0.6	^	^	^	^	–	–
Education	1.1	1.2	1.5	2.1	3.0	3.0	4.9
Welfare, relig. serv.	0.5	0.8	1.0	0.9	0.4	0.9	1.5
Nonprofit org.	–	–	–	–	0.4	0.4	0.2
Postal service	1.1	1.1	1.5	1.7	1.8	–	–
Government	2.1	2.2	4.1	5.3	8.6	7.7	9.5
Misc. social services	0.1	0.2	0.6	–	–	0.5	2.8
VI Personal services	7.7	7.8	6.9	6.4	7.4	6.1	6.3
Domestic serv.	4.4	4.0	3.2	1.5	0.5	0.4	0.2
Hotel	2.1	2.4	2.2	2.6	2.9	2.8	2.7
Eating, drinking places	^	^	^	^	^	^	^
Repair services	–	–	–	–	1.1	1.0	1.1
Laundry	0.2	–	–	0.6	0.5	0.5	0.2
Barber, beauty shops	0.4	0.7	0.8	0.9	0.9	0.9	1.0
Entertainment	0.4	0.5	0.1	–	0.4	0.4	0.9
Misc. personal serv.	0.1	0.2	0.6	0.8	0.4	0.1	0.1

^ Signifies that the figure is included in the category immediately above.
The numbers may not add up due to rounding.
Sources: (a) Singelmann (1978); (b) Statistiches Bundesamt, Volkszählung

Table 4.4 France: percentage distribution of employment by industrial sector and intermediate industry group, 1921–1989

Industry	(a) 1921–68						(b) 1968–89					
	1921	1931	1946	1954	1962	1968	1968	1970	1975	1980	1985	1989
I Extractive	43.6	38.3	40.2	30.9	23.0	17.0	15.6	13.5	10.3	8.7	7.6	6.4
Agriculture	42.4	36.6	38.8	28.6	20.6	15.9	14.8	12.9	9.9	8.4	7.4	6.3
Mining	1.2	1.7	1.4	2.3	2.4	1.1	0.2	0.6	0.4	0.3	0.2	0.1
II Transformative	29.7	32.8	29.6	35.2	37.7	39.3	39.4	38.0	37.3	34.8	30.9	29.5
Construction	3.0	4.2	5.1	7.4	8.7	10.3	9.5	9.5	8.9	8.5	7.1	7.2
Utilities	0.2	0.0	0.6	0.7	0.8	0.8	0.8	0.8	0.8	0.9	1.0	1.0
Manufacturing	26.4	28.5	23.8	27.2	28.0	26.0	27.0	27.7	27.6	25.5	22.9	21.3
Food	2.3	2.6	2.2	3.2	3.1	3.0	3.0	3.0	2.9	2.9	2.9	2.8
Textiles	9.4	4.4	2.5	6.0	4.9	2.3	3.8	3.6	3.1	2.5	2.1	1.7
Metal	0.6	2.1	7.3	0.9	1.1	1.5	5.0	5.1	5.0	4.3	3.6	3.5
Machinery	–	–	<	0.9	1.2	1.3	4.9	5.3	5.6	5.2	4.8	4.5
Chemical	0.9	1.1	1.1	1.3	1.4	1.5	1.8	1.9	1.9	1.8	1.7	1.6
Misc. mfg	13.2	18.3	10.7	14.9	16.3	18.5	8.4	8.8	9.1	8.7	7.7	7.3
III Distributive services	14.4	13.6	15.1	14.2	16.4	15.5	18.8	18.7	19.2	19.9	20.2	20.5
Transportation	5.6	5.1	6.1	4.2	4.3	4.3	4.2	4.1	4.1	4.1	4.2	4.3
Communication	0.7	<	<	1.3	1.7	0.1	1.8	1.8	2.0	2.1	2.3	2.2
Wholesale	8.1	8.5	9.1	2.3	3.2	3.6	3.7	3.8	4.0	4.4	4.4	4.5
Retail	<	<	<	6.5	7.3	7.5	9.1	9.0	9.2	9.3	9.3	9.5
IV Producer services	1.6	2.1	1.9	2.6	3.2	5.5	5.0	5.5	6.5	7.8	8.5	10.0
Banking	0.6	0.9	1.2	0.8	1.1	2.0	1.3	1.4	1.8	2.0	2.8	2.0
Insurance	0.2	0.3	0.4	0.5	0.7	0.8	0.5	0.5	0.6	0.7	0.7	0.8
Real estate	0.0	0.0	0.0	0.4	0.2	0.4	0.1	0.2	0.3	0.3	0.3	0.3
Engineering	0.5	0.7	–	0.9	1.1	0.3	–	–	–	–	–	–

Accounting	<	<	–	<	<	1.6	–	–	–	–	–	–
Misc. business serv.	<	<	–	<	<	<	3.1	3.4	3.8	4.9	5.3	6.9
Legal services	0.3	0.3	0.3	–	–	0.4	–	–	–	–	–	–
V Social services	5.3	6.1	6.8	9.4	12.3	14.5	15.1	15.6	16.4	17.1	19.8	19.5
Medical, health serv.	0.9	1.1	1.2	2.2	2.9	1.0	–	–	–	–	–	–
Hospital	<	<	<	<	<<	2.2	–	–	–	–	–	–
Education	1.3	1.4	1.5	2.4	3.5	4.4	–	–	–	–	–	–
Welfare, relig. serv.	0.5	0.5	0.7	0.6	1.1	1.1	–	–	–	–	–	–
Nonprofit org.	–	–	–	–	1.0	0.7	–	–	–	–	–	–
Postal service	2.3	2.8	3.2	4.0	3.4	1.8	–	–	–	–	–	–
Government	<	<	<	<	<	3.3	–	–	–	–	–	–
Misc. social services	0.2	0.2	0.1	0.2	0.4	0.0	–	–	–	–	–	–
VI Personal services	5.6	7.2	6.4	7.4	7.4	7.9	8.2	8.7	10.2	11.6	13.1	14.1
Domestic serv.	3.7	3.8	1.3	3.1	3.0	2.7	–	–	–	–	–	–
Hotel	1.5	2.8	1.4	1.5	1.6	0.9	2.7	2.7	2.7	2.8	3.1	3.5
Eating, drinking places	<	<	<	1.4	1.2	1.8	<	<	<	<	<	<
Repair services	–	–	–	–	0.3	1.1	–	–	–	–	–	–
Laundry	–	–	0.2	1.0	1.2	0.5	–	–	–	–	–	–
Barber, beauty shops	0.3	–	–	<	<	0.7	–	–	–	–	–	–
Entertainment	0.1	0.2	0.3	0.4	0.2	0.2	–	–	–	–	–	–
Misc. personal serv.	0.0	0.5	0.5	–	0.0	0.0	5.6	6.0	7.4	8.8	10.0	10.6

< Signifies the figure is included in the category immediately above.
The numbers may not add up due to rounding.
1989 figures are preliminary. Communication includes postal services.
Miscellaneous services includes all non-profit services in 1968–89.
Sources: (a) Singelmann (1978); (b) INSEE, Annuaire statistique de la France

Table 4.5 Italy: percentage distribution of employment by industrial sector and intermediate industry group, 1921–1990

Industry	(a) 1921–61				(b) 1961–90			
	1921	1931	1951	1961	1961	1971	1981	1990
I Extractive	57.1	48.1	42.9	29.8	29.8	17.2	11.7	9.5
Agriculture	56.7	47.7	42.5	29.1	29.1	17.2	11.4	9.5
Mining	0.4	0.4	0.4	0.7	0.7	–	0.3	–
II Transformative	24.3	29.0	31.8	40.0	39.9	44.3	40.5	29.7
Constructive	4.1	6.0	7.6	12.0	12.0	10.8	9.4	7.0
Utilities	0.3	0.6	0.5	0.6	0.6	0.9	0.9	0.8
Manufacturing	19.9	22.4	23.7	27.4	27.3	32.7	30.2	21.8
Food	1.2	1.5	2.4	2.4	–	–	1.8	1.6
Textiles	3.2	4.2	3.7	3.4	–	–	6.3	5.0
Metal	1.8	4.4	1.2	1.5	–	–	7.0	4.7
Machinery	1.5	<	1.4	1.8	–	–	4.8	3.3
Chemical	0.4	1.0	1.1	1.4	–	–	1.4	1.3
Misc. mfg	11.8	11.3	13.9	16.9	–	–	8.8	5.9
III Distributive services	8.6	10.1	10.6	13.0	15.3	18.7	16.2	25.8
Transportation	3.9	4.2	3.4	4.1	4.9	5.3	4.9	5.2
Communication	0.4	0.5	0.6	0.8	<	<	1.5	1.3
Wholesale	4.3	5.4	1.2	1.4	10.3	13.4	3.6	17.3
Retail	<	<	5.4	6.7	<	<	6.1	<
IV Producer services	1.2	1.8	1.9	2.0	–	–	4.6	–
Banking	0.2	0.5	0.8	0.9	1.1	1.5	1.7	1.8
Insurance	<	0.1	0.1	0.2	<	<	0.5	<
Real estate	<	<	<	0.0	–	–	0.0	–
Engineering	0.8	<	<	0.3	–	–	1.4	–

Accounting	<	1.0	0.7	<	–	–	0.4	–
Misc. business serv.	<	<	<	0.2	–	–	0.1	–
Legal services	0.2	0.2	0.3	0.4	–	–	0.4	–
V Social services	4.1	5.1	7.9	9.3	–	–	19.1	–
Medical, health serv.	0.6	0.8	1.1	0.7	–	–	1.7	–
Hospital	<	<	<	0.9	–	–	2.6	–
Education	1.0	1.1	2.0	2.7	–	–	7.4	–
Welfare, relig. serv.	0.6	0.7	1.2	0.2	–	–	0.2	–
Nonprofit org.	–	0.1	0.1	–	–	–	0.3	–
Postal service	1.3	2.1	3.4	4.8	–	–	–	–
Government	<	<	<	<	6.9	6.5	6.5	15.5
Misc. social services	0.6	0.3	0.1	–	–	–	0.4	–
VI Personal services	4.6	5.6	4.7	5.9	–	–	7.9	–
Domestic serv.	2.4	3.2	2.2	2.2	–	–	1.2	–
Hotel	0.2	0.6	1.4	0.7	–	–	0.9	4.1
Eating, drinking places	0.8	0.7	<	1.4	–	–	2.0	<
Repair services	–	–	–	0.2	–	–	2.0	–
Laundry	0.3	0.2	0.1	0.2	–	–	0.3	–
Barber, beauty shops	0.4	0.7	0.6	0.9	–	–	1.0	–
Entertainment	0.0	0.1	0.3	0.3	–	–	0.5	–
Misc. personal serv.	0.5	0.1	0.1	0.2	–	–	0.1	–
All other services					7.0	11.8	15.6	15.6

^ Signifies that the figure is included in the category immediately above.
The numbers may not add up due to rounding.
1990 figures may not be comparable to figures from earlier years due to the difference in sources.
Sources: (a) Singelmann (1978); (b) 1961–81: Istituto Centrale di statistica, Censimento generale della popolazione; 1990: Istituto nazionale di statistica, Annuario Statistico Italiano, 1991

Table 4.6 United Kingdom: percentage distribution of employment by industrial sector and intermediate industry group, 1921–1992

Industry	(a) England and Wales 1921–71					(b) UK (employees) 1970–90					(c) Great Britain (employees) 1970–92						(d) Great Britain (employed) 1971–81	
	1921	1931	1951	1961	1971	1970	1975	1980	1985	1990	1970	1971	1980	1981	1990	1992	1971	1981
I Extractive	14.2	11.8	8.9	6.6	4.3	3.6	3.3	4.7	4.4	3.3	3.6	3.4	4.3	4.9	3.2	1.8	4.3	3.9
Agriculture	7.1	6.1	5.0	3.5	2.6	1.7	1.8	1.6	1.6	1.3	1.7	1.6	1.6	1.6	1.2	1.2	2.7	2.3
Mining	7.1	5.7	3.9	3.1	1.7	1.9	1.6	3.2	2.8	2.0	1.9	1.9	3.2	3.3	2.0	0.5	1.6	1.6
II Transformative	42.2	39.3	45.4	46.0	43.8	46.7	40.3	35.7	29.8	27.3	46.6	45.9	35.7	33.7	27.3	26.3	42.8	35.6
Construction	4.4	5.2	6.5	6.9	7.1	6.3	5.8	5.5	4.8	4.8	6.2	6.0	5.4	5.2	4.8	4.0	7.0	7.0
Utilities	1.0	1.3	1.7	1.7	1.6	1.7	1.6	–	–	–	1.7	1.7	–	–	–	1.2	1.5	1.5
Manufacturing	36.8	32.9	37.2	37.4	34.9	38.7	33.0	30.2	25.0	22.5	38.8	38.2	30.3	28.5	22.5	21.1	34.2	27.1
Food	3.3	3.4	3.0	3.0	3.0	3.9	3.2	3.2	2.8	2.4	3.8	3.8	3.1	3.1	2.9	2.9	3.1	3.0
Textiles	5.9	5.9	4.5	3.4	2.4	3.1	2.1	1.5	1.1	0.9	3.0	2.8	1.5	1.5	0.9	0.8	2.5	1.3
Metal	2.8	2.1	2.7	2.7	2.3	5.4	4.6	6.8	3.6	3.1	5.5	5.3	6.9	6.2	3.2	2.7	4.8	4.1
Machinery	1.6	1.4	3.0	3.2	4.8	9.2	7.7	7.9	6.8	6.1	9.3	9.1	8.0	7.6	6.2	5.8	8.3	7.1
Chemical	1.1	1.1	2.1	2.3	2.0	2.3	2.1	–	1.6	1.4	2.4	2.4	–	–	1.5	1.4	2.2	1.7
Misc. mfg	22.1	19.0	21.9	22.8	20.4	14.8	13.1	10.8	9.2	8.6	14.8	14.8	10.8	10.2	8.5	8.0	13.4	10.0
III Distributive services	19.3	21.6	19.2	19.7	17.9	18.7	18.9	19.9	20.4	20.6	18.8	18.7	20.2	20.4	20.4	20.7	19.3	20.3
Transportation	7.3	7.0	6.4	5.7	4.8	4.9	4.7	6.5	4.2	4.1	4.9	5.0	6.5	6.6	4.2	4.3	4.8	4.6
Communication	–	–	–	–	–	2.0	2.0	<	2.0	1.9	2.0	2.1	<	<	1.9	1.9	1.8	1.9
Wholesale	12.0	14.6	12.8	14.0	3.4	2.3	3.7	4.0	4.5	4.5	2.3	2.4	4.1	4.2	4.3	4.5	2.1	3.9
Retail	<	<	<	<	9.6	9.5	8.4	9.5	9.7	10.1	9.5	9.3	9.5	9.6	10.1	10.0	10.7	9.8
IV Producer services	2.6	3.1	3.2	4.5	5.6	5.0	5.7	7.5	9.7	12.0	5.1	5.2	7.5	8.0	12.1	12.3	5.6	7.9
Banking	0.8	0.8	0.9	1.2	1.6	1.6	1.9	2.0	2.4	2.8	1.6	1.7	2.0	2.2	2.8	2.8	1.6	2.1
Insurance	0.7	0.9	0.9	1.1	1.2	1.3	1.2	0.9	1.1	1.2	1.3	1.3	1.0	1.0	1.2	1.2	1.2	1.1

Real estate	–	0.3	0.3	0.3	0.4	0.3	0.4	–	0.6	0.6	0.3	0.3	–	–	0.6	0.7	0.4	0.4
Engineering	0.2	0.2	0.2	–	0.4	0.4	0.4	–	–	–	–	–	–	–	–	–	0.5	–
Accounting	0.0	0.3	0.3	0.4	0.4	0.4	0.4	–	–	–	0.4	0.4	–	–	–	0.8	0.4	–
Misc. business serv.	0.4	0.2	0.1	1.1	1.0	1.0	1.4	4.5	5.6	7.4	1.1	1.1	4.5	4.8	7.5	5.9	1.1	4.3
Legal services	0.4	0.4	0.4	0.4	0.5	0.5	0.5	–	–	–	0.5	0.5	–	–	–	1.0	0.5	–
V Social services	8.9	9.7	12.1	14.1	19.4	17.7	22.1	24.2	26.8	27.2	17.7	18.3	23.9	24.9	27.2	28.9	18.9	22.8
Medical, health serv.	1.0	1.1	2.9	3.4	0.8	4.5	5.5	6.8	7.8	8.1	4.4	4.6	6.8	7.1	8.1	8.7	1.0	6.3
Hospital	^	^	^	^	3.1	–	–	^	^	^	^	^	^	^	^	^	3.2	–
Education	2.1	2.2	2.4	3.9	5.8	6.4	8.5	7.6	8.1	8.3	6.4	6.7	7.5	7.8	8.2	8.7	6.2	6.7
Welfare, relig. serv.	0.6	0.6	0.6	0.7	1.0	0.1	0.1	2.5	3.5	3.9	0.1	0.1	2.4	2.6	3.2	3.4	1.1	–
Nonprofit org.	0.1	0.1	–	0.0	0.2	–	–	–	–	–	–	–	–	–	–	–	0.1	–
Postal service	1.1	1.2	1.6	1.6	1.8	–	–	–	–	–	–	–	–	–	–	–	–	–
Government	3.8	4.3	4.2	4.0	6.0	6.2	7.3	7.3	7.4	6.8	6.2	6.4	7.2	7.4	7.0	7.4	6.8	7.2
Misc. social services	0.2	0.2	0.4	0.6	0.6	0.6	0.6	–	–	–	0.6	0.5	–	–	0.6	0.7	0.4	2.6
VI Personal services	12.9	14.5	11.3	9.0	9.0	8.1	9.7	8.1	9.0	9.7	8.1	8.1	7.9	8.1	9.8	9.7	8.4	8.9
Domestic serv.	7.5	8.2	2.4	1.6	1.0	0.4	–	–	–	–	0.4	0.4	–	–	–	–	1.0	0.4
Hotel	2.4	2.2	4.2	2.7	1.6	1.2	1.1	4.3	4.9	5.6	1.2	1.2	4.3	4.4	1.2	1.3	1.0	4.1
Eating, drinking places	0.8	1.3	^	^	1.0	1.3	2.5	^	^	^	1.3	1.3	^	^	4.4	4.0	1.9	^
Repair services	–	–	1.4	1.8	2.1	1.8	1.9	0.9	1.0	1.0	1.8	1.9	0.9	0.9	1.0	1.1	2.1	1.5
Laundry	0.8	0.9	0.8	0.7	0.4	0.5	0.4	–	–	–	0.5	0.5	–	–	–	–	0.4	–
Barber, beauty shops	0.3	0.5	0.4	0.7	1.1	0.4	0.4	–	–	–	0.4	0.4	–	–	–	–	0.6	–
Entertainment	0.7	0.9	1.1	1.0	1.1	1.1	1.3	1.9	2.3	2.3	1.1	1.1	1.9	2.0	2.3	2.3	1.1	1.9
Misc. personal serv.	0.5	0.3	1.0	0.5	0.8	1.3	2.1	1.0	0.9	0.9	1.3	1.4	0.8	0.8	0.9	0.9	0.2	1.1
Unclassifiable	–	–	–	–	–	0.2	0.0	0.0	–	–	0.2	0.3	–	–	0.0	0.3	0.7	0.6

^ Signifies that the figure is included in the category immediately above.
The numbers may not add up due to rounding.
The data for Great Britain are of the employed, while the data for United Kingdom are of employees in employment.
Postal service is included in Communication.
From 1980 UK figures, utilities is included under Mining. Chemical is included in Metal in 1980.
Sources: (a) Singelmann (1978); (b)–(d) 1970–92: Annual Abstract of Statistics, and Employment Gazette; 1971–81: Office of Population Censuses and Surveys, Census Reports

Table 4.7 Canada: percentage distribution of employment by industrial sector and intermediate industry group, 1921–1992

Industry	(a) 1921–71						(b) 1971–92		
	1921	1931	1941	1951	1961	1971	1971	1981	1992
I Extractive	36.9	34.4	31.7	21.6	14.7	9.1	8.3	7.1	5.7
Agriculture	35.2	32.5	29.5	19.7	12.8	7.4	6.6	5.3	4.4
Mining	1.6	1.9	2.2	1.9	1.9	1.7	1.6	1.8	1.3
II Transformative	26.1	24.7	28.2	33.7	31.1	30.0	27.1	26.8	22.3
Construction	9.0	6.8	5.3	6.9	7.0	6.9	6.3	6.5	6.3
Utilities	–	1.5	0.6	1.2	1.1	1.1	1.0	1.1	1.2
Manufacturing	17.0	16.4	22.3	25.6	23.0	22.0	19.7	19.2	14.9
Food	1.2	2.2	3.4	3.1	3.7	3.2	2.9	2.7	–
Textiles	2.7	2.6	3.7	1.6	1.3	0.9	1.0	0.7	–
Metal	2.9	1.9	2.3	3.9	3.2	1.5	3.0	3.4	–
Machinery	<	0.7	0.9	<	0.8	1.0	2.3	2.2	–
Chemical	0.2	0.4	0.8	1.3	1.4	1.0	1.2	1.1	–
Misc. mfg	10.0	8.6	11.2	15.7	12.6	14.4	9.3	9.0	14.9
III Distributive services	19.2	18.4	17.7	21.8	23.9	23.0	20.8	22.9	24.0
Transportation	8.5	7.2	5.8	6.8	6.6	5.4	5.0	4.8	4.1
Communication	–	0.9	0.7	1.1	2.1	2.1	1.9	2.1	2.1
Wholesale	10.7	1.6	2.4	3.8	4.7	4.5	4.1	4.8	4.5
Retail	<	8.7	8.8	10.1	10.5	11.0	9.8	11.1	13.2
IV Producer services	3.7	3.3	2.7	3.9	5.3	7.3	6.6	9.7	11.3
Banking	1.2	1.2	0.9	1.3	1.8	2.4	2.2	2.7	3.7
Insurance	<	1.0	0.9	1.1	1.9	2.2	2.0	0.9	<
Real estate	<	0.2	0.3	0.4	<	<	<	1.7	2.2
Engineering	2.3	–	–	0.2	0.4	0.7	0.6	0.9	–

Accounting	<	0.1	0.1	0.2	0.3	0.4	0.4	0.5	—
Misc. business serv.	<	0.4	0.2	0.4	0.5	1.1	1.0	2.3	5.4
Legal services	0.2	0.4	0.3	0.3	0.4	0.5	0.4	0.6	—
V Social services	7.5	8.9	9.4	11.3	15.4	21.1	22.0	24.0	22.6
Medical, health serv.	1.1	1.8	2.2	3.1	0.9	1.0	1.8	2.0	9.1
Hospital	<	<	<	<	3.7	4.7	4.1	4.0	<
Education	2.0	2.7	2.7	2.9	4.4	7.3	6.0	6.6	7.0
Welfare, relig. serv.	0.9	1.0	0.7	1.1	1.3	1.4	1.3	1.9	—
Nonprofit org.	—	—	—	—	—	0.2	0.2	0.2	—
Postal service	3.0	0.5	0.5	0.6	5.1	5.4	—	—	—
Government	<	2.6	2.8	3.4	<	<	7.4	7.6	6.5
Misc. social services	0.5	0.3	0.5	0.2	—	—	1.1	1.6	—
VI Personal services	6.7	10.2	10.2	7.8	9.5	9.6	7.5	9.5	13.5
Domestic serv.	—	4.2	4.5	1.6	1.6	0.7	0.6	0.4	—
Hotel	—	2.8	1.6	1.5	3.9	1.7	1.5	5.7	6.5
Eating, drinking places	—	<	1.3	1.6	<	2.6	2.2	—	<
Repair services	—	0.5	1.1	1.1	1.1	0.9	1.0	1.1	—
Laundry	—	0.5	0.5	0.7	0.6	0.5	0.5	0.3	—
Barber, beauty shops	—	0.6	0.6	0.5	0.7	0.7	0.6	0.5	—
Entertainment	—	0.4	0.4	0.5	0.6	1.0	0.9	1.2	—
Misc. personal serv.	—	1.2	0.2	0.3	1.0	1.5	0.3	0.3	7.0
Unclassifiable	—	—	—	—	—	—	7.3	—	0.7

^ Signifies that the figure is included in the category immediately above.

The numbers may not add up due to rounding.

1992 figures may not be comparable to the earlier years due to the difference in sources.

Sources: (a) Singelmann (1978); (b) 1971–81: Population Census; 1992: Statistics Canada, *The Labour Force*, May

Table 4.8 United States: employment statistics by industry, 1920–1991

	(a) 1920–70							(b) 1970–91				
	1920	1930	1940	1950	1960	1970	1970	1980	1985	1990	1991
Industry (%)	48.0	43.3	37.9	39.2	38.2	33.6	34.0	30.5	27.7	25.8	24.9
Services (%)	52.0	56.7	62.1	60.8	61.8	66.4	66.0	69.5	72.3	74.2	75.1
Goods handling (%)	73.3	69.0	67.4	69.3	65.8	61.1	61.2	57.3	54.7	52.6	51.7
Information handling (%)	26.7	31.0	32.5	30.6	34.0	38.9	39.0	42.7	45.3	47.4	48.3
Services : industry	1.1	1.3	1.6	1.6	1.6	2.0	1.9	2.3	2.6	2.9	3.0
Information : goods	0.4	0.5	0.5	0.4	0.5	0.6	0.6	0.7	0.8	0.9	0.9

Industry = mining, construction, manufacturing.
Services = remaining categories.
Goods handling = mining, construction, manufacturing, transportation, wholesale/retail trade.
Information handling = communications; finance, insurance, and real estate (FIRE); services; government.
Services : industry = ratio between services and industry employment.
Information : goods = ratio between information handling and goods handling employment.
Source: See table 4.1

Table 4.9 Japan: employment statistics by industry, 1920–1990

	(a) 1920–70						(b) 1970–90			
	1920	1930	1940	1950	1960	1970	1970	1980	1985	1990
Industry (%)	46.3	40.7	47.8	43.1	43.4	42.1	42.1	37.4	36.3	35.8
Services (%)	53.7	59.3	52.2	56.9	56.6	57.9	57.9	62.6	63.7	64.2
Goods handling (%)	76.8	75.8	77.3	72.9	73.8	73.2	73.0	69.6	67.9	65.9
Information handling (%)	23.2	24.0	22.5	27.1	26.4	27.0	26.9	30.4	31.9	33.4
Services : industry	1.2	1.5	1.1	1.3	1.3	1.4	1.4	1.7	1.8	1.8
Information : goods	0.3	0.3	0.3	0.4	0.4	0.4	0.4	0.4	0.5	0.5

Industry = mining, construction, manufacturing.
Services = remaining categories.
Goods handling = mining, construction, manufacturing, transportation, wholesale/retail trade.
Information handling = communications, finance, insurance, and real estate (FIRE); services; government.
Services : industry = ratio between services and industry employment.
Information : goods = ratio between information handling and goods handling employment.
Source: See table 4.2

Table 4.10 Germany: employment statistics by industry, 1925–1987

	(a) 1925–70					(b) 1970–87	
	1925	1933	1950	1961	1970	1970	1987
Industry (%)	59.1	56.6	57.3	56.2	51.2	51.4	41.5
Services (%)	40.9	43.4	42.7	43.8	48.8	48.6	58.5
Goods handling (%)	78.8	77.1	78.1	76.5	71.4	71.6	60.8
Information handling (%)	21.2	22.9	21.9	23.5	29.1	28.4	39.2
Services : industry	0.7	0.8	0.7	0.8	1.0	0.9	1.4
Information : goods	0.3	0.3	0.3	0.3	0.4	0.4	0.6

Industry = mining, construction, manufacturing.
Services = remaining categories.
Goods handling = mining, construction, manufacturing, transportation, wholesale/retail trade.
Information handling = communications; finance, insurance, and real estate (FIRE); services; government.
Services : industry = ratio between services and industry employment.
Information : goods = ratio between information handling and goods handling employment.
Source: See table 4.3

Table 4.11 France: employment statistics by industry, 1921–1989

	(a) 1921–68						(b) 1968–89					
	1921	1931	1946	1954	1962	1968	1968	1970	1975	1980	1985	1989
Industry (%)	53.1	54.3	49.7	51.8	49.5	47.3	43.8	43.4	41.0	37.4	32.5	30.6
Services (%)	46.9	45.7	50.3	48.2	50.5	52.7	56.2	56.6	59.0	62.6	67.5	69.4
Goods handling (%)	79.8	80.2	77.8	73.1	71.2	67.7	67.8	66.8	64.1	60.8	56.3	54.9
Information handling (%)	20.2	19.8	22.4	27.0	29.0	32.3	32.2	33.2	35.9	39.2	43.7	45.1
Services : industry	0.9	0.8	1.0	0.9	1.0	1.1	1.3	1.3	1.4	1.7	2.1	2.3
Information : goods	0.3	0.2	0.3	0.4	0.4	0.5	0.5	0.5	0.6	0.6	0.8	0.8

Industry = mining, construction, manufacturing.
Services = remaining categories.
Goods handling = mining, construction, manufacturing, transportation, wholesale/retail trade, hotels/lodging places.
Information handling = communications; finance, insurance, and real estate (FIRE); services; government.
Services : industry = ratio between services and industry employment.
Information : goods = ratio between information handling and goods handling employment.
Source: See table 4.4

Table 4.12 Italy: employment statistics by industry, 1921–1990

	(a) 1921–61					(b) 1961–90			
	1921	1931	1951	1961		1961	1971	1981	1990
Industry (%)	56.5	55.4	55.3	56.6		56.4	52.5	45.0	31.9
Services (%)	43.5	44.6	44.7	43.4		43.6	47.5	55.0	68.1
Goods handling (%)	76.6	76.2	76.1	75.6		78.8	76.1	63.6	62.2
Information handling (%)	23.4	23.8	23.9	24.4		21.2	23.9	36.4	37.8
Services : industry	0.8	0.8	0.8	0.8		0.8	0.9	1.2	2.1
Information : goods	0.3	0.3	0.3	0.3		0.3	0.3	0.6	0.6

Industry = mining, construction, manufacturing,
Services = remaining categories.
Goods handling = mining, construction, manufacturing, transportation, wholesale/retail trade, hotels/lodging places.
Information handling = communications; finance, insurance and real estate (FIRE); services; government.
Services : industry = ratio between services and industry employment.
Information : goods = ratio between information handling and goods handling employment.
1990 figures may not be comparable to figures from earlier years due to the difference in sources.
Source; See table 4.5

Table 4.13 United Kingdom: employment statistics by industry, 1921–1990

	(a) England and Wales, 1921–71					(b) UK, 1970–90					
	1921	1931	1951	1961	1971	1970	1975	1980	1985	1990
Industry (%)	53.0	47.9	51.8	50.9	46.7	49.4	42.6	39.4	33.1	29.6
Services (%)	47.0	52.1	48.2	49.1	53.3	50.6	57.4	60.6	66.9	70.4
Goods handling (%)	76.3	73.3	76.4	74.2	66.6	67.6	61.0	64.0	56.7	54.2
Information handling (%)	23.7	26.7	23.6	25.8	33.3	32.2	39.0	36.0	43.3	45.8
Services : industry	0.9	1.1	0.9	1.0	1.1	1.0	1.3	1.5	2.0	2.4
Information : goods	0.3	0.4	0.3	0.3	0.5	0.5	0.6	0.6	0.8	0.8

Industry = mining, construction, manufacturing.
Services = remaining categories.
Goods handling = mining, construction, manufacturing, transportation, wholesale/retail trade, hotels/lodging places.
Information handling = communications; finance, insurance, and real estate (FIRE); services; government.
Services : industry = ratio between services and industry employment.
Information : goods = ratio between information handling and goods handling employment.
Source: see table 4.6

Table 4.14 Canada: employment statistics by industry, 1921–1992

	(a) 1921–71						(b) 1971–92		
	1921	1931	1941	1951	1961	1971	1971	1981	1992
Industry (%)	42.7	37.2	42.3	42.8	36.6	33.0	29.8	29.0	23.5
Services (%)	57.3	62.8	57.7	57.2	63.4	67.0	70.2	71.0	76.5
Goods handling (%)	72.3	69.6	69.6	71.9	67.4	58.6	52.8	58.1	54.3
Information handling (%)	27.6	30.4	30.4	28.1	32.6	41.4	47.2	41.9	45.7
Services : industry	1.3	1.7	1.4	1.3	1.7	2.0	2.4	2.4	3.3
Information : goods	0.4	0.4	0.4	0.4	0.5	0.7	0.9	0.7	0.8

Industry = mining, construction, manufacturing.
Services = remaining categories.
Goods handling = mining, construction, manufacturing, transportation, wholesale/retail trade, hotels/lodging places.
Information handling = communications; finance, insurance, and real estate (FIRE); services; government.
Services : industry = ratio between services and industry employment.
Information : goods = ratio between information handling and goods handling employment.
1992 figures may not be comparable to figures from previous years due to the difference in sources.
Source: See table 4.7

Table 4.15 Occupational structure of selected countries (%)

Categories	USA 1991	Canada 1992	UK 1990	France 1989	Germany 1987	Japan 1990
Managers	12.8	13.0	11.0	7.5	4.1	3.8
Professionals	13.7	17.6	21.8	6.0	13.9	11.1
Technicians	3.2	^	^	12.4	8.7	^
Subtotal	29.7	30.6	32.8	25.9	26.7	14.9
Sales	11.9	9.9	6.6	3.8	7.8	15.1
Clerical	15.7	16.0	17.3	24.2	13.7	18.6
Subtotal	27.6	25.9	23.9	28.0	21.5	33.7
Crafts and operators	21.8	21.1	22.4	28.1	27.9	31.8
Semi-skilled service workers	13.7	13.7	12.8	7.2	12.3	8.6
Semi-skilled transport workers	4.2	3.5	5.6	4.2	5.5	3.7
Subtotal	17.9	17.2	18.4	11.4	17.3	12.3
Farm workers and managers	3.0	5.1	1.6	6.6	3.1	7.2
Unclassified	—	—	1.0	—	3.0	—

^ Signifies that figure is included in the category immediately above.
The numbers may not add up due to rounding.
Source: Author's elaboration; see Appendix B

Table 4.16 United States: percentage distribution of employment by occupation, 1960–1991 (%)

Occupational category	1960	1970	1980	1985	1990	1991
Managerial	11.1	10.5	11.2	11.4	12.6	12.8
Professional	11.8	14.2	16.1	12.7	13.4	13.7
Technicians	^	^	^	3.0	3.3	3.2
Sales	7.3	6.2	6.3	11.8	12.0	11.9
Clerical	14.8	17.4	18.6	16.2	15.8	15.7
Crafts and operators	30.2	32.2	28.1	23.9	22.5	21.8
Semi-skilled service workers	13.0	12.4	13.3	13.5	13.4	13.7
Semi-skilled transport workers	4.9	3.2	3.6	4.2	4.1	4.2
Farm workers and managers	7.0	4.0	2.8	3.2	2.9	3.0

^ Signifies that figure is included in the category immediately above.
Figures are seasonally adjusted annual data except the 1960 data, which are those of December.
Source: Labor Statistics: Employment and Earnings (various issues)

Table 4.17 Japan: percentage distribution of employment by occupation, 1955–1990

Occupational category	1955	1960	1965	1970	1975	1980	1985	1990
Managerial	2.2	2.1	2.8	2.6	4.0	4.0	3.6	3.8
Professional	4.6	5.0	5.0	5.8	7.0	7.9	9.3	11.1
Technicians	^	^	^	^	^	^	^	^
Sales	13.3	13.4	13.0	13.0	14.2	14.4	14.9	15.1
Clerical	9.0	11.2	13.4	14.8	15.7	16.7	17.7	18.6
Crafts and operators	27.0	29.5	31.4	34.2	33.3	33.1	33.2	31.8
Semi-skilled service workers	5.4	6.7	7.5	7.6	8.8	9.1	8.7	8.6
Semi-skilled transport workers	1.7	2.3	3.7	4.6	4.5	4.5	3.9	3.7
Farm workers and managers	36.7	29.8	23.1	17.3	12.5	10.3	8.7	7.2

^ Signifies that figure is included in the category immediately above.
Sweepers and garbage collectors are included in semi-skilled service category between 1970 and 1980. From 1985, they are included in crafts and operators category.
Source: Statistical Yearbook of Japan, 1991

Table 4.18   Germany: percentage distribution of employment by occupation 1976–1989 (%)

Occupational category	1976	1980	1985	1989
Managerial	3.8	3.2	3.9	4.1
Professional	11.0	11.1	12.6	13.9
Technicians	7.0	7.2	7.8	8.7
Sales	7.6	7.6	7.5	7.8
Clerical	13.1	14.2	12.5	13.7
Crafts and operators	31.8	32.0	28.3	27.9
Semi-skilled service workers	12.5	12.5	15.8	12.3
Semi-skilled transport workers	6.3	6.1	5.5	5.5
Farm workers and managers	5.8	4.8	3.9	3.1
Not classifiable	1.1	1.2	2.1	3.0

^ Signifies that figure is included in the category immediately above.
Source: 1976–89: *Statistisches Bundesamt, Statistisches Jahrbuch* (various issues)

Table 4.19   France: percentage distribution of employment by occupation, 1982–1989 (%)

Occupational category	1982	1989
Managerial	7.1	7.5
Professional	4.8	6.0
Technicians	12.3	12.4
Sales	3.3	3.8
Clerical	22.8	24.2
Crafts and operators	30.9	28.1
Semi-skilled service workers	6.2	7.2
Semi-skilled transport workers	4.6	4.2
Farm workers and managers	8.0	6.6
Not classifiable		

^ Signifies that figure is included in the category immediately above.
Source: 1982: *Enquête sur l'emploi de mars 1982*; 1989 *Enquête sur l'emploi de mars 1989*

Table 4.20   Great Britain: percentage distribution of employment by occupation, 1961–1990 (%)

Occupational category	1961	1971	1981	1990
Managerial	2.7	3.7	5.3	11.0
Professional	8.7	8.6	11.8	21.8
Technicians	^	2.4	2.0	^
Sales	9.7	8.9	8.8	6.6
Clerical	13.3	14.1	14.8	17.3
Crafts and operators	43.1	34.2	27.9	22.4
Semi-skilled service workers	11.9	12.7	14.0	12.8
Semi-skilled transport workers	6.5	10.0	9.1	5.6
Farm workers and managers	4.0	2.9	2.4	1.6
Not classifiable		2.6	3.8	1.0

^ Signifies that figure is included in the category immediately above.
Source: Census, 1961, 1971, 1981; 1990: (Spring) *Labour Force Survey 1991*

Table 4.21   Canada: percentage distribution of employment by occupation, 1950–1992 (%)

Occupational category	1950	1970	1980	1985	1992
Managerial	8.4	10.0	7.7	11.4	13.0
Professional	7.0	13.6	15.6	17.1	17.6
Technicians	1.5	^	^	^	^
Sales	6.9	7.1	10.8	9.6	9.9
Clerical	10.6	14.8	17.5	17.3	16.0
Crafts and operators	28.2	29.6	26.0	22.3	21.1
Semi-skilled service workers	8.8	12.3	13.1	13.7	13.7
Semi-skilled transport workers	6.9	5.3	4.1	3.8	3.5
Farm workers and managers	21.7	7.4	5.3	4.7	5.1

^ Signifies that figure is included in the category immediately above. 1950 figures were taken on March 4, 1950; 1980 and 1985 figures are those of January. 1992 figures are those of July.
Source: *Statistics Canada, The Labour Force* (various issues)

Table 4.22 Foreign resident population in Western Europe, 1950–1990 (in thousands and as % of total population)

Country	1950		1970		1982[a]		1990	
	No.	%	No.	%	No.	%	No.	%
Austria	323	4.7	212	2.8	303	4.0	512	6.6
Belgium	368	4.3	696	7.2	886	9.0	905	9.1
Denmark	–		–		102	2.0	161	3.1
Finland	11	0.3	6	0.1	12	0.3	35	0.9
France	1765	4.1	2621	5.3	3680	6.8	3608	6.4
Germany, Fed. Rep.	568	1.1	2977	4.9	4667	7.6	5242	8.2
Greece	31	0.4	93	1.1	60	0.7	70	0.9
Ireland	–		–		69	2.0	90	2.5
Italy	47	0.1	–		312	0.5	781	1.4
Liechtenstein	3	19.6	7	36.0	9	36.1	–	
Luxembourg	29	9.9	63	18.4	96	26.4	109	28.0
Netherlands	104	1.1	255	2.0	547	3.9	692	46
Norway	16	0.5	–		91	2.2	143	3.4
Portugal	21	0.3	–		64	0.6	108	1.0
Spain	93	0.3	291	0.9	418	1.1	415	1.1
Sweden	124	1.8	411	1.8	406	4.9	484	5.6
Switzerland	285	6.1	1080	17.2	926	14.7	1100	16.3
United Kingdom	–		–		2137	3.9	1875	3.3
Total[b]	5100	1.3	10200	2.2	15000	3.1	16600	4.5

[a] 1982 is a reference year, rather than 1980, since the data are better for 1982.
[b] Includes interpolated figures for the missing (—) data.
Source: Fassman and Münz (1992)

Table 4.23   Employment in manufacturing by major countries and regions, 1970–1997 (thousands)

Year	United States	European Union[a]	Japan	Brazil	Mexico	China	India[b]	Republic of Korea
1970	19,367	38,400	–	2,499	–	–	4,594	887
1975	18,323	36,600	13,400	3,953	–	42,840	5,087	2,678
1980	20,285	35,200	13,670	7,425	2,581	67,140	5,872	2,955
1985	19,245	30,700	14,530	7,907	–	83,490	6,183	3,504
1990	19,076	30,200	15,050	9,410	4,493	96,970	6,118	4,911
1993	18,075	30,344[c]	15,300	8,539	4,960	92,950	n.a.	4,652
1995	18,468	28,000	14,560	8,548	4,932	98,000	6,767	4,773
1997	18,657	29,919	14,420	8,407[c]	6,125	96,100	n.a.	4,474

[a] The European Union includes the Europe 15 (Sweden not included).
[b] Public employees and private employees in establishments with 10 or more employees.
[c] In 1991, the German series changed to include workers from the former Democratic Republic of Germany. This increased the number of manufacturing workers by 2.8 million in 1991. This implies a "real" number of manufacturing workers in the EU (without the DRG) of about 28.8 million by 1993 and by 1997, about 28 million (c.1996).
Sources: International Labour Office, *Statistical Yearbook*, 1986, 1988, 1994, 1995, 1996, 1997; OECD, *Labour Force Statistics, 1977–1997* (Paris: OECD, 1998); OECD, *Main Economic Indicators: Historical Statistics, 1962–1991* (Paris: OECD, 1993), compiled and elaborated by Carnoy (2000)

Table 4.24 Employment shares by industry/occupation and ethnic/gender group of all workers in the United States, 1960–1998 (percent)

	1960	1970	1980	1988	1990	1998
Total employed						
I (High wage)	24.6	25.5	28.2	32.4	32.9	33.0
II (Middle wage)	44.7	43.8	34.4	38.1	38.2	34.6
III (Low wage)	31.6	30.8	37.4	29.5	28.8	32.4
White males						
I	28.4	29.4	32.3	37.2	39.5	37.7
II	48.0	45.8	43.6	39.7	37.2	36.2
III	23.6	24.9	24.2	23.1	23.2	26.0
Black males						
I	7.9	9.1	13.8	16.3	18.0	20.6
II	36.2	45.2	47.9	42.8	40.9	40.5
III	56.0	45.8	38.2	40.9	41.0	38.5
Latino males						
I	10.5	13.9	16.2	16.9	15.6	16.7
II	42.2	45.8	44.2	43.1	38.2	37.9
III	47.2	40.2	39.6	42.0	46.2	45.0
White females						
I	19.2	20.2	24.6	30.5	32.1	35.5
II	47.5	46.0	43.7	39.4	38.8	31.9
III	33.2	33.8	31.7	30.4	29.1	32.3
Black females						
I	9.1	13.5	17.8	18.8	20.4	24.0
II	19.0	33.3	42.2	41.1	40.7	33.9
III	71.8	53.1	40.0	40.2	38.9	40.5
Latina females						
I	5.2	11.5	13.6	17.3	18.2	19.8
II	50.0	52.3	46.1	42.5	43.0	34.1
III	44.9	36.2	40.3	40.3	38.9	45.6

Source: US Department of Commerce, Bureau of the Census, *1 Percent Sample, US Population Census, 1960, 1970*, compiled by Carnoy (2000)

Table 4.25 Information technology spending per worker (1987–1994), employment growth (1987–1994), and unemployment rate (1995) by country

Country	Information technology spending per worker (US$ PPP)		Employment growth 1987–94 (%/yr)	Unemployment rate 1995 (%)
	1987	1994		
Australia	647.9	949.4	1.9	8.5
Austria	303.0	540.5	0.8	5.9
Belgium	469.6	945.9	0.5	13
Canada	525.0	772.7	1.6	9.5
Denmark	395.2	717.1	0.2	10
Finland	414.9	650.0	−1.6	17.2
France	540.5	871.6	0.1	11.6
Germany	519.2	722.2	0.7	9.4
Greece	54.9	79.2	0.5	10.0
Ireland	272.7	341.9	0.4	12.9
Italy	428.6	606.1	0.0	12.0
Japan	350.0	604.6	1.2	3.1
Netherlands	578.9	873.0	1.8	7.1
New Zealand	431.6	833.3	0.3	6.3
Norway	410.2	750.0	0.3	4.9
Portugal	186.0	204.5	0.3	7.2
Spain	294.1	440.7	0.6	22.9
Sweden	559.4	891.3	−0.6	7.7
Switzerland	497.1	981.4	1.5	4.2
United Kingdom	595.2	873.0	0.6	8.2
United States	973.0	1487.8	1.8	5.6

Sources: OECD, *Information Technology Outlook, 1995* (Paris: OECD, 1996, figure 2.1); OECD, *Labour Force Statistics, 1974–1994* (for employment growth); OECD, *Employment Outlook* (July 1996) (for unemployment rates), compiled and elaborated by Carnoy (2000)

Table 4.26 Main telephone lines per employee (1986 and 1993) and Internet hosts per 1,000 population (January 1996) by country

Country	Main telephone lines per employee		Internet Hosts per 1,000 population (Jan. 1996)
	1986	*1993*	
Australia	71.3	118.3	17.5
Austria	154.1	198.6	6.6
Belgium	120.7	169.8	3.1
Canada	123.2	188.0	13.0
Denmark	137.0	182.8	10.0
Finland	106.9	182.2	41.2
France	144.7	200.0	2.4
Germany	122.2	159.7	5.6
Greece	111.2	180.0	0.8
Ireland	49.1	89.5	4.2
Italy	165.6	210.2	1.3
Japan	151.9	235.7	2.2
Netherlands	203.2	238.6	11.4
New Zealand	55.0	159.4	15.4
Norway	105.2	166.7	20.5
Portugal	65.0	154.7	0.9
Spain	155.2	191.7	1.4
Sweden	123.9	226.1	17.2
Switzerland	180.5	222.4	12.4
United Kingdom	99.2	170.8	7.8
United States	147.3	223.4	23.5

Sources: ITU Statistical Yearbook, 1995, pp. 270–5; Sam Paltridge, "How competition helps the Internet," *OECD Observer*, no. 201 (August–September), 1996, p. 201; OECD, *Information Technology Outlook*, 1995, figure 3.5, compiled and elaborated by Carnoy (2000)

Table 4.27   Men's and women's employment/population ratios, 15–64 years old, 1973–1998 (percent)

Country	Men			Women		
	1973	1983	1998	1973	1983	1998
Australia	89.9	77.5	75.2	46.4	47.0	59.2
Austria	82.4	79.4	75.9	47.7	47.1	59.0
Belgium	81.6	69.2	67.0	39.9	39.8	47.5
Canada	81.9	77.8	74.7	44.1	55.0	63.3
Denmark	89.0	78.3	80.2	61.2	65.0	70.2
Finland	78.1	77.4	68.2	62.3	69.0	61.2
France	83.8	73.4	66.5	47.9	48.3	52.3
Germany	88.8	76.6	72.5	49.7	47.8	55.6
Greece	81.8	75.3	71.0	31.2	35.6	39.6
Ireland	86.5	73.8	71.4	32.8	33.6	48.2
Italy	81.6	75.7	65.1	29.9	34.2	36.7
Japan[a]	88.8	86.7	81.7	53.4	55.7	57.2
Luxembourg	93.1	84.0	74.6	35.9	40.9	45.6
Netherlands	83.5	69.1	79.9	28.6	34.7	59.4
New Zealand	89.1	80.3	77.1	39.1	42.8	62.1
Norway	85.6	84.4	82.7	49.3	63.0	73.5
Portugal	99.2	82.8	75.8	30.5	49.8	58.1
Spain	90.5	67.9	67.0	32.5	26.5	35.7
Sweden	86.2	83.0	73.5	60.8	73.9	69.4
Switzerland	100.0	92.7	87.2	54.1	54.7	71.0
United Kingdom	90.3	75.9	78.1	52.7	52.6	64.2
United States	82.8	76.5	80.5	48.0	56.2	67.4

[a] Japanese series changes from 1996 to 1998 *Employment Outlook.*
Sources: OECD, *Employment Outlook* (July, 1996, table A); OECD, *Employment Outlook* (June, 1999, table B), compiled and elaborated by Carnoy (2000)

Table 4.28 Percentage of standard workers in the *chuki koyo* system of Japanese firms

(A) Size of the firm, education of workers, and *chuki koyo* membership (% calculated on the total of workers in each cell)

	No. of employees		
	>1,000	100–999	10–99
Elementary/new junior high	8.4	4.9	3.9
Old junior high/new senior high	24.3	11.7	4.8
Professional high/2-year college	14.1	7.2	2.8
University	53.2	35.0	15.7

(B) Percentage of workers in firms with over 1,000 employees included in *chuki koyo* system, according to their age and education

Education	Age (years)							
	20–24	25–29	30–34	35–39	40–44	45–49	50–54	55–59
Elementary/new junior high	13.1	13.1	27.9	32.5	25.6	17.1	8.4	6.2
Old junior high/new senior high	53.4	50.3	42.9	52.6	41.4	39.1	24.3	14.3
Professional high/2-year college	50.8	34.1	31.3	37.2	30.9	15.8	14.1	8.6
University	88.9	59.5	57.1	49.9	58.9	53.4	53.2	31.7

Source: Nomura (1994)

Table 4.29 Concentration of stock ownership by income level in the United States, 1995 (percent)

Income level (in thousands)[a]	Share of households	% who own	% of stock owned	
			Shares	Cumulative
Publicly traded stock				
Over 250	1.0	56.6	41.9	41.9
100–250	5.4	41.4	23.2	65.1
75–100	5.8	33.9	9.1	74.2
50–75	13.7	24.4	11.2	85.4
25–50	31.1	14.0	8.7	94.1
15–25	19.1	10.4	3.7	97.8
Under 15	23.9	3.4	2.3	100.0
Total	100.0	15.2	100.0	
Stock in pension plans[b]				
Over 250	1.0	65.0	17.5	17.5
100–250	5.4	61.7	31.3	48.8
75–100	5.8	58.9	14.8	63.6
50–75	13.7	50.8	18.1	81.7
25–50	31.1	35.1	14.3	96.0
15–25	19.1	16.8	3.1	99.1
Under 15	23.9	3.2	0.9	100.0
Total	100.0	29.2	100.0	
All stock[c]				
Over 250	1.0	84.6	28.0	28.0
100–250	5.4	80.7	26.2	54.2
75–100	5.8	75.6	11.9	66.1
50–75	13.7	63.7	14.6	80.7
25–50	31.1	47.7	13.0	93.7
15–25	19.1	28.1	4.6	98.3
Under 15	23.9	7.9	1.7	100.0
Total	100.0	40.4	100.0	

[a] Constant 1995 dollars.
[b] All defined contribution stock plans including 401(k) plans.
[c] All stock directly or indirectly held in mutual funds, IRAs, or Keogh plans and defined contribution pension plans.
Source: Unpublished analysis of SCF data by Wolff, compiled and elaborated by Mishel et al. (1999)

Appendix B:

Methodological Note and Statistical References for the Analysis of Employment and Occupational Structure of G-7 Countries, 1920–2005

Three sets of statistics have been compiled to illustrate the development of the service and information sectors. Data have been collected for seven countries (Canada, France, Germany, Italy, Japan, the United Kingdom, and the United States) beginning from the 1920s up to the most recently available date. The following describes each set of statistics compiled for this exercise.

Percentage distribution of employment by industrial sector and intermediate industry group

Employment statistics by industry have been compiled for seven countries. Industries are classified into six industrial sectors and 37 intermediate industry groups, according to the classification developed and used by Singelmann (1978). The six industrial sectors are:

I   Extractive
II   Transformative
III   Distributive services
IV   Producer services
V   Social services
VI   Personal services

Within each sector, two to eight intermediate industry groups are included, as shown in table A4.1. Employment statistics with detailed industrial breakdown, from national census or statistical abstracts, have been aggregated and reclassified into these categories.

Instead of reconstructing the database from the 1920s, we chose to

Table A.4.1   Classification of industrial sectors and intermediate industry groups

I Extractive	V Social services
Agriculture	Medical, health services
Mining	Hospital
II Transformative	Education
Construction	Welfare, religious services
Utilities	Nonprofit organizations
Manufacturing	Postal service
Food	Government
Textiles	Miscellaneous social services
Metal	VI Personal services
Machinery	Domestic services
Chemicals	Hotel
Miscellaneous manufacturing	Eating, drinking places
III Distributive services	Repair services
Transportation	Laundry
Communication	Barber, beauty shops
Wholesale	Entertainment
Retail	Miscellaneous personal services
IV Producer services	
Banking	
Insurance	
Real estate	
Engineering	
Accounting	
Miscellaneous business services	
Legal services	

Source: Singelmann (1978)

build upon Singelmann's work by extending his database beyond 1970. We put the best possible effort into making our classification of industries identical to that used by Singelmann, so that the database would be comparable in time series.

For the purpose of clarification, table A4.2 shows the industrial breakdown we used in updating the employment distribution by industry. The table lists all detailed industrial categories included in each intermediate industrial group for the seven countries. Any major variations from other countries concerning the classification is noted in each statistical table produced. For all countries, figures that represent annual averages of the number of employed persons (including self-employed, nonsalaried employees) by industry have been used for this analysis.

Note that the sectoral categories (categories I through VI) do not take into account detailed industries which may be included in an-

Table A4.2 Classification of industries by countries

	Canada	France	Germany	Italy	Japan	United Kingdom	United States
Agriculture	Agriculture, forestry, fishing, trapping	Agriculture, forestry, fisheries	Agriculture, forestry, fisheries, gardening	Agriculture, forestry, fisheries	Agriculture, forestry fisheries	Agriculture, forestry, fishing	Agriculture, forestry, fisheries
Mining	Mining, quarries oil wells	Solid mineral extraction/coking	Coal mining, ore mining, petroleum/gas extraction	Extraction of combustible solids, liquids	Mining	Coal extraction, solid fuels, electricity/gas	Metal, coal mining, crude petroleum and natural gas extraction
Construction	Construction	Building/civil engineering/ agricole	Construction	Construction	Construction	Construction	Construction
Food	Food/beverage, tobacco	Food, meat/milk	Food, beverage, tobacco	Food, beverage, tobacco	Food, beverage, tobacco, feed	Food, drink, tobacco	Food/kindred prods, tobacco manufactures
Textiles	Textiles, knitting mills	Textiles, clothing	Textiles	Textiles	Textiles	Textiles	Textile mill prods
Metal	Primary metal, metal fabricating	Ferrous metals, steel, construction materials, foundry	Foundry, metal, steel	Nonferrous metal, fabricated metal, foundry	Nonferrous metal, fabricated metal, iron/steel	Metal, nonmetallic mineral prods	Primary metal, fabricated metal
Machinery	Machinery, electrical products	Machinery, electric/electronic prods, household appliances	Machinery, electrical, office equipment	Machinery, electrical/ electronics machinery	Machinery, electrical/ electronic products	Mechanical engineering, data-processing equip., electrical/electronic engineering	Machinery, electrical machinery
Chemical	Chemical petroleum/coal products	Basic chemical/artificial fibers, pharmaceutical	Chemical/fibers	Chemical	Basic chemical, petroleum/coal prods	Chemical/man-made fibers	Chemical/allied prods, petroleum/coal prods
Miscellaneous manufacturing	Rubber/plastic, leather, clothing, wood, furniture/fixtures, paper, printing/ publishing, transp. equipment, nonmetallic mineral products, misc. manufacturing	Automobiles, ships/aerospace/ military mfg, apparel, misc. mfg, wood, plastic, glass, paper/ printing/ publishing, shoe/ leather prods	Stone/clay, rubber, transport equip., aircraft/ shipbldg, wood, plastic, glass, paper, printing/ publishing, leather, music instr., clothing	Leather, transport equip., clothing/ footwear, paper/ printing/ publishing, rubber/plastic, misc. mfg	Apparel/other fabric prods, transp. equip., precision instr., misc. mfg, lumber/wood/ furniture, plastic, rubber, pulp/ paper, printing/ publishing, leather/fur, ceramic/stone/ clay prods	Motor vehicle/ parts, other transp. equip., instrument engineering, footwear/clothing, timber/wood furniture/paper/ printing/publishing, rubber/plastics, other mfg	Transportation equip., apparel, prof. photographic equipment/watches, toys/sporting goods, lumber/wood, furniture/fixtures, stone/clay/glass, paper, publishing/printing, rubber/plastic, leather, misc. mfg

Utilities	Electric power, gas, water utilities	Electricity production/distrib., gas/water distrib.	Electricity, gas, water supply	Electricity, gas, water	Electricity distr., water/gas/heat supply	Gas/electricity/ water	Utilities/sanitary serv.
Transportation	Transportation, storage	Transport	Railways, water transport	Railways, air transport	Railways, road passenger/freight, water/air, auto. rel. serv., parking	Railways, other inland transport, sea, air transport, supporting serv.	Railroads, bus/urban transit, taxicab trucking, water/air transp., warehousing
Communication	Communications	Telecommunications/ postal services	Communications, postal services	Communications	Communication	Communications/ postal services	Communications, broadcasting
Wholesale	Wholesale trade	Food wholesale, non-food wholesale	Wholesale	Wholesale	Wholesale, warehousing	Wholesale	Wholesale trade
Retail	Retail trade	Food retail, non-food retail, auto repair/sales	Retail	Retail	Retail	Retail	Retail trade
Banking	Banks, credit agencies, security brokers/dealers	Financial organizations	Financial institutions	Financial institutions, securities	Financing/ insurance	Banking/finance	Banking, S&L, credit agencies, security brokerage
Insurance	Insurance carriers/ agencies/real estate	Insurance	Insurance	Insurance	Insurance	Insurance, except social security	Insurance
Real estate	n.a.	Real estate rental/ finance	Real estate, rental	Real estate	Real estate	Owning/dealing real estate	Real estate, real estate insurance law offices
Engineering	Engineering/ scientific services	n.a.	Technical consulting	Technical services	Civil engineering, architecture	n.a.	Engineering/ architectural/survey
Accounting	Accountants	n.a.	n.a.	Accounting	Accounting	Accounting	Accounting/auditing
Misc. business services	Services to business management	Services to enterprises	Legal/accounting/ other business services	Other business services, renting	Goods rental/ leasing, info. serv./research/ advertising, professional serv.	Business services, renting of movables	Advertising, commercial R&D, personnel supply serv., bus. mgmt consulting, computer serv., detective serv., bus. serv.
Legal services	Office of lawyers/ notaries	n.a.	n.a.	Legal	Legal services	Legal	Legal serv.

	Canada	France	Germany	Italy	Japan	United Kingdom	United States
Medical, health services	Office of physicians/surgeons, paramedical, dentists, etc.	n.a.	Health/veterinary	Health services, veterinary	Medical/health serv., public health serv.	Medical/other health serv., sanitary serv.	Health serv. except hospitals
Hospital	Hospitals	n.a.	n.a.	Hospitals	Hospitals	n.a.	Hospitals
Education	Education and related services	n.a.	Education, science/research institutions	Education, research, museums, botanical/zoological gardens	Education, science research institutions	Education, research and development	Schools, libraries, vocational schools, educational serv.
Welfare, religious services	Welfare, religious organizations	n.a	Social serv./employment offices	Religious organizations	Welfare/social insurance, religion	Other serv. incl. social welfare	Religious organizations
Nonprofit organizations	Labor organizations, trade associations	n.a.	Nonprofit organizations	Economic org., professional associations	Co-ops, pol./bus./cultural organizations	n.a.	Membership organizations
Postal service	n.a.	n.a	n.a.	Postal services	n.a.	n.a.	Postal serv.
Government	Public administration defense	n.a	Public administration	Public administration, armed forces, international organizations	National gov't serv., local gov't serv., foreign gov'ts/int'l org.	Public administration and defense	Public administration, defense, justice, public order
Misc. social services	Miscellaneous services	n.a.	Trash removal, residential institutions	Other social services	Waste treatment, other services	Other professional/scientific services	Misc. prof. and related serv.
Domestic services	Private households	n.a.	Private households	Domestic services	Domestic services	n.a.	Private households
Hotel	Hotels/motels lodging houses/residential clubs, camping grounds	Hotels/cafés/restaurants	Hotels/restaurants	Hotels (with or without restaurants)	Hotels/lodging places	Hotels/catering (restaurants, cafés, clubs/canteens)	Hotels/motels, lodging places
Eating, drinking places	Restaurants/caterers/taverns	n.a.	n.a.	Restaurants, camping	Eating/drinking places	Restaurants/cafés/snack bars	Eating/drinking pl.

Repair services	Repair of shoe, auto, jewelry electrical appliance	n.a.	Auto/bicycle repair	Repair	Repair services	Repair of consumer goods/vehicles	Auto, electrical, misc. repair
Laundry	Laundries/cleaners/presser, self-service laundries	n.a.	Laundry/cleaning	Laundry	Laundry	Laundry/dry cleaning	Laundry/cleaning
Barber, beauty shops	Barber/beauty shops	n.a.	Barber/body care businesses	Barber/beauty shops	Barber/beauty shops	Hairdressing/manicure	Beauty shops, barber shops
Entertainment	Amusement/recreational services	n.a.	Culture/sports/entertainment	Entertainment, cinema, broadcasting, sports	Motion pictures, recreation, broadcasting, amusement	Recreation/cultural services	Entertainment, theaters/movies, bowling alleys/billiard/pool places
Misc. personal services	Funeral services misc. personal services	All for-profit personal services	Other personal services	Cemetery administration	Misc. personal services	Personal services	Funeral service/crematories

other sector. For instance, when a country's statistics include eating and drinking places in retail services, but cannot be disaggregated due to the lack of detailed breakdown, the percentage for distributive services (III) becomes overestimated and personal services (VI) becomes underestimated. As a result, proportions for certain industrial sectors may be inflated or deflated.

Also, priority was given to comparability across countries rather than to strict breakdown of detailed industry by our classification. This was done to avoid assigning industries to different categories in each country, which would have disturbed the comparability of the shares of employment in the large categories (I through VI). This was due to the fact that data from some countries combined various sectors and we were unable to disaggregate them. For instance, many countries regarded paper, printing and publishing as one sector, and we have allocated it to miscellaneous manufacturing, although it was theoretically favorable to consider publishing as business services. As a result, we have allocated publishing statistics from all countries under miscellaneous manufacturing, even those countries which provide disaggregated data on publishing, in order to maintain cross-national comparability.

For the same reasons, the following industries are allotted to the following detailed categories.

- products that are made from textiles or fabrics, including apparel, shoes, and clothing are classified as "miscellaneous manufacturing;"
- transport equipment (including automobile, shipbuilding and aerospace industry products) are classified under "miscellaneous manufacturing;"
- scientific equipment, including optical, photography, and precision instruments are classified under "miscellaneous manufacturing;"
- printing and publishing are classified under "miscellaneous manufacturing;"
- depending on the breakdown available in each country, broadcasting (radio and TV) is classified under either "communication" or "entertainment;"
- miscellaneous professional and related services may be classified in any miscellaneous services, depending on the country. After carefully analyzing the data and finding some further disaggregated data, "other professional services" was classified as "business services" for Japan. For the United States, it was classified as "miscellaneous social services."

In addition, the following specificities should be noted for the countries studied.

Canada

The 1971 figures are based on the census data for persons 15 years and over who worked in 1970. The 1981 figures are based on the 20 percent sample data from the 1981 census on the labor force 15 years and over. Due to the unavailability of the breakdown of the labor force in detailed industry from the results of the 1991 census as of November 1992, we have used the latest statistics available (May 1992) from Statistics Canada, published in the monthly report, *The Labour Force*. The figures are derived from the sample of about 62,000 representative households across the country (excluding the Yukon and Northwest Territories). The survey was designed to represent all persons in the population 15 years of age and over residing in the provinces of Canada, with the exception of the following: persons living on Indian reserves; full-time members of the armed forces; and people living in institutions (that is, inmates of penal institutions and patients in hospitals or nursing homes who have resided in the institution for more than six months). The 1992 figures reflect the labor force in May 1992, and have been based on the 1980 Standard Industrial Classification since 1984 (Statistics Canada, 1992).

France

Figures are based on the employed population on December 31 of every year, published in the annual statistical abstract. The 1989 figures are preliminary. Problems have been encountered due to the general lack of detailed breakdown of statistics on service sector employment. Whenever a detailed breakdown of service industries is unavailable, the category "not-for-profit services" is classified as miscellaneous social services, and "for-profit services" is classified as miscellaneous personal services. However, the data from the annual statistical abstract was used instead of the census data since the most recent results currently available to us from the census are those of 1982.

Germany

In this analysis we used the former Federal Republic of Germany prior to unification as a unit of analysis. The figures are based on the census data on the employed for 1970 and 1987. No census was conducted in Germany between these years.

Italy

Figures are based on the census data on labor force in 1971 and 1981; 1990 figures may not be directly comparable to the data in earlier years due to the difference in sources. Since the 1991 census figures were not available at the time of our analysis, the 1990 figures were used as a rough indicator of recent trends.

Japan

Figures are based on the census data from October 1970, 1980, and 1990 on employed persons 15 years of age and over. The 1970 and 1980 figures are that of a 20 percent sample tabulation, and the 1990 figures are that of a 1 percent sample tabulation.

United Kingdom

Figures for England and Wales are used for the years between 1921 and 1971. From 1971 onwards, figures for employees in employment for the whole of the United Kingdom in June every year are used. These figures are chosen in preference to the census data on employed persons due to the unavailability of 1991 census results at the time of our analysis, and the 1971 and 1981 figures available to us do not include the entire United Kingdom. In addition, careful comparisons of the census data on the employed and the Department of Employment data on employees in employment for Great Britain revealed that differences are minor in terms of employment distribution.[152] Thus we have decided that the employees-in-employment figures would serve as a rough estimate of the trends in the United Kingdom between 1970 and 1990. These figures exclude private domestic servants and a small number of employees of agricultural machinery contractors but include seasonal and temporary workers. Family workers are included in the figures for Great Britain but not for Northern Ireland. The figures on the employees in employment also excludes the self-employed. The figures are from censuses of employment conducted in Great Britain by the Department of Employment and for the United Kingdom include information from similar censuses conducted in Northern Ireland by the Department of Manpower Services.

---

152   There is a tendency, however, for share of agricultural employment to be estimated lower than that of the entire employed population, as shown in table 4.16.

United States

The detailed breakdown of employment from the current population survey for 1970 was not published in the *Employment and Earnings* issues. Thus we have substituted the 1970 data with that of the census, since the intercensal statistics provided by the current population survey are, in general, designed to be comparable with the decennial statistics (see p. vii of 1970 census, volume 2: 7B, Subject Reports: Industrial Characteristics). The US figures are based on all civilians who, during the survey week, did any work at all as paid employees, in their own business, profession, or on their own farm, or who worked 15 hours or more as unpaid workers in an enterprise operated by a member of a family; and all those who were not working but who had jobs or businesses from which they were temporarily absent because of illness, bad weather, vacation, labor–management disputes, or personal reasons, whether they were paid for the time off or were working in other jobs. Members of the armed forces stationed in the United States are also included in the employed total. Each employed person is counted only once. Those who held more than one job are counted in the job at which they worked the greatest number of hours during the survey week. Included in the total are employed citizens of foreign countries who are temporarily in the United States but not living on the premises of an embassy. Excluded are persons whose only activity consisted of work around the house (painting, repairing, or own-home housework) or volunteer work for religious, charitable, and similar organizations (Department of Labor Statistics 1992). Due to the reclassification of the SIC codes for the 1980 census, figures before and after that date may not be strictly comparable.

Employment statistics by industry

Hall proposes two ways of dividing employment sectors: industry versus services, and goods handling versus information handling (Hall 1988). "Industry" includes all mining, construction, and manufacturing sectors, and "services"' includes all remaining categories. "Goods handling" sector includes mining, construction, manufacturing, transportation, wholesale/retail trade; "Information handling" sector includes communications, finance, insurance and real estate (FIRE), all remaining services and government.

In our analysis, employment statistics with Singelmann's classification have been aggregated and reorganized to fit into Hall's classification.[153] Further, the ratio between services and industry employment, as well as the ratio between information handling and goods handling employment, have been derived from the data used in tables 4.8 through 4.14.

Employment by occupations

Standard occupational classifications of most countries habitually confuse sectoral activities with skill levels, and thus are unfavorable for our use. However, after careful consideration based on the available data from the countries, it became clear that a reconfiguration of occupational classifications would be a major project by itself. Since our primary purpose in this appendix excludes such analysis, we decided to use the existing classification as a rough indicator for the occupational breakdown of these countries. As a result, the following rough breakdown of occupations has been determined:

- managerial
- professional
- technicians
- sales
- clerical
- crafts and operators
- semi-skilled service workers
- semi-skilled transport workers
- farm workers and managers

For most countries, it was impossible to separate professional and technician categories. Also, in some countries, craft workers and operators are mixed, thus we have collapsed these categories into one in order to avoid misleading conclusions from the data. The same applies to the collapse of farm workers and farm managers into one category. "Crafts and operators" also includes laborers, handlers, and miners. Those categorized as service workers have been included in semi-skilled service workers.

The specificity for each country is described as follows:

Canada

Figures are based on the occupational classification of the employed. Professional and technician categories also includes those whose pro-

---

153   In order to comply with the standard classification of services, eating and drinking places are included in retail trade.

fessions are in natural science, social science, teaching, medicine/health and artistic/recreational. Crafts and operators category also includes mining/quarrying, machining, processing, construction trades, materials handling, and other crafts/equipment operating. Farm workers and managers also includes agriculture, fishing/hunting/trapping and forestry/logging.

France

Figures are based on the occupational classification of the population aged 15 years and over, excluding unemployed, retired, students, and others who have never worked, according to employment surveys, the results of which are included in the statistical abstract. Managerial category also includes high-level public officials and high-level administrative/commercial workers in business enterprises. Professional category includes professors/scientific occupations, information/art, and engineers/technical workers. Technicians includes intermediate professions, workers in religion, and social/health mid-level workers. Clerical category includes civil servants and administrative workers. Crafts and operators category includes qualified and unqualified workers in industries.

Germany

Figures are based on the occupational classification of the employed persons, according to the statistical abstract. Managerial category includes accountants, public officials, and entrepreneurs. Professional category includes engineers, scientists, artists, and health service workers. Crafts and operators includes most industrial workers. Technicians includes social workers. Farm workers and managers category includes workers in forestry and fisheries.

Japan

Figures are based on the occupational classification of employed persons, according to Labour Force Survey, the results of which are included in the statistical abstract. Farm workers and managers includes workers in forestry and fisheries. Semi-skilled service workers category also includes protective service workers. Semi-skilled transport workers includes communications occupations.

United Kingdom

Figures are based on the 10 percent sample of Great Britain, derived from the censuses. Professional category includes judges, economists, environmental health officers, etc. Technicians includes estimators, welfare occupations, medical technicians, draughtsmen, foremen, tracers, supervisors of tracers, and technician engineers. Crafts and operators includes most industrial workers. Semi-skilled transport workers includes warehousemen/storekeepers/packers/bottlers. Semi-skilled service workers includes sport/recreation workers and protective services. The 1990 figures are based on the Labour Force Survey (1990 and 1991) conducted by the Office of Censuses and Surveys. The 1990 figures are not directly comparable to previous years due to the different survey methodology and categories employed. However, since the 1991 census data were not available at the time of this analysis, the 1990 figures provide a rough estimate of employment structure in Great Britain.

United States

Figures are based on the annual averages of employed persons according to the household survey, conducted as part of the Current Population Survey by the Bureau of the Census for the Department of Labor. Managerial category includes executive and administrative occupations. Clerical category includes administrative support. Semi-skilled service worker category includes private household and protective services. Crafts and operators category includes precision production, repair, machine operators/assemblers/inspectors, handlers, equipment cleaners, helpers, and laborers. Semi-skilled transport workers includes material-moving occupations. Farm workers and managers includes forestry and fishing.

Distribution of employment status

The status of employed persons are broadly categorized as employees, self-employed, and family workers. When figures for family workers are not available, they may be included within the self-employed categories. Self-employed generally include employers, unless otherwise noted.

The following lists the specificity for each country.

Canada

Those employers who are paid workers (rather than the self-employed) are included in the employees category.

France

Figures are based on civilian employment, indicated in OECD Labour Force Statistics.

Germany

Figures are based on the annual statistical abstract.

Italy

Figures are based on civilian employment, indicated in OECD Labour Force Statistics.

Japan

Figures are based on the Labour Force Survey on employed persons, included in the annual statistical abstract.

United Kingdom

Figures are based on civilian employment, indicated in OECD Labour Force Statistics.

United States

Figures are based on the annual averages of employed civilians in agriculture and non-agricultural industries.

Statistical references

Canada

Statistics Canada. *1971 Census of Canada*, vol. 3: *Economic Characteristics*, 1973.
—— *1981 Census of Canada: Population, Labor Force – Industry by demographic and educational characteristics, Canada, provinces, urban, rural, nonfarm and rural farm*, January 1984.

—— *The Labour Force*, various issues.
—— *Labour Force: Annual Averages, 1975–1983*, January 1984.

France

Institut national de la statistique et des études économiques (INSEE). *Annuaire statistique de la France 1979: résultats de 1978*, Ministère de l'économie, des finances et du budget, Paris: INSEE, 1979.
—— *Recensement général de la population de 1982: résultats définitifs*, par Pierre-Alain Audirac, no. 483 des Collections de l'INSEE, série D, no. 103, Ministère de l'économie, des finances et du budget, Paris: INSEE, 1985.
—— *Enquêtes sur l'emploi de 1982 et 1983: résultats redressés*, no. 120, February 1985.
—— *Enquêtes sur l'emploi de mars 1989: résultats détaillés*, no. 28–29, October 1989.
—— *Annuaire statistique de la France 1990: résultats de 1989*, vol. 95, nouvelle série no. 37, Ministère de l'économie, des finances et du budget, Paris: INSEE, 1990.

Germany

Statistisches Bundesamt. *Statistisches Jahrbuch 1977: für die Bundesrepublik Deutschland*, Metzler-Poeschel Verlag Stuttgart, 1977.
—— *Statistisches Jahrbuch 1991: für die Bundesrepublik Deutschland*, Metzler-Poeschel Verlag Stuttgart, 1991.
—— *Bevölkerung und Kultur:Volkszählung vom 27. Mai 1970*, Heft 17, Erwerbstätige in wirtschaftlicher Gliederung nach Wochenarbeitszeit und weiterer Tätigkeit, Fachserie A, Stuttgart and Mainz: Verlag W. Kohlhammer.
—— *Volkszählung vom 25 Mai 1987*, Bevölkerung und Erwerbstätigkeit, Stuttgart: Metzler-Poeschel, 1989.

Italy

Istituto Centrale di Statistica. *10° Censimento Generale della Popolazione, 15 Ottobre 1961, Vol. IX: Dati Generali Riassuntivi*, Rome, 1969.
—— *11° Censimento Generale della Popolazione, 24 Ottobre,1971*, vol. VI: *Professioni e Attività Economiche*, Tomo 1: *Attività Economiche*, Rome, 1975.
—— *12° Censimento Generale della Popolazione, 25 Ottobre, 1981*, vol. II: *Dati sulle caratteristiche strutturali della popolazione e delle abitazioni*, Tomo 3: *Italia*, Rome, 1985.
Istituto Nazionale di Statistica (ISTAT). *Annuario Statistico Italiano*, edizione 1991.

Japan

Statistics Bureau, Management and Coordination Agency (1977) *Japan Statistical Yearbook*, Tokyo.
—— (1983) *Japan Statistical Yearbook*, Tokyo.
—— (1991) *Japan Statistical Yearbook*, Tokyo.
Bureau of Statistics, Office of the Prime Minister. *Summary of the Results of 1970 Population Census of Japan*, Tokyo: Bureau of Statistics, 1975.
—— *1980 Population Census of Japan*, Tokyo: Bureau of Statistics, 1980.
—— *1990 Population Census of Japan*, Prompt report (results of 1 percent sample tabulation), Tokyo: Bureau of Statistics, 1990.

United Kingdom

Office of Population Censuses and Surveys, General Registrar Office. *Census 1971: Great Britain, Economic Activity*, Part IV (10 percent Sample), London: HMSO, 1974.
—— *Census 1981: Economic Activity, Great Britain*, London: HMSO, 1984.
—— *Labour Force Survey 1990 and 1991: A Survey Conducted by OPCS and the Department of Economic Development in Northern Ireland on behalf of the Employment Department and the European Community*, Series LFS no. 9, London: HMSO, 1992.
Central Statistical Office. *Annual Abstract of Statistics: 1977*, London: HMSO, 1977.
—— *Annual Abstract of Statistics: 1985*, London: HMSO, 1985.
—— *Annual Abstract of Statistics: 1992*, no. 128, London: HMSO, 1992.
Department of Employment. *Employment Gazette* vol. 100, no. 8 (August 1992).

United States

United States Department of Labor. *Handbook of Labor Statistics*, Bulletin 2175, Bureau of Labor Statistics, December.
—— *Labor Force Statistics: Derived from the Current Population Survey, 1948–87*, Bureau of Labor Statistics, August 1988.
—— *Handbook of Labor Statistics*, Bulletin 2340, Bureau of Labor Statistics, March, 1990.
—— *Employment and Earnings*, various issues.

Other

Eurostat. *Labour Force Sample Survey*, Luxembourg: Eurostat, various issues.
—— *Labour Force Survey*, Theme 3, Series C, *Population and Social Statistics, Accounts, Surveys and Statistics*, Luxembourg: Eurostat, various issues.

Hall, Peter (1988) "Regions in the transition to the information economy," in G. Sternlieb and J.W. Hughes (eds), *America's New Market Geography: Nation, Region and Metropolis*, Rutgers, NJ: State University of New Jersey, Center for Urban Policy Research, New Brunswick, pp. 137–59.

Mori, K. (1989) *Hai-teku shakai to rōdō: naniga okite iruka*, Iwanami Shinsho no. 70, Tokyo: Iwanami Shoten.

Organization for Economic Cooperation and Development (OECD) (1991) *OECD Labour Force Statistics: 1969–1989*, Paris: OECD.

—— (1992a) *OECD Economic Outlook: Historical Statistics: 1960–90*, Paris: OECD.

—— (1992b) *OECD Economic Outlook*, no. 51, June.

5

The Culture of Real Virtuality: the Integration of Electronic Communication, the End of the Mass Audience, and the Rise of Interactive Networks

Around 700BC a major invention took place in Greece: the alphabet. This conceptual technology, it has been argued by leading classics scholars such as Havelock, was the foundation for the development of Western philosophy and science as we know it today. It made it possible to bridge the gap from spoken tongue to language, thus separating the spoken from the speaker, and making possible conceptual discourse. This historical turning point was prepared for by about 3,000 years of evolution in oral tradition and non-alphabetic communication, until Greek society reached what Havelock calls a new state of mind, "the alphabetic mind," which prompted the qualitative transformation of human communication.[1] Widespread literacy did not occur until many centuries later, after the invention and diffusion of the printing press and the manufacturing of paper. Yet it was the alphabet that, in the

1 Havelock (1982: esp. 6–7).

West, provided the mental infrastructure for cumulative, knowledge-based communication.

However, the new alphabetic order, while allowing rational discourse, separated written communication from the audiovisual system of symbols and perceptions, so critical for the fully fledged expression of the human mind. By implicitly and explicitly establishing a social hierarchy between literate culture and audiovisual expression, the price paid for the foundation of human practice in the written discourse was to relegate the world of sounds and images to the backstage of the arts, dealing with the private domain of emotions and with the public world of liturgy. Of course, audiovisual culture took an historical revenge in the twentieth century, first with film and radio, then with television, overwhelming the influence of written communication in the hearts and souls of most people. Indeed, this tension between noble, alphabetic communication and sensorial, non-reflective communication underlies the intellectuals' frustration with the influence of television that still dominates the social critique of mass media.[2]

A technological transformation of similar historic dimensions is taking place 2,700 years later, namely the integration of various modes of communication into an interactive network. Or, in other words, the formation of a hypertext and a meta-language which, for the first time in history, integrate into the same system the written, oral, and audiovisual modalities of human communication. The human spirit reunites its dimensions in a new interaction between the two sides of the brain, machines, and social contexts. For all the science fiction ideology and commercial hype surrounding the emergence of the so-called "information superhighway," we can hardly underestimate its significance.[3] The potential integration of text, images, and sounds in the same system, interacting from multiple points, in chosen time (real or delayed) along a global network, in conditions of open and affordable access, does fundamentally change the character of communication. And communication decisively shapes culture, because, as Postman writes, "we do not see . . . reality . . . as 'it' is, but as our languages are. And our languages are our media. Our media are our metaphors. Our

2   For a critical presentation of these ideas, see Postman (1985).
3   For a documented exposition of technological trends in advanced communication systems, see Sullivan-Trainor (1994); Conseil d'Etat (1998); Dutton (1999); Owen (1999). For a political economic overview of the issues discussed in this chapter, see Schiller (1999). For a scholarly synthesis of the main findings of research on the media, see Croteau and Haynes (2000). For a worldwide perspective on the evolution of communication, with emphasis on new communication technologies, see UNESCO (1999). For an insightful theoretical elaboration, see De Kerckhove (1997).

metaphors create the content of our culture."[4] Because culture is mediated and enacted through communication, cultures themselves – that is, our historically produced systems of beliefs and codes – become fundamentally transformed, and will be more so over time, by the new technological system. At the time of writing, such a new system is not fully in place, and its development will occur at an uneven pace and with uneven geography in the coming years. Yet it is a certainty that it will develop and embrace at least the dominant activities and the core segments of the population of the whole planet. Furthermore, it already exists in bits and pieces, in the new media system, in the rapidly changing telecommunications systems, in the networks of interaction already formed around the Internet, in the imagination of people, in the policies of governments, and on the drawing boards of corporate offices. The emergence of a new electronic communication system characterized by its global reach, its integration of all communication media, and its potential interactivity is changing and will change forever our culture. However, the issue arises of the actual conditions, characteristics, and effects of such change. Given the still embryonic development of an otherwise clearly identified trend, how can we assess its potential impact without falling into the excesses of futurology from which this book tries to depart sharply? On the other hand, without analyzing the transformation of cultures under the new electronic communication system, the overall analysis of the information society would be fundamentally flawed. Fortunately, while there is technological discontinuity, there is in history a great deal of social continuity that allows analysis of tendencies on the basis of the observation of trends that have prepared the formation of the new system over the past two decades. Indeed, one of the major components of the new communication system, the mass media of communication, structured around television, have been studied in minute detail.[5] Their evolution toward globalization and decentralization was foreseen in the early 1960s by McLuhan, the great visionary who revolutionized thinking in communications in spite of his unrestrained use of hyperbole.[6] In this chapter I shall first retrace the formation of the mass media, and their interplay with culture and social behavior. Then I shall assess their transformation during the 1980s, with the emergence of decentralized and diversified "new media" which prepared the formation of a multi-media system in the 1990s. I shall later turn my attention to a

4   Postman (1985: 15).
5   See the evolution of media research synthesized in Williams et al. (1988).
6   For a retrospective of McLuhan's theories, see his posthumous book: McLuhan and Powers (1989).

different system of communication, organized around computer networking, with the emergence of the Internet and the surprising, spontaneous development of new kinds of virtual communities. While this
is a relatively new phenomenon, we have enough empirical observations, both from France and from the United States, to formulate some
hypotheses on reasonable grounds. Finally, I shall try to bring together
what we know about the two systems to speculate on the social dimension of their coming merger, and the impact of such a merger on
the pro-cesses of communication and cultural expression. I argue that
through the powerful influence of the new communication system,
mediated by social interests, government policies, and business strategies, a new culture is emerging: the *culture of real virtuality*, whose
content, dynamics, and significance will be presented and analyzed in
the following pages.

From the Gutenberg Galaxy to the McLuhan Galaxy: the Rise of Mass Media Culture

The diffusion of television in the three decades following World War
II (in different times and with variable intensity depending on countries) created a new galaxy of communication, if I may use the
McLuhanian terminology.[7] Not that other media disappeared, but they
were restructured and reorganized in a system whose heart was made
of vacuum tubes and whose appealing face was a television screen.[8]
Radio lost its centrality but won in pervasiveness and flexibility, adapting modes and themes to the rhythm of people's everyday lives. Films
transformed themselves to fit television audiences, with the exceptions
of government-subsidized art and of special-effects shows on large
screens. Newspapers and magazines specialized in deepening their content or targeting their audience, while being attentive to providing
strategic information to the dominant TV medium.[9] As for books, they
remained books, although the unconscious desire behind many books
was to become a TV script; the best-sellers' lists soon became filled
with titles referring to TV characters or to TV-popularized themes.

   Why television became such a prevailing communication mode is
still the object of raging debate among scholars and media critics.[10] W.
Russell Neuman's hypothesis, which I would rephrase as being the

---

7 McLuhan (1964).
8 Ball-Rokeach and Cantor (1986).
9 Postman (1985).
10 Withey and Abeles (1980); Ferguson (1986).

consequence of the basic instinct of a lazy audience, seems to be a plausible explanation with regard to available evidence. In his own words: "The key finding from the realm of research on educational and advertising effects that must be dealt with candidly if we are to understand the nature of low-salience learning in regard to politics and culture is simply that people are attracted to the path of least resistance."[11] He grounds his interpretation in the broader psychological theories by Herbert Simon and Anthony Downs, emphasizing the psychological costs of obtaining and processing information. I would be inclined to place the roots of such logic not in human nature, but in the conditions of home life after long days of strenuous work, and in the lack of alternatives for personal/cultural involvement.[12] Yet social conditions in our societies being as they are, the minimum-effort syndrome that seems to be associated with TV-mediated communication could explain the rapidity and pervasiveness of its dominance as a communication medium as soon as it appeared on the historical scene.[13] For instance, according to media studies,[14] only a small proportion of people choose in advance the program they will view. In general, the first decision is to watch television, then programs are scanned until the most attractive is selected or, more often, the least boring.

The TV-dominated system could be easily characterized as mass media.[15] A similar message was simultaneously emitted from a few centralized senders to an audience of millions of receivers. Thus, the content and format of messages were tailored to the lowest common denominator. In the case of private TV, predominant in the original TV country, the US, it was the lowest common denominator of the audience as evaluated by marketing experts. For most of the world, dominated by government television until at least the 1980s, the standard was the lowest common denominator in the minds of bureaucrats in control of broadcasting, although increasingly audience ratings played a role. In both cases, the audience was seen as largely homogeneous, or susceptible to being made homogeneous.[16] The notion of mass culture, arising from mass society, was a direct expression of the media system resulting from the control of new electronic communication technology by governments and corporate oligopolies.[17]

11   Neuman (1991: 103).
12   Mattelart and Stourdze (1982); Trejo Delarbre (1992).
13   Owen (1999).
14   Neuman (1991).
15   Blumler and Katz (1974).
16   Botein and Rice (1980).
17   Neuman (1991).

What was fundamentally new in television? The novelty was not so much its centralizing power and its potential as a propaganda instrument. After all, Hitler showed how radio could be a formidable instrument of resonance for one-way single-purpose messages. What TV represented, first of all, was the end of the Gutenberg Galaxy – that is, of a system of communication essentially dominated by the typographic mind and the phonetic alphabet order.[18] For all his critics (generally turned off by the obscurity of his mosaic language), Marshall McLuhan struck a universal chord when, in all simplicity, he declared that the "medium is the message":

> The mode of TV image has nothing in common with film or photo, except that it offers also a nonverbal gestalt or posture of forms. With TV, the viewer is the screen. He is bombarded with light impulses that James Joyce called "The Charge of the Light Brigade". . . The TV image is not a still shot. It is not a photo in any sense, but a ceaselessly forming contour of things limned by the scanning-finger. The resulting plastic contour appears by light through, not light on, and the image so formed has the quality of sculptures and icon, rather than a picture. The TV image offers some three million dots per second to the receiver. From these he accepts only a few dozen each instant, from which to make an image.[19]

Because of the low definition of TV, McLuhan argued, viewers have to fill in the gaps in the image, thus becoming more emotionally involved in the viewing (what he, paradoxically, characterized as a "cool medium"). Such involvement does not contradict the hypothesis of the least effort because TV appeals to the associative/lyrical mind, not involving the psychological effort of information retrieving and analyzing to which Herbert Simon's theory refers. This is why Neil Postman, a leading media scholar, considers that television represents an historical rupture with the typographic mind. While print favors systematic exposition, TV is best suited to casual conversation. To make the distinction sharply, in his own words: "Typography has the strongest possible bias towards exposition: a sophisticated ability to think conceptually, deductively and sequentially; a high valuation of reason and order; an abhorrence of contradiction; a large capacity for detachment and objectivity; and a tolerance for delayed response."[20] While for television, "entertainment is the supra-ideology of all discourse on television. No matter what is depicted or from what point

18   McLuhan (1962).
19   McLuhan (1964: 313).
20   Postman (1985: 87).

of view, the overarching presumption is that it is there for our amusement and pleasure."[21] Beyond the discrepancies in the social/political implications of this analysis, from McLuhan's belief about the universal communitarian potential of television to the Luddite attitudes of Jerry Mander[22] and some of the critics of mass culture,[23] the diagnoses converge toward two fundamental points: a few years after its development television became the cultural epicenter of our societies;[24] and the television modality of communication is a fundamentally new medium, characterized by its seductiveness, its sensorial simulation of reality, and its easy communicability along the lines of least psychological effort.

Led by television, there has been in the past three decades a communication explosion throughout the world.[25] In the most TV-oriented country, the United States, in the late 1980s TV presented 3,600 images per minute per channel. According to the Nielsen report, the average American home had the TV set on for about seven hours a day, and actual viewing was estimated at 4.5 hours daily per adult. To this had to be added radio, which offered 100 words per minute and was listened to an average of two hours a day, mainly in the car. An average daily newspaper offered 150,000 words, and it was estimated to take between 18 and 49 minutes of daily reading time, while magazines were browsed over for about 6–30 minutes, and book reading, including schoolwork-related books, took about 18 minutes per day.[26] Media exposure is cumulative. According to some studies, US homes with cable TV watch more network TV than homes without cable. All in all, the average adult American uses 6.43 hours a day in media attention.[27] This figure can be contrasted (although in rigor it is not comparable) to other data which give the figure of 14 minutes per day and per person for interpersonal interaction in the household.[28] In Japan in 1992, the weekly average of television watching time per household was 8 hours and 17 minutes per day, up by 25 minutes from 1980.[29] Other countries seem to be less intensive consumers of media: for example, in the late 1980s French adults watched TV only about three hours a day.[30] Still, the predominant pattern of behavior

21 Postman(1985: 87).
22 Mander (1978).
23 Mankiewicz and Swerdlow (1979).
24 See Williams (1974); Martin and Chaudhary (1983).
25 Williams (1982).
26 Data from various sources, reported by Neuman (1991).
27 Data reported by Sabbah (1985); Neuman (1991).
28 Sabbah (1985).
29 Dentsu Institute for Human Studies/DataFlow International (1994: 67).
30 Neuman (1991); for Japan, see Sato et al. (1995).

around the world seems to be that in urban societies media consumption is the second largest category of activity after work, and certainly the predominant activity at home.[31] This observation must, however, be qualified to truly understand the role of media in our culture: media watching/listening is by no means an exclusive activity. It is generally mixed with the performance of home tasks, with shared meals, with social interaction. It is the almost constant background presence, the fabric of our lives. We live with the media and by the media. McLuhan used the expression of technological media as staples or natural resources.[32] Rather, the media, particularly radio and television, have become the audiovisual environment with which we interact endlessly and automatically. Very often television, above all, is a presence in the home. A precious feature in a society where increasing numbers of people live alone: in the 1990s, 25 percent of American households were formed by one single person. Although the situation is not so extreme in other societies, the trend toward decreasing size of households is similar in Europe.

This pervasive, powerful presence of such subliminally provoking messages of sounds and images could be assumed to produce dramatic impacts on social behavior. Yet most available research points to the opposite conclusion. After reviewing the literature, W. Russell Neuman concludes that "the accumulated findings from five decades of systematic social science research reveal that mass media audience, youthful or otherwise, is not helpless, and the media are not all-powerful. The evolving theory of modest and conditional media effects helps to put in perspective the historical cycle of moral panic over new media."[33] Furthermore, the barrage of advertising messages received through the media seems to have limited effect. According to Draper,[34] although in the US the average person is exposed to 1,600 advertising messages per day, people respond (and not necessarily positively) to only about 12 of them. Indeed, McGuire,[35] after reviewing accumulated evidence on the effects of media advertising, concluded that there is no substantial evidence of specific impacts by media advertising on actual behavior, an ironic conclusion for an industry that spent at that time US$50 billion a year. Why, then, do companies keep insisting on advertising? For one thing, companies pass on the cost of advertising to consumers: according to *The Economist* in 1993,

---

31   Sorlin (1994).
32   McLuhan (1964: 21).
33   Neuman (1991: 87).
34   Roger Draper, "The Faithless Shepard," *New York Review of Books*, June 26, reported by Neuman (1991).
35   McGuire (1986).

"free TV" in the US cost every American household $30 per month. Yet a substantive answer to such an important question requires that we first analyze the mechanisms through which television and other media influence behavior.

The key issue is that while mass media are a one-way communication system, the actual process of communication is not, but depends on the interaction between the sender and the receiver in the interpretation of the message. Researchers have found evidence of the significance of what they call the "active audience." In the words of Croteau and Haynes, "there are three basic ways in which media audiences have been seen as active: through individual interpretation of media products, through collective interpretation of media, and through collective political action."[36] And they go on to provide a wealth of data and illustrations to support their claim of the relative autonomy of the audience *vis à vis* messages received from the media. Indeed, this is a well-established tradition in media studies. Thus, Umberto Eco provided an insightful perspective to interpret media effects in his 1977 seminal paper titled "Does the Audience have Bad Effects on Television?" As Eco wrote:

> There exist, depending on sociocultural circumstances, a variety of codes, or rather of rules of competence and interpretation. The message has a signifying form that can be filled with different meanings . . . So the suspicion grew that the sender organized the televisual image on the basis of his own codes, which coincided with those of the dominant ideology, while the addressees filled it with "aberrant" meanings according to their particular cultural codes.[37]

The consequence of this analysis is that: "One thing we do know is that there doesn't exist a Mass Culture in the sense imagined by the apocalyptic critics of mass communications because this model competes with others (constituted by historical vestiges, class culture, aspects of high culture transmitted through education etc.)."[38] While historians and empirical researchers of the media would find this statement pure common sense, in fact, taking it seriously, as I do, it decisively undermines a fundamental aspect of critical social theory from Marcuse to Habermas. It is one of the ironies of intellectual history that it is precisely those thinkers who advocate social change who often view people as passive receptacles of ideological manipulation,

---

36 Croteau and Haynes (2000: 263).
37 Eco (1977: 90).
38 Eco (1977: 98).

in fact precluding the notions of social movements and social change except under the mode of exceptional, singular events generated outside the social system. If people have some level of autonomy in organizing and deciding their behavior, the messages sent through the media should interact with their receivers, and thus the notion of mass media refers to a technological system, not to a form of culture, the mass culture. Indeed, some experiments in psychology found that even if TV presents 3,600 images per minute per channel, the brain responds consciously to only one sensory stimulus among each million stimuli being sent.[39]

Yet to emphasize the autonomy of the human mind and of individual cultural systems in filling in the actual meaning of the messages received does not imply that the media are neutral institutions, or that their effects are negligible. What empirical studies show is that the media are not independent variables in inducing behavior. Their messages, explicit or subliminal, are worked out, processed by individuals placed in specific social contexts, thus modifying what was the intended effect of the message. But the media, and particularly audiovisual media in our culture, are indeed the basic material of communication processes. We live in a media environment, and most of our symbolic stimuli come from the media. Furthermore, as Cecilia Tichi has shown in her wonderful book *The Electronic Hearth*,[40] the diffusion of television took place in a television environment; that is, a culture in which objects and symbols are referred to television, from the shapes of home furniture to acting styles and themes of conversation. The real power of television, as Eco and Postman have also argued, is that it sets the stage for all processes that intend to be communicated to society at large, from politics to business, including sports and art. Television frames the language of societal communication. If advertisers keep spending billions in spite of reasonable doubts about the actual direct impact of advertising on their sales, it may be because an absence of television usually means conceding name recognition in the mass market to those competitors who do advertise. While the effects of television on political choices is highly diverse, politics and politicians who are not on television in advanced societies simply do not stand a chance of obtaining people's support, since people's minds are informed fundamentally by the media, with television being foremost among such media.[41] The social impact of television works in the binary mode: to be or not to be. Once a message is on television, it can be changed, transformed, or even subverted. But in a society

39   Neuman (1991: 91).
40   Tichi (1991).
41   Lichtenberg (1990).

organized around mass media, the existence of messages that are out-side the media is restricted to interpersonal networks, thus disappear-ing from the collective mind. However, the price to be paid for a message to be on television is not just money or power. It is to accept being mixed in a multi-semantic text whose syntax is extremely lax. Thus, information and entertainment, education and propaganda, relaxa-tion and hypnosis are all blurred in the language of television. Because the context of the viewing is controllable and familiar to the receiver, all messages are absorbed into the reassuring mode of the home or quasi-home situation (for instance, sports bars as one of the few real extended families left . . .).

This normalization of messages, where atrocious images of real war can almost be absorbed as part of action movies, does have a funda-mental impact: the leveling of all content into each person's frame of images. Thus, because they are the symbolic fabric of our life, the media tend to work on consciousness and behavior as real experience works on dreams, providing the raw material out of which our brain works. It is as if the world of visual dreams (the information/enter-tainment provided by television) would give back to our conscious-ness the power to select, recombine, and interpret the images and sounds that we have generated through our collective practices or by our in-dividual preferences. It is a system of feedbacks between distorting mirrors: the media are the expression of our culture, and our culture works primarily through the materials provided by the media. In this fundamental sense, the mass media system fulfilled most of the feat-ures suggested by McLuhan in the early 1960s: it was the McLuhan Galaxy.[42] Yet the fact that the audience is not a passive object but an interactive subject opened the way to its differentiation, and to the subsequent transformation of the media from mass communication to segmentation, customization and individualization, from the moment technology, corporations, and institutions allowed such moves.

The New Media and the Diversification of Mass Audience

During the 1980s new technologies transformed the world of media.[43] Newspapers were written, edited, and printed at a distance, allowing

42   I label the mass media electronic communication system the McLuhan Galaxy in hom-age to the revolutionary thinker who visualized its existence as a distinctive mode of cogni-tive expression. It should be emphasized, however, that we are entering a new communication system, clearly distinct from the one McLuhan envisaged, as this chapter tries to argue.
43   This section relies partly on the information and ideas on new developments in the

for simultaneous editions of the same newspaper tailored to several major areas (for example, *Le Figaro* in several French cities; *The New York Times* in parallel East Coast/West Coast editions; *International Herald Tribune*, printed daily in several locations in three continents, and so on). Walkman devices made personally selected music a portable audio environment, allowing people, particularly teenagers, to build walls of sounds against the outside world. Radio became increasingly specialized, with thematic and sub-thematic stations (such as 24–hour easy-listening music or exclusive dedication to a singer or pop group for several months until the new hit comes in). Radio's hosted talk-shows filled the time of commuters and flexible workers. VCRs exploded all over the world and became in many developing countries a major alternative to boring, official television broadcasting.[44] Although the multiplicity of potential uses of VCRs were not fully exploited because of lack of consumers' technological skills, and because of rapid commercialization of its use by video rental stores, their diffusion provided a great deal of flexibility to the use of visual media. Films survived in the form of video-cassettes. Music video, accounting for over 25 percent of total video production, became a new cultural form that shaped the images of a whole generation of youth, and actually changed the music industry. The ability to record TV programs and watch them at selected times changed the habits of TV audiences and reinforced their selective viewing, counteracting the pattern of least resistance that I discussed above. On the basis of VCRs, any future diversification of television offerings was amplified in its effects by the second-step choice of the recording audience, further segmenting it.

People started to tape their own events, from vacation to family celebrations, thus producing their own images beyond the photo album. For all the limits of this self-production of images, it actually modified the one-way flow of images and reintegrated life experience and the screen. In many countries, from Andalusia to southern India, local community video technology allowed for the blossoming of rudimentary local broadcasting which mixed diffusion of video films with local events and announcements, often on the fringes of communications regulations.

But the decisive move was the multiplication of television channels,

---

media worldwide provided by Manuel Campo Vidal, leading television journalist in Spain and Latin America, vice-president of Antena-3 Television; see Campo Vidal (1996). For projections on these trends elaborated in the academic world during the 1980s, see also Rogers (1986). For a visionary analysis of media diversification in an historical perspective, I recall de Sola Pool (1983).

44   Alvarado (1988).

leading to their increasing diversification.[45] Development of cable television technologies, fostered in the 1990s by fiber-optics and digitization, and of direct satellite broadcasting, dramatically expanded the spectrum of transmission and put pressure on the authorities to deregulate communications in general and television in particular. An explosion of cable television programming followed in the United States and of satellite television in Europe, Asia, and Latin America. Soon, new networks were formed that came to challenge the established ones, and in Europe governments lost control of much of television. In the US the number of independent TV stations grew during the 1980s from 62 to 330. Cable systems in major metropolitan areas feature up to 60 channels, mixing network TV, independent stations, cable networks, most of them specialized, and pay TV. In the countries of the European Union, the number of TV networks increased from 40 in 1980 to 150 by the mid-1990s, one-third of them being satellite broadcasted. In Japan, the NHK public network has two terrestrial networks and two specialized satellite services; in addition there are five commercial networks. From 1980 to the mid-1990s, the number of satellite-TV stations grew from 0 to 300.

According to UNESCO, in 1992 there were over 1 billion TV sets in the world (35 percent of which were in Europe, 32 percent in Asia, 20 percent in North America, 8 percent in Latin America, 4 percent in the Middle East, and 1 percent in Africa). Ownership of TV sets was expected to grow at 5 percent per year up to the year 2000, with Asia leading the charge. The impact of such a proliferation of television offerings on the audience was deep in all contexts. In the US, while the three major networks controlled 90 percent of prime-time audience in 1980, their share went down to 65 percent in 1990, and the trend has accelerated since: it was at about 60 percent in 1995, and went down to about 55 percent in 1999. CNN established itself as the major global news producer worldwide to the point that in emergency situations in countries around the world politicians and journalists alike turn on CNN full time. Direct satellite television is making a major penetration of the Asian market, broadcasting from Hong Kong to the whole Asian Pacific. Indian media are being increasingly globalized.[46] Hubbard Communications and Hughes Corporation launched in 1994 two competing direct satellite broadcasting systems that sell 'à la carte' almost any program from anywhere to anywhere in the US, the Asian Pacific, and Latin America. Chinese communities in the US can watch daily Hong Kong news while Chinese in China may have access to

45   Doyle (1992); Dentsu Institute for Human Studies/DataFlow International (1994).
46   Chatterjee (forthcoming).

American soap operas (*Falcon Crest* recorded 450 million viewers in China). Thus, as Françoise Sabbah wrote in 1985, in one of the best and earliest assessments of new trends in the media:

> In sum, the new media determine a segmented, differentiated audience that, although massive in terms of numbers, is no longer a mass audience in terms of simultaneity and uniformity of the message it receives. The new media are no longer mass media in the traditional sense of sending a limited number of messages to a homogeneous mass audience. Because of the multiplicity of messages and sources, the audience itself becomes more selective. The targeted audience tends to choose its messages, so deepening its segmentation, enhancing the individual relationship between sender and receiver.[47]

Youichi Ito, analyzing the evolution of media uses in Japan, has also concluded that there is evolution from a mass society to a "segmented society" (*bunshu shakai*), as a result of new communication technologies which focus on diversified, specialized information, so that the audience becomes increasingly segmented by ideologies, values, tastes, and lifestyles.[48]

Thus, because of the diversity of media and the possibility of targeting the audience, we can say that in the new media system, the message is the medium. That is, the characteristics of the message will shape the characteristics of the medium. For instance, if feeding the musical environment of teenagers is the message (a very explicit one), MTV will be tailored to the rites and language of this audience, not only in the content but in the whole organization of the station and in the technology and design of image production/broadcasting. Or, again, to produce a 24–hour world news service requires a different setting, programming, and broadcasting, such as weather report shows of global and continental scope. This is indeed the present and future of television: decentralization, diversification, and customization. Within the broader parameters of the McLuhanian language, the message of the medium (still operating as such) is shaping different media for different messages.

Yet diversification of messages and media expressions does not imply loss of control by major corporations and governments over television. Indeed, it is the opposite trend that has been observed during the past decade.[49] Investment has poured into the communications field,

---

47   Sabbah (1985: 219).
48   Ito (1991b).
49   See, for instance, data cited in *The Economist* (1994a); also Trejo Delarbre (1988); Doyle (1992); Campo Vidal (1996).

as mega-groups have been formed and strategic alliances have been established to carve out market shares in a market in complete transformation. In the period 1980–95, the three major US TV networks changed ownership, two of them twice: the merger of Disney and ABC in 1995 was a turning point in integrating TV into the emerging multimedia business. TF1, the leading French channel was privatized. Berlusconi took control of all private TV stations in Italy, organizing them in three private networks. Private television flourished in Spain, with the development of three private networks, and made significant inroads in the UK and in Germany, always under the control of powerful financial groups, both national and international. Russian television became diversified, including private, "independent" television channels, controlled by rival oligarchs. Latin American television experienced a process of concentration around a few major players. The Asian Pacific became the most hotly contested terrain for new television mavericks, such as Murdoch's Star channel, as well as for "old television hands" such as the new, global BBC, pitted in competition against CNN. In Japan, the government's NHK was joined in competition by private networks: Fuji TV, NTV, TBS, TV Asahi, and TV Tokyo, as well as by cable and direct satellite broadcasting operations. In 1993–5, about US$80 billion were spent on television programming worldwide, and spending was rising by 10 percent a year. In the late 1990s, mergers and strategic alliances continued to characterize the media industry, as companies tried to use economies of scale to find synergies between different segments of the communications market.[50] Figure 5.1 shows the level of concentration of business for the ten largest multimedia groups in the world, and figure 5.2. shows the complex pattern of interlinkages between various media groups in the European market in 1998.[51] While the profile of the industry will undoubtedly change in the coming years, the logic of networking and competitive partnerships is likely to characterize the multimedia world for a long time. Indeed, the web of alliances and the strategies of competition will be even more complex, as media firms come into cooperation and conflict with telecommunication operators, cable operators, satellite operators, and Internet service providers.

The net result of this business competition and concentration is that while the audience has been segmented and diversified, television has become more commercialized than ever, and increasingly oligopolistic at the global level. The actual content of most programming is not substantially different from one network to the other, if we consider

50   Schiller (1999).
51   See figures in *The Economist* (1999c: 62).

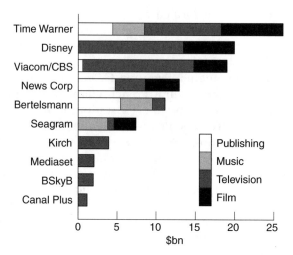

Figure 5.1 Media sales in 1998 for major media groups (in billions of US dollars)
(*Author's note*: In January 2000, Time Warner merged with the Internet service provider America On-Line, forming the largest multimedia group in the world)
Sources: Company reports; Veronis, Suhler and Associates; Zenith Media; Warburg Dillon Read, elaborated by *The Economist* (1999c: 62)

the underlying semantic formulae of most popular programs as a whole. Yet the fact that not everybody watches the same thing at the same time, and that each culture and social group has a specific relationship to the media system, does make a fundamental difference *vis-à-vis* the old system of standardized mass media. In addition, the widespread practice of "surfing" (simultaneously watching several programs) allows the audience to create its own visual mosaics. While the media have become indeed globally interconnected, and programs and messages circulate in the global network, *we are not living in a global village, but in customized cottages globally produced and locally distributed.*

However, the diversification of the media, because of the conditions of their corporate and institutional control, did not transform the unidirectional logic of their message, nor truly allow the audience's feedback except in the most primitive form of market reaction. While the audience received more and more diverse raw material from which to construct each person's own image of the universe, the McLuhan Galaxy was a world of one-way communication, not of interaction. It was, and still is, the extension of mass production, industrial logic

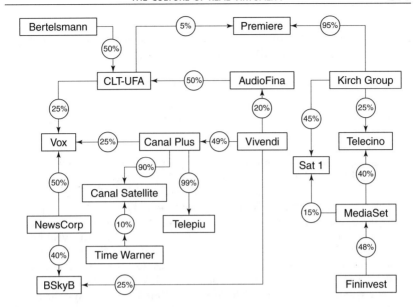

Figure 5.2 Strategic alliances between media groups in Europe, 1999
Source: Warburg Dillon Read, elaborated by *The Economist* (1999c: 62)

into the realm of signs, and it fell short, McLuhan's genius notwithstanding, of expressing the culture of the Information Age. This is because information processing goes far beyond one-way communication. Television needed the computer to be free from the screen. But their coupling, with major potential consequences for society at large, came after a long detour taken by computers in order to be able to talk to television only after learning to talk to each other. Only then could the audience speak up.

Computer-mediated Communication, Institutional Control, Social Networks, and Virtual Communities

History will recall that the two first large-scale experiments of what Ithiel de Sola Pool labeled "technologies of freedom" were induced by the state: the French Minitel, as a device to steer France into the information society; and the American ARPANET, predecessor of the Internet, as a military strategy to enable communication networks to survive a nuclear attack aimed at destroying the command and control centers. They were very different, both being deeply rooted in the culture and institutions of their respective societies. Leo Scheer has highlighted their contrasting logic in a synthetic view of each system's features:

> Both announced the information superhighways, but their differences are full of lessons. First of all, Internet links up computers while Minitel links, via Transpac, server centers that can be questioned by terminals with low capacity of memory. Internet is an American initiative of world-wide scope, initiated, with military support, by computer companies, financed by the American government, to create a world club of computer users and data banks. Minitel is a French system that, until now [1994] could never go beyond its national boundaries because of [foreign] regulatory constraints. It is the product of the boldest imagination from high level state technocrats in their effort to remedy the weakness of French electronic industries. On the side of Internet: the random topology of local networks of computer fanatics. On the side of Minitel: the orderly arrangement of the telephone book. Internet: an anarchic tariff system of uncontrollable services. Minitel: a kiosk system that allows for homogeneous tariffs and a transparent sharing of revenues. On the one hand, the uprooting and the phantasm of generalized connections beyond boundaries and cultures; on the other hand, the electronic version of communal roots.[52]

The comparative analysis of the development of these two systems, in relation to their social and institutional environments, helps to shed some light on the characteristics of the emerging, interactive communication system.[53]

The Minitel story: l'état et l'amour

Teletel, the network feeding Minitel terminals, is a videotex system designed in 1978 by the French Telephone Company and introduced to the market in 1984, after years of localized experiments. The earliest and largest of such systems in the world, in spite of its primitive technology, almost unchanged for 15 years, it won a wide acceptance among French households and grew to phenomenal proportions. By the mid-1990s, it was offering 23,000 services, and billing FFr7 billion to 6.5 million Minitel terminals in service, being used in one out of four French households and by one-third of the adult population.[54]

---

52   Scheer (1994: 97–8), my translation.
53   Case (1994).
54   Myers (1981); Lehman (1994); Thery (1994).

This success is particularly striking when contrasted to the general failure of videotex systems such as Prestel in Britain and Germany, and Japan's Captain, and to the limited receptivity to Minitel or other videotex networks in the United States.[55] Such success came in spite of very limited video and transmission technology: thus, until the early 1990s it transmitted at 1,200 baud speed, to be compared with typical computer information services at the same time in the US operating at 9,600 bauds.[56] Behind the success of Minitel lie two fundamental reasons: the first was the commitment of the French government to the experiment as an element of the challenge presented by the Nora–Minc report on the "informatization of society" prepared in 1978 at the request of the prime minister.[57] The second was the simplicity of its use, and the straightforwardness of its kiosk billing system which made it accessible and trustworthy to the average citizen.[58] Still, people needed an extra incentive to use it and this is the most revealing part of the Minitel story.[59]

The government's commitment, through French Telecom, was spectacularly shown in the launching of the program: each household was given the option of the delivery of a free Minitel terminal in place of the usual telephone book. Furthermore, the telephone company subsidized the system until it broke even for the first time in 1995. It was a way of stimulating telecommunications usage, creating a captive market for the troubled French electronics industry and, above all, inducing familiarity with the new medium for both companies and people.[60] However, the most intelligent strategy from French Telecom was to open the system wide to private providers of services, and first of all to French newspapers, which quickly became the defenders and popularizers of Minitel.[61]

But there was a second, major reason for the widespread use of Minitel: the appropriation of the medium by the French people for their personal expression. The first services provided by Minitel were the same as were available via traditional telephone communication: telephone directory, weather reports, transportation information and reservations, advance purchase of tickets for entertainment and cultural events, and so on. As the system and people became more sophisticated, and thousands of providers of services came on line, advertising,

55 McGowan and Compaine (1989).
56 Rosenbaum (1992); Preston (1994); Thery (1994).
57 Nora and Minc (1978).
58 McGowan (1988).
59 Mehta (1993).
60 For a comprehensive analysis of the policy that led to the development of Minitel, see Cats-Baril and Jelassi (1994).
61 Preston (1994).

tele-shopping, tele-banking, and various business services were offered through Minitel. Yet the social impact of Minitel was limited in the early stages of its development.[62] In terms of volume, the telephone directory accounted for over 40 percent of total calls; in terms of value, in 1988 36 percent of Minitel revenues came from 2 percent of its users, which were businesses.[63] The system caught fire with the introduction of chat-lines or *messageries*, most of which quickly specialized in sex offerings or in sex-related conversations (*les messageries roses*), which by 1990 accounted for more than half of the calls.[64] Some of these services were commercial porno-electronic conversations, equivalent to the phone sex so pervasive in other societies. The main difference was the accessibility of such services over the videotex network, and their massive advertising in public places. But most of the erotic uses of Minitel were initiated by people themselves over the general-purpose chat-lines. Yet there was not a generalized sex bazaar, but a democratized sexual fantasy. More often than not (source: author's participant observation), the on-line exchanges were based on impersonation of ages, genders, and physical characteristics, so that Minitel became the vehicle of sexual and personal dreams rather than the substitute for pick-up bars. This infatuation with the intimate use of Minitel was critical to ensure its rapid diffusion among the French people, in spite of the solemn protests of prudish puritans. By the early 1990s, the erotic uses of Minitel dwindled down, as the fashion faded away, and the rudimentary character of the technology limited its sex appeal: chat-lines came to account for less than 10 percent of the traffic.[65] Once the system was fully settled, the fastest growing services in the 1990s were developed by businesses for their internal use, with the highest growth being that of high value-added services, such as legal services, accounting for over 30 percent of the traffic.[66] Yet the hooking-up of a substantial proportion of the French people to the system needed the detour through their personal psyche, and the partial fulfillment of their communication needs, at least for a while.

When in the 1990s Minitel emphasized its role as service provider, it also made evident its built-in limitations as a means of communication.[67] Technologically, it was relying on ages-old video and transmission technology whose overhaul would end its basic appeal as a free electronic device. Furthermore, it was not based on personal comput-

62 Mehta (1993).
63 Honigsbaum (1988).
64 Maital (1991); Rheingold (1993).
65 Wilson (1991).
66 Wilson (1991).
67 Dalloz and Portnoff (1994).

ing but, by and large, on dumb terminals, thus substantially limiting autonomous capacity for information processing. Institutionally, its architecture, organized around a hierarchy of server networks, with little capacity for horizontal communication, was too inflexible for a society as culturally sophisticated as France, once new realms of communication were available beyond Minitel. The obvious solution adopted by the French system was to offer the option, at a price, of linking up with the Internet worldwide. In so doing, Minitel became internally split between a bureaucratic information service, a networked system of business services, and the tributary gateway to the vast communication system of the Internet constellation.

The Internet constellation

The Internet (whose process of formation I analyzed in chapter 1) is the backbone of global computer-mediated communication (CMC): it is the network that links up most computer networks. According to sources collected and elaborated by Vinton Cerf, in June 1999 the Internet connected about 63 million computer hosts, 950 million telephone terminations, five million level 2 domains, 3.6 million web sites, and was used by 179 million people in more than 200 countries. United States and Canada accounted for over 102 million users, Europe for over 40 million, Asia and the Asian Pacific for almost 27 million, Latin America for 23.3 million, Africa for 1.14 million and the Middle East for 0.88 million. Projections in mid-1999 were for growth in the number of connected hosts to almost 123 million by 2001 and to 878 million in 2007 (see figure 5.3), and for users to reach a number somewhere between 300 million and 1 billion by December 2000.[68] Some analysts think Cerf's figures, because of Cerf's customary caution, may underestimate the diffusion of the Internet in 1999/2000.[69] My own personal guess is that the number of users will be in the vicinity of 700 million by mid-2001. This is to be compared with the Internet's size in earlier stages of development: in 1973, there were 25 computers in the network; through the 1970s, it could only support 256 computers; in the early 1980s, after substantial enhancement, it was still limited to about 25 networks with only a few hundred primary computers and a few thousand users.[70] In terms of users, two surveys in August and November 1995 estimated the number of users in the United States at

68　Cerf (1999).
69　Zook (2000c).
70　Hafner and Markoff (1991); *Business Week* (1994a); Sullivan-Trainor (1994); *El Pais/ World Media* (1995); McLeod (1996).

Figure 5.3 Internet hosts, 1989–2006 (in thousands)
The figures (in thousands) for each year were as follows: 1989: 157;
1990: 376; 1991: 727; 1992: 1,313; 1993: 2,217; 1994: 5,846; 1995:
14,352; 1996: 21,819; 1997: 29,670; 1998: 43,230; 1999: 62,987; 2000:
91,774; 2001: 122,717; 2002: 194,830; 2003: 283,872; 2004: 413,610;
2005: 602,641; 2006: 878,065
Source: Cerf (1999)

9.5 million and at 24 million.[71] This means that in just four years the
number of Internet users in North America increased by a factor of
either 10.7 or 4.25. Since network connections tend to increase their
rate of growth with the expansion of the network (see chapter 1), the
notion of 1 billion computer hosts connected via the Internet and well
over 2 billion Internet users before 2010 does not appear to be far-
fetched. Indeed, in computer-mediated communication the sky is not
the limit: in 1999, Vinton Cerf, one of the fathers of ARPANET, then
of the Internet, was advising NASA on the design of an interplanetary
Internet backbone, which included the possibility of a manned Mars
station by 2030, and the ultimate wish upon a star: a stable interplanetary Internet backbone by 2040.[72] Down to earth, the Internet,

71   For documented and intelligent analyses of the origins, development, and characteristics of the Internet and other CMC networks, see Hart et al. (1992); Rheingold (1993). For
an empirical study of the growth of the Internet, see Batty and Barr (1994). For a discussion
of Internet's prospects, see a study by the Rand Corporation available only on-line at the
time of writing: Rand Corporation (1995).
72   Cerf (1999).

in its different incarnations and unfolding manifestations, is already the universal, interactive computer communication medium of the Information Age.[73]

There are, however, important inequalities in the Internet. Considering data from various sources around 1998–2000, industrialized countries, with about 15 percent of the population of the planet, accounted for 88 percent of Internet users. There was considerable regional disparity in the diffusion of the Internet. While only 2.4 percent of world population had access to Internet, the percentage was 28 percent in Finland (the most Internet-oriented society in the world at the turn of the century), 26.3 percent in the US, and 6.9 percent in OECD countries, excluding the United States. Within countries, social, racial, gender, age, and spatial inequality in Internet access was substantial. Worldwide, 30 percent of Internet users had a university degree, and the proportion increased to 55 percent in Russia, 67 percent in Mexico, and 90 percent in China. In Latin America, 90 percent of Internet users came from upper income groups. In China only 7 percent of Internet users were women. Age was a major discriminating factor. The average age of Internet users in the US was 36 years, and in the UK and in China was below 30. In Russia, only 15 percent of Internet users were older than 45. In the United States, households with income of $75,000 and higher were 20 times more likely to have Internet access than those at the lowest level of income. People with a four-year college degree had a usage rate of 61.6 percent, while the rate for those with elementary education or less was just 6.6 percent. Men accessed the Internet more than women, by three percentage points. African-American and Hispanics were one-third as likely to have access to the Internet as Asians, and two-fifths as likely as whites. Gaps in Internet access between white and Hispanic households and whites and African-American households were six percentage points larger in December 1998 than in December 1994. However, for Americans with incomes higher than $75,000 the racial gap considerably narrowed in 1998, thus pointing to income and education, rather than race *per se*, as the sources of inequality. Spatial inequality in Internet access is one of the most striking paradoxes of the Information Age, given the supposedly placeless characteristic of the technology. Yet, the pioneering work of Matthew Zook provides evidence of the high concentration of commercial Internet domains in some metropolitan hubs (see figures 5.4–5.7).[74] In the US, controlling by income, urban residents were more than twice as likely to have Internet access as

---

73   Kahn (1999).
74   Zook (2000c).

Figure 5.4 Internet CONE and country code domain names by city worldwide, July 1999 (represents 8,766,072 Internet domain names)

Note: The maps in figures 5.4–5.7 show the location of registration addresses for domain names such as nytimes.com or nokia.com mapped to the city level. The methodology for obtaining and mapping domain names is outlined in Zook (2000a, b). These maps include two types of domain name: (a) CONE (.com, .ord, .net, and .edu) top-level domains (TLDs) originally designed to be used by businesses, non-profit organizations, computer networks, and educational institutions; and (b) country code (CC) TLDs, such as ".de" for Germany and ".jp" for Japan, which were for Internet use in their respective countries. Due to the enormous number of CONE domains, the July 1999 data are based on a randomly selected 4 percent sample of CONE domain names.
Source: Zook (2000c)

Figure 5.5 Internet CONE and country code domain names by city in North America, July 1999 (combined, the United States and Canada contain 60.1 percent of the world's domains) (see figure 5.4 for further explanation of map)
Source: Zook (2000c)

Cities.shp

. 175–10,175
· 10,175–34,900
● 34,900–87,475
● 87,475–204,900
● 204,900–553,325

0   500   1000   1500 miles

Cities.shp

• 175–10,175
• 10,175–34,900
● 34,900–87,475
● 87,475–204,900
● 204,900–553,325

0   500   1000 miles

Figure 5.6 Internet CONE and country code domain names by city in Europe, July 1999 (Europe contains 25.1 percent of the world's domains) (see figure 5.4 for further explanation of map)
Source: Zook (2000c)

Figure 5.7 Internet CONE and country code domain names by city in Asia, July 1999 (see figure 5.4 for further explanation of map)
Source: Zook (2000c)

rural residents – another counterintuitive finding that rejects the popular image of rural life in cyberspace. In Russia, in 1998 50 percent of Internet users were in Moscow, and over 75 percent were concentrated in the three largest cities (Moscow, St Petersburg, and Yekaterinburg), in spite of the communication needs of a population scattered in a vast territory.[75]

On the other hand, the rate of diffusion of the Internet in 1999 was so high everywhere that it was clear that widespread access would be the norm in the advanced countries in the early years of the twenty-first century. For instance, in the US, in 1997–8, the racial gap in Internet access did increase, but Internet access grew in one year by 48 percent for Hispanic households, and by 52 percent for African-American households, in comparison with 52.8 percent for white households. Indeed, among college students the racial and gender difference in the use of the Internet was disappearing by the end of the century. And in 2000, 95 percent of US public schools had access to the Internet, although only one-third of them had a technically competent staff able to train teachers and students in the uses of the Internet. The Internet has posted the fastest rate of penetration of any communication medium in history: in the United States, the radio took 30 years to reach 60 million people; TV reached this level of diffusion in 15 years; the Internet did it in just three years after the development of the world wide web. The rest of the world is lagging behind North America and the developed countries, but Internet access and use were catching up rapidly in the main metropolitan centers in all continents.[76] Yet, it is not unimport-ant who had earlier access, and to what, because, unlike television, Internet consumers are also its producers, by providing content, and shaping the web. Thus the vastly unequal arrival time of societies into the Internet constellation will have lasting consequences on the future pattern of the world's communication and culture.[77]

Millions of computer networks exist today around the world, covering the whole spectrum of human communication, from politics and religion to sex and research – with e-commerce as the centerpiece of the contemporary Internet.[78] By the turn of the century, the large majority of these networks were connected to the Internet, but they were keeping their own identity and enforcing their own rules of behavior. And a growing share of the Internet was becoming, as I showed in chapter 2, a vast marketplace.

75   UNDP (1999); UNESCO (1999); US Department of Commerce (1999b); Castells and Kiselyova (2000); Zook (2000a).
76   See, for instance, Comision de nuevas tecnologias (1999).
77   Dutton (1999); UNESCO (1999).
78   Zook (2000b).

Yet the capacity of the network of networks (the Net) is such that a sizeable proportion of the communication taking place on the Internet is still largely spontaneous, unorganized, and diversified in purpose and membership. In fact, commercial and government interests co-incide in favoring the expanding use of the network: the greater the diversity of messages and participants, the higher the critical mass in the network, and the higher the value. The peaceful coexistence of various interests and cultures in the Net took the form of the world wide web (www), a flexible network of networks within the Internet where institutions, businesses, associations, and individuals create their own "sites," on the basis of which everybody with access can produce her/his/its "home page," made of a variable collage of text and images (see chapter 1).

The web allowed for groupings of interests and projects in the Net, overcoming the time-costly chaotic browsing of the pre-www Internet. On the basis of these groupings, individuals and organizations were able to interact meaningfully on what has become, literally, a world wide web of individualized, interactive communication.[79] The price to pay for such diverse and widespread participation is to let spontane-ous, informal communication flourish at the same time. The commer-cialization of cyberspace will be closer to the historical experience of merchant streets which sprout out from vibrant urban culture than to the shopping centers spread in the dullness of anonymous suburbs.

The two sources of the Net, the military/science establishment and the personal computing counterculture, did have a common ground: the university world. As I reported in chapter 1, the first ARPANET node was set up in 1969 at UCLA, and six other nodes were added in 1970–1 at UC Santa Barbara, SRI, University of Utah, BBN, MIT, and Harvard. From there, they spread primarily over the academic com-munity, with the exception of the internal networks of large electronic corporations. This university origin of the Net has been, and is, de-cisive for the development and diffusion of electronic communica-tion throughout the world. The large-scale initiation to computer-mediated communication in the United States took place among gradu-ate students and faculties of universities in the early 1990s. And a similar process took place only a few years later in the rest of the world. In Spain, in the mid-1990s the largest contingent of early "internetters" came from the computer networks built around the various universities in Madrid and Barcelona. In Russia, computer-mediated communication (CMC) appeared in the late 1980s as a semi-legal grass-roots movement from researchers in the institutes of the

79   Markoff (1995).

Academy of Sciences, and universities.The story seems to be the same around the world. This university-based process of diffusion is significant because it has the highest potential for spreading both the know-how and the habits of CMC. Indeed, contrary to the assumption of social isolation suggested by the image of the ivory tower, universities are major agents of diffusion of social innovation because generation after generation of young people go through them, becoming aware of and accustomed to new ways of thinking, managing, acting, and communicating. As CMC becomes pervasive in the university system on an international scale, the graduates that will take over companies and institutions in the early twenty-first century will bring with them the message of the new medium into the mainstream of society.

The process of the formation and diffusion of the Internet, and related CMC networks, in the last quarter of the century shaped for ever the structure of the new medium, in the architecture of the network, in the culture of the networkers, and in the actual patterns of communication.[80] The architecture of the network is, and will remain, technologically open, enabling widespread public access and seriously limiting governmental or commercial restrictions to such access, although social inequality will powerfully manifest itself in the electronic domain. This openness is the consequence, on the one hand, of the original design conceived partly for the above-mentioned military strategic reasons, partly because the scientists managing military research programs wanted to set up such a new system, both to show technological prowess and as a utopian endeavor. On the other hand, the openness of the system also results from the constant process of innovation and free accessibility enacted by early computer hackers and the network hobbyists who still populate the Net by the hundreds of thousands. For instance, in the late 1990s, the free diffusion over the Net of Linux software, designed by Linus Torvalds, a young, brilliant computer scientist at the University of Helsinki, to run on Unix Internet applications, posed a major challenge to Microsoft software domination. But the significant factor in the success of Linux was its relentless improvement as a result of the contribution of thousands of users, finding new uses, and perfecting the software, then posting their improvements on the Net, free of charge, thus reciprocating the technical gift they had received in the first place. This constant, multi-sided effort to improve the communicability of the network is a remarkable example of how the technological productivity of cooperation through the Net ended up enhancing the Net itself.[81]

80   De Kerckhove (1997).
81   Harmon (1999); Linus Torvalds (personal communication, 1999).

The culture of first-generation users, with its utopian, communal, and libertarian undercurrents, shaped the Net in two opposite directions. On the one hand, it tended to restrict access to a minority of computer hobbyists, the only people able and willing to spend time and energy living in cyberspace. From this era there remains a pioneering spirit that looks with distrust at the commercialization of the network, and watches with apprehension how the realization of the dream of generalized communication for the people brings with it the limits and misery of humankind as it is. But as the heroics of early computer tribes recedes under the relentless flow of "newbies," what remains from the countercultural origins of the network is the informality and self-directedness of communication, the idea that many contribute to many, and yet each one has her own voice and expects an individualized answer.[82] The multipersonalization of CMC does express to some extent the same tension that arose in the 1960s between the "me culture" and the communal dreams of each individual.[83] In fact, there are more bridges than communication experts usually acknowledge between the countercultural origins of CMC and the mainstream Internetters of today, as is shown by the business acceptance of *Wired* magazine, which was created as a countercultural outfit, but became the hottest expression of Internet culture and how-to advice in the mid-1990s.

Thus, in spite of all efforts to regulate, privatize, and commercialize the Internet and its tributary systems, CMC networks, inside and outside the Internet, are characterized by their pervasiveness, their multifaceted decentralization, and their flexibility. They sprawl as colonies of micro-organisms.[84] They will increasingly reflect commercial interests, as they will extend the controlling logic of major public and private organizations into the whole realm of communication. But unlike the mass media of the McLuhan Galaxy, they have technologically and culturally embedded properties of interactivity and individualization. However, do these potentialities translate into new patterns of communication? What are the cultural attributes emerging from the process of electronic interaction? Let us turn to an examination of the meager empirical record on this matter.

The interactive society

Internet-mediated communication is too recent a social phenomenon to have provided the opportunity for scholarly research to reach firm

---

82 Himannen (2001).
83 Gitlin (1987); Rand Corporation (1995).
84 To follow Rheingold's (1993) biological image.

conclusions on its social meaning. Moreover, the meager empirical record is still marked by the kind of questions arising in the pre-www era, that is before 1995, when computer-mediated communication was a small affair of a few hundreds of thousands of devoted users. This is particularly the case for the question that dominated the debate on the social dimensions of the Internet during the 1990s: does the Internet favor the development of new communities, virtual communities, or, instead, is it inducing personal isolation, severing people's ties with society, and ultimately, with their "real" world? Howard Rheingold, in his pioneering book *Virtual Communities* marked the tone of the debate by forcefully arguing for the birth of a new form of community, bringing people together on-line around shared values and interests.[85] Furthermore, on the basis of his own experience with WELL, a cooperative computer network in the San Francisco Bay area, he proposed the notion that communities built on-line could develop, as in his own case, into physical meetings, friendly parties, and material support for members of their virtual community. A virtual community, in line with Rheingold's argument, is generally understood as a self-defined electronic network of interactive communication organized around a shared interest or purpose, although sometimes communication becomes the goal in itself. Such communities may be relatively formalized, as in the case of hosted conferences or bulletin boards systems, or be spontaneously formed by social networks which keep logging into the network to send and retrieve messages in a chosen time pattern (either delayed or in real time). Tens of thousands of such "communities" were created throughout the world in the 1990s, most of them based in the US but increasingly reaching out on a global scale. It is, however, still unclear how much sociability is taking place in such electronic networks, and what are the cultural effects of such a new form of sociability, in spite of the efforts of a growing body of researchers.[86]

The legendary John Perry Barlow, rock singer, co-founder of the libertarian Electronic Frontier Foundation, Internet prophet, and champion of humanitarian causes, was hopeful that "we are now creating a space in which people of the planet can have [a new] kind of communication relationship: I want to be able to completely interact with the consciousness that's trying to communicate with me."[87] In a more scholarly approach, William Mitchell has convincingly argued that new forms of sociability, and new forms of urban life, adapted to our new

85 Rheingold (1993).
86 Rheingold (1993); Turkle (1995); Jones (1995, 1997, 1998); Kiesler (1997).
87 Barlow (1995: 40).

technological environment, are emerging on-line.[88] And in one of the first psychoanalytical studies of Internet users (actually of members of a Multi Users Dungeons group – MUDs) Sherry Turkle showed that, yes, users were playing roles and building identities on-line. But this did create a feeling of community, if ephemeral, and probably brought some solace to people in need of communication and self-expression. However, she concludes that "the notion of the real fights back. People who live parallel lives on the screen are nevertheless bound by the desires, pain, and mortality of their physical selves. Virtual communities offer a dramatic new context in which to think about human identity in the age of the Internet."[89]

On the other hand, social critics, such as Mark Slouka, have chastised the de-humanization of social relationships brought about by computers, as life on-line appears to be an easy way to escape real life.[90] And in France, Dominique Wolton, a respected sociologist, has called upon intellectuals to resist the dominant, technocratic ideology as embodied in the Internet.[91] Furthermore, rigorous, academic research seems to indicate that, under certain conditions, use of the Internet increases the chances of loneliness, feelings of alienation, or even depression. In a highly publicized study, a team of psychology researchers at Carnegie Mellon University examined the social and psychological impact of the Internet on social involvement and psychological well-being by measuring their behavior and attitudes during their first one or two years on-line, in 1995 and in 1996. In this sample, greater use of the Internet was associated with a decline in participants' communication with family members in the household, a decline in the size of their social circle, and an increase in their depression and loneliness.[92]

Trying to make sense of the confusing diversity of the record, the leading empirical researcher on the sociology of the Internet, Barry Wellman, and his collaborators analyzed, in a series of articles in 1996–9, the main findings concerning the emergence of virtual communities on the Internet, from a broad variety of sources.[93] Wellman's key point is to remind us that "virtual communities" do not have to be opposed to "physical communities": they are different forms of community, with specific rules and dynamics, which interact with other forms of community. Besides, too often, social critics refer implicitly to an idyllic notion of community, a tightly bounded, spatially defined, culture

88   Mitchell (1995, 1999).
89   Turkle (1995: 267).
90   Slouka (1995).
91   Wolton (1998).
92   Kraut et al. (1998).
93   Wellman et al. (1996); Wellman (1997); Wellman and Gulia (1999).

of support and belonging, which probably did not exist in rural societies, and which has certainly disappeared in advanced, industrialized
countries.[94] Instead, Wellman has shown in a stream of consistent findings over the years that what has emerged in advanced societies is
what he calls "personal communities": "an individual's social network
of informal, interpersonal ties, ranging from a half-dozen intimates to
hundreds of weaker ties. . . . Both group communities and personal
communities operate on-line as well as off-line."[95] In this perspective,
social networks substitute for communities, with locally based communities being one of the many possible alternatives for the creation
and maintenance of social networks, and the Internet providing another such alternative. With this in mind, what do we know of what is
happening on the Internet?

   Wellman and Gulia show that, as in physical personal networks,
most virtual community ties are specialized and diversified, as people
build their own "personal portfolios." Internet users join networks or
on-line groups on the basis of shared interests, and values, and since
they have multidimensional interests, so are their on-line memberships.
However, over time, many networks that start as instrumental and
specialized end up providing personal support, both material and af-
fective, as it was, for instance, in the case of the SeniorNet, for people
of old age, or the case of "Systers," a network of female computer
scientists. So, ultimately, Internet interaction seems to be both special-
ized/functional and broad/supportive, as interaction in the networks
broadens the scope of communication over time.

   A key distinction in the analysis of sociability is that between weak
ties and strong ties. The Net is particularly suited to the development
of multiple weak ties. Weak ties are useful in providing information
and opening up opportunities at a low cost. The advantage of the Net
is that it allows the forging of weak ties with strangers, in an egalitarian pattern of interaction where social characteristics are less influential in framing, or even blocking, communication. Indeed, off-line and
on-line, weak ties facilitate linking of people with different social
characteristics, thus expanding sociability beyond the socially defined
boundaries of self-recognition. In this sense, the Internet may contribute to expanding social bonds in a society that seems to be in the
process of rapid individualization and civic disengagement.[96] Virtual
communities seem to be stronger than observers usually give them
credit for. There is substantial evidence of reciprocal supportiveness

94   Castells (1972); Wellman (1979); Fischer (1982).
95   Wellman and Gulia (1999: 355).
96   Putnam (1995).

on the Net, even between users with weak ties to each other. In fact, on-line communication fosters uninhibited discussion, thus allowing sincerity in the process. The cost, however, is the high mortality rate of on-line friendships, as an unhappy sentence may be sanctioned by clicking away the connection – for ever.

As for the impact of Internet communication on physical intimacy and sociability, Wellman and collaborators consider that the fears of the impoverishment of social life are misplaced. They point to the fact that there is no zero-sum game, and that, in fact, in some of the networks they have studied, more Internet use leads to more social ties, including physical ties. Here again, pundits seem to be opposing sociability on the Internet to a mythical notion of a tight community-based society. Yet, "current research suggests that North Americans usually have more than one thousand inter-personal ties. Only half a dozen of them are intimate and no more than fifty are significantly strong. Yet, taken together a person's other 950+ ties are important sources of information, support, companionship and sense of belonging."[97] The Internet favors the expansion and intensity of these hundreds of weak ties that create a fundamental layer of social interaction for people living in a technologically developed world.

So, in the end, are virtual communities real communities? Yes and no. They are communities, but not physical ones, and they do not follow the same patterns of communication and interaction as physical communities do. But they are not "unreal," they work in a different plane of reality. They are interpersonal social networks, most of them based on weak ties, highly diversified and specialized, still able to generate reciprocity and support by the dynamics of sustained interaction. As Wellman puts it, they are not imitations of other forms of life, they have their own dynamics: the Net is the Net. They transcend distance, at low cost, they are usually of asynchronous nature, they combine the fast dissemination of mass media with the pervasiveness of personal communication, and they allow multiple memberships in partial communities. Besides, they do not exist in isolation of other forms of sociability. They reinforce the trend toward the "privatization of sociability" – that is, the rebuilding of social networks around the individual, the development of personal communities, both physically and on-line. Cyberlinks provide the opportunity of social links for people who, otherwise, will live more limited social lives, because their ties are increasingly spatially dispersed.

Furthermore, within the segment of regular users of CMC, it appears that the medium favors uninhibited communication and

97 Wellman and Gulia (1999: 350).

stimulates participation from lower-status workers in company-based networks.[98] Along the same line of argument, women, and other oppressed groups in society, seem to be more likely to express themselves openly through the protection of the electronic medium, although we must keep in mind that, as a whole, women were a minority of users up to 1999.[99] It seems as though the symbolism of power embedded in face-to-face communication has not yet found its language in the new CMC. Because of the historical newness of the medium and the relative improvement in the relative status of power for traditionally subordinated groups, such as women, CMC could offer a chance to reverse traditional power games in the communication process.

Shifting the analysis from the *users* to the *uses*, it must be emphasized that *the overwhelming proportion of CMC activity takes place at work or in work-related situations*. I have discussed in chapters 3 and 4 the critical importance of the computer medium for the new form of networked organization and for the specific labor conditions of the networkers. In the context of the present analysis of cultural impacts, what should be considered is the symbolic isomorphism in the processes of work, home, services, and entertainment in the new structure of communication. Is the relationship to the computer specific enough to connect work, home, and entertainment into the same system of symbol processing? Or, on the contrary, does the context determine the perception and uses of the medium? We do not have enough reliable research on the matter at this point, but some preliminary observations by Penny Gurstein[100] seem to indicate that while people using computers at home enjoy their self-reliance in the management of time and space, they resent the lack of distinct separation between work and leisure, family and business, personality and function. Alesia Montgomery, studying in 1998 the uses of the Internet in work situations, found that for her interviewees "their on-line access, skills and contacts seem shaped to some extent by their work spaces, and their on-line interactions primarily involve people they also see face-to-face: family, friends, and colleagues."[101] Nancy Baym, studying the emergence of an on-line community on the basis of her ethnographic study of r.a.t.s. (a news group discussing soap operas), analyzes the relationship between social contexts of on-line interaction and the meaning and content of on-line exchanges. She suggests that the "reality seems to be that many, probably most social users of CMC create

98   Sproull and Kiesler (1991); Rand Corporation (1995).
99   Hiltz and Turoff (1993); Sato et al. (1995), US Department of Commerce (1999).
100   Gurstein (1990).
101   Montgomery (1999: 15).

on-line selves consistent with their off-line identities."[102] Let us say, as a hypothesis, that the convergence of experience in the same medium blurs somewhat the institutional separation of domains of activity, and confuses codes of behavior.

Beyond the performance of professional tasks, the uses of CMC already reach the whole realm of social activity.[103] Tele-banking is being imposed upon customers by both incentives and penalties from the banks. On-line shopping is exploding, not in opposition to the shopping malls, but in connection with them, although some traditional stores (for example, bookstores, record stores, perhaps car dealers) will be either phased out or transformed by on-line competition. Universities are slowly but surely entering an era of articulation between personal interface and on-line teaching.[104] Personal communication by e-mail, the most usual CMC activity outside work, is growing exponentially.[105] In fact, its widespread use does not substitute for interpersonal communication but for telephone communication, since answering machines and voice-phone services have created a communication barrier that makes e-mail the best alternative for direct communication at a chosen time. Computer sex is another major use of CMC, and is expanding quickly. While there is a fast-growing business market in computerized sexual stimulation, increasingly associated with virtual reality technology,[106] most computer sex takes place on conversation lines, either on specialized BBSs or as a spontaneous derivation of personal interaction. The interactive power of new networks made this activity more dynamic in 1990s' California than it was in 1980s' French Minitel.[107] Increasingly afraid of contagion and of personal aggression, people search for alternatives to express their sexuality, and in our culture of symbolic overstimulation CMC certainly offers avenues to sexual fantasy, particularly as long as the interaction is not visual and identities can be concealed.

Politics is also a growing area of utilization of CMC.[108] On the one hand, e-mail is being used for mass diffusion of targeted political propaganda with the possibility of interaction. Electoral compaigns in all countries start their work by setting up their web sites. Politicians display their promises on their Internet home pages. Christian fundamentalist groups, the American militia in the US, and the *Zapatistas* in

102 Baym (1998: 55).
103 Dyson (1998).
104 US Library of Congress (1999).
105 Lanham (1993); Rand Corporation (1995).
106 Specter (1994).
107 Armstrong (1994).
108 Abramson et al. (1988); Epstein (1995).

Mexico pioneered this political technology.[109] On the other hand, local democracy is being enhanced through experiments in electronic citizen participation, such as the PEN program organized by the City of Santa Monica, California,[110] through which citizens debate public issues and make their feelings known to the city government: a raging debate on homelessness (with electronic participation by the homeless themselves!) was one of the most highly publicized results of this experiment in the early 1990s. Amsterdam's Digital City, created in the 1990s through a shared initiative by former leaders of the squatters movement and of the municipal government, showed the extraordinary potential of computer communication networks as instruments of grassroots self-organizing and public debate at the local level.[111] In the 1990s, community activists in Seattle, and other cities in the United States, were building community-based, on-line networks with the aim of providing information, stimulating citizens' debate, and reasserting democratic control over environmental issues and local politics.[112] In the international arena, new trans-border social movements, rising to defend women's causes, human rights, environmental preservation, and political democracy, are making the Internet an essential tool for disseminating information, organizing, and mobilizing.[113]

How specific is the language of CMC as a new medium? To some analysts, CMC, and particularly e-mail, represents the revenge of the written medium, the return to the typographic mind, and the recuperation of the constructed, rational discourse. For others, on the contrary, the informality, spontaneity, and anonymity of the medium stimulates what they call a new form of "orality," expressed by an electronic text.[114] If we can consider such behavior as informal, unconstructed writing in real-time interaction, in the mode of a synchronist chat (a writing telephone), perhaps we can foresee the emergence of a new medium, mixing forms of communication which were previously separated in different domains of the human mind. As De Kerckhove writes, "The message of the medium of cyberspace is touch, body, identity. These are precisely the three areas of our being that pessimistic critics say we are losing to technology. But isn't it clear, too, that to put them in jeopardy is also to bring them out in the open?"[115]

Overall, when assessing the social and cultural impacts of CMC we

---

109   Castells et al. (1996).
110   Ganley (1991); Varley (1991).
111   Patrice Riemens (personal communication – face to face, handwritten mail, electronic mail – 1997/99).
112   Schuler (1996).
113   Keck and Sikkink (1998).
114   December (1993), cited and summarized by Benson (1994).
115   De Kerckhove (1997: 51).

must keep in mind the accumulated sociological research on the social uses of technology.[116] More to the point, the masterful work by Claude Fischer on the social history of the telephone in America to 1940 shows the high social elasticity of any given technology.[117] Thus, the northern California communities he studied adopted the telephone to enhance their existing social networks of communication, and to reinforce their deep-rooted social habits. The telephone was adapted, not just adopted. People shape technology to fit it to their own needs, as I have argued above in relation to the personal and contextual reception of television messages by the audience, and as is clearly shown by the adoption of Minitel by French people to fulfill their sexual fantasy needs. The many-to-many electronic communication mode represented by CMC has been used in different ways and for different purposes, as many as in the range of social and contextual variation among its users. What is common to CMC is that, according to the few existing studies on the matter, it does not substitute for other means of communication: it reinforces pre-existing social patterns. It adds to telephone and transportation communication, it expands the reach of social networks, and makes it possible for them to interact more actively and in chosen time patterns. Because access to CMC is culturally, educationally, and economically restrictive, and will be so for a long time, the most important cultural impact of CMC could be potentially the reinforcement of culturally dominant social networks, as well as the increase in their cosmopolitanism and globalization. This is not because CMC *per se* is more cosmopolitan: as Fischer showed, early telephone networks favored local over long-distance communication. In some of the virtual communities, for instance in the San Francisco Bay area's SFNET, the majority of their "regulars" are local residents, and some of them periodically celebrate face-to-face parties, in order to nurture their electronic intimacy.[118] Yet, in spite of their potential usefulness for social movements, the influence of electronic networks at large in the cultural realm may well be to reinforce the cosmopolitanism of the new professional and managerial classes living symbolically in a global frame of reference, unlike most of the population in any country. Thus, CMC could be a powerful medium to strengthen the social cohesion of the cosmopolitan elite, providing material support to the meaning of a global culture, from the chic of an e-mail address to the rapid circulation of fashionable messages.[119] In contrast, for the majority of the population in all countries, beyond

116 Dutton (1999).
117 Fischer (1992).
118 Rheingold (1993).
119 Castells and Kiselyova (2000).

the workplace, and besides on-line shopping, the experience and uses of CMC will be increasingly intertwined with the new world of communication associated with the emergence of multimedia.

The Grand Fusion: Multimedia as Symbolic Environment

In the second half of the 1990s a new electronic communication system started to be formed out of the merger of globalized, customized mass media and computer-mediated communication. As I mentioned above, the new system is characterized by the integration of different media and by its interactive potential. Multimedia, as the new system was hastily labeled, extend the realm of electronic communication into the whole domain of life, from home to work, from schools to hospitals, from entertainment to travel. By the mid-1990s governments and companies around the world were in a frantic race to position themselves in setting up the new system, considered to be a tool of power, a potential source of huge profits, and a symbol of hypermodernity. In the US, Vice-president Albert Gore launched the National Information Infrastructure program, to renew America's leadership in the twenty-first century.[120] In Japan, the Telecommunications Council proposed the necessary "Reforms toward the Intellectually Creative Society of the Twenty-first Century," and the Ministry of Posts and Telecommunications obliged with a strategy to create a multimedia system in Japan, to overcome the lagging of the nation behind the United States.[121] The French Prime Minister commissioned a report in 1994 on *"autoroutes de l'information,"* which concluded that it was to the potential advantage of France in the field, building on the society's experience with Minitel and on French advanced technology, to foster the next stage of multimedia, putting emphasis on providing a media content less dependent on Hollywood.[122] European technology programs, particularly Esprit and Eureka, stepped up efforts to develop a European standard of high-definition television, as well as telecommunication protocols that could integrate different communication systems across the borders.[123] In February 1995 the G-7 club held a special meeting in Brussels to jointly address the issues involved in the transition to the "information society." In early 1995, Brazil's

120   Sullivan-Trainor (1994).
121   Telecommunications Council (1994).
122   Thery (1994).
123   Banegas (1993).

new president, distinguished sociologist Fernando Henrique Cardoso, decided, as one of the key measures of his new administration, to over-haul Brazil's communication system, to link up with the emerging glo-bal superhighway. And in the first semester of 2000, under the presidency of Portugal, the European Union placed the construction of a European Information Society at the top of its strategic agenda.

Yet business, not governments, was shaping the new multimedia system.[124] Indeed, the scale of investment in infrastructure prevented any government from acting by itself: for the United States alone, the estimates for the launch phase of the so-called information superhigh-way were $US 400 billion. Companies from all over the world were positioning themselves to enter a market that could become, in the early twenty-first century, the equivalent of what the automobile–oil–rubber–highway industrial complex was in the first half of the twenti-eth century. Furthermore, because the actual technological shape of the system is uncertain, whoever controls its first stages could decis-ively influence its future evolution, thus acquiring structural com-petitive advantage. Because of technological convergence between computers, telecommunications, and mass media in all its modalities, global/regional consortia were formed, and dissolved, on a gigantic scale.[125] Telephone companies, cable TV operators, TV satellite broad-casting, movie studios, music recording companies, publishing houses, newspapers, computer firms, and Internet service providers were both competing and merging to hedge the risks of the new market.[126] Com-puter companies were hurrying to provide "the box," the magic de-vice that would embody the potential to hook up the electronic home to a new galaxy of communication, while providing people with a navigating and self-programming capability in a "user-friendly" mode – it was hoped by just speaking to "it."[127] Software companies, from Microsoft to Japanese video games creators, such as Nintendo and Saga, were generating the new interactive know-how that would un-leash the fantasy of immersion in the virtual reality of the electronic environment.[128] Television networks, music companies, and movie studios were cranking up their production to feed an entire world sup-posedly hungry for info-entertainment and audiovisual product lines.[129] And Internet service providers were trying to link up the media world

---

124   See, among a myriad of business sources on the matter, Bird (1994); Bunker (1994); Dalloz and Portnoff (1994); Herther (1994).
125   *The Economist* (1994a).
126   Schiller (1999).
127   *Business Week* (1994h).
128   Elmer-Dewwit (1993); Poirier (1993); *Business Week* (1994d).
129   *New Media Markets* (1993).

by providing a variety of technologies, and a diversity of content that could supplement, if not replace, television and stored video. In the late 1990s, while the broadcast of regular TV signals over the Internet, while technologically possible, seemed to be a long-term possibility because of the huge transmission capacity that would be required to ensure standard quality video, other forms of technological integration were emerging:[130] WebTV, in which a television is linked to both a computer and a telephone line, allowing reception in the same screen of both TV signals and Internet services – this is, in fact, a user-friendly integration of two separate technologies which could still function independently; web pages transmitted over the telephone line with content complementary to a video broadcast, and displayed either on a TV screen or a computer monitor; transmission by a broadcast medium of Internet content via cable directly to homes employing cable modems; Internet-transmitted video information incorporated as a window within web pages; information complementary to TV broadcasts made available via the Internet from servers maintained by local TV stations (the "CityWeb" concept). TV channels can be used, when they are off the air, to transmit video or information to storage devices from where they can be retrieved by computers. This development could link up with high-quality, stereo digital video (DVD), operated by computer and displayed on a high-definition screen, increasing the potential of stored video as an additional component of the multimedia system.

However, the process of formation of the new system is likely to be slower, and more contradictory, than anticipated. In 1994, there were several experiments with multimedia interactive systems in a number of areas: in Kansai Science City in Japan; a coordinated program in eight European telecommunication networks, to test the asymmetrical digital subscriber loop (ASDL);[131] and in several areas of the United States, from Orlando to Vermont, from Brooklyn to Denver.[132] The results did not match the expectations. Major technological problems were still unsolved by the end of the century. The big promise of multimedia, standard-quality video on demand, through an interactive mode, by using the magic set-top box with the proper software, would require a major increase in transmission capacity. According to Owen, such an offer to millions of ordinary viewers would result in the collapse of the distribution systems as of 1998. He asserts that "the

---

130   Owen (1999: ch.17).
131   Ministry of Posts and Telecommunications (1994); *New Media Markets* (1994).
132   Kaplan (1992); Sellers (1993); Booker (1994); *Business Week* (1994e); Lizzio (1994); Wexler (1994).

interactive integrated video future requires much more capacity than we have, not only in national backbones, but in local distribution systems that link up with individual households."[133] While "video-on-demand" companies advertise unlimited possibilities, the technological ability to handle requests still does not go too far beyond the range of choice provided by existing cable and satellite-based systems or online servers. However, counting on rapid technological change, particularly in digital compression, bandwidth could be dramatically broadened, given the necessary investment – which would be significant, and would only pay off if there is enough demand for it. Therefore, the possibility of the emergence of an integrated multimedia system in the early twenty-first century does exist. But its fully fledged development requires not only a huge investment in infrastructure and in programming content, but also the clarification of the regulatory environment, still entangled in disputes between entrenched business interests, political constituencies, and government regulators. Under such conditions, only very powerful groups, resulting from alliances between media companies, communication operators, Internet service providers, and computer companies, will be in a position to master the economic and political resources necessary for the diffusion of multimedia. Thus, there will be a multimedia system but, in all likelihood, it will be decisively shaped by the commercial interests of a few major conglomerates around the world. The issue then arises about the ability of these conglomerates to identify accurately what people really want from the media system. Indeed, unlike standard television, which people did not have to pay for, except in terms of their time as forced advertising viewers, most of the multimedia broadcast will come in pay-per-view form to recover the costs of the huge investment necessary for their diffusion. Thus, the connection (or lack of connection) between the interests of media business and people's taste and resources will shape the future of communication. The issue is not whether a multimedia system will develop (it will) but when and how, and under what conditions in different countries, because the cultural meaning of the system will be deeply modified by the timing and shape of the technological trajectory.

Business control over the first stages of development of multimedia systems will have lasting consequences on the characteristics of the new electronic culture. For all the ideology of the potential of new communication technologies in education, health, and cultural enhancement, the prevailing strategy aims at developing a giant electronic entertainment system, considered the safest investment from a business

133   Owen (1999: 313).

perspective. Indeed, in the pioneer country, the United States, entertainment in all its forms was in the mid-1990s the fastest growing
industry, with over $350 billion of consumer spending per year, and
about 5 million workers, with employment increasing at 12 percent
per year.[134] In Japan, a 1992 national market survey on the distribution of multimedia software by product category found that entertainment accounted for 85.7 percent of the value, while education
represented only 0.8 percent.[135] Thus, while governments and futurologists speak of wiring classrooms, doing surgery at a distance, and
tele-consulting the *Encyclopedia Britannica*, most of the actual construction of the new system focuses on "video-on-demand," tele-gam-
bling, and virtual reality theme parks. In the analytical vein of this
book, I am not opposing the noble goals of new technologies to their
mediocre materialization. I am simply indicating that their actual use
in the early stages of the new system will considerably shape the uses,
perceptions, and ultimately the social consequences of multimedia.

Furthermore, the expectations of unlimited demand for entertainment seem to be overstated and heavily influenced by the ideology of
the "leisure society." While entertainment spending appears to be re-
cession-resilient, payment for the full range of possibilities proposed
on-line clearly exceeds the expected evolution of households' income
in the near future. Time is also a scarce resource. There are indications
that in the United States leisure time decreased by 37 percent between
1973 and 1994. In addition, media viewing time declined in the second half of the 1980s: between 1985 and 1990 total time spent reading and watching TV and movies declined by 45 hours per year; hours
spent watching TV declined by 4 percent; and hours watching network TV declined by 20 percent.[136] In another estimate, in the US,
broadcast and cable TV viewing by the average person peaked at 20.4
hours per week in 1984, and declined slightly from then until, at least,
1998.[137] Although decreasing media exposure seems to be linked more
to an overworked society (dual-job families) than to lack of interest,
multimedia business is betting on another interpretation: lack of suffi-
ciently attractive content. Indeed, most experts of the media industry
consider that the real bottleneck for the expansion of multimedia is
that content does not follow the technological transformation of the
system: the message is lagging the medium.[138] A dramatic expansion
of broadcasting capacity, coupled with interactive choice, will fall short

134   *Business Week* (1994f).
135   Dentsu Institute for Human Studies (1994: 117).
136   Martin (1994).
137   Owen (1999: 4).
138   Bunker (1994); *Business Week* (1994f); Cuneo (1994); *The Economist* (1994a).

of its potential if there is no real choice in terms of the content: the on-line availability of 500 distinct-but-similar sex/violence movies does not justify the dramatic broadening of transmission capacity. This is why the acquisition of Hollywood studios, movie companies, and TV documentary archives is a must for any global multimedia consortium. Entrepreneurial creators, such as Steven Spielberg, seem to have understood that, *in the new system, because of the potential diversity of contents, the message is the message*: it is the ability to differentiate a product that yields the greatest competitive potential. Thus, any conglomerate with sufficient financial resources could have access to multimedia technology and, in an increasingly deregulated context, could access almost any market. But whoever controls Bogart's films or the capacity to generate the new electronic Marilyn or the next Jurassic Park episode will be in the position to supply the much-needed commodity to whichever communication support.

However, it is not certain that what people want, even if given the time and resources, is more entertainment with an increasingly sophisticated format, from sadistic video-games to endless sports events. Although there is scant evidence on the matter, some indications point to a more complex demand pattern. One of the most complete surveys on multimedia demand, carried out by Charles Piller on a national sample of 600 adults in 1994 in the United States,[139] revealed a much deeper interest in using multimedia for information access, community affairs, political involvement, and education, than in adding television and movies to their choice. Only 28 percent of consumers considered video-on-demand as highly desirable, and the lack of interest in entertainment was equally strong among Internet users. On the other hand, political uses were highly valued: 57 percent would like to participate in electronic town-hall meetings; 46 percent wanted to use e-mail to send messages to their representatives; and about 50 percent valued the possibility of voting electronically. Additional services in high demand were: educational/instructional courses; interactive reports on local schools; access to reference materials; and access to information about government services. Respondents were ready to back up their opinions with their pocket: 34 percent were ready to pay an additional $10 a month for distant learning, while only 19 percent were ready to pay that amount for additional entertainment choice. Also, experiments conducted by multimedia companies for video-on-demand in local markets have shown that people are not ready for a substantial increase in their entertainment dose. Thus, the 18-month experiment conducted by US West/ATT video in Littleton, Colorado,

139　Piller (1994).

in 1993–4 showed that households had indeed switched from standard video viewing to customized video offerings, but they did not increase the number of films they were viewing: it stayed at 2.5 movies
per month, priced at $3 per movie.[140]

Taking into consideration the large-scale success of Internet service
providers in offering services and information rather than entertainment, and the fast diffusion of personal communication on the Internet,
observation tends to suggest that mass-produced, diversified entertainment on demand may not be the obvious choice for multimedia users,
although it is clear that this is the strategic choice of business firms
shaping the field. It may result in an increasing tension between
infotainment products, guided by the ideology of what people are, as
imagined in marketing think-tanks, and the need for personal communication and information enhancement that asserts itself with great
determination in CMC networks, and could expand as well in a new
kind of television.[141] It may well also be that this tension is diluted
through the social stratification of different multimedia expressions, a
critical theme to which I shall return.

Because of the newness of multimedia, it is difficult to assess their
implications for the culture of society, beyond acknowledging that
fundamental changes are indeed underway. Nevertheless, scattered
empirical evidence and informed commentary on the different components of new communications systems provide a basis to ground
some hypotheses on the emerging social and cultural trends. Thus, a
"scanning report" by the European Foundation for the Improvement
of Living and Working Conditions on the development of the "electronic home" emphasizes two critical features of the new lifestyle: its
"home centredness," and its individualism.[142] On the one hand, the
increasing electronic equipment in European homes has increased their
comfort and stepped up their self-sufficiency, enabling them to link up
with the whole world from the safety of the home. Together with the
increase in the size of housing units and the decrease in size of the
household, more space per person is available, making home a cozier
place. Indeed, time spent at home went up in the early 1990s. On the
other hand, the new electronic home and portable communication
devices increase the chances of individual members of the family to
organize their own time and space. For instance, microwave ovens,
allowing for individual consumption of precooked food, has reduced
the incidence of collective family dinners. Individual TV dinner sets

140 Tobenkin (1993); Martin (1994).
141 Van der Haak (1999).
142 Moran (1993).

represent a growing market. VCRs and walkman devices, together with the decrease in the price of TV sets, radios, and CD players, allow a large segment of the population to be individually hooked into sel-ected audiovisual worlds. Family care is also helped/transformed by electronics: children are monitored from a distance through remote control; studies show the increased use of TV as a baby-sitter while parents do their housework; elderly persons living alone are provided with alarm systems for emergency situations. Yet some social features seem to endure beyond the technological revolution: the sharing of home tasks between genders (or, rather, lack of it) is unaffected by electronic means; VCR use and the handling of remote control devices reflect the authority structure in the family; and the use of electronic devices is differentiated along gender and age lines, with men more often using computers, women handling electrical home maintenance and telematic services, and children obsessed with video games.

New electronic media do not depart from traditional cultures: they absorb them. A case in point is the Japanese invention of *karaoke*, rapidly diffusing all over Asia in the 1990s, and most likely spreading to the rest of the world in the near future. In 1991, *karaoke* dissemination in Japan reached 100 percent of recreational hotels and inns, and about 90 percent of bars and clubs, to which should be added an explosion of specialized *karaoke* rooms, from under 2,000 in 1989 to over 107,000 in 1992. In 1992, about 52 percent of Japanese participated in *karaoke*, including 79 percent of all teenage women.[143] At first sight, *karaoke* extends and amplifies the traditional habit of singing together in bars, something as popular in Japan as it was (and is) in Spain or the UK, thus escaping the world of electronic communication. Yet what in fact it does is to integrate this habit into a preprogrammed machine, whose musical rhythms and repertoire have to be followed by the singer, reciting the words that appear on the screen. Indeed, competition with friends to reach a higher score depends on the reward given by the machine to whoever best follows its pace. The *karaoke* machine is not a musical instrument: the singer is swallowed by the machine to supplement its sounds and images. While in the *karaoke* room we become part of a musical hypertext, we physically enter the multimedia system, and we separate our singing from that of our friends waiting their turn to substitute a linear sequence of performance for the disorderly chorus of traditional pub singing.

Overall, in Europe as in America or in Asia, multimedia appear to be supporting, even in their early stage, a social/cultural pattern characterized by the following features. First, *widespread social and*

143   Dentsu Institute for Human Studies (1994: 140–3).

cultural differentiation, leading to the segmentation of the users/viewers/readers/listeners. Not only are the messages segmented by markets following senders' strategies, but they are also increasingly diversified by users of the media, according to their interests, taking advantage of interactive capacities. As some experts put it, in the new system, *"prime time is my time."*[144] The formation of virtual communities is but one of the expressions of such differentiation.

Secondly, *increasing social stratification among the users.* Not only will choice of multimedia be restricted to those with time and money to access, and to countries and regions with enough market potential, but cultural/educational differences will be decisive in using interaction to the advantage of each user. The information about what to look for and the knowledge about how to use the message will be essential to truly experience a system different from standard customized mass media. *Thus, the multimedia world will be populated by two essentially distinct populations: the interacting and the interacted,* meaning those who are able to select their multidirectional circuits of communication, and those who are provided with a restricted number of prepackaged choices. And who is what will be largely determined by class, race, gender, and country. The unifying cultural power of mass television (from which only a tiny cultural elite had escaped in the past) is now replaced by a socially stratified differentiation, leading to the coexistence of a customized mass media culture and an interactive electronic communication network of self-selected communes.

Thirdly, the communication of all kinds of messages in the same system, even if the system is interactive and selective (in fact, precisely because of this), induces an *integration of all messages in a common cognitive pattern.* Accessing audiovisual news, education, and shows on the same medium, even from different sources, takes one step further the blurring of contents that was already taking place in mass television. From the perspective of the medium, different communication modes tend to borrow codes from each other: interactive educational programs look like video games; newscasts are constructed as audiovisual shows; trial cases are broadcast as soap operas; pop music is composed for MTV; sports games are choreographed for their distant viewers, so that their messages become less and less distinguishable from action movies; and the like. From the perspective of the user (both as receiver and sender, in an interactive system), the choice of various messages under the same communication mode, with easy switching from one to the other, reduces the mental distance between various sources of cognitive and sensorial involvement. The issue at

144 Negroponte (1995).

stake is not that the medium is the message: messages are messages. And because they keep their distinctiveness as messages, while being mixed in their symbolic communication process, they blur their codes in this process, creating a multifaceted semantic context made of a random mixture of various meanings.

Finally, perhaps *the most important feature of multimedia is that they capture within their domain most cultural expressions, in all their diversity.* Their advent is tantamount to ending the separation, and even the distinction, between audiovisual media and printed media, popular culture and learned culture, entertainment and information, education and persuasion. Every cultural expression, from the worst to the best, from the most elitist to the most popular, comes together in this digital universe that links up in a giant, non-historical hypertext, past, present, and future manifestations of the communicative mind. By so doing, they construct a new symbolic environment. They make virtuality our reality.

The Culture of Real Virtuality

Cultures are made up of communication processes. And all forms of communication, as Roland Barthes and Jean Baudrillard taught us many years ago, are based on the production and consumption of signs.[145] Thus there is no separation between "reality" and symbolic representation. In all societies humankind has existed in and acted through a symbolic environment. Therefore, what is historically specific to the new communication system, organized around the electronic integration of all communication modes from the typographic to the multisensorial, is not its inducement of virtual reality but the construction of real virtuality. I shall explain, with the help of the dictionary, according to which: "*virtual*: being so in practice though not strictly or in name," and "*real*: actually existing."[146] Thus reality, as experienced, has always been virtual because it is always perceived through symbols that frame practice with some meaning that escapes their strict semantic definition. It is precisely this ability of all forms of language to encode ambiguity and to open up a diversity of interpretations that makes cultural expressions distinct from formal/logical/mathematical reasoning. It is through the polysemic character of our discourses that the complexity and even contradictory quality of messages of the human mind manifest themselves. This range of cultural

145 Baudrillard (1972); Barthes (1978).
146 *Oxford Dictionary of Current English* (1992).

variation of the meaning of messages is what enables us to interact with each other in a multiplicity of dimensions, some explicit, some implicit. Thus, when critics of electronic media argue that the new symbolic environment does not represent "reality," they implicitly refer to an absurdly primitive notion of "uncoded" real experience that never existed. All realities are communicated through symbols. And in human, interactive communication, regardless of the medium, all symbols are somewhat displaced in relation to their assigned semantic meaning. In a sense, all reality is virtually perceived.

What is then a communication system that, in contrast to earlier historical experience, generates *real virtuality? It is a system in which reality itself (that is, people's material/symbolic existence) is entirely captured, fully immersed in a virtual image setting, in the world of make believe, in which appearances are not just on the screen through which experience is communicated, but they become the experience.* All messages of all kinds become enclosed in the medium because the medium has become so comprehensive, so diversified, so malleable that it absorbs in the same multimedia text the whole of human experience, past, present, and future, as in that unique point of the Universe that Jorge Luis Borges called "Aleph." Let me give an example, which is only that, an example to help communicate ideas.

In the 1992 American presidential campaign, the then Vice-president, Dan Quayle, wanted to make a stand in defense of traditional family values. Armed with his moral convictions he initiated an unusual debate with Murphy Brown. Murphy Brown, played by a fine actress, Candice Bergen, was the main character of a popular television soap opera who (re)presented the values and problems of a new kind of woman: the single, working professional woman with her own criteria about life. Around the time of the presidential campaign, Murphy Brown (not Candice Bergen) decided to have a child out of wedlock. Vice-president Quayle hurried to condemn her behavior as improper, prompting national outrage, particularly among working women. Murphy Brown (not just Candice Bergen) retaliated: in her next episode, she appeared watching the television interview in which Vice-president Quayle was criticizing her, and she spoke up, sharply criticizing politicians' interference with women's life, and defending her right to a new morality. Eventually *Murphy Brown* increased its share of the audience and Dan Quayle's outdated conservatism contributed to the electoral defeat of President Bush, both events being real and, to some extent, socially relevant. In 1999, vying again in the primary elections to become the republican nominee for President, Dan Quayle opened his campaign defiantly, asserting he was still there while Murphy Brown was now off the screen. To no avail: in the first contest in the primaries he scored so poorly that he had to withdraw his candidacy. Thus a new text of the real and the imaginary had been composed throughout the dialogue. The unsolicited presence of Murphy Brown's imaginary world in the real-life presidential campaign induced the transformation of Quayle (or rather, of his "real" television image) into a character of Murphy Brown's imaginary life: a supertext had been made, blending in the same discourse passionately argued messages emitted from both levels of experience. In this case, virtuality (that is Murphy Brown being in practice what many women were, without being so in the name of any woman) had become real, in the sense that it had actually interacted, with some significant impact, with the process of election to the most powerful political office on earth. Granted, the example is extreme and unusual, but I believe it illustrates my analysis, helping to reduce the obscurity of its abstraction. Hoping that such is the case, let me be more precise.

What characterizes the new system of communication, based in the digitized, networked integration of multiple communication modes, is its inclusiveness and comprehensiveness of all cultural expressions. Because of its existence, all kinds of messages in the new type of society work in a binary mode: presence/absence in the multimedia communication system. Only presence in this integrated system permits communicability and socialization of the message. All other messages are reduced to individual imagination or to increasingly marginalized face-to-face subcultures. From society's perspective, *electronically based communication (typographic, audiovisual, or computer-mediated)* is *communication*. Yet it does not follow that there is homogenization of cultural expressions and full domination of codes by a few central senders. It is precisely because of the diversification, multimodality, and versatility of the new communication system that it is able to embrace and integrate all forms of expression, as well as the diversity of interests, values, and imaginations, including the expression of social conflicts. But the price to pay for inclusion in the system is to adapt to its logic, to its language, to its points of entry, to its encoding and decoding. This is why it is so critical for different kinds of social effects that there should be the development of a multinodal, horizontal network of communication, of Internet type, instead of a centrally dispatched multimedia system, as in the video-on-demand configuration. The setting of barriers to entry into this communication system, and the creation of passwords for the circulation and diffusion of messages throughout the system, are critical cultural battles for the new society, the outcome of which predetermines the fate of symbolically mediated conflicts to be fought in this new historical environment. Who are the *interacting* and who are the *interacted* in the new system, to use the terminology whose meaning I suggested above, largely frames the system of domination and the processes of liberation in the informational society.

The inclusion of most cultural expressions within the integrated communication system based in digitized electronic production, distribution, and exchange of signals has major consequences for social forms and processes. On the one hand, it weakens considerably the symbolic power of traditional senders external to the system, transmitting through historically encoded social habits: religion, morality, authority, traditional values, political ideology. Not that they disappear, but they are weakened unless they recode themselves in the new system, where their power becomes multiplied by the electronic materialization of spiritually transmitted habits: electronic preachers and interactive fundamentalist networks are a more efficient, more penetrating form of indoctrination in our societies than face-to-face transmission of distant, charismatic authority. But by having to concede the earthly coexistence of transcendental messages, on-demand pornography, soap operas, and chat-lines within the same system, superior spiritual powers still conquer souls but lose their suprahuman status. The final step of the secularization of society follows, even if it sometimes takes the paradoxical form of conspicuous consumption of re-ligion, under all kinds of generic and brand names. Societies are finally and truly disenchanted because all wonders are on-line and can be combined into self-constructed image worlds.

On the other hand, the new communication system radically transforms space and time, the fundamental dimensions of human life. Localities become disembodied from their cultural, historical, geographical meaning, and reintegrated into functional networks, or into image collages, inducing a space of flows that substitutes for the space of places. Time is erased in the new communication system when past, present, and future can be programmed to interact with each other in the same message. The *space of flows* and *timeless time* are the material foundations of a new culture that transcends and includes the diversity of historically transmitted systems of representation: the culture of real virtuality where make-believe is belief in the making.

6

The Space of Flows

Space and time are the fundamental, material dimensions of human life. Physicists have unveiled the complexity of such notions, beyond their fallacious intuitive simplicity. School children know that space and time are related. And superstring theory, the latest fashion in physics, advances the hypothesis of a hyperspace that articulates ten dimensions, including time.[1] There is of course no place for such a discussion in my analysis, strictly concerned with the *social meaning of space and time*. But my reference to such complexity goes beyond rhetorical pedantry. It invites us to consider social forms of time and space that are not reducible to what have been our perceptions to date, based upon socio-technical structures superseded by current historical experience.

Since space and time are intertwined in nature and in society, so they will be in my analysis, although for the sake of clarity I shall focus sequentially first on space, in this chapter, and then on time in the next one. The ordering in the sequence is not random: unlike most classical social theories, which assume the domination of space by time, I propose the hypothesis that space organizes time in the network society. This statement will, I hope, make more sense at the end of the intellectual journey I propose to the reader in these two chapters.

Both space and time are being transformed under the combined effect of the information technology paradigm, and of social forms and processes induced by the current process of historical change, as presented in this book. However, the actual profile of this transformation sharply departs from common-sense extrapolations of technological determinism. For instance, it appears to be obvious that

1 Kaku (1994).

advanced telecommunications would make location of offices ubiquitous, thus enabling corporate headquarters to quit expensive, congested,
and unpleasant central business districts for custom-made sites in beautiful spots around the world. Yet Mitchell Moss's empirical analysis
of the impact of telecommunications on Manhattan's business in the
1980s found that these new, advanced telecommunications facilities
were among the factors responsible for slowing down corporate relocation away from New York, for reasons that I shall expose below.
Or, to use another example on a different social domain, home-based
electronic communication was supposed to induce the decline of dense
urban forms, and to diminish spatially localized social interaction. Yet
the first mass diffused system of computer-mediated communication,
the French Minitel, described in chapter 5, originated in the 1980s in
an intense urban environment, whose vitality and face-to-face interaction was hardly undermined by the new medium. Indeed, French
students used Minitel to successfully stage *street* demonstrations against
the government. In the early 1990s telecommuting – that is, working
at home on-line – was practiced by a very small fraction of the labor
force, in the United States (between 1 and 2 percent on a given day),
Europe, or Japan, if we except the old, customary practice of professionals to keep working at home or to organize their activity in flexible time and space when they have the leisure to do so.[2] While working
at home part-time seems to be emerging as a mode of professional
activity in the future, it develops out of the rise of the network enterprise and of the flexible work process, as analyzed in preceding chapters, not as the direct consequence of available technology. The
theoretical and practical consequences of such precisions are critical.
It is this complexity of the interaction between technology, society,
and space that I shall address in the following pages.

   To proceed in this direction, I shall examine the empirical record on
the transformation of location patterns of core economic activities under
the new technological system, both for advanced services and for manufacturing. Afterwards, I shall try to assess the scarce evidence on the
interaction between the rise of the electronic home and the evolution
of the city, and I shall elaborate on the recent evolution of urban forms
in various contexts. I shall then synthesize the observed tendencies
under a new spatial logic that I label *space of flows*. I shall oppose to
such logic the historically rooted spatial organization of our common

2   For an excellent overview of the interaction between telecommunications and spatial
processes, see Graham and Marvin (1996). For evidence of the impact of telecommunications on business districts, see Moss (1987, 1991, 1992: 147–58). For a summary of the
evidence on teleworking and telecommuting in advanced societies, see Korte et al. (1988);
and Qvortup (1992).

experience: *the space of places*. And I shall refer to the reflection of such dialectical opposition between the space of flows and the space of places in current debates in architecture and urban design. The purpose of this intellectual itinerary is to draw the profile of this new spatial process, the space of flows, that is becoming the dominant spatial manifestation of power and function in our societies. In spite of all my efforts to anchor the new spatial logic in the empirical record, I am afraid it is unavoidable, toward the end of the chapter, to confront the reader with some fundamentals of a social theory of space, as a way to approach the current transformation of the material basis of our experience. Yet my ability to communicate a rather abstract theorization of new spatial forms and processes will, I hope, be enhanced by a brief survey of available evidence on recent spatial patterning of dominant economic functions and social practices.[3]

Advanced Services, Information Flows, and the Global City

The informational, global economy is organized around command and control centers able to coordinate, innovate, and manage the intertwined activities of networks of firms.[4] Advanced services, including finance, insurance, real estate, consulting, legal services, advertising, design, marketing, public relations, security, information gathering, and management of information systems, but also R&D and scientific innovation, are at the core of all economic processes, be it in manufacturing, agriculture, energy, or services of different kinds.[5] They all can be reduced to knowledge generation and information flows.[6] Thus, advanced telecommunications systems could make possible their

---

3   To a large extent, the empirical basis and the analytical foundations of this chapter rely on the research work I did in the 1980s, summarized and elaborated in my book *The Informational City: Information Technology, Economic Restructuring, and the Urban–Regional Process* (Castells 1989b). Although this chapter contains updated, additional information on various countries, as well as further theoretical elaboration, I still refer the reader to the cited book for more detailed analysis and empirical support of the analysis presented here. Accordingly, *I shall not repeat here the empirical sources that have been used and cited in the above-mentioned book*. This note should be considered as a generic reference to the sources and material contained in *The Informational City*. For an up-to-date discussion on these matters, see also Graham and Marvin (1996; 2000). For an historical, analytical, and cultural overview of the evolution of cities, see the masterpiece by Sir Peter Hall (1998). For an international perspective on urbanization, see Borja and Castells (1997).
4   For an excellent overview of current transformations of spatial forms and processes at the global level, see Hall (1995: 3–32).
5   Daniels (1993).
6   Norman (1993).

scattered location around the globe. Yet more than a decade of studies on the matter have established a different spatial pattern, characterized by the simultaneous dispersion and concentration of advanced services.[7] On the one hand, advanced services have substantially increased their share in employment and GNP in most countries, and they display the highest growth in employment and the highest investment rates in the leading metropolitan areas of the world.[8] They are pervasive, and they are located throughout the geography of the planet, excepting the "black holes" of marginality. On the other hand, there has been a spatial concentration of the upper tier of such activities in a few nodal centers of a few countries.[9] This concentration follows a hierarchy between tiers of urban centers, with the higher-level functions, in terms of both power and skill, being concentrated in some major metropolitan areas.[10] Saskia Sassen's classic study of the global city has shown the joint dominance of New York, Tokyo, and London in international finance, and in most consulting and business services of international scope.[11] These three centers together cover the spectrum of time zones for the purpose of financial trading, and work largely as a unit in the same system of endless transactions. But other centers are important, and even more pre-eminent in some specific segments of trade, for example Chicago and Singapore in futures' contracts (in fact, first practiced in Chicago in 1972). Hong Kong, Osaka, Frankfurt, Zurich, Paris, Los Angeles, San Francisco, Amsterdam, and Milan are also major centers both in finance and in international business services.[12] And a number of "regional centers" are rapidly joining the network, as "emerging markets" develop all over the world: Madrid, São Paulo, Buenos Aires, Mexico, Taipei, Moscow, Budapest, among others.

As the global economy expands and incorporates new markets it also organizes the production of advanced services required to manage the new units joining the system, and the conditions of their ever-changing linkages.[13] A case in point which illustrates this process is Madrid, relatively a backwater of the global economy until 1986. In that year Spain joined the European Community, opening up fully to foreign capital investment in the stock exchange markets, in banking operations, and in acquisition of companies equity, as well as in real

---

7   Graham (1994).
8   Enderwick (1989).
9   Daniels (1993).
10   Thrift (1986); Thrift and Leyshon (1992).
11   Sassen (1991).
12   Daniels (1993).
13   Borja et al. (1991).

estate. As shown in our study,[14] in the 1986–90 period foreign direct investment in Madrid and in Madrid's stock exchange fueled a period of rapid regional economic growth, together with a boom in real estate and a fast expansion of employment in business services. Acquisitions of stocks in Madrid by foreign investors between 1982 and 1988 jumped from 4,494 million pesetas (pts) to 623,445 million pts. Foreign direct investment in Madrid went up from 8,000 million pts in 1985 to almost 400,000 million pts in 1988. Accordingly, office construction in downtown Madrid, and high-level residential real estate, went in the late 1980s through the same kind of frenzy experienced in New York and London. The city was deeply transformed both through the saturation of valuable space in the core city, and through a process of massive suburbanization which, until then, had been a somewhat limited phenomenon in Madrid.

Along the same line of argument, a study by Cappelin on services networking in European cities shows the increasing interdependence and complementarity between medium-sized urban centers in the European Union. He concluded that: "The relative importance of the city–region relationships seems to decrease with respect to the importance of the relationships which interlink various cities of different regions and countries . . . New activities concentrate in particular poles and that implies an increase of disparities between the urban poles and their respective hinterlands."[15] Thus, the global city phenomenon cannot be reduced to a few urban cores at the top of the hierarchy. It is a process that connects advanced services, producer centers, and markets in a global network, with different intensity and at a different scale depending upon the relative importance of the activities located in each area *vis-à-vis* the global network. Inside each country, the networking architecture reproduces itself into regional and local centers, so that the whole system becomes interconnected at the global level. Territories surrounding these nodes play an increasingly subordinate function, sometimes becoming irrelevant or even dysfunctional; for example, Mexico City's *colonias populares* (originally squatter settlements) that account for about two-thirds of the megapolitan population, without playing any distinctive role in the functioning of Mexico City as an international business center.[16] Furthermore, globalization stimulates regionalization. In his studies on European regions in the 1990s, Philip Cooke has shown, on the basis of available evidence, that the growing internationalization of economic activities through-

14 For a summary of the research report, see Castells (1991).
15 Cappelin (1991): 237.
16 Davis (1994).

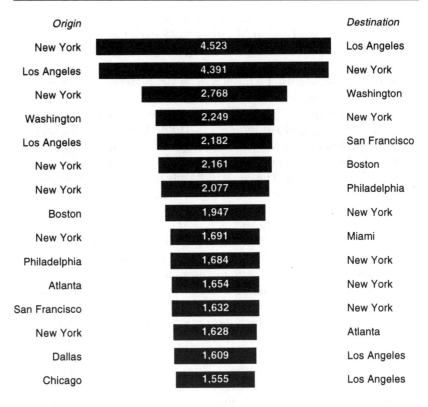

Figure 6.1 Largest absolute growth in information flows, 1982 and 1990
Source: Federal Express data, elaborated by Michelson and Wheeler (1994)

out Europe has made regions more dependent on these activities. Accordingly, regions, under the impulse of their governments and business elites, have restructured themselves to compete in the global economy, and they have established networks of cooperation between regional institutions and between region-based companies. Thus, regions and localities do not disappear, but become integrated in international networks that link up their most dynamic sectors.[17]

An approximation to the evolving architecture of information flows in the global economy has been obtained by Michelson and Wheeler on the basis of data analysis of traffic for one of the leading business couriers, Federal Express Corporation.[18] They studied the 1990s' move-

17   Cooke and Morgan (1993); Cooke (1994).
18   Michelson and Wheeler (1994).

Figure 6.2 Exports of information from the United States to major world regions and centers
Source: Federal Express data, 1990, elaborated by Michelson and Wheeler (1994)

ment of overnight letters, packages, and boxes between US metropolitan areas, as well as between the US major sending centers and international destinations. The results of their analysis, illustrated in figures 6.1 and 6.2 show two basic trends: (a) dominance of some nodes, particularly New York, followed by Los Angeles, increasing over time; (b) selected national and international circuits of connection. As they conclude:

> All indicators point to a strengthening of the hierarchical structure of command-and-control functions and the resulting exchange of information . . . The locational concentration of information results from high levels of uncertainty, driven in turn by technological change, market demassification, deregulation and market globalization. . . . [However] as the current epoch unfolds, the importance of flexibility as a basic coping mechanism, and of agglomeration economies as the preeminent locational force will persist. The importance of the city as a center of gravity for economic transactions thus will not vanish. But with the impending regulation of international markets . . . with less uncertainty about the rules of the economic game and the players involved, the concentration of the information industry will slow and certain aspects of production and distribution will filter into lower levels of an internationalized urban hierarchy.[19]

Indeed, the hierarchy in the network is by no means assured or stable: it is subject to fierce inter-city competition, as well as to the venture of highly risky investments in both finance and real estate. Thus, P. W. Daniels, in one of the most comprehensive studies of the matter, explains the partial failure of the major redevelopment project of Canary Wharf in London's Docklands as the result of the overextended strategy of its developer, the notorious Canadian firm Olympia & York, unable to absorb the office development glut of the early 1990s, in the wake of retrenchment of financial services employment in both London and New York. He concludes that:

> The expansion of services into the international market place has therefore introduced a greater degree of flexibility, and ultimately competition, into the global urban system than was the case in the past. As the experience with Canary Wharf has shown, it also made the outcome of large-scale planning and redevelopment within cities a hostage to external international factors over which they can have limited control.[20]

Thus, in the early 1990s, while business-led explosive urban growth

19   Michelson and Wheeler (1994: 102–3).
20   Daniels (1993: 166).

was experienced in cities such as Bangkok, Taipei, Shanghai, Mexico DF, or Bogota, on the other hand, Madrid, along with New York, London, and Paris, went into a slump that triggered a sharp downturn in real-estate prices and halted new construction. Then, in the late 1990s, London's and New York's real estate revalued substantially, while the urban cores of major Asian cities were severely struck by a financial crisis, partly induced by the bursting of the bubble of their real-estate markets (see volume III). This urban roller-coaster at different periods, across areas of the world, illustrates both the dependence and vulnerability of any locale, including major cities, to changing global flows.

But why must these advanced service systems still be dependent on agglomeration in a few large metropolitan nodes? Here again, Saskia Sassen, capping years of field work research by herself and other researchers in different contexts, offers convincing answers. She argues that:

> The combination of spatial dispersal and global integration has created a new strategic role for major cities. Beyond their long history as centers for international trade and banking, these cities now function in four new ways: first, as highly concentrated command points in the organization of the world economy; second, as key locations for finance and for specialized service firms . . . ; third, as sites of production, including the production of innovation in these leading industries; and fourth, as markets for the products and innovations produced.[21]

These cities, or rather, their business districts, are information-based, value-production complexes, where corporate headquarters and advanced financial firms can find both the suppliers and the highly skilled, specialized labor they require. They constitute indeed networks of production and management, whose flexibility needs *not* to internalize workers and suppliers, but to be able to access them when it fits, and in the time and quantities that are required in each particular instance. Flexibility and adaptability are better served by this combination between agglomeration of core networks, and global networking of these cores, and of their dispersed, ancillary networks, via telecommunications and air transportation. Other factors seem also to contribute to strengthen concentration of high-level activities in a few nodes: once they are constituted, heavy investment in valuable real estate by corporations explains their reluctance to move because such a move would devalue their fixed assets; also, face-to-face contacts for critical

21   Sassen (1991: 3–4).

decisions are still necessary in the age of widespread eavesdropping, since, as Saskia Sassen reports that a manager confessed to her during an interview, sometimes business deals are, of necessity, marginally illegal.[22] And, finally, major metropolitan centers still offer the greatest opportunities for the personal enhancement, social status, and individual self-gratification of the much-needed upper-level professionals, from good schools for their children to symbolic membership at the heights of conspicuous consumption, including art and entertainment.[23]

Nevertheless, advanced services, and even more so services at large, do indeed disperse and decentralize to the periphery of metropolitan areas, to smaller metropolitan areas, to less-developed regions, and to some less-developed countries.[24] New regional centers of service processing activities have emerged in the United States (for example, Atlanta, Georgia, or Omaha, Nebraska), in Europe (for example, Barcelona, Nice, Stuttgart, Bristol), or in Asia (for example, Bombay, Bangkok, Shanghai). The peripheries of major metropolitan areas are bustling with new office development, be it Walnut Creek in San Francisco or Reading near London. And in some cases, new major service centers have sprung up on the edge of the historic city, Paris's La Défense being the most notorious and successful example. Yet, in almost all instances, decentralization of office work affects "back offices;" that is, the mass processing of transactions that execute strategies decided and designed in the corporate centers of high finance and advanced services.[25] These are precisely the activities that employ the bulk of semi-skilled office workers, most of them suburbanite women, many of them replaceable or recyclable, as technology evolves and the economic roller-coaster goes on.

What is significant about this spatial system of advanced service activities is neither their concentration nor decentralization, since both processes are indeed taking place at the same time throughout countries and continents. Nor is it the hierarchy of their geography, since this is in fact tributary to the variable geometry of money and information flows. After all, who could predict in the early 1980s that Taipei, Madrid, or Buenos Aires could emerge as important international financial and business centers? I believe that the megalopolis Hong Kong–Shenzhen–Guangzhou–Zhuhai–Macau will be one of the major

---

22 Personal notes, reported by Sassen over a glass of Argentinian wine, Harvard Inn, April 22, 1994.
23 For an approximation to the differentiation of social worlds in global cities, using New York as an illustration, see the various essays collected in Mollenkopf (1989); and Mollenkopf and Castells (1991); see also Zukin (1992).
24 For evidence on spatial decentralization of services, see Marshall et al. (1988); Castells (1989b: ch. 3); Daniels (1993: ch. 5).
25 See Castells (1989b: ch.3); and Dunford and Kafkalas (1992).

financial and business capitals in the early twenty-first century, thus inducing a major realignment in the global geography of advanced services.[26] But for the sake of the spatial analysis I am proposing here, it is secondary if I miss my prediction. Because, while the actual location of high-level centers in each period is critical for the distribution of wealth and power in the world, from the perspective of the spatial logic of the new system what matters is the versatility of its networks. The global city is not a place, but a process. A process by which centers of production and consumption of advanced services, and their ancillary local societies, are connected in a global network, while simultaneously downplaying the linkages with their hinterlands, on the basis of information flows.

The New Industrial Space

The advent of high-technology manufacturing, namely microelectronics-based, computer-aided manufacturing, ushered in a new logic of industrial location. Electronic firms, the producers of new information technology devices, were also the first to practice the locational strategy both allowed and required by the information-based production process. During the 1980s, a number of empirical studies conducted by faculty and graduate students at the University of California Berkeley's Institute of Urban and Regional Development provided a solid grasp on the profile of "the new industrial space."[27] It is characterized by the technological and organizational ability to separate the production process in different locations while reintegrating its unity through telecommunications linkages, and micro-electronics-based precision and flexibility in the fabrication of components. Furthermore, geographical specificity of each phase of the production process is made advisable by the singularity of the labor force required at each stage, and by the different social and environmental features involved in the living conditions of highly distinct segments of this labor force. This is because high-technology manufacturing presents an occupational composition very different from traditional manufacturing: it is organized in a bipolar structure around two predominant groups of roughly similar size; a highly skilled, science- and technology-based labor force, on the one hand; and a mass of unskilled workers engaged in routine assembly and auxiliary operations,

26 See Henderson (1991); Kwok and So (1992, 1995).
27 For an analytical summary of the evidence gathered by these studies on new patterns of manufacturing location, see Castells (1988a). See also Scott (1988); Henderson (1989).

on the other hand. While automation has increasingly enabled companies to eliminate the lower tier of workers, the staggering increase in the volume of production still employs, and will for some time, a considerable number of unskilled and semi-skilled workers whose location in the same areas as scientists and engineers is neither economically feasible nor socially suitable, in the prevailing social context. In between, skilled operators also represent a distinctive group that can be separated from the high levels of high-technology production. Because of the light weight of the final product, and because of easy communication linkages developed by companies throughout the globe, electronics firms, particularly American, developed from the beginnings of the industry (as early as Fairchild's plant location in Hong Kong in 1962) a locational pattern characterized by the international spatial division of labor.[28] Roughly speaking, both for micro-electronics and computers, four different types of location were sought for each one of the four distinctive operations in the production process:

1   R&D, innovation, and prototype fabrication were concentrated in highly innovative industrial centers in core areas, generally with good quality of life before their development process degraded the environment to some extent.
2   Skilled fabrication in branch plants, generally in newly industrializing areas in the home country, which in the case of the US generally meant in medium-sized towns in the Western states.
3   Semi-skilled, large-scale assembly and testing work that from the very beginning was located offshore in a substantial proportion, particularly in South-East Asia, with Singapore and Malaysia pioneering the movement of attracting factories of American electronics corporations.
4   Customization of devices and aftersales maintenance and technical support, which was organized in regional centers throughout the globe, generally in the area of major electronics markets, originally in America and Western Europe, although in the 1990s the Asian markets rose to equal status.

European companies, used to cozy locations on their protected home turfs, were pushed to decentralize their production systems in a similar global chain, as markets opened up, and they started to feel the pinch of competition from Asian-based operations, and from American and Japanese technological advantage.[29] Japanese companies tried

28   Cooper (1994).
29   Chesnais (1994).

to resist for a long time quitting "fortress Japan," both for reasons of nationalism (at the request of their government) and because of their close dependence on "just-in-time" networks of suppliers. However, unbearable congestion and sky-rocketing prices of operation in the Tokyo–Yokohama area forced first regional decentralization (helped by MITI's Technopolis Program) in less-developed areas of Japan, particularly in Kyushu;[30] and then, from the late 1980s, Japanese companies proceeded to follow the locational pattern initiated by their American competitors two decades earlier: offshore production facilities in South-East Asia, searching for lower labor costs and looser environmental constraints, and dissemination of factories throughout the main markets in America, Europe, and Asia in order to pre-empt future protectionism.[31] Thus, the end of Japanese exceptionalism confirmed the accuracy of the locational model that, together with a number of colleagues, we proposed to understand the new spatial logic of high-technology industry. Figure 6.3 displays schematically the spatial logic of this model, elaborated on the basis of empirical evidence gathered by a number of researchers in different contexts.[32]

A key element in this locational pattern is the decisive importance of technological innovation production complexes for the whole system. This is what Peter Hall and I, as well as the pioneer in this field of research, Philippe Aydalot, called "milieux of innovation."[33] By milieu of innovation I understand a specific set of relationships of production and management, based on a social organization that by and large shares a work culture and instrumental goals aimed at generating new knowledge, new processes, and new products. Although the concept of milieu does not necessarily include a spatial dimension, I argue that in the case of information technology industries, at least in this century, spatial proximity is a necessary material condition for the existence of such milieux because of the nature of the interaction in the innovation process. What defines the specificity of a milieu of innovation is its capacity to generate synergy; that is, the added value resulting not from the cumulative effect of the elements present in the

30 Castells and Hall (1994).
31 Aoyama (1995).
32 Castells (1989b: ch. 2).
33 The concept of milieu of innovation, as applied to technological/industrial development, emerged in the early 1980s in a series of exchanges, in Berkeley, between Peter Hall, the late Philippe Aydalot, and myself. We were also influenced by some economic writings on the matter, around the same time, by B. Arthur and by A. E. Anderson. Peter Hall and I, in separate papers, attempted formulations of the concept in 1984 and subsequent years; and in Europe the research network originally organized by Philippe Aydalot, the Groupe de Recherche sur les Milieux Innovateurs (GREMI), undertook systematic research on the matter, published in 1986 and subsequent years. Among GREMI researchers, Roberto Camagni provided, in my personal opinion, the most precise analysis on this topic.

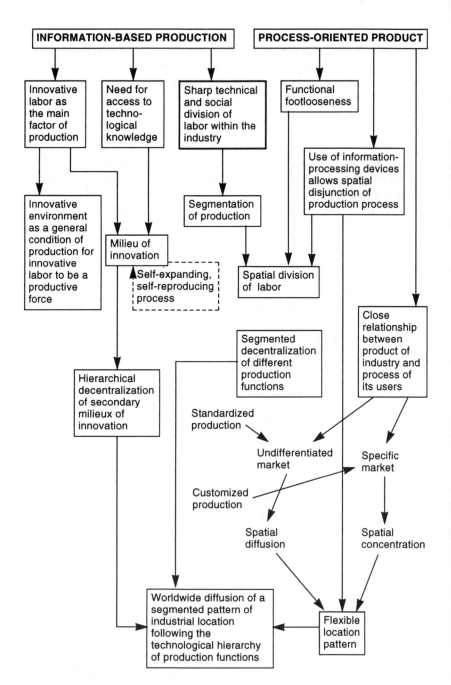

Figure 6.3 System of relationships between the characteristics of information technology manufacturing and the industry's spatial pattern
Source: Castells (1989a)

milieu but from their interaction. Milieux of innovation are the fundamental sources of innovation and of generation of value added in the process of industrial production in the Information Age. Peter Hall and I studied for several years the formation, structure, and dynamics of the main technological milieux of innovation around the world, both actual and supposed. The results of our inquiry added some elements to the understanding of the locational pattern of information technology industry.[34]

First of all, high-technology-led industrial milieux of innovation, which we called "technopoles," come in a variety of urban formats. Most notably, it is clear that in most countries, with the important exceptions of the United States and, to some extent, Germany, the leading technopoles are in fact contained in the leading metropolitan areas: Tokyo, Paris-Sud, London–M4 Corridor, Milan, Seoul–Inchon, Moscow–Zelenograd, and at a considerable distance Nice–Sophia Antipolis, Taipei–Hsinchu, Singapore, Shanghai, São Paulo, Barcelona, and so on. The partial exception of Germany (after all, Munich is a major metropolitan area) relates directly to political history: the destruction of Berlin, the pre-eminent European science-based industrial center, and the relocation of Siemens from Berlin to Munich in the last months of the Third Reich, under the anticipated protection of American occupation forces and with the subsequent support of the Bavarian CSU party. Thus, against the excessive imagery of upstart technopoles there is indeed continuity in the spatial history of technology and industrialization in the Information Age: major metropolitan centers around the world continue to cumulate innovation-inducing factors and to generate synergy, in manufacturing as in advanced services.

However, some of the most important innovation centers of information technology manufacturing are indeed new, particularly in the world's technological leader, the United States. Silicon Valley, Boston's Route 128 (rejuvenating an old, traditional manufacturing structure), the southern California technopole, North Carolina's research triangle, Seattle, and Austin, among others, were by and large linked to the latest wave of information-technology-based industrialization. We have shown that their development resulted from the clustering of specific varieties of the usual factors of production: capital, labor, and raw material, brought together by some kind of institutional entrepreneur, and constituted by a particular form of social organization. Their raw material was made up of new knowledge, related to strategically important fields of application, produced by

34 Castells and Hall (1994).

major centers of innovation, such as Stanford University, CalTech, or MIT schools of engineering research teams, and the networks built around them. Their labor, distinct from the knowledge factor, required the concentration of a large number of highly skilled scientists and engineers, from a variety of locally based schools, including those mentioned above but also others, such as Berkeley, San Jose State, or Santa Clara, in the case of Silicon Valley. Their capital was also specific, willing to take the high risks of investing in pioneering high-tech: either because of the military imperative on performance (defense-related spending), or else because of the high stakes of venture capital betting on the extra rewards of risk-taking investments. The articulation of these production factors was generally the fact, at the onset of the process, of an institutional actor, such as Stanford University launching the Stanford Industrial Park that induced Silicon Valley; or the Air Force commanders who, relying on Los Angeles boosterism, won for southern California the defense contracts that would make the new Western metropolis the largest high-technology defense complex in the world. Finally, social networks, of different kinds, powerfully contributed to the consolidation of the milieu of innovation, and to its dynamism, ensuring the communication of ideas, the circulation of labor, and the cross-fertilization of technological innovation and business entrepreneurialism.

What our research on the new milieux of innovation, in the US or elsewhere, shows is that while there is indeed spatial continuity in metropolitan dominance, it can also be reversed given the right conditions. And that the right conditions concern the capacity to spatially concentrate the proper ingredients for inducing synergy. If such is the case, as our evidence seems to support, then we do have a new industrial space marked by fundamental discontinuity: milieux of innovation, new and old, constitute themselves on the basis of their internal structure and dynamics, later attracting firms, capital, and labor to the seedbed of innovation they constituted. Once established, milieux of innovation both compete and cooperate between different regions, creating a network of interaction that brings them together in a common industrial structure beyond their geographical discontinuity. Research by Camagni and the research teams organized around the GREMI network[35] shows the growing interdependence of these milieux of innovation all over the globe, while at the same time emphasizing how decisive for its fate is the capacity of each milieu to enhance its synergy. Finally, milieux of innovation command global networks of production and distribution that extend their reach all over the

35 Camagni (1991).

planet. This is why some researchers, such as Amin and Robins, argue that the new industrial system is neither global nor local but "a new articulation of global and local dynamics."[36]

However, to have a clear vision of the new industrial space constituted in the Information Age we must add some precision. This is because too often the emphasis of the analysis has been placed on the hierarchical spatial division of labor between different functions located in different territories. This is important, but not essential in the new spatial logic. Territorial hierarchies can be blurred, and even reversed, as the industry expands throughout the world, and as competition enhances or depresses entire agglomerations, including milieux of innovation themselves. Also, secondary milieux of innovation are constituted, sometimes as decentralized systems spun off from primary centers, but they often find their niches in competition with their original matrices, examples to the point being Seattle *vis-à-vis* Silicon Valley and Boston in software, or Austin, Texas, *vis-à-vis* New York or Minneapolis in computers. Furthermore, in the 1990s, the development of the electronics industry in Asia, mainly under the impulse of American–Japanese competition, has complicated extraordinarily the geography of the industry in its mature stage, as shown in the analyses by Cohen and Borrus and by Dieter Ernst.[37] On the one hand, there has been substantial upgrading of the technological potential of American multinationals' subsidiaries, particularly in Singapore, Malaysia, and Taiwan, and this upgrading has trickled down to their local subsidiaries. On the other hand, Japanese electronics firms, as mentioned above, have massively decentralized their production in Asia, both to export globally and to supply their onshore parent plants. In both cases, a substantial supply base has been built in Asia, thus rendering obsolete the old spatial division of labor in which South-East and East Asian subsidiaries occupied the bottom level of the hierarchy.

Furthermore, on the basis of the review of available evidence up to 1994, including his own company surveys, Richard Gordon convincingly argues for the emergence of a new spatial division of labor, one characterized by its variable geometry, and its back and forth linkages between firms located in different territorial complexes, including the leading milieux of innovation. His detailed analysis of developments in 1990s' Silicon Valley shows the importance of extra-regional relationships for the most technologically sophisticated and transaction-intensive interactions of regional high-technology firms. Thus he argues that

---

36 Amin and Robins (1991).
37 Ernst (1994c); Cohen and Borrus (1995a).

in this new global context, localized agglomeration, far from constituting an alternative to spatial dispersion, becomes the principal basis for
participation in a global network of regional economies . . . Regions
and networks in fact constitute interdependent poles within the new
spatial mosaic of global innovation. Globalization in this context involves not the leavening impact of universal processes but, on the contrary, the calculated synthesis of cultural diversity in the form of
differentiated regional innovation logics and capabilities.[38]

The new industrial space does not represent the demise of old, established metropolitan areas and the rising sun of new, high-tech regions. Nor can it be apprehended under the simplistic opposition
between automation at the center and low-cost manufacturing at the
periphery. It is organized in a hierarchy of innovation and fabrication
articulated in global networks. But the direction and architecture of
these networks are submitted to the endless changing movements of
cooperation and competition between firms and between locales, sometimes historically cumulative, sometimes reversing the established pattern through deliberate institutional entrepreneurialism. What does
remain as the characteristic logic of the new industrial location is its
geographical discontinuity, paradoxically made up of territorial production complexes. The new industrial space is organized around flows
of information that bring together and separate at the same time –
depending upon cycles or firms – their territorial components. And as
the logic of information technology manufacturing trickles down from
the producers of information technology devices to the users of such
devices in the whole realm of manufacturing, so the new spatial logic
expands, creating a multiplicity of global industrial networks whose
intersections and exclusions transform the very notion of industrial
location from factory sites to manufacturing flows.

Everyday Life in the Electronic Cottage: the End of Cities?

The development of electronic communication and information systems allows for an increasing disassociation between spatial proxim-
ity and the performance of everyday life's functions: work, shopping,
entertainment, healthcare, education, public services, governance, and
the like. Accordingly, futurologists often predict the demise of the city,
or at least of cities as we have known them until now, once they are

38 Gordon (1994: 46).

voided of their functional necessity. Processes of spatial transformation are of course much more complicated, as history shows. Therefore, it is worthwhile to consider the scant empirical record on the matter.[39]

A dramatic increase of teleworking is the most usual assumption about the impact of information technology on cities, and the last hope for metropolitan transportation planners before surrendering to the inevitability of the mega-gridlock. Yet, in 1988, a leading European researcher on telecommuting could write, without the shadow of a joke, that "There are more people doing research on telework than there are actual teleworkers."[40] In fact, as noted by Qvortup, the whole debate is biased by the lack of precision in defining telework, leading to considerable uncertainty when measuring the phenomenon.[41] After reviewing available evidence, he adequately distinguishes between three categories: (a) "Substitutors, those who substitute work done at home for work done in a traditional work setting" (these are telecommuters in the strict sense); (b) self-employed, working on-line from their homes; (c) supplementers, "bringing supplementary work home from their conventional office." Furthermore, in some cases this "supplementary work" takes most of the working time; for example, according to Kraut,[42] in the case of university professors. By most reliable accounts, the first category, telecommuters *stricto sensu* employed regularly to work on-line at home, is very small overall, and is not expected to grow substantially in the foreseeable future.[43] In the United States the highest estimates evaluated in 1991 about 5.5 million home-based telecommuters, but of this total only 16 percent telecommuted 35 hours or more per week, 25 percent telecommuted less than one day a week, with two days a week being the most common pattern. Thus, the percentage of workers who on any given day are telecommuting ranges, depending on estimates, between 1 and 2 percent of total labor force, with major metropolitan areas in California displaying the highest percentages.[44] On the other hand, what seems to be emerging is telecommuting from telecenters; that is, networked computer facilities scattered in the suburbs of metropolitan areas for workers to work on-line with their companies.[45] If these trends are confirmed, homes would not become workplaces, but work activity could spread con-

39 For sources on topics covered in this section, see Graham and Marvin (1996); Wheeler and Aoyama (2000).
40 Steinle (1988: 8).
41 Qvortup (1992: 8).
42 Kraut (1989).
43 Nilles (1988); Rijn and Williams (1988); Huws et al. (1990).
44 Mokhtarian (1991a, b); Handy and Mokhtarian (1995).
45 Mokhtarian (1991b).

siderably throughout the metropolitan area, increasing urban decentralization. Increase in home work may also result as a form of electronic outworking by temporary workers, paid by the piece of information processing under an individualized subcontracting arrangement.[46] Interestingly enough, in the United States, a 1991 national survey showed that fewer than a half of home telecommuters used computers: the rest worked with a telephone, pen, and paper.[47] Examples of such activities are social workers and welfare fraud investigators in Los Angeles County.[48] What is certainly significant, and on the rise, is the development of self-employment, and of "supplementers," either full-time or part-time, as part of the broader trend toward the disaggregation of labor and the formation of virtual business networks, as indicated in previous chapters. This does not imply the end of the office, but the diversification of working sites for a large fraction of the population, and particularly for its most dynamic, professional segment. Increasingly mobile telecomputing equipment will enhance this trend toward the office-on-the-run, in the most literal sense.[49]

How do these tendencies affect cities? Scattered data seem to indicate that transportation problems will get worse, not better, because increasing activity and time compression allowed by new networking organization translate into higher concentration of markets in certain areas, and into greater physical mobility for a labor force that was previously confined to its working sites during working hours.[50] Work-related commuting time is kept at a steady level in the US metropolitan areas, not because of improved technology, but because of a more decentralized location pattern of jobs and residences that allows easier, suburb-to-suburb traffic flows. In those cities, particularly in Europe, where a radioconcentric pattern still dominates daily commuting (such as Paris, Madrid, or Milan), commuting time is sharply up, particularly for stubborn automobile addicts.[51] As for the new, sprawling metropolises of Asia, their coming into the Information Age runs parallel to their discovery of the most awesome traffic jams in history, from Bangkok to Shanghai.[52]

Teleshopping was slow to live up to its promise, and ultimately was pushed out by the Internet's competition. It supplemented rather than replaced commercial areas.[53] However, e-commerce, with billions of

46   See Lozano (1989); Gurstein (1990).
47   "Telecommuting data form link resources corporation," cited by Mokhtarian (1991b).
48   Mokhtarian (1992:12).
49   "The New Face of Business," in *Business Week* (1994a: 99ff).
50   I have relied on a balanced evaluation of impacts by Vessali (1995).
51   Cervero (1989, 1991); Bendixon (1991).
52   Lo and Yeung (1996).
53   Miles (1988); Schoonmaker (1993); Menotti (1995).

dollars of on-line sales in the US over Christmas 1999, is a major, new development (see chapter 2). Nevertheless, the growing importance of on-line transactions does not imply the disappearance of shopping centers and retail stores. In fact, the trend is the opposite: shopping areas proliferate around the urban and suburban landscape, with show-rooms that address customers to on-line ordering terminals to get the actual goods, often home-delivered.[54] A similar story can be told for most on-line consumer services. For instance, telebanking[55] is spreading fast, mainly under the impulse of banks interested in eliminating branch offices and replacing them by on-line customer services and automated-teller machines. However, the consolidated bank branches continue as service centers, to sell financial products to their customers through a personalized relationship. Even on-line, cultural features of localities may be important as locational factors for information-oriented transactions. Thus, First Direct, the telephone banking branch of Midland Bank in Britain, located in Leeds because its research "showed West Yorkshire's plain accent, with its flat vowel sounds but clear diction and apparent classlessness, to be the most easily under-stood and acceptable throughout the UK – a vital element of any tele-phone-based business."[56] Thus, it is the system of branch office sellers, automated tellers, customer service-by-telephone, and on-line trans-actions that constitutes the new banking industry.

Health services offer an even more interesting case of the emerging dialectics between concentration and centralization of people-oriented services. On the one hand, expert systems, on-line communications, and high-resolution video transmission allow for the distant intercon-nection of medical care. For instance, in a practice that has become usual, if not yet routine, in 1995, highly skilled surgeons supervise by videoconference surgery performed at the other end of the country or of the world, literally guiding the less-expert hand of another surgeon into a human body. Regular health checks are also conducted via com-puter and telephone on the basis of patients' computerized, updated information. Neighborhood healthcare centers are backed by infor-mation systems to improve the quality and efficiency of their primary-level attention. Yet, on the other hand, in most countries major medical complexes emerge in specific locales, generally in large metropolitan areas. Usually organized around a big hospital, often connected to medical and nursing schools, they include in their physical proxim-ity private clinics headed by the most prominent hospital doctors,

54 *Business Week* (1999d).
55 Castano (1991); Silverstone (1991).
56 Fazy (1995).

radiology centers, test laboratories, specialized pharmacists, and, not infrequently, gift shops and mortuaries, to cater for the whole range of possibilities. Indeed, such medical complexes are a major economic and cultural force in the areas and cities where they are located, and tend to expand in their surrounding vicinity over time. When forced to relocate, the whole complex moves together.[57]

Schools and universities are paradoxically the institutions least affected by the virtual logic embedded in information technology, in spite of the foreseeable quasi-universal use of computers in the classrooms of advanced countries. But they will hardly vanish into virtual space. In the case of elementary and secondary schools, this is because they are as much childcare centers and/or children's warehouses as they are learning institutions. In the case of universities, this is because the quality of education is still, and will be for a long time, associated with the intensity of face-to-face interaction. Thus, the large-scale experiences of "distant universities," regardless of their quality (bad in Spain, good in Britain), seem to show that they are second-option forms of education which could play a significant role in a future, enhanced system of adult education, but which could hardly replace current higher-education institutions. What is emerging, however, in good-quality universities is the combination of on-line, distant learning and on-site education. This means that the future higher-education system will not be on-line, but on networks between nodes of information, classrooms' sites, and students' individual locations. Computer-mediated communication is diffusing around the world, although with an extremely uneven geography, as mentioned in chapter 5. Thus, some segments of societies across the globe, for the time being concentrated in the upper professional strata, interact with each other, reinforcing the social dimension of the space of flows.[58]

There is no point in exhausting the list of empirical illustrations of the actual impacts of information technology on the spatial dimension of everyday life. What emerges from different observations is a similar picture of simultaneous spatial dispersion and concentration via information technologies. People increasingly work and manage services from their home, as the 1993 survey of the European Foundation for the Improvement of Living and Working Conditions shows.[59] Thus, "home centeredness" is an important trend of the new society. Yet it does not mean the end of the city. Because workplaces, schools, medi-

57   Moran (1990); Lincoln et al. (1993); Miller and Swensson (1995).
58   Batty and Barr (1994); Graham and Marvin (1996); Wellman (1999).
59   Moran (1993).

cal complexes, consumer services outlets, recreational areas, commercial streets, shopping centers, sports stadiums, and parks still exist and will exist, and people will shuttle between all these places with increasing mobility precisely because of the newly acquired looseness of working arrangements and social networking: as time becomes more flexible, places become more singular, as people circulate among them in an increasingly mobile pattern.

However, the interaction between new information technology and current processes of social change does have a substantial impact on cities and space. On the one hand, the urban form is considerably transformed in its layout. But this transformation does not follow a single, universal pattern: it shows considerable variation depending upon the characteristics of historical, territorial, and institutional contexts. On the other hand, the emphasis on interactivity between places breaks up spatial patterns of behavior into a fluid network of exchanges that underlies the emergence of a new kind of space, the space of flows. On both counts, I must tighten the analysis and raise it to a more theoretical level.

The Transformation of Urban Form: the Informational City

The Information Age is ushering in a new urban form, the informational city. Yet, as the industrial city was not a worldwide replica of Manchester, the emerging informational city will not copy Silicon Valley, let alone Los Angeles. On the other hand, as in the industrial era, in spite of the extraordinary diversity of cultural and physical contexts there are some fundamental common features in the transcultural development of the informational city. I shall argue that, because of the nature of the new society, based upon knowledge, organized around networks, and partly made up of flows, the informational city is not a form but a process, a process characterized by the structural domination of the space of flows. Before developing this idea, I think it is first necessary to introduce the diversity of emerging urban forms in the new historical period, to counter a primitive technological vision that sees the world through the simplified lenses of endless freeways and fiber-optic networks.

America's last suburban frontier

The image of a homogeneous, endless suburban/ex-urban sprawl as the city of the future is belied even by its unwilling model, Los

Angeles, whose contradictory complexity is revealed by Mike Davis's marvelous *City of Quartz*.[60] Yet it does evoke a powerful trend in the relentless waves of suburban development in the American metropolis, West and South as well as North and East, toward the end of the millennium. Joel Garreau has captured the similarities of this spatial model across America in his journalistic account of the rise of *Edge City*, as the core of the new urbanization process. He empirically defines Edge City by the combination of five criteria:

> Edge City is any place that: (a) Has five million square feet or more of leasable office space – the work place of the Information Age . . . (b) Has 600,000 square feet or more of leasable retail space . . . (c) Has more jobs than bedrooms (d) Is perceived by the population as one place . . . (e) Was nothing like 'city' as recently as thirty years ago.[61]

He reports the mushrooming of such places around Boston, New Jersey, Detroit, Atlanta, Phoenix, Texas, southern California, San Francisco Bay area, and Washington, DC. They are both working areas and service centers around which mile after mile of increasingly dense, single-family dwelling residential units organize the "home centeredness" of private life. He remarks that these ex-urban constellations are:

> tied together not by locomotives and subways, but by freeways, jetways, and rooftop satellite dishes thirty feet across. Their characteristic monument is not a horse-mounted hero, but the atria reaching for the sun and shielding trees perpetually in leaf at the core of corporate headquarters, fitness centers, and shopping plazas. These new urban areas are marked not by the penthouses of the old urban rich or the tenements of the old urban poor. Instead, their landmark structure is the celebrated single-family detached dwelling, the suburban home with grass all around that made America the best housed civilization the world has ever known.[62]

Naturally, where Garreau sees the relentless frontier spirit of American culture, always creating new forms of life and space, James Howard Kunstler sees the regrettable domination of the "geography of nowhere,"[63] thus reigniting a decades-long debate between partisans and detractors of America's sharp spatial departure from its European ancestry. Yet, for the purpose of my analysis, I will retain just two major points of this debate.

60   Davis (1990).
61   Garreau (1991: 6–7).
62   Garreau (1991: 4).
63   Kunstler (1993).

First, the development of these loosely interrelated ex-urban con-stellations emphasizes the functional interdependence of different units and processes in a given urban system over very long distances, mini-mizing the role of territorial contiguity, and maximizing the commu-nication networks in all their dimensions. Flows of exchange are at the core of the American Edge City.[64]

Secondly, this spatial form is indeed very specific to the American experience because, as Garreau acknowledges, it is embedded in a classic pattern of American history, always pushing for the endless search for a promised land in new settlements. While the extraordinary dyna-mism that this represents did indeed build one of the most vital na-tions in history, it did so at the price of creating, over time, staggering social and environmental problems. Each wave of social and physical escapism (for example, the abandonment of inner cities, leaving the lower social classes and ethnic minorities trapped in their ruins) deep-ened the crisis of American cities,[65] and made more difficult the man-agement of an overextended infrastructure and of an overstressed society. Unless the development of private "jails-for-rent" in Western Texas is considered a welcome process to complement the social and physical disinvestment in American inner cities, the *"fuite en avant"* of American culture and space seems to have reached the limits of refusing to face unpleasant realities. Thus, the profile of America's informational city is not fully represented by the Edge City phenom-enon, but by the relationship between fast ex-urban development, in-ner-city decay, and obsolescence of the suburban built environment.[66]

European cities have entered the Information Age along a different line of spatial restructuring linked to their historical heritage, although finding new issues, not always dissimilar to those emerging in the American context.

The fading charm of European cities

A number of trends constitute together the new urban dynamics of major European metropolitan areas in the 1990s.[67] The business center is, as in America, the economic engine of the city, networked in the global economy. The business center is made up of an infrastructure of telecommunications, communications, advanced services, and of-fice space, based upon technology-generating centers and educational

64 See the collection of papers gathered in Caves (1994).
65 Goldsmith and Blakely (1992).
66 Gottdiener (1985); Fainstein et al. (1992).
67 For developments on European cities, see Borja et al. (1991); Deben et al. (1993); Martinotti (1993); Siino (1994); Hall (1995); Borja and Castells (1997).

institutions. It thrives upon information processing and control functions. It is usually complemented by tourism and travel facilities. It is a
node of the inter-metropolitan network.[68] Thus, the business center
does not exist by itself but by its connection to other equivalent locales organized in a network that forms the actual unit of management, innovation, and work.[69]

The new managerial–technocratic–political elite does create exclusive spaces, as segregated and removed from the city at large as the
bourgeois quarters of the industrial society, but, because the professional class is larger, on a much larger scale. In most European cities
(Paris, Rome, Madrid, Amsterdam), unlike in America – if we except
New York, the most un-American of US cities – the truly exclusive
residential areas tend to appropriate urban culture and history, by
locating in rehabilitated or well-preserved areas of the central city. By
so doing, they emphasize the fact that when domination is clearly established and enforced (unlike in *nouveau-riche* America) the elite does
not need to go into suburban exile to escape the populace. This trend
is, however, limited in the case of the UK where the nostalgia for the
life of the gentry in the countryside translates into up-scale residence
in selected suburbs of metropolitan areas, sometimes urbanizing charming historic villages in the vicinity of a major city.

The suburban world of European cities is a socially diversified space;
that is, segmented in different peripheries around the central city. There
are the traditional working-class suburbs, often organized around large,
public housing estates, lately in home ownership. There are the new
towns, French, British, or Swedish, inhabited by a younger population
of the middle classes, whose age made it difficult for them to penetrate
the housing market of the central city. And there are also the peripheral ghettos of older public housing estates, exemplified by Paris's La
Courneuve, where new immigrant populations and poor working families experience exclusion from their "right to the city." Suburbs are
also the locus of manufacturing production in European cities, both
for traditional manufacturing and for new, high-technology industries
that locate in the newest and environmentally most desirable peripheries of metropolitan areas, close enough to the communication centers
but removed from old industrial districts.

Central cities are still shaped by their history. Thus, traditional working-class neighborhoods, increasingly populated by service workers,
constitute a distinctive space, a space that, because it is the most vulnerable, becomes the battleground between the redevelopment efforts

68   Dunford and Kafkalas (1992); Robson (1992).
69   Tarr and Dupuy (1988).

of business and the upper middle class, and the invasion attempts of countercultures (Amsterdam, Copenhagen, Berlin) trying to reappropriate the use value of the city. Thus, they often become defensive spaces for workers who only have their home to fight for, being at the same time meaningful popular neighborhoods and likely bastions of xenophobia and localism.

The new professional middle class in Europe is torn between attraction to the peaceful comfort of boring suburbs and the excitement of a hectic, and often too expensive, urban life. The trade-offs between the differential spatial patterns of work of dual-job families often determine the location of their household.

The central city, in Europe as well, is also the focus for the ghettos of immigrants. However, unlike American ghettos, most of these areas are not so economically deprived because immigrant residents are generally workers, with strong family ties, thus counting on a very strong support structure that makes European ghettos family-oriented communities, unlikely to be taken over by street crime. England again seems exceptional in this regard, with some ethnic-minority neighborhoods in London (for example, Tower Hamlets or Hackney) being closer to the American experience than to Paris's La Goutte d'Or. Paradoxically, it is in the core administrative and entertainment districts of European cities, be it Frankfurt or Barcelona, where urban marginality makes its presence felt. Its pervasive occupation of the busiest streets and public transportation nodal points is a survival strategy destined to be present, so that they can receive public attention or private business, whether it be welfare assistance, a drug transaction, a prostitution deal, or the customary police attention.

Major European metropolitan centers present some variation around the urban structure I have outlined, depending upon their differential role in the European network of cities. The lower their position in the new informational network, the greater the difficulty of their transition from the industrial stage, and the more traditional will be their urban structure, with old-established neighborhoods and commercial quarters playing the determinant role in the dynamics of the city. On the other hand, the higher their position in the competitive structure of the new European economy, the greater the role of their advanced services in the business district, and the more intense will be the restructuring of urban space.

The critical factor in the new urban processes, in Europe as elsewhere, is the fact that urban space is increasingly differentiated in social terms, while being functionally interrelated beyond physical contiguity. There follows the separation between symbolic meaning, location of functions, and the social appropriation of space in the metropolitan area. This is the trend underlying the most important transformation of urban forms worldwide, with particular force in the newly industrializing areas: the rise of mega-cities.

Third millennium urbanization: mega-cities

The new global economy and the emerging informational society have indeed a new spatial form, which develops in a variety of social and geographical contexts: mega-cities.[70] Mega-cities are, certainly, very large agglomerations of human beings, all of them (13 in the United Nations classification) with over 10 million people in 1992 (see figure 6.4), and four of them projected to be well over 20 million in 2010. But size is not their defining quality. They are the nodes of the global economy, concentrating the directional, productive, and managerial upper functions all over the planet: the control of the media; the real politics of power; and the symbolic capacity to create and diffuse messages. They have names, most of them alien to the still dominant European/North American cultural matrix: Tokyo, São Paulo, New York, Ciudad de Mexico, Shanghai, Bombay, Los Angeles, Buenos Aires, Seoul, Beijing, Rio de Janeiro, Calcutta, Osaka. In addition, Moscow, Jakarta, Cairo, New Delhi, London, Paris, Lagos, Dacca, Karachi, Tianjin, and possibly others, are in fact members of the club.[71] Not all of them (for example, Dacca or Lagos) are dominant centers of the global economy, but they do connect to this global system huge segments of the human population. They also function as magnets for their hinterlands; that is, the whole country or regional area where they are located. Mega-cities cannot be seen only in terms of their size, but as a function of their gravitational power toward major regions of the world. Thus, Hong Kong is not just its six million people, and Guangzhou is not just its six and a half million people: what is emerging is a mega-city of 40–50 million people, connecting Hong Kong, Shenzhen, Guangzhou, Zhuhai, Macau, and small towns in the Pearl River Delta, as I shall develop below. Mega-cities articulate the global economy, link up the informational networks, and concentrate the world's power. But they are also the depositories of all these segments of the population who fight to survive, as well as of those groups who want to make visible their dereliction, so that they will not die ignored in areas bypassed by communication networks. Mega-cities concen-

70   The notion of mega-cities has been popularized by several urban experts in the international arena, most notably by Janice Perlman, founder and director of the New York-based "Mega-cities Project." For a journalistic account of her vision, see *Time* (1993), which also offers basic data on the topic.
71   See Borja and Castells (1997).

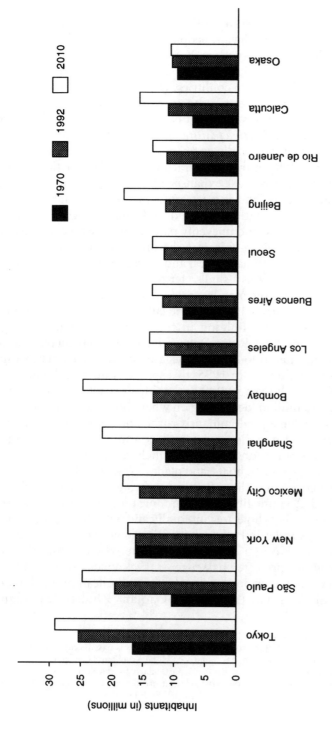

Figure 6.4 The world's largest urban agglomerations (> 10 million inhabitants in 1992)
Source: United Nations (1992)

trate the best and the worst, from the innovators and the powers that be to their structurally irrelevant people, ready to sell their irrelevance or to make "the others" pay for it. Yet what is most significant about mega-cities is that they are connected externally to global networks and to segments of their own countries, while internally disconnecting local populations that are either functionally unnecessary or socially disruptive. I argue that this is true of New York as well as of Mexico or Jakarta. *It is this distinctive feature of being globally connected and locally disconnected, physically and socially, that makes mega-cities a new urban form.* A form that is characterized by the functional linkages it establishes across vast expanses of territory, yet with a great deal of discontinuity in land-use patterns. Mega-cities' functional and social hierarchies are spatially blurred and mixed, organized in retrenched encampments, and unevenly patched by unexpected pockets of undesirable uses. Mega-cities are discontinuous constellations of spatial fragments, functional pieces, and social segments.[72]

To illustrate my analysis I shall refer to a mega-city in the making that is not even yet on the map but that, in my opinion, will be one of the pre-eminent industrial, business, and cultural centers of the twenty-first century, without indulging in futurology: the Hong Kong–Shenzhen–Canton–Pearl River Delta–Macau–Zhuhai metropolitan regional system.[73] Let us look at the mega-urban future from this vantage point (see figure 6.5). In 1995, this spatial system, still without a name, extended itself over 50,000 km², with a total population of between 40 and 50 million, depending on where boundaries are defined. Its units, scattered in a predominantly rural landscape, were functionally connected on a daily basis, and communicated through a multimodal transportation system that included railways, freeways, country roads, hovercrafts, boats, and planes. New superhighways were under construction, and the railway was being fully electrified and double-tracked. An optic fiber telecommunications system was in process of connecting the whole area internally and with the world, mainly via earth stations and cellular telephony. Five new airports were under construction in Hong Kong, Macau, Shenzhen, Zhuhai, and Guangzhou, with a projected passenger traffic capacity of 150 million per year. New container ports were also being built in North Lantau (Hong Kong), Yiantian (Shenzhen), Gaolan (Zhuhai), Huangpo

72   Mollenkopf and Castells (1991); Lo and Yeung (1996).
73   My analysis on the emerging southern China metropolis is based, on the one hand, on my personal knowledge of the area, particularly of Hong Kong and Shenzhen, where I conducted research in the 1980s; on the other hand, particularly for developments in the 1990s, on a number of sources of which the most relevant are the following: Sit (1991); Leung (1993); Lo (1994); Hsing (1995); Kwok and So (1995); Ling (1995).

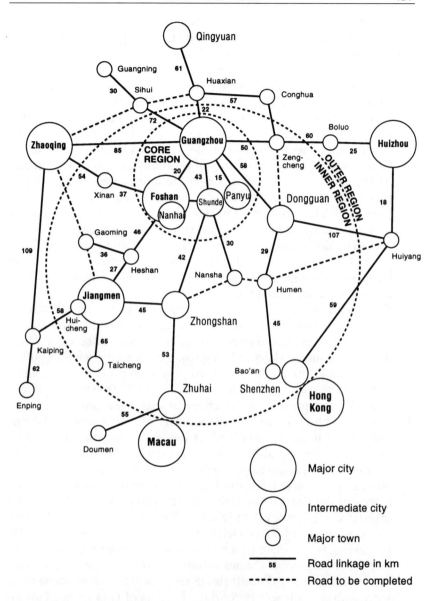

Figure 6.5 Diagrammatic representation of major nodes and links in the urban region of the Pearl River Delta
Source: Woo (1994)

(Guangzhou) and Macau, adding up to the world's largest port capacity in a given location. At the heart of such staggering metropolitan development are three interlinked phenomena:

1   The economic transformation of China, and its link-up to the global economy, with Hong Kong being one of the nodal points in such connection. Thus, in 1981–91, Guandong province's GDP grew at 12.8 percent per year in real terms. Hong Kong-based investors accounted at the end of 1993 for US$40 billion invested in China, representing two-thirds of total foreign direct investment. At the same time, China was also the largest foreign investor in Hong Kong, with about US$25 billion a year (compared with Japan's US$12.7 billion). The management of these capital flows was dependent upon the business transactions operated in, and in between, the various units of this metropolitan system. Thus, Guanghzou was the actual connecting point between Hong Kong business and the governments and enterprises not only of Guandong province, but of inland China.

2   The restructuring of Hong Kong's economic basis in the 1990s led to a dramatic shrinkage of Hong Kong's traditional manufacturing basis, to be replaced by employment in advanced services. Thus, manufacturing workers in Hong Kong decreased from 837,000 in 1988 to 484,000 in 1993, while employees in trading and business sectors increased, in the same period, from 947,000 to 1.3 million. Hong Kong developed its functions as a global business center.

3   However, Hong Kong's manufacturing exports capacity did not fade away: it simply modified its industrial organization and its spatial location. In about ten years, between the mid-1980s and the mid-1990s, Hong Kong's industrialists induced one of the largest-scale processes of industrialization in human history in the small towns of the Pearl River Delta. By the end of 1994, Hong Kong investors, often using family and village connections, had established in the Pearl River Delta 10,000 joint ventures and 20,000 processing factories, in which were working about 6 million workers, depending upon various estimates. Much of this population, housed in company dormitories in semi-rural locations, came from surrounding provinces beyond the borders of Guandong. This gigantic industrial system was being managed on a daily basis from a multilayered managerial structure, based in Hong Kong, regularly traveling to Guangzhou, with production runs being supervised by local managers throughout the rural area. Materials, technology, and managers were being sent from Hong Kong and Shenzhen, and manufactured goods were generally exported from

Hong Kong (actually surpassing the value of Hong Kong-made exports), although the building of new container ports in Yiantian and Gaolan aimed at diversifying export sites.

This accelerated process of export-oriented industrialization and business linkages between China and the global economy led to an unprecedented urban explosion. Shenzhen Special Economic Zone, on the Hong Kong border, grew from zero to 1.5 million inhabitants between 1982 and 1995. Local governments in the whole area, full of cash from overseas Chinese investors, embarked on the construction of major infrastructural projects, the most amazing of which, still in the planning stage at the time of writing, was the decision by Zhuhai's local government to build a 60 km bridge over the South China Sea to link by road Zhuhai and Hong Kong.

The southern China metropolis, still in the making but a sure reality, is a new spatial form. It is not the traditional megalopolis identified by Gottman in the 1960s on the north-eastern seaboard of the United States. Unlike this classical case, the Hong Kong–Guandong metropolitan region is not made up of the physical conurbation of successive urban/suburban units with relative functional autonomy in each one of them. It is rapidly becoming an interdependent unit, economically, functionally, and socially, even more so after Hong Kong and Macau rejoined China. But there is considerable spatial discontinuity within the area, with rural settlements, agricultural land, and undeveloped areas separating urban centers, and industrial factories being scattered all over the region. The internal linkages of the area and the indispensable connection of the whole system to the global economy via multiple communication links are the real backbone of this new spatial unit. Flows define the spatial form and processes. Within each city, within each area, processes of segregation and segmentation take place, in a pattern of endless variation. But such segmented diversity is dependent upon a functional unity marked by gigantic, technology-intensive infrastructures, which seem to know as their only limit the amount of fresh water that the region can still retrieve from the East River area. The southern China metropolis, only vaguely perceived in most of the world at this time, is likely to become the most representative urban face of the twenty-first century.

Current trends point in the direction of another Asian mega-city on an even greater scale when, in the early twenty-first century, the corridor Tokyo–Yokohama–Nagoya (already a functional unit) links up with Osaka–Kobe–Kyoto, creating the largest metropolitan agglomeration in human history, not only in terms of population, but in economic and technological power. Thus, in spite of all their social, urban and environmental problems, mega-cities will continue to grow, both in their size and in their attractiveness for the location of high-level functions and for people's choice. The ecological dream of small, quasi-rural communes will be pushed away to countercultural marginality by the historical tide of mega-city development. This is because mega-cities are:

- centers of economic, technological, and social dynamism, in their countries and on a global scale; they are the actual development engines; their countries' economic fate, be it the United States or China, depends on mega-cities' performance, in spite of the small-town ideology still pervasive in both countries;
- centers of cultural and political innovation;
- connecting points to the global networks of every kind; the Internet cannot bypass mega-cities: it depends on the telecommunications and on the "telecommunicators" located in those centers.

To be sure, some factors will slow down their pace of growth, depending on the accuracy and effectiveness of policies designed to limit mega-cities' growth. Family planning is working, in spite of the Vatican, so we can expect a continuation of the decline in the birthrate already taking place. Policies of regional development may be able to diversify the concentration of jobs and population to other areas. And I foresee large-scale epidemics, and disintegration of social control that will make mega-cities less attractive. However, overall, mega-cities will grow in size and dominance, because they keep feeding themselves on population, wealth, power, and innovators, from their extended hinterland. Furthermore, they are the nodal points connecting to the global networks. Thus, in a fundamental sense, the future of humankind, and of each mega-city's country, is being played out in the evolution and management of these areas. Mega-cities are the nodal points, and the power centers of the new spatial form/process of the Information Age: the space of flows.

Having laid out the empirical landscape of new territorial phenomena, we now have to come to grips with the understanding of such a new spatial reality. This requires an unavoidable excursus through the uncertain trails of the theory of space.

The Social Theory of Space and the Theory of the Space of Flows

Space is the expression of society. Since our societies are undergoing structural transformation, it is a reasonable hypothesis to suggest that new spatial forms and processes are currently emerging. The purpose of the analysis presented here is to identify the new logic underlying such forms and processes.

The task is not an easy one because the apparently simple acknowledgement of a meaningful relationship between society and space hides a fundamental complexity. This is because space is not a reflection of society, it is its expression. In other words: space is not a photocopy of society, it is society. Spatial forms and processes are formed by the dynamics of the overall social structure. This includes contradictory trends derived from conflicts and strategies between social actors playing out their opposing interests and values. Furthermore, social processes influence space by acting on the built environment inherited from previous socio-spatial structures. Indeed, *space is crystallized time.* To approach in the simplest possible terms such a complexity, let us proceed step by step.

What is space? In physics, it cannot be defined outside the dynamics of matter. In social theory, it cannot be defined without reference to social practices. This area of theorizing being one of my old trades, I still approach the issue under the assumption that "space is a material product, in relationship to other material products – including people – who engage in [historically] determined social relationships that provide space with a form, a function, and a social meaning."[74] In a convergent and clearer formulation, David Harvey, in his book *The Condition of Postmodernity,* states that "from a materialist perspective, we can argue that objective conceptions of time and space are necessarily created through material practices and processes which serve to reproduce social life . . . It is a fundamental axiom of my enquiry that time and space cannot be understood independently of social action."[75] Thus, we have to define, at a general level, what space is, from the point of view of social practices; then, we must identify the historical specificity of social practices, for example those in the informational society that underlie the emergence and consolidation of new spatial forms and processes.

From the point of view of social theory, *space is the material support of time-sharing social practices.* I immediately add that any material support bears always a symbolic meaning. By time-sharing social practices I refer to the fact that space brings together those practices that are simultaneous in time. It is the material articulation of this simultaneity that gives sense to space *vis-à-vis* society. Traditionally, this notion was assimilated to contiguity. Yet it is fundamental that

74 Castells (1972: 152) (my own translation).
75 Harvey (1990: 204).

we separate the basic concept of material support of simultaneous practices from the notion of contiguity, in order to account for the possible
existence of material supports of simultaneity that do not rely on physical contiguity, since this is precisely the case of the dominant social
practices of the Information Age.

I have argued in the preceding chapters that our society is constructed
around flows: flows of capital, flows of information, flows of technology, flows of organizational interaction, flows of images, sounds, and
symbols. Flows are not just one element of the social organization:
they are the expression of processes *dominating* our economic, political, and symbolic life. If such is the case, the material support of the
dominant processes in our societies will be the ensemble of elements
supporting such flows, and making materially possible their articulation in simultaneous time. Thus, I propose the idea that there is a new
spatial form characteristic of social practices that dominate and shape
the network society: the space of flows. *The space of flows is the material organization of time-sharing social practices that work through
flows.* By flows I understand purposeful, repetitive, programmable
sequences of exchange and interaction between physically disjointed
positions held by social actors in the economic, political, and symbolic
structures of society. Dominant social practices are those which are
embedded in dominant social structures. By dominant structures I
understand those arrangements of organizations and institutions whose
internal logic plays a strategic role in shaping social practices and social consciousness for society at large.

The abstraction of the concept of the space of flows can be better
understood by specifying its content. The space of flows, as the material form of support of dominant processes and functions in the informational society, can be described (rather than defined) by the
combination of at least three layers of material supports that, together,
constitute the space of flows. *The first layer, the first material support
of the space of flows, is actually constituted by a circuit of electronic
exchanges* (micro-electronics-based devices, telecommunications, computer processing, broadcasting systems, and high-speed transportation – also based on information technologies) that, together, form the
material basis for the processes we have observed as being strategically crucial in the network of society. This is indeed a material support of simultaneous practices. Thus, it is a spatial form, just as it
could be "the city" or "the region" in the organization of the merchant society or of the industrial society. The spatial articulation of
dominant functions does take place in our societies in the network of
interactions made possible by information technology devices. In this
network, no place exists by itself, since the positions are defined by

the exchanges of flows in the network. Thus, the network of communication is the fundamental spatial configuration: places do not disappear, but their logic and their meaning become absorbed in the network. The technological infrastructure that builds up the network defines the new space, very much like railways defined "economic regions" and "national markets" in the industrial economy; or the boundary-specific, institutional rules of citizenry (and their technologically advanced armies) defined "cities" in the merchant origins of capitalism and democracy. This technological infrastructure is itself the expression of the network of flows whose architecture and content is determined by the powers that be in our world.

The second layer of the space of flows is constituted by its nodes and hubs. The space of flows is not placeless, although its structural logic is. It is based on an electronic network, but this network links up specific places, with well-defined social, cultural, physical, and functional characteristics. Some places are exchangers, communication hubs playing a role of coordination for the smooth interaction of all the elements integrated into the network. Other places are the nodes of the network; that is, the location of strategically important functions that build a series of locality-based activities and organizations around a key function in the network. Location in the node links up the locality with the whole network. Both nodes and hubs are hierarchically organized according to their relative weight in the network. But this hierarchy may change depending upon the evolution of activities processed through the network. Indeed, in some instances, some places may be switched off the network, their disconnection resulting in instant decline, and thus in economic, social and physical deterioration. The characteristics of nodes are dependent upon the type of functions performed by a given network.

Some examples of networks, and their corresponding nodes, will help to communicate the concept. The easiest type of network to visualize as representative of the space of flows is the network constituted by decision-making systems of the global economy, particularly those relative to the financial system. This refers to the analysis of the global city as a process rather than a place, as presented in this chapter. The analysis of the "global city" as the production site of the informational, global economy has shown the critical role of these global cities in our societies, and the dependence of local societies and economies upon the directional functions located in such cities. But beyond the main global cities, other continental, national, and regional economies have their own nodes that connect to the global network. Each one of these nodes requires an adequate technological infrastructure, a system of ancillary firms providing the support services, a specialized labor market, and the system of services required by the professional labor force.

As I showed above, what is true for top managerial functions and financial markets is also applicable to high-technology manufacturing (both to industries producing high technology and to those using high technology, that is all advanced manufacturing). The spatial division of labor that characterizes high-technology manufacturing translates into the worldwide connection between the milieux of innovation, the skilled manufacturing sites, the assembly lines, and the market-oriented factories, with a series of intra-firm linkages between the different operations in different locations along the production lines; and another series of inter-firm linkages among similar functions of production located in specific sites that become production complexes. Directional nodes, production sites, and communication hubs are defined along the network and articulated in a common logic by communication technologies and programmable, micro-electronics-based, flexible integrated manufacturing.

The functions to be fulfilled by each network define the characteristics of places that become their privileged nodes. In some cases, the most unlikely sites become central nodes because of historical specificity that ends up centering a given network around a particular locality. For instance, it was unlikely that Rochester, Minnesota, or the Parisian suburb of Villejuif would become central nodes of a world network of advanced medical treatment and health research, in close interaction with each other. But the location of the Mayo Clinic at Rochester and of one of the main centers for cancer treatment of the French health administration at Villejuif, in both cases for accidental, historical reasons, have articulated a complex of knowledge generation and advanced medical treatment around these two odd locales. Once established, they attracted researchers, doctors, and patients from around the world: they became a node in the world's medical network.

Each network defines its sites according to the functions and hierarchy of each site, and to the characteristics of the product or service to be processed in the network. Thus, one of the most powerful networks in our society, narcotics production and distribution (including its money-laundering component), has constructed a specific geography that has redefined the meaning, structure, and culture of societies, regions, and cities connected in the network.[76] Thus, in cocaine production and trade, the coca production sites of Chapare or Alto Beni in Bolivia or Alto Huallanga in Peru are connected to the refiner-

---

76   Arrieta et al. (1991); Laserna (1995).

ies and management centers in Colombia, which were subsidiary, until 1995, to the Medellin or Cali headquarters, themselves connected to financial centers such as Miami, Panama, the Cayman Islands, and Luxembourg, and to transportation centers, such as the Tamaulipas or Tijuana drug traffic networks in Mexico, then finally to distribution points in the main metropolitan areas of America and Western Europe. None of these localities can exist by itself in such a network. The Medellin and Cali cartels, and their close American and Italian allies, would have been out of business a long time before being dismantled by repression without the raw materials produced in Bolivia or Peru, without the chemicals (precursors) provided by Swiss and German laboratories, without the semi-legal financial networks of free-banking paradises, and without the distribution networks starting in Miami, Los Angeles, New York, Amsterdam, or La Coruña.

Therefore, while the analysis of global cities provides the most direct illustration of the place-based orientation of the space of flows in nodes and hubs, this logic is not limited by any means to capital flows. The main dominant processes in our society are articulated in networks that link up different places and assign to each one of them a role and a weight in a hierarchy of wealth generation, information processing, and power making that ultimately conditions the fate of each locale.

The third important layer of the space of flows refers to the spatial organization of the dominant, managerial elites (rather than classes) that exercise the directional functions around which such space is articulated. The theory of the space of flows starts from the implicit assumption that societies are asymmetrically organized around the dominant interests specific to each social structure. The space of flows is not the only spatial logic of our societies. It is, however, the dominant spatial logic because it is the spatial logic of the dominant interests/functions in our society. But such domination is not purely structural. It is enacted, indeed conceived, decided, and implemented by social actors. Thus, the technocratic–financial–managerial elite that occupies the leading positions in our societies will also have specific spatial requirements regarding the material/spatial support of their interests and practices. The spatial manifestation of the informational elite constitutes another fundamental dimension of the space of flows. What is this spatial manifestation?

The fundamental form of domination in our society is based on the organizational capacity of the dominant elite that goes hand in hand with its capacity to disorganize those groups in society which, while constituting a numerical majority, see their interests partially (if ever) represented only within the framework of the fulfillment of the domi-

nant interests. Articulation of the elites, segmentation and disorgani-
zation of the masses seem to be the twin mechanisms of social domination in our societies.[77] Space plays a fundamental role in this
mechanism. In short: elites are cosmopolitan, people are local. The
space of power and wealth is projected throughout the world, while
people's life and experience is rooted in places, in their culture, in their
history. Thus, the more a social organization is based upon ahistorical
flows, superseding the logic of any specific place, the more the logic of
global power escapes the socio-political control of historically specific
local/national societies.

On the other hand, the elites do not want and cannot become flows
themselves, if they are to preserve their social cohesion, develop the
set of rules and the cultural codes by which they can understand each
other and dominate the others, thus establishing the "in" and "out"
boundaries of their cultural/political community. The more a society
is democratic in its institutions, the more the elites have to become
clearly distinct from the populace, so avoiding the excessive penetration of political representatives into the inner world of strategic decision-making. However, my analysis does not share the hypothesis
about the improbable existence of a "power elite" à la Wright Mills.
On the contrary, the real social domination stems from the fact that
cultural codes are embedded in the social structure in such a way that
the possession of these codes opens the access to the power structure
without the elite needing to conspire to bar access to its networks.

The spatial manifestation of this logic of domination takes two main
forms in the space of flows. On the one hand, the elites form their own
society, and constitute symbolically secluded communities, retrenched
behind the very material barrier of real-estate pricing. They define their
community as a spatially bound, interpersonally networked subcul-
ture. I propose the hypothesis that the space of flows is made up of
personal micro-networks that project their interests in functional macro-
networks throughout the global set of interactions in the space of flows.
This is a well-known phenomenon in the financial networks: major
strategic decisions are taken over business luncheons in exclusive restaurants, or in country house week-ends over golf playing, as in the
good old days. But such decisions will be executed in instant decision-
making processes over telecommunicated computers which can trigger their own decisions to react to market trends. Thus, the nodes of
the space of flows include residential and leisure-oriented spaces which,
along with the location of headquarters and their ancillary services,
tend to cluster dominant functions in carefully segregated spaces, with

77   See Zukin (1992).

easy access to cosmopolitan complexes of arts, culture, and entertainment. Segregation happens both by location in different places and by security control of certain spaces open only to the elite. From the pinnacles of power and their cultural centers, a series of symbolic sociospatial hierarchies is organized, so that lower levels of management can mirror the symbols of power and appropriate such symbols by constructing second-order spatial communities that will also tend to isolate themselves from the rest of society, in a succession of hierarchical segregation processes that, together, are tantamount to sociospatial fragmentation. At the limit, when social tensions rise, and cities decay, elites take refuge behind the walls of "gated communities," a major phenomenon around the world in the late 1990s, from southern California to Cairo and from São Paulo to Bogota.[78]

A second major trend of cultural distinctiveness of the elites in the informational society is to create a lifestyle and to design spatial forms aimed at unifying the symbolic environment of the elite around the world, thus superseding the historical specificity of each locale. Thus, there is the construction of a (relatively) secluded space across the world along the connecting lines of the space of flows: international hotels whose decoration, from the design of the room to the color of the towels, is similar all over the world to create a sense of familiarity with the inner world, while inducing abstraction from the surrounding world; airports' VIP lounges, designed to maintain distance *vis-à-vis* society in the highways of the space of flows; mobile, personal, on-line access to telecommunications networks, so that the traveler is never lost; and a system of travel arrangements, secretarial services, and reciprocal hosting that maintains a close circle of the corporate elite together through the worshipping of similar rites in all countries. Furthermore, there is an increasingly homogeneous lifestyle among the information elite that transcends the cultural borders of all societies: the regular use of SPA installations (even when traveling), and the practice of jogging; the mandatory diet of grilled salmon and green salad, with *udon* and *sashimi* providing a Japanese functional equivalent; the "pale chamois" wall color intended to create the cozy atmosphere of the inner space; the ubiquitous laptop computer, and Internet access; the combination of business suits and sportswear; the unisex dressing style, and so on. All these are symbols of an international culture whose identity is not linked to any specific society but to membership of the managerial circles of the informational economy across a global cultural spectrum.

The call for cultural connectedness of the space of flows between its

78   Blakely and Snyder (1997).

different nodes is also reflected in the tendency toward the architectural uniformity of the new directional centers in various societies. Paradoxically, the attempt by postmodern architecture to break the molds and patterns of architectural discipline has resulted in an overimposed postmodern monumentality which became the generalized rule of new corporate headquarters from New York to Kaoshiung during the 1980s. Thus, the space of flows includes the symbolic connection of homogeneous architecture in the places that constitute the nodes of each network across the world, so that architecture escapes from the history and culture of each society and becomes captured into the new imaginary, wonderland world of unlimited possibilities that underlies the logic transmitted by multimedia: the culture of electronic surfing, as if we could reinvent all forms in any place, on the sole condition of leaping into the cultural indefinition of the flows of power. The enclosure of architecture into an historical abstraction is the formal frontier of the space of flows.

The Architecture of the End of History

Nomada, sigo siendo un nomada.

Ricardo Bofill[79]

If the space of flows is truly the dominant spatial form of the network society, architecture and design are likely to be redefined in their form, function, process, and value in the coming years. Indeed, I would argue that all over history, architecture has been the "failed act" of society, the mediated expression of the deeper tendencies of society, of those that could not be openly declared but yet were strong enough to be cast in stone, in concrete, in steel, in glass, and in the visual perception of the human beings who were to dwell, deal, or worship in such forms.

Panofsky on Gothic cathedrals, Tafuri on American skyscrapers, Venturi on the surprisingly kitsch American city, Lynch on city images, Harvey on postmodernism as the expression of time/space compression by capitalism, are some of the best illustrations of an intellectual tradition that has used the forms of the built environment as one of the most signifying codes to read the basic structures of society's dominant values.[80] To be sure, there is no simple, direct inter-

---

79 Opening statement of Ricardo Bofill's architectural autobiography, *Espacio y Vida* (Bofill 1990).
80 Panofsky (1957); Lynch (1960); Tafuri (1971); Venturi et al. (1977); Harvey (1990).

pretation of the formal expression of social values. But as research by scholars and analysts has revealed, and as works by architects have demonstrated, there has always been a strong, semiconscious connection between what society (in its diversity) was saying and what architects wanted to say.[81]

Not any more. My hypothesis is that the coming of the space of flows is blurring the meaningful relationship between architecture and society. Because the spatial manifestation of the dominant interests takes place around the world, and across cultures, the uprooting of experience, history, and specific culture as the background of meaning is leading to the generalization of ahistorical, acultural architecture.

Some tendencies of "postmodern architecture," as represented for instance by the works of Philip Johnson or Charles Moore, under the pretext of breaking down the tyranny of codes, such as modernism, attempt to cut off all ties with specific social environments. So did modernism in its time, but as the expression of an historically rooted culture that asserted the belief in progress, technology and rationality. In contrast, postmodern architecture declares the end of all systems of meaning. It creates a mixture of elements that searches formal harmony out of transhistorical, stylistic provocation. Irony becomes the preferred mode of expression. Yet, in fact what most postmodernism does is to express, in almost direct terms, the new dominant ideology: the end of history and the supersession of places in the space of flows.[82] Because only if we are at the end of history can we now mix up everything we knew before (see figure 6.6). Because we do not belong any longer to any place, to any culture, the extreme version of postmodernism imposes its codified code-breaking logic anywhere something is built. The liberation from cultural codes hides in fact the escape from historically rooted societies. In this perspective, postmodernism could be considered the architecture of the space of flows.[83]

The more that societies try to recover their identity beyond the global logic of uncontrolled power of flows, the more they need an architecture that exposes their own reality, without faking beauty from a transhistorical spatial repertoire. But at the same time, oversignificant architecture, trying to give a very definite message or to express directly the codes of a given culture, is too primitive a form to be able to

---

81 See Burlen (1972).
82 I find my own understanding of postmodernism and postmodern architecture very close to David Harvey's analysis. But I shall not take responsibility for using his work in support of my position.
83 For a balanced, intelligent discussion of the social meaning of postmodern architecture, see Kolb (1990); for a broader discussion of the interaction between globalization/informationalization processes and architecture, see Saunders, (1996).

Figure 6.6 Downtown Kaoshiung (photograph: Professor Hsia Chu-joe)

penetrate our saturated visual imaginary. The meaning of its messages will be lost in the culture of "surfing" that characterizes our symbolic behavior. This is why, paradoxically, the architecture that seems most charged with meaning in societies shaped by the logic of the space of flows is what I call "the architecture of nudity." That is, the architecture whose forms are so neutral, so pure, so diaphanous, that they do not pretend to say anything. And by not saying anything they confront the experience with the solitude of the space of flows. Its message is the silence.

For the sake of communication, I shall use two examples drawn from Spanish architecture, an architectural milieu that is widely recognized as being currently at the forefront of design. Both concern, not by accident, the design of major communication nodes, where the space of flows materializes ephemerally. The Spanish festivities of 1992 provided the occasion for the construction of major functional buildings designed by some of the best architects. Thus, the new Barcelona airport, designed by Bofill, simply combines beautiful marble floor, dark glass façade, and transparent glass separating panels in an immense, open space (see figure 6.7). No cover up of the fear and anxiety

Figure 6.7   The entrance hall of Barcelona airport
Source: Original drawing by Ricardo Bofill; reproduced by kind permission of
Ricardo Bofill

that people experience in an airport. No carpeting, no cozy rooms, no
indirect lighting. In the middle of the cold beauty of this airport pas-
sengers have to face their terrible truth: they are alone, in the middle
of the space of flows, they may lose their connection, they are suspended in the emptiness of transition. They are, literally, in the hands
of Iberia Airlines. And there is no escape.

Let us take another example: the new Madrid AVE (high-speed train)
station, designed by Rafael Moneo. It is simply a wonderful old station, exquisitely rehabilitated, and made into an indoor palm-tree park,
full of birds that sing and fly in the enclosed space of the station. In a
nearby structure, adjacent to such a beautiful, monumental space, there
is the real station with the high-speed train. Thus, people go to the
pseudo-station, to visit it, to walk through its different levels and paths,
as they go to a park or a museum. The too-obvious message is that we
are in a park, not in a station; that in the old station, trees grew, and
birds nested, operating a metamorphosis. Thus, the high-speed train
becomes the oddity in this space. And this is in fact the question everybody in the world asks: what is a high-speed train doing there, just to
go from Madrid to Seville, with no connection whatsoever with the
European high-speed network, at a cost of US$4 billion? The broken
mirror of a segment of the space of flows becomes exposed, and the

Figure 6.8 The waiting room at D.E. Shaw and Company: no ficus trees, no sectional sofas, no corporate art on the walls
Source: Muschamp (1992)

use value of the station recovered, in a simple, elegant design that does not say much but makes everything evident.

Some prominent architects, such as Rem Koolhas, the designer of the Lille Grand Palais Convention Center, theorize the need to adapt architecture to the process of de-localization, and to the relevance of communication nodes in people's experience: Koolhas actually sees his project as an expression of the "space of flows." Or, in another instance of a growing self-awareness of architects about the structural transformation of space, the American Institute of Architects' award-winning design of D.E. Shaw and Company's offices by Steven Holl in New York's West 45th Street (figure 6.8):

> offers [in Herbert Muschamp's words] a poetic interpretation of . . . the space of flows . . . Mr Holl's design takes the Shaw offices to a place as novel as the information technology that paid to build them. When we walk in the door of D.E. Shaw we know we are not in 1960s Manhat-

tan or Colonial New England. For that matter, we have left even much of present day New York far below on the ground. Standing inside the Holl atrium we have got our head in the clouds and our feet firmly planted on solid air.[84]

Granted we may be forcing Bofill, Moneo, and even Holl into discourses that are not theirs.[85] But the simple fact that their architecture would allow me, or Herbert Muschamp, to relate forms to symbols, to functions, to social situations, means that their strict, retained architecture (in rather formally different styles) is in fact full of meaning. Indeed, architecture and design, because their forms either resist or interpret the abstract materiality of the dominant space of flows, could become essential devices of cultural innovation and intellectual autonomy in the informational society through two main avenues. Either the new architecture builds the palaces of the new masters, thus exposing their deformity hidden behind the abstraction of the space of flows; or it roots itself into places, thus into culture, and into people.[86] In both cases, under different forms, architecture and design may be digging the trenches of resistance for the preservation of meaning in the generation of knowledge. Or, which is the same, for the reconciliation of culture and technology.

Space of Flows and Space of Places

The space of flows does not permeate down to the whole realm of human experience in the network society. Indeed, the overwhelming majority of people, in advanced and traditional societies alike, live in places, and so they perceive their space as place-based. *A place is a locale whose form, function, and meaning are self-contained within the boundaries of physical contiguity.* A place, to illustrate my argument, is the Parisian *quartier* of Belleville.

Belleville was, as for so many immigrants throughout its history, my entry point to Paris, in 1962. As a 20–year-old political exile, without

---

84 Muschamp (1992).
85 For Bofill's own interpretation of Barcelona airport (whose formal antecedent, I believe, is his design for Paris's Marché St Honoré), see his book: Bofill (1990). However, in a long personal conversation, after reading the draft of my analysis, he did not disagree with my interpretation of the project of an "architecture of nudity," although he conceived it rather as an innovative attempt to bring together high-tech and classic design. We both agreed that the new architectural monuments of our epoch are likely to be built as "communication exchangers" (airports, train stations, intermodal transfer areas, telecommunication infrastructures, harbors, and computerized trading centers).
86 For a useful debate on the matter, see Lillyman et al. (1994).

Figure 6.9   Belleville, 1999: a multicultural, urban place
(photograph: Irene Castells and Jose Bailo)

much to lose except my revolutionary ideals, I was given shelter by a
Spanish construction worker, an anarchist union leader, who introduced me to the tradition of the place. Nine years later, this time as a
sociologist, I was still walking Belleville, working with immigrant
workers' committees, and studying social movements against urban
renewal: the struggles of what I labeled "*La Cité du Peuple*," reported
in my first book.[87] More than thirty years after our first encounter,
both Belleville and I have changed. But Belleville is still a place, while
I am afraid I look more like a flow. The new immigrants (Asians,
Yugoslavs) have joined a long-established stream of Tunisian Jews,
Maghrebian Muslims, and southern Europeans, themselves the suc-
cessors of the intra-urban exiles pushed into Belleville in the nineteenth
century by the Hausmannian design of building a bourgeois Paris.
Belleville itself has been hit by several waves of urban renewal, intensified in the 1970s.[88] Its traditional physical landscape of a poor but
harmonious historic *faubourg* has been messed up with plastic

87   Castells (1972: 496ff).
88   For an updated social and spatial, illustrated history of Belleville, see the delightful
book by Morier (1994); on urban renewal in Paris in the 1970s, see Godard et al. (1973).

Figure 6.10   Las Ramblas, Barcelona, 1999: city life in a liveable place (photograph: Jordi Borja and Zaída Muxi)

postmodernism, cheap modernism, and sanitized gardens on top of a still somewhat dilapidated housing stock. And yet, Belleville in 1999 is a clearly identifiable place, both from the outside and from the inside (see figure 6.9). Ethnic communities that often degenerate into hostility toward each other coexist peacefully in Belleville, although keeping track of their own turf, and certainly not without tensions. New middle-class households, generally young, have joined the neighborhood because of its urban vitality, and powerfully contribute to its survival, while self-controlling the impacts of gentrification. Cultures and histories, in a truly plural urbanity, interact in the space, giving meaning to it, linking up with the "city of collective memory" *à la* Christine Boyer.[89] The landscape pattern swallows and digests substantial physical modifications, by integrating them in its mixed uses and active street life. Yet Belleville is by no means the idealized version of the lost community, which probably never existed, as Oscar Lewis demonstrated in his revisit of Tepoztlan. Places are not necessarily communities, although they may contribute to community-building. But the life of their inhabitants is marked by their characteristics, so that they are indeed good and bad places depending on the value judgement

89   Boyer (1994).

0   1 Mile

0   1000   2000   3000   4000   5280 Feet

0   500   1000   1609 Meters

Figure 6.11   Barcelona: Paseo de Gracia
Source: Jacobs (1993)

of what a good life is (see figure 6.10). In Belleville, its dwellers, without loving each other, and while certainly not being loved by the police, have constructed throughout history a meaningful, interacting space, with a diversity of uses and a wide range of functions and expressions. They actively interact with their daily physical environment. In between home and the world, there is a place called Belleville.

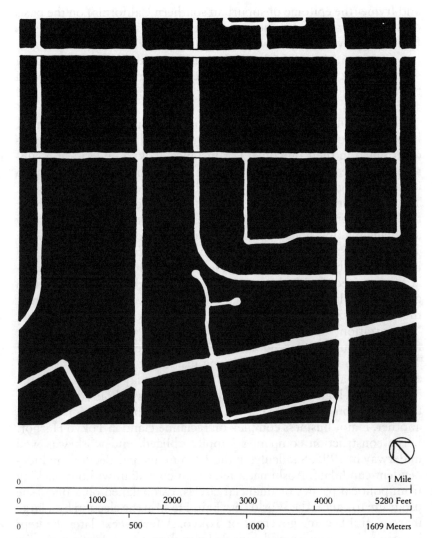

0 ─── 1 Mile

0 ──── 1000 ──── 2000 ──── 3000 ──── 4000 ──── 5280 Feet

0 ──────── 500 ──────── 1000 ──────── 1609 Meters

Figure 6.12   Irvine, California: business complex
Source: Jacobs (1993)

Not all places are socially interactive and spatially rich. It is precisely because their physical/symbolic qualities make them different that they are places. Thus Allan Jacobs, in his great book about *Great Streets*,[90] examines the difference in urban quality between Barcelona

90   Jacobs (1993).

and Irvine (the epitome of suburban southern California) on the basis of the number and frequency of intersections in the street pattern: his findings go even beyond what any informed urbanist could imagine (see figures 6.11 and 6.12). So Irvine is indeed a place, although a special kind of place, where the space of experience shrinks inward toward the home, as flows take over increasing shares of time and space.

The relationships between the space of flows and the space of places, between simultaneous globalization and localization, are not pre-determined in their outcome. For instance, Tokyo underwent a sub-stantial process of urban restructuring during the 1980s to live up to its role as "a global city," a process fully documented by Machimura. The city government, sensitive to the deep-seated Japanese fear about the loss of identity, added to its business-oriented restructuring policy an image-making policy of singing the virtues of old Edo, pre-Meiji Tokyo. An historical museum (*Edo-Tokyo Hakubutsakan*) was opened in 1993, a public relations magazine was published, exhibitions regu-larly organized. As Machimura writes, "Although these views seem to go in totally different directions, both of them seek for redefinition of the Westernized image of the city in more domestic ways. Now, "Japanization" of the Westernized city provides an important context for the discourse about "global city" Tokyo after modernism."[91] Yet Tokyo citizens were not complaining just about the loss of historical essence, but about the reduction of their everyday life's space to the instrumental logic of the global city. A project symbolized this logic: the celebration of a World City Fair in 1997, a good occasion to build another, major business complex on reclaimed land in Tokyo Harbor. Large construction companies happily obliged, and work was well underway in 1995. Suddenly, in the 1995 municipal election, an inde-pendent candidate, Aoshima, a television comedian without backing from political parties or financial circles, campaigned on a one-issue program: to cancel the World City Fair. He won the election by a large margin, and became governor of Tokyo. A few weeks later, he kept his campaign promise and canceled the World City Fair to the dis-belief of the corporate elite. The local logic of civil society was catch-ing up with, and contradicting, the global logic of international business.

Thus, people do still live in places. But because function and power in our societies are organized in the space of flows, the structural domi-nation of its logic essentially alters the meaning and dynamic of places. Experience, by being related to places, becomes abstracted from power,

---

91 Machimura (1995: 16). See his book on the social and political forces underlying the restructuring of Tokyo: Machimura (1994).

and meaning is increasingly separated from knowledge. There follows a structural schizophrenia between two spatial logics that threatens to break down communication channels in society. The dominant tendency is toward a horizon of networked, ahistorical space of flows, aiming at imposing its logic over scattered, segmented places, increasingly unrelated to each other, less and less able to share cultural codes. Unless cultural, political, *and physical* bridges are deliberately built between these two forms of space, we may be heading toward life in parallel universes whose times cannot meet because they are warped into different dimensions of a social hyperspace.

7

The Edge of Forever: Timeless Time

We are embodied time, and so are our societies, made out of history. Yet the simplicity of this statement hides the complexity of the concept of time, one of the most controversial categories in the natural and social sciences alike, whose centrality is underlined by current debates in social theory.[1] Indeed, the transformation of time under the information technology paradigm, as shaped by social practices, is one of the foundations of the new society we have entered, inextricably linked to the emergence of the space of flows. Furthermore, according to the illuminating essay by Barbara Adam on time and social theory, research in physics and biology seems to converge with social sciences in adopting a contextual notion of human time.[2] All time, in nature as in society, seems to be specific to a given context: time is local. Focusing on the emerging social structure, I argue, in the tradition of Harold Innis, that "the fashionable mind is the time-denying mind,"[3] and that this new "time regime" is linked to the development of communication technologies. Thus, in order to appreciate the transformation of human time under the new social socio-technical context

---

1   The analysis of time plays a central role in the thought of Anthony Giddens, one of the leading sociological theorists of our intellectual generation. See, particularly, Giddens (1981, 1984). An extremely stimulating theorization of the relationship between time, space, and society is the work by Lash and Urry (1994); see also Young (1988). Adam (2000) offers a most innovative analysis of time-frames in relation to social debates, as epitomized by the conflicts over genetically modified food. For a more traditional, empirical approach to the social analysis of time, see Kirsch et al. (1988). For debates on various perspectives, see Friedland and Boden (1994). Of course, for sociologists, the classic references on social time continue to be Durkheim (1912) and Sorokin and Merton (1937). See also the pioneering work by Innis (1950, 1951, 1952) on regimes of time and space as defining historical epochs.
2   Adam (1990: 81, 87–90).
3   Innis (1951: 89ff); see also Innis (1950).

it may be helpful to introduce briefly a historical perspective on the changing relationship between time and society.

Time, History, and Society

In a classic book, Whitrow has shown how conceptions of time have varied considerably throughout history, from the determination of human fate under the Babylonian horoscopes, to the Newtonian revolution of absolute time as an organizing principle of nature.[4] And Nigel Thrift has reminded us of the fact that time in medieval societies was a loose notion, with some major events (religious celebrations, market fairs, the coming of the seasons) becoming time markers around which most of daily life went by without precise timing.[5] To illustrate the wide contextual variation of such an apparently simple fact of life, let us recall in a few paragraphs the transformation of the notion of time in Russian culture in two critical historical periods: the reforms of Peter the Great, and the rise and fall of the Soviet Union.[6]

Traditional, popular Russian culture viewed time as eternal, without beginning or end. Writing in the 1920s, Andrey Platonov emphasized this deep-seated notion of Russia as a timeless society. Yet Russia was periodically shaken by statist modernization efforts to organize life around time. The first deliberate attempt at timing life came from Peter the Great. Upon his return from a long trip abroad to educate himself about ways and means in more advanced countries, he decided to bring Russia, literally, to a new departure, by shifting to the Western European (Julian) calendar, and starting the new year in January instead of September, as had been the case until then. On December 19 and 20, 1699, he issued two decrees that would start the eighteenth century in Russia a few days later. He prescribed detailed instructions about celebrating the new year, including the adoption of the Christmas tree, and adding a new holiday to entice the traditionalists. While some people marveled at the Czar's power to alter the course

---

4   Whitrow (1988). For a good example of cultural/historical variation of time and time measures, see the fascinating book by Zerubavel (1985).
5   Thrift (1990).
6   The plural source for this analysis of the evolution of time in Russian culture is the set of unpublished presentations and discussions at the Conference on Time and Money in Russian Culture, organized by the University of California at Berkeley's Center for Slavic and Eastern European Studies, and Stanford University's Center for Russian and East European Studies, held at Berkeley on March 17, 1995 (personal notes and summary of the proceedings by Emma G. Kiselyova). Among the various significant contributions to this conference, I have used Zhivov (1995). Additionally, for the time implications of Peter the Great's reforms, see Waliszewski (1990); Anisimov (1993); Kara-Murza and Polyakov (1994).

of the sun, many were concerned about offending God: was not September 1 the day of the Creation in 5508BC? And was it not supposed to be so because the daring act of Creation had to take place in warm weather, an occurrence extremely unlikely in the Russian January? Peter the Great argued personally with his critics, in his customary pedagogic mode, indulging in teaching them about global time geography. His stubbornness was rooted in his reformist motivation to homogenize Russia with Europe, and to emphasize time-measured obligations of people toward the state. Although these decrees focused strictly on calendar changes, Peter the Great's reforms, in broader terms, introduced a distinction between the time of religious duty and secular time to be given to the state. Measuring and taxing people's time, and giving his own personal example of an intense, timed work schedule, Peter the Great inaugurated a centuries-old tradition of associating service to the country, submission to the state, and the timing of life.

In the early stages of the Soviet Union, Lenin shared with Henry Ford an admiration for Taylorism and the "scientific organization of work," based on measuring working time to the smallest movement in the assembly line. But time compression under communism came with a decisive ideological twist.[7] While under Fordism the speeding up of work was associated with money, by increasing pay, under Stalinism not only was money evil, in line with Russian tradition, but time should be accelerated by ideological motivation. Thus, Stakhanovism meant working more per unit of time as a service to the country, and five-year plans were fulfilled in four years as a proof of the ability of the new society to revolutionize time. In May 1929, at the Fifth Congress of the Soviets of the Union which marked the triumph of Stalin, an even more extreme acceleration of time was attempted: the uninterrupted *(nepreryvka)* work week. Although increase in production was the explicit goal of the reform, the destruction of the weekly rhythm of religious observance was an even greater motivation, in the tradition of the French Revolution. So, in November 1931, a resting day was introduced every sixth day, but the traditional seven-day cycle was still denied. Protests from families separated by differences in schedules between their members brought the seven-day week back in 1940, particularly after it was realized that cities were on the six-day pattern, but most of the countryside was still observing the traditional week, introducing a dangerous cultural cleavage between peasants and industrial workers. Indeed, while forced collectivization of agriculture aimed at eliminating the communal notion of slow-paced time, rooted

---

7   For analysis of time in the Soviet Union, see Hanson (1991); Castillo (1994); on developments related to "uninterrupted workweek" under Stalin, see Zerubavel (1985: 35–43).

in nature, family, and history, social and cultural resistance to such a brutal imposition was widespread, showing the depth of the time foundation of social life. Yet, while compressing time at the workplace, the time horizon of communism was always in the long term and to some extent eternal, as expressed in Lenin's embodied immortality, and in Stalin's attempt to make an idol of himself during life. Accordingly, in the 1990s, the collapse of communism shifted Russians, and particularly the new professional classes, from the long-term horizon of historical time to the short term of monetized time characteristic of capitalism, thus ending the centuries-old statist separation between time and money. By so doing Russia joined the West at the very moment that advanced capitalism was revolutionizing its own time-frame.

Contemporary societies are still by and large dominated by the notion of clock time, a mechanical/categorical discovery that E. P. Thompson,[8] among others, considers to be critical to the constitution of industrial capitalism. Modernity can be conceived, in material terms, as the dominance of clock time over space and society, a theme that has been developed by Giddens, Lash and Urry, and Harvey. Time as repetition of daily routine, as Giddens proposes,[9] or as "the mastery of nature, as all sorts of phenomena, practices and places become subjected to the disembedding, centralizing and universalizing march of time," in the words of Lash and Urry,[10] is at the core of both industrial capitalism and statism. Industrial machinism brought the chronometer to the assembly lines of Fordist and Leninist factories almost at the same moment.[11] Long-distance travel in the West became organized by the late nineteenth century around Greenwich Mean Time, as the materialization of the hegemony of the British Empire. While, half a century later, the constitution of the Soviet Union was marked by the organization of an immense territory around Moscow time, with time zones arbitrarily decided at the bureaucrats' convenience without proportion to geographical distance. Significantly, the first act of defiance of the Baltic Republics during Gorbachev's *perestroika* was to vote for the adoption of Finland's time zone as the official time in their territories.

This linear, irreversible, measurable, predictable time is being shattered in the network society, in a movement of extraordinary historical significance. But we are not just witnessing a relativization of time according to social contexts or alternatively the return to time reversibility as if reality could become entirely captured in cyclical myths.

8 Thompson (1967).
9 Giddens (1984).
10 Lash and Urry (1994: 229).
11 Castillo (1994).

The transformation is more profound: it is the mixing of tenses to create a forever universe, not self-expanding but self-maintaining, not cyclical but random, not recursive but incursive: timeless time, using technology to escape the contexts of its existence, and to appropriate selectively any value each context could offer to the ever-present. James Gleick has documented the acceleration of "just about everything" in our societies, in a relentless effort to compress time in all domains of human activity.[12] Compressing time to the limit is tantamount to make time sequence, and thus time, disappear. I argue that this is happening now not only because capitalism strives to free itself from all constraints, since this has been the tendency of the capitalist system all along, without being able fully to realize it.[13] Nor is it sufficient to refer to the cultural and social revolts against clock time, since they have characterized the history of the past century without actually reversing its domination, indeed furthering its logic by including the clock time distribution of life in the social contract.[14] Capital's freedom from time and culture's escape from the clock are decisively facilitated by new information technologies, and embedded in the structure of the network society.

Having said these words, I shall proceed with the specification of their meaning, so that by the end of this chapter sociological analysis has a chance to replace metaphorical statements. To do so, without annoying repetition, I shall rely on the empirical observations presented in other chapters of this book on the transformation of various domains of social structure, while adding illustrations or analyses where necessary to complete our understanding. Thus, I shall sequentially explore the effects on time of transformations occurring in the economic, political, cultural, and social spheres, and end with an attempt at reintegrating time and space in their new, contradictory relationship. In this exploration of the ongoing transformation of time in very different social spheres, I shall be somewhat schematic in my statements, since it is materially impossible to develop fully in a few pages the analysis of domains as complex and diverse as global finance, working time, the life-cycle, death, war-making, and the media. However, by dealing with so many and different matters I shall try to extract, beyond such diversity, the shared logic of new temporality manifesting itself in the whole range of human experience. Thus, the purpose of this chapter is not to summarize the transformation of social life in all its dimensions, but, rather, to show the consistency of

12   Gleick (1999).
13   As Harvey (1990) shows.
14   Hinrichs et al. (1991); see also Rifkin (1987).

patterns in the emergence of a new concept of temporality, which I call *timeless time*.

Another word of caution must be added. The transformation of time as surveyed in this chapter does not concern all processes, social groupings, and territories in our societies, although it does affect the entire planet. What I call *timeless time* is only the emerging, *dominant* form of social time in the network society, as the space of flows does not negate the existence of places. It is precisely my argument that social domination is exercised through the selective inclusion and exclusion of functions and people in different temporal and spatial frames. I shall return to this theme at the end of the chapter after having explored the profile of time in its new, dominant form.

Time as the Source of Value: the Global Casino

David Harvey adequately represents current transformations in capitalism under the formula of "time–space compression."[15] Nowhere is this logic more evident than in the circulation of capital at the global level. As we analyzed in chapter 2, during the 1990s the convergence of global deregulation of finance and the availability of new information technologies and new management techniques transformed the nature of capital markets. For the first time in history, a unified global capital market, *working in real time,* has emerged.[16] The explanation, and the real issue, of the phenomenal volume of trans-border financial flows, as shown in chapter 2, lies in the *speed* of the transactions.[17] The same capital is shuttled back and forth between economies in a matter of hours, minutes, and sometimes seconds.[18] Favored by deregulation, disintermediation, and the opening of domestic financial markets, powerful computer programs and skillful financial analysts/ computer wizards, sitting at the global nodes of a selective telecommunications network, play games, literally, with billions of dollars.[19] The main card room in this electronic casino is the currency market, which has exploded in the past decade, taking advantage of floating exchange rates. In 1998, US$1.3 trillion were exchanged every day in the currency market.[20] These global gamblers are not obscure

15   See Harvey (1990: 284–5).
16   O'Brien (1992); Chesnais (1994); Held et al. (1999).
17   Reynolds (1992); Javetski and Glasgall (1994); Castells in Giddens and Hutton (2000).
18   Breeden (1993); Shirref (1994).
19   Jones (1993); *Time* (1994). For a revealing "financial fiction" allegory, enjoy reading Kimsey (1994).
20   *The Economist* (1995b).

speculators, but major investment banks, pension funds, multinational corporations (of course including manufacturing corporations), and mutual funds organized precisely for the sake of financial manipulation.[21] François Chesnais identified about 50 major players in the global financial markets.[22] Yet, as argued above, once turbulences are generated in the market, flows take over, as central banks have repeatedly learned to their heavy cost. Time is critical to the profit-making of the whole system. It is the speed of the transaction, sometimes automatically preprogrammed in the computer to make quasi-instantaneous decisions, that generates the gain – or the loss. But it is also the time circularity of the process, a relentless sequence of buying and selling, that characterizes the system. The architecture of global finance is indeed constructed around time zones, with London, New York, and Tokyo anchoring the three shifts of capital, and a number of financial maverick centers working on the slight discrepancies between market values at their opening and closing times.[23] Furthermore, a significant and growing number of financial transactions are based on making value out of the capture of future time in present transactions, as in the futures, options, and other derivative capital markets.[24] Together these new financial products dramatically increase the mass of nominal capital *vis-à-vis* bank deposits and assets, so that it can be said properly that time creates money, as everybody bets on and with future money anticipated in computer projections.[25] The very process of marketing future development affects these developments, so that the time-frame of capital is constantly dissolved into its present manipulation after being given a fictitious value for the purpose of monetizing it. Thus capital not only compresses time: it absorbs it, and lives out of (that is, generates rent) its digested seconds and years.

The material consequences of this apparently abstract digression on time and capital are increasingly felt in economies and daily lives around the world: recurrent monetary crises, ushering in an era of structural economic instability and actually jeopardizing European integration; the inability of capital investment to anticipate the future, thus undermining incentives for productive investment; the wrecking of companies, and of their jobs, regardless of performance because of sudden, unforeseen changes in the financial environment in which they operate; the increasing gap between profits in the production of goods and services and rents generated in the sphere of circulation, thus shift-

21 Heavey (1994); Giddens and Hutton (2000).
22 Chesnais (1994).
23 Lee and Schmidt-Marwede (1993).
24 *Asian Money Supplement* (1993–4); Fager (1994); Lee et al. (1994).
25 Chesnais (1994).

ing an increasing share of world savings to financial gambling; the growing risks for pension funds and private insurance liabilities, thus introducing a question mark over the hard-bought security of working people around the world; the dependence of entire economies, and particularly those of developing countries, on movements of capital largely determined by subjective perception and speculative turbulence; the destruction in the collective experience of societies of the deferred-gratification pattern of behavior, in favour of the "quick buck" common ideology, emphasizing individual gambling with life and the economy; and the fundamental damage to the social perception of the correspondence between production and reward, work and meaning, ethics and wealth. Puritanism seems to have been buried in Singapore in 1995 along with the venerable Barings Bank.[26] And Confucianism will last in the new economy only as long as "blood is thicker than water;"[27] that is, while family ties still provide social cohesion beyond pure speculation in the brave new world of gambling finance. The annihilation and manipulation of time by electronically managed global capital markets are at the source of new forms of devastating economic crises, looming into the twenty-first century.

Flex-time and the Network Enterprise

The supersession of time is also at the core of the new organizational forms of economic activity that I have identified as the *network enterprise*. Flexible forms of management, relentless utilization of fixed capital, intensified performance of labor, strategic alliances, and inter-organizational linkages, all come down to shortening time per operation and to speeding up turnover of resources. Indeed, the "just-in-time" inventory management procedure has been the symbol of lean production, even if, as I mentioned above, it belongs to a pre-electronic age of manufacturing technology. Yet, in the informational economy, this time compression does not primarily rely on extracting more time from labor or more labor from time under the clock imperative. Because the value-making potential of labor and organizations is highly dependent on the autonomy of informed labor to make decisions in real time, the traditional disciplinary management of labor does not fit the new production system.[28] Instead, skilled labor is required to manage its own time in a flexible manner, sometimes adding

---

26   *The Economist* (1995a).
27   Hsing (1994).
28   See the discussion of the matter in Freeman (1994).

more work time, at other times adjusting to flexible schedules, in some instances reducing working hours, and thus pay. This new time-oriented management of labor could be called, as John Urry suggests, "just-in-time labor."[29]

For the networked firm, the time-frame of its adaptability to market demand and technology changes is also at the root of its competitiveness. Thus, the showcase of networking production, the Italian knitwear multinational firm, Benetton, was overtaken in 1995 by its American competitor Gap mainly because of its inability to follow Gap's speed in introducing new models according to evolving consumer taste: every two months, as compared with twice a year for Benetton.[30] Another example: in the software industry in the mid-1990s firms started to give away their products for free, over the line, in order to attract customers at a faster pace.[31] The rationale behind this final dematerialization of software products is that profits are to be made in the long term, mainly out of customized relationships with users over development and improvements of a given program. But the initial adoption of such a program depends on the advantage of solutions offered by a product over other products in the market, thus putting a premium on the quick availability of new breakthroughs, as soon as they are generated by a firm or an individual. The flexible management system of networked production relies on flexible temporality, on the ability to accelerate or slow down product and profit cycles, on the time-sharing of equipment and personnel, and on the control of time lags of available technology vis-à-vis the competition. Time is managed as a resource, not under the linear, chronological manner of mass production, but as a differential factor with reference to the temporality of other firms, networks, processes, or products. Only the networked form of organization and increasingly powerful and mobile information-processing machines are able to ensure the flexible management of time as the new frontier of high-performance firms.[32] Under such conditions time is not only compressed: it is processed.

The Shrinking and Twisting of Life Working Time

Work is, and will be for the foreseeable future, the nucleus of people's life. More specifically, in modern societies, *paid working time* struc-

29 Lash and Urry (1994).
30 *Business Week* (1995d).
31 *Business Week* (1995c).
32 Benveniste (1994).

Table 7.1 Annual hours worked per person, 1870–1979

	1870	1880	1890	1900	1913	1929	1938	1950	1960	1970	1979
Canada	2,964	2,871	2,789	2,707	2,605	2,399	2,240	1,967	1,877	1,805	1,730
France	2,945	2,852	2,770	2,688	2,588	2,297	1,848	1,989	1,983	1,888	1,727
Germany	2,941	2,848	2,765	2,684	2,584	2,284	2,316	2,316	2,083	1,907	1,719
Italy[1]	2,886	2,795	2,714	2,634	2,536	2,228	1,927	1,997	2,059	1,768	1,556
Japan	2,945	2,852	2,770	2,688	2,588	2,364	2,391	2,272	2,432	2,252	2,129
United Kingdom	2,984	2,890	2,807	2,725	2,624	2,286	2,267	1,958	1,913	1,735	1,617
United States	2,964	2,871	2,789	2,707	2,605	2,342	2,062	1,867	1,794	1,707	1,607

[1] For Italy, 1978 figure is used for 1979.
Source: Maddison (1982); Bosch et al. (1994: 8, table 1)

Table 7.2 Potential lifelong working hours, 1950–1985

	1950	1960	1979	1980	1985
East Germany	108,252	n.a.	97,046	93,698	93,372
France	113,729	107,849	101,871	92,708	77,748
Hungary	97,940	96,695	92,918	85,946	78,642
Italy	n.a.	n.a.	n.a.	n.a.	82,584
Japan	109,694	109,647	100,068	95,418	93,976
United Kingdom	n.a.	n.a.	n.a.	n.a.	82,677
USA	n.a.	n.a.	n.a.	n.a.	93,688
USSR	n.a.	n.a.	n.a.	n.a.	77,148
West Germany	114,170	104,076	93,051	87,367	85,015

n.a. = not available
Source: Schuldt (1990: 43), cited in Bosch et al. (1994: 15)

tures social time. Working time in industrialized countries has experienced a secular decline in the past 100 years, measured in annual working hours *per person,* as shown in the study by Maddison (see table 7.1).[33] I should remind the reader that this reduction in working time hides in fact a substantial increase in total labor, as a result of the increase in the number of jobs since, as I showed in chapter 4, aggregate employment is less a function of technology than of the expansion of investment and demand, depending on social and institutional organization. Calculations on the potential lifelong working hours per person also show a significant reduction in the past four decades, although with important variations in the number of hours between countries (see table 7.2).[34]

The number of working hours and their distribution in the life-cycle and in the annual, monthly, and weekly cycles of people's lives, are a central feature of how they feel, enjoy, and suffer. Their differential evolution in various countries and historical periods reflects economic organization, the state of technology, the intensity of social struggles, and the outcomes of social contracts and institutional reforms.[35] French workers were the first in Europe to conquer the 40–hour week and the right to paid vacation, after bitter social struggles and the election to government of the Popular Front in 1936. The UK, the USA, and Japan have been the bastions of business-imposed Stakhanovism, with workers having half or one-third less vacation time than workers in Germany, France, or Spain, with no apparent effect on productivity (actually, in terms of productivity growth in the past 30 years, if we except Japan, vacation time seems to correlate positively with growth in labor productivity). Yet overall, for more than a century, between 1870 and 1980, we could observe two related trends in industrialized economies toward decreasing labor time per person and per worker, and toward increasing homogenization and regulation of working time as part of the social contract underlying the welfare state. However, recently these trends have been modified toward an increasingly complex and variable pattern (see table 7.3).[36] The key phenomenon seems to be the increasing diversification of working time and working schedules, reflecting the trend toward the disaggregation of labor in the work process, as analyzed in chapter 4. Thus the 1994 ILO study on the evolution of working time in 14 industrialized countries synthesizes its observations as follows:

33   Maddison (1982).
34   Schuldt (1990), cited in Bosch et al. (1994: 15).
35   Hinrichs et al. (1991).
36   Bosch et al. (1994).

Table 7.3 Duration and reduction of working time, 1970–1987

	Agreed working hours	Reduction of agreed hours (%)		Actual working hours per employee			Working hours per person, working age 55–64 years			Working hours per person
		1970–80	1980–7	1980	1987	Change (%) 1980–7	1980	1987	Change (%) 1980–7	
Belgium	1,759 (6)	−9.2 (1)	−5.0 (5)	1,590 (3)	1,550 (3)	−3.0 (5)	925 (2)	875 (2)	−5.4 (3)	601 (1)
Denmark	1,733 (4)	−2.6 (6)	−6.0 (4)	1,720 (4)	1,596 (4)	−7.2 (2)	1,246 (8)	1,211 (8)	−2.8 (4)	812 (8)
Finland	1,720 (3)	0 (8)	−7.5 (1)	1,818 (8)	1,782 (10)	−2.0 (6)	1,299 (9)	1,305 (10)	+0.5 (6)	890 (10)
France	1,767 (7)	0 (8)	−4.6 (7)	1,850 (9)	1,696 (7)	−3.3 (1)	1,122 (5)	1,001 (3)	−10.8 (1)	672 (5)
Germany	1,712 (1)	−5.9 (5)	−4.7 (6)	1,736 (7)	1,672 (6)	−3.7 (4)	1,090 (3)	1,020 (4)	−6.4 (2)	712 (4)
Japan	2,121 (11)	−5.9 (5)	0 (8)	2,113 (10)	2,085 (11)	−1.3 (8)	1,446 (10)	1,469 (11)	+1.6 (7)	1,020 (11)
Netherlands	1,744 (5)	−9.1 (2)	−7.0 (2)	1,720 (4)	1,645 (5)	−4.5 (3)	881 (1)	864 (1)	−1.9 (5)	603 (2)
Norway	1,714 (2)	−6.2 (4)	−6.6 (3)	1,563 (2)	1,537 (2)	−1.7 (7)	1,131 (6)	1,210 (7)	+7.0 (9)	788 (7)
Sweden	1,796 (9)	−8.2 (3)	0 (8)	1,438 (1)	1,482 (1)	+3.1 (10)	1,133 (7)	1,188 (6)	+4.9 (8)	770 (6)
United Kingdom	1,782 (8)	−2.1 (7)	−4.6 (7)	–	1,730 (8)	–	–	1,183 (5)	–	765 (5)
USA	1,916 (10)	0 (8)	0 (8)	1,735 (6)	1,770 (9)	+2.0 (9)	1,106 (4)	1,231 (9)	+11.3 (10)	832 (9)

The table is based on Eurostat figures. It is assumed that hours of part-timers are 25% lower than those of full-time employees and that hours outside industry are 2.5% longer than in industry.
Figures in brackets are rankings.
Source: Pettersson (1989)

In the long term, the reduction of working time obviously is the dominant trend. Also, in the last 20 years working hours were reduced in
most countries, but by very different combinations of increasing part
time work, reducing agreed and actual weekly and yearly working hours
and lifetime hours. However, in analyzing this main trend one easily
overlooks some manifest tendencies towards an extension of hours at
least in some countries and for some groups of workers within different
countries. *These tendencies may indicate the increasing differentiation
of the duration of working hours between and within countries after a
long period of standardization and harmonization of working hours.*[37]

What are the sources of this diversity? On the one hand, there are
institutional differences in the regulation of labor markets, with the
US, Japan, and the European Union displaying clear-cut contrasting
logics. On the other hand, within countries, longer working hours are
concentrated in two groups: high-level professionals and unskilled service workers. The former, because of their value-making contribution,
the latter because of their weak bargaining power, often associated
with immigrant status or informal work arrangements. As for shorter
working time and atypical schedules, they are linked to part-time and
temporary work, and concern mainly women and low-educated youth.
The massive entry of women into the labor force is, to some extent,
associated with the diversification of work status and working schedules. As a result, as shown above in chapter 4, between one-quarter
and one-half of the employed population of major industrialized countries (including self-employment) does not follow the classic pattern of
a full-time job with a regular working schedule. The number of workers in variable job assignments is rapidly increasing everywhere. In
addition, a considerable proportion of full-time workers (probably a
majority of the professional labor force) are heading toward flexible
time schedules, generally increasing their workload. The technological ability to reintegrate in a network of stored information contributions from various workers at various times induces the constant
variation of the actual time of work performance, undermining the
structuring capacity of working time over everyday life. Thus, in his
insightful analysis on the transformation of work and firms in France,
Frederic de Conninck focuses on the fact that "the enterprise is affected by plural and divergent temporalities," "the economy is dominated more and more by the search for flexibility, or organized around
short run time," with the result that "today, the individual is overwhelmed by the various temporalities he has to confront;" thus, while
work remains integrated, society tends toward its *éclatement,* out of

37   Bosch et al. (1994: 19) (my italics).

the unmanageable development of contradictory temporalities within the same structure.[38]

Therefore, the real issue in our societies is not so much that technology allows us to work less for the same unit of output: it does so, but the impact of this technological fact on actual working time and schedules is undetermined. What is at stake, and what appears to be the prevailing trend in most advanced sectors of most advanced societies, is the general diversification of working time, depending on firms, networks, jobs, occupations, and characteristics of the workers. Such diversity ends up, in fact, being measured in terms of each worker's and each job's differential capacity to manage time. Without anticipating my analysis of the evolution of the family (in volume II), it seems that the heterogeneity of working schedules in a society with similar participation by both genders in the labor force, imposes a dramatic readjustment of household arrangements. Not necessarily for the worst, since in fact added work-time flexibility could provide the basis for time-sharing in the household. Yet new household partnerships would have to be built on the ruins of patriarchal family rules.[39] Since flex-time and part-time have penetrated the contractual structures of working time on the basis of women's work, largely to accommodate women's needs to combine their child-rearing endeavors and their working lives, the extension of this logic to men and to other domains of social life other than child-rearing could actually introduce (it is in fact already introducing in many instances)[40] a new articulation of life time and work time at different ages and under different conditions, for both men and women. Thus, under such new arrangements, working time may lose its traditional centrality throughout the life-cycle.

A convergent trend pointing in the same direction comes from the dramatic shortening of actual working *years* in major industrialized countries, precisely at the moment of a substantial increase in life expectancy. This is, on the one hand, because the age of entry into the labor force, both for men and women, is increasingly higher, as a greater proportion of the population attends universities: a trend that results from cultural expectations, the tightening of labor markets, and employers' increasing requirement for higher education credentials in the labor force.[41] On the other hand, Anne Marie Guillemard has conducted comparative studies that show the dramatic decline of actual

38   De Conninck (1995); quotes are, in sequential order, from pp. 200, 193, and 193 (my translation).
39   Martin Carnoy and I have jointly elaborated on this theme in Carnoy and Castells (1996).
40   Hewitt (1993).
41   Carnoy and Levin (1985).

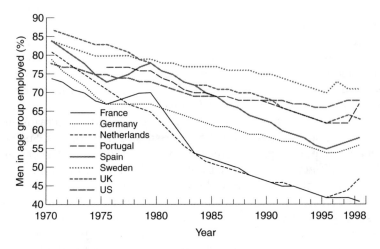

Figure 7.1 Labor force participation rate (%) for men 55–64 years old in eight countries, 1970–1998
Sources: Guillemard (1993); Carnoy (2000), re-elaborated by Carnoy

employment for the labor force over 50 years, and specially over 55 years.[42] As figure 7.1 shows, the rate of activity of men between 55 and 64 years declined significantly between 1970 and 1998 in major industrialized economies, and in 1998 was down to 68 percent in the US, 64 percent in the UK, 56 percent in Germany, 48 percent in The Netherlands, and 41 percent in France. For these countries, whether by early retirement, disability, permanent unemployment, attrition, or discouragement, between one-third and over one-half of the male labor force *permanently* quits the labor market in their early fifties. Guillemard puts forward a solid argument for the fact that this tendency is not temporary but rooted in short-sighted government and business policies and in the belief that the aged worker is unable to adapt to the current speed of technological and organizational innovation.[43] Under such circumstances, the actual working lifetime could be shortened to about 30 years (from 24 to 54) in a real lifetime span of about 75–80 years. Then, not only working time loses its centrality *vis-à-vis* life in general, but the accounting system on which pensions and healthcare are calculated collapses, not because there are too many elderly persons, but because the proportion between contributing workers and non-working recipients becomes unbearable, unless pro-

42   Guillemard (1993).
43   Guillemard and Rein (1993).

ductivity increases are dramatic and society accepts a massive intergenerational redistribution.[44]

Thus, the real challenge of the new relationship between work and technology does not concern mass unemployment, as I tried to discuss in chapter 4, but the overall shortening of life working time for a substantial proportion of the population. Unless the basis of calculation for social benefits is modified through a new social contract, the shrinkage of valuable working time and the accelerated obsolescence of labor will bring to an end the institutions of social solidarity, ushering in the age wars.

The Blurring of the Life-cycle: Toward Social Arrhythmia?

It seems that all living beings, including us, are biological clocks.[45] Biological rhythms, whether individual, related to the species, or even cosmic, are essential to human life. People and societies ignore them at their peril.[46] For millenniums, the rhythm of human life was constructed in close relationship to the rhythms of nature, generally with little bargaining power against hostile natural forces, so that it seemed reasonable to go with the flow, and to model the life-cycle in accordance with a society where most babies would die as infants, where women's reproductive power had to be used early, where youth was ephemeral (Ronsard), where growing elderly was such a privilege that it brought with it the respect due to a unique source of experience and wisdom, and where plagues would periodically wipe out a sizeable share of the population.[47] In the developed world, the industrial revolution, the constitution of medical science, the triumph of reason, and the affirmation of social rights have altered this pattern in the past two centuries, prolonging life, overcoming illness, regulating births, alleviating death, calling into question the biological determination of roles in society, and constructing the life-cycle around social categories, among which education, working time, career patterns, and the right to retirement became paramount. However, although the principle of a sequential life shifted from being bio-social to becoming socio-biological, there was (indeed, there still is) a life-cycle pattern to which advanced societies tend to conform, and toward which developing

44 Lenoir (1994).
45 Berger (1984), cited by Adam (1990).
46 Schor (1991).
47 McNeill (1977).

countries try to evolve. Now, organizational, technological, and cultural developments characteristic of the new, emerging society are decisively undermining this orderly life-cycle without replacing it with an alternative sequence. *I propose the hypothesis that the network society is characterized by the breaking down of the rhythms, either biological or social, associated with the notion of a life-cycle.*

I have already examined one of the reasons for this new trend, namely the variable chronology of working time. But an even more important development is the increasing ability to control, within obvious limits, the reproduction of our species, and the average duration of the life of its individuals (see chapter 1). Although the upper limit of longevity has a biological boundary, the prolongation of the average duration of life to the late seventies (early eighties for women), and the increasing share of the population reaching well beyond the average, into the eighties age group, have considerable consequences for our societies and for the ways in which we conceive of ourselves. While old age was once considered a homogeneous last stage of life, in fact dominated by "social death," as demonstrated in the French study that Anne Marie Guillemard conducted many years ago with my collaboration,[48] it is now a highly diverse universe, made up of early retirees, average retirees, able elders, and elders with various degrees and forms of disability. So, suddenly, the "third age" is extended toward younger and older groups, and substantially redefines the life-cycle in three ways: it denies the exit from the labor market as the defining criterion, since for a substantial proportion of the population about one-third of their life may occur after this event; it differentiates the elderly fundamentally in terms of their level of disability, not always correlating with age, thus assimilating to some extent their disabled condition to other disabled groups of a younger age, thus inducing a new social category; and it compels the distinction between several age groups, whose actual differentiation will greatly depend on their social, cultural, and relational capital accumulated throughout their lives.[49] Depending on each one of these variables, the social attributes of these distinct old ages will differ considerably, thus breaking down the relationship between social condition and biological stage at the roots of the life-cycle.

Simultaneously, this relationship is being called into question at the other end: reproduction is coming under increasing control around the world. In advanced societies the norm is birth control, although social marginality and religious beliefs constitute areas of resistance to

---

48   Castells and Guillemard (1971); Guillemard (1972).
49   Guillemard (1988).

Table 7.4 Principal demographic characteristics by main regions of the world, 1970–1995[a]

	Total fertility rate			Life expectancy at birth			Infant mortality rate		
	1970–5	1980–5	1990–5	1970–5	1980–5	1990–5	1970–5	1980–5	1990–5
World	4.4	3.5	3.3	57	60	65	93	78	62
More-developed regions	2.2	2.0	1.9	71	73	75	22	16	12
Less-developed regions	5.4	4.1	3.6	54	57	62	104	88	69
Africa	6.5	6.3	6.0	46	49	53	142	112	95
Americas	3.6	3.1	–	64	67	68	64	49	–
Latin	–	–	3.1	–	–	–	–	–	47
Northern	–	–	2.0	–	–	–	–	–	8
Asia	5.1	3.5	3.2	56	59	65	97	83	62
Europe	2.2	1.9	1.7	71	73	75	24	15	10
Oceania	3.2	2.7	2.5	66	68	73	39	31	22
USSR	2.4	2.4	2.3	70	71	70	26	25	21

[a] Data for 1990–5 all projections.
Sources: United Nations, World Population Prospects. Estimates and Projections as Assessed in 1984; United Nations, World Population at the Turn of the Century, 1989, p. 9, table 3; United Nations Population Fund, The State of World Population: Choices and Responsibilities, 1994

Table 7.5 Total fertility rates of some industrialized countries, 1901–1985

	Denmark	Finland	France	Germany[a]	Italy	Netherlands	Portugal	Sweden	Switzerland	United Kingdom	United States
1901–05	4.04	4.22	2.78	4.74	—	4.48	—	3.91	3.82	3.40	—
1906–10	3.83	4.15	2.59	4.25	—	4.15	—	3.76	3.56	3.14	—
1911–15	3.44	3.68	2.26	3.19	—	3.79	—	3.31	3.02	2.84	—
1916–20	3.15	3.49	1.66	2.13	—	3.58	—	2.94	2.46	2.40	3.22
1921–25	2.85	3.33	2.43	2.49	—	3.47	—	2.58	2.43	2.39	3.08
1926–30	2.41	2.88	2.29	2.05	—	3.08	—	2.08	2.10	2.01	2.65
1931–35	2.15	2.41	2.18	1.86	3.06	2.73	3.88	1.77	1.91	1.79	2.21
1936–40	2.17	2.38	2.07	2.43	3.00	2.58	3.45	1.82	1.80	1.80	2.14
1941–45	2.64	2.60	2.11	2.05	2.56	2.85	3.43	2.35	2.38	2.00	2.45
1946–50	2.75	2.86	2.99	2.05	2.78	3.48	3.29	2.45	2.52	2.38	2.97
1951–55	2.55	2.99	2.73	2.09	2.30	3.05	3.05	2.23	2.30	2.19	3.27
1956–60	2.54	2.78	2.70	2.34	2.32	3.11	3.02	2.24	2.40	2.52	3.53
1961–65	2.59	2.58	2.83	2.50	2.56	3.15	3.10	2.33	2.61	2.83	3.16
1966–70	2.20	2.06	2.60	2.33	2.50	2.74	2.91	2.12	2.29	2.56	2.41
1971–75	1.96	1.62	2.26	1.62	2.31	1.99	2.64	1.89	1.82	2.06	1.84
1976–80	1.65	1.67	1.88	1.41	1.88	1.59	2.32	1.66	1.51	1.76	1.69
1981–85	1.38	1.74	1.82	1.32	1.53	1.47	1.97	1.61	1.50	1.75	1.66

[a] German figures include both FRG and GDR.

Sources: J. Bourgeois-Pichat, "Comparative fertility trends in Europe," in *Causes and Consequences of Non-Replacement Fertility* (Hoover Institution, 1985); United Nations, *World Population at the Turn of the Century*, 1989, p. 90, table 21

Table 7.6 First live births per 1,000 women by age group of mother (30–49 years) and by race in the United States, 1960 and 1990

	Age (years)			
	30–34	*35–39*	*40–44*	*45–49*
Total				
1960	8.6	3.2	0.8	0.0
1990	21.2	6.7	1.0	0.0
White				
1960	8.9	3.3	0.8	0.0
1990	21.6	6.8	1.0	0.0
Black				
1964	5.4	2.2	0.6	0.0
1990	12.9	4.0	0.7	0.0
All other				
1960	6.9	2.9	0.7	0.1
1990	19.1	6.3	1.1	0.1

Note the dramatic increase in the first live birth rate between 1960 and 1990: an increase of 146.5% for the 30–34 year age group, and of 109% for the 35–39 year age group.
Sources: U.S. Bureau of the Census, *Historical Statistics of the United States: Colonial Times to 1970*, vol. 1, p. 50, Series B 11–19, 1975; US Dept of Health and Human Services. *Vital Statistics of the United States: 1990*, vol. 1, section 1, table 1.9, 1994

planned motherhood. In close interaction with the cultural and professional emancipation of women, the development of reproductive rights has altered the demographic structure and biological rhythms of our societies in just two decades (see tables 7.4 and 7.5). Overall, the most industrialized countries have entered an era of low birth rates (below the reproduction rate for the native population), of delayed time for marriage and reproduction, and of variable stages for women to have children throughout their life-cycle, as they strive to combine education, work, personal life, and children in an increasingly individualized pattern of decision-making (see table 7.6). Together with the transformation of the family and the increasing diversification of lifestyles (see volume II), we observe a substantial modification of the time and forms for mothering and fathering in the life-cycle, where the new rule is, increasingly, that there are few rules. Furthermore, new reproductive technologies and new cultural models make it possible, to a considerable extent, to disassociate age and biological condition from reproduction and from parenthood. In strictly technical terms it is possible today to differentiate the legal parent(s) of a child; whose is the sperm; whose is the egg; where and how the fertilization is performed, in real or delayed time, even after the death of the father; and whose is the womb which gives birth to the child. *All combinations are possible and are socially decided.* Our society has already reached the technological capacity to separate social reproduction and biological reproduction of the species. I am obviously referring to exceptions to the rule, but to tens of thousands of exceptions throughout the world. Some of them are showcases of the possibility for aged women (in their late fifties or early sixties) actually to give birth. Others are soap opera happenings about a dead lover whose frozen sperm is fought over by irate heirs. Most are secluded events often whispered over dinner in high-tech California or in gossipy Madrid. Since these developments are related to very simple reproductive technologies which do not involve genetic engineering, it is plausible to imagine a much greater range for the possible manipulation of reproductive ages and reproduction conditions when human genetic engineering ends up finding a legal and ethical accommodation in society, as all technologies do in the long term.

Since I am not speculating on future projections but elaborating on well-known facts of our everyday life, I believe it is legitimate to think about the consequences of these developments for human life, and particularly for the life-cycle. It is very simple: they lead to the final blurring of the biological foundation of the life-cycle concept. Sixty-year-old parents of infants; children of different marriages enjoying brothers and sisters 30 years older with no intermediate age groups; men and women deciding to procreate, with or without coupling, at whatever age; grandmothers giving birth to the baby originated in her daughter's egg (also cases in real life); posthumous babies; and an increasing gap between social institutions and reproductive practices (children born out of wedlock represent about 50 percent of all births in Sweden, and about 40 percent in France). It is essential that we do not include a value judgment in this observation. What for traditionalists amounts to challenging the divine wrath, for cultural revolutionaries is the triumph of individual desire, and indeed the ultimate affirmation of women's rights over their bodies and their lives. Yet what is essential is that we are not on the fringes of society, even if these are still embryos of a new relationship between our social and biological condition. These are growing social trends, whose technological and cultural diffusion seems unstoppable, except under conditions of a new theocracy. And their direct implication is another form of the annihilation of time, of human biological time, of the time rhythm by which our species has been regulated since its origins. Regardless of our opinion, we may have to live without the clock that told our parents when they were supposed to procreate us, and that told us when, how, and if to pass our life on to our children. A secular biological rhythm has been replaced by a moment of existential decision.

Death Denied

The belief in the probability of death with dignity is our, and society's attempt to deal with the reality of what is all too frequently a series of destructive events that involve by their very nature the disintegration of the dying person's humanity. I have not often seen much dignity in the process by which we die. The quest to achieve true dignity fails when our bodies fail . . . The greatest dignity to be found in death is the dignity of the life that preceded it.

Sherwin B. Nuland[50]

Time in society and life is measured by death. Death is and has been the central theme of cultures throughout history, either revered as God's will or defied as the ultimate human challenge.[51] It has been exorcised in the rites destined to calm the living, accepted with the resignation of the serene, tamed in the carnivals of the simple, fought with the desperation of the romantics, but never denied.[52] It is a distinctive feature of our new culture, the attempt to exile death from our lives. Although the matrix of this attempt lies in the rationalist belief in almighty progress, it is the extraordinary breakthroughs in medical technology and biological research in the past two decades that provide a material basis for the oldest aspiration of humankind: to live as if death did not exist, in spite of its being our only certainty. By so doing, the ultimate subversion of the life-cycle is accomplished, and life becomes this flat landscape punctuated by chosen moments of high and low experiences, in the endless boutique of customized feelings. So when death does happen it is simply an additional blip on the screen of distracted spectators. If it is true that, as Ionesco said, "each of us is the first one to die,"[53] social mechanisms make sure that we are also the last, namely that the dead are truly alone, and do not take away the vital energy of the living. Yet this old, and healthy, aspiration to survival, documented by Philippe Aries as being present in Western culture since the Middle Ages,[54] takes a new turn under the biological revolution. Because we

50 Nuland (1994: xvii, 242).
51 Morin (1970).
52 Thomas (1985, 1988).
53 Quoted by Thomas (1988: 17).
54 Aries (1977, 1983).

are so close to unveiling the secrets of life, two major trends have diffused from the medical sciences toward the rest of the society: obsessive prevention, and the fight to the end.

According to the first trend, every biological study, every medical exploration relating human health to the environment becomes quickly translated into hygienic advice or mandatory prescription (for example, the anti-smoking crusade in the US, the same country in which submachine guns can be purchased by mail) which increasingly transforms society into a symbolically sanitized environment, with the full cooperation of the media. Indeed, newscasters have found in the health crusade an endless source of public attention, more so since the results of studies are periodically refuted and replaced by new specific instructions. A whole "healthy living" industry is directly related to this crusade, from hygienized food to fashionable sportswear and to mainly irrelevant vitamin pills. This perverted use of medical research is particularly pathetic when contrasted to the indifference of health insurance companies and mainstream business toward primary care and occupational safety.[55] Thus, an increasing proportion of people in advanced societies, and the professional classes throughout the world, spend considerable time, money, and psychological energy all through their lives pursuing health fashions in ways and with outcomes only slightly different from traditional shaman rites. For instance, while recent studies show that weight is largely linked to genetically programmed metabolism, and that people oscillate in a 10–15 percent range around their age and size average regardless of their efforts,[56] diet is a social obsession, either real or manipulated. True, personal aesthetics and the relationship to the body is also linked to the culture of individualism and narcissism, but the hygienist view of our societies adds a decisive instrumental twist to it (indeed, it is often linked with rejecting the objectification of woman's body). It aims at delaying and fighting death and aging every minute of life, with the support of medical science, the health industry, and media information.

Yet the real offensive against death is the good-faith, all-out medical struggle to push back the ineluctable as much as humanly possible. Sherwin B. Nuland, a surgeon and historian of medicine, writes in his soul-shaking book *How We Die:*

> Every medical specialist must admit that he has at times convinced patients to undergo diagnostic or therapeutic measures at a point in illness so far beyond reason that The Riddle might better remained unsolved.

55   Navarro (1994a).
56   Kolata (1995).

Figure 7.2   Ratio of hospitalized deaths to total deaths (%), by year, 1947–1987, Japan
Source: Koichiri Kuroda, "Medicalization of death: changes in site of death in Japan after World War Two," Hyogo: Kobe College, Department of Intercultural Studies, 1990, unpublished research paper

> Too often near the end, were the doctor able to see deeply within himself, he might recognize that his decisions and advice are motivated by his inability to give up The Riddle and admit defeat as long as there is any chance of solving it. Though he be kind and considerate of the patient he treats, he allows himself to push his kindness aside because the seduction of The Riddle is so strong and the failure to solve it renders him so weak.[57]

This medical impulse to repulse death has nothing to do with capitalism. In fact, some insurance companies would rather welcome euthanasia, and would like to send patients home as soon as possible, a cynical view daily fought against by doctors. Without this relentless will to reject the inevitable, valuable lessons would be lost, and our collective ability to survive and overcome suffering would be hampered. Yet the societal impact of such efforts, along with less-noble enterprises of using terminal patients as experimental subjects, is tantamount to the denial of death until its very last act. So strong is the

57   Nuland (1994: 249).

temporal and spatial confinement of death that the overwhelming majority of deaths (80 percent in the US, and a growing proportion in all countries: see figure 7.2 for Japan, a society with a strong family culture) takes place in hospital, very often in special intensive care units, with the bodies already removed from their social and emotional environments. In spite of some limited movements in defense of humane hospices for terminally ill patients, and even more limited tendencies toward bringing the dying back home, our last episode is increasingly sanitized, and our loved ones do not have the courage to object: it is too messy, too dirty, too painful, too inhuman, too degrading in fact. Life is interrupted at the threshold of the last possible smile, and death becomes visible only for a brief, ceremonial moment, after specialized image-makers perform their soothing *mise-en-scène*. Afterwards, mourning is going out of fashion in our societies, both as a reaction against traditional social hypocrisy, and as a down-to-earth philosophy of survival. Yet psychoanalysts and anthropologists have shown the social functions and individual benefits of mourning, both in its ritual and in its feeling.[58] But forfeiting mourning is the price to pay for accessing eternity in our lifetime through the denial of death.

The dominant trend in our societies, as an expression of our technological ambition, and in line with our celebration of the ephemeral, is to erase death from life, or to make it meaningless by its repeated representation in the media, always as the other's death, so that our own is met with the surprise of the unexpected. By separating death from life, and by creating the technological system to make this belief last long enough, we construct eternity in our life span. Thus, eternal we become except for that brief moment when embraced by the light.

Instant Wars

Death, war, and time are secular historical associates. It is one of the most striking characteristics of the emerging technological paradigm that this association is essentially altered, at least for the decisive warfare of dominant powers. Indeed, the advent of nuclear technology, and the possibility of planetary holocaust, had the paradoxical effect of canceling large-scale, global warfare between major powers, superseding a condition that marked the first half of the twentieth century as the most destructive, lethal period in history.[59] However, geopolitical interests and societal confrontations continue to fuel international,

58 Thomas (1975).
59 Van Creveld (1989); Tilly (1995).

inter-ethnic, and ideological hostility to the limit of aiming at physical destruction:[60] the roots of war, we must acknowledge, are in human nature, at least as historically experienced.[61] Yet in the past two decades, democratic, technologically advanced societies, in North America, Western Europe, Japan, and Oceania, have come to reject warfare and to oppose extraordinary resistance to governments' calling their citizens to the ultimate sacrifice. The Algerian War in France, the Vietnam War in the United States, and the Afghanistan War in Russia[62] were turning points in the capacity of states to commit their societies to destruction for not so compelling reasons. Since warfare, and the credible threat of resorting to it, is still at the core of state power, since the end of the Vietnam War strategists have been busy finding ways still to make war. Only under this condition can economic, technological,

---

60   For some useful information, of questionable conceptualization, see US House of Representatives, Committee on Armed Services, Readiness Subcommittee (1990). See also Harff (1986); Gurr (1993).

61   I have to confess that my understanding of war, and of the social context of warfare, is influenced by what is probably the oldest military treatise on strategy: Sun Tzu's *On the Art of War* (c.505–496BC). If the reader suspects that I indulge in exoticism, I invite her or him to read it, on the condition of having the patience to extract the logic embedded in the analysis from its historical context. Read a sample of it: "The art of war is of vital importance to the State. It is a matter of life and death, a road either to safety or ruin. Hence it is a subject of inquiry which can on no account be neglected. The art of war, then, is governed by five constant factors, to be taken into account in one's deliberations, when seeking to determine the conditions obtaining in the field. These are (1) The Moral Law (2) Heaven (3) Earth (4) The Commander (5) Method and Discipline. The Moral Law causes the people to be in complete accord with their ruler, so that they will follow him regardless of their lives. Heaven signifies night and day, cold and heat, times and seasons. Earth comprises distances, great and small; danger and security; open ground and narrow passes; the chances of life and death. The Commander stands for the virtues of wisdom, sincerity, benevolence, courage, and strictness. By Method and Discipline are to be understood the marshalling of the army in its proper subdivisions, the gradations of rank among the officers, the maintenance of roads by which supplies may reach the army, and *the control of military expenditure.*" (pp.1–3; my emphasis).

62   Public opinion in Russia is probably, with Japan and Germany, one of the most pacifist in the world, since in the twentieth century Russian people suffered more from war than anyone else in the world. This pacifism could not express itself in the open until the 1980s for obvious reasons, but widespread discontent with the war in Afghanistan was an important factor in inducing Gorbachev's *perestroika*. Furthermore, although the war in Chechnya in 1994 seemed to belie this statement, in fact it provoked the disaffection of a large proportion of the population *vis-à-vis* Yeltsin's policies, and precipitated the split between the Russian President and many of the democrats who had supported him in the past. On the basis of my personal knowledge of Russia and of some survey data, I would propose the admittedly optimistic hypothesis that Russia's military lobby will face in the future as serious a popular opposition to war-making as Western countries do, thus inducing a shift to technological emphasis in warfare. (*Author's note, December 1999*: I have not revised this footnote, as written in early 1996, in order to show how risky specific predictions are in political matters. At the end of 1999, after a series of mysterious, murderous bombings in Moscow, the Russian public was fully supporting an all-out assault by federal troops on the Russian republic of Chechnya. Yet, I would not change my statement to a new prediction since this also can change once the human toll of war begins to mount.)

and demographic power be translated into domination over other states, the oldest game in humankind. Three conclusions were rapidly reached in advanced, democratic countries, regarding the conditions necessary to make war more acceptable to society:[63]

1 It should not involve common citizens, thus being enacted by a professional army, so that the mandatory draft should be reserved for truly exceptional circumstances, perceived as unlikely.
2 It should be short, even instantaneous, so that the consequences would not linger on, draining human and economic resources, and raising questions about the justification for military action.
3 It should be clean, surgical, with destruction, even of the enemy, kept within reasonable limits and as hidden as possible from public view, with the consequence of linking closely information-handling, image-making, and war-making.

Dramatic breakthroughs in military technology in the past two decades provided the tools to implement this socio-military strategy. Well-trained, well-equipped, full-time, professional armed forces do not require the involvement of the population at large in the war effort, except for viewing and cheering from their living rooms a particularly exciting show, punctuated with deep patriotic feelings.[64] Professional management of news reporting, in an intelligent form that understands the needs of the media while monitoring them, can bring the war live to people's homes with limited, sanitized perception of killing and suffering, a theme that Baudrillard has elaborated thoroughly.[65] Most importantly, communications and electronic weapons technology allow for devastating strikes against the enemy in extremely brief time spans. The Gulf War was, of course, the general rehearsal for a new type of war, and its 100 hours' denouement, against a large, and well-equipped Iraqi army, was a demonstration of the decisiveness of new military powers when an important issue is at stake (the West's oil

63 See the reassessment of American military strategy, in fact initiated in the late 1970s, in an important report from a blue-ribbon Commission for the US Defense Department: Ikle and Wohlsletter (1988). See my elaboration on the impact of technology on military strategy in Castells and Skinner (1988).
64 Most Western European countries still had no strictly professional armed forces in the mid-1990s. Yet, although a time-limited draft (less than a year in general) was still practiced, actual military operations were in the hands of a core of professional soldiers with appropriate technological training and readiness to fight. Indeed, given widespread opposition to risking life for the sake of the country, the more an army relies on the draft the less these troops are likely to be engaged in combat. The overall trend points clearly to a purely symbolic military service for the large majority of the population in advanced, democratic societies.
65 Baudrillard (1991).

supply in that case).[66] Of course, this analysis, and the Gulf War itself, would require some lengthy qualifications. The US and its allies did send half a million soldiers for several months to launch a ground attack, although many experts suspect that this was in fact due to internal politics in the Defense Department, not yet ready to concede to the Air Force that wars can be won from the air and the sea. This was indeed the case, since land forces did not in practice meet much resistance after the punishment inflicted on the Iraqis at a distance. True, the allies did not press their drive into Baghdad, yet this decision was not because of serious military obstacles, but because of their political calculation in keeping Iraq as a military power in the area, to check Iran and Syria. The lack of support from a major state (Russia or China) made the Iraqis particularly vulnerable. Yet, other "quasi-instant wars" may be waged against more powerful countries, with stronger political support. Thus, the 1999 war against Yugoslavia (orginally intended for two days) could proceed with almost three months of daily bombings of an industrialized country, in spite of the strong opposition of Russia and China, because NATO forces had no casualties in combat, Western powers won the media battle in their countries, and US technological power kept at bay any serious challenge to the aerial assault. The key to NATO's military success was its ability to inflict substantial damage on Yugoslavia without engaging ground troops in the conflict.

Technologically equivalent powers would have greater difficulty going after each other. However, given the mutual cancellation of nuclear exchange between major military powers, their potential wars, and the wars between their surrogate states, are likely to depend on rapid exchanges that set the real state of technological imbalance between the warring forces. Massive destruction, or a quick demonstration of its possibility, in minimum time seems to be the accepted strategy to fight advanced wars in the Information Age.

However, this military strategy can only be pursued by dominant technological powers, and it contrasts sharply with numerous, endless internal and international violent conflicts that have plagued the world since 1945.[67] This temporal difference in war-making is one of the most striking manifestations of the difference in temporality that characterizes our segmented global system, a theme on which I shall elaborate below.

In dominant societies, this new age of warfare has considerable impact on time, and on the notion of time, as experienced in history.

66 See, for instance, Morrocco (1991).
67 Carver (1980); Holsti (1991); Tilly (1995).

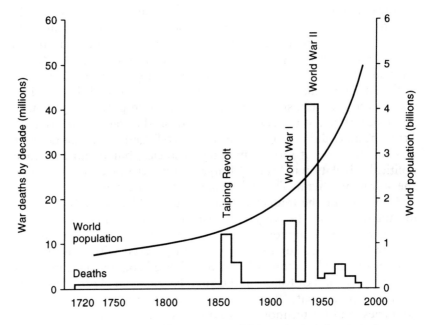

Figure 7.3 War deaths relative to world population, by decade,
1720–2000
Source: Kaye et al. (1985)

Extraordinarily intense moments of military decision-making will
emerge as shaping instants over long periods of peace or restrained
tension. For instance, according to an historical quantitative study on
armed conflicts, conducted for the Canadian Defense Ministry, the
duration of conflicts in the first half of the 1980s was reduced, on
average, by more than half in comparison to the 1970s, and by more
than two-thirds with reference to the 1960s.[68] Relying on the same
source, figure 7.3 displays the decrease in the scale of death as the
result of war *in recent years,* particularly when compared to the size
of world population. However, observation of the same figure shows
the extent to which war has been historically a way of life, with particular intensity in the first half of the twentieth century. Other sources
indicate that per capita deaths from war in Western Europe, North
America, Japan, and Latin America were much lower in 1945–89 than
in 1815–1913.[69] Under the new warfare temporality, induced by the

68   Kaye et al. (1985).
69   Tilly (1995), citing Derriennic (1990).

convergence of technology and the pressure from civil societies in advanced countries, it seems likely that war will recede to the background of these dominant societies, to flare up from time to time in a sudden reminder of human nature.

In several societies, this disappearance of war from the life-cycle of most people has already decisively impacted on culture and behavior. In industrialized, democratic countries, if we except a minority of the population for a short period of time in France, in Portugal, and in the United States, the generations born after the Second World War are the first in history not to have experienced war in their lifetime, with the exception of the lucky Swedes and Swiss. This is a fundamental discontinuity in the human experience. Indeed, this essentially affects masculinity and the culture of manhood. Up to these generations, in the life of all men it was assumed that at some point something terrible would happen: they would be sent to be killed, to be killers, to live with death and the destruction of bodies, to experience dehumanization on a large scale, and yet be proud of it, or else be banned from the esteem of their society and, frequently, of their families. It is impossible to understand women's extraordinary patience in the traditional, patriarchal family without reference to this moment of truth, to the male's atrocious fate, to which mothers, wives, and daughters paid their respect, a recurrent theme in the literature of all countries.[70] Anyone who has grown up, as in my case, in the first generation without war in their life, knows how decisive the experience of war was for our fathers, how much childhood and the life of the family was filled with the wounds and the reconstructed memories of those years, sometimes only months, but still shaping men's personality for ever, and with it, the personality of their families throughout the life-cycle. This acceleration of time by cohabitation with death, regularly experienced by generation after generation for most of human history, is now over in some societies.[71] And this truly ushers in a new age in our experience.

However, we must be strongly reminded that instant, surgical, secluded, technology-driven wars are the privilege of technologically dominant nations. All around the world, half-ignored, cruel wars

70   This theme has been elaborated by French feminist writer Annie Leclerc. Although I discovered this idea through our personal conversations, it is also present in some of her essays; see especially Leclerc (1975).
71   In his cultural study of post-World War II Japanese youth, Inoue Syun found that the "non-war" generation differed sharply from its fathers in thinking of life apart from death. He writes: "We might very loosely label the war-time generation as death-acceptors and the non-war generation as death-defiers" (Syun 1975). For a broader analysis on the matter, see Freud (1947).

linger on for years and years, often fought with primitive means, although global diffusion of high-tech weaponry is also catching up in this market. In the 1989–92 period alone the United Nations counted 82 armed conflicts in the world, of which 79 were internal to a nation.[72] The Indian guerrillas of Guatemala, the endless revolutionary struggles in Colombia and Peru, the Christian rebellion of southern Sudan, the liberation struggles of Kurdish people, the Muslim rebellion of Mindanao, the mixing of drug traffic and national struggles in Myanmar and Thailand, the tribal/ideological wars in Angola, and in Congo, the warlords' confrontations in Somalia or Liberia, the ethnic civil wars of Rwanda and Burundi, the Sahara resistance to Morocco, the civil war in Algeria, the civil war in Afghanistan, the civil war in Sri Lanka, the civil war in Bosnia, and Kosovo, the decades-old Arab–Israeli wars and struggles, the wars in the Caucasus, and so many other armed confrontations and wars that last for years and decades, clearly demonstrate that slow-motion, debilitating wars are still, and will be for the foreseeable future, the hideous sign of our destructive capacity.[73] It is precisely the asymmetry of various countries in their relationship to power, wealth, and technology that determines different temporalities, and particularly the time of their warfare. Furthermore, the same country may shift from slow-motion wars to instant wars depending on its relationship to the global system and to the interests of dominant powers. Thus, Iran and Iraq fought for seven years an atrocious war, carefully fed by Western countries supporting both sides of the carnage (US and France helping Iraq, Israel helping Iran, Spain selling chemical weapons to both), so that their reciprocal destruction would undermine the capacity of either of them to jeopardize the oil supply. When Iraq, with a well-equipped, combat-hardened army, went on to affirm its leadership in the region (indeed, counting on the acquiescence of Western powers), it found itself confronted by instant war technology, in a demonstration of force that was intended as a warning of future world disorder. Or elsewhere, the lingering, atrocious war in Bosnia, the shame of the European Union, was transformed in a few days, and a peace process was imposed at Dayton, Ohio, in August 1995, once the NATO countries settled their differences, and shifted the technological mode to a few days of selective, devastating strikes that crippled the Bosnian Serbs' fighting capacity. When and if a conflict becomes included in the high-priority plans of world powers, it shifts to a different tempo.

To be sure, even for dominant societies, the end of war does not

---

72　*The Economist* (1993).
73　Tillema (1991).

mean the end of violence and of violent confrontation with political apparatuses of various kinds. The transformation of war ushers in new forms of violent conflict, terrorism being foremost among them. Potential nuclear, chemical, and bacteriological terrorism, in addition to indiscriminate massacres and hostage-taking, with the media as the focus of the action, are likely to become the expressions of warfare in advanced societies. Yet even these violent acts, susceptible to affecting everybody's psyche, are experienced as discontinuous instants in the course of peaceful normality. This is in striking contrast to the pervasiveness of state-induced violence in much of the planet.[74]

Instant wars, and their technologically induced temporality, are an attribute of informational societies, but, as with other dimensions of the new temporality, they characterize the forms of domination of the new system, to the exclusion of countries and events that are not central to the emerging, dominant logic.

Virtual Time

I wrote in my notebook that December: "more and more I find I want to be living in a Big Here and a Long Now". I guess part of the reason the idea attracted me is that it offered justification for the type of music I was starting to make at the time – a music which was sort of suspended in an eternal present tense.

Brian Eno, cited by Brand[75]

The culture of real virtuality associated with an electronically integrated multimedia system, as argued in chapter 5, contributes to the transformation of time in our society in two different forms: simultaneity and timelessness. On the one hand, instant information throughout the globe, mixed with live reporting from across the neighborhood, provides unprecedented temporal immediacy to social events and cultural expressions.[76] To follow minute by minute in real time the collapse of the Soviet state in August 1991, with simultaneous translation of Russian political debates, introduced a new era of communication, when the making of history can be directly witnessed, provided it is deemed interesting enough by the controllers of information. Also, computer-mediated communication makes possible real-time dialogue, bringing people together around their interests, in interactive, multilateral chat writing. Time-delayed answers can be easily overcome, as

74   Tilly (1995).
75   Brand (1999: 28).
76   Wark (1994); Campo Vidal (1996).

new communication technologies provide a sense of immediacy that conquers time barriers, as much as the telephone did but with greater flexibility, with the communicating parties able to lapse for a few seconds, or minutes, to bring in other information, to expand the realm of communication, without the pressure of the telephone, ill-adapted to long silences.

On the other hand, the mixing of times in the media, within the same channel of communication and at the choice of the viewer/interactor, creates a temporal collage, where not only genres are mixed, but their timing becomes synchronous in a flat horizon, with no beginning, no end, no sequence. The timelessness of multimedia's hypertext is a decisive feature of our culture, shaping the minds and memories of children educated in the new cultural context. History is first organized according to the availability of visual material, then submitted to the computerized possibility of selecting seconds of frames to be pieced together, or split apart, according to specific discourses. School education, media entertainment, special news reports, or advertising organize temporality as it fits, so that the overall effect is a non-sequential time of cultural products available from the whole realm of human experience. If encyclopedias have organized human knowledge by alphabetical order, electronic media provide access to information, expression, and perception according to the impulses of the consumer or to the decisions of the producer. By so doing, the whole ordering of meaningful events loses its internal, chronological rhythm, and becomes arranged in time sequences depending upon the social context of their utilization. Thus, *it is a culture at the same time of the eternal and of the ephemeral*. It is eternal because it reaches back and forth to the whole sequence of cultural expressions. It is ephemeral because each arrangement, each specific sequencing, depends on the context and purpose under which any given cultural construct is solicited. We are not in a culture of circularity, but in a universe of undifferentiated temporality of cultural expressions.

I have discussed the relationship between the ideology of the end of history, the material conditions created under the logic of the space of flows, and the emergence of postmodern architecture, where all cultural codes can be mixed without sequencing or ordering, since we are in a world of finite cultural expressions. Eternal/ephemeral time also fits in this particular cultural mode, as it transcends any particular sequencing. David Harvey, along similar lines of argument, has brilliantly shown the interaction between postmodern culture, be it in architecture, cinema, art, or philosophy, and what he calls the "postmodern condition" induced by space–time compression. Although I believe that he gives to capitalist logic more responsibility than it deserves for current processes of cultural transformation, his analysis unveils the social sources of the sudden convergence of cultural expressions toward the negation of meaning and the affirmation of irony as the supreme value.[77] Time is compressed and ultimately denied in culture, as a primitive replica of the fast turnover in production, consumption, ideology, and politics on which our society is based. A speed only made possible because of new communication technologies.

Yet culture does not simply reproduce in all its manifestations the logic of the economic system. The historical correspondence between the political economy of signs and the signs of political economy is not a sufficient argument to characterize the emergence of timeless time in postmodernism. I think we must add something else: the specificity of new cultural expressions, their ideological and technological freedom to scan the planet and the whole history of humankind, and to integrate, and mix, in the supertext any sign from anywhere, from the rap culture of American ghettos, mimicked a few months later in the pop groups of Taipei or Tokyo, to Buddhist spiritualism transformed in electronic music. The eternal/ephemeral time of the new culture does fit with the logic of flexible capitalism and with the dynamics of the network society, but it adds its own, powerful layer, installing individual dreams and collective representations in a no-time mental landscape.

Perhaps New Age music, so characteristic of the taste of today's professionals throughout the world, is representative of the timeless dimension of the emerging culture, bringing together reconstructed Buddhist meditation, electronic sound-making, and sophisticated Californian composition. The electric harp of Hillary Staggs, modulating the range of elementary notes in an endless variation of a simple melody, or the long pauses and sudden volume alterations of Ray Lynch's painful serenity, combine within the same musical text a feeling of distance and repetition with the sudden surge of restrained sentiment, as blips of life in the ocean of eternity, a feeling often underscored by background sound of ocean waves or of the desert's wind in many New Age compositions. Assuming, as I do, that New Age is the classic music of our epoch, and observing its influence in so many different contexts but always among the same social groups, it can be suggested that the manipulation of time is the recurrent theme of new cultural expressions. A manipulation obsessed with the binary reference to instantaneity and eternity: me and the universe, the self and the Net. Such reconciliation, actually fusing the biological individual into the cosmological whole, can only be achieved under the condition of the

---

77 Harvey (1990: 284ff).

merger of all times, from the creation of ourselves to the end of the universe. Timelessness is the recurrent theme of our age's cultural expressions, be it in the sudden flashes of video clips or in the eternal echoes of electronic spiritualism.

Time, Space, and Society: the Edge of Forever

So, in the end, what is time, this elusive notion that bewildered St Augustine, misled Newton, inspired Einstein, obsessed Heidegger? And how is it being transformed in our society?

For the sake of my exploration, I find it helpful to call upon Leibniz, for whom time is the order of succession of "things," so that without "things" there would be no time.[78] Current knowledge on the concept of time in physics, biology, history, and sociology does not seem to be contradicted by such clear, synthetic conceptualization. Furthermore, we may better understand the ongoing transformation of temporality by reference to the Leibnizian notion of time. I propose the idea that *timeless time*, as I label the dominant temporality of our society, *occurs when the characteristics of a given context, namely, the informational paradigm and the network society, induce systemic perturbation in the sequential order of phenomena performed in that context*. This perturbation may take the form of compressing the occurrence of phenomena, aiming at instantaneity, or else by introducing random discontinuity in the sequence. Elimination of sequencing creates undifferentiated time, which is tantamount to eternity.

The specific analyses presented in this chapter provide illustrations of the substantive issues involved under such abstract characterization. Split-second capital transactions, flex-time enterprises, variable life working time, the blurring of the life-cycle, the search for eternity through the denial of death, instant wars, and the culture of virtual time, all are fundamental phenomena, characteristic of the network society, which systemically mix tenses in their occurrence.

However, this characterization does not refer to all time in human

---

78 Although the analysis of space and time is embedded in the whole philosophical vision of Leibniz, one of the most clear formulations of his thinking is the following paragraph, extracted from his correspondence with Clark (1715–16): "I have more than once stated that I held *space* to be something purely relative, like *time*; *space being an order of co-existences as time is an order of successions*. For space denotes in terms of possibility an order of things which exist at the same time, in so far as they exist together, and is not concerned with their particular ways of existing: and when we see several things together we perceive this order of things among themselves . . . The same is true of time . . . *Instants apart from things are nothing, and they only consist in the successive order of things*" (quoted from Parkinson 1973: 211–12, my added emphasis).

experience. In fact, in our world, most people and most spaces live in a different temporality. I mentioned the dramatic contrast between instant wars and the elimination of war in the life horizon of most people in the dominant countries, on the one hand, and the endless, daily war-making in places scattered all over the planet, on the other hand. A similar argument may be extended to each instance associated with the new temporality. Infant mortality rates in Uruguay and in the former USSR are more than twice the average of those in the US, but so are the rates for infant mortality in Washington, DC (see table 7.7). Death and illness are being pushed back throughout the world, yet in 1990 people from the least-developed countries were expected to live 25 years less than those in the most advanced areas. Flex-time, networked production, and self-management of time in northern Italy or Silicon Valley have very little meaning for the millions of workers brought into the clock-run assembly lines of China and South-East Asia. Flexible schedules still mean for the vast majority of the world's urban population their survival in unpredictable work patterns of the informal economy, where the notion of unemployment is strange to a system where you work or you die. For instance, mobile telephony adds time/space flexibility to personal and professional connections, but in the streets of Lima, in 1995, it spurred a new form of informal business, nicknamed *cholular*,[79] in which street communication vendors wandered around carrying cellular phones, offering rental calls to people walking by: maximum flexibility in endless working days of unpredictable future. Or, again, virtual culture is still associated for a large segment of people with passive TV viewing at the end of exhausting days, with the mind captured in images of soap operas about Texas millionaires, strangely equally familiar to youngsters in Marrakesh and to housewives in Barcelona where, naturally proud of their identity, they watch it in Catalan.

Timeless time belongs to the space of flows, while time discipline, biological time, and socially determined sequencing characterize places around the world, materially structuring and destructuring our segmented societies. Space shapes time in our society, thus reversing an historical trend: flows induce timeless time, places are time-bounded.[80] The idea of progress, at the roots of our culture and society for the past two centuries, was based on the movement of history, indeed on

---

79 "Cholo" is the common language name received by the people of the coast in Peru. "Cholular" plays with the linguistic integration between cellular telephony and Lima's identity.

80 This conceptualization has some similarity with the construction of space–time regimes proposed by Innis (1950, 1951). I do not claim, however, an intellectual lineage with his theory, since I believe he would probably have disagreed with my overall analysis of time.

Table 7.7   Comparisons of infant mortality rates, selected countries, 1990–1995 (estimates)

	Deaths per 1,000 live births
United States	9
Black	18
White	8
Other	16
Counties and cities	
Norfolk City, VA	20
Portsmouth City, VA	19
Suffolk City, VA	25
New York City, NY	12
Bronx	13
Orleans, LA	17
Los Angeles Co., CA	8
Wayne Co. (Detroit), MI	16
Washington, DC	21
Africa	95
Algeria	61
Egypt	57
Kenya	66
Morocco	68
Nigeria	96
South Africa	53
Tanzania	102
Zaire	93
Asia	62
Europe	10
Latin America	47
Northern America	8
Oceania	22
USSR (former)	21
Other countries	
Bulgaria	14
Canada	7
Chile	17
China	27
Costa Rica	14
France	7
Germany	7
Hong Kong	6
Jamaica	14
Japan	5
Korea	21
Malaysia	14

Poland	15
Singapore	8
Thailand	26
Ukraine	14
United Kingdom	7
Uruguay	20

Sources: United Nations Population Fund, *The State of World Population*, 1994; US Dept of Health and Human Services, *Vital Statistics of the United States: 1990*, vol. II section 2, table 2-1, 1994

the predetermined sequence of history following the lead of reason and with the impulse of productive forces, escaping the constraints of spatially bounded societies and cultures. The mastery of time, the control of rhythmicity, colonized territories and transformed space in the vast movement of industrialization and urbanization accomplished by the twin historical processes of formation of capitalism and statism. *Becoming* structured *being*, time conformed space.

The dominant trend in our society displays the historical revenge of space, structuring temporality in different, even contradictory logics according to spatial dynamics. The space of flows, as analyzed in the preceding chapter, dissolves time by disordering the sequence of events and making them simultaneous, thus installing society in eternal ephemerality. The multiple space of places, scattered, fragmented, and disconnected, displays diverse temporalities, from the most primitive domination of natural rhythms to the strictest tyranny of clock time. Selected functions and individuals transcend time,[81] while downgraded activities and subordinate people endure life as time goes by. While the emerging logic of the new social structure aims at the relentless supersession of time as an ordered sequence of events, most of society, in a globally interdependent system, remains on the edge of the new universe. Timelessness sails in an ocean surrounded by time-bound shores, from where still can be heard the laments of time-chained creatures.

Furthermore, the logic of timelessness is not displayed without resistance in society. As places and localities aim at regaining control over the social interests embedded in the space of flows, so time-conscious social actors try to bring under control the ahistorical domination of timelessness. Precisely because our society reaches the

81　It would seem counterintuitive to argue that the professional elite in our societies is time-transcendent. Are not they (we) constantly running against the clock? My argument is that this behavioral pattern is precisely the consequence of aiming at the relentless supersession of time and of the rhythmicity of the life-cycle (aging, career advancement), induced by our culture/organization, and apparently facilitated by new technological means. What can be more time stressful than the daily battle against time?
82　Lash and Urry (1994: 243).
83　Brand (1999: 2).

understanding of material interactions for the whole environment, science and technology provide us with the potential to foresee a new kind of temporality, also placed within the framework of eternity, but taking into account historical sequences. This is what Lash and Urry call "glacial time," a notion in which "the relation between humans and nature is very long-term and evolutionary. It moves back out of immediate human history and forwards into a wholly unspecifiable future."[82] In fact, the opposition between the management of glacial time and the search for timelessness anchors in contradictory positions in the social structure the environmentalist movement and the powers that be in our society, as I shall elaborate further in volume II.

Concerned with the disappearance of the long-term view of time in our culture, in 1998 a group of scientists, artists, and business people in the San Francisco Bay area established The Long Now Foundation to promote an alternative conception of time based upon two main questions: "How do we make long-term thinking automatic and common instead of difficult and rare? How do we make the taking of long-term responsibility inevitable?"[83] Besides establishing a web site, building a Long Now library, and organizing seminars and conferences to debate time and future making, the Foundation concentrated its effort on designing and manufacturing a new kind of clock, on the basis of an idea by computer designer Daniel Hillis. This would be a gigantic, mechanical Clock of the Long Now, programmed to record time for 10,000 years, giving its sound signals once a year, once a century, and once a millennium. It may be perhaps as large as Stonehenge, and it could be settled in the American Western desert. In late 1999, a sizeable prototype was being completed, and scheduled to be displayed in 2000 at San Francisco's Presidio International Center. This clock was explicitly conceived as a cultural artifact, to counter the notion of instant time, to slow down our time experience to the pace of our cosmological being, and of our historical becoming. Ultimately, it aims at materializing our temporal responsibility *vis-à-vis* future generations.

What must be retained from the discussion at this point is the conflictive differentiation of time, understood as the impact of opposed social interests on the sequencing of phenomena. Such differentiation concerns, on the one hand, the contrasting logic between timelessness, structured by the space of flows, and multiple, subordinate temporalities, associated with the space of places. On the other hand, the contradictory dynamics of society opposes the search for human eternity, through the annihilation of time in life, to the realization of cosmological eternity, through the respect of glacial time. Between subdued temporalities and evolutionary nature the network society rises on the edge of forever.

Conclusion:
the Network Society

Our exploration of emergent social structures across domains of human activity and experience leads to an over-arching conclusion: as an historical trend, dominant functions and processes in the Information Age are increasingly organized around networks. Networks constitute the new social morphology of our societies, and the diffusion of networking logic substantially modifies the operation and outcomes in processes of production, experience, power, and culture. While the networking form of social organization has existed in other times and spaces, the new information technology paradigm provides the material basis for its pervasive expansion throughout the entire social structure. Furthermore, I would argue that this networking logic induces a social determination of a higher level than that of the specific social interests expressed through the networks: the power of flows takes precedence over the flows of power. Presence or absence in the network and the dynamics of each network *vis-à-vis* others are critical sources of domination and change in our society: a society that, therefore, we may properly call the network society, characterized by the pre-eminence of social morphology over social action.

To clarify this statement, I shall try to link up the main lines of analysis presented in this volume with the broader theoretical perspective outlined in the Prologue. It should, however, be kept in mind that I cannot address the full range of theoretical questions introduced at the outset of this inquiry until after examining (in volumes II and III) fundamental issues such as gender relationships, the construction of identity, social movements, the transformation of political process, and the crisis of the state in the Information Age. It is only after treating these matters, and observing their actual expression in the macroprocesses reshaping societies at this turn of the millennium, that I shall try to propose some exploratory hypotheses to interpret the new society in the making. Nevertheless, enough information and ideas have been submitted to the reader's attention in this volume to be able to reach some provisional conclusions concerning the new structure of dominant functions and processes, a necessary starting-point to understand the overall dynamics of society.

I shall first define the concept of network, since it plays such a central role in my characterization of society in the Information Age.[1] A network is a set of interconnected nodes. A node is the point at which a curve intersects itself. What a node is, concretely speaking, depends on the kind of concrete networks of which we speak. They are stock exchange markets, and their ancillary advanced services centers, in the network of global financial flows. They are national councils of ministers and European Commissioners in the political network that governs the European Union. They are coca fields and poppy fields, clandestine laboratories, secret landing strips, street gangs, and money-laundering financial institutions in the network of drug traffic that penetrates economies, societies, and states throughout the world. They are television systems, entertainment studios, computer graphics milieux, news teams, and mobile devices generating, transmitting, and receiving signals in the global network of the new media at the roots of cultural expression and public opinion in the Information Age. The topology defined by networks determines that the distance (or intensity and frequency of interaction) between two points (or social positions) is shorter (or more frequent, or more intense) if both points are nodes in a network than if they do not belong to the same network. On the other hand, within a given network, flows have no distance, or the same distance, between nodes. Thus, distance (physical, social, economic, political, cultural) for a given point or position varies between zero (for any node in the same network) and infinite (for any point external to the network). The inclusion/exclusion in networks, and the architecture of relationships between networks, enacted by light-speed-operating information technologies, configure dominant processes and functions in our societies.

Networks are open structures, able to expand without limits, integrating new nodes as long as they are able to communicate within the network, namely as long as they share the same communication codes (for example, values or performance goals). A network-based social structure is a highly dynamic, open system, susceptible to innovating

---

1 I am indebted for my conceptualization of networks to my continuing intellectual dialogue with François Bar. For further theoretical elaboration on networks, and on the network society, see Castells (2000).

without threatening its balance. Networks are appropriate instruments for a capitalist economy based on innovation, globalization, and decentralized concentration; for work, workers, and firms based on flexibility and adaptability; for a culture of endless deconstruction and reconstruction; for a polity geared toward the instant processing of new values and public moods; and for a social organization aiming at the supersession of space and the annihilation of time. Yet the network morphology is also a source of dramatic reorganization of power relationships. Switches connecting the networks (for example, financial flows taking control of media empires that influence political processes) are the privileged instruments of power. Thus, the switchers are the power-holders. Since networks are multiple, the inter-operating codes and switches between networks become the fundamental sources in shaping, guiding, and misguiding societies. The convergence of social evolution and information technologies has created a new material basis for the performance of activities throughout the social structure. This material basis, built in networks, earmarks dominant social processes, thus shaping social structure itself.

So observations and analyses presented in this volume seem to indicate that the new economy is organized around global networks of capital, management, and information, whose access to technological know-how is at the roots of productivity and competitiveness. Business firms and, increasingly, organizations and institutions are organized in networks of variable geometry whose intertwining supersedes the traditional distinction between corporations and small business, cutting across sectors, and spreading along different geographical clusters of economic units. Accordingly, the work process is increasingly individualized, labor is disaggregated in its performance, and reintegrated in its outcome through a multiplicity of interconnected tasks in different sites, ushering in a new division of labor based on the attributes/capacities of each worker rather than on the organization of the task.

However, this evolution toward networking forms of management and production does not imply the demise of capitalism. The network society, in its various institutional expressions, is, for the time being, a capitalist society. Furthermore, for the first time in history, the capitalist mode of production shapes social relationships over the entire planet. But this brand of capitalism is profoundly different from its historical predecessors. It has two fundamental distinctive features: it is global, and it is structured to a large extent around a network of financial flows. Capital works globally as a unit in real time; and it is realized, invested, and accumulated mainly in the sphere of circulation, that is as finance capital. While finance capital has generally been among the dominant fractions of capital, we are witnessing the emergence of something different: capital accumulation proceeds, and its value-making is generated, increasingly, in the global financial markets enacted by information networks in the timeless space of financial flows. From these networks, capital is invested, globally, in all sectors of activity: information industries, media business, advanced services, agricultural production, health, education, technology, old and new manufacturing, transportation, trade, tourism, culture, environmental management, real estate, war-making and peace-selling, religion, entertainment, and sports. Some activities are more profitable than others, as they go through cycles, market upswings and downturns, and segmented global competition. Yet whatever is extracted as profit (from producers, consumers, technology, nature, and institutions) is reverted to the meta-network of financial flows, where all capital is equalized in the commodified democracy of profit-making. In this electronically operated global casino specific capitals boom or bust, settling the fate of corporations, household savings, national currencies, and regional economies. The net result sums to zero: the losers pay for the winners. But who are the winners and the losers changes by the year, the month, the day, the second, and permeates down to the world of firms, jobs, salaries, taxes, and public services – to the world of what is sometimes called "the real economy," and of what I would be tempted to call the "unreal economy," since in the age of networked capitalism the fundamental reality, where money is made and lost, invested or saved, is in the financial sphere. All other activities (except those of the dwindling public sector) are primarily the basis to generate the necessary surplus to invest in global flows, or the result of investment originated in these financial networks.

Financial capital needs, however, to rely for its operation and competition on knowledge and information generated and enhanced by information technology. This is the concrete meaning of the articulation between the capitalist mode of production and the informational mode of development. Thus, capital that would remain purely speculative is submitted to excessive risk, and ultimately washed out by simple statistical probability in the random movements of the financial markets. It is in the interaction between investment in profitable firms and using accumulated profits to make them fructify in the global financial networks that the process of accumulation lies. So it depends on productivity, on competitiveness, and on adequate information on investment and long-term planning in every sector. High-technology firms depend on financial resources to go on with their endless drive toward innovation, productivity, and competitiveness. Financial capital, acting directly through financial institutions or indirectly through the dynamics of stock exchange markets, conditions the fate of high-technology industries. On the other hand, technology and information are decisive tools in generating profits and in appropriating market shares. Thus, financial capital and high-technology, industrial capital are increasingly interdependent, even if their modes of operation are specific to each industry. Hilferding and Schumpeter were both right, but their historical coupling had to wait until it was dreamed of in Palo Alto and consummated in Ginza.

Thus, capital is either global or becomes global to enter the accumulation process in the electronically networked economy. Firms, as I have tried to show in chapter 3, are increasingly organized in networks, both internally and in their relationship. So capital flows, and their induced production/management/distribution activities are spread in interconnected networks of variable geometry. Under these new technological, organizational, and economic conditions, who are the capitalists? They are certainly not the legal owners of the means of production, who range from your/my pension fund to a passer-by at a Singapore ATM suddenly deciding to buy stock in Buenos Aires' emergent market. But this has been to some extent true since the 1930s, as shown by Berle and Means's classic study on control and ownership in United States corporations. Yet nor are the corporate managers, as suggested in their study, and, thereafter, by other analysts. For managers control specific corporations, and specific segments of the global economy, but do not control, and do not even know about, the actual, systemic movements of capital in the networks of financial flows, of knowledge in the information networks, of strategies in the multi-faceted set of network enterprises. Some actors at the top of this global capitalist system are indeed managers, as in the case of Japanese corporations. Others could still be identified under the traditional category of bourgeoisie, as in the overseas Chinese business networks, who are culturally bonded, often family or personally related, share values and, sometimes, political connections. In the United States, a mixture of historical layers provides to the capitalist characters a colorful array of traditional bankers, *nouveau-riche* speculators, self-made geniuses-turned-entrepreneurs, global tycoons, and multinational managers. In other cases, public corporations (as in French banking or electronics firms) are the capitalist actors. In Russia, survivors of communist *nomenklatura* compete with wild young capitalists in recycling state property in the constitution of the newest capitalist province. And all over the world, money-laundering from miscellaneous criminal businesses flows toward this mother of all accumulations that is the global financial network.

So all these are capitalists, presiding over all sorts of economies, and people's lives. But a capitalist class? There is not, sociologically and economically, such a thing as a global capitalist class. But there is an integrated, global capital network, whose movements and variable logic ultimately determine economies and influence societies. Thus, above a diversity of human-flesh capitalists and capitalist groups there is a faceless collective capitalist, made up of financial flows operated by electronic networks. This is not simply the expression of the abstract logic of the market because it does not truly follow the law of supply and demand: it responds to the turbulences, and unpredictable movements, of non-calculable anticipations, induced by psychology and society, as much as by economic processes. This network of networks of capital both unifies and commands specific centers of capitalist accumulation, structuring the behavior of capitalists around their submission to the global network. They play their competing, or converging, strategies by and through the circuits of this global network, and so they are ultimately dependent upon the non-human capitalist logic of an electronically operated, random processing of information. It is indeed capitalism in its pure expression of the endless search for money by money through the production of commodities by commodities. But money has become almost entirely independent from production, including the production of services, by escaping into the networks of higher-order electronic interactions barely understood by its managers. While capitalism still rules, capitalists are randomly incarnated, and the capitalist classes are restricted to specific areas of the world where they prosper as appendixes to a mighty whirlwind which manifests its will by spread points and futures options ratings in the global flashes of computer screens.

What happens to labor, and to the social relationships of production, in this brave new world of informational, global capitalism? Workers do not disappear in the space of flows, and, down to earth, work is plentiful. Indeed, belying apocalyptic prophecies of simplistic analyses, there are more jobs and a higher proportion of working-age people employed than at any time in history. This is mainly because of the massive incorporation of women into paid work in all industrialized societies, an incorporation that has generally been absorbed, and to a large extent induced, by the labor market without major disruptions. So the diffusion of information technologies, while certainly displacing workers and eliminating some jobs, has not resulted, and it does not seem that it will result in the foreseeable future, in mass unemployment. This in spite of the rise of unemployment in European economies, a trend that is related to social institutions rather than to the new production system. But, if work, workers, and working classes exist, and even expand, around the world, the social relationships between capital and labor are profoundly transformed. At its core, capital is global. As a rule, labor is local. Informationalism, in its historical reality, leads to the concentration and globalization of capital, precisely by using the decentralizing power of networks. Labor is disaggregated in its performance, fragmented in its organization, diversified in its existence, divided in its collective action. Networks converge toward a meta-network of capital that integrates capitalist interests at the global level and across sectors and realms of activity: not without conflict, but under the same over-arching logic. Labor loses its collective identity, becomes increasingly individualized in its capacities, in its working conditions, and in its interests and projects. Who are the owners, who the producers, who the managers, and who the servants becomes increasingly blurred in a production system of variable geometry, of teamwork, of networking, outsourcing, and subcontracting. Can we say that the producers of value are the computer nerds who invent new financial instruments to be dispossessed from their work by corporate brokers? Who is contributing to value creation in the electronics industry: the Silicon Valley chip designer, or the young woman on the assembly line of a South-East Asian factory? Certainly both, albeit in quite substantially different proportions. Thus, are they jointly the new working class? Why not include in it the Bombay computer consultant subcontracted to program this particular design? Or the flying manager who commutes or telecommutes between California and Singapore customizing chip production and electronics consumption? There is unity of the work process throughout the complex, global networks of interaction. But there is at the same time differentiation of work, segmentation of workers, and disaggregation of labor on a global scale. So while capitalist relationships of production still persist (indeed, in many economies the dominant logic is more strictly capitalist than ever before), capital and labor increasingly tend to exist in different spaces and times: the space of flows and the space of places, instant time of computerized networks versus clock time of everyday life. Thus, they live by each other, but do not relate to each other, as the life of global capital depends less and less on specific labor, and more and more on accumulated, generic labor, operated by a small brains trust inhabiting the virtual palaces of global networks. Beyond this fundamental dichotomy a great deal of social diversity still exists, made up of investors' bids, workers' efforts, human ingenuity, human suffering, hirings and lay-offs, promotions and demotions, conflicts and negotiations, competition and alliances: working life goes on. Yet, at a deeper level of the new social reality, social relationships of production have been disconnected in their actual existence. Capital tends to escape in its hyperspace of pure circulation, while labor dissolves its collective entity into an infinite variation of individual existences. Under the conditions of the network society, capital is globally coordinated, labor is individualized. The struggle between diverse capitalists and miscellaneous working classes is subsumed into the more fundamental opposition between the bare logic of capital flows and the cultural values of human experience.

Processes of social transformation summarized under the ideal type of the network society go beyond the sphere of social and technical relationships of production: they deeply affect culture and power as well. Cultural expressions are abstracted from history and geography, and become predominantly mediated by electronic communication networks that interact with the audience and by the audience in a diversity of codes and values, ultimately subsumed in a digitized, audiovisual hypertext. Because information and communication circulate primarily through the diversified, yet comprehensive media system, politics becomes increasingly played out in the space of media. Leadership is personalized, and image-making is power-making. Not that all politics can be reduced to media effects, or that values and interests are indifferent to political outcomes. But whoever the political actors and whatever their orientations, they exist in the power game through and by the media, in the whole variety of an increasingly diverse media system, which includes computer-mediated communication networks. The fact that politics has to be framed in the language of electronically based media has profound consequences for the characteristics, organization, and goals of political processes, political actors, and political institutions. Ultimately, the powers that are in the media networks take second place to the power of flows embodied in the structure and language of these networks.

At a deeper level, the material foundations of society, space, and time are being transformed, organized around the space of flows and timeless time. Beyond the metaphorical value of these expressions, supported by a number of analyses and illustrations in preceding chapters, a major hypothesis is put forward: dominant functions are organized in networks pertaining to a space of flows that links them up around the world, while fragmenting subordinate functions, and people, in the multiple space of places, made of locales increasingly segregated and disconnected from each other. Timeless time appears to be the result of the negation of time, past and future, in the networks of the space of flows. Meanwhile clock time, measured and valued differentially for each process according to its position in the network, continues to characterize subordinate functions and specific locales. The end of history, enacted in the circularity of computerized financial flows or in the instantaneity of surgical wars, overpowers the biological time of poverty or the mechanical time of industrial work. The social construction of new dominant forms of space and time develops a meta-network that switches off non-essential functions, subordinate social groups, and devalued territories. By so doing, infinite social distance is created between this meta-network and most individuals, activities, and locales around the world. Not that people, locales, or activities disappear. But their structural meaning does, subsumed in the unseen logic of the meta-network where value is produced, cultural codes are created, and power is decided. The new social order, the network society, increasingly appears to most people as a meta-social disorder. Namely, as an automated, random sequence of events, derived from the uncontrollable logic of markets, technology, geopolitical order, or biological determination.

In a broader historical perspective, the network society represents a qualitative change in the human experience. If we refer to an old sociological tradition according to which social action at the most fundamental level can be understood as the changing pattern of relationships between nature and culture, we are indeed in a new era. The first model of relationship between these two fundamental poles of human existence was characterized for millenniums by the domination of nature over culture. The codes of social organization almost directly expressed the struggle for survival under the uncontrolled harshness of nature, as anthropology taught us by tracing the codes of social life back to the roots of our biological entity. The second pattern of the relationship established at the origins of the modern age, and associated with the industrial revolution and with the triumph of reason, saw the domination of nature by culture, making society out of the process of work by which humankind found both its liberation from natural forces and its submission to its own abysses of oppression and exploitation.

We are just entering a new stage in which culture refers to culture, having superseded nature to the point that nature is artificially revived ("preserved") as a cultural form: this is in fact the meaning of the environmental movement, to reconstruct nature as an ideal cultural form. Because of the convergence of historical evolution and technological change we have entered a purely cultural pattern of social interaction and social organization. This is why information is the key ingredient of our social organization and why flows of messages and images between networks constitute the basic thread of our social structure. This is not to say that history has ended in a happy reconciliation of humankind with itself. It is in fact quite the opposite: history is just beginning, if by history we understand the moment when, after millenniums of a prehistoric battle with nature, first to survive, then to conquer it, our species has reached the level of knowledge and social organization that will allow us to live in a predominantly social world. It is the beginning of a new existence, and indeed the beginning of a new age, the Information Age, marked by the autonomy of culture *vis-à-vis* the material bases of our existence. But this is not necessarily an exhilarating moment. Because, alone at last in our human world, we shall have to look at ourselves in the mirror of historical reality. And we may not like the vision.

To be continued.

Summary of the Contents of Volumes II and III

Throughout this first volume of *The Information Age: Economy, Society and Culture*, reference has been made to the themes presented in Volumes II and III of this work. An outline of their contents is given below.

Volume II: *The Power of Identity*

Our World, our Lives

1 Communal Heavens: Identity and Meaning in the Network Society
2 The Other Face of the Earth: Social Movements against the New Global Order
3 The Greening of the Self: the Environmental Movement
4 The End of Patriarchalism: Social Movements, Family, and Sexuality in the Information Age
5 A Powerless State?
6 Informational Politics and the Crisis of Democracy
Conclusion: Social Change in the Network Society

Volume III: *End of Millennium*

A Time of Change

1 The Crisis of Industrial Statism and the Collapse of the Soviet Union
2 The Rise of the Fourth World: Informational Capitalism, Poverty, and Social Exclusion

Bibliography

Abbate, Janet (1999) *Inventing the Internet*, Cambridge, MA: MIT Press.
Abegglen, J.C. and Stalk, G. (1985) *Kaisha: the Japanese Corporation*, New York: Basic Books.
Abolaffia, Michael Y. and Biggart, Nicole W. (1991) "Competition and markets: an institutional perspective", in Amitai Etzioni and Paul R. Lawrence (eds), *Socio-economics: Towards a New Synthesis*, Armonk, NY: M.E. Sharpe, pp. 211–31.
Abramson, Jeffrey B., Artertone, F. Christopher and Orren, Cary, R. (1988) *The Electronic Commonwealth: the Impact of New Media Technologies in Democratic Politics*, New York: Basic Books.
Adam, Barbara (1990) *Time and Social Theory*, Cambridge: Polity Press.
—— (2000) "The temporal gaze: the challenge for social theory in the context of GM food", *British Journal of Sociology*, 51(1): 125–42.
Adler, Gerald (1999) "Relationships between Israel and Silicon Valley in the software industry", unpublished masters thesis, Berkeley, CA: University of California.
Adler, Glenn and Suarez, Doris (1993) *Union Voices: Labor's Responses to Crisis*, Albany, NY: State University of New York Press.
Adler, Paul S. (1992) *Technology and the Future of Work*, New York: Oxford University Press.
Agence de l'Informatique (1986) *L'Etat d'informatisation de la France*, Paris: Economica.
Aglietta, Michel (1976) *Régulation et crise du capitalisme: l'expérience des Etats-Unis*, Paris: Calmann-Levy.
Alarcon, Rafael (1998) "Mexican engineers in Silicon Valley", unpublished PhD dissertation, Berkeley, CA: University of California.
Allen, G.C. (1981a) *The Japanese Economy*, New York: St Martin's Press.
—— (1981b) *A Short Economic History of Modern Japan*, London: Macmillan.
Allen, Jane E. (1995) "New computers may use DNA instead of chips", *San Francisco Chronicle*, May 13: B2.

Alvarado, Manuel (ed.) (1988) *Video World-wide*, London and Paris: John Libbey.

Amin, Ash and Robins, Kevin (1991) "These are not Marshallian times", in Roberto Camagni (ed.), *Innovation Networks: Spatial Perspectives*, London: Belhaven Press, pp. 105–20.

Amsdem, Alice (1979) "Taiwan's economic history: a case of étatisme and a challenge to dependency theory", *Modern China*, 5(3): 341–80.

—— (1985) "The state and Taiwan's economic development", in Peter B. Evans, Dietrich Rueschemeyer and Theda Skocpol (eds), *Bringing the State Back In*, Cambridge: Cambridge University Press.

—— (1989) *Asia's Next Giant: South Korea and Late Industrialization*, New York: Oxford University Press.

—— (1992) "A theory of government intervention in late industrialization", in Louis Putterman and Dietrich Rueschemeyer (eds), *State and Market in Development: Synergy or Rivalry?*, Boulder, CO: Lynne Rienner.

Anderson, A.E. (1985) *Creativity and Regional Development*, Laxenburg: International Institute for Applied Systems Analysis, working paper 85/14.

Anderson, K. and Norheim, H. (1993) "Is world trade becoming more regionalized?", *Review of International Economics*, 1.

Anisimov, Evgenii (1993) *The Reforms of Peter the Great: Progress through Coercion in Russia*, Armonk, NY: M.E. Sharpe.

Aoki, Masahiko (1988) *Information, Incentives, and Bargaining in the Japanese Economy*, Cambridge: Cambridge University Press.

Aoyama, Yuko (1995) "Locational strategies of Japanese multinational corporations in electronics", unpublished PhD dissertation, Berkeley, CA: University of California.

Appelbaum, Eileen (1984) *Technology and the Redesign of Work in the Insurance Industry*, research report, Stanford, CA: Stanford University Institute of Research on Educational Finance and Governance.

—— and Schettkat, Ronald (eds) (1990) *Labor Markets, Adjustments to Structural Change and Technological Progress*, New York: Praeger.

Appelbaum, Richard P. and Henderson, Jeffrey (eds) (1992) *States and Development in the Asian Pacific Rim*, London: Sage.

Archibugi, D. and Michie, J. (eds) (1997) *Technology, Globalization, and Economic Performance*, Cambridge: Cambridge University Press.

Aries, Philippe (1977) *L'homme devant la mort*, Paris: Seuil.

—— (1983) *Images de l'homme devant la mort*, Paris: Seuil.

Armstrong, David (1994) "Computer sex: log on; talk dirty; get off", *San Francisco Examiner*, April 10.

Aron, Raymond (1963) *Dix-huit leçons sur la société industrielle*, Paris: Idées-Gallimard.

Aronowitz, Stanley and Di Fazio, Williams (1994) *The Jobless Future*, Minneapolis: University of Minnesota.

Arrieta, Carlos G. et al. (1991) *Narcotrafico en Colombia: dimensiones politicas, economicas, juridicas e internacionales*, Bogota: Tercer Mundo Editores.

Arthur, Brian (1985) *Industry Location and the Economics of Agglomera-*

tion: Why a Silicon Valley?, Stanford, CA: Stanford University Center for Economic Policy Research, working paper.

—— (1986) *Industry Location Patterns and the Importance of History*, Stanford, CA: Stanford University Food Research Institute, research paper.

—— (1989) "Competing technologies, increasing returns, and lock-in by historical events", *Economic Journal*, 99: 116–31.

—— (1998) *Increasing Returns and Path Dependence in the Economy*, Ann Arbor: University of Michigan Press.

Ashton, Thomas S. (1948) *The Industrial Revolution, 1760–1830*, Oxford: Oxford University Press.

Asian Money, Asian Issuers and Capital Markets Supplement (1993/1994) "Derivatives: making more room to manoeuvre", December–January: 30–2.

Aydalot, Philippe (1985) "L'aptitude des milieux locaux a promouvoir innovation technologique", communication au symposium *Nouvelles technologies et regions en crise*, Association de Science Régionale de Langue Française, Brussels, April 22–23.

Aznar, Guy (1993) *Travailler moins pour travailler tous*, Paris: Syros.

Bailey, Paul, Parisotto, Aurelio and Renshaw, Geoffrey (eds) (1993) *Multinationals and Employment: the Global Economy of the 1990s*, Geneva: International Labour Organization.

Baker, Hugh (1979) *Chinese Family and Kinship*, New York: Columbia University Press.

Balaji, R. (1994) "The formation and structure of the high technology industrial complex in Bangalore, India", unpublished PhD dissertation, Berkeley, CA: University of California.

Ball-Rokeach, Sandra J. and Cantor, Muriel (eds) (1986) *Media, Audience and Social Structure*, Beverly Hills, CA: Sage.

Banegas, Jesus (ed.) (1993) *La industria de la información: situación actual y perspectivas*, Madrid: Fundesco.

Bar, François (1990) "Configuring the telecommunications infrastructure for the computer age: the economics of network control", unpublished PhD dissertation, Berkeley, CA: University of California.

—— (1992) "Network flexibility: a new challenge for telecom policy", *Communications and Strategies*, special issue, June: 111–22.

—— and Borrus, M. (1993) *The Future of Networking*, Berkeley, CA: University of California, BRIE working paper.

—— and —— with Coriat, Benjamin (1991) *Information Networks and Competitive Advantage: Issues for Government Policy and Corporate Strategy Development*, Brussels: Commission of European Communities, DGIII–BRIE–OECD Research Program.

Baran, Barbara (1985) "Office automation and women's work: the technological transformation of the insurance industry", in Manuel Castells (ed.), *High Technology, Space, and Society*, Beverly Hills, CA: Sage, pp. 143–71.

—— (1989) "Technological innovation and deregulation: the transformation of the labor process in the insurance industry", unpublished PhD dissertation, Berkeley, CA: University of California.

Baranano, Ana M. (1994) "La empresa española en los programas europeos de cooperación tecnológica", unpublished thesis, Madrid: Universidad Autonoma de Madrid.

Barboza, David (1999a) "Measuring floorspace and cyberspace", *The New York Times*: January 10 (weekend review): 4.

—— (1999b) "Chicago faces the future, reluctantly: Board of Trade battles new electronic rivals", *The New York Times*, November 23: C1–C14.

Barglow, Raymond (1994) *The Crisis of the Self in the Age of Information: Computers, Dolphins, and Dreams*, London: Routledge.

Barlow, John Perry et al. (1995) "What are we doing on line?" *Harper's*, August: 40.

Barthes, Roland (1978) *Leçon inaugurale de la chaire de sémiologie littéraire du Collège de France, prononcée le 7 Janvier 1977*, Paris: Seuil.

Basalla, George (1988) *The Evolution of Technology*, Cambridge: Cambridge University Press.

Batty, Michael and Barr, Bob (1994) "The electronic frontier: exploring and mapping cyberspace", *Futures*, 26(7): 699–712.

Baudrillard, Jean (1972) *Pour une critique de l'économie politique du signe*, Paris: Gallimard.

—— (1991) *La Guerre du Golfe n'a pas eu lieu*, Paris: Fayard.

Baumgartner, Peter and Payr, Sabine (eds) (1995) *Speaking Minds: Interviews with Twenty Eminent Cognitive Scientists*, Princeton, NJ: Princeton University Press.

Baumol, W.J., Blackman S.A.B. and Wolf, E.N. (1989) *Productivity and American Leadership: the Long View*, Cambridge, MA: MIT Press.

Baym, Nancy (1998) "The emergence of on-line community", in Steven G. Jones (ed.), *Cybersociety 2.0: Revisiting Computer-mediated Communication and Community*, Thousand Oaks, CA: Sage, pp. 35–68.

Beasley, W.G. (1990) *The Rise of Modern Japan*, London: Weidenfeld and Nicolson.

Bedi, Hari (1991) *Understanding the Asian Manager*, Sydney: Allen and Unwin.

Bell, Daniel (1976) *The Coming of Post-industrial Society: a Venture in Social Forecasting*, New York: Basic Books, 2nd edn.

Belussi, Fiorenza (1992) "La flessibilita si fa gerarchia: la Benetton", in F. Belussi (ed.), *Nuovi modelli d'impresa, gerarchie organizzative e imprese rete*, Milan: Franco Angeli.

Bendixon, Terence (1991) "El transporte urbano", in Jordi Borja et al. (eds), *Las grandes ciudades en la decada de los noventa*, Madrid: Editorial Sistema, pp. 427–53.

Beniger, James R. (1986) *The Control Revolution: Technological and Economic Origins of the Information Society*, Cambridge, MA: Harvard University Press.

Benner, Chris (2000) "Labor market intermediaries and flexible employment in Silicon Valley', unpublished PhD dissertation, Berkeley, CA: University of California.

——, Brownstein, Bob and Dean, Amy B. (1999) *Negotiating Work in the New Economy*, San Jose, CA: Working Partnerships USA and Economic Policy Institute.

Bennett, A. (1990) *The Death of Organization Man*, New York: William Morrow.

Benson, Rod (1994) "Telecommunications and society: a review on the research literature on computer-mediated communication", Berkeley, CA: University of California, Berkeley Roundtable on the International Economy, Compuscript.

Benveniste, Guy (1994) *Twenty-first Century Organization: Analyzing Current Trends, Imagining the Future*, San Francisco, CA: Jossey Bass.

Berger, J. (1984) *And our Faces, my Heart, Brief as Photos*, London: Writers and Readers.

Berger, Peter (1987) *The Capitalist Revolution*, London: Wildwood.

—— and Hsiao, M. (eds) (1988) *In Search of an East Asian Development Model*, New Brunswick, NJ: Transaction Books.

Bernstein, Michael A. and Adler, David E. (1994) *Understanding American Economic Decline*, New York: Cambridge University Press.

Bertazzoni, F. et al. (1984) *Odissea Informatica. Alle soglie della nuova era: intinerario nelle societa informatiche*, Milan: Istituto A. Gemelli per I Problemi della Comunicazione, Gruppo Editoriale Jackson.

Bessant, John (1989) *Microelectronics and Change at Work*, Geneva: International Labour Organization.

Bettinger, Cass (1991) *High Performance in the 1990s: Leading the Strategic and Cultural Revolution in Banking*, Homewood, IL: Business One Irwin.

Bianchi, Patrizio, Carnoy, Martin and Castells, Manuel (1988) *Economic Modernization and Technology Policy in the People's Republic of China*, Stanford, CA: Stanford University Center for Education Research, research monograph.

Bielenski, Harald (ed.) (1994) *New Forms of Work and Activity: Survey of Experience at Establishment Level in Eight European Countries*, Dublin: European Foundation for the Improvement of Living and Working Conditions.

Biggart, Nicole Woolsey (1990a) *Charismatic Capitalism*, Chicago, IL: University of Chicago Press.

—— (1990b) "Institutionalized patrimonialism in Korean business", *Comparative Social Research*, 12: 113–33.

—— (1991) "Explaining Asian economic organization: toward a Weberian institutional perspective", *Theory and Society*, 20: 199–232.

—— (1992) "Institutional logic and economic explanation", in Jane Marceau (ed.), *Reworking the World: Organizations, Technologies, and Cultures in Comparative Perspective*, Berlin: Walter de Gruyter, pp. 29–54.

—— and Hamilton, G.G. (1992) "On the limits of a firm-based theory to explain business networks: the western bias of neoclassical economics", in Nitin Nohria and Robert G. Ecckles (eds), *Networks and Organizations: Structure, Form, and Action*, Boston, MA: Harvard Business School Press.

Bijker, Wiebe E., Hughes, Thomas P. and Pinch, Trevor (eds) (1987) *The Social Construction of Technological Systems: New Directions in the Sociology and History of Technology*, Cambridge, MA: MIT Press.

Birch, David L. (1987) *Job Generation in America*, New York: Free Press.

Bird, Jane (1994) "Dial M for multimedia", *Management Today*, July: 50–3.

Bishop, Jerry E. and Waldholz, Michael (1990) *Genome*, New York: Simon and Schuster.

Bison, I. and Esping-Andersen, G. (2000) "Income packaging, poverty and unemployment in Europe", in D. Gallie and S. Paugham (eds), *The Experience of Unemployment in Oxford*, Oxford: Oxford University Press.

Blakely, Edward J. and Snyder, Mary Gail (1997) *Fortress America: Gated Communities in the United States*, Washington, DC: Brookings Institution Press.

——, Scotchmer, S. and Levine, J. (1988) *The Locational and Economic Patterns of California's Biotech Industry*, Berkeley, CA: University of California Institute of Urban and Regional Development, Biotech Industry Research Group Report.

Blazejczak, Jurgen, Eber, Georg and Horn, Gustav A. (1990) "Sectoral and macroeconomic impacts of research and development on employment", in Egon Matzner and Michael Wagner (eds), *The Employment Impact of New Technology: the Case of West Germany*, Aldershot, Hants: Avebury, pp. 221–33.

Bluestone, Barry and Harrison, Bennett (1988) *The Great American Job Machine: the Proliferation of Low-wage Employment in the US Economy*, New York: Basic Books.

Blumler, Jay G. and Katz, Elihu (eds) (1974) *The Uses of Mass Communications*, Newport Beach, CA: Sage.

Bofill, Ricardo (1990) *Espacio y Vida*, Barcelona: Tusquets Editores.

Booker, Ellis (1994) "Interactive TV comes to public broadcasting", *Computerworld*, 28(3): 59.

Borja, Jordi and Castells, Manuel (1996) *The Local and the Global: Cities in the Information Age*, report commissioned by the United Nations Habitat Center for Habitat II – United Nations Conference *The City Summit*, Istanbul, 1996.

—— and —— (1997) *Local and Global: Management of Cities in the Information Age*, London: Earthscan.

—— et al. (eds) (1991) *Las grandes ciudades en la decada de los noventa*, Madrid: Editorial Sistema.

Borjas, George F., Freeman, Richard B. and Katz, Lawrence F. (1991) *On the Labour Market Effects of Immigration and Trade*, Cambridge, MA: National Bureau of Economic Research.

Bornstein, Lisa (1993) "Flexible production in the unstable state: the Brazilian information technology industry", unpublished PhD dissertation, Berkeley, CA: University of California.

Borrus, Michael G. (1988) *Competing for Control: America's Stake in Microelectronics*, Cambridge, MA: Ballinger.

—— and Zysman, John (1997) "Wintelism and the changing terms of global competition: prototype of the future", Berkeley, CA: University of California, BRIE working paper.

Bosch, Gerhard (1995) *Flexibility and Work Organization: Report of Expert*

Working Group, Brussels: European Commission, Directorate General for Employment, Industrial Relations, and Social Affairs.

——, Dawkins, Peter and Michon, François (eds) (1994) *Times are Changing: Working Time in 14 Industrialised Countries*, Geneva: International Labour Organization.

Botein, Michael and Rice, David M. (eds) (1980) *Network Television and the Public Interest*, Lexington, MA: Lexington Books.

Boureau, Allain et al. (1989) *The Culture of Print: Power and the Uses of Print in Early Modern Europe*, ed. Roder Chartier, Princeton, NJ: Princeton University Press.

Bouvier, Leon F. and Grant, Lindsay (1994) *How Many Americans? Population, Immigration, and the Environment*, San Francisco, CA: Sierra Club Books.

Bower, J.L. (1987) *When Markets Quake*, Boston, MA: Harvard Business School Press.

Boyer, Christine (1994) *The City of Collective Memory*, Cambridge, MA: MIT Press.

Boyer, Robert (ed.) (1986) *Capitalismes fin de siècle*, Paris: Presses Universitaires de France.

—— (1988a) "Is a new socio-technical system emerging?", paper prepared for the Conference on Structural Change and Labour Market Policy, Var, Gard, 6–9 June.

—— (1988b) "Technical change and the theory of regulation", in G. Dosi et al. (eds), *Technical Change and Economic Theory*, London: Pinter, pp. 67–94.

—— (1990) "Assessing the impact of R&D on employment: puzzle or consensus?", in E. Matzner and M. Wagner (eds), *The Employment Impact of New Technology: the Case of West Germany*, Aldershot, Hants: Avebury, pp. 234–54.

—— and Mistral, J. (1988) "Le bout du tunnel? Stratégies conservatrices et nouveau régime d'accumulation", paper delivered at the International Conference on the Theory of Regulation, Barcelona, June 16–18.

—— and Ralle, P. (1986a) "Croissances nationales et contrainte extérieure avant et après 1973", *Economie et société*, P29.

—— and —— (1986b) "L'Insertion internationale conditionne-t-elle les formes nationales d'emploi? Convergences ou différentiations des pays européens", *Economie et société*, P29.

Boyett, Joseph H. and Conn, Henry P. (1991) *Workplace 2000: the Revolution Reshaping American Business*, New York: Dutton.

Braddock, D.J. (1992) "Scientific and technical employment, 1900–2005", *Monthly Labor Review*, February: 28–41.

Brand, Stewart (1999) *The Clock of the Long Now: Time and Responsibility*, New York: Basic Books.

Braudel, Fernand (1967) *Civilisation matérielle et capitalisme. XVᵉ–XVIIᵉ siècle*, Paris: Armand Colin.

Braun, Ernest and Macdonald, Stuart (1982) *Revolution in Miniature: the History and Impact of Semiconductor Electronics Re-explored*, 2nd edn,

Cambridge: Cambridge University Press.

Braverman, Harry (1973) *Labor and Monopoly Capital*, New York: Monthly Review Press.

Breeden, Richard C. (1993) "The globalization of law and business in the 1990s", *Wake Forest Law Review*, 28(3): 509–17.

BRIE (1992) *Globalization and Production*, Berkeley, CA: University of California, BRIE working paper 45.

Broad, William J. (1985) *Star Warriors*, New York: Simon and Schuster.

Bronson, P. (1999) *Nudist on the Late Shift and Other True Tales of Silicon Valley*, New York: Random House.

Brooks, Harvey (1971) "Technology and the ecological crisis", lecture given at Amherst, May 9.

Brusco, S. (1982) "The Emilian model: productive decentralization and social integration", *Cambridge Journal of Economics* 6(2): 167–84.

Brynjolfsson, Erik (1997) "Information technology and the reorganization of work", paper delivered at a conference on "Vernetzung als Wettbewerbsfaktor", Johann Wolfgang Goethe Universitat, Frankfurt, September 4.

Buitelaar, Wout (ed.) (1988) *Technology and Work: Labour Studies in England, Germany and the Netherlands*, Aldershot, Hants: Avebury.

Bunker, Ted (1994) "The multimedia infotainment I-way: telephone, cable, and media companies are pursuing video-on-demand, interactive education, multimedia politicking, and more", *LAN Magazine*, 9(10): S24.

Burawoy, Michael (1979) *Manufacturing Consent*, Chicago: University of Chicago Press.

Bureau of Labor Statistics (1994) *Occupational Projections and Training Data*, Statistical and Research Supplement to the 1994–5 *Occupational Outlook Handbook*, Bulletin 2451, May.

Burlen, Katherine (1972) "La réalisation spatiale du désir et l'image spatialisée du besoin", *Espaces et sociétés*, 5: 145–59.

Bushnell, P. Timothy (1994) *The Transformation of the American Manufacturing Paradigm*, New York: Garland.

Business Week (1993a) "The horizontal corporation", October 28.

—— (1993b) "Asia's wealth: special report", November 29.

—— (1994a) "The information technology revolution: how digital technology is changing the way we work and live", special issue.

—— (1994b) "The new face of business", in special issue on "The Information Revolution", pp. 99ff.

—— (1994c) "China: birth of a new economy", January 31: 42–8.

—— (1994d) "Sega: it's blasting beyond games and racing to build a high-tech entertainment empire", February 21: cover story.

—— (1994e) "Interactive TV: not ready for prime time", March 14: 30.

—— (1994f) "The entertainment economy", March 14: 58–73.

—— (1994g) "How the Internet will change the way you do business", November 14.

—— (1994h) "Home computers: sales explode as new uses turn PCs into all-purpose information appliances", November 28: 89ff.

—— (1995a) "The networked corporation", special issue.

—— (1995b) "Mexico: can it cope?", January 16.

—— (1995c) "Software industry", February 27: 78–86.

—— (1995d) "Benetton's new age", April 14.

—— (1995e) "The gene kings", May 8: 72ff.

—— (1996) "Sun's rise", January 22.

—— (1998) "Log on, link up, save big", June 22: 132–8.

—— (1999a) "Gene therapy", July 12: 94–104.

—— (1999b) "The great DNA chip derby", October 25: 90–2.

—— (1999c) "The wild new workforce", December 6: 39–44.

—— (1999d) The Internet age", October 4.

—— (1999e) "Cisco: John Chambers' new plan to rule the Internet", special report: 129–54.

Calderon, Fernando and Laserna, Roberto (1994) *Paradojas de la modernidad: sociedad y cambios en Bolivia*, La Paz: Fundacion Milenio.

Calhoun, Craig (ed.) (1994) *Social Theory and the Politics of Identity*, Oxford: Blackwell.

Camagni, Roberto (1991) "Local milieu, uncertainty and innovation networks: towards a new dynamic theory of economic space", in Roberto Camagni (ed.), *Innovation Networks: Spatial Perspectives*, London: Belhaven Press, pp. 121–44.

Campbell, Duncan (1994) "Foreign investment, labor immobility and the quality of employment", *International Labour Review*, 2: 185–203.

Campo Vidal, Manuel (1996) "La transición audiovisual", Madrid: Antena-3 TV (unpublished).

Campos Alvarez, Tostado (1993) *El Fondo Monetario y la dueda externa mexicana*, Mexico: Plaza y Valdes Editores.

Canals, Jordi (1997) *Universal Banking: International Comparisons and Theoretical Perspectives*, Oxford: Oxford University Press.

Canby, E.T. (1962) *A History of Electricity*, Englewood Cliffs, NJ: Prentice-Hall.

Cappelin, Riccardo (1991) "International networks of cities", in Roberto Camagni (ed.), *Innovation Networks: Spatial Perspectives*, London: Belhaven Press.

Cappelli, Peter (1997) *Change at Work*, New York: Oxford University Press.

—— and Rogovsky, Nicolai (1994) "New work systems and skill requirements", *International Labour Review*, 133(2): 205–20.

Capra, Fritjof (1996) *The Web of Life*, New York: Random House.

—— (1999a) Personal communication, Berkeley, October.

—— (1999b) "Complexity theory", unpublished presentation at the University of California, Berkeley, November.

Carey, M. and Franklin, J.C. (1991) "Outlook: 1990–2005 industry output and job growth continues slow into next century", *Monthly Labor Review*, November: 45–60.

Carnoy, Martin (1989) *The New Information Technology: International Diffusion and its Impact on Employment and Skills. A Review of the Literature*, Washington, DC: World Bank, PHREE.

—— (1993) "Multinational corporations in the global economy", in Carnoy et al. (1993b).

—— (1994) *Faded Dreams: The Politics and Economics of Race in America*, New York: Cambridge University Press.

—— (2000) *Sustaining Flexibility: Work, Family and Community in the Information Age*, Cambridge, MA: Harvard University Press.

—— and Castells, Manuel (1996) "Sustainable flexibility: work, family, and society in the information age", Berkeley: University of California, Center for Western European Studies.

—— and Fluitman, Fred (1994) "Training and the reduction of unemployment in industrialized countries", Geneva: International Labour Organization, unpublished report.

—— and Levin, Henry (1985) *Schooling and Work in the Democratic State*, Stanford, CA: Stanford University Press.

——, Pollack, Seth and Wong, Pia L. (1993a) *Labor Institutions and Technological Change: a Framework for Analysis and Review of the Literature*, Stanford, CA: Stanford University International Development Education Center, report prepared for the International Labour Organization, Geneva.

—— et al. (eds) (1993b) *The New Global Economy in the Information Age*, University Park, PA: Penn State University Press.

Carre, Jean-Jacques, Dubois, Paul and Malinvaud, Edmond (1984) *Abrégé de la croissance française: un essai d'analyse économique causale de l'après guerre*, Paris: Editions du Seuil.

Carver, M. (1980) *War since 1945*, London: Weidenfeld and Nicolson.

Case, Donald O. (1994) "The social shaping of videotex: how information services for the public have evolved", *Journal of the American Society for Information Science*, 45(7): 483–9.

Castano, Cecilia (1991) *La Informatizacion de la banca en Espana*, Madrid: Ministerio de Economia/Universidad Autónoma de Madrid.

—— (1994a) *Nuevas Tecnologias, Trabajo y Empleo en Espana*, Madrid: Alianza Editorial.

—— (1994b) *Tecnologia, empleo y trabajo en Espana*, Madrid: Alianza Editorial.

Castells, Manuel (1972) *La Question urbaine*, Paris: François Maspero.

—— (1976a) "The service economy and the postindustrial society: a sociological critique", *International Journal of Health Services*, 6(4): 595–607.

—— (1976b) *La crise economique et la société americaine*, Paris: Presses Universitaires de France.

—— (1980) *The Economic Crisis and American Society*, Princeton, NJ: Princeton University Press/Oxford: Blackwell.

—— (1985) *High Technology, Space and Society*, Beverley Hills, CA: Sage.

—— (1988a) "The new industrial space: information technology manufacturing and spatial structure in the United States", in G. Sternlieb and J. Hughes (eds), *America's New Market Geography: Nation, Region and Metropolis*, New Brunswick, NJ: Rutgers University.

—— (director) (1988b) *The State and Technology Policy: a Comparative*

Analysis of US Strategic Defense Initiative, Informatics Policy in Brazil, and Electronics Policy in China, Berkeley, CA: University of California, Berkeley Roundtable on the International Economy (BRIE), research monograph.

—— (1989a) "High technology and the new international division of labor", *Labour Studies*, October.

—— (1989b) *The Informational City: Information Technology, Economic Restructuring, and the Urban–Regional Process*, Oxford: Blackwell.

—— (1989c) "Notes of field work in the industrial areas of Taiwan", unpublished.

—— (1991) "Estrategias de desarrollo metropolitano en las grandes ciudades españolas: la articulación entre crecimiento economico y calidad de vida", in Jordi Borja et al. (eds), *Las grandes ciudades en la decada de los noventa*, Madrid: Editorial Sistema, pp. 17–64.

—— (1992) "Four Asian tigers with a dragon head: a comparative analysis of the state, economy, and society in the Asian Pacific Rim", in Richard Appelbaum and Jeffrey Henderson (eds), *States and Development in the Asian Pacific Rim*, Newbury Park, CA: Sage, pp. 33–70.

—— (1993) "The informational economy and the new international division of labor", in Carnoy et al. (1993b): 15–45.

—— (1994) "Paths towards the informational society: employment structure in G-7 countries, 1920–1990", *International Labour Review*, 133(1): 5–33 (with Yuko Aoyama).

—— (1996) "The net and the self: working notes for a critical theory of informational society", *Critique of Anthropology*, 16(1): 9–38.

—— (2000) "Materials for an exploratory theory of the network society", *British Journal of Sociology*, special millennium issue, 1.

—— and Guillemard, Anne Marie (1971) "Analyse sociologique des pratiques sociales en situation de retraite", *Sociologie du travail*, 3: 282–307.

—— and Hall, Peter (1994) *Technopoles of the World: the Making of 21st Century Industrial Complexes*, London: Routledge.

—— and Kiselyova, Emma (1998) "Russia as a network society", paper presented at Stanford University's Symposium on Russia at the End of the Twentieth Century, Stanford, November 1–3.

—— and —— (2000) "Russia in the information age", in Victoria Bonnell and George Breslauer (eds), *Russia at the End of the 20th Century*, Boulder, CO: Westview Press.

—— and Skinner, Rebecca (1988) "State and technological policy in the US: the SDI program", in Manuel Castells (director), *The State and Technological Policy: a Comparative Analysis*, Berkeley, CA: University of California, BRIE research monograph.

—— and Tyson, Laura d'Andrea (1988) "High technology choices ahead: restructuring interdependence", in John W. Sewell and Stuart Tucker (eds), *Growth, Exports, and Jobs in a Changing World Economy*, New Brunswick, NJ: Transaction Books.

—— and —— (1989) "High technology and the changing international division of production: implications for the US economy", in Randall B. Purcell (ed.), *The Newly Industrializing Countries in the World Economy: Challenges for US Policy*, Boulder, CO: Lynne Rienner, pp. 13–50.

—— et al. (1986) *Nuevas tecnologias: economia y sociedad en España*, 2 vols, Madrid: Alianza Editorial.

—— Gamella, Manuel, De la Puerta, Enrique, Ayala, Luis and Matias, Carmen (1991) *La industria de las tecnologias de informacion (1985–90). España en el contexto mundial*, Madrid: Fundesco.

——, Goh, Lee and Kwok, R.W.Y. (1990) *The* Shek Kip Mei *Syndrome: Economic Development and Public Housing in Hong Kong and Singapore*, London: Pion.

——, Yazawa, Shujiro and Kiselyova, Emma (1996) "Insurgents against the global order: a comparative analysis of Chiapas Zapatistas, American militia movement, and Aum Shinrikyo", *Berkeley Journal of Sociology*.

Castillo, Gregory (1994) "Henry Ford, Lenin, and the scientific organization of work in capitalist and soviet industrialization", Berkeley, CA: University of California, Department of City and Regional Planning, seminar paper for CP 275, unpublished.

Cats-Baril, William L. and Jelassi, Tawfik (1994) "The French videotex system Minitel: a successful implementation of a national information technology infrastructure", *MIS Quarterly*, 18(1): 1–20.

Caves, Roger W. (1994) *Exploring Urban America*, Thousand Oaks, CA: Sage.

Centre d'Etudes Prospectives et d'Informations Internationales (CEPII) (1992) *L'Economie mondiale 1990–2000: l'impératif de la croissance*, Paris: Economica.

—— and OFCE (1990) Mimosa: une modelisation de l'économie mondiale, *Observations et diagnostics économiques*, 30 January.

Cerf, Vinton (1999) "History and future of the Internet", presentation at the University of Washington Conference on the Internet and Global Political Economy, Seattle, September 19–20.

Ceruzzi, Paul (1998) *A History of Modern Computing, 1945–1995*, Cambridge, MA: MIT Press.

Cervero, Robert (1989) *America's Suburban Centers: the Land Use–Transportation Link*, Boston, MA: Unwin Hyman.

—— (1991) "Changing live–work spatial relationships: implications for metropolitan structure and mobility", in John Brotchie et al. (eds), *Cities in the 21st Century: New Technologies and Spatial Systems*, Melbourne: Longman and Cheshire, pp. 330–47.

Chandler, Alfred D. (1977) *The Visible Hand: the Managerial Revolution in American Business*, Cambridge, MA: Harvard University Press.

—— (1986) "The evolution of modern global competition", in M.E. Porter (ed.), *Competition in Global Industries*, Boston, MA: Harvard Business School Press, pp. 405–48.

Chatterjee, Anshu (forthcoming) "Globalization of media and cultural identity in India", unpublished PhD dissertation, Berkeley, CA: University of California.

Chen, Edward K.Y. (1979) *Hypergrowth in Asian Economies: a Compara-*

tive Analysis of Hong Kong, Japan, Korea, Singapore and Taiwan, London: Macmillan.

Chesnais, François (1994) *La Mondialisation du capital*, Paris: Syros.

Chida, Tomohei and Davies, Peter N. (1990) *The Japanese Shipping and Shipbuilding Industries: a History of their Modern Growth*, London: Athlone Press.

Child, John (1986) "Technology and work: an outline of theory and research in the western social sciences", in Peter Grootings (ed.), *Technology and Work: East–West Comparison*, London: Croom Helm, pp. 7–66.

Chin, Pei-Hsiung (1988) *Housing Policy and Economic Development in Taiwan*, Berkeley, CA: University of California, IURD.

Chizuko, Ueno (1987) "The position of Japanese women reconsidered." *Current Anthropology*, 28(4): 75–84.

—— (1988) "The Japanese women's movement: the counter-values to industrialism", in Grakan McCormack and Yoshio Sugimoto (eds), *Modernization and Beyond: the Japanese Trajectory*, Cambridge: Cambridge University Press, pp. 167–85.

Chung, K.H., Lee H.C. and Okumura, A. (1988) "The managerial practices of Korean, American, and Japanese firms", *Journal of East and West Studies*, 17: 45–74.

Cisco Systems (1999) "The global networked business: a model for success", on-line report, posted on Cisco Systems' Web Site, July 20.

Clark, R. (1979) *The Japanese Company*, New Haven, CT: Yale University Press.

Clegg, Stewart (1990) *Modern Organizations: Organization Studies in the Postmodern World*, London: Sage.

—— (1992) "French bread, Italian fashions, and Asian enterprises: modern passions and postmodern prognoses", in Jane Marceau (ed.), *Reworking the World*, Berlin: Walter de Gruyter, pp. 55–94.

—— and Redding, S. Gordon (eds) (1990) *Capitalism in Contrasting Cultures*, Berlin: Walter de Gruyter.

Clow Archibald and Clow, Nan L. (1952) *The Chemical Revolution*, London: Batchworth Press.

Coclough, Christopher and Manor, James (eds) (1991) *States or Markets? Neo-liberalism and the Development Policy Debate*, Oxford: Clarendon Press.

Cohen Stephen (1990) "Corporate nationality can matter a lot", testimony before the US Congress Joint Economic Committee, September.

—— (1993) "Geo-economics: lessons from America's mistakes", in Martin Carnoy et al. (eds), *The New Global Economy in the Information Age*, University Park, PA: Penn State University Press, pp. 97–147.

—— (1994) "Competitiveness: a reply to Krugman", *Foreign Affairs*, 73: 3.

—— and Borrus, Michael (1995a) *Networks of American and Japanese Electronics Companies in Asia*, Berkeley, CA: University of California, BRIE research paper.

—— and —— (1995b) *Networks of Companies in Asia*, Berkeley, CA: University of California, BRIE research paper.

—— and Guerrieri, Paolo (1995) "The variable geometry of Asian trade", in Eileen M. Doherty (ed.), *Japanese Investment in Asia*, Berkeley, CA: University of California, BRIE–Asia Foundation, pp. 189–208.

—— and Zysman, John (1987) *Manufacturing Matters: the Myth of Postindustrial Economy*, New York: Basic Books.

—— et al. (1985) *Global Competition: the New Reality*, vol. III of John Young (chair), *Competitiveness: the Report of the President's Commission on Industrial Competitiveness*, Washington, DC: Government Printing Office, p. 1.

Cohendet, P. and Llerena, P. (1989) *Flexibilité, information et décision*, Paris: Economica.

Colas, Dominique (1992) *La Glaive et le fléau: genéalogie du fanatisme et de la société civile*. Paris: Grasset.

Collective Author (1994) *The State of Working Women: 1994 Edition*, Tokyo: 21 Seiki Zoidan (in Japanese).

Comision de nuevas tecnologias de informacion y comunicacion de la presidencia de la Republica de Chile (1999) *Chile: hacia la sociedad de la informacion*, Informe al Presidente de la Republica, Santiago de Chile.

Commission of the European Communities (1994) *Growth, Competitiveness, Employment: the Challenges and Ways Forward into the 21st Century, White Paper*, Luxembourg: Office of the European Communities.

Conference on Time and Money in the Russian Culture (1995), organized by the University of California at Berkeley's Center for Slavic and Eastern European Studies, and the Stanford University's Center for Russian and Eastern European Studies, held at Berkeley on March 17 1995, unpublished presentations and discussions (personal notes and summary of the proceedings by Emma G. Kiselyova).

Conseil d'Etat (1998) *The Internet and Digital Networks*, Paris: La Documentation Française.

Cooke, Philip (1994) "The cooperative advantage of regions", paper prepared for Harold Innis Centenary Celebration Conference *Regions, Institutions and Technology*, University of Toronto, September 23–25.

—— and Morgan, K. (1993) "The network paradigm: new departures in corporate and regional development", *Society and Space*, 11: 543–64.

Cooper, Charles (ed.) (1994) *Technology and Innovation in the International Economy*, Aldershot, Hants.: Edward Elgar and United Nations University Press.

Cooper, James C. (1995) "The new golden age of productivity", *Business Week*, September 26: 62.

Coriat, Benjamin (1990) *L'Atelier et le robot*, Paris: Christian Bourgois Editeur.

—— (1994) "Neither pre- nor post-fordism: an original and new way of managing the labour process", in K. Tetsuro and R. Steven (eds), *Is Japanese Management Post-Fordism?*, Tokyo: Mado-sha, p. 182.

Council of Economic Advisers (1995) *Economic Report to the President of the United States. Transmitted to the Congress, February 1995*, Washington, DC: Government Printing Office, pp. 95–127.

Crick, Francis (1994) *The Astonishing Hypothesis: the Scientific Search for the Soul*, New York: Charles Scribner.

CREC (Center for Research in Electronic Commerce) (1999a) "The Internet economy indicators – October 1999 report", Austin: University of Texas, Graduate School of Business (on-line report).

—— (1999b) "The Internet economy indicators: key findings. November 17 report", Austin: University of Texas, Graduate School of Business (on-line report).

Croteau, David and Haynes, William (2000) *Media/Society: Industries, Images, and Audiences*, 2nd edn, Thousand Oaks, CA: Pine Forge Press.

Cuneo, Alice (1994) "Getting wired in the Gulch: creative and coding merge in San Francisco's multimedia community", *Advertising Age*, 65(50).

Cusumano, M. (1985) *The Japanese Automobile Industry: Technology and Management at Nissan and Toyota*, Cambridge, MA: Harvard University Press.

Cyert, Richard M. and Mowery, David C. (eds) (1987) *Technology and Employment: Innovation and Growth in the US Economy*, Washington, DC: National Academy Press.

Dalloz, Xavier and Portnoff, Andre-Yves (1994) "Les promesses de l'unimedia", *Futuribles*, 191: 11–36.

Daniel, W. (1987) *Workplace Survey of Industrial Relations*, London: Policy Studies Institute.

Daniels, P.W. (1993) *Service Industries in the World Economy*, Oxford: Blackwell.

Danton de Rouffignac, Peter (1991) *Europe's New Business Culture*, London: Pitman.

Darbon, Pierre and Robin, Jacques (eds) (1987) *Le Jaillissement des biotechnologies*, Paris: Fayard-Fondation Diderot.

David, P.A. (1975) *Technical Choice Innovation and Economic Growth: Essays on American and British Experience in the Nineteenth Century*, London: Cambridge University Press.

—— and Bunn, J.A. (1988) "The economics of gateways' technologies and network evolution: lessons from the electricity supply industry", *Information Economics and Policy*, 3 (April): 165–202.

David, Paul (1989) *Computer and Dynamo: the Modern Productivity Paradox in Historical Perspective*, Stanford, CA: Stanford University Center for Economic Policy Research, working paper No. 172.

Davis, Diane (1994) *Urban Leviathan: Mexico in the 20th Century*, Philadelphia, PA: Temple University Press.

Davis, Mike (1990) *City of Quartz*, London: Verso.

Dean, James W., Yoon, Se Joon and Susman, Gerald I. (1992) "Advanced manufacturing technology and organization structure: empowerment or subordination?", *Organization Science*, 3(2): 203–29.

De Anne, Julius (1990) *Global Companies and Public Policy: the Growing Challenge of Foreign Direct Investment*, New York: Council of Foreign Relations Press.

De Bandt, J. (ed.) (1985) *Les Services dans les sociétés industrielles avancées*, Paris: Economica.

Deben, Leon et al. (eds) (1993) *Understanding Amsterdam: Essays on Economic Vitality, City Life, and Urban Form*, Amsterdam: Het Spinhuis.

December, John (1993) "Characteristics of oral culture in discourse on the Net", unpublished paper.

De Conninck, Frederic (1995) *Société éclatée: travail intégré*, Paris: Presses Universitaires de France.

De Kerckhove, Derrick (1997) *Connected Intelligence: The Arrival of the Web Society*, Toronto: Somerville.

Denison, Edward F. (1967) *Why Growth Rates Differ: Postwar Experience in Nine Western Countries*, Washington, DC: Brookings Institution.

—— (1974) *Accounting for United States Economic Growth, 1929–69*, Washington, DC: Brookings Institution.

—— (1979) *Accounting for Slower Economic Growth: the United States in the 1970s*, Washington, DC: Brookings Institution.

Dentsu Institute for Human Studies/DataFlow International (1994) *Media in Japan*, Tokyo: DataFlow International.

Derriennic, J.P. (1990) "Tentative de polémologie nécrométrique", Quebec: Université Laval, unpublished paper.

Deyo, Frederick (ed.) (1987) *The Political Economy of New Asian Industrialism*, Ithaca, NY: Cornell University Press.

Dicken, Peter (1998) *Global Shift*, London: Chapman.

Dickens, William T., Tyson, Laura D'Andrea and Zysman, John, (eds) (1988) *The Dynamics of Trade and Employment*, Cambridge, MA: Ballinger Press.

Dickinson, H.W. (1958) "The steam engine to 1830", in C. Singer (ed.), *A History of Technology*, vol. 4: *The Industrial Revolution, 1750–1850*, Oxford: Oxford University Press, pp. 168–97.

Dizard, Wilson P. (1982) *The Coming Information Age*, New York: Longman.

Dodgson, M. (ed.) (1989) *Technology Strategy and the Firm: Management and Public Policy*, Harlow, Essex: Longman.

Dohse, K., Jurgens, V. and Malsch, T. (1985) "From Fordism to Toyotism? The social organization of the labour process in the Japanese automobile industry", *Politics and Society*, 14(2): 115–46.

Dondero, George (1995) "Information, communication, and vehicle technology", Berkeley, CA: University of California Department of City and Regional Planning, Spring, unpublished seminar paper for CP-298I.

Dordick, Herbert S. and Wang, Georgette (1993) *The Information Society: a Retrospective View*, Newbury Park, CA: Sage.

Dosi, Giovanni (1988) "The nature of the innovative process", in G. Dosi et al. (ed.), *Technical Change and Economic Theory*, London: Pinter, pp. 221–39.

——, Freeman, Christopher, Nelson, Richard, Silverberg, Gerald and Soete Luc (eds) (1988a) *Technical Change and Economic Theory*, London: Pinter.

—— Pavitt, K and Soete, L. (1988b) *The Economics of Technical Change and International Trade*, Brighton, Sussex: Wheatsheaf.

Dower, John W. (ed.) (1975) *Origins of the Modern Japanese State: Selected Writings of E. H. Norman*, New York: Pantheon Books.

Doyle, Marc (1992) *The Future of Television: a Global Overview of Programming, Advertising, Technology and Growth*, Lincolnwood, IL: NTC Business Books.

Drexler, K. Eric and Peterson, Chris (1991) *Unbounding the Future: the Nanotechnology Revolution*, New York: Quill/William Morrow.

Drucker, Peter F. (1988) "The coming of the new organization", *Harvard Business Review*, 88: 45–53.

Duarte, Fabio (1998) *Global e local no mundo contemporaneo*, São Paulo: Editora Moderna.

Dubois, Pierre (1985) "Rupture de croissance et progrès technique", *Economie et statistique*, 181.

Dunford, M. and Kafkalas, G. (eds) (1992) *Cities and Regions in the New Europe: the Global–Local Interplay and Spatial Development Strategies*, London: Belhaven Press.

Dunning, John (1993) *Multinational Enterprises and the Global Economy*, Reading, MA: Addison-Wesley.

—— (1997) *Alliance Capitalism and Global Business*, London: Routledge.

Dupas, Gilberto (1999) *Economia global e exclusao social*, São Paulo: Paz e Terra.

Durlabhji, Subhash and Marks, Norton (eds) (1993) *Japanese Business: Cultural Perspectives*, Albany, NY: State University of New York Press.

Dutton, William (1999) *Society on the Line: Information Politics and the Digital Age*, Oxford: Oxford University Press.

Dy, Josefina (ed.) (1990) *Advanced Technology in Commerce, Offices, and Health Service*, Aldershot, Hants: Avebury.

Dyson, Esther (1998) *Release 2.1: A Design for Living in the Digital Age*, London: Penguin.

Ebel, K. and Ulrich, E. (1987) *Social and Labour Effects of CAD/CAM*, Geneva: International Labour Organization.

Eco, Umberto (1977) "Dalla periferia dell'impero", cited in the English translation as "Does the audience have bad effects on television?", in Umberto Eco, *Apocalypse Postponed*, Bloomington: Indiana University Press, 1994, pp. 87–102.

Edquist, Charles and Jacobsson, Stefan (1989) *Flexible Automation: the Global Diffusion of New Technologies in the Engineering Industry*, Oxford: Blackwell.

Egan, Ted (1995) "The development and location patterns of software industry in the US", unpublished PhD dissertation, Berkeley, CA: University of California.

Eichengreen, Barry (1996) *Globalizing Capital: A History of the International Monetary System*, Princeton, NJ: Princeton University Press.

Elkington, John (1985) *The Gene Factory: Inside the Business and Science of Biotechnology*, New York: Carroll and Graf.

Elmer-Dewwit, Philip (1993) "The amazing video game boom", *Time*, September 27: 67–72.

El Pais/World Media (1995) "Habla el futuro", March 9: supplement.

Enderwick, Peter (ed.) (1989) *Multinational Service Firms*, London: Routledge.

Epstein, Edward (1995) "Presidential contender's campaign online", *San Francisco Chronicle*, November 27.

Ernst, Dieter (1994a) *Carriers of Regionalization? The East Asian Production Networks of Japanese Electronics Firms*, Berkeley, CA: University of California, BRIE working paper 73.

—— (1994b) *Inter-firms Networks and Market Structure: Driving Forces, Barriers and Patterns of Control*, Berkeley, CA: University of California, BRIE research paper.

—— (1994c) *Networks in Electronics*, Berkeley, CA: University of California, BRIE research monograph.

—— (1995) "International production networks in Asian electronics: how do they differ and what are their impacts?", unpublished paper presented at the BRIE–Asia Foundation Conference on Competing Production Networks in Asia, San Francisco, 27–28 April.

—— (1997) "From partial to systemic globalization: international production networks in the electronic industry", Berkeley: University of California, BRIE working paper.

—— and O'Connor, David (1992) *Competing in the Electronics Industry: the Experience of Newly Industrializing Economies*, Paris: OECD.

Esping-Andersen, G. (ed.) (1993) *Changing Classes*, London: Sage.

—— (1999) *Social Foundations of Postindustrial Economies*, Oxford: Oxford University Press.

Estefania, Joaquin (1996) *La nueva economia: La globalizacion*, Madrid: Editorial Debate.

Evans, Peter (1995) *Embedded Autonomy: States and Industrial Transformation*, Princeton, NJ: Princeton University Press.

Fager, Gregory (1994) "Financial flows to the major emerging markets in Asia", *Business Economics*, 29(2): 21–7.

Fainstein, Susan S., Gordon, Ian and Harloe, Michael (eds.) (1992) *Divided Cities*, Oxford: Blackwell.

Fajnzylber, Fernando (1990) *Unavoidable Industrial Restructuring in Latin America*, Durham, NC: Duke University Press.

Fassmann H. and Münz, R. (1992) "Patterns and trends of international migration in Western Europe", *Population and Development Review*, 18(3).

Fazy, Ian Hamilton (1995) "The superhighway pioneers", *The Financial Times*, June 20.

Ferguson, Marjorie (ed.) (1986) *New Communications Technologies and the Public Interest: Comparative Perspectives on Policies and Research*, Newbury Park, CA: Sage.

Feuerwerker, Albert (1984) "The state and economy in late imperial China", *Theory and Society*, 13: 297–326.

Fischer, Claude (1982) *To Dwell Among Friends*, Berkeley, CA: University of California Press.

—— (1985) "Studying technology and social life", in Manuel Castells (ed.),

High Technology, Space, and Society, Beverly Hills, CA: Sage (*Urban Affairs Annual Reviews*, 28: 284–301).

—— (1992) *America Calling: a Social History of the Telephone to 1940*, Berkeley, CA: University of California Press.

Flynn, P.M. (1985) *The Impact of Technological Change on Jobs and Workers*, paper prepared for the US Department of Labor, Employment Training Administration.

Fontana, Josep (1988) *La fin de l'Antic Regim i l'industrialitzacio, 1787–1868*, vol. V of Pierre Vilar (director), *Historia de Catalunya*, Barcelona: Edicions 62.

Foray, Dominique (1999) "Science, technology and the market", in *World Social Science Report 1999*, Paris: Unesco, pp. 246–56.

—— and Freeman, Christopher (eds) (1992) *Technologie et richesse des nations*, Paris: Economica.

Forbes, R.J. (1958) "Power to 1850", in C. Singer (ed.), *A History of Technology*, vol. 4: *The Industrial Revolution, 1750–1850*, Oxford: Oxford University Press.

Forester, Tom (ed.) (1980) *The Microelectronics Revolution*, Oxford: Blackwell.

—— (ed.) (1985) *The Information Technology Revolution*, Oxford: Blackwell.

—— (ed.) (1987) *High-tech Society*, Oxford: Blackwell.

—— (ed.) (1988) *The Materials Revolution*, Oxford: Blackwell Business.

—— (ed.) (1989) *Computers in the Human Context*, Oxford: Blackwell.

—— (1993) *Silicon Samurai: How Japan Conquered the World Information Technology Industry*, Oxford: Blackwell.

Fouquin, Michel, Dourille-Feer, Evelyne and Oliveira-Martins, Joaquim, (1992) *Pacifique: le recentrage asiatique*, Paris: Economica.

Frankel, J.A. (1991) "Is a yen bloc forming in Pacific Asia?", in R. O'Brien (ed.), *Finance and the International Economy*, 5, New York: Oxford University Press.

—— (ed.) (1994) *The Internationalization of Equity Markets*, Chicago: University of Chicago Press.

Freeman, Christopher (1982) *The Economics of Industrial Innovation*, London: Pinter.

—— (ed.) (1986) *Design, Innovation, and Long Cycles in Economic Development*, London: Pinter.

—— and Soete, Luc (1994) *Work for All or Mass Unemployment?* London: Pinter.

——, Sharp, Margaret and Walker, William (eds) (1991) *Technology and the Future of Europe*, London: Pinter.

Freeman, Richard (ed.) (1994) *Working under Different Rules*, Cambridge, MA: Harvard University Press.

French, W. Howard (1999) "Economy's ebb in Japan spurs temporary jobs", *The New York Times*, August 12: A1–A4.

Freud, Sigmund (1947) "Thoughts for the times on war and death", in his *On War, Sex, and Neurosis*, New York: Arts and Science Press, pp. 243–76.

Friedland, Roger and Boden, Deirdre (eds) (1994) *Nowhere: Space, Time, and Modernity*, Berkeley, CA: University of California Press.

Friedman, D. (1988) *The Misunderstood Miracle*, Ithaca, NY: Cornell University Press.

Friedman, Milton (1968) *Dollars and Deficits: Living with America's Economic Problems*, Englewood Cliffs, NJ: Prentice-Hall.

Friedmann, Georges (1956) *Le Travail en miettes*, Paris: Gallimard.

—— (1957) *Countries in the World Economy: Challenges for US Policy*, Boulder, CO: Lynne Reinner, pp. 159–86.

—— and Naville, Pierre (eds) (1961) *Traité de sociologie du travail*, Paris: Armand Colin.

Friedmann, Thomas L. (1999) *The Lexus and the Olive Tree*, New York: Times Books.

Fulk, J. and Steinfield, C. (eds) (1990) *Organizations and Communication Technology*, Newbury, CA: Sage.

Gallie, D. and Paugham, S. (eds) (2000) *The Experience of Unemployment in Oxford*, Oxford: Oxford University Press.

Ganley, Gladys D. (1991) "Power to the people via electronic media", *Washington Quarterly*, Spring: 5–22.

Garratt, G.R.M. (1958) "Telegraphy", in C. Singer (ed.), *A History of Technology*, vol. 4: *The Industrial Revolution, 1750–1850*, Oxford: Oxford University Press, pp. 644–62.

Garreau, Joel (1991) *Edge City: Life on the New Frontier*, New York: Doubleday.

Garton, Laura and Wellman, Barry (1995) "Social impacts of electronic mail in organizations: a review of the research literature", in Brant E. Burleson (ed.), *Communications Yearbook*, *18*, Thousand Oaks, CA: Sage, pp. 434–53.

GATT (General Agreement on Tariffs and Trade) (1994) *International Trade*, Geneva: GATT, Trends and Statistics.

Gelb, Joyce and Lief Palley, Marian (eds) (1994) *Women of Japan and Korea: Continuity and Change*, Philadelphia, PA: Temple University Press.

Gelernter, David (1991) *Mirror Worlds*, New York: Oxford University Press.

Gereffi, Gary (1993) *Global Production Systems and Third World Development*, Madison: University of Wisconsin Global Studies Research Program, working paper series, August.

—— (1999) "International trade and industrial upgrading in the apparel commodity chain", *Journal of International Economics*, 48: 37–70.

—— and Wyman, Donald (eds) (1990) *Manufacturing Miracles: Paths of Industrialization in Latin America and East Asia*, Princeton, NJ: Princeton University Press.

Gerlach, Michael L. (1992) *Alliance Capitalism: the Social Organization of Japanese Business*, Berkeley, CA: University of California Press.

Geroski, P. (1995) "Markets for technology: knowledge, innovation and appropriability", in P. Stoneman (ed.), *Handbook of the Economics of Innovation and Technological Change*, Oxford: Blackwell, pp. 91–131.

Gershuny, J.I. and Miles, I.D. (1983) *The New Service Economy: the Transformation of Employment in Industrial Societies*, London: Pinter.

Ghoshal, Sumantra and Bartlett, Christopher (1993) "The multinational corporation as an inter-organizational network", in Sumantra Ghoshal and D. Eleanor Westney (eds), *Organization Theory and Multinational Corporations*, New York: St Martin's Press, pp. 77–104.

—— and Westney, E. Eleanor (eds) (1993) *Organization Theory and Multinational Corporations*, New York: St Martin's Press.

Gibson, David G. and Rogers, Everett (1994) *R&D: Collaboration on Trial. The Microelectronics Computer Technology Corporation*, Boston, MA: Harvard Business School Press.

Giddens, A. (1981) *A Contemporary Critique of Historical Materialism*, Berkeley, CA: University of California Press.

—— (1984) *The Constitution of Society: Outline of a Theory of Structuration*, Cambridge: Polity Press.

—— (1998) *The Third Way: the Renewal of Social Democracy*, Oxford: Blackwell.

Gille, Bertrand (1978) *Histoire des techniques: technique et civilisations, technique et sciences*, Paris: Gallimard.

Gitlin, Todd (1987) *The Sixties: Years of Hope, Days of Rage*, Toronto and New York: Bantam Books.

Gleick, James (1987) *Chaos*, New York: Viking Penguin.

—— (1999) *Faster: The Acceleration of Just About Everything*, New York: Pantheon.

Godard, Francis et al. (1973) *La Renovation urbaine à Paris*, Paris: Mouton.

Gold, Thomas (1986) *State and Society in the Taiwan Miracle*, Armonk, NY: M.E. Sharpe.

Goldsmith, William W. and Blakely, Edward J. (1992) *Separate Societies: Poverty and Inequality in US Cities*, Philadelphia, PA: Temple University Press.

Goodman, P.S., Sproull, L.S. et al. (1990) *Technology and Organization*, San Francisco, CA: Jossey-Bass.

Gordon, Richard (1994) *Internationalization, Multinationalization, Globalization: Contradictory World Economies and New Spatial Divisions of Labor*, Santa Cruz, CA: University of California Center for the Study of Global Transformations, working paper 94.

Gordon, Robert (1999) "Has the 'new economy' rendered the productivity slow-down obsolete?", Northwestern University, Department of Economics, on-line report.

Gorgen, Armelle and Mathieu, Rene (1992) "Developing partnerships: new organizational practices in manufacturer–supplier relationships in the French automobile and aerospace industry", in Jane Marceau (ed.), *Reworking the World: Organizations, Technologies, and Cultures in Comparative Perspective*, Berlin: Walter de Gruyter, pp. 171–80.

Gottdiener, Marc (1985) *The Social Production of Urban Space*, Austin TX: University of Texas Press.

Gould, Stephen J. (1980) *The Panda's Thumb: More Reflections on Natural History*, New York: W.W. Norton.

Gourevitch, Peter A. (ed.) (1984) *Unions and Economic Crisis: Britain, West*

Germany and Sweden, Boston, MA: Allen and Unwin.

Graham, E. (1996) *Global Corporations and National Governments*, Washington, DC: Institute for International Economics.

Graham, Stephen (1994) "Networking cities: telematics in urban policy – a critical review", *International Journal of Urban and Regional Research*, 18(3): 416–31.

—— and Marvin, Simon (1996) *Telecommunications and the City: Electronic Spaces, Urban Places*, London: Routledge.

—— and —— (2000) *Splintering Networks, Fragmenting Cities: Urban Infrastructure in a Global–Local Age*, London: Routledge.

Granovetter, M. (1985) "Economic action and social structure: the problem of embeddedness", *American Journal of Sociology*, 49: 323–34.

Greenhalgh, S. (1988) "Families and networks in Taiwan's economic development", in E.A. Winckler and S. Greenhalgh (eds), *Contending Approaches to the Political Economy of Taiwan*, Armonk, NY: M.E. Sharpe.

Greenspan, Alan (1998) "The semi-annual monetary policy report before the Committee on Banking and Financial Services of the US House of Representatives", February 24.

Guerrieri, Paolo (1993) "Patterns of technological capability and international trade performance: an empirical analysis", in M. Kreinin (ed.), *The Political Economy of International Commercial Policy: Issues for the 1990s*, London: Taylor & Francis.

Guile, Bruce R. (ed.) (1985) *Information Technologies and Social Transformation*, Washington DC: National Academy of Engineering, National Academy Press.

—— and Brooks, Harvey (eds) (1987) *Technology and Global Industry: Companies and Nations in the World Economy*, Washington, DC: National Academy of Engineering.

Guillemard, Anne Marie (1972) *La Retraite: une mort sociale*, Paris: Mouton.

—— (1988) *Le Déclin du social*, Paris: Presses Universitaires de France.

—— (1993) "Travailleurs vieillissants et marché du travail en Europe", *Travail et emploi*, Sept.: 60–79.

—— and Rein, Martin (1993) "Comparative patterns of retirement: recent trends in developed societies", *Annual Review of Sociology*, 19: 469–503.

Gurr, T.R. (1993) *Minorities at Risk: a Global View of Ethnopolitical Conflicts*, Washington, DC: US Institute of Peace Press.

Gurstein, Penny (1990) "Working at home in the live-in office: computers, space, and the social life of household", unpublished PhD dissertation, Berkeley, CA: University of California.

Gutner, Todi (1999) "Special report: the e-bond revolution", *Business Week*, November 15: 270–80.

Hafner, Katie and Markoff, John (1991) *Cyberpunk: Outlaws and Hackers in the Computer Frontier*, New York: Touchstone.

Hall, Carl (1999a) "Tiny switch could shrink computers: microscopic machines with the power of a billion PCs", *San Francisco Chronicle*, July 16: 1–8.

—— (1999b) "Brave new nano-world lies ahead", *San Francisco Chronicle*, July 19: 1–8.

Hall, Nina (ed.) (1991) *Exploring Chaos: a Guide to the New Science of Disorder*, New York: W.W. Norton.

Hall, Peter (1995) "Towards a general urban theory", in John Brotchie et al. (eds), *Cities in Competition: Productive and Sustainable Cities for the 21st Century*, Sydney: Longman Australia, pp. 3–32.

—— (1998) *Cities in Civilization*, New York: Pantheon Books.

—— and Preston, Pascal (1988) *The Carrier Wave: New Information Technology and the Geography of Innovation, 1846–2003*, London: Unwin Hyman.

—— et al. (1987) *Western Sunrise: the Genesis and Growth of Britain's Major High Technology Corridor*, London: Allen and Unwin.

——, Bornstein, Lisa, Grier, Reed and Webber, Melvin (1988) *Biotechnology: the Next Industrial Frontier*, Berkeley, CA: University of California Institute of Urban and Regional Development, Biotech Industry Research Group Report.

Hall, Stephen S. (1987) *Invisible Frontiers: the Race to Synthesize a Human Gene*, New York: Atlantic Monthly Press.

Hamelink, Cees (1990) "Information imbalance: core and periphery", in C. Downing et al., *Questioning the Media*, Newbury Park: Sage, pp. 217–28.

Hamilton, Gary G. (1984) "Patriarchalism in Imperial China and Western Europe", *Theory and Society*, 13: 293–426.

—— (1985) "Why no capitalism in China? Negative questions in historical comparative research", *Journal of Asian Perspectives*, 2: 2.

—— (1991) *Business Networks and Economic Development in East and Southeast Asia*, Hong Kong: University of Hong Kong, Centre of Asian Studies.

—— and Biggart, N.W. (1988) "Market, culture, and authority: a comparative analysis of management and organization in the Far East", in C. Winship and S. Rosen (eds), *Organization and Institutions: Sociological Approaches to the Analysis of Social Structure*, Chicago, IL: University of Chicago Press, American Journal of Sociology Supplement, pp. S52–S95.

—— and Kao, C.S. (1990) "The institutional foundation of Chinese business: the family firm in Taiwan", *Comparative Social Research*, 12: 95–112.

——, Zeile, W. and Kim, W.J. (1990) "The networks structures of East Asian economies", in Stewart R. Clegg and S. Gordon Redding (eds), *Capitalism in Contrasting Cultures*, Berlin: Walter de Gruyter.

Hammer, M. and Camphy, J. (1993) *Re-engineering the Corporation*, New York: The Free Press.

Handelman, Stephen (1995) *Comrade Criminal: Russia's New Mafiya*, New Haven, CT: Yale University Press.

Handinghaus, Nicolas H. (1989) "Droga y crecimiento economico: el narcotrafico en las cuentas nacionales", *Nueva Sociedad* (Bogota), no. 102.

Handy, Susan and Mokhtarian, Patricia L. (1995) "Planning for telecommuting", *Journal of the American Planning Association*, 61(1): 99–111.

Hanks, Roma S. and Sussman, Marvin B. (eds) (1990) *Corporations, Businesses and Families*, New York: Haworth Press.

Hanson, Stephen E. (1991) "Time and Soviet industrialization", unpublished PhD dissertation, Berkeley, CA: University of California.

Harff, B. (1986) "Genocide as state terrorism", in Michael Stohl and George A. Lopez (eds) *Government Violence and Repression*, Westport, CT: Greenwood Press.

Harmon, Amy (1999) "The rebel code", *The New York Times Magazine*, February 21: 34–7.

Harper-Anderson, Elsie (forthcoming) "Differential career patterns of the professional labor force in the new economy: the case of the San Francisco Bay Area", unpublished PhD dissertation, Berkeley, CA: University of California.

Harrington, Jon (1991) *Organizational Structure and Information Technology*, New York: Prentice-Hall.

Harris, Nigel (1987) *The End of the Third World*, Harmondsworth, Middx.: Penguin.

Harrison, Bennett (1994) *Lean and Mean: the Changing Landscape of Corporate Power in the Age of Flexibility*, New York: Basic Books.

Hart, Jeffrey A., Reed, Robert R. and Bar, François (1992) *The Building of Internet*, Berkeley, CA: University of California, BRIE working paper.

Hartman, Amir and Sifonis, John, with Kador, John (2000) *Net Ready*, New York: McGraw-Hill.

Hartmann, Heidi (ed.) (1987) *Computer Chips and Paper Clips: Technology and Women's Employment*, Washington, DC: National Academy Press.

Harvey, David (1990) *The Condition of Postmodernity*, Oxford: Blackwell.

Havelock, Eric A. (1982) *The Literate Revolution in Greece and its Cultural Consequences*, Princeton, NJ: Princeton University Press.

Heavey, Laurie (1994) "Global integration", *Pension World*, 30(7): 24–7.

Held, David, McGrew, Anthony, Goldblatt, David and Perraton, Jonathan (1999) *Global Transformations: Politics, Economics and Culture*, Stanford, CA: Stanford University Press.

Henderson, Jeffrey (1989) *The Globalisation of High Technology Production: Society, Space and Semiconductors in the Restructuring of the Modern World*, London: Routledge.

—— (1990) *The American Semiconductors Industry and the New International Division of Labor*, London: Routledge.

—— (1991) "Urbanization in the Hong Kong–South China region: an introduction to dynamics and dilemmas", *International Journal of Urban and Regional Research*, 15(2): 169–79.

Herman, Robin (1990) *Fusion: the Search for Endless Energy*, Cambridge: Cambridge University Press.

Herther, Nancy K. (1994) "Multimedia and the 'information superhighway' ", *Online*, 18(5): 24.

Hewitt, P. (1993) *About Time: the Revolution in Work and Family Life*, London: IPPR/Rivers Oram Press.

Hill, Christopher (ed.) (1996) *The Actors in Europe's Foreign Policy*, London: Routledge.

Hiltz, Starr Roxanne and Turoff, Murray (1993) *The Network Nation: Human Communication via Computer*, Cambridge, MA: MIT Press.

Hiltzik, Michael (1999) *Dealers of Lightning: Xerox Parc and the Dawn of the Computer Age*, New York: Harper.

Himannen, Pekka (2001) *The Hackers' Ethic and the Spirit of Informationalism*, New Haven: Yale University Press, forthcoming.

Hinrichs, Karl, Roche, William and Sirianni, Carmen (eds) (1991) *The Political Economy of Working Hours in Industrial Nations*, Philadelphia, PA: Temple University Press.

Hirschhorn, Larry (1984) *Beyond Mechanization: Work and Technology in a Postindustrial Age*, Cambridge, MA: MIT Press.

—— (1985) "Information technology and the new services game", in Manuel Castells (ed.), *High Technology, Space and Society*, Beverly Hills, CA: Sage, pp. 172–90.

Ho, H.C.Y. (1979) *The Fiscal System of Hong Kong*, London: Croom Helm.

Hockman, E. and Kostecki, G. (1995) *The Political Economy of the World Trading System: From GATT to WTO*, Oxford: Oxford University Press.

Hoffman, Abbie (1999) "Globalization and networking: the Cisco Systems' strategy", Berkeley, CA: California, Department of City and Regional Planning, research paper for CP 229.

Hohenberg, Paul (1967) *Chemicals in Western Europe, 1850–1914*, Chicago, IL: Rand-McNally.

Holsti, K.J. (1991) *Peace and War: Armed Conflicts and International Order, 1648–1989*, Cambridge: Cambridge University Press.

Honigsbaum, Mark (1988) "Minitel loses fads image, moves toward money", *MIS Week*, 9(36): 22.

Hoogvelt, Ankie (1997) *Globalisation and the Postcolonial World: The New Political Economy of Development*, London: Macmillan.

Howell, David (1994) "The skills myth", *American Prospect*, 18 (Summer): 81–90.

—— and Wolff, Edward (1991) "Trends in the growth and distribution of skills in the US workplace, 1960–85", *Industrial and Labor Relations Review*, 44(3): 486–502.

Howell, J. and Woods, M. (1993) *The Globalization of Production and Technology*, London: Belhaven Press.

Hsing, You-tien (1994) "Blood thicker than water: networks of local Chinese officials and Taiwanese investors in Southern China", paper delivered at the Conference sponsored by the University of California Institute on Global Conflict and Cooperation, The Economies of the China Circle, Hong Kong, September 1–3.

—— (1995) *Migrant Workers, Foreign Capital, and Diversification of Labor Markets in Southern China*, Vancouver: University of British Columbia, Asian Urban Research Networks, working paper series.

—— (1996) *Making Capitalism in China: the Taiwan Connection*, New York: Oxford University Press.

Hutton, Will (1995) *The State We Are In*, London: Jonathan Cape.

—— and Giddens, A. (eds) (2000) *On the Edge*, London: Jonathan Cape.

Huws, U., Korte, W.B. and Robinson, S. (1990) *Telework: Towards the Elusive Office*, Chichester, Sussex: John Wiley.

Hyman, Richard and Streeck, Wolfgang (eds) (1988) *New Technology and Industrial Relations*, Oxford: Blackwell.

Ikle, Fred C. and Wohlsletter, Albert (co-chairmen) (1988) *Discriminate Deterrence: Report of the Commission on Integrated Long-term Strategy to the Secretary of Defense*, Washington, DC: US Government Printing Office.

Imai, Ken'ichi (1980) *Japan's Industrial Organization and its Vertical Structure*, Kunitachi: Hitotsubashi University, Institute of Business Research, discussion paper no. 101.

—— (1990a) *Joho netto waku shakai no tenbo* [The information network society], Tokyo: Chikuma Shobo.

—— (1990b) *Jouhon Network Shakai no Tenkai* [The development of information network society], Tokyo: Tikuma Shobou.

—— and Yonekura, Seiichiro (1991) "Network and network-in strategy", paper presented at the International Conference between Bocconi University and Hitotsubashi University, Milan, September 20.

Innis, Harold A. (1950) *Empire and Communications*, Oxford: Oxford University Press.

—— (1951) *The Bias of Communication*, Toronto: University of Toronto Press.

—— (1952) *Changing Concepts of Time*, Toronto: University of Toronto Press.

Inoki, Takenori and Higuchi, Yoshio (eds) (1995) *Nihon no Koyou system to Iodo shijo* [Japanese employment system and labor market], Tokyo: Nihon Keizai Shinbunsha.

International Labor Organization (ILO) (1988) *Technological Change, Work Organization and Pay: Lessons from Asia*, Geneva: ILO Labor-Management Relations Series, no. 68.

—— (1993 and 1994) *World Labor Report*, Geneva: International Labor Organization.

Ito, Youichi (1991a) "Birth of *joho shakai* and *johoka* concepts in Japan and their diffusion outside Japan", *Keio Communication Review*, 13: 3–12.

—— (1991b) "*Johoka* as a driving force of social change", *Keio Communication Review*, 12: 33–58.

—— (1993) "How Japan modernised earlier and faster than other non-western countries: an information sociology approach", *Journal of Development Communication*, 4 (2).

—— (1994) "Japan", in Georgette Wang (ed.), *Treading Different Paths: Informatization in Asian Nations*, Norwood, NJ: Ablex, pp. 68–97.

Jackson, John H. (1989) *The World Trading System*, Cambridge, MA: MIT Press.

Jacobs, Allan (1993) *Great Streets*, Cambridge, MA: MIT Press.

Jacobs, N. (1985) *The Korean Road to Modernization and Development*, Urbana, IL: University of Illinois Press.

Jacoby, S. (1979) "The origins of internal labor markets in Japan", *Industrial Relations*, 18: 184–96.

James, William E., Naya, Seiji and Meier, Gerald M. (1989) *Asian Development: Economic Success and Policy Lessons*, Madison, WIS: University of Wisconsin Press.

Janelli, Roger (with Yim, Downhee) (1993) *Making Capitalism: the Social and Cultural Construction of a South Korean Conglomerate*, Stanford, CA: Stanford University Press.

Japan Informatization Processing Center (1994) *Informatization White Paper*, Tokyo: JIPDEC.

Japan Institute of Labour (1985) *Technological Innovation and Industrial Relations*, Tokyo: JIL.

Jarvis, C.M. (1958) "The distribution and utilization of electricity", in Charles Singer et al., *A History of Technology*, vol. 5: *The Late Nineteenth Century*, Oxford: Clarendon Press, pp. 177–207.

Javetski, Bill and Glasgall, William (1994) "Borderless finance: fuel for growth", *Business Week*, November 18: 40–50.

Jewkes, J., Sawers, D. and Stillerman, R. (1969) *The Sources of Invention*, New York: W.W. Norton.

Johnson, Chalmers (1982) *MITI and the Japanese Miracle*, Stanford, CA: Stanford University Press.

—— (1985) "The institutional foundations of Japanese industrial policy", *California Management Review*, 27(4).

—— (1987) "Political institutions and economic performance: the government–business relationship in Japan, South Korea, and Taiwan", in Frederick Deyo (ed.), *The Political Economy of New Asian Industrialism*, Ithaca, NY: Cornell University Press, pp. 136–64.

—— (1995) *Japan: Who Governs? The Rise of the Developmental State*, New York: W.W. Norton.

——, Tyson, L. and Zysman, J. (eds) (1989) *Politics and Productivity: How Japan's Development Strategy Works*, New York: Harper Business.

Johnston, William B. (1991) "Global labor force 2000: the new world labor market", *Harvard Business Review*, March–April.

Jones, Barry (1982) *Sleepers, Wake! Technology and the Future of Work*, Melbourne: Oxford University Press (references are to the 1990 rev. edn).

Jones, David (1993) "Banks move to cut currency dealing costs", *Financial Technology International Bulletin*, 10(6): 1–3.

Jones, Eric L. (1981) *The European Miracle*, Cambridge: Cambridge University Press.

—— (1988) *Growth Recurring: Economic Change in World History*, Oxford: Clarendon Press.

Jones, L.P. and Sakong, I. (1980) *Government Business and Entrepreneurship in Economic Development: the Korean Case*, Cambridge, MA: Council on East Asian Studies.

Jones, Steven G. (ed.) (1995) *Cybersociety: Computer Mediated Communication and Community*, Thousand Oaks, CA: Sage.

—— (ed.) (1997) *Virtual culture*, London: Sage.

—— (ed.) (1998) *Cybersociety 2.0: Revisiting Computer-mediated Communication and Community*, Thousand Oaks, CA: Sage.

Jorgerson, Dale W. and Griliches, Z. (1967) "The explanation of productivity growth", *Review of Economic Studies*, 34 (July): 249–83.

Jost, Kennet (1993) "Downward mobility", *CQ Researcher*, 3(27): 627–47.

Joussaud, Jacques (1994) "Diversité des statuts des travailleurs et flexibilité des entreprises au Japon", *Japan in Extenso*, 31: 49–53.

Kahn, Robert E. (1999) "Evolution of Internet", in UNESCO (1999): 157–64.

Kaku, Michio (1994) *Hyperspace: a Scientific Odyssey through Parallel Universes, Time Warps, and the 10th Dimension*, New York: Oxford University Press.

Kamatani, Chikatoshi (1988) *Gijutsu Taikoku Hyakunen no Kei: Nippon no Kindaika to Kokuritsu Kenkyu Kikan* [The road to techno-nationalism: Japanese modernization and national research institutes from the Meiji era], Tokyo: Heibonsha.

Kaplan, David (1999) *The Silicon Boys and their Valley of Dreams*, San Francisco: McGraw-Hill.

Kaplan, Rachel (1992) "Video on demand", *American Demographics*, 14(6): 38–43.

Kaplinsky, Raphael (1986) *Microelectronics and Work Revisited: a Review*, report prepared for the International Labor Organization, Brighton: University of Sussex Institute of Development Studies.

Kara-Murza, A.A. and Polyakov, L.V. (1994) *Reformator. Opyt analiticheskoy antologii*, Moscow: Institut Filosofii Rossiiskoi Akademii Nauk, Flora.

Katz, Jorge (ed.) (1987) *Technology Generation in Latin American Manufacturing Industries*, London: Macmillan.

Katz, Raul L. (1988) *The Information Society: an International Perspective*, New York: Praeger.

Kay, Ron (1990) *Managing Creativity in Science and High-tech*, Berlin: Springer Verlag.

Kaye, G.D., Grant, D.A. and Emond, E.J. (1985) *Major Armed Conflicts: a Compendium of Interstate and Intrastate Conflict, 1720 to 1985*, Ottawa: Operational Research and Analysis Establishment, Report to National Defense, Canada.

Keck, Margaret E. and Sikkink, Kathryn (1998) *Activists beyond Borders*, Ithaca and London: Cornell University Press.

Kelley, Maryellen (1986) "Programmable automation and the skill question: a re-interpretation of the cross-national evidence", *Human Systems Management*, 6.

—— (1990) "New process technology, job design and work organization: a contingency model", *American Sociological Review*, 55 (April): 191–208.

Kelly, Kevin (1995) *Out of Control: the Rise of Neo-biological Civilization*, Menlo Park, CA: Addison-Wesley.

Kendrick, John W. (1961) *Productivity Trends in the United States*, National Bureau of Economic Research, Princeton, NJ: Princeton University Press.

—— (1973) *Postwar Productivity Trends in the United States, 1948–69*, National Bureau of Economic Research New York: Columbia University Press.

—— (1984) *International Comparisons of Productivity and Causes of the Slowdown*, Cambridge, MA: Ballinger.

—— and Grossman, E. (1980) *Productivity in the United States: Trends and Cycles*, Baltimore, MD: Johns Hopkins University Press.

Kenney, Martin (1986) *Biotechnology: The University–Industrial Complex*, New Haven, CT: Yale University Press.

Kepel, G. (ed.) (1993) *Les Politiques de Dieu*, Paris: Seuil.

Khoury, Sarkis and Ghosh, Alo (1987) *Recent Developments in International Banking and Finance*, Lexington, MA: D.C. Heath.

Kiesler, Sara (ed.) (1997) *The Culture of the Internet*, Hillsdale, NJ: Erlbaum.

Kim, E.M. (1989) "From domination to symbiosis: state and chaebol in Korea", *Pacific Focus*, 2: 105–21.

Kim, Jong-Cheol (1998) "Asian financial crisis and the state", unpublished MA thesis, Berkeley, CA: University of California, Department of Sociology.

Kim, Kyong-Dong (ed.) (1987) *Dependency Issues in Korean Development*, Seoul: Seoul National University Press.

Kimsey, Stephen (1994) "The virtual flight of the cyber-trader", *Euromoney*, June: 45–6.

Kincaid, A. Douglas and Portes, Alejandro (eds) (1994) *Comparative National Development: Society and Economy in the New Global Order*, Chapel Hill, NC: University of North Carolina Press.

Kindleberger, Charles (1964) *Economic Growth in France and Britain, 1851–1950*, Cambridge, MA: Harvard University Press.

King, Alexander (1991) *The First Global Revolution: a Report by the Council of the Club of Rome*, New York: Pantheon Books.

Kirsch, Guy, Nijkamp, Peter and Zimmermann, Klaus (eds) (1988) *The Formulation of Time Preferences in a Multidisciplinary Perspective*, Aldershot, Hants: Gower.

Klam, Matthew (1999) "The solitary obsessions of a day trader", *New York Times Sunday Magazine*, November 21: 72–92.

Koike, Kazuo (1988) *Understanding Industrial Relations in Modern Japan*, London: Macmillan.

Kolata, Gina (1995) "Metabolism found to adjust for a body's natural weight", *The New York Times*, March 9: A1–A11.

Kolb, David (1990) *Postmodern Sophistications: Philosophy, Architecture and Tradition*, Chicago, IL: University of Chicago Press.

Koo, H. and Kim, E.M. (1992) "The developmental state and capital accumulation in South Korea", in Richard P. Appelbaum and Jeffrey Henderson (eds), *States and Development in the Asian Pacific Rim*, London: Sage, pp. 121–49.

Korte, W.B., Robinson, S. and Steinle, W.K. (eds) (1988) *Telework: Present Situation and Future Development of a New Form of Work Organization*, Amsterdam: North-Holland.

Kotter, John P. and Heskett, James L. (1992) *Corporate Culture and Performance*, New York: Free Press.

Kranzberg, M. (1985) "The information age: evolution or revolution?", in Bruce R. Guile (ed.), *Information Technologies and Social Transformation*, Washington, DC: National Academy of Engineering.

—— (1992) "The scientific and technological age", *Bulletin of Science and Technology Society*, 12: 63–5.

—— and Pursell, Carroll W. Jr (eds) (1967) *Technology in Western Civilization*, 2 vols, New York: Oxford University Press.

Kraut, R.E. (1989) "Tele-commuting: the trade-offs of home-work", *Journal of Communications*, 39: 19–47.

Kraut, Robert, Patterson, Michael, Lundmark, Vicki, Kiesler, Sara, Mukopadhyay, Tridas, and Scherlis, William (1998) "Internet paradox: a social technology that reduces social involvement and psychological well-being?", *American Psychologist*, September: 1017–31.

Kristoff, Nicholas (1999) "World ills are obvious, the cures much less so", *The New York Times*, February 18: 1 and 14–15.

—— and Sanger, David E. (1999) "How US wooed Asia to let cash flow in", *The New York Times*, February 16: 1 and 10–11.

—— and WuDunn, Sheryl (1999) "Of world markets, none an island", *The New York Times*, February 17: 1 and 8–9.

—— and Wyatt, Edward (1999) "Who went under in the world's sea of cash", *The New York Times*, February 15: 1 and 10–11.

Krugman, Paul (1990) *The Age of Diminished Expectations*, Cambridge, MA: MIT Press.

—— (1994a) *Peddling Prosperity: Economic Sense and Nonsense in the Age of Diminished Expectations*, New York: W.W. Norton.

—— (1994b) "Competitiveness: a dangerous obsession", *Foreign Affairs*, 73(2): 28–44.

—— (1995) "Growing world trade: causes and consequences", *Brookings Papers on Economic Activity*: 327–62.

—— and Lawrence, Robert Z. (1994) "Trade, jobs and wages", *Scientific American*, April: 44–9.

Kuhn, Thomas (1962) *The Structure of Scientific Revolutions*, Chicago, IL: University of Chicago Press.

Kumazawa, M. and Yamada, J. (1989) "Jobs and skills under the lifelong Nenko employment practice", in Stephen Wood (ed.), *The Transformation of Work?: Skill, Flexibility and the Labour Process*, London: Unwin Hyman.

Kunstler, James Howard (1993) *The Geography of Nowhere: the Rise and Decline of America's Man Made Landscape*, New York: Simon and Schuster.

Kuo, Shirley W.Y. (1983) *The Taiwan Economy in Transition*, Boulder, CO: Westview Press.

Kutscher, R.E. (1991) "Outlook 1990–2005: new BLS projections: findings and implications", *Monthly Labor Review*, November: 3–12.

Kuttner, Robert (1983) "The declining middle", *Atlantic Monthly*, July: 60–72.

Kuwahara, Yasuo (1989) *Japanese Industrial Relations System: a New Interpretation*, Tokyo: Japan Institute of Labour.

Kwok, R. and So, Alvin (eds) (1995) *The Hong Kong–Guandong Link: Part-nership in Flux*, Armonk, NY: M.E. Sharpe.

——, Yin-Wang and So, Alvin (1992) *Hong Kong–Guandong Interaction: Joint Enterprise of Market Capitalism and State Socialism*, Manoa: University of Hawaii, research paper.

Landau, Ralph and Rosenberg, Nathan (eds) (1986) *The Positive Sum Strategy: Harnessing Technology for Economic Growth*, Washington, DC: National Academy Press.

Landes, David (1969) *The Unbound Prometheus: Technical Change and Industrial Development in Western Europe from 1750 to the Present*, London: Cambridge University Press.

Lanham, Richard A. (1993) *The Electronic Ward*, Chicago, IL: University of Chicago Press.

Laserna, Roberto (1995) "Regional development and coca production in Cochabamba, Bolivia", unpublished PhD dissertation, Berkeley, CA: University of California.

—— (1996) *El circuito coca-cocaine y sus implicaciones*, La Paz: ILDIS.

Lash, Scott (1990) *Sociology of Postmodernism*, London: Routledge.

—— and Urry, John (1994) *Economies of Signs and Space*, London: Sage.

Lawrence, Robert Z. (1984) "The employment effects of information technologies: an optimistic view", paper delivered at the OECD Conference on the Social Challenge of Information Technologies, Berlin, November: 28–30.

Leal, Jesus (1993) *La desigualdad social en España*, 10 vols, Madrid: Universidad Autonóma de Madrid, Instituto de Sociologia de Nuevas Tecnologias, Research Monograph.

Leclerc, Annie (1975) *Parole de femme*, Paris: Grasset.

Lee, Peter and Townsend, Peter (1993) *Trends in Deprivation in the London Labour Market: a Study of Low Incomes and Unemployment in London between 1985 and 1992*, Geneva: International Institute of Labour Studies, discussion paper 59/1993.

——, King, Paul, Shirref, David and Dyer, Geof (1994) "All change", *Euromoney*, June: 89–101.

Lee, Roger and Schmidt-Marwede, Ulrich (1993) "Interurban competition? Financial centres and the geography of financial production", *International Journal of Urban and Regional Research*, 17(4): 492–515.

Lehman, Yves (1994) "Videotex: a Japanese lesson", *Telecommunications*, 28(7): 53–4.

Lenoir, Daniel (1994) *L'Europe sociale*, Paris: La Découverte.

Leo, P.Y. and Philippe, J. (1989) "Réseaux et services aux entreprises: marchés locaux et développement global", papers of Seminar 32, 1989–II, CEP, pp. 79–103.

Leontieff, Wassily and Duchin, Faye (1985) *The Future Impact of Automation on Workers*, New York: Oxford University Press.

Lethbridge, Henry J. (1978) *Hong Kong: Stability and Change*, Hong Kong: Oxford University Press.

Leung, Chi Kin (1993) "Personal contacts, subcontracting linkages, and development in the Hong Kong–Zhujiang Delta Region", *Annals of the Association of American Geographers*, 83(2): 272–302.

Levy, Pierre (1994) *L'Intelligence collective: pour une anthropologie du cyberspace*, Paris: La Découverte.

Levy, R.A., Bowes, M. and Jondrow, J.M. (1984) "Technical advance and other sources of employment change in basic industry", in E.L. Collins and L.D. Tanner (eds), *American Jobs and the Changing Industrial Base*, Cambridge, MA: Ballinger, pp. 77–95.

Levy, Stephen (1984) *Hackers: Heroes of the Computer Revolution*, Garden City, NY: Doubleday.

Lewis, Michael (2000) *The New New Thing: a Silicon Valley Story*, New York: W. W. Norton.

Lichtenberg, Judith (ed.) (1990) *Democracy and Mass Media*, New York: Cambridge University Press.

Lillyman, William, Moriarty, Marilyn F. and Neuman, David J. (eds) (1994) *Critical Architecture and Contemporary Culture*, New York: Oxford University Press.

Lim, Hyun-Chin (1982) *Dependent Development in Korea (1963–79)*, Seoul: Seoul National University Press.

Lin, T.B., Mok, V. and Ho, Y.P. (1980) *Manufactured Exports and Employment in Hong Kong*, Hong Kong: Chinese University Press.

Lincoln, Edward J. (1990) *Japan's Unequal Trade*, Washington, DC: Brookings Institution.

Lincoln, Thomas L. and Essin, Daniel J. (1993) "The electronic medical record: a challenge for computer science to develop clinically and socially relevant computer systems to coordinate information for patient care and analysis", *Information Society*, 9: 157–88.

——, —— and Ware, Willis H. (1993) "The electronic medical record", *Information Society*, 9(2): 157–88.

Ling, K.K. (1995) "A case for regional planning: the Greater Pearl River Delta: a Hong Kong perspective", unpublished research seminar paper, CP 229, Berkeley, CA: University of California, Department of City and Regional Planning.

Lizzio, James R. (1994) "Real-time RAID storage: the enabling technology for video on demand", *Telephony*, 226(21): 24–32.

Lo, C.P. (1994) "Economic reforms and socialist city structure: a case study of Guangzhou, China", *Urban Geography*, 15(2) 128–49.

Lo, Fu-chen and Yeung, Yue-man (eds) (1996) *Emerging World Cities in the Pacific Asia*, Tokyo: United Nations University Press.

Lorenz, E. (1988) "Neither friends nor strangers: informal networks of subcontracting in French industry", in D. Gambetta, (ed.), *Trust: Making and Breaking Cooperative Relations*, Oxford: Blackwell, pp. 194–210.

Lovins, Amory B. and Lovins, L. Hunter (1995) "Reinventing the wheels", *Atlantic Monthly*, January: 75–86.

Lozano, Beverly (1989) *The Invisible Work Force: Transforming American Business with Outside and Home-based Workers*, New York: Free Press.

Lynch, Kevin (1960) *The Image of the City*, Cambridge, MA: MIT Press.

Lyon, David (1988) *The Information Society: Issues and Illusions*, Cambridge: Polity Press.

—— (1994) *Postmodernity*, Oxford: Blackwell.

Lyon, Jeff and Gorner, Peter (1995) *Altered Fates: Gene Therapy and the Retooling of Human Life*, New York: W.W. Norton.

Machimura, T. (1994) *Sekai Toshi Tokyo no Kozo* [The structural transformation of a global city Tokyo], Tokyo: Tokyo University Press.

—— (1995) *Symbolic Use of Globalization in Urban Politics in Tokyo*, Kunitachi: Hitotsubashi University Faculty of Social Sciences, Research Paper.

McGowan, James (1988) "Lessons learned from the Minitel phenomenon", *Network World*, 5(49): 27.

—— and Compaine, Benjamin (1989) "Is Minitel a good model for the North American market?", *Network World*, 6(36).

McGuire, William J. (1986) "The myth of massive media impact: savagings and salvagings", in George Comstock (ed.), *Public Communication and Behavior*, Orlando, FLA: Academic Press, pp. 173–257.

Machlup, Fritz (1962) *The Production and Distribution of Knowledge in the United States*, Princeton, NJ: Princeton University Press.

—— (1980) *Knowledge: its Creation, Distribution, and Economic Significance*, vol. I: *Knowledge and Knowledge Production*, Princeton, NJ: Princeton University Press.

—— (1982) *Knowledge: its Creation, Distribution and Economic Significance*, vol. II: *The Branches of Learning*, Princeton, NJ: Princeton University Press.

—— (1984) *Knowledge: its Creation, Distribution and Economic Significance*, vol. III, *The Economics of Information and Human Capital*, Princeton, NJ: Princeton University Press.

Mackie, J.A.C. (1992a) "Changing patterns of Chinese big business in Southeast Asia", in Ruth McVey (ed.), *Southeast Asian Capitalists*, Ithaca, NY: Cornell University, Southeast Asian Program.

—— (1992b) "Overseas Chinese entrepreneurship", *Asian Pacific Economic Literature*, 6(1): 41–64.

McKinsey Global Institute (1992) *Service Sector Productivity*, Washington, DC: McKinsey Global Institute.

—— (1993) *Manufacturing Productivity*, Washington, DC: McKinsey Global Institute.

McLeod, Roger (1996) "Internet users abandoning TV, survey finds", *San Francisco Chronicle*, January 12: 1, 17.

McLuhan, Marshall (1962) *The Gutenberg Galaxy: the Making of Typographic Man*, Toronto: University of Toronto Press.

—— (1964) *Understanding Media: the Extensions of Man*, New York: Macmillan.

—— and Powers, Bruce R. (1989) *The Global Village: Transformations in World Life and Media in the 21st Century*, New York: Oxford University Press.

McMillan, C. (1984) *The Japanese Industrial System*, Berlin: De Gruyter.

McNeill, William H. (1977) *Plagues and People*, New York: Doubleday.

Maddison, A. (1982) *Phases of Capitalised Development*, New York: Oxford University Press.

—— (1984) "Comparative analysis of the productivity situation in the advanced capitalist countries", in John W. Kendrick (ed.), *International Comparisons of Productivity and Causes of the Slowdown*, Cambridge, MA: Ballinger.

Maital, Shlomo (1991) "Why the French do it better", *Across the Board*, 28(11): 7–10.

Malinvaud, Edmond et al. (1974) *Fresque historique du système productif français*, Paris: Collections de l'INSEE, Séries E, 27 (October).

Mallet, Serge (1963) *La Nouvelle classe ouvrière*, Paris: Seuil.

Malone, M.S. (1985) *The Big Score: the Billion-dollar Story of Silicon Valley*, Garden City, NY: Doubleday.

Mandel, Michael J. (1999a) "Handling the hot-rod economy", *Business Week*, July 12: 30–2.

—— (1999b) "Meeting the challenge of the new economy", in *Blueprint: Ideas for a New Century*, Winter issue (on-line edition): 1–14.

Mander, Jerry (1978) *Four Arguments for the Elimination of Television*, New York: William Morrow.

Mankiewicz, Frank and Swerdlow, Joel (eds) (1979) *Remote Control: Television and the Manipulation of American Life*, New York: Ballantine.

Mansfield, Edwin (1982) *Technology Transfer, Productivity, and Economic Policy*, Englewood Cliffs, NJ: Prentice-Hall.

Marceau, Jane (ed.) (1992) *Reworking the World: Organisations, Technologies, and Cultures in Comparative Perspective*, Berlin: Walter De Gruyter.

Markoff, John (1995) "If the medium is the message, the message is the Web", *The New York Times*, 20 November: A1, C5.

—— (1999a) "Tiniest circuits hold prospects of explosive computer speeds", *The New York Times*, July 16: A1–C17.

—— (1999b) "A renaissance in computer science: chip designers search for life after silicon", *The New York Times*, July 19: C1–C8.

Marshall, Alfred (1919) *Industry and Trade*, London: Macmillan.

Marshall, J.N. et al. (1988) *Services and Uneven Development*, Oxford: Oxford University Press.

Marshall, Jonathan (1994) "Contracting out catching on: firms find it's more efficient to farm out jobs", *San Francisco Chronicle*, August 22: D2–D3.

Martin, L. John and Chaudhary, Anja Grover (eds) (1983) *Comparative Mass Media Systems*, New York: Longman.

Martin, Patricia (1994) "The consumer market for interactive services: observing past trends and current demographics", *Telephony*, 226(18): 126–30.

Martinotti, Guido (1993) *Metropoli. La Nuova morfologia sociale della citta*, Bologna: Il Mulino.

Marx, Jean L. (ed.) (1989) *A Revolution in Biotechnology*, Cambridge: Cambridge University Press for the International Council of Scientific Unions.

Massey, Douglas R. et al. (1999) *Worlds in Motion: Understanding International Migration at the End of the Millennium*, Oxford: Clarendon Press.

Matsumoto, Miwao and Sinclair, Bruce (1994) "How did Japan adapt itself to scientific and technological revolution at the turn of the 20th Century?", *Japan Journal for Science, Technology, and Society*, 3: 133–55.

Mattelart, Armand and Stourdze, Yves (1982) *Technologie, culture et communication*, Paris: La Documentation française.

Matzner, Egon and Wagner, Michael (eds) (1990) *The Employment Impact of New Technology: the Case of West Germany*, Aldershot, Hants.: Avebury.

Mazlish, Bruce (1993) *The Fourth Discontinuity: the Co-evolution of Humans and Machines*, New Haven, CT: Yale University Press.

Mehta, Suketu (1993) "The French connection", *LAN Magazine*, 8(5).

Menotti, Val (1995) "The transformation of retail social space: an analysis of virtual shopping's impact on retail centers", unpublished research paper for seminar CP298I, University of California, Berkeley, Department of City and Regional Planning.

Michelson, Ronald L. and Wheeler, James O. (1994) "The flow of information in a global economy: the role of the American urban system in 1990", *Annals of the Association of American Geographers*, 84 (1): 87–107.

Miles, Ian (1988) *Home Informatics: Information Technology and the Transformation of Everyday Life*, London: Pinter.

Millan, Jose del Rocio et al. (2000) "Robust EEG-based recognition of mental tasks", *Clinical Neuropsychology* (forthcoming).

Miller, Richard L. and Swensson, Earl S. (1995) *New Directions in Hospital and Health Care Facility Design*, New York: McGraw-Hill.

Miller, Steven, M. (1989) *Impacts of Industrial Robotics: Potential Effects of Labor and Costs within the Metalworking Industries*, Madison, WIS: University of Wisconsin Press.

Miners, N. (1986) *The Government and Politics of Hong Kong*, Hong Kong: Oxford University Press.

Mingione, Enzo (1991) *Fragmented Societies*, Oxford, Blackwell.

Ministry of Labor [Japan] (1991) *Statistical Yearbook*, Tokyo: Government of Japan.

Ministry of Posts and Telecommunications (Japan) (1994) *Communications in Japan 1994*, Part 3: *Multimedia: Opening up a New World of Infocommunication*, Tokyo: Ministry of Posts and Telecommunications.

—— (1995) *Tsushin Hakusho Heisei 7 nenban* [White Paper on Communication in Japan], Tokyo: Yusei shou.

Mishel, Lawrence and Bernstein, Jared (1993) *The State of Working America*, Armonk NY: M.E. Sharpe.

—— and —— (1994) *The State of Working America 1994–95*, Washington, DC: Economic Policy Institute.

—— and Teixeira, Ruy A. (1991) *The Myth of the Coming Labor Shortage: Jobs, Skills, and Incomes of America's Workforce 2000*, Washington, DC: Economic Policy Institute Report.

——, Bernstein, Jared and Schmitt, John (1999) *The State of Working America, 1998–1999*, Ithaca, NY: Cornell University Press.

Mitchell, William J. (1995) *City of Bits: Space, Place and the Infobahn*, Cambridge, MA: MIT Press.

—— (1999) *E-topia: Urban Life, Jim – But Not as We Know It*, Cambridge, MA: MIT Press.

Mokhtarian, Patricia L. (1991a) "Defining telecommuting", *Transportation Research Record*, 1305: 273–81.

—— (1991b) "Telecommuting and travel: state of the practice, state of the art", *Transportation*, 18: 319–42.

—— (1992) "Telecommuting in the United States: letting our fingers do the commuting", *Telecommuting Review: the Gordon Report*, 9(5): 12.

Mokyr, Joel (1990) *The Lever of Riches: Technological Creativity and Economic Progress*, New York: Oxford University Press.

—— (ed.) (1985) *The Economics of the Industrial Revolution*, Totowa, NJ: Rowman and Allanheld.

Mollenkopf, John (ed.) (1989) *Power, Culture, and Place: Essays on New York City*, New York: Russell Sage Foundation.

—— and Castells, Manuel (eds) (1991) *Dual City: Restructuring New York*, New York: Russell Sage Foundation.

Monk, Peter (1989) *Technological Change in the Information Economy*, London: Pinter.

Montgomery, Alesia F. (1999) "New metropolis? online use, work, space and social ties", unpublished masters thesis, Berkeley, CA: University of California.

Moran, R. (1990) "Health environment and healthy environment", in R. Moran, R. Anderson and P. Paoli (eds), *Building for People in Hospitals, Workers, and Consumers*, Dublin: European Foundation for the Improvement of Living and Working Conditions.

—— (1993) *The Electronic Home: Social and Spatial Aspects. A Scoping Report*, Dublin: European Foundation for the Improvement of Living and Working Conditions.

Morier, Françoise (ed.) (1994) *Belleville, Belleville: visages d'un planète*, Paris: Editions Creaphis.

Morin, Edgar (1970) *L'homme et la mort*, Paris: Seuil.

Morrocco, John D. (1991) "Gulf War boosts prospects for high-technology weapons", *Aviation Week and Space Technology*, 134(11): 45–7.

Moss, Mitchell (1987) "Telecommunications, world cities, and urban policy", *Urban Studies*, 24: 534–46.

—— (1991) "The new fibers of economic development", *Portfolio*, 4: 11–18.

—— (1992) "Telecommunications and urban economic development", in OECD, *Cities and New Technologies*, Paris: OECD, pp. 147–58.

Mowery, David (ed.) (1988) *International Collaborative Ventures in US Manufacturing*, Cambridge, MA: Ballinger.

—— and Henderson, Bruce E. (eds) (1989) *The Challenge of New Technology to Labor–Management Relations*, Washington, DC: Dept of Labor, Bureau of Labor Management Relations.

—— and Rosenberg, Nathan (1998) *Paths of Innovation: Technological Change in 20th Century America*, Cambridge: Cambridge University Press.

Mowshowitz, Abbe (1986) "Social dimensions of office automation", in *Advances in Computers*, vol. 25, New York: Academic Press.

Mulgan, G.J. (1991) *Communication and Control: Networks and the New Economies of Communication*, New York: Guilford Press.

Murphy, Kevin M. and Welch, Finis (1993) "Inequality and relative wages", *American Economic Review*, May.

Muschamp, Herbert (1992) "A design that taps into the 'Informational City' ", *Sunday New York Times*, August 9, Architecture View Section: 32.

Mushkat, Miron (1982) *The Making of the Hong Kong Administrative Class*, Hong Kong: University of Hong Kong Centre of Asian Studies.

Myers, Edith (1981) "In France it's Teletel", *Datamation*, 27(10): 78–88.

Nadal, Jordi and Carreras, Albert (eds) (1990) *Pautas regionales de la industrializacion española. Siglos XIX y XX*, Barcelona: Ariel.

National Science Board (1991) *Science and Engineering Indicators, 1991*, 10th edn (NSB 91–1), Washington, DC: US Government Printing Office.

Naughton, John (1999) *A Brief History of the Future: The Origins of the Internet*, London: Weidenfeld and Nicolson.

Navarro, Vicente (1994a) *The Politics of Health Policy*, Oxford: Blackwell.

—— (1994b) "La economia y el Estado de bienestar", unpublished paper presented at the 10th Meeting on the Future of the Welfare State, Madrid.

Needham, Joseph (1954–88) *Science and Civilization in China*, Cambridge: Cambridge University Press.

—— (1969) *The Grand Titration*, Toronto: Toronto University Press.

—— (1981) *Science in Traditional China*, Cambridge, MA: Harvard University Press.

Negroponte, Nicholas (1995) *Being Digital*, New York: Alfred A. Knopf.

Nelson, Richard (1980) "Production sets, technological knowledge, and R&D: fragile and overworked constructs for analysis of productivity growth?", *American Economic Review*, 70(2): 62–7.

—— (1981) "Research on productivity growth and productivity differences: dead ends and new departures", *Journal of Economic Literature*, 19(3): 1029–64.

—— (1984) *High Technology Policies: A Five Nations Comparison*, Washington, DC: American Enterprise Institute.

—— (1988) "Institutions supporting technical change in the United States", in G. Dosi et al. (eds), *Technical Change and Economic Theory*, London: Pinter, pp. 312–29.

—— (1994) "An agenda for formal growth theory", New York: Columbia University Department of Economics, unpublished paper (communicated by the author).

—— and Winter, S.G. (1982) *An Evolutionary Theory of Economic Change*, Cambridge, MA: Harvard University Press.

Neuman, W. Russell (1991) *The Future of Mass Audience*, New York: Cambridge University Press.

New Media Markets (1993) "Video on demand will provide Hollywood studios with much-needed boost", 11(10): 13–15.

—— (1994) "Video-on-demand trials planned across Europe", 12(1): 8.

Newsweek (1993) "Jobs", special issue, June 14.

Nicol, Lionel (1985) "Communications technology: economic and social impacts", in Manuel Castells (ed.), *High Technology, Space and Society*, Beverly Hills, CA: Sage.

NIKKEIREN [Japan Federation of Employers Associations] (1993) *The Current Labor Economy in Japan*, Tokyo: NIKKEIREN, Information Report.

Nilles, J.M. (1988) "Traffic reduction by telecommuting: a status review and selected bibliography", *Transportation Research A*, 22A(4): 301–17.

Noble, David F. (1984) *Forces of Production: a Social History of Industrial Automation*, New York: Alfred A. Knopf.

Nolan, Peter and Furen, Dong (eds) (1990) *The Chinese Economy and its Future: Achievements and Problems of Post-Mao Reform*, Cambridge: Polity Press.

Nomura, Masami (1994) *Syushin Koyo*, Tokyo: Iwanami Shoten.

Nonaka, Ikujiro (1990) *Chisiki souzou no keiei* [Knowledge creation: epistemology of the Japanese firms], Tokyo: Nikkei shinbunsha.

—— (1991) "The knowledge-creating company", *Harvard Business Review*, November–December: 96–104.

—— (1994) "A dynamic theory of organizational knowledge creation", *Organization Science*, 5(1): 14–37.

—— and Takeuchi, Hirotaka (1994) *The Knowledge-creating Company: How Japanese Companies Created the Dynamics of Innovation*, New York: Oxford University Press.

Nora, Simon and Minc, Alain (1978) *L'Informatisation de la société*. Paris: La Documentation française.

Norman, Alfred Lorn (1993) *Informational Society: an Economic Theory of Discovery, Invention and Innovation*, Boston/Dordrecht/London: Kluwer Academic Publishers.

Norman, E. Herbert (1940) *Japan's Emergence as a Modern State: Political and Economic Problems of the Meiji Period*, New York: Institute of Pacific Relations.

North, Douglas (1981) *Structure and Change in Economic History*, New York: W.W. Norton.

Northcott, J. (1986) *Microelectronics in Industry*, London: Policy Studies Institute.

Nuland, Sherwin B. (1994) *How We Die: Reflections on Life's Final Chapter*, New York: Alfred A. Knopf.

O'Brien, Richard (1992) *Global Financial Integration: the End of Geography*, London: Pinter.

OECD (1994a) *Employment Outlook*, July, Paris: OECD.

—— (1994b) *Employment/Unemployment Study: Policy Report*, Paris: OECD.

—— (1994c) *The OECD Jobs Study*, Paris: OECD.

—— (1994d) *The Performance of Foreign Affiliates in OECD Countries*, Paris: OECD.

—— (1995) *Economic Outlook*, June, Paris: OECD.

—— (1997) *Second European Report on Scientific and Technological Indicators*, Paris: OECD.

Office of Technology Assessment (OTA) (US Congress) (1984) *Computer-*

ized Manufacturing Automation: Employment, Education, and the Workplace, Washington, DC: US Government Printing Office.

—— (1986) *Technology and Structural Unemployment*, Washington, DC: US Government Printing Office.

Ohmae, Kenichi (1990) *The Borderless World: Power and Strategy in the Interlinked Economy*, New York: Harper.

Osterman, Paul (1999) *Securing Prosperity. The American Labor Market: How it has Changed and What to do About it*, Princeton, NJ: Princeton University Press.

Owen, Bruce M. (1999) *The Internet Challenge to Television*, Cambridge, MA: Harvard University Press.

Ozaki, Muneto et al. (1992) *Technological Change and Labour Relations*, Geneva: International Labour Organization.

Pahl, Ray (ed.) (1988) *On Work: Historical, Comparative, and Theoretical Approaches*, Oxford: Blackwell.

Panofsky, Erwin (1957) *Gothic Architecture and Scholasticism*, New York: Meridian Books.

Park, Young-bum (1992) *Wage-fixing Institutions in the Republic of Korea*, Geneva: International Institute of Labour Studies, discussion paper 51/1992.

Parkinson, G.H.R. (ed.) (1973) *Leibniz: Philosophical Writings*, London: J.M. Dent.

Parsons, Carol A. (1987) "Flexible production technology and industrial restructuring: case studies of the metalworking, semiconductor, and apparel industries, unpublished PhD dissertation, Berkeley, CA: University of California.

Patel, S.J. (1992) "In tribute to the Golden Age of the South's development", *World Development*, 20(5): 767–77.

Perez, Carlotta (1983) "Structural change and the assimilation of new technologies in the economic and social systems", *Futures*, 15: 357–75.

Petrella, Ricardo (1993) *Un techno-monde en construction: synthèse des résultats et des recommendations FAST 1989–1992/93*, Brussels: European Commission: FAST Programme.

Pettersson, L.O. (1989) "Arbetstider i tolv Lander", *Statens offentliga utrednigar*, 53, cited in Bosch et al. (eds) (1994).

Pfeffer, Jeffrey (1998) *The Human Equation: Building Profits by Putting People First*, Cambridge, MA: Harvard Business School Press.

Picciotto, Sol and Mayne, Ruth (eds) (1999) *Regulating International Business: Beyond the MAI*, Oxford: Oxfam.

Piller, Charles (1994) "Dreamnet", *Macworld*, 11(10): 96–9.

Piore, Michael J. and Sabel, Charles F. (1984) *The Second Industrial Divide: Possibilities for Prosperity*, New York: Basic Books.

PNUD (Programa de Naciones Unidas para el Desarrollo) (1998a) *Desarrollo humano en Chile*, Santiago de Chile: Naciones Unidas.

—— (1998b) *Desarrollo humano en Bolivia*, La Paz: Naciones Unidas.

Poirier, Mark (1993) "The multimedia trail blazers", *Catalog Age*, 10(7): 49.

Pool, Ithiel de Sola (1983) *Technologies of Freedom: on Free Speech in the Electronic Age*, Cambridge, MA: Belknap Press of Harvard University Press.

—— (1990) *Technologies Without Boundaries*, ed. Eli M. Noam, Cambridge, MA: Harvard University Press.

Porat, Marc (1977) *The Information Economy: Definition and Measurement*, Washington, DC: US Department of Commerce, Office of Telecommunications, publication 77-12 (1).

Porter, Michael (1990) *The Competitive Advantage of Nations*, New York: Free Press.

Portes, Alejandro, Castells, Manuel and Benton, Lauren (eds) (1989) *The Informal Economy: Studies on Advanced and Less Developed Countries*, Baltimore, MD: Johns Hopkins University Press.

Postman, Neil (1985) *Amusing Ourselves to Death: Public Discourse in the Age of Show Business*, New York: Penguin Books.

—— (1992) *Technopoly*, New York: Pantheon.

Poulantzas, Nicos (1978) *L'Etat, le pouvoir, le socialisme*, Paris: Presses Universitaires de France.

Powell, Walter W. (1990) "Neither market nor hierarchy: network forms of organization", in Barry M. Straw and Larry L. Cummings (eds), *Research in Organizational Behavior*, Greenwich, CT: JAI Press, pp. 295–336.

Preston, Holly H. (1994) "Minitel reigns in Paris with key French connection", *Computer Reseller News*, 594: 49–50.

Putnam, Robert (1995) "Bowling alone: America's declining social capital", *Journal of Democracy*, 6: 65–78.

Pyo, H. (1986) *The Impact of Microelectronics and Indigenous Technological Capacity in the Republic of Korea*, Geneva: International Labour Organization.

Qian, Wen-yuan (1985) *The Great Inertia: Scientific Stagnation in Traditional China*, London: Croom Helm.

Qingguo Jia (1994) "Threat or opportunity? Implications of the growth of the China Circle for the distribution of economic and political power in the Asia Pacific Region", paper delivered at the Conference sponsored by the University of California Institute on Global Conflict and Cooperation, The Economics of the China Circle, Hong Kong, September 1–3.

Quinn, James Brian (1987) "The impacts of technology in the services sector", in Bruce R. Guile and Harvey Brooks (eds), *Technology and Global Industry: Companies and Nations in the World Economy*, Washington, DC: National Academy Press, pp. 119–159.

—— (1988) "Technology in services: past myths and future challenges", in Bruce R. Guile and James B. Quinn (eds), *Technology in Services*, Washington, DC: National Academy Press, pp. 16–46.

Qvortup, Lars (1992) "Telework: visions, definitions, realities, barriers", in OECD, *Cities and New Technologies*, Paris: OECD, pp. 77–108.

Ramamurthy, K. (1994) "Moderating influences of organizational attitude and compatibility on implementation success from computer-integrated manufacturing technology", *International Journal of Production Research*, 32(10): 2251–73.

Rand Corporation (1995) *Universal Access to E-Mail: Feasibility and Social*

Implications, world wide web, (ttp://www.rand.org/publications/MR/
MR650/).

Randlesome, Collin, Brierly, William, Bruton, Kevin, Gordon, Colin and King,
Peter (1990) *Business Cultures in Europe*, Oxford: Heinemann.

Redding, S. Gordon (1990) *The Spirit of Chinese Capitalism*, Berlin: Walter
de Gruyter.

Rees, Teresa (1992) *Skill Shortages, Women, and the New Information Technologies*, Report of the Task Force of Human Resources, Education, Training, and Youth, Brussels: Commission of the European Communities,
January.

Reich, Robert (1991) *The Work of Nations*, New York: Random House.

Reid, Robert H. (1997) *Architects of the Web*, New York: John Wiley.

Reynolds, Larry (1992) "Fast money: global markets change the investment
game", *Management Review*, 81(2): 60–1.

Rheingold, Howard (1993) *The Virtual Community*, Reading, MA: Addison-
Wesley.

Rice, Ronald E. "Issues and concepts on research on computer-mediated communication systems", *Communication Yearbook*, 12: 436–76.

Rifkin, Jeremy (1987) *Time Wars: The Primary Conflict in Human History*,
New York: Henry Holt.

—— (1995) *The End of Work*, New York: Putnam.

Rijn, F.V. and Williams, R. (eds) (1988) *Concerning Home Telematics*, Amsterdam: North-Holland.

Roberts, Edward B. (1991) *Entrepreneurs in High Technology: MIT and Beyond*, New York: Oxford University Press.

Robinson, Olive (1993) "Employment in services: perspectives on part-time
employment growth in North America", *Service Industries Journal*, 13(3):
1–18.

Robson, B. (1992) "Competing and collaborating through urban networks",
Town and Country Planning, September: 236–8.

Rodgers, Gerry (ed.) (1994) *Workers, Institutions, and Economic Growth in
Asia*, Geneva: International Institute of Labour Studies.

Rogers, Everett M. (1986) *Communication Technology: the New Media in
Society*, New York: Free Press.

—— and Larsen, Judith K. (1984) *Silicon Valley Fever: Growth of High Technology Culture*, New York: Basic Books.

Rohozinski, Rafal (1998) "Mapping Russian cyberspace: a perspective on
democracy and the Net", paper delivered at the United Nations Research
Institute on Social Development Conference on Globalization and Inequality, Geneva, June 22.

Rosen, Ken et al. (1999) "The multimedia industry in San Francisco's South
of Market area", Berkeley, University of California, Haas School of Business, Centre for Real Estate Economics, research report.

Rosenbaum, Andrew (1992) "France's Minitel has finally grown up", *Electronics*, 65(6).

Rosenberg, Nathan (1976) *Perspectives on Technology*, Cambridge: Cambridge University Press.

—— (1982) *Inside the Black Box: Technology and Economics*, Cambridge: Cambridge University Press.

—— and Birdzell, L.E. (1986) *How the West Grew Rich: the Economic Transformation of the Industrial World*, New York: Basic Books.

Rostow, W.W. (1975) *How It All Began*, New York: McGraw Hill.

Roszak, Theodore (1986) *The Cult of Information*, New York: Pantheon.

Rothstein, Richard (1993) *Workforce Globalization: a Policy Response*, Washington, DC: Economic Policy Institute, Report prepared for the Women's Bureau of the US Department of Labor.

—— (1994) "The global hiring hall: why we need worldwide labor standards", *American Prospect*, 17: 54–61.

Rumberger, R.W. and Levin, H.M. (1984) *Forecasting the Impact of New Technologies on the Future Job Market*, Stanford, CA: Stanford University School of Education, Research Report.

Russell, Alan M. (1988) *The Biotechnology Revolution: an International Perspective*, Brighton, Sussex: Wheatsheaf Books.

Sabbah, Françoise (1985) "The new media", In Manuel Castells (ed.), *High Technology, Space, and Society*, Beverly Hills, CA: Sage.

Sabel, C. and Zeitlin, J. (1985) "Historical alternatives to mass production: politics, markets, and technology in 19th century industrialization", *Past and Present*, 108 (August): 133–76.

Sachs, Jeffrey (1998a) "International economics: unlocking the mysteries of globalization", *Foreign Policy*, spring: 97–111.

—— (1998b) "Proposals for reform of the global financial architecture", paper prepared for the United Nations Development Programme meeting on the reform of global financial architecture, New York, December 8.

—— (1998c) "The IMF and the Asian flu", *The American Prospect*, March–April: 16–21.

—— (1999) "Helping the world's poorest", *The Economist*, August 14: 17–20.

Saez, Felipe et al. (1991) *Tecnologia y empleo en España: situación y perspectivas*, Madrid: Universidad Autónoma de Madrid–Instituto de Sociologia de Nuevas Tecnologias y Ministerio de Economia–Instituto de Estudios de Prospectiva.

Salomon, Jean-Jacques (1992) *Le Destin technologique*, Paris: Editions Balland.

Salvaggio, Jerry L. (ed.) (1989) *The Information Society: Economic, Social, and Structural Issues*, Hillsdale, NJ: Lawrence Erlbaum.

Sandholtz, Wayne et al. (1992) *The Highest Stakes: the Economic Foundations of the Next Security System*, New York: Oxford University Press (a BRIE Project).

Sandkull, Bengdt (1992) "Reorganizing labour: the Volvo experience", in Jane Marceau (ed.), *Reworking the World: Organisations, Technologies, and Cultures in Comparative Perspective*, Berlin: Walter de Gruyter, pp. 399–409.

Sapolsky, Robert (2000) "It's not 'all in the genes'" *Newsweek*, April 10: 68.

Sassen, Saskia (1991) *The Global City: New York, London, Tokyo*, Princeton, NJ: Princeton University Press.

Sato, Takeshi et al. (1995) *Johoza to taisyu bunka* [Informationalization and mass culture], Kunitachi: Hitotsubashi University Department of Social Psychology, Research Report.

Saunders, William (ed.) (1996) *Architectural Practices in the 1990s*, Princeton, NJ: Princeton University Press.

Saussois, Jean-Michel (1998) "Knowledge production, mediation and use in learning economies and societies", report prepared for OECD–CERI meeting, Centre for Educational Research and Innovation, Stanford University, September 10–11.

Sautter, Christian (1978) "L'efficacité et la rentabilité de l'économie française de 1954 à 1976", *Economie et statistique*, 68.

Saxby, Stephen (1990) *The Age of Information*, London: Macmillan.

Saxenian, Anna L. (1994) *Regional Advantage: Culture and Competition in Silicon Valley and Route 128*, Cambridge, MA: Harvard University Press.

—— (1999) *Silicon Valley's New Immigrant Entrepreneurs*, San Francisco: Public Policy Institute of California.

Sayer, Andrew and Walker, Richard (1992) *The New Social Economy: Reworking the Division of Labor*, Oxford: Blackwell.

Schaff, Adam (1992) *El Socialismo del Futuro*, no. 4: Special Issue on the Future of Labor.

Scheer, Leo (1994) *La Démocratie virtuelle*, Paris: Flammarion.

Schettkat, R. and Wagner, M. (eds) (1990) *Technological Change and Employment Innovation in the German Economy*, Berlin: Walter De Gruyter.

Schiatarella, R. (1984) *Mercato di Lavoro e struttura produttiva*, Milan: Franco Angeli.

Schiffer, Jonathan (1983) *Anatomy of a Laissez-faire Government: the Hong Kong Growth Model Reconsidered*, Hong Kong: University of Hong Kong Centre for Asian Studies.

Schiller, Dan (1999) *Digital Capitalism: Networking in the Global Market System*, Cambridge, MA: MIT Press.

Schoettle, Enid C.B. and Grant, Kate (1998) *Globalisation: A Discussion Paper*, New York: The Rockefeller Foundation.

Schofield Clark, Nancy (1998) "Dating on the net: teens and the rise of "pure relationships", in Jones (1998): 159–83.

Schon, Don, Sanyal, Bishmal, and Mitchell, William J. (eds) (1998) *High Technology and Low Income Communities*, Cambridge, MA: MIT Press.

Schoonmaker, Sara (1993) "Trading on-line: information flows in advanced capitalism", *Information Society*, 9(1): 39–49.

Schor, Juliet (1991) *The Overworked American*, New York: Basic Books.

Schuldt, K. (1990) "Soziale und ökonomische Gestaltung der Elemente der Lebensarbeitzeit der Werktätigen", unpublished dissertation, Berlin; cited in Bosch et al. (1994).

Schuler, Douglas (1996) *New Community Networks: Wired for Change*, New York: ACM Press.

Schumpeter, J.A. (1939) *Business Cycles: a Theoretical, Historical, and Statistical Analysis of the Capitalist Process*, New York: McGraw-Hill.

Schweitzer, John C. (1995) "Personal computers and media use", *Journalism*

Quarterly, 68(4): 689–97.

Schwitzer, Glenn E. (1995) "Can research and development recover in Russia?", *Business World of Russia Weekly*, May 15–20: 10–12; reprinted from *Journal of Technology and Society*, 17(2).

Scott, Allen (1988) *New Industrial Spaces*, London: Pion.

—— (1998) *Regions in the World Economy*, Oxford: Oxford University Press.

Seidman, Steven and Wagner, David G. (eds) (1992) *Postmodernism and Social Theory*, Oxford: Blackwell.

Seki, Kiyohide (1988) *Summary of the National Opinion Survey of Family in Japan*, Tokyo: Nihon University Research Center, Research Paper.

Sellers, Patricia (1993) "The best way to reach buyers", *Fortune*, 128(13): 14–17.

Sengenberger, Werner and Campbell, Duncan (eds) (1992) *Is the Single Firm Vanishing? Inter-enterprise Networks, Labour, and Labour Institutions*, Geneva: International Institute of Labour Studies.

—— and —— (eds) (1994) *International Labour Standards and Economic Interdependence*, Geneva: International Institute of Labour Studies.

——, Loveman, Gary and Piore, Michael (eds) (1990) *The Re-emergence of Small Enterprises: Industrial Restructuring in Industrialized Countries*, Geneva: International Institute for Labour Studies.

Servon, Lisa and Horrigan, John B. (1998) "Urban poverty and access to information technology: a role for local government", *Journal of Urban Technology*, 4(3): 61–81.

Shaiken, Harley (1985) *Work Transformed: Automation and Labor in the Computer Age*, New York: Holt, Rinehart and Winston.

—— (1990) *Mexico in the Global Economy: High Technology and Work Organization in Export Industries*, La Jolla, CA: University of California at San Diego, Center for US–Mexican Studies.

—— (1993) "Beyond lean production", *Stanford Law and Policy Review*, 5(1): 41–52.

—— (1995) "Experienced workers and high performance work organization: a case study of two automobile assembly plants", unpublished paper presented at the Industrial Relations Research Association Annual Meeting, Washington, DC, January 6.

Shapira, Phillip (1990) *Modernizing Manufacturing*, Washington, DC: Economic Policy Institute.

Shapiro, Carl and Varian, Hal (1999) *Information Rules: A Strategic Guide to the Network Economy*, Cambridge, MA: Harvard Business School Press.

Sharlin, Harold I. (1967) "Electrical generation and transmission", in Melvin Kranzberg and Carroll W. Pursell Jr (eds), *Technology in Western Civilization*, 2 vols, New York: Oxford University Press, vol. 2, pp. 578–91.

Shin, E.H. and Chin S.W. (1989) "Social affinity among top managerial executives of large corporations in Korea", *Sociological Forum*, 4: 3–26.

Shinotsuka, Eiko (1994) "Women workers in Japan: past, present, and future", in Joyce Gelb and Marian Lief Palley (eds), *Women of Japan and Korea: Continuity and Change*, Philadelphia, PA: Temple University Press, pp. 95–119.

Shirref, David (1994) "The metamorphosis of finance", *Euromoney*, June: 36–42.

Shoji, Kokichi (1990) *Le Nipponisme comme méthode sociologique. Originalité, particularité, universalité*, Tokyo: Tokyo University Department of Sociology, discussion paper.

Shujiro Urata (1993) "Changing patterns of direct investment and its implications for trade and development", in C. Fred Bergsten and Marcus Noland (eds), *Pacific Dynamism and the International Economic System*, Washington, DC: Institute for International Economics, pp. 273–99.

Siddell, Scott (1987) *The IMF and Third World Political Instability*, London: Macmillan.

Siino, Corinne (1994) "La ville et le chomage", *Revue d'économie régionale et urbaine*, 3: 324–52.

Silverstone, R. (1991) *Beneath the Bottom Line: Households and Information and Communication Technologies in the Age of the Consumer*, London: Brunel University Center for Research on Innovation, Culture, and Technology.

Silvestri, George T. (1993) "The American work force, 1992–2005: occupational employment, wide variations in growth", *Monthly Labor Review*, November: 58–86.

—— and Lukasiewicz, J. (1991) "Outlook 1990–2005: occupational employment projections", *Monthly Labor Review*, November.

Singelmann, Joachim (1978) *The Transformation of Industry: from Agriculture to Service Employment*, Beverly Hills, CA: Sage.

Singer, Charles et al. (1957) *A History of Technology*, vol. 3: *From the Renaissance to the Industrial Revolution*, Oxford: Clarendon Press.

——, Holmyard, E.J., Hall, A.R. and Williams, Trevor I. (eds) (1958) *A History of Technology*, vol. 4: *The Industrial Revolution, c.1750 to c.1850*, Oxford: Clarendon Press.

Singh, Ajit (1994) "Global economic changes, skills, and international competitiveness", *International Labour Review*, 133(2): 107–83.

Sit, Victor Fueng-Shuen (1991) "Transnational capital flows and urbanization in the Pearl River Delta, China", *Southeast Asian Journal of Social Science*, 19(1–2): 154–79.

—— and Wong, S.L. (1988) *Changes in the Industrial Structure and the Role of Small and Medium Industries in Asian Countries: the Case of Hong Kong*, Hong Kong: University of Hong Kong Centre of Asian Studies.

——, Wong, Sin Lun and Kiang, Tsiu-Sing (1979) *Small-scale Industry in a Laissez-faire Economy: a Hong Kong Case Study*, Hong Kong: University of Hong Kong, Centre of Asian Studies.

Slouka, Mark (1995) *War of the Worlds: Cyberspace and the High-tech Assault on Reality*, New York: Basic Books.

Smith, Merrit Roe and Marx, Leo (eds) (1994) *Does Technology Drive History? The Dilemma of Technological Determinism*, Cambridge, MA: MIT Press.

Smith, Michael P. and Guarnizo, Luis E. (eds) (1998) *Transnationalism from Below*, New Brunswick, NJ: Transaction Books.

Solow, Robert M. (1956) "A contribution to the theory of economic growth", *Quarterly Journal of Economics*, 70: 65–94.

—— (1957) "Technical change and the aggregate production function", *Revue of Economics and Statistics*, 39: 214–31.

Sorlin, Pierre (1994) *Mass Media*, London: Routledge.

Sorokin, P.A. and Merton, R.K. (1937) "Social time: a methodological and functional analysis", *American Journal of Sociology*, 42: 615–29.

Soros, George (1998) *The Crisis of Global Capitalism: Open Society Endangered*, New York: Perseus.

Southern, R.W. (1995) *Scholastic Humanism and the Unification of Europe*, vol. 1: *Foundations*, Oxford: Blackwell.

Soysal, Yasemin Nuhoglu (1994) *Limits of citizenship: Migrants and Postnational Membership in Europe*, Chicago, IL: University of Chicago Press.

Specter, Michael (1994) "Russians' newest space adventure: cyberspace", *The New York Times*, March 9: C1–C2.

Sproull, Lee and Kiesler, Sara (1991) *Connections: New Ways of Working in the Networked Organization*, Cambridge, MA: MIT Press.

Stalker, Peter (1994) *The Work of Strangers: a Survey of International Labour Migration*, Geneva: International Labour Organization.

—— (1997) *Global Nations: The Impact of Globalization on International Migration*, Geneva: International Labour Office, Employment and Training Department.

Stanback, T.M. (1979) *Understanding the Service Economy: Employment, Productivity, Location*, Baltimore, MD: Johns Hopkins University Press.

Steers, R.M., Shin, Y.K. and Ungson, G.R. (1989) *The Chaebol*, New York: Harper and Row.

Steinle, W.J. (1988) "Telework: opening remarks and opening debate", in W.B. Korte, S. Robinson and W.K. Steinle (eds), *Telework: Present Situation and Future Development of a New Form of Work Organization*, Amsterdam: North-Holland.

Stevens, Barrie and Michalski, Wolfgang (1994) *Long-term Prospects for Work and Social Cohesion in OECD Countries: an Overview of the Issues*, Paris: Report to the OECD Forum for the Future.

Stevenson, Richard W. (1999) "Greenspan calls recent rate of US growth unsustainable", *The New York Times*, October 29: C6.

Stonier, Tom (1983) *The Wealth of Information*, London: Methuen.

Stourdze, Yves (1987) *Pour une poignée d'électrons*, Paris: Fayard.

Stowsky, Jay (1992) "From spin-off to spin-on: redefining the military's role in American technology development", in Wayne Sandholtz, Michael Borrus and John Zysman et al., *The Highest Stakes: The Economic Foundations of the Next Security System*, New York: Oxford University Press.

Strange, S. (1996) *The Retreat of the State: The Diffusion of Power in the World Economy*, Cambridge: Cambridge University Press.

Strassman, Paul A. (1985) *Information Payoff: The Transformation of Work in the Electronic Age*, New York: Free Press.

Sullivan-Trainor, Michael (1994) *Detour: The Truth about the Information SuperHighway*, San Mateo, CA: IDG Books.

Sun Tzu (*c.* 505–496BC) *On the Art of War*, trans. from Chinese with critical notes by Lionel Giles, Singapore: Graham Brash, 1988 (first published in English in 1910).

Swann, J. (1986) *The Employment Effects of Microelectronics in the UK Service Sector*, Geneva: International Labour Organization.

Syun, Inoue (1975) The loss of meaning in death. *Japan Interpreter*, 9(3): 336.

Tafuri, Manfredo (1971) *L'urbanistica del riformismo*, Milan: Franco Angeli.

Takenori, Inoki and Higuchi, Yoshio (eds) (1995) *Nihon no Koyou system to lodo shijo* [Japanese employment system and labour market], Tokyo: Nihon Keizai Shinbunsha.

Tan, Augustine H.H. and Kapur, Basant (eds) (1986) *Pacific Growth and Financial Interdependence*, Sydney: Allen & Unwin.

Tapscott, Don (ed.) (1998) *Blueprint to the Digital Economy: Wealth Creation in the Era of E-business*, New York: McGraw-Hill.

Tardanico, Richard and Rosenberg, Mark B. (eds) (2000) *Poverty of Development: Global Restructuring and Regional Transformations in the US South and the Mexican South*, New York: Routledge.

Tarr, J. and Dupuy, G. (eds) (1988) *Technology and the Rise of the Networked City in Europe and North America*, Philadelphia, PA: Temple University Press.

Teitelman, Robert (1989) *Gene Dreams: Wall Street, Academia, and the Rise of Biotechnology*, New York: Basic Books.

Teitz, Michael B., Glasmeier, Amy and Shapira, Philip (1981) *Small Business and Employment Growth in California*, Berkeley, CA: Institute of Urban and Regional Development, working paper no. 348.

Telecommunications Council (Japan) (1994) *Reforms Toward the Intellectually Creative Society of the 21st Century: Program for the Establishment of High-performance Info-communications Infrastructure*, report–response to inquiry no. 5, 1993, Tokyo: May 31 (unofficial translation, July 1994).

Tetsuro, Kato and Steven, Rob (eds) (1994) *Is Japanese Management Post-Fordism?*, Tokyo: Mado-sha.

Thach, Liz and Woodman, Richard W. (1994) "Organizational change and information technology: managing on the edge of cyberspace", *Organizational Dynamics*, 1: 30–46.

The Economist, (1993) 7 July 27.

—— (1994a) "Feeling for the future: survey of television", February 12: special report.

—— (1994b) "Sale of the century", May 14: 67–9.

—— (1995a) "The bank that disappeared", February 27.

—— (1995b) "Currencies in a spin", March 11: 69–70.

—— (1997) "A connected world: survey of telecommunications", September 13: 1–14.

—— (1999a) "The new economy: work in progress", July 24: 21–4.

—— (1999b) "Share without the other bit: in corporate America paying dividends has gone out of fashion", November 20: 93.

—— (1999c) "European media: flirtation and frustration", December 11: 61–3.

Thery, Gérard (1994) *Les autoroutes de l'information. Rapport au Premier Ministre*, Paris: La Documentation française.

Thomas, Hugh (1993) *The Conquest of Mexico*, London: Hutchinson.

Thomas, Louis-Vincent (1975) *Anthropologie de la mort*, Paris: Payot.

—— (1985) *Rites de mort pour la paix des vivants*, Paris: Fayard.

—— (1988) *La Mort*, Paris: Presses Universitaires de France.

Thompson, E.P. (1967) "Time, work-discipline, and industrial capitalism", *Past and Present*, 36: 57–97.

Thrift, Nigel J. (1986) *The "Fixers": the Urban Geography of International Financial Capital*, Lampeter: University of Wales Department of Geography.

—— (1990) "The making of capitalism in time consciousness", in J. Hassard (ed.), *The Sociology of Time*, London: Macmillan, pp. 105–29.

—— and Leyshon, A. (1992) "In the wake of money: the City of London and the accumulation of value", in L. Budd and S. Whimster (eds), *Global Finance and Urban Living: A Study of Metropolitan Change*, London: Routledge, pp. 282–311.

Thurow, Lester (1992) *Head to Head: the Coming Economic Battle among Japan, Europe, and America*, New York: William Morrow.

—— (1995) "How much inequality can a democracy take?", *New York Times Magazine*, special issue: *The Rich*, November 19: 78.

Tichi, Cecilia (1991) *Electronic Hearth: Creating an American Television Culture*, New York: Oxford University Press.

Tillema, H.K. (1991) *International Armed Conflict Since 1945: a Bibliographic Handbook of Wars and Military Intervention*, Boulder, CO: Westview Press.

Tilly, Charles (1995) "State-incited violence, 1900–1999", *Political Power and Social Theory*, 9: 161–79.

Time (1993) Special issue on mega-cities, January 11.

—— (1994) "Risky business in Wall Street: high-tech supernerds are playing dangerous games with money", special report, April 11: 24–35.

Tirman, John (ed.) (1984) *The Militarization of High Technology*, Cambridge, MA: Ballinger.

Tobenkin, David (1993) "Customers respond to video on demand", *Broadcasting and Cable*, 123(48): 16.

Touraine, Alain (1955) *L'Evolution du travail ouvrier aux usines Renault*, Paris: Centre National de la Recherche Scientifique.

—— (1959) "Entreprise et bureaucratie", *Sociologie du travail*, 1: 58–71.

—— (1969) *La Société post-industrielle*, Paris: Denoel.

—— (1987) *La Parole et le sang. Politique et société en Amerique Latine*, Paris: Odile Jacob.

—— (1991) "Existe-t-il encore une société française?", *Contemporary French Civilization*, 15: 329–52.

—— (1992) *Critique de la modernité*, Paris: Fayard.

—— (1994) *Qu'est-ce que la démocratie?*, Paris: Fayard.

Trejo Delarbre, Raul (1992) *La Sociedad Ausente: comunicacion, democracia y modernidad*, Mexico: Cal y Arena.

—— (ed.) (1988) *Las Redes de Televisa*, Mexico: Como/Rotativo.

Tuomi, Ilkka (1999) *Corporate Knowledge: Theory and Practice of Intelligent Organizations*, Helsinki: Metaxis.

Turkle, Sherry (1995) *Life on the Screen: Identity in the Age of the Internet*, New York: Simon and Schuster.

Tyson, Laura d'Andrea (1992) *Who's Bashing Whom? Trade Conflict in High-technology Industries*, Washington, DC: Institute of International Economics.

—— and Zysman, John (1983) *American Industry in International Competition*, Ithaca, NY: Cornell University Press.

——, Dickens, William T. and Zysman, John (eds) (1988) *The Dynamics of Trade and Employment*, Cambridge, MA: Ballinger.

Ubbelhode, A.R.J.P. (1958) "The beginnings of the change from craft mystery to science as a basis for technology", in C. Singer et al., *A History of Technology*, vol. 4: *The Industrial Revolution, 1750–1850*, Oxford: Clarendon Press.

Uchida, Hoshimi (1991) "The transfer of electrical technologies from the US and Europe to Japan, 1869–1914", in David J. Jeremy (ed.), *International Technology Transfer: Europe, Japan, and the USA, 1700–1914*, Aldershot, Hants: Edward Elgar, pp. 219–41.

Uchitelle, Louis (1999) "Big increases in productivity by workers", *The New York Times*, November 13: B1–B14.

UCSF/Field Institute (1999) *The 1999 California Work and Health Survey*, San Francisco, CA: Institute for Health Policy Studies, University of California at San Francisco, and The Field Institute.

UNESCO (1999) *World Communication and Information Report, 1999–2000*, Paris: UNESCO.

United Nations Center on Transnational Corporations (1991) *Transnational Banks and the External Indebtedness of Developing Countries*, New York: United Nations, UNCTC Current Studies, Series A, No.22.

United Nations Conference on Trade and Development (UNCTAD) (1993) *World Investment Report 1993: Transnational Corporations and Integrated International Production*, New York: United Nations.

—— (1994) *World Investment Report 1994: Transnational Corporations, Employment and the Workplace*, report by the UNCTAD Secretariat to the Commission on Transnational Corporations, 2–11 May.

—— (1995) *World Investment Report 1995: Transnational Corporations and Competitiveness*, New York: United Nations.

—— (1996) *World Investment Report 1996: Investment, Trade, and International Policy Arrangements*, New York: United Nations.

—— (1997) *World Investment Report 1997: Transnational Corporations, Market Structure and Competition Policy*, New York: United Nations.

United Nations Development Program (UNDP) (1999) *Human Development Report 1999: Globalization with a Human Face*, New York: United Nations.

UNISDR (United Nations Institute for Social Development Research) (1998) "Proceedings of the International Conference on Globalization and Inequality, Geneva, June (published on-line).

US Congress, Office of Technology Assessment (1991) *Biotechnology in a Global Economy*, Washington, DC: US Government Printing Office.

US Department of Commerce (1999a) "The emerging digital economy", Washington, DC: National Technical Information Service (on-line report).

—— (1999b) "The emerging digital economy II", Washington, DC: National Technical Information Service (on-line report).

US House of Representatives, Committee on Armed Services, Readiness Subcommittee (1990) *US Low-intensity Conflicts, 1899–1990*, a study by the Congressional Research Service, Library of Congress, Washington, DC: US Government Printing Office.

US Library of Congress (1999) "Proceedings of the Conference on Frontiers of the Mind in the 21st Century", posted on the library's web site.

US National Science Board (1991) *Science and Engineering Indicators: 1991*, 10th edn, Washington, DC: US Government Printing Office.

Vaill, P.B. (1990) *Managing as a Performing Art: New Ideas for a World of Chaotic Change*, San Francisco, CA: Jossey-Bass.

Van Creveld, Martin (1989) *Technology and War from 2000 BC to the Present*, New York: Free Press.

Van der Haak, Bregtje (1999) "Television and the digital revolution", *Archis*, 6: 12–18.

Van Tulder, Rob and Junne, Gerd (1988) *European Multinationals in Core Technologies*, New York: John Wiley.

Varley, Pamela (1991) "Electronic democracy", *Technology Review*, Nov/Dec: 43–51.

Velloso, Joao Paulo dos Reis (1994) "Innovation and society: the modern bases for development with equity", in Colin I. Bradford (ed.), *The New Paradigm of Systemic Competitiveness: Toward More Integrated Policies in Latin America*, Paris: OECD, pp. 97–118.

Venturi, Robert et al. (1977) *Learning from Las Vegas: the Forgotten Symbolism of Architectural Form*, Cambridge, MA: MIT Press.

Vessali, Kaveh V. (1995) "Transportation, urban form, and information technology", Berkeley, CA: University of California, unpublished seminar paper for CP 298 I.

Wade, Richard (1990) *Governing the Market: Economic Theory and the Role of Government in East Asian Industrialization*, Princeton, NJ: Princeton University Press.

Waldrop, M. Mitchell (1992) *Complexity: the Emerging Science at the Edge of Order and Chaos*, New York: Simon and Schuster.

Waliszewski, Kasimierz (1900) *Peter the Great*, New York: D. Appleton and Co.

Wall, Toby D. et al. (eds) (1987) *The Human Side of Advanced Manufacturing Technology*, Chichester, Sussex: John Wiley.

Wallerstein, Immanuel (1974) *The Modern World System*, New York: Academic Press.

Wang, Georgette (ed.) (1994) *Treading Different Paths: Informatization in Asian Nations*, Norwood, NJ: Ablex.

Wang, Yeu-fain (1993) *China's Science and Technology Policy, 1949–1989*, Brookfield, VT: Avebury.

Wark, McKenzie (1994) *Virtual Geography: Living with Global Media Events*, Bloomington, IN: Indiana University Press.

Warme, Barbara et al. (eds) (1992) *Working Part-time: Risks and Opportunities*, New York: Praeger.

Warnken, Jurgen and Ronning, Gerd (1990), "Technological change and employment structures", in R. Schettkat and M. Wagner (eds), *Technological Change and Employment Innovation in the German Economy*, Berlin: Walter De Gruyter, pp. 214–53.

Watanabe, Susumu (1986) "Labour-saving versus work-amplifying effects of microelectronics", *International Labour Review*, 125(3): 243–59.

—— (ed.) (1987) *Microelectronics, Automation, and Employment in the Automobile Industry*, Chichester, Sussex: John Wiley.

Watanuki, Joji (1990) *The Development of Information Technology and its Impact on Japanese Society*, Tokyo: Sophia University Institute of International Relations, Research Paper.

Watts, Duncan J. (1999) *Small Worlds: The Dynamics of Networks between Order and Randomness*, Princeton, NJ: Princeton University Press.

Weber, Marx (1958) *The Protestant Ethic and the Spirit of Capitalism*, trans. Talcott Parsons, New York: Charles Scribner (first published 1904–5).

Webster, Andrew (1991) *Science, Technology, and Society: New Directions*, London: Macmillan.

Weiss, Linda (1988) *Creating Capitalism: the State and Small Business since 1945*, Oxford: Blackwell.

—— (1992) "The politics of industrial organization: a comparative view", in Jane Marceau (ed.), *Reworking the World: Organizations, Technologies, and Cultures in Comparative Perspective*, Berlin: Walter De Gruyter, pp. 95–124.

Wellman, Barry (1979) "The community question", *American Journal of Sociology*, 84: 1201–31.

—— (1997) "An electronic group is virtually a social network", in Kiesler (ed.) (1997): 179–205.

—— (ed.) (1999) *Networks in the Global Village*, Boulder, CO: Westview Press.

—— and Gulia, Milena (1999) "Netsurfers don't ride alone: virtual communities as communities", in Barry Wellman (ed.), *Networks in the Global Village*, Boulder, CO: Westview Press, pp. 331–66.

—— et al. (1996) "Computer networks as social networks: collaborative work, telework and virtual community", *Annual Reviews of Sociology*, 22: 213–38.

Wexler, Joanie (1994) "ATT preps service for video on demand", *Network World*, 11(25): 6.

Wheeler, James O. and Aoyama, Yuko (eds) (2000) *Cities in the Telecommunications Age*, London: Routledge.

Whightman, D.W. (1987) "Competitive advantage through information technology", *Journal of General Management*, 12(4).

Whitaker, D.H. (1990) "The end of Japanese-style employment", *Work, Employment and Society*, 4(3): 321–47.

Whitley, Richard (1993) *Business Systems in East Asia: Firms, Markets, and Societies*, London: Sage.

Whitrow, G.J. (1988) *Time in History: the Evolution of our General Awareness of Time and Temporal Perspective*, Oxford: Oxford University Press.

Wieczorek, Jaroslaw (1995) *Sectoral Trends in World Employment*, Working Paper 82, Geneva: International Labour Organization, Industrial Activities Branch.

Wieviorka, Michel (1993) *La Démocratie à l'épreuve: nationalisme, populisme, ethnicité*, Paris: La Découverte.

Wilkinson, B. (1988) "A comparative analysis", in *Technological Change, Work, Organization and Pay: Lessons from Asia*, Geneva: International Labour Organization.

Wilkinson, Barry, Morris, Jonathan and Nich, Oliver (1992) "Japanizing the world: the case of Toyota", in Jane Marceau (ed.), *Reworking the World: Organizations, Technologies, and Cultures in Comparative Perspective*, Berlin: Walter de Gruyter, pp. 133–50.

Williams, Frederick (1982) *The Communications Revolution*, Beverly Hills, CA: Sage.

—— (ed.) (1988) *Measuring the Information Society*, Beverly Hills, CA: Sage.

—— (1991) *The New Telecommunications: Infrastructure for the Information Age*, New York: Free Press.

——, Rice, Ronald E. and Rogers, Everett M. (1988) *Research Methods and the New Media*, New York: Free Press.

Williams, Raymond (1974) *Television: Technology and Cultural Form*, New York: Schocken Books.

Williamson, Oliver E. (1975) *Markets and Hierarchies: Analysis and Antitrust Implications*, New York: Free Press.

—— (1985) *The Economic Institutions of Capitalism*, New York: Free Press.

Willmott, W.E. (ed.) (1972) *Economic Organization in Chinese Society*, Stanford, CA: Stanford University Press.

Wilson, Carol (1991) "The myths and magic of Minitel", *Telephony*, 221(23): 52.

Withey, Stephen B. and Abeles, Ronald P. (eds) (1980) *Television and Social Behavior*, Hillsdale, NJ: Lawrence Erlbaum.

Wolton, Dominique (1998) *Au dela de l'Internet*, Paris: La Decouverte.

Wong, Siulun (1988) *Emigrant Entrepreneurs: Shanghai Industrialists in Hong Kong*, Hong Kong: Oxford University Press.

Wong, S.L. (1985) "The Chinese family firm: a model", *British Journal of Sociology*, 36: 58–72.

Woo, Edward S.W. (1994) "Urban development", in Y.M. Yeung and David K.Y. Chu (eds), *Guandong: Survey of a Province Undergoing Rapid Change*, Hong Kong: Chinese University Press.

Wood, Adrian (1994) *North–South Trade, Employment and Inequality*, Oxford: Clarendon Press.
Wood, Stephen (ed.) (1989) *The Transformation of Work*, London: Unwin Hyman.
Woodward, Kathleen (ed.) (1980) *The Myths of Information: Technology and Postindustrial Culture*, London: Routledge and Kegan Paul.
World Bank (1995) *World Development Report, 1995*, Washington, DC: World Bank.
—— (1998) *World Development Report, 1998/99: Knowledge and Development*, Washington, DC: The World Bank.
World Trade Organization (WTO) (1997) *Annual Report*, Geneva: WTO.
—— (1998) *Annual Report*, Geneva: WTO.
Ybarra, Josep-Antoni (1989) "Informationalization in the Valencian economy: a model for underdevelopment", in A. Portes, M. Castells and L. Benton (eds), *The Informal Economy*, Baltimore, MD: Johns Hopkins University Press.
Yergin, Daniel and Stanislaw, Joseph (1998) *The Commanding Heights: The Battle between Goverment and the Marketplace that is Remaking the Modern World*, New York: Simon and Schuster.
Yoo, S. and Lee, S.M. (1987) "Management style and practice in Korean chaebols", *California Management Review*, 29: 95–110.
Yoshihara, K. (1988) *The Rise of Ersatz Capitalism in South East Asia*, Oxford: Oxford University Press.
Yoshino, Kosaku (1992) *Cultural Nationalism in Contemporary Japan*, London: Routledge.
Yoshino, M.Y. and Lifson, T.B. (1986) *The Invisible Link: Japan's Sogo Shosha and the Organization of Trade*, Cambridge, MA: MIT Press.
Young, K. and Lawson, C. (1984) "What fuels US job growth? Changes in technology and demand on employment growth", paper prepared for the Panel on Technology and Employment of the National Academy of Sciences, Washington, DC.
Young, Michael (1988) *The Metronomic Society*, Cambridge, MA: Harvard University Press.
Youngson, A.J. (1982) *Hong Kong: Economic Growth and Policy*, Hong Kong: Oxford University Press.
Zaldivar, Carlos Alonso (1996) *Variaciones sobre un mundo en cambio*, Madrid: Alianza Editorial.
—— and Castells, Manuel (1992) *España, fin de siglo*, Madrid: Alianza Editorial.
Zaloom, Caitlin (forthcoming) "Risk, rationality and technology: prediction and calculative rationality in global financial markets", unpublished PhD dissertation, Berkeley, CA: University of California.
Zerubavel, Eviatar (1985) *The Seven Day Circle: the History and Meaning of the Week*, New York: Free Press.
Zhivov, Victor M. (1995) "Time and money in Imperial Russia", unpublished paper delivered at the Conference on Time and Money in the Rus-

sian Culture, University of California at Berkeley, Center for Slavic and Eastern European Studies, March 17.

Zook, Matthew (1998) "The web of consumption: the spatial organization of the Internet industry in the United States", paper delivered at the Association of Collegiate Schools of Planning Conference, Pasadena, California, November 5–8 (it can be downloaded from: http://www.socrates. berkeley.edu/-zook/pubs/acsp1998.html).

—— (2000a) "The web of production: the economic geography of commercial Internet content production in the United States", *Environment and Planning A*, 32.

—— (2000b) "Old hierarchies or new networks of centrality: the global geography of the Internet content market", submitted for a special issue of the *American Behavioral Scientist*.

—— (2000c) "The role of regional venture capital in the development of the Internet commerce industry: the San Francisco Bay region and the New York Metropolitan area", unpublished PhD dissertation, Berkeley, CA: University of California.

Zuboff, Shoshana (1988) *In the Age of the Smart Machine*, New York: Basic Books.

Zukin, Sharon (1992) *Landscapes of Power*, Berkeley, CA: University of California Press.

Index